1987
Buying Guide Issue

THIS IS THE DECEMBER 1986 ISSUE OF CONSUMER REPORTS
VOLUME 51, NO.12

CONSUMER REPORTS (ISSN 0010-7174) is published monthly by Consumers Union of United States Inc., 256 Washington St., Mount Vernon, N.Y. 10553. Second-class postage paid at Mount Vernon, N.Y., and at additional mailing offices. Canadian postage paid at Niagara Falls, Ontario, Canada. Title CONSUMER REPORTS registered in U.S. Patent Office. CU is a member of the International Organization of Consumers Unions (IOCU).

CONSUMERS UNION is a nonprofit organization, established in 1936 and chartered under the Not-For-Profit Corporation Law of the State of New York. It derives its income solely from the sale of CONSUMER REPORTS and other publications. In addition, expenses of occasional public-service efforts may be met, in part, by nonrestrictive, noncommercial grants and fees. CU accepts no advertising or product samples, and is not beholden in any way to any commercial interest. Its Ratings and product reports are solely for the use of readers of CONSUMER REPORTS. Neither the Ratings nor the reports may be used in advertising or for any commercial purpose. CU will take all steps open to it to prevent or prosecute any such uses of its material, its name, or the name of CONSUMER REPORTS.

THE PURPOSES OF CONSUMERS UNION are to provide consumers with information and counsel on consumer goods and services, to give information on all matters relating to the expenditure of the family income, and to initiate and to cooperate with individual and group efforts seeking to create and maintain decent living standards.

READERS' LETTERS about editorial content should be sent to The Editors, CONSUMER REPORTS, P.O. Box 1111, Mount Vernon, N.Y. 10551.

SUBSCRIBERS: For subscription service or to change address, write CONSUMER REPORTS, P.O. Box 2480, Boulder, Colo. 80322. Please attach or copy your address label from the back cover of a regular monthly issue. With an address change, include both old and new zip codes; please allow six weeks for change to take effect.

SUBSCRIPTION RATES: U.S. only, $16 for 1 year, $26 for 2 years, $36 for 3 years, $56 for 5 years. All other countries, add $4.50 per year. Back issues up to 11 months old are available as supplies permit. Single copies are $4. The December Buying Guide Issue is $7: Order from Back Issue Dept., Consumers Union, P.O. Box 2485, Boulder, Colo. 80322. School Order Program: 50¢ per copy, minimum 20 copies per issue (September to May, except December).

SUBSCRIBERS MAY BECOME MEMBERS of Consumers Union either on written application or by voting in the annual election of CU's Directors; ballots are mailed to all subscribers. There is no financial or other obligation.

CU'S STAFF operates under a contract between CU and The Newspaper Guild of New York, Local 3, The Newspaper Guild, AFL-CIO. Printed in U.S.A.

POSTMASTER: Send address changes to CONSUMER REPORTS, P.O. Box 2480, Boulder, Colo. 80322.

Contents

How to use the Buying Guide Issue

Here, in one handy source volume, we have gathered the major test reports, brand-and-model Ratings, and general buying guidance from the last several years of CONSUMER REPORTS. Major product reports from the 1986 magazine issues have been summarized, and earlier summaries have been carefully reviewed and, where necessary, revised.

1. To find the report on a specific type of product, look in the Index to the Buying Guide on page 388. That's where you'll find the page number if this issue has a Ratings report or a discussion of that product.

2. If you're not looking specifically for something but are generally interested in a product area, consult the Contents in the front of the book. There we have listed all the Rated products in nine categories of consumer interest. If, for instance, you're interested in improving your physical fitness, look through the items in the chapter Personal Products. This year's entries include running shoes, various equipment for exercising at home, touring bicycles, and a fun new type of bike called an "ATB," or all-terrain bicycle.

3. Articles from the November 1986 issue will be summarized for the 1988 Buying Guide. We do not attempt to summarize general articles on economics and medicine. Copies of January-through-November issues up to 11 months old may be purchased, as supplies permit, by sending $3.00 per copy to Back Issue Department, Consumers Union, P.O. Box 2485, Boulder, Colo. 80322. Issues are available on microfilm from the following: Bell & Howell, Micro Photo Div., Old Mansfield Rd., Wooster, Ohio 44691; NCR, 3100 Valleywood Dr., Dayton, Ohio 45429; Xerox University Microfilms, 300 N. Zeeb Rd., Ann Arbor, Mich. 48106. Your local library may have back issues or bound volumes of CONSUMER REPORTS on file.

4. Detailed background and technical information concerning many of the Buying Guide's entries can be found in past monthly issues of CONSUMER REPORTS. We commend them (and our regular 1987 issues) to you as further resources.

How CU selects products for testing

In determining what products to purchase and test at a given time, we consider a number of elements, including patterns of consumer expenditures, expressions of reader interest, the extent of a product's availability in the marketplace, and the special nature of a new product or of a significantly altered existing product.

For one reason or another, not all products lend themselves equally well to useful testing and reporting. The category in which a product falls may be dominated by unbranded models readers cannot identify; adequate test methods may not have been developed; or applicable tests would cost too much for the amount of useful information they could yield. Where comparative Ratings would not be valid, CU often provides general guidance about competing types of products and their generic differences.

CU's Ratings are based on laboratory tests, controlled use tests, and expert judgments of the purchased samples. Although CU exercises meticulous care to insure accuracy in its reports, errors may occur. Such errors are promptly corrected. But because quality may vary within brands and products may change behind their names, no test results can provide infallible guidance. A Rating of a given model should not be considered a Rating of other models of the same brand unless so specified.

How up-to-date are the Ratings?

Buying Guide Issue Ratings are based on CU's latest tests of each product. These tests are reported in full in the regular monthly issues of CONSUMER REPORTS. The date of the original report is noted in most Guide entries—just below the title.

Because of the time required for testing and reporting, all of those Ratings may not be of the latest models. But new CU tests are continually being made, so check the new regular monthly issues of CONSUMER REPORTS, as well as this Guide, before you buy in 1987.

Up-to-date information on the availability of each model mentioned in this Guide would require the kind of checking that goes well beyond CU's staff resources. But some checks on availability can be and are made. Products that had been discontinued by their manufacturers but were still available at the time our judgments of them were originally published in CONSUMER REPORTS are included in the Ratings in this Buying Guide but are designated with the symbol [D].

[D] is also used in a second check on availability. Sometimes a product sold by a mail-order house may be dropped from the mail-order house catalog, for seasonal or other reasons, after CU has rated the product in a regular test report. The model may still be available in the mail-order company's retail stores or can still be ordered. When we are unable to find such a model in the latest catalog available to us, that product is designated in the Buying Guide's Ratings with a [D].

When CU becomes aware that a large number of models tested have been superseded, the detailed comments on them may be curtailed or eliminated, and lower-rated models, or even all models, may be omitted. However, whether brands and models are given in full, in part, or not at all, CU strives to give general buying advice on each product in the Buying Guide Issue.

What the prices mean

Because prices change, most prices cited in this Guide will differ from those the consumer will encounter in the marketplace. Unfortunately, it is impossible for CU to provide up-to-date prices on the thousands of brands and models included in the Guide—and even if we could, as of press time, such prices would soon be obsolete.

Prices given, unless otherwise indicated at the head of the Ratings, are list prices, dating from the original report. Of course, the meaning of "list price" is highly variable. Not only are discounts from list frequently available, but the list price itself is sometimes a fiction designed to enable the seller to appear to be offering a bargain.

In some cases, national price surveys by CU shoppers can provide the best indications of current prices. Where list prices are available, however, we usually include them—if only for purposes of comparison among models.

CU's objectivity

As a nonprofit organization which abjures any form of commercialism, CU accepts no advertising and no product samples from anyone. All products tested are bought by CU's shoppers from retail sources. CU takes all steps open to it to stop any commercial usage of its work, including the use of its name or allusions to its findings in the promotion of any product or service.

New from CU: Product Features Service

Modern high-tech products often come in a bewildering thicket of models. A single maker, Panasonic for instance, might offer a dozen models of video cassette recorders, each differing from the others mainly in the choice of built-in features. How do you know which to choose? Starting January, 1987, CU will offer a way out of the thicket with a new, computerized Product Features Service. For selected products, we will sell computer printouts that list the brands on the market and show each model's important features.

The Product Features Service is an outgrowth of the information CONSUMER REPORTS already publishes on such products. The Features Service will go beyond our published work in that it will cover more brands—not just the ones tested—and it will be updated frequently to offer current information. The service will initially be available for:

Video cassette recorders
Microwave ovens
Telephone-answering machines
Refrigerator freezers

Other products will be added to the service throughout the year—e.g., TV's and compact-disc players. See the monthly issues of CONSUMER REPORTS to stay up to date.

The charge for a printout will be $8; if printouts for more than one product are ordered at one time, the additional printouts will cost $6 apiece. If you wish to order one of the printouts listed above, send your request with a check to: **Product Features Service, Box 17003, Hauppauge NY 11788.**

Kitchen and laundry

Microwave ovens

Condensed from CONSUMER REPORTS, November, 1985

Fully half the homes in the country, it's estimated, are equipped with a microwave oven. There are essentially two reasons for the microwave boom: smaller sizes and lower prices. While an elaborate, full-sized oven sells for $600 or more, some of the smallest, most-basic models now sell for as little as $150. The models we tested for this report, with prices of $189 to $365, fell between those extremes.

To a certain extent, an oven that's small on the inside is small on the outside. But some ovens have been designed to use space more efficiently than others. We made our own measurements of capacity, because a manufacturer's stated capacity isn't always a reliable guide to usable space. For the *Samsung* and *Sanyo*, for example, we measured 0.6 cubic feet, not 0.9 and 1.0 cubic feet, as their manufacturers claim. Models with a turntable (the *Panasonic* and the *Sharp*, among those we tested) also overstate capacity, claiming as usable space the entire interior volume of the oven instead of just the interior space above the turntable.

To relate cubic-foot capacity to real cooking chores, we used our plastic turkey, which is about the size of a 14-pound bird. Ovens with a usable capacity of 1.0 cubic foot accommodated the bird with a lot of room to spare. Whether the turkey easily fit into the smaller-capacity models depended on the shape of their cooking compartment. The 0.8-cubic-foot *Frigidaire* and *Toshiba* and the 0.7-cubic-foot *General Electric* have an elongated compartment that accommodated the turkey easily, but it was a tight squeeze in models with a square compartment.

The oven that used space most efficiently was the *GE* model sold under the *Spacemaker II* name. With an exterior roughly 12 by 24 by 13 inches, it still had a usable capacity of 0.7 cubic feet. It makes the most of that space by having a full-width door opening, so it's easy to slide a big item in and out.

PERFORMANCE. Another difference between large and small microwave ovens is the amount of microwave energy that they produce. As a rule, big ones cook faster than small ones. That rule was generally confirmed in our heating-speed tests. The *Amana*, one of the largest ovens we tested and close in size to the full-size oven, was fastest. The *Whirlpool*, one of the smallest, was the slowest. In terms of cooking time, the slower ovens took about a quarter to a third longer than the faster ovens.

A big criticism of microwave ovens concerns the unevenness with which they cook. And it is true that the pattern of energy distribution within an oven isn't easily predictable. Most of the tested models employ a rotating reflector, a sort of microwave "stirrer," that disperses the cooking energy somewhat. That stirrer seems to do all right with many foods; we got good results cooking chicken legs, bacon, small casseroles, carrot cakes, and stews.

But foods that graphically demonstrate the strange cooking patter of microwaves are brownies and cheese melted on slices of bread. With those foods, we found that using a turntable in the oven provided the most even cooking patterns. The *Panasonic* and the *Sharp* were the only models we tested that come with a built-in turntable instead of a rotating reflector. However, it is possible to buy a separate rotating turntable for just about any oven. (We tested several: the *Micro-Go-Round* and the slightly smaller *Merry-Go-Round Plus* by Nordic Ware, the *Microware Compact Turntable* by Anchor Hocking, and the *Imperial* by Regal. Although they functioined well enough, we think some cautions are in order. Avoid placing foods directly on the turntable without a suitable glass, ceramic, or plastic dish; use a turntable only when its needed—with dishes where cooking uniformity is a problem; and don't use them when heating food with a low moisture content.)

Even so, a turntable isn't always the solution to the problem of uneven cooking. Overall, baking brownies on a turntable improved them. But since a turntable rotates only in a horizontal plane, food can cook in a bull's-eye pattern. That happened with the brownies. They were consistently overdone or underdone at the center when cooked on a turntable. Also, a turntable takes up oven space that may be needed to accommodate larger items. The *Panasonic* and the *Sharp*, for example, could hold our plastic turkey, but their turntables wouldn't have been able to turn if we had tried to cook it.

CONTROLS. As on other appliances, the controls on microwave ovens constitute a major area in which the brands and models differ from one another. And the differences in controls often result in differences in price. All the tested ovens come with relatively fancy electronic touch-pad controls that are nicely precise and easy to clean. You could save $100 or more in some brand lines by buying a simpler version—one with mechanical, not electronic, controls. There's not much of a difference in function, one way or another.

The number of "power levels" often tracks with the price of a model. All our fancy models have at least five power levels; some have as many as 10 or even 100 levels. We've found that four or five power levels are ample for handling just about any cooking tasks.

All the tested models can be programmed to cook food at a certain power setting for a certain length of time. Most can be programmed to stop cooking another way—by reacting to the temperature of the food. The feature that allows that is a temperature probe, which works rather like a meat thermometer in a conventional oven. The probe, attached to a cable that plugs into the oven wall, is inserted into the food, and the desired internal temperature is selected on the touch panel. As the food cooks, the oven's display shows the current internal temperature, usually changing the display with every five-degree change in temperature. Most probes and displays were accurate to within five degrees in measuring and reporting the internal temperature of the food.

Text continued on page 13

Ratings of microwave ovens

Listed in groups by size, based on exterior dimensions. Within groups, listed in order of estimated overall quality based on performance and convenience.

Except as noted, prices are list; * indicates price is approx. Discounts are usually available. Ⓓ indicates model has been discontinued.

Excellent	Very good	Good	Fair	Poor
⊜	⊖	○	◒	●

Brand and model	Price	Dimensions (HxWxD, in.)	Weight (lb.)	Usable capacity (cu. ft.)	Heating speed, large load	Heating speed, small load	Power levels	Advantages	Disadvantages	Comments
Small ovens										
GE JEM31E	$295*	11¾x23¾x13¼	44	0.7	Good	Good	5	A,B,C,D	d	*F,I,L,O*
LITTON 1455	259	11½x21¾x14¼	40	0.7	Good	Good	10	—	d,g,i	*D,M,T*
ⒹWHIRLPOOL MW3500X	269	12¾x20½x16	42	0.7	Fair	Fair	10	F	d,f,i	*B,D*
Medium ovens										
■ *The following ovens were judged about equal in quality. Listed alphabetically*										
ⒹFRIGIDAIRE MC400A	189	14x22x17	57	0.8	Good	Very good	9	B,G,H	j	*G,T*

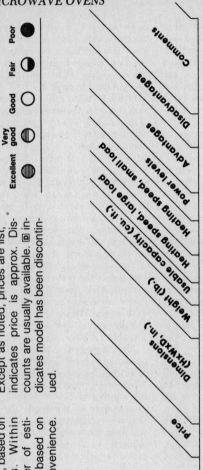

HOTPOINT RE86	255*	13x20½x18½	57	0.6	○	○	5	D,G,H	k	*I,K,Y*
[D]J.C. PENNEY 5645	200	13¾x21x17¼	43	1.0	○	○	10	B	e	*D,G,J,N,Y*
MAGIC CHEF M41AGP	269	15¼22x16	62	1.0	○	○	10	B,C,D,H	h	*D,X*
[D]MONTGOMERY WARD 8135	228	14x21¾x15½	46	0.7	○	○	5	D	j	*I,J,K,R,Y*
PANASONIC NE6960	360	13¾x21x17¼	43	0.6	○	○	6	E	a,g	*J,Q,W,Y*
[D]QUASAR MQ6674XW	330	13½x21x17¾	43	1.0	○	○	6	B	—	*D,G,J,Q,Y*
SAMSUNG RE620TC	250	13x20½x18½	56	0.6	◐	○	10	—	k	*G,I,J,K,P,S,V,Y*
SANYO EM2520S	300	13¾x20½x18½	48	0.6	○	○	100	—	j,l	*E,K,X*
[D]SEARS 87750	[1]	13¾x20½x18	48	0.6	○	◐	100	D	j	*E,K,R*
[D]SHARP R4850	319	14¾x22x16	47	0.6	○	◐	5	E	a,j	*J,O,S,Y*
[D]TAPPAN 56247310	249	15x21½x15½	51	0.7	◐	◐	10	—	c,g,j	*C,D,H,Z*
TOSHIBA ER175BT	299	14x22x17¾	57	0.8	◐	○	9	B,G,H	j	*G,P,T*
Large ovens										
AMANA RR920	365*	15¼x22¾x18¼	68	1.0	●	●	10	B	g	*A,C,O*
MAYTAG CME500	300*	15x25x18¾	78	1.0	◐	○	10	B	b,d	*C,G,O,U,X,Z*

[1] *Price varies from store to store. CU paid $270.*

Keys to Ratings on next page

Keys to microwave oven Ratings

FEATURES IN COMMON

All have touch-panel controls.

Except as noted, all: come with a removable glass tray; beep when a touch pad is activated; employ a rotating reflector to disperse microwave energy; operate on full power unless otherwise programmed; cannot be set to start cooking automatically at some later time; can be programmed for 2 cooking stages; have a time-of-day clock; will not easily hold a medium turkey; have a probe that allows temperature-controlled cooking with settings in 1-degree increments ranging from a low of 90° to 110° F to a high of 190° to 200° (displayed in 5-degree increments); shut off when set temperature is reached; provide only a dim view of food that is cooking; can be built into a wall or cabinet using optional hardware; have a basic 1-yr. in-home repair warranty, which covers all parts and labor, and a 5-yr. warranty covering magnetron parts only.

KEY TO ADVANTAGES

A – Design uses space more efficiently than other models.
B – Medium-sized turkey easily fits inside oven.
C – Has removable metal shelf that increases capacity for small items (but may complicate cooking if one dish shields another or if foods cook at different rates).
D – Exceptionally clear control display.
E – Comes with turntable instead of rotating reflector; provides predictable microwave distribution during cooking (but see Disadvantage a).
F – Comes with particularly clear operating instructions.
G – Window offers relatively clear view.
H – Fan is quieter than most.

KEY TO DISADVANTAGES

a – Holds turkey, but, when it does, turntable cannot rotate; thus judged inadequate for cooking such large items.
b – Does not beep when touch pads are activated; judged more prone to programming errors than models that beep.
c – Separate On/Off switch must be activated to operate oven.
d – End-of-cycle signal is barely audible.
e – Needs extra step to run on full power.
f – LED display is relatively dim.
g – Fan is noisier than most.
h – Inconvenient recessed door handle.
i – Door did not always latch when closed.
j – Cabinet must be disassembled to change light bulb, requiring service call.
k – Sharp edges on sheet metal surround light bulb.
l – Glass tray slides forward too easily.

KEY TO COMMENTS

A – Has highest heating rate, over 600 watts.
B – Has lowest heating rate, under 450 watts.
C – Draws close to 1500 watts; more likely than most to overload circuit.
D – No removable glass tray.
E – Temperature-probe range relatively narrow, 115° to 185°.
F – Temperature probe can be set down to 80°.
G – Temperature can be set only in 5° or 10° increments.
H – Temperature-probe setting less accurate than others; off by more than 10° at low- and middle-range settings.
I – Temperature displayed in 1° increments.
J – Door opens at push of button or lever, occasionally an inconvenience.
K – Installation hardware not available.
L – Comes with hardware for under-cabinet installation and very good installation instructions. Hardware for installing in cabinets or on wall not available.
M – Hardware for installing under cabinets or on wall available as option.
N – 1-yr parts-and-labor warranty.
O – 2-yr. parts-and-labor warranty (in-home).
P – 2-yr. parts-and-labor warranty (carry-in).
Q – 5-yr. parts-and-labor warranty (carry-in).
R – Magnetron warranty (5-yr.) includes labor.
S – 7-yr. magnetron warranty.
T – 10-yr. magnetron warranty.
U – 5-yr. parts-and-labor warranty for magnetorn and other major electronic components, such as touch panel.
V – Has alarm that can be set to repeat at the same time each day.
W – Instead of temperature probe, has moisture-sensor system, which worked well.
X – Only 1 cooking stage.
Y – 3 cooking stages.
Z – Has no time-of-day clock.

The *Panasonic* offers yet another way for an oven to tell when the cooking is done. Its "Auto Sensor" feature is a humidity-sensing device that turns the oven off when the rate of moisture evaporating within a covered dish indicates that the food is cooked. The Auto Sensor worked well with a variety of foods. It was especially useful for heating leftovers, which are easy to overcook in a microwave oven.

Many models allow programmed cooking in more than one stage—defrosting a casserole at a lower power level, for instance, and then cooking it at a high level. Most of the tested ovens can be programmed for two stages; some for three.

Since instructing a microwave oven can mean a lot of touch-pad touching, some models have a few programs built in. On the *Penney*, for example, you can recall the instructions for common tasks by pushing just one button. On the *Samsung*, you can program in your own cooking directions for easy recall.

RECOMMENDATIONS. Most of the microwave ovens tested for this report come pretty close, we think, to striking an ideal compromise between exterior size and interior capacity. They're small enough to avoid overwhelming the average kitchen and large enough to handle most microwave-cooking chores.

But a line of relatively small ovens sold under the *General Electric Spacemaker II* label manages to use space more efficiently than the other models we tested. Designed to be installed under cabinets, the *Spacemakers* need not tie up any counter space at all. With suggested prices ranging from $235 to $295, the GE line is about as cheap as any in our selection.

Gas barbecue grills

Condensed from CONSUMER REPORTS, June 1986

Gas grills promise to make outdoor cookery simple and clean. Just open a valve, twist a knob, press a button, and relax as the grill heats. But the promise comes at a price. The 22 gas barbecue grills that we tested list for $149 to $509. There may be an element of danger, too. We judged three models Not Acceptable, because they may allow a hazardous gas buildup.

In the firebox of most grills are a couple of burners fueled by LP gas. A grid above the burners holds a layer of lava rocks that distribute the heat. Above the rocks are the cooking grid and a hinged hood. The whole business sits on a wheeled cart or stand that also supports the fuel tank.

COOKING. Only the fastest-heating models could preheat the grills in 15 minutes or less, despite the makers' claims; the slowest took nearly 30 minutes. Some manufacturers' claims for maximum heat output—up to 40,000 Btu per hour—are also too optimistic, we reckoned. But it doesn't really matter. Some lower-output grills cooked better than higher-output grills.

We cooked pairs of 1¾-pound pieces of London broil at each grill's hottest setting, with the hood closed. We wanted the meat to be seared but not charred on the outside and rare and juicy in the middle. (A grill that succeeds here can also produce medium or well-done meat with a longer cooking time at

Text continued on page 17

Ratings of gas barbecue grills

Listed in order of estimated overall quality. Except as noted, prices are list; + indicates that shipping is extra; * indicates that price is approximate. Discounts are generally available. D indicates that model has been discontinued.

⊜ ⊖ ○ ◒ ●
Better ⟷ Worse

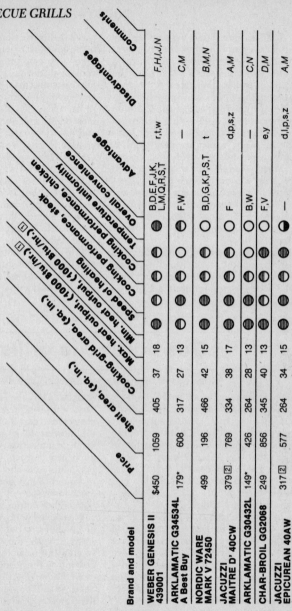

Brand and model	Price	Shelf area, (sq. in.)	Cooking-grid area, (sq. in.)	Max. heat output, (1000 Btu/hr.) [1]	Min. heat output, (1000 Btu/hr.) [1]	Speed of heating	Cooking performance, steak	Cooking performance, chicken	Temperature uniformity	Overall convenience	Advantages	Disadvantages	Comments
WEBER GENESIS II 439001	$450	1059	405	37	18	⊜	⊖	⊖	⊖	⊜	B,D,E,F,J,K, L,M,Q,R,S,T	r,t,w	*F,H,I,J,N*
ARKLAMATIC G34534L A Best Buy	179*	608	317	27	13	⊖	⊜	⊖	○	⊖	F,W	—	*C,M*
NORDIC WARE MARK V 72450	499	196	466	42	15	⊜	⊜	⊖	⊖	○	B,D,G,K,P,S,T	t	*B,M,N*
JACUZZI MAITRE D' 40CW	379 [2]	769	334	38	17	⊜	⊜	⊖	⊖	○	F	d,p,s,z	*A,M*
ARKLAMATIC G30432L	149*	426	264	28	13	⊜	⊜	⊖	○	○	B,W	—	*C,N*
CHAR-BROIL GG2068	249	856	345	40	13	⊜	⊖	⊖	⊜	○	F,V	e,y	*D,M*
JACUZZI EPICUREAN 40AW	317 [2]	577	264	34	15	⊜	⊜	⊖	⊜	◒	—	d,l,p,s,z	*A,M*

Ⓓ SEARS 700 Cat. No. 10755	280+	649	356	37	13	◍	◍	⊖	◍	○	—	a,b,d,m,y	E,M
CHARMGLOW CROWN CLASSIC 537X	359	586	364	35	22	◍	◍	⊖	○	○	—	—	B,M
STRUCTO GOLDEN CLASSIC 77608	199	694	313	35	11	◍	⊖	○ [3]	⊖	⊖	F	—	C,M
DUCANE 2002HLPE	509 [2]	216	303	23	14	●	⊖	◍	◍	◒	A,K,L,N,P,Q,T	d,i,m,o,t,z	B
CHAR-BROIL GG1466	199	743	299	31	13	◍	⊖	⊖	⊖	○	F	p	D,M
SUNBEAM 3385P	365	590	296	30	17	○	⊖	⊖	⊖	○	P,T	—	C,M
CHARMGLOW CROWN CLASSIC 535X	299	754	300	31	21	◍	⊖	○ [3]	◒	○	F	m	B,M
Ⓓ SEARS 600 Cat. No. 10651	240+	450	322	31	15	◍	⊖	⊖	○	◒	—	d,m	E,M
TURCO CARLYLE 55641	249	592	352	40	18	○	⊖	⊖	⊖	◒	—	n,v	C,M
HARDWICK LB3530KOT	300 [2]	294	317	29	15	○	◍	⊖	⊖	●	C,L,N,O,T	d,f,g,k,l,t,u,z	C
JOHN DEERE 44G	369 [4]	139	412	39	18	◍	⊖	⊖	⊖	●	L	g,i,n,t,z	E
DUCANE 1200HLPE	298 [2]	—	303	23	13	●	⊖	◍	⊖	●	K,N,P,Q,T	d,h,l,m,o,t,z	B

Not Acceptable

■ *The following two models were rated Not Acceptable because closing the lid often blew out the flame, creating a possible hazard at re-ignition.*

HAPPY COOKER SCC502	399	679	363	36	6	◍	⊖	○	◍	◒	B,H,I,K,U	a,d,m,q,r,x	B,I,L,N
SEARS Cat. No. 10859	300+	679	363	36	6	◍	⊖	○	◍	◒	B,H,I,K,U	a,d,m,q,r,x	G,I,N

■ *The following was rated Not Acceptable because igniter did not light burner reliably, allowing gas to collect and thus creating a possible hazard at ignition.*

WEBER 611001 [6]	299	611	363	22	14	○	⊖	⊖	◍	●	K,R	c,e,j,k, m,q,r	E,I,J,K

[1] *As calculated by CU.*
[2] *Fuel tank, about $25, not included.*
[3] *Performance improved when preheat was eliminated.*
[4] *Price includes $79 for optional wheel and fuel-tank kit.*

Keys to Ratings on next page

Ratings keys for gas barbecue grills

FEATURES IN COMMON

Except as noted, all have: 20-lb. refillable fuel tank; rectangular cast-aluminum firebox; 2 burners with independent controls; 2-piece cooking grid; provision for drip can; mechanical igniter, plus provision for lighting with match; warming rack; 2 side shelves; 1 center-mounted or 2 side-mounted lid handles; fuel gauge; 2 wheels.

KEY TO ADVANTAGES

A-Raised third burner and rotisserie set.
B-Temperature gauge, a minor convenience.
C-Judged easy to assemble.
D-Comes with detailed cookbook.
E-Convenient grease-collection arrangement.
F-Fold-down front shelf.
G-Removable front shelf/serving tray/cutting board.
H-Porcelainized steel cart.
I-Bell timer, a minor convenience.
J-Grill judged easy to clean.
K-Handwheel allows gas regulator to be installed without tools.
L-Removable side shelf or shelves.
M-3 main burners with separate controls.
N-Judged easy to see if burners are lit.
O-Judged easy to light with match.
P-Igniter can light either burner independently.
Q-Wide cooking grids that are easier to clean than most.
R-Fuel tank easy to secure.
S-Controls judged conveniently placed; remained cooler than most during cooking.
T-Controls have click-stops for 3 burner settings.
U-Self-cleaning model; feature worked well.
V-2 casters can be locked to keep grill in place.
W-Relatively low cooking costs, judged by CU's tests.

KEY TO DISADVANTAGES

a-Cooked chicken very slowly on low heat.
b-Removable front shelf is flimsy.
c-Hood not hinged; slides to side through slot in cart. Obstructive in open position. Can be removed, but hard to store when hot.
d-No fuel gauge.
e-Judged difficult to assemble.
f-No igniter; optional igniter kit, $20.
g-Judged less stable than most.
h-No shelves.
i-Only 1 side shelf.
j-No warming rack.
k-Post-mounted controls judged inconvenient.
l-Handle on only 1 side of hood.
m-1-piece cooking grid.
n-Cooking grids slipped from supports when being brushed clean.
o-No drip-can provision.
p-No cooking instructions.
q-Only 1 burner.
r-Judged hard to see if burner(s) were lit.
s-Wide cooking grids that are harder to clean than most.
t-Judged awkward to move.
u-Fuel tank hard to secure.
v-No detailed ignition warnings on front panel.
w-CU's sample lacked match hole.
x-Very low heat output on Low setting.
y-Among the highest in cooking costs, judging by CU's tests.
z-Comes without fuel tank.

KEY TO COMMENTS

A-Lifetime warranty on firebox; 3 yr. on burners; 1 yr. on other parts.
B-5-yr. warranty on firebox and burners; 1 yr. on other parts.
C-5-yr. warranty on firebox; 3 yr. on burners; 1 yr. on other parts.
D-5-yr. warranty on firebox; 2 yr. on burner; 6 mo. on other parts.
E-1-yr. warranty on all parts.
F-1-yr. warranty on "grill"; 3 yr. on burners, valves, tank, and regulator; 5 yr. on other parts.
G-5-yr. warranty on lid and kettle only.
H-Uses steel bars in place of lava rock.
I-Firebox made of porcelainized steel (steel and cast aluminum on **Weber 439001**).
J-Final four digits of model no. vary to indicate color: **-1001** (black), **-4001** (red), **-9001,** (chocolate).
K-Not Acceptable judgment also applies to pedestal-mounted version, **211101.**
L-Not Acceptable judgment also applies to **Happy Cooker SCC501.**
M-Firebox has viewing window.
N-Has temperature gauge.

lower heat.) All the grills gave us steaks judged at least very good, typically in about 10 minutes.

To check the low setting of each model's temperature range, we grilled 2½-pound split chickens, cooked bone-side down with the hood closed. Chicken is rather fatty, and too much heat makes the fat flare up, burning the outside of the bird before it can cook through to the bone. The two *Ducanes* did the best job; they turned out fully cooked chicken with a crisp, brown skin.

We did preheat all the grills before analyzing their cooking surfaces for temperature uniformity. We used an infrared camera to see the surface heat directly, then corroborated the results by cooking batches of real hamburgers. The grills with poor scores turned out uneven batches ranging from very rare burgers to overdone.

Even the least efficient of our gas grills was much cheaper to run than a kettle-type charcoal grill of similar size. Assuming a price of 45 cents a pound for LP fuel, the cost of gas to cook a couple of steaks at high heat ranged from 14 to 38 cents; the cost of cooking chicken slowly on low heat ranged from 19 to 46 cents.

IGNITION—SAFE OR NOT? All the grills can be lighted with a match, but most have igniters that proved handier for that task. The starting procedure for most grills goes something like this: You raise the hood, turn on the gas from the tank and, in two-burner models, turn the right-hand control knob to High. Then you press a button a few times or turn a knob to make the igniter produce a spark. If all goes well, the burner will light; the other burner lights from that flame when you turn its control to High. Most grills lit in one or two tries.

But the igniter of the *Weber 611001*, which is located so that you must crouch to reach it with your face near the open kettle, often failed to light the grill in as many as a dozen straight tries. And when it did eventually spark the burner, enough gas had collected to set off a flash of flame from the grill. Replacement burners and igniters didn't help.

Although, as with all the grills, the instructions warn against attempting repeated ignitions with the gas on, that *Weber's* provocations may prove too strong. We believe that some owners would sooner or later keep pushing the igniter button while gas accumulated in the cooker. We therefore judged the *Weber 611001* Not Acceptable. The same judgment applies to three other versions of that model—the *614001*, the *619001*, and the *211101*. If you already own one of those grills, we advise you to remove the igniter and make a practice of lighting the burner only with a long match, following the manufacturer's directions.

Serious ignition problems also showed up with two "self-cleaning" grills, the *Happy Cooker SCC502* and the *Sears Cat. No. 10859*. With the burner set anywhere from Low to Medium, closing the lid was enough to blow out the flame. The gas, however, would continue to flow, setting up a very hazardous situation. We judged those models Not Acceptable.

CONVENIENCE. Most grills have two burners with separate controls, which is useful for cooking two foods at different heats. The versatile *Weber 439001* has three burners. The *Ducane 2002HLPE* has a third burner for use with its rotisserie. That rotisserie did a nice job with roasts, but it didn't produce the flaring that can give meat a smoked or barbecued flavor. (In contrast, the optional rotisserie for the *Sears 10755* let drippings flare so high that a roast quickly charred on the outside.)

The Ratings list the cooking-grid area

of all the tested models. They differ considerably, but even the smaller of the tested grills have enough cooking area to serve almost any family cookout. Most grids are made of steel rods, coated with porcelain to protect them from rust.

Many grills have their controls on a panel in front of the firebox. That's convenient, but the knobs and the panel tend to get hot. Some grills are designed to keep the controls cool. The Ratings note the presence or absence of other considerations, such as shelves, warming trays, fuel gauges, temperature gauges, handles, and drip-catchers.

None of the grills come fully assembled. Most took roughly 2½ hours to set up. Even if you're mechanically adept, you might be wise to have a dealer assemble your grill; some will do it at no cost. More than a third of our models arrived with missing or damaged parts, a problem that a dealer should be better able to cope with than you are.

Six of the tested models come without a gas tank. If you choose one of them, figure on spending about $25 for a 20-lb.-capacity LP tank.

RECOMMENDATIONS. Actually, there wasn't much difference in the quality of the cooking by one grill or another. The large variations in price seem chiefly to reflect differences in features. So if you're feeling flush enough to insist on a grill with all the amenities, the top-rated *Weber 439001,* which lists at $450, might make a nice choice. It's designed to make fuel-tank changes easy; it's easy to clean; and it has the cleverest arrangement we've seen for collecting meat drippings. On the other hand, it won't cook any better than the *Arklamatic G34534L,* a Best Buy at approximately $179. Don't be swayed by such frills as a window on the lid, a temperature gauge, or a timer. More important are handy shelves and racks, easy-to-change fuel tanks, and split cooking grills.

Freezers

Condensed from CONSUMER REPORTS, February 1985

If you consider a freezer's life as being 15 years, and add in its operating costs to the purchase price, the appliance is more likely to be a convenience than an economy. Even so, we didn't select luxury models. None of the tested freezers, for example, are self-defrosting.

PERFORMANCE. A good freezer should keep everything inside it at a temperature of 0° F, give or take a couple of degrees, even on hot summer days.

Theoretically, a chest-freezer has an advantage over an upright freezer in maintaining uniform cold temperatures. In a chest freezer, the freezer coils are within the walls, surrounding the food. The door is on top; cold air, which tends to sink below warm air, naturally wants to stay in the chest.

In the best chest models, only the top of the storage compartment was a few degrees above zero; the rest was closer to zero.

The design of an upright freezer, while convenient, is at odds with physics. Cold air within that tall, narrow cabinet tends to sink to the bottom, letting warmer air collect at the top. Each time the door is opened, cold air spills out from the bottom while warm air comes in at the top.

Still, some upright models did nearly

as well in the test at normal home temperatures as the chest freezers.

Our test for reserve capacity, run at 110°, gives a measure of a freezer's performance on really torrid days. It also provides an indication of how well a freezer will endure through the years.

Important, too, is a freezer's ability to hold a constant inside temperature despite fluctuations in the outside temperature. To test for that ability, we stabilized each freezer's inside temperature at 0° and raised the chamber's temperature from 70° to 90°.

A final performance test was for resistance to condensation in humid weather. Most of the freezers are designed so that "hot tubes," which carry the heat extracted by the refrigeration process, run through the walls. A few models have electric heating elements instead; you can switch the elements on to discourage condensation—or off to save energy. But when we ran the test-chamber temperature up to 90° and operated each tested model first with relative humidity at 75 percent, then at 90 percent, condensation on the door and around the gaskets was somewhat worse than average with the models having electric heaters.

CONVENIENCE. You'd probably have to defrost any of the upright freezers we tested at least twice a year, the frequency depending on the humidity and on how often you open the door. With a chest freezer, however, you might be able to go for 12 to 18 months between defrostings, especially if you occasionally scrape off the ice that builds up around the rim.

Most models have a drain to draw off the water coming from the melted ice. Uprights generally have a hose attached to the drain. Most chests are designed so a hose can be attached.

Chest freezers are relatively easy to defrost and clean. They have a smooth interior and removable wire baskets or dividers instead of shelves. You can use an ice scraper to hasten defrosting and then swab down the walls.

You must be more patient when defrosting an upright, waiting for the ice to melt around the coils in the shelves. Using tools to speed the process could puncture the coils.

Space organizers are minimal in chest freezers—a wire basket and maybe a divider. Most uprights have three fixed shelves in the main compartment. At the bottom of the typical upright is a bin area, with a wire gate to keep the contents from spilling out.

RECOMMENDATIONS. There's something to say for each type of freezer. The typical chest model costs less and needs less defrosting; its design helps keep food more uniformly cold throughout the freezing compartment. The typical upright model is more convenient when it comes to stashing, locating, and removing food, and it takes up less floor space. Overall, we'd say that a chest freezer has the edge over an upright model—if you have space for it.

Ratings on next page

How to use the Buying Guide

- Look in the index for specific reports.
- Look in the Contents for general subject areas.
- Look on pages 5 to 7 for explanations of check-ratings and Best Buys, and of why some products are included and others not.

Ratings of freezers

Listed by types; within types, listed in order of estimated overall quality. Differences in quality between closely ranked models were slight. Prices are approximate retail; discounts are generally available. D indicates model has been discontinued.

◍ ⊜ ○ ◒ ●

Better ← → Worse

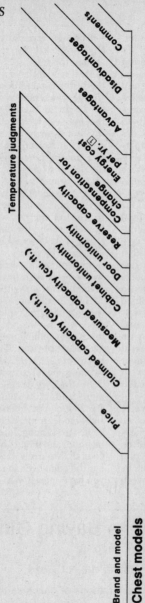

Brand and model	Price	Claimed capacity (cu. ft.)	Measured capacity (cu. ft.)	Temperature judgments: Cabinet uniformity	Temperature judgments: Door uniformity	Temperature judgments: Reserve capacity	Temperature judgments: Compensation for change	Energy cost per yr. [1]	Advantages	Disadvantages	Comments
Chest models											
WARDS 8523	$299	15.7	15.1	⊜	—	◒	◒	$62	C	d	B,J
FRIGIDAIRE CF16J	570	15.6	15.1	⊜	—	◒	◒	62	—	d	B
KELVINATOR HFS156SM	659	15.6	15.1	⊜	—	◒	◒	62	C	b,d	—
WHITE-WESTINGHOUSE FC164D	520	15.6	15.1	⊜	—	◒	◒	62	C	b,d	—
GENERAL ELECTRIC CB15DF	419	15.6	15.1	⊜	—	◒	◒	62	—	b,d	—
GIBSON FH16M2WM	360	15.7	15.1	⊜	—	◒	◒	62	—	b,d	A
AMANA C15B1	450	15.0	14.8	○	—	○	●	58	C	d,e	B
MAGIC CHEF C15D	369	15.2	14.8	◒	—	◍	⊜	63	—	d	—
D SEARS 14152	335	15.1	14.5	◒	—	○	○	57	—	b,d	—
WHIRLPOOL EH150CXL	400	15.2	14.5	◒	—	○	○	57	—	b,d	—

Upright models

AMANA ESU15C	540	15.0	13.7	⊜	◒	⊜	⊜	62	B,D,E	f	*C*
ADMIRAL DF15	540	15.2	12.9	⊜	●	⊜	○	72	B	f	*E*
MAGIC CHEF DF15	399	15.2	12.9	⊜	●	⊜	○	72	B	f	*E*
D SEARS 24152	335	15.1	13.2	○	●	⊜	⊜	62	B	a,b,d,f	*E,I*
GIBSON FV16M5WN	430	16.0	14.3	◒	○	○	◒	71	C	—	*G*
GENERAL ELECTRIC CA16DF	469	16.0	14.3	◒	○	○	◒	71	—	—	*H*
WHITE-WESTINGHOUSE FU166E	580	16.0	14.3	◒	○	○	◒	71	—	—	*D,H*
KELVINATOR UFS161SM	669	16.0	14.3	◒	○	○	◒	71	—	b	*H*
FRIGIDAIRE UF16	590	16.0	14.3	◒	○	○	◒	71	—	—	*H*
WARDS 4633	339	16.0	14.3	◒	○	○	◒	71	—	c	*G,J*
WHIRLPOOL EV160FXK	480	15.9	13.0	○	⊜	●	○	90	A,C	a,f	*F,G,I*

[1] *Cost figured at 8.2¢ per kilowatt-hour.*

FEATURES IN COMMON
Except as noted, all have: painted steel interior; interior light; drain and hose or pan to dispose of defrost water.
All chests: are between 35 and 37 in. high, 41 and 45 in. wide, and 28 and 31 in. deep; have a lid that opens to a maximum height above the floor of between 61 and 63 in.; and have 1 suspended storage basket.
All uprights: are between 59 and 66 in. high, 28 and 30 in. wide, and 28 and 32 in. deep; have a door that opens out to a total depth from wall of between 55 and 59 in.
Except as noted, all uprights have: 3 fixed wire shelves in main compartment (judged somewhat difficult to clean) and 5 shelves in door; door stop to keep door opening more than 180°; gate across bin area at bottom of storage compartment.

KEY TO ADVANTAGES
A – Interior is porcelain on steel.
B – Interior is plastic.
C – Outside light indicates power on.
D – Judged easiest upright to clean.
E – Sliding basket at bottom of storage compartment.

KEY TO DISADVANTAGES
a – Somewhat more condensation on exterior than most in humid, conditions.
b – No interior light.
c – No defrost drain.
d – No defrost hose or pan.
e – Defrost drain lacks adapter and will not accept standard hose adapter.
f – No stop to prevent door from opening more than 180°.

KEY TO COMMENTS
A – 1 adjustable, removable divider.
B – 1 single-position, removable divider.
C – 4 main-compartment shelves.
D – 1 main-compartment shelf can be adjusted to 3 positions or removed completely.
E – 4 door shelves.
F – 6 door shelves, 2 sized for juice cans.
G – 2 door shelves are sized for juice cans.
H – 1 door shelf is sized for juice cans.
I – Trivet occupies bin area at bottom of storage compartment; no gate across front.
J – Catalog price is higher than store price (indicated in table); $430 plus shipping for **Cat. No. 8523**; $490 plus shipping for **Cat. No. 4633**.

Ice-cream makers

Condensed from CONSUMER REPORTS, July 1986

Judged objectively, homemade ice cream doesn't always taste better than the store-bought kind. It isn't always cheaper, either. A quart of ice cream cost us $1.78 to make, not including ice and salt—just about what you would expect to pay at the store. But some people think making ice cream is more fun than merely buying it. Our test of 14 ice-cream makers show that you can make America's favorite dessert without a great deal of fuss.

The more you spend on an ice-cream maker, of course, the less hard work you have to do. If you have around $400 handy, you can buy an electric Italian model that does virtually all the work; we tested three that are essentially small refrigerators, which makes them rather large countertop appliances. We also tested seven models patterned after the old-fashioned churn but with an electric motor to do the cranking; they require some effort to set up, but some of the better ones were priced at less than $50. Finally, we tested four manual models, listing at $20 to $76.

HOW EASY? The basic ingredients of ice cream are sugar and cream. Most recipes also call for eggs or unflavored gelatin to make the ice cream smoother. The mixture of ingredients is poured into a cold metal container surrounded by a refrigerant of some kind and frozen quickly. All the ice-cream makers have a paddle for stirring the mix as it chills. Constant agitation lightens ice cream by allowing air to enter the mix; it also prevents large ice crystals from forming.

Most ice-cream makers use a combination of ice and salt as the refrigerant. The resulting brine, a liquid but lower than 32°F, freezes the ice-cream mixture efficiently. But the Italian models have a built-in refrigeration system to chill the mix. The *Simac* has its refrigerant sealed inside the unit. So do the *Gaggia* and the *Bialetti,* but their instructions suggest pouring a small amount of alcohol and water into the permanent tub before putting in the removable ice-cream container. The alcohol/water mixture transmits the chilling effect between the two containers.

That system worked fine in the *Gaggia.* However, when we poured a full, recommended measure of the alcohol solution into the *Bialetti,* the solution welled up and spilled into the inner container that holds the ice-cream mixture. When we tried using less solution, the alcohol still managed to work its way into the ice cream. (The instructions call for denatured or rubbing alcohol, but we used vodka just to be safe.) We traced the leak to a knob that holds the mixing blade in place, and we couldn't stop the leak unless we tightened the knob so hard that it threatened to damage the sleeve over the blade shaft. Since it goes without saying that a food-processing machine shouldn't ruin the food that it's processing, we judged the *Bialetti 300 Exclusive* ice-cream maker Not Acceptable.

Most of the other models have to be assembled and loaded with ice and salt. Some permit the convenience of using ice cubes; others call for crushed ice. Some allow the use of table salt; others insist on rock salt.

Of all the tested models, the *Sears* took longest to churn a batch of ice cream—as long as one and three-quarters hours. (The *Sears* operates in the freezer and does not require ice and salt.) The other Acceptable electric models took between 20 and 45 minutes, and with most of them, we occasionally needed to add more ice and salt before the end of a run. It took us from 19 to 25 minutes to hand-crank ice cream, but only the last five minutes or so were hard work. Two people are required to churn with the *Sunbeam*, one to crank and one to hold down the lightweight plastic tub.

With an unassuming quart-sized model called the *Donvier*, there's no need to use ice and salt or to churn vigorously. The secret of that little manual model is a refrigerant sealed inside the aluminum tub walls. Once the tub has been stored in the freezer for seven hours, its ready to be set into a plastic bucket. Into the tub go the ice-cream ingredients, to be topped by a plastic lid that holds the paddle and its crank handle. The crank then has to be turned only a couple of times every few minutes for about half an hour. (The instructions say 15 to 20 minutes, but it never worked that quickly for us.) The *Donvier* is not only easy to use, we found, but it's quite versatile, too. It can make frozen drinks in less than five minutes and frozen yogurt in less than ten. We know people who bring the frozen tub right to the dinner table to make dessert there.

HOW GOOD? Following a basic vanilla recipe, we made ice cream in each machine and dished it up freshly churned, while it was still soft and creamy, to a panel of trained tasters. The only significant differences our panel found were in texture. Ice cream should be smooth, cold but not too cold, and creamy. Our panelists faulted ice creams that seemed too icy and felt rough against the tongue.

The *Simac*, the *Gaggia*, and the *White Mountain* electric models made the smoothest ice cream, very nearly up to the level of the best store-bought products we've tasted. They also made rather dense ice cream, in particular contrast to the *Sears*, which made very fluffy stuff with the consistency of marshmallow cream.

Our basic vanilla recipe called for an egg mixed in with the cream and sugar. We found that adding more eggs and cooking them first with the other ingredients into a sort of custard made a smoother, richer ice cream. Conversely, if you're trying to cut down on fat, you can make ice milk by substituting milk for cream. Some recipes we tried directed us to add chocolate bits and cookie pieces after the ice cream was formed but not completely frozen. That was easy with the Italian machines but too much of a bother with most of the others. We also tried, with some success, ices made with fresh fruit.

RECOMMENDATIONS. It's pointless to touch on the economics of homemade ice cream. True, if you pay $300 to $400, depending on available discounts, for one of the top-rated Italian ice-cream makers, you can make ice cream almost as good as the best ice cream you can buy at the store for about the same cost and for not much more effort. But people who decide to buy the *Simac II Gelataio Super 185* or the *Gaggia Gelatiera IC-2* surely won't reason that way. They'll think of the fun they can have. And doubtless, the same kind of motivation, though on a lesser fiscal scale, will lead others to less expensive but perhaps equally entertaining ice-cream makers.

Ratings on next page

Ratings of ice-cream makers

Listed by types; within types, listed in order of estimated quality. Except where separated by heavy lines, closely ranked models were judged to differ little in quality. Prices are list; + indicates shipping is extra; discounts are available.

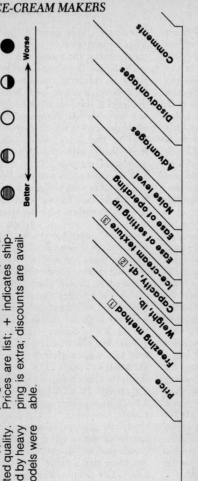

◍ ⊖ ○ ◒ ●

Better ⟷ Worse

Brand and model	Price	Freezing method [1]	Weight, lb.	Capacity, qt. [2]	Ice-cream texture [3]	Ease of setting up	Ease of operating	Noise level	Advantages	Disadvantages	Comments
Electric models											
SIMAC IL GELATAIO SUPER 185	$450	S	33	1½	⊖	◍	◍	○	E,G,H,I,M	j	*D,N,P,T,V*
GAGGIA GELATIERA IC-2	375	S,A	28½	1½	⊖	⊖	◍	◒	A,E,G	c,i,j	*D,O,R,S,V*
WARING ICE CREAM PARLOR CF520-1	47	I	4¼	2	○	○	⊖	◒	C,J,K	—	*C,J,O,S*
WHITE MOUNTAIN 69204	147	I	14½	4	⊖	◒	⊖	●	L	d,g,l	*B,F,H,L,Q,T,V*
OSTER QUICK FREEZE 768	44	I	5¼	2	○	○	○	◒	B,C,E,J	d,e	*C,O,S*
SEARS KENMORE Cat. No. 8001	100+	F	4	2	○	○	◍	◍	H	b	*K,Q,S,X*
RICHMOND CEDAR WORKS 76E	23	I	4¼	2	○	◒	⊖	◒	D	l	*B,O,U,Y*
SUNBEAM PACER 8457-3	29	I	5¼	4	◒	◒	⊖	◒	—	l	*B,P,U,Y*
RICHMOND CEDAR WORKS EFKW4	50	I	9	4	◒	◒	⊖	◒	—	f,k,l	*B,L,P,U,Y*

Not Acceptable

■ *The following was rated Not Acceptable because alcohol/water coolant can contaminate ice cream (see story).*

BIALETTI 300 EXCLUSIVE	455	S,A	39	2	○	⊜	⊜	◒	E	h,i,j	*E,G,M,Q,S,V,Y,Z*

Manual models

DONVIER	40	PF	5¾	1	◒	⊜	⊜	⊜	G,H,J,M	a	*A,I,S,W*
WHITE MOUNTAIN 64302	76	I	10¾	2	○	◒	○	○	F,L	I	*F,H,T,Y*
RICHMOND CEDAR WORKS FKW4	34	I	7	4	○	◒	◒	○	—	f,l	*L,U,Y*
SUNBEAM PACER 8455-3	20	I	3¾	4	◒	◒	●	○	—	I	*U*

[1] *S = self-contained refrigeration system; A = alcohol/water used as coolant; I = ice and salt used as coolant; F = freezer as the place in which unit operates; PF = prefrozen container.*

[2] *As claimed by manufacturer. But all except* **Bialetti** and **Donvier** made somewhat less than claimed.

[3] *Judged in terms of smoothness or relative absence of ice crystals in ice cream made from CU's recipe.*

FEATURES IN COMMON

All: have at least 1 removable metal container in which ingredients are chilled and churned.

Except as noted, all have: a lid that is difficult to manipulate for adding ingredients; plastic housing or outer tub; plastic mixing blade; clear plastic lid; adequate instructions and recipes; 1-yr. repair-or-replacement warranty.

Except as noted, all electric models: turn on when plugged in and stop when unplugged; have overload protector for the motor; take from 20 to 45 min. to make a batch.

Except as noted, all manual models: must be churned constantly during operation; are easier to churn if tub is held down by second person as ice cream forms; take from 19 to 25 min., including packing of ice and salt, to make a batch.

KEY TO ADVANTAGES

A – Has 2 removable containers and well-marked measuring container for alcohol/water coolant.
B – On/Off switch.
C – Unit may be packed with ice cubes and table salt, according to instructions, instead of crushed ice and rock salt. But Oster requires small ice cubes.
D – Uses ice cubes and table salt or rock salt.
E – Adding extra ingredients judged easy.
F – Wooden tub.
G – Filled ice-cream container easier to move than most.
H – Judged easier to clean than most.
I – Parts may be washed in dishwasher.
J – Judged easier than most to move and store.
K – Cord-storage provision.
L – 5-yr. warranty on ice-cream container.
M – Instructions and recipes judged excellent.

KEY TO DISADVANTAGES

a – Ice-cream container must be chilled at least 7 hr. in freezer before each use.
b – Takes up freezer space during operation, and takes more time than any other model to make full batch.
c – No specified settings on timer.
d – No overload protector or timer.
e – Small openings on tub lid make it hard to add extra ice and salt.
f – Opaque lid hides ice cream in the making.
g – Motor and gear assembly harder to remove than any other.
h – Filled ice-cream container could not be removed from unit.
i – Alcohol/water coolant must be cleaned from unit after every use, a messy job.

Keys continued on next page

Ratings keys for ice-cream makers continued

j-Large unit; hard to move.
k-No handle; unit hard to carry.
l-Has at least 1 part judged likely to rust.

KEY TO COMMENTS

A-Handle needs to be turned only a few times every 2 to 3 min. for about 30 min.
B-Top-mounted motor.
C-Motor in base.
D-Controls for chill, mix, and timer.
E-Control for timer, but no overload protector.
F-Unit should be packed with rock salt, according to manufacturer.
G-Has 1-liter blender for mixing ingredients.
H-Cast-metal led and cast-metal mixer with wooden scrapers.
I-No warranty (to cover, for instance, small piece that broke off lid of 1 sample).
J-Ingredients can be added through hole in lid, but only in tiny pieces.
K-Synthesized voice announces that machine is operating and when it has finished.
L-Wooden tub, but it leaked somewhat.
M-Took about 1 hr. to make full batch.
N-Release lever must be opened to remove container.
O-Cord 2½ to 4 ft. long.
P-Cord about 5 ft. long.
Q-Cord about 6 ft. long.
R-1 Sample did not chill properly at first; unit should not be used for 24 hr. after moving, we were advised by salesperson.
S-Aluminum ice-cream container.
T-Stainless-steel container.
U-Tin-plated steel container.
V-Ice cream denser than most.
W-Texture improved when making only 1 qt.
X-90-day warranty.

Toasters

Condensed from CONSUMER REPORTS, February 1986

Very little has ever been expected of a toaster. It merely has to cook slices of bread to the shade of brown one likes, and perhaps do the same to an occasional English muffin or bagel. Pop-up toasters have been doing that quite well for decades.

We emphasized the traditional for this report on two-slice and four-slice toasters. Most that we tested are fundamentally no different from ones your parents might have used. You'll see 25 models in the Ratings, but the majority are made by two companies. Toastmaster accounts for five models, and Proctor-Silex (also sold under the *Sears*, *J.C. Penney*, *Farberware*, and *Panasonic* names) accounts for 12.

PERFORMANCE. Because manufacturers have pretty much perfected toaster technology, you can expect most models on the market today to make toast to your liking. Indeed, all but one model—the *Vivalp V17*, a unique but discontinued design—performed well in our tests. In those tests, each model was evaluated for three achievements: toasting a single slice of supermarket white bread; toasting a batch of bread slices; and toasting six consecutive batches.

In the single-slice test, the *Sunbeam 20030* and the *Proctor-Silex T330W* two-slice models did the best job, browning both sides of the toast evenly. But only the fussiest individual would object to the toast from most of the other models.

In the full-batch test, we tried making toast with just a hint of golden color and toast that was very dark but short of burnt. Each model's color control was sensitive enough to yield toast through a wide light-to-dark range. But with all the toasters, we discovered, it takes some trial and error before one learns how to achieve precisely the desired degree of doneness.

Once the color control is set, a toaster should be able to produce batch after batch of toast to just the selected shade of brown. We toasted batches in quick succession to find out how consistent these appliances could be. The *Sunbeam 20030* and the *General Electric T88* two-slice models were best at that test.

The two-slice models averaged 1½ minutes to toast a full batch; the four-slice models averaged slightly less than two minutes. The *GE T88* was the slowest of the two-slicers, requiring about two minutes per batch. The *GE 128* was the fastest four-slicer, turning out a batch in less than a minute and a half.

Performance generally didn't change much when we tried toasting whole-wheat bread and English muffins. All the toasters required a bit more toasting time, however. A few models have a "pastry" or "bakery" setting for toaster pastries. But all models did a nice job with such pastries, special setting or no.

CONVENIENCE. Most models have the familiar push-down lever that lowers bread into the toaster slots and pops up with the bread-turned toast. The elegant *Sunbeam 20030* has no lever; it quietly lowers the bread into the slots by itself.

The four-slice models that have their slots lined up side by side have two levers, so you can toast two slices of bread without heating up all four elements. They also have two color controls, so, if you're toasting four slices at once, you can make two light and two dark, if you wish.

Toasting in most models can be interrupted by flipping up the push-down lever. Moving the color control to a lighter shade raises the toast in the *Sunbeam 20030*; it never "pops" up, even when left to rise automatically. The *Proctor-Silex T330W* has a keep-warm feature that will keep toast in the slots, basking in residual heat without becoming darker in color.

English muffins fit into all the toasters without having to be crammed in, but only the *Vivalp* could accommodate slices of bread 1 ⅜ inches thick. Among the other toasters, the *GE T88* and the two-slice *Toastmasters* had the most generously sized slots; they could hold bread a trifle larger than most toasters could.

RECOMMENDATIONS. The top-rated *Sunbeam 20030* is an excellent toaster, but, at $74 list or any discount close to that, it's not three times as good as most of the other tested models. The second-rated *GE T88*, at $32, is a very able toaster, too, but some of the other models would appear to give better value. The *Sears 4800*, the *Panasonic NT-124*, the *Proctor-Silex T620B*, and the *Penney 3133* two-slice toasters look to be bargains, priced as they are at less than $20.

Ratings on next page

What about prices?

The Buying Guide Issue usually notes prices as given in the full report cited at the beginning of each article. Unless otherwise stated, prices are list or suggested retail, current at the time of original publication. In many cases, inflation will have increased prices, but the price relationships among models is stable enough to be informative to consumers.

Ratings of toasters

Listed by types; within types, listed by groups in order of estimated overall quality; within groups, listed in order of increasing price. Prices are list; + indicates shipping is extra. Discounts are usually available. [D] indicates model was discontinued at original publication.

⊜ ⊖ ○ ◒ ●

Better ⟵⟶ **Worse**

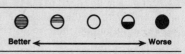

Brand and model	Price	Overall toasting performance	Advantages	Disadvantages	Comments
Two-slice toasters					
SUNBEAM 20030	$74	⊜	A,B,H,J,L	—	*D,L,O*
GENERAL ELECTRIC T88	32	⊖	A,F,L	c	*C,J,N,P*
SEARS Cat. No. 4800	15+	○	—	d	—
PANASONIC NT-124	16	○	J	—	*J*
PROCTOR-SILEX T620B	18	○	—	d,f	—
J.C. PENNEY 3133	19	○	—	d,f	*M*
TOASTMASTER B705	20	○	F	—	—
SEARS Cat. No. 63078	20+	○	—	f,g	*D,M*
GENERAL ELECTRIC T17B	21	○	I	—	*J*
SUNBEAM 20170	23	○	J	b	—
PROCTOR-SILEX T239AL	24	○	I	—	*M*
TOASTMASTER B708	27	○	F,I	—	*F,M*
PROCTOR-SILEX T330W	32	○	B	f	*D,H*
FARBERWARE 292	35	○	M	e	—
TOASTMASTER B720	35	○	F,I	—	*C,E,G*
[D]VIVALP V17	45	●	D,G,J,M	a,h	*C,F,I,K,M*
Four-slice toasters					
GENERAL ELECTRIC T128	45	○	C,I,K,M	—	*A,D,J,N*

Brand and model	Price	Overall toasting performance	Advantages	Disadvantages	Comments
SEARS Cat. No. 4812	$40+	○	K,N	—	*A,D,N*
[D]TOASTMASTER D137	48	○	I,K	i	*A,C,D,J*
PROCTOR-SILEX T009N	49	○	K,N	—	*A,D,N*
PANASONIC NT-140	28	○	—	—	*B*
J.C. PENNEY 3326	28	○	—	d,f	*B,M*
SUNBEAM 20190	31	○	E	—	*C*
PROCTOR-SILEX T522B	32	○	—	f	*B*
TOASTMASTER D182	32	○	E	b	*J*

FEATURES IN COMMON

All have 1-yr. repair or replacement warranty. *Except as noted,* 2-slice models draw $5^1/_2$ to 9 amps and 4-slice models draw 11 to 14 amps. *Except as noted, all have:* color-control lever on side of unit; slots to accommodate standard slices of supermarket bread; very hot exterior when in operation; easy-to-open crumb tray, but with at least 1 sharp edge; chrome finish; 25- to 29-in. cord.

KEY TO ADVANTAGES

A - Better than most when making consecutive batches of toast.
B - Better than most when making single slices of toast.
C - Produced full batch of toast faster than other four-slice toasters.
D - Single $8^1/_2$-in. slot will accommodate 1 long slice of bread or 2 standard-sized slices.
E - Elongated toaster with 2 $9^1/_2$-in. slots; each accommodates 1 long slice of bread or 2 standard-sized slices.
F - Toast slots of $5^3/_8$ in. will accommodate larger slices than most.
G - Holds bread up to $1^3/_8$ in. thick.
H - Lowers toast automatically.
I - Very clear markings on color control.
J - Color control very easy to use.
K - Separate controls for each pair of toast slots.
L - Very safe to move when still quite warm.
M - Fairly safe to move when still quite warm.
N - Cord must be unplugged from toaster before crumb trays can be removed.

KEY TO DISADVANTAGES

a - Toast was blotchy, ranging from white in some areas to dark brown in others.
b - Toast was consistently lighter on one side.
c - Produced batch of medium-brown toast more slowly than other two-slice toasters.
d - Color controls lack graduated markings.
e - Color control judged awkwardly placed.
f - Color control moved somewhat stiffly.
g - Toaster poorly balanced; pressure on push-down lever tended to topple the unit.
h - No crumb tray.
i - Latches on crumb tray difficult to open.

KEY TO COMMENTS

A - Square model; side-by-side slots.
B - Elongated model; end-to-end slots.
C - Rotary-knob color control.
D - Controls on front.
E - Has control to adjust width of slots.
F - Automatically adjusts width of slots.
G - Bakery switch for toaster pastries.
H - Hold-warm feature.
I - Eject button.
J - Cord about 3 ft. long.
K - Cord about 6 ft. long.
L - Length of cord varied with sample.
M - Painted finish.
N - Simulated wood panels on housing. **GE T88** has plastic exterior, others are chrome.
O - Draws $11^1/_2$ amps.
P - 2 of 4 samples were defective when purchased, but did not pose safety hazard.

Toaster ovens and toaster-oven/broilers

Condensed from CONSUMER REPORTS, March 1986

As every home chef well knows, there's considerable overlap among the functions of modern kitchen appliances. In addition to making toast, toaster ovens can heat frozen dinners, bake potatoes or a small meatloaf, warm rolls, and do many of the chores that a regular oven does, but of course on a smaller scale. Toaster-oven/broilers can do those baking chores and broil, too. Of the two types, toaster-oven/broilers are the more common; they account for 11 of the 13 models tested for this report.

PERFORMANCE. Despite the promise implicit in the names of these appliances, most people, it seems, prefer the old-fashioned toaster for bread. Our tests showed why. None of the toaster ovens and toaster-oven/broilers could toast a single slice of bread to an even, medium brown on both sides. For the most part, the bread came out evenly toasted on top and striped on bottom. Nearly all the regular pop-up toasters we've tested have done a better toasting job.

Our readers have told us that they use their toaster ovens and toaster-oven/broilers fairly often to bake potatoes and heat frozen entrees. We included those dishes in our baking tests, and we cooked hamburgers and steaks to see how well these appliances broil.

All models did a fine job with potatoes—nicely done inside, with a crispy skin. Most needed an hour to an hour and a quarter to bake a batch of four potatoes.

We heated chicken pot pies, which took about 40 minutes. The results were acceptable, although the pies didn't brown as evenly as they did in a conventional oven.

Only the two *Toastmaster* oven/broilers baked a cake that rose well, browned evenly, and had a light texture. Cake from the other models was blotchy and sometimes had a wavy-looking top, suggesting that it hadn't risen evenly.

All the broilers could handle six quarter-pound hamburgers at a time. And by and large, all did a good job. The burgers they produced were medium brown outside and rare to medium rare inside. But we could cook even better burgers, and quicker, in an aluminum skillet with a nonstick finish; they were crisp outside and nice and rare inside.

T-bone steaks that we cooked in the oven/broilers came out medium brown on the outside and rare to medium rare inside in about 14 to 20 minutes. The steaks were good, but they would have been better if the broilers had crisped the outside of the meat.

DESIGN. Toaster ovens and toaster-oven/broilers are small appliances meant for small jobs. Most occupy a space about 10 by 15 inches. The Ratings note the relative capacity of each model.

On most models, an easy-to-use temperature control activates the baking or broiling element; the *Black & Decker* and the *GE T93B* have a separate On/Off or Start switch. The controls are marked much like those on conventional ovens, in 25- or 50-degree increments. While those controls were convenient, they were less than precise. We had to fiddle to get the food to come out right, especially when baking.

Each oven has a toasting rack held by grooves or projections along the walls. All the racks except the one in the *GE T93B* can be removed. In six ovens the

Text continued on page 32

Ratings of toaster ovens and toaster-oven/broilers

Listed by types; within types, listed by groups in order of estimated overall quality; within groups, listed in order of increasing price. Prices are list; + indicates shipping is extra. Discounts are usually available.

⊜ ⊖ ○ ◒ ●

Better ⟷ Worse

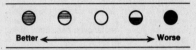

Brand and model	Price	Dimensions (HxWxD, in.)	Toasting performance	Capacity	Advantages	Disadvantages	Comments
Toaster-oven broilers							
PANASONIC NT850U	$58	8¼x16¾x10¼	○	○	A,C,I,L	a,d	E
GENERAL ELECTRIC T26	63	7½x15½x10	◒	○	D,G,L	—	E
BLACK & DECKER S02500 SPACEMAKER	123	9½x17x12	◒	⊜	G,H,K,M,Q	k	A,C
MUNSEY T85	60	7x13¼10¾	◒	○	F,H,J,K	i,k	—
J.C. PENNEY CAT. NO. 3857	60+	7¾x15¾x10½	◒	○	D	k	—
SEARS CAT. NO. 4822	60+	7¾x15¾x10¾	◒	○	B,D	h,k	—
PROCTOR-SILEX 0229B	67	7¾x15½x10½	◒	○	D	h,k	E
GENERAL ELECTRIC T50	70	7¾x15½x10	○	○	G,O	d	—
PROCTOR-SILEX 0234AL	82	7¾x15½x10¾	◒	○	D	k	—
TOASTMASTER 321	63	8½x15½x11½	◒	⊖	E,K,M,P	c,f,g,h,j,l,n	E
TOASTMASTER 330	73	8½x15½x11½	◒	⊖	E,K,M,P	c,f,g,h,j,l,n	—
Toaster ovens							
GENERAL ELECTRIC T104	55	7½x15½x10	○	○	G,I	d	E
GENERAL ELECTRIC T93B	52	7½x13¾x9	○	●	D,G,H, M,N,O	b,e,m	A,B,D,E

Keys to Ratings on next page

Ratings Keys for toaster ovens and toaster-oven broilers

FEATURES IN COMMON

All: have door with glass window that can become hot enough to cause burn; have at least 1-yr. repair or replacement warranty. *All broilers* were judged good at broiling.

Except as noted, all: are counter-top models; were judged fair at baking; have 1 removable toast rack; have 1 metal oven pan (with broiling rack insert on broilers); have crumb tray; hold at least 4 slices of bread; hold 8-in. round cake pan, 6-cupcake pan, or large frozen dinner; broil up to 6 hamburgers at a time; have light that indicates when oven is on; do not shut off heating elements automatically when door is opened; have continuous-clean interior.

KEY TO ADVANTAGES

A-60-min. timer initiates baking and broiling. Oven shuts off when time is up.
B-Holds 2 racks, but clearance between them is only $1^1/_4$ in. Has additional baking pan.
C-Oven pan judged sturdier than others.
D-Toast rack advances when door opens, improving access.
E-Oven pan easier to grasp than most.
F-Oven-on light judged very visible.
G-Elements shut off when door is opened.
H-Toaster and oven cannot operate at the same time.
I-Exterior stays cooler than that of others.
J-Nonstick interior; judged easiest to clean.
K-Door can be removed for cleaning.
L-Uses less energy than most when baking potatoes.
M-Full batch of toast fit easily.
N-Better than others at making dark toast.
O-Better than most at making consecutive batches of toast.
P-Made an excellent single-layer cake.
Q-Can also be installed under wall cabinet; comes with mounting hardware, which increases installed dimensions to $10^1/_4$x$17^1/_2$x$13^1/_2$ in.

KEY TO DISADVANTAGES

a-Full batch of toast is a very tight fit.
b-Nonremovable toast rack makes cleaning harder.
c-Toast rack lacks back guard.
d-Does not hold 8-in. round cake pan.
e-Does not hold 8-in. round cake pan, 6-cupcake pan, or medium-size frozen dinner.
f-Broiler insert was difficult to remove.
g-No crumb tray.
h-No oven-operating signal light.
i-No carrying handles.
j-Door fit poorly on some samples.
k-Toast sensor left white area on 1 toast slice.
l-Toast became lighter after third consecutive batch.
m-Baked poor cake (in loaf pan).
n-Baked potatoes more slowly than most.

KEY TO COMMENTS

A-Separate On/Off or Start switch.
B-Door opens and rack advances when toasting is done.
C-Holds 6 slices of bread.
D-Holds only 2 slices of bread.
E-Uncoated metal interior.

---

rack advances automatically when the door is opened.

The ovens draw between 10 and 13 $^1/_2$ amps. Using another appliance (particularly one that heats up, like an electric frying pan) on the same circuit could blow a fuse or trip a circuit breaker. But the cost in energy for using one of these appliances is measured in pennies. At average electricity rates, it would cost something like five to seven cents to bake a batch of potatoes—about the same as it would cost to bake them in a conventional oven.

RECOMMENDATIONS. Toaster-oven/broilers are more versatile than toaster ovens, and may cost no more, especially under the price-leveling influence of substantial discounts often offered for both types of appliance. In the top Ratings group, the *Panasonic* ($58 list) was the best toaster; it's well designed besides, and it stayed relatively cool on the outside while cooking. The *Black & Decker* oven/broiler (at $123, the most expensive model tested) was big enough to manage six slices of toast at a time. Yet it can be installed under a cabinet so that it takes up no counter space at all.

Clothes dryers

Condensed from CONSUMER REPORTS, May 1986

We've tested and rated 25 full-sized dryers, choosing in most cases the top-of-the-line model and, for big sellers, the next-to-the-top. We wanted to evaluate whether the frills added to costly dryers were worth the dollars you pay for them.

We tested 19 electric models and 6 gas dryers. Nine of these top-of-the-line models control the dryness of clothes loads through moisture-sensing. That's a more direct method than the technique of monitoring dryness by the temperature-sensing of a thermostat. It tends to be a slightly more accurate method, too.

PERFORMANCE. Clothes dryers have to handle a wide range of natural, synthetic, and blended fabrics, some of which can stand more heat than others. All-cotton shrink-resistant fabrics can usually tolerate the highest heat setting—180°F or more in some dryers. Permanent-press fabrics must be heated to at least 150° to release their wrinkles—but not to more than 180°. Delicate fabrics may be unable to tolerate temperatures higher than 140°, and rubberized items often can't take that much heat.

All the tested dryers offer two or three drying temperatures, besides an unheated Fluff or Air setting. With each model, we measured the temperature of the clothes inside the drum at every available temperature setting and with various-sized loads.

We loaded each machine with about 16½ pounds of wet cotton/polyester cloths, set it on its longest timed cycle and highest heat, and waited until the loads had lightened to their dry weight of 10½ pounds. That test told us not only how quickly each dryer worked, but also how much energy it used. All the electric models dried the test load in 25 to 30 minutes and used about 21 cents worth of electricity (at national average rates) doing it. The gas dryers took about the same amount of time, but used only about 6½ cents worth of energy.

If permanent-press items are at room temperature by the time a dryer stops tumbling, they're less likely to wrinkle, should they remain in the dryer for a while. In some dryers, the laundry remained too warm. We downrated those models.

Most models allow you to extend the period of cool tumbling beyond the end of the automatic dry cycle. Called "Press Guard," "Wrinkle Guard," or some such name, the feature extends the tumbling for anywhere from 15 minutes to 2½ hours, continuously in some machines and intermittently in others.

We used three test loads—one of mixed regular fabrics and two different-sized loads of permanent-press fabrics— to determine dryness range. Practically speaking, that's an indicator of the ability to provide totally dry as well as rather damp laundry. With one exception, the moisture-sensing models scored higher than the others in producing the desired dryness. Machines that scored poorly in this category weren't very good at leaving laundry slightly damp.

FEATURES. Instead of the familiar timer dial and switches found on most dryers, four models—two *Sears* and two *Whirlpools*—have electronic controls with "membrane" push buttons. Those controls may amaze, but they don't inform

Text continued on page 38

Ratings of clothes dryers

Listed by types; within types, listed in order of estimated quality. Differences in quality between closely ranked models were judged slight. Prices are the average quoted to CU shoppers in a 12-city survey for models with white finish.

◍ ◓ ○ ◒ ●

Better ⟷ Worse

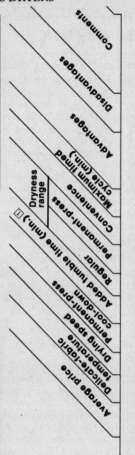

Brand and model	Average price	Delicate-fabric temperature	Drying speed	Permanent-press cool-down	Added tumble time (min.) [1]	Dryness range: Regular	Dryness range: Permanent-press	Convenience	Maximum timed cycle (min.)	Advantages	Disadvantages	Comments
Electric models												
SEARS KENMORE 65921	$402	◒	◓	◓	45	◓	◓	◍	50	A,C,E,F,G	—	*A,C,D*
SEARS KENMORE 62941	550	◒	◓	○	75	◓	◓	◍	80	C,D,E,F,G,H	a	*A,C,D,F,L,P*
WHIRLPOOL LE9805XP	478	○	◓	○	150	○	◓	◍	80	C,E,G	a	*A,C,D,F,H,P*
GENERAL ELECTRIC DDE9200G	412	◒	◓	◓	15	◓	○	◓	70	A,G,I	c,e,i	*B,G,H*
GENERAL ELECTRIC DDE8200G	397	○	◓	◓	20	◓	●	◓	70	A,I	c,e,i	*B,G,H*
HOTPOINT DLB2880D	379	◒	◓	○	50	◒	◓	◓	50	A,I	f,i	*B,G,H*
MONTGOMERY WARD 7635	368	○	◓	◍	20	●	◓	○	120	B	d,h,k	*B,K,Q*
AMANA TEA800	409	○	◓	○	20	◒	○	○	70	A,E	h,k	*I,J,Q*
SPEED QUEEN HE7003	393	○	◓	○	20	◒	○	○	70	A,E	h,k	*Q*
MAGIC CHEF YE20E4	329	○	◓	◍	60	◒	○	◒	120	E	d,h,k	*B,Q*
WHITE-WESTINGHOUSE DE800E	363	○	○	◍	45	●	◓	◒	60	A,I	e,j	—

FRIGIDAIRE DECIM	371	◒	⊖	○	75	◒	○	○	100	—	d,e,h	*B*
ADMIRAL DE20F8	372	○	⊖	⊜	60	⊖	●	◒	110	E	c,d,h,k	*B,Q*
KELVINATOR DEA900C	359	◒	⊖	◒	0	◒	⊖	○	100	—	b,g	*B,I*
NORGE DEF208	420	○	⊖	⊜	60	●	○	◒	110	E	c,d,h,k	*B,Q*
MAYTAG DE712	492	◒	⊖	⊜	40	◒	●	◒	60	G,H	—	*E,G,I,J,Q*
MAYTAG DE612	465	◒	⊖	○	30	●	○	◒	60	H	—	*E,G,J,Q*
GIBSON DE28A6WP	340	○	⊖	◒	0	◒	⊖	◒	90	—	b,e,g	*B,M*
WHIRLPOOL LE7805XP	394	◒	⊖	○	45	◒	●	◒	60	C	g	*A,C,D,F,H,N*
Gas models												
SEARS KENMORE 75921	437	◒	⊖	⊜	45	⊖	⊖	⊜	50	A,C,E,F,G	—	*A,C,D,F*
SEARS KENMORE 72941	595	◒	⊖	⊖	75	⊖	⊖	⊜	80	C,D,E,F,G,H	a	*A,C,D,F,L,P*
WHIRLPOOL LG9806XP	489	◒	⊖	⊖	150	⊖	⊖	⊜	80	E,G	a	*A,C,D,F,H,P*
GENERAL ELECTRIC DDG9280G	448	◒	⊖	⊖	20	○	⊜	⊖	70	A,G,I	e,i	*B,G,H*
HOTPOINT DLL2880D	397	◒	○	○	50	◒	○	⊖	50	A,I	f,i	*B,G,H*
WHIRLPOOL LG7806XP	424	◒	⊖	⊖	45	●	●	◒	60	C	g	*A,C,D,F,H,O*

[1] *At end of automatic permanent-press cycle.*

FEATURES IN COMMON
All have: automatic dryness-control cycle; safety-start switch (which may be incorporated in other console controls); no-heat (Air Fluff) setting; 4 leveling legs.
Except as noted, all have: 3 temperature settings; continuously adjustable timed cycle; rotary timer dial; satisfactory permanent-press cycle; automatic cycle at each temperature setting; end-of-cycle buzzer, beep, or bell, not adjustable for loudness; drum light; round drum opening; door that opens to right; venting from rear, side, or bottom; 1-yr. warranty on parts and labor.

KEY TO ADVANTAGES
A – Loudness of end-of-cycle signal is adjustable.
B – End-of-cycle signal can be turned off.
C – Signal indicates when lint filter is full.
D – Lighted dial.
E – Rack for drying items without tumbling.
F – Rack for holding hangers.
G – Moisture sensor.
H – Porcelain top.
I – Porcelain drum.

KEY TO DISADVANTAGES
a – Cycle not continuously adjustable.
b – No added tumble time.
c – Drying temperature somewhat low with large permenent-press loads.
d – Cycle-selector dial turns only 1 way.
e – Drying temperature very high with regular load (but O.K. at lower setting).
f – Drying temperature somewhat high with regular load (but O.K. at lower setting).
g – No drum light.
h – Drum light is fairly dim.
i – Lint filter may fall out when laundry is unloaded.

Keys to Ratings continued on next page

Keys to Ratings of clothes dryers continued

j-Lint filter secured by 2 screws; awkward to clean while in place.
k-Lint filter can be put in improperly, preventing door from closing.

KEY TO COMMENTS

A-During added tumble, drum turns for about 10 sec. every 5 min.
B-Semicircular door opening.
C-Lint filter accessible from top.
D-Door opens down.
E-Door opens to left.
F-Vents from rear only.
G-Vents from rear, left, or bottom.
H-Manufacturer offers special help for do-it-yourself repairs.
I-2-yr. parts warranty.
J-5-yr. warranty against rust on certain parts.
K-30-day parts-and-labor warranty on defective porcelain parts.
L-5-yr. warranty on parts and labor and against rust.
M-Has been replaced by essentially similar model **DE28A6WS.**
N-Has been replaced by model **LE7810XP,** essentially similar except for interior finish.
O-Has been replaced by model **LE7811XP,** essentially similar except for interior finish.
P-Electronic controls.
Q-2 temperature settings.

Clothes-dryer features compared

Charted below are key features of tested and similar models. Prices given here are approximate list. See the Ratings for the actual prices of tested models, which are indicated here by a dot (•).

Brand and model	Price	Moisture sensor	Electronic controls	No. of temperatures	Drum light	Porcelain top	Porcelain drum
Electric models							
ADMIRAL DE20F5	$400	—	—	2	—	—	—
• DE20F8	430	—	—	2	✓	—	—
AMANA TEA600	369	—	—	2	—	—	—
• TEA800	389	—	—	2	✓	—	—
FRIGIDAIRE DEIM	326	—	—	3	—	—	—
• DECIM	384	—	—	3	✓	—	—
GENERAL ELECTRIC							
• DDE8200G	411	—	—	3	✓	—	✓
• DDE9200G	434	✓	—	3	✓	—	✓
GIBSON • DE28A6WP [1]	330	—	—	3	—	—	—
HOTPOINT • DLB2880D	394	—	—	3	✓	—	✓
KELVINATOR • DEA900C	331	—	—	3	—	—	—
MAGIC CHEF • YE20E4	450	—	—	2	✓	—	—

Brand and model	Price	Moisture sensor	Electronic controls	No. of temperatures	Drum light	Porcelain top	Porcelain drum
MAYTAG DE412	$420	—	—	2	—	✔	—
DE512	430	—	—	2	—	✔	—
• DE612	460	—	—	2	✔	✔	—
• DE712	490	✔	—	2	✔	✔	—
NORGE DEF204	400	—	—	2	—	—	—
• DEF208	430	—	—	2	✔	—	—
SEARS KENMORE 65811	380	✔	—	2	—	—	—
65831	440	✔	—	2	✔	—	—
• 65921	480	✔	—	3	✔	—	—
• 62941	600	✔	✔	3	✔	✔	—
SPEED QUEEN HE5003	379	—	—	2	—	—	—
HE6003	399	—	—	2	—	—	—
• HE7003	419	—	—	2	✔	—	—
MONTGOMERY WARD 7435	420	—	—	2	—	—	—
• 7635	450	—	—	2	✔	—	—
7835	490	—	—	2	✔	—	—
WHIRLPOOL • LE7805XP [1]	379	—	—	3	—	—	—
• LE9805XP	449	✔	✔	3	✔	—	—
WHITE-WESTINGHOUSE							
DE700E	320	—	—	3	—	—	✔
• DE800E	367	—	—	3	✔	—	✔
Gas models							
GENERAL ELECTRIC							
DDG8280G	464	—	—	3	✔	—	✔
• DDG9280G	474	✔	—	3	✔	—	✔
HOTPOINT • DLL2880D	451	—	—	3	✔	—	✔
SEARS KENMORE 75811	420	✔	—	2	—	—	—
75831	480	✔	—	2	✔	—	—
• 75921	520	✔	—	3	✔	—	—
• 72941	640	✔	✔	3	✔	✔	—
WHIRLPOOL • LG7806XP	419	—	—	3	—	—	—
• LG9806XP [1]	489	✔	✔	3	✔	—	—

[1] *See Ratings Comments for change in model designation.*

very well. They don't tell, for example, how far into a cycle the dryer has progressed, as the position of a rotary knob would. And they don't give a continuously variable choice of lengths to timed cycles, as the turning of a rotary knob does. The *Whirlpools* give you a choice of 20, 30, 60, or 80 minutes—nothing in between. The *Sears* models offer still fewer choices.

Although no tested machine has more than three drying temperatures, some models pretend to have more. The *Amana* and the *Speed Queen* electric models, for example, show settings labeled Heavy, Normal, Permanent Press, and Delicate. But Heavy is the same temperature as Normal, and Permanent Press is the same as Delicate. Similarly, the *Sears 62941* and *72941* have nine temperature buttons but only three different temperatures.

RECOMMENDATIONS. If natural gas is available to you, we suggest that you buy a gas-heated dryer rather than an electric one—especially if the gas lines are already in place from a previous installation. Operating costs for the gas models are about a third as high as those for the electrics. Yet the performance of the high-rated gas and electric models was nearly identical. Gas versions may cost more initially, perhaps $50 or so, but they should soon make up that difference in energy savings.

Heading our Ratings lists of both electric and gas clothes dryers are two *Sears Kenmore* models followed by a *Whirlpool* model. All six are moisture-sensing models, which would seem to be a plus. And four have electronic push-button controls instead of rotary mechanical dials, which is a drawback to the extent that you can't dial "in-between" settings. Though we did prefer the cheaper of the two *Sears* models we tested, we can't say that even-cheaper brandmates would perform as well since they have only two drying temperatures instead of three. We much preferred the more expensive *Whirlpool* and *General Electric* clothes dryers with their moisture sensors.

Among other models, as the features table shows, cheaper variants share major components—drums, motors, and types of controls—with the tested models. They just have fewer features.

Washing machines

Condensed from CONSUMER REPORTS, June 1985 and August 1986

Still widely available—and therefore, for our purposes, still ratable—are nine large-tub, top-of-the-line washers tested for our June 1985 report. Seven are top-loaders; two are front-loaders.

(General Electric replaced the models we originally tested and now offer two widely advertised *Spotscrubber* washing machines, which have a "mini-basket" accessory that fits over the agitator and a special spot-removing wash cycle in which the mini-basket is used. We tested the higher-priced version, model *WWA8600G*, which lists at $479, and got good but not great results from that feature. Because we weren't geared up for testing that *GE* model further, we haven't rated it. But if it's like the last *GE* washer that we tested fully, it should do regular laundry just fine).

The models with the greatest capacity turned out to be top-loaders, some of which could hold as much as 16 pounds of mixed, dry laundry. That was about half again as much as either front-loader held. (Note, though, that our judgments of capacity are based on tub volume. And since laundry varies considerably by size and weight, our determinations of capacity can be considered no better than rough estimates.)

Lots of bells and whistles distinguish these expensive models from some cheaper ones. But the important features are those affecting performance: wash cycles, wash and spin speeds, water temperatures, and water levels.

The wash cycle can be either regular, permanent-press, delicate, or knit. Permanent-press cycles are usually slightly shorter than regular cycles and have a slower spin speed and a cool-down phase to minimize wrinkles. A typical regular or permanent-press cycle takes approximately 40 minutes. A typical delicate cycle takes approximately 30 minutes.

Speed controls, separate or incorporated as part of the cycle selector, are to be found on the typical top-loader. They allow for gentler handling of delicate fabrics and slower spinning of permanent-press fabrics. Front-loaders don't offer multiple speeds; they run at a slow speed for wash and a higher speed for spin.

A water-level control is important. By letting you adjust the level of water to the size of the wash load, it enables you to save water, detergent, and energy. All the rated models have such a control that can be preset over a continuous range of fill.

PERFORMANCE. The front-loading machines conserved water best. Fully filled, a front-loader used 25 to 30 gallons. Top-loaders used anywhere from 40 to 57 gallons. Since the top-loaders hold as much as 50 percent more laundry than the front-loaders, we compared gallons used with laundry done to arrive at our water-efficiency judgments. But even by that reckoning, the front-loaders were still the more water-efficient washing machines.

The Ratings scores for hot-water efficiency indicate the relative cost of operating the machines. (The greatest cost of running a washing machine is the cost of heating the water it uses; the cost of electricity to run the motor is negligible.) Again, the front-loaders showed themselves to be more efficient—by significant amounts.

Only the *White-Westinghouse* models and the *Wards* coped well with unbalanced loads. Most machines vibrated in complaint. Some protested by banging the tub against the outer cabinet. The *Sears* was overly sensitive; it shut down under only a moderate load.

The amount of water left in the clothes after they're spun out determines drying time, whether in a dryer or on a clothesline. The best models in this respect left about five pounds of water in our test load; the worst left about seven pounds of water.

FEATURES. The washer controls are usually centered on a conventional rotary dial. Most models prevent movement of the dial forward while the machine is running to save needless wear on the components. The *Whirlpool* boasts an electronic touch panel, which we judged well thought out but of no certain advantage over a dial.

Some models have a prewash feature that provides an extra period of agitation. Most also have a soak cycle for dealing with heavily soiled clothes. The *White-Westinghouse* models are equipped with a crude built-in scale for weighing laundry.

Most of the washers minimize the risk of tangling hands with the spinning tub by halting the spin within a few seconds after the lid is opened. The *Maytag* was the slowest; it took five seconds to stop. Some washers reduce the risk instead

Text continued on page 42

Ratings of washing machines

Listed by types; within types, listed in order of estimated quality.

Prices are list. Discounts may be available.

◍	⊖	○	◒	●
Better ←				→ Worse

Brand and model	Price	Water efficiency [1]: Total, regular cycle	Water efficiency [1]: Total, perm. press	Water efficiency [1]: Hot, all cycles	Unbalanced-load handling	Capacity	Water extraction	Linting	Noise	Brand Frequency of Repair	Advantages	Disadvantages	Comments
Top-loaders													
MAYTAG A712	$609	⊖	○	⊖	○	◍	○	⊖	◍	◍	A,B,D,K,O	g	*A,C,D,E*
WHIRLPOOL LA9800XP	569	⊖	⊖	⊖	○	◍	◒	○	⊖	⊖	A,M	f	*A,D,K,M, N,P*
SEARS 23921	599	⊖	⊖	⊖	◒	◍	◒	⊖	⊖	⊖	A,I,K,L,M	d,h	*A,D,E, F,K,M*
GIBSON WA28D7WP	454	○	◒	○	○	⊖	○	⊖	○	[2]	F,H,J,O	d	*D,I,L*
SPEED QUEEN HA7001	499	○	◒	⊖	○	○	○	○	○	●	A,D,G,J,O	b	*M*
HOTPOINT WLW5700B	474	◒	○	○	◒	⊖	○	○	⊖	⊖	D	e	*C,J,K,M,P*
WHITE-WESTINGHOUSE LA800E	569	●	●	◒	⊖	◒	●	◒	○	○	F,J,M,N	c,i	*B,D,G,J*

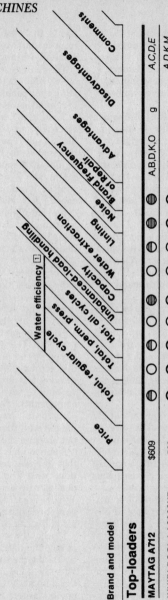

Front-loaders

WHITE-WESTINGHOUSE LT800E	739	◍	◍	◍	⊖	●	◒	⊖	◍	◒	C,E,F,M,N,O	a,h,i,j,k	*C,D,G,H,M*
WARDS 6514 [1]	690	◍	◍	◍	⊖	●	◒	⊖	◍	◒	C,E,F,O	a,i,k	*A,C,G,H,I, L,M,O*

[1] *Measured at maximum fill.* [2] *Insufficient data.*

FEATURES IN COMMON

All have: continuously variable water-level control; occupy floor space of, at most, 29 in. (width) by 28 in. (depth).

Except as noted, all have: automatic agitation/spin speed settings for regular (normal/normal), permanent press (normal/slow), delicate (slow/slow), and knit (slow/normal) cycles; 40-45 min. regular cycle; 35-45 min. permanent-press cycle; 5 wash/rinse temperature options (hot/cold, warm/cold, cold/cold, hot/warm, and warm/warm); safety switch that stops spin action only; timer that cannot be rotated when machine is on; bleach dispenser (for wash); softener dispenser (for rinse); lint filter that needs periodic cleaning; finish of porcelain enamel on top, lid, and tub; baked-enamel finish on rest of cabinet.

PERFORMANCE NOTES

Excepted as noted, all were judged average in handling permanent-press clothes for line drying, and average in sand disposal.

KEY TO ADVANTAGES

A – Better than average in handling permanent-press clothes for line drying.
B – Motor uses less electricity than most.
C – Safety switch stops all action.
D – Safety switch stops agitation and spin.
E – Better than average in sand disposal.
F – Lid or door locks during spin.
G – Stainless-steel tub.
H – Plastic tub.
I – Water-temperature selection is manual or automatic.
J – Washer speed and temperature combinations can be set independently.
K – 1 cycle has automatic second rinse.
L – Top-mounted dispensers for detergent, bleach, and softener.
M – Prewash setting.
N – Built-in weighing scale.
O – Allows front access for repairs.

KEY TO DISADVANTAGES

a – Range of fill controls very narrow.
b – Range of fill controls fairly narrow.
c – Worse than average in sand disposal.
d – Timer can be rotated forward with machine on, causing component wear.
e – Changing cycle speed with machine on may cause damage.
f – No speed setting for knit cycle (slow agitation, normal spin).
g – Tub took longer to stop than others when lid was opened during spin.
h – Open lid does not lie flat; access from left is hampered.
i – Low-sudsing detergent may be required.
j – Top has intrusive projections.
k – Painted finish on top; easily scratched.

KEY TO COMMENTS

A – Regular cycle shorter than most.
B – Regular cycle longer than most.
C – Permanent-press cycle shorter than most.
D – Timed-soak option.
E – Timed-soak option; can advance automatically to regular wash cycle.
F – Split agitator, with top and bottom sections moving independently.
G – No hot/warm temperature option (and none really needed, in CU's judgment).
H – No choice of speeds; same speed for all washing, and higher speed for spin.
I – No bleach dispenser.
J – Separate agitator for small loads or gentle action.
K – Extra-rinse cycle option.
L – No softener dispenser.
M – "Self-cleaning" lint filter; convenient, but lint discharged into drain may lead to blockages.
N – Electronic touch-panel controls; well thought out, but not necessarily advantageous.
O – Stackable model; requires top (painted top approx. $20 extra) to be free-standing.
P – Manufacturer offers toll-free number for do-it-yourself repair information.

by locking the door or lid during spin or by stopping agitation if the door or lid is opened.

RECOMMENDATIONS. If conserving water or energy is a primary concern, choose a front-loader. If, however, you're more interested in coping with any size of laundry in the fewest possible steps, choose a top-loader. Models of that type can hold more than front-loaders and still adjust to smaller loads.

Another consideration should be a brand's reliability. According to our Frequency-of-Repair data, *Maytag* models have been the most trouble-free washers. The records of other brands on which we have sufficient information are noted in the Ratings.

If you're willing to sacrifice a few features, you may be able to get the repair record and the performance offered by some brands for less money. Though not quite as fancy as the top-loaders in the Ratings, the following models (with list prices in parentheses) should perform about as well as their respective brandmates: *Maytag A612* ($575), *Whirlpool LA5800XP* ($459) and *LA7800XP* ($469), *Sears 23801* ($520), *Gibson WA28D5WS* ($439), *Speed Queen HA6001* ($469), *Hotpoint WLW3700B* ($434) and *WLW4700B* ($454), and *White-Westinghouse LA600E* ($469) and *LA700E* ($499). Similarly, two cheaper alternatives to the front-loading *White-Westinghouse LT800E* are models *LT600E* ($639) and *LT700E* ($699).

Laundry bleaches

Condensed from CONSUMER REPORTS, August 1985

Liquid chlorine bleach has an established position in the laundry room, bathroom, and kitchen for whitening, disinfecting, and removing stains and mildew. But, when used improperly, chlorine bleach can cause faded splotches, frayed fabrics, and dissolved stitching. Excessive use may slow down natural decomposition of sewage in a septic tank.

Both chlorine and nonchlorine bleaches use an oxidizing agent (usually sodium hypochlorite or sodium perborate) that reacts with the help of a detergent to lift out a stain. Our laboratory analysis of the liquid chlorine bleaches we bought showed that they all had about the same amount of active ingredient and that there was little difference from brand to brand.

PERFORMANCE. To prepare for our whitening tests, we stained white nylon fabric by washing swatches with brand-new blue denim, and we soaked fabrics of nylon and cotton/polyester in tea. Chlorine bleach whitened best, removing nearly all traces of the indigo (the dye in denim) and tea stains. Except on grease stains, the all-fabric powdered bleaches didn't do nearly as well. The all-fabric liquid bleaches whitened scarcely better than detergent alone.

We ran the wash loads four times with each of the bleaches. We tried them in hot water (140°F) instead of the warm water (100°) we had been using. Some of those recourses—including doubling the dose of dry bleaches—improved the whitening performance of the better all-fabric products considerably, but not to the point where they equalled that of a single dose of chlorine bleach.

Text continued on page 44

Ratings of laundry bleaches

Listed by types; within types, listed in order of bleaching ability. Bracketed products were judged equal; listed alphabetically. Prices are the average of those paid by CU shoppers.

Excellent | Very good | Good | Fair | Poor

Product	Size (fl. oz. or oz.)	Price	Cost per use	Whitening	Wine stains	Oil stains	Blood stains
Liquid chlorine bleaches							
■ *The following 2 brands rated are the chlorine bleaches that were actually wash-tested by CU, but, since there are no real differences among brands, judgments apply to 12 other liquid chlorine bleaches that CU bought and tested; Acme, Alpha Beta, A & P, Bright, Cost Cutter, Econo Buy, Grand Union, Hilex, Lady Lee, P & Q, Pathmark, and White Magic.*							
Clorox	64	$ .94	6¢	Excellent	Fair	Poor	Very good
Purex	64	.91	6	Excellent	Fair	Poor	Very good
Powdered all-fabric bleaches							
Clorox 2	40	1.79	20	Good	Very good	Very good	Very good
Lady Lee	61	1.51	9	Good	Good	Very good	Good
Alpha Beta	61	1.61	12	Good	Good	Good	Good
P & Q	40	.87	11	Good	Good	Very good	Good
Bright	40	1.29	14	Good	Good	Good	Very good
Purex	40	1.34	15	Good	Good	Good	Very good
Acme	40	.99	11	Good	Fair	Good	Very good
White Magic	40	1.51	17	Good	Good	Very good	Fair
A & P	40	1.17	13	Good	Good	Good	Good
Cost Cutter	61	1.39	9	Good	Good	Good	Very good
Scotch Buy	40	1.59	16	Good	Good	Good	Fair
Biz	30	2.77	23	Good	Good	Poor	Very good
Econo Buy	61	1.45	12	Good	Poor	Fair	Fair
Climalene	55	1.59	12	Fair	Good	Good	Fair
Snowy	40	2.94	13	Fair	Fair	Poor	Good
Borateem	40	1.77	16	Poor	Fair	Poor	Good
Liquid all-fabric bleaches							
Snowy	64	2.24	14	Poor	Poor	Poor	Fair
Vivid	64	2.31	14	Poor	Poor	Poor	Fair

To prepare for our tests for stain removal, we daubed four infamous stains—spaghetti sauce, red wine, motor oil, and blood—onto swatches of nylon knit, a notorious stain-holding fabric. None of the bleaches, chlorine or nonchlorine, could completely remove spaghetti sauce.

To measure color loss, we repeatedly washed and bleached a bright cotton print. Initially, none of the bleaches had a noticeable effect on the brightness of the colors. After four washings, however, the chlorine began taking its toll. Slight fading became evident and then, after eight washings, objectionable. On the other hand, even after 13 washings with all-fabric bleach, the print remained bright.

Another concern with chlorine bleach is its tendency to weaken a fabric. But after 13 chlorine-bleach washings, swatches of cotton—a fabric that's more likely to degrade than a synthetic—showed no significant loss of fiber strength. Nevertheless, we advise against washing with a chlorine bleach repeatedly and routinely.

RECOMMENDATIONS. Chlorine bleach, when used properly, is still the most effective way to whiten clothes, including many synthetics.

The all-fabric powdered bleaches have the advantage of being safe with most fabrics and dyes, even over the long term. The highest-rated ones are fairly effective at removing greasy stains.

Waffle makers

Condensed from CONSUMER REPORTS, July 1985

Appliance manufacturers recognize the preferences of two populations of waffle lovers: traditionalists who favor a waffle with smallish indentations; and others who favor the Belgian waffle, with its larger, deeper indentations. We too recognized those preferences in our selection and tests of 18 waffle makers: 11 make traditional waffles; 7 make Belgian waffles.

Most of the traditional-waffle makers have multipurpose grids. Some grids can be flipped to provide a flat surface for grilling sandwiches or hamburgers; some have a round, patterned surface on the flip side, used for baking the kind of wafer cookies known as pizzelles.

PERFORMANCE. As a group, the traditional-waffle makers did the best job. The best of the Belgian-waffle makers also made very good waffles. Most models needed about half an hour, from preheat to finish, to make six waffles.

Text continued on page 46

Ratings of waffle makers

Listed by types; within types, listed in order of estimated overall quality. Bracketed models were judged approximately equal in quality and are listed in order of increasing price. Except as noted, prices are list; * indicates approx. price; + indicates shipping is extra. Discounts are generally available. [D] indicates model has been discontinued.

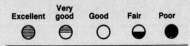

Excellent	Very good	Good	Fair	Poor
⊜	⊖	○	◒	●

Brand and model	Price	Size of waffle grills (in.)	Performance [1]	Extra functions [2]	Advantages	Disadvantages
Traditional-waffle makers						
GENERAL ELECTRIC G48T	$53	8x8	⊜	G	A,B,C,H,I	—
TOASTMASTER 269	67	9x9	⊜	G	B,C,G,L,N	n
BROIL KING 785	70	9¼x5½	⊜	G,P,S	B,C,D,F,K	a,d,h
BROIL KING 736	60	9x9	⊖	G	B,C,N	a,n
RIVAL 9705	60	9x5¼	⊖	P	A,D	l
TOASTMASTER W252	34	7dia.	⊜	—	A,G	i,m,o,p
MUNSEY WC-1	33*	8x8	◒	—	A	c,g,k,o,p
Not acceptable						
■ *The following models were judged Not Acceptable because lid handles do not protect user adequately from burns.*						
TOASTMASTER 270	54	8x8	⊖	G	B,C,H,I	e,j
[D] SEARS Cat. No. 48238	44+	8x8	⊖	P	E,H,I	e,j,p
TOASTMASTER 290	58	8x8	⊖	P	E,H,I	e,j,p
[D] SEARS Cat. No. 64778	42+	8x8	◒	G	B,C,H,I	e,j
Belgian-waffle makers						
[D] SEARS Cat. No. 64861	25+	7¼ dia.	⊖	—	—	b,i,m,o,p
J.C. PENNEY Cat. No. 4616	35+	7¼ dia.	⊖	—	—	b,i,m,o,p
TOASTMASTER 250	37	7¼ dia.	⊖	—	—	b,i,m,o,p
BROIL KING 780	50	9x4¾	○	—	A,J	o
RIVAL 9710	60	9¼x5½	○	—	P	f,l
OSTER 712-06	46	8¼x4	◒	—	A,H,M,O	f,o,p
MUNSEY BW-2	26*	5¾x5¾	◒ [3]	—	—	b,c,f,g,k, o,p

[1] *Based on 6 consecutive batches of medium-brown waffles, which usually took 30 min. for preheating and baking.*

[2] *G = Grill with range of temperature settings. P = Pizzelles. S = Sandwich maker.*

[3] *Performance improved to ○ when making dark brown, crisp waffles.*

Keys to Ratings on next page

FEATURES IN COMMON
All have plastic feet or stands and non-stick-coated grids.

KEY TO ADVANTAGES
A - Faster than most.
B - Hamburgers cooked with grill closed judged excellent or very good; those cooked on open grill judged good.
C - Grilled-cheese sandwiches cooked on open grill judged excellent; those cooked on closed grill judged good.
D - Pizzelles judged very good.
E - Pizzelles judged good.
F - Makes 2 filled, divided sandwiches per batch; judged very good.
G - On/off control.
H - Easy-to-see light indicates when unit is hot enough to begin cooking.
I - Light indicates when waffles are cooked to specified degree.
J - Large, effective overflow rim.
K - Long plastic lid handle provides excellent protection against burns.
L - Plastic lid handle provides very good protection against burns.
M - Luggage-like lid handle provides very good protection against burns and safe, easy way to carry unit after cooking.
N - Plastic carrying handles judged very safe for carrying unit even when it's still warm.
O - Rubber inserts in feet for extra stability.
P - Only Belgian-waffle maker with removable grids for easy cleaning.

KEY TO DISADVANTAGES
a - Slower than most.
b - Waffle grid is not sectioned for serving-sized portions.
c - Lacks signal light to indicate when unit is hot enough for cooking.
d - Controls are relatively inaccessible.
e - Small overflow rim.
f - No overflow rim.
g - Lid handle provides less protection from burns than most.
h - Lid handle doubles as carrying handle and, as such, is awkward to use.
i - Plastic carrying handles become hot during cooking; must be allowed to cool before carrying unit.
j - Fairly narrow carrying handles provide little protection against burns.
k - Very narrow carrying handles provide minimal protection against burns.
l - No carrying handles.
m - Easily tipped when lid is raised.
n - Grids somewhat difficult to remove and replace.
o - Grids cannot be removed for cleaning.
p - Lid does not open flat for cleaning.

Many models have a browning control and a signal light. But browning, we found, could best be controlled by turning to the darkest setting and timing for the desired degree of doneness accordingly. It's usually necessary to time the waffles anyway. With most models, the signal light indicated only that the waffle maker had come up to temperature, and was ready to cook, not that the waffles were cooked.

The waffle makers that double as grills can be used two ways: open flat with the lid and the base used as grilling surfaces; or closed, so both sides of the food are cooked at the same time. The first side of hamburgers cooked on the open grills came out nicely browned, but the second side hardly browned at all. Inside, the meat wasn't very evenly cooked. Hamburgers that we cooked in the closed grills came out much better—nicely browned outside and rare or medium-rare inside.

Grilled-cheese sandwiches came out better when we cooked them on the open grills. Closing the lid compressed the sandwiches so that the cheese oozed out.

SAFETY. The plastic handle used to open and close a waffle maker's lid during cooking should be large enough to provide a good grip, so that your fingers won't touch a surface that can reach nearly 300°F. The handle should also be designed to shield fingers from escaping steam. Most handles were well enough designed to do an adequate job on both counts.

But the lid handle of the four models judged Not Acceptable has too narrow a grasping area. One's instinctive tendency is to reach for the top of the handle and, in doing so, touch the hot metal lid of the waffle maker. In addition, the handle doesn't protrude far enough, so fingers can easily be burned by escaping steam.

Kitchen knives

Condensed from CONSUMER REPORTS, November 1983

For many years, carbon steel was believed to be the best material for knife blades because it sharpens easily and well. But it darkens and stains with use, and, if not thoroughly dried right after washing, it rusts. Stainless steel, although it rarely loses its good looks, is harder to sharpen and keep sharp.

Today, most blades are made of a steel that manufacturers call high-carbon stainless (or no-stain) steel. It's said to combine the sharpness of carbon steel with the easy care of stainless. Knives with blades of high-carbon stainless can be obtained that are very high in quality.

Knife blades can be made in a number of different cross-section configurations. The common configurations include fully tapered, partially tapered, and hollow ground. But the taper of a knife blade provides little information about how a knife will perform. Modern manufacturing techniques make it possible to achieve equally fine edges on blades of different configurations.

The secret of good performance is, rather, in the angle of the cutting edge. On most kitchen knives, the angle ranges from about 35 degrees to about 60 degrees. In use, a narrow angle is generally perceived as sharper than a wide one. A narrow angle is desirable for slicing meat, vegetables, and the like. A sturdier, wider angle is generally more appropriate for chopping chores.

The cutting edge on most knives is angled on both sides, so the knives can be used with equal ease on either side. If a knife is angled on only one side, the blade may tend to work outward or inward during slicing, producing uneven slices.

Serrated blades are useful primarily for slicing foods that have a relatively hard surface and soft interior, such as bread and tomatoes. Cooks who don't want to be bothered with sharpening their knives may prefer a serrated blade for many chores.

In addition to the cutting edge, the handle should also be taken into account when buying a knife. The handle should be generously sized to fit the hand and leave clearance beneath the handle for chopping purposes. A metal extension of the knife blade, called a tang, attaches a knife blade to its handle. On high-quality knives, this metal extension runs the full length of the knife's handle, and generally insures a strong blade-to-handle assembly and provides some balance as well.

CHEF'S KNIVES. The best chef's knives are hefty, with good balance, and generous, comfortable handles with ample clearance beneath them. A slight curve of the blade on all the tested chef's knives make them well suited for the rocking-chopping motion that many experienced cooks use to chop onions and such.

PARING KNIVES. For little jobs that require precision—removing potatoes' eyes, making radish flowers, trimming strawberries—a paring knive is the tool of choice. Paring knives come in a variety of shapes, but the shape of the blade didn't seem to matter as much as its length. Consumers Union's testers generally preferred models with 3-inch blades to those with 3½ or 4-inch blades.

SLICING KNIVES. These are the long knives of kitchen cutting—generally, the longer, the better. Most have a pointed tip on the blade, which is handy for cutting around bones.

UTILITY KNIVES. For odd jobs, when a chef's knife seems too large and a paring knife too small, a utility knife is called for. It should be able to dice, chop, slice, and pare. And it should be as effective on meat and hard vegetables as it is on soft bread and tomatoes.

RECOMMENDATIONS. Good knives can be expensive. However, cheaper lines can perform well enough for most home uses. Note also that knives don't have to be purchased in matching sets. There's nothing to prevent you from selecting different types of knives from different brand lines, whether you're shopping for one knife or several.

Ratings of kitchen knives

Listed by brand and line in order of estimated overall quality. Overall brand Rating is based on the compiled scores of the individual knives, with emphasis on chef's and paring knives. Differences between closely ranked models were slight. Prices are suggested retail, rounded to nearest dollar; * means price is approximate; discounts are often available.

Excellent	Very good	Good	Fair	Poor
⊜	⊖	○	◒	●

Brand and line	Overall Rating
✔GERBER BALANCE PLUS	Excellent
CHICAGO CUTLERY PLUS THREE	Very good
CHICAGO CUTLERY WALNUT A Best Buy	Very good
J.A. HENCKELS FOUR STAR	Very good
IMPERIAL MIGHTY OAK	Very good
J.A. HENCKELS PROFESSIONAL	Very good
WUSTHOF-TRIDENT FORGED STAINLESS	Very good
HOFFRITZ TOP OF THE LINE	Very good
HOFFRITZ SABATIER	Good
J.A. HENCKELS SUPERFECTION	Good
CASE OLD FORGE	Good
CARVEL HALL COSMOPOLITAN	Good
IMPERIAL THE PROFESSIONALS	Good
WILKINSON SWORD SELF-SHARPENING	Good
WASHINGTON FORGE FORGECRAFT HI-CARBON	Good
EKCO FORGE	Good
CARVEL HALL CITATION	Good
GINSU II	Fair
WASHINGTON FORGE FORGECRAFT	Fair
EKCO 29000	Fair

For the full story

The date of the original article in CONSUMER REPORTS appears directly below its title. For a more complete report, consult the original version. (For back issues, see page 5.)

Meat thermometers

Condensed from Consumer Reports, March 1985

Most meat thermometers are basically dials mounted on a metal stem. Within the stem is a twisted strip of two different metals, bonded together and connected to a pointer on the dial. When heated, each metal expands at a different rate, causing the dial's pointer to rotate.

A few models are essentially glass tubes containing liquid that expands as it heats. The level of that liquid is read against a temperature scale.

A "professional," or "chef's," model needs to be inserted only momentarily in meat to check its temperature. A "regular" thermometer should be left in place as long as the meat remains in the oven.

Dial thermometers have certain advantages over tube models. They're more durable, and they're easier to use. Glass-tube models generally can't be inserted into the meat without first making a pilot hole, lest the tube break. (Most tube models provide a skewer for that purpose.)

Ratings of meat thermometers

Listed by types; within types, listed in order of estimated overall quality. Prices are list. D indicates model was discontinued at original publication.

Regular models

The following models were the most accurate regular thermometers tested.

TEL-TRU BP40, TAYLOR 5939 [1], ACU-RITE 00670, TEL-TRU RM36.

The following models were less accurate than the ones above.

COOPER 323, SPRINGFIELD 303, TAYLOR 5937 [1], D OHIO 4631, ACU-RITE 00762.

The following models were the least accurate regular thermometers tested.

SPRINGFIELD 613, TRU-TEMP 290, TRU-TEMP 121, D OHIO 4632.

Professional models (All were accurate)

COOPER MICRO-THERM 2236, TEL-TRU MT39R, CUISINART BA711, TAYLOR 6081 PROFESSIONAL [1], SPRINGFIELD 813, H-B 21105, TAYLOR 5982 [1].

[1] *A later designation is* **Sybron/Taylor**.

Kitchen scales

Condensed from CONSUMER REPORTS, August 1984

Dieters are instructed to use a scale so that calorie intake can be monitored closely, but a kitchen scale can be handy for ordinary cooking, too.

ACCURACY. Nearly two-thirds of the tested models were judged very accurate; they erred by less than a half-ounce over their entire weight range.

CONVENIENCE. The digital scales were very quick and easy to read. With some nondigital models, clearly identifiable weight graduations—neither too few nor too many, and properly spaced—made it easy to get precise readings.

RECOMMENDATIONS. Undoubtedly, the best scales in our tests—highly accurate and legible to small fractions of an ounce—were three digital models; the small-capacity *American Family Tanita Electronic 3500* and *Hoan Electronic 21200* (later designated *213200*), and the medium-capacity *Soehnle Digita S 8003*. But they were priced at $80 to $90.

Many of the other tested scales, at a third to a tenth of those prices, would be almost as useful—if not as convenient—for most kitchen and diet purposes. If you need a larger-capacity scale, the balance-beam *Terraillon T565*, at $48, is worth considering; it was quite accurate.

Ratings of kitchen scales

Listed by groups according to capacity; within groups, listed in order of estimated overall quality. Models in parentheses were judged approximately equal in overall quality and are listed alphabetically. Prices are suggested retail; + indicates shipping is extra.

Small-capacity (up to 2 lb.)

(✓ **AMERICAN FAMILY TANITA ELECTRONIC COOKING/DIET 3500,** $80; ✓ **HOAN ELECTRONIC DIET/KITCHEN 21200,** 90;) **SOEHNLE DIETETIC 1301,** 22; **SOEHNLE DIETETIC AND LETTER 8600,** 24; **TERRAILLON DIET D200,** 30; **(AMERICAN FAMILY 3120,** 11; **HANSON DIET CALCULATOR 185,** 11;) **HANSON FOOD PORTION 1523,** 40; **(AMERICAN FAMILY DIET 3100,** 7; **COOKS TOOLS DIET 21679,** 7; **IDL SKINNY 33300,** 7;) **HOAN DIET WATCHER'S 410,** 8.

Medium-capacity (up to 11 lb.)

✓ **SOEHNLE DIGITA S 8003,** 85; **(COMPUCAL PERSONAL DIET/KITCHEN COMPUTER PDC1R,** 135; **KRUPS ADDIGRAMM M844,** 30;) **SOEHNLE 1230,** 25; **EVA 28510,** 38; **TERRAILLON BA5000,** 32; **TERRAILLON MURALE 3000,** 38; **SOEHNLE 1140,** 35; **COOKS TOOLS WAYMASTER 21681,** 20; **(HANSON 4400,** 17; **HOAN 411,** 20.)

Large-capacity (up to 26 lb.)

TERRAILLON T565, 48; **HOAN BALANCE 427,** 35; **(AMERICAN FAMILY KITCHEN/CANNING 3000,** 16; **SEARS Cat. No. 8886,** 13+.)

Dishwashing liquids

Condensed from CONSUMER REPORTS, July 1984

The selling price of a dishwashing liquid doesn't always reflect cleaning power, which varies from brand to brand. A low-priced but inefficient detergent may cost more to use than an expensive, efficient brand.

EFFICIENCY. In the chemistry lab, we recreated what happens in the kitchen to find out how much greasy soil the detergents could handle. Some detergents lasted nearly five times as long as others. We assigned to the best cleaners an efficiency factor of 1 and to the worst cleaners a factor of 4.7. The groups of dishwashing detergents in between were assigned efficiency factors of 1.4 and 2.7.

REAL COST. To determine a detergent's real cost, multiply its price per ounce (or per quart) by the efficiency factor.

Ratings of dishwashing liquids

Listed by groups in order of estimated cleaning efficiency in hard water. Within groups, listed in order of real cost (see story).

The following products had an efficiency factor of 1.

Kroger; Brocade [1]; Ajax; Dawn; Ivory Liquid; Joy; Palmolive; Sun Light; Lady Lee [2].

The following products had an efficiency factor of 1.4.

Von's [3]; Dermassage; Dove; White Magic [1]; Su-Purb [1].

The following products had an efficiency factor of 2.7.

Octagon; Cost Cutter [4]; Lilac; Crystal White; Tryst [2]; Ahoy [5]; Econo Buy [6]; Missy [4]; IGA; Sweet Heart; Grand Union; Gaylord; Gentle Fels; Janet Lee [7]; Pathmark; A&P; Trend; Alpha Beta; Lux.

The following products had an efficiency factor of 4.7.

No Frills [8]; Scotch Buy [1].

[1] *Sold at Safeway stores.*
[2] *Sold at Lucky stores.*
[3] *Sold at Von's stores.*
[4] *Sold at Kroger stores.*
[5] *Sold at A&P stores.*
[6] *Sold at Alpha Beta and Acme stores.*
[7] *Sold at Albertsons stores.*
[8] *Sold at Pathmark stores.*

Autos

Buying a new car

Buying a new car is really two separate operations: selecting the best model for you within your price range; then making the best deal you can with the dealer. It's unrealistic to expect the dealer to work in your best interest toward either goal.

As a starting point, you might decide on the general size or type of car you want. In our Ratings, we have sorted passenger cars into four size classifications: small, compact, medium and large. To those, we add what we call "sporty" cars—those whose appeal is based on racy looks or hot performance rather than on practical considerations of size. And we've added small vans.

SMALL CARS. The main appeal of a small car such as the *Toyota Corolla* or *Honda Civic* is low cost, both in the initial price and in the operating costs. But small cars today run the gamut of price from the basic, bare-bones versions to highly-trimmed models with luxury appointments that rival larger cars. Small cars seat two in comfort; their rear seats are usually substandard in space. Hatchback versions offer more versatility, some sedans have fold-down rear seats. In our experience, small cars are at their best when equipped with manual transmissions.

COMPACT CARS. The compact category has grown to where it encompasses a wide range of cars both in dollars and in performance. Compacts generally claim to seat five. The newest breed of compacts are wider and have the capability to serve a family as its only car.

MEDIUM CARS. These models represent the traditional basic family car; most are domestic products. Many are capable of carrying six persons, some can do it with a reasonable degree of comfort. The newer models are front-wheel-drive and a four-cylinder engine or small V6 is adequate for normal use. The new *Ford Taurus* and *Mercury Sable* front-wheel-drive models are good examples of this breed of family-sized cars.

LARGE CARS. This group of cars is shrinking in numbers but not in popularity. The traditional large Fords, Mercury, and Lincoln models are still around, as are the Chevrolet, and Cadillac rear-wheel-drive big cars. GM modernized its *Buick Le Sabre* and *Oldsmobile 88 Royale* models last year; they are now front-wheel-drive and in exterior size, little different from the medium models. One advantage of the older models is their ability to tow a relatively heavy trailer—something the new, front-wheel-drive models cannot do.

SPORTY CARS. This category is a variant of the other size categories. We classify cars as sporty if they are available as a two-door with a unique body, chassis, or powertrain. Some sporty cars are two-seaters; the rest have rear seats that are barely habitable. Low roof lines make entry and exit awkward, and luggage space may be very limited.

SMALL VANS. This new category has become very important. Buyers are discovering that the added space and versatility of a van needn't come in the bulky and clumsy body of a truck. The front-wheel-drive *Dodge Caravan/ Plymouth Voyager* are the most like passenger cars.

After settling on the general size or type of car you want, you'll have to determine how you want it equipped. Some luxury cars are sold with most of the options already installed, so there's little left for you to decide. Typically, however, you'll be faced with choosing from a long list of options, all of which will be charged for separately and added to the sticker price.

Detroit commonly "bundles" several option packages that you can choose among. That practice may give you a price break over buying each option separately, but you may also get an option or two that you wouldn't have bought if you'd had a choice.

CU's views on the most common options follow:

ENGINES. Avoid an engine that's larger than standard unless you use your car to pull a trailer. A standard four- or six-cylinder engine offers adequate power, even with air-conditioning. A larger engine consumes more fuel.

A diesel engine offers excellent drivability and extraordinary fuel mileage—25 to 60 percent better than a gasoline engine of similar size. But diesels are presently unpopular, now that fuel is relatively cheap and plentiful, and resale could be a problem.

Turbo-boosted engines produce very impressive power. But they also imbibe impressive quantities of fuel. And they're too new in passenger cars for their reliability to have been convincingly determined.

TRANSMISSIONS. On most medium-sized and large domestic cars, the automatic transmission has been changed to help improve fuel economy. But a manual transmission still delivers better gasoline mileage than an automatic.

The manual transmission on most imports is convenient to use. But on many domestic cars, the shift linkage and the long-travel clutch make shifting clumsy and awkward. On large cars, an overdrive automatic transmission is usually the best choice for fuel economy.

Many cars now offer a five-speed manual transmission as standard. The fifth speed is often an overdrive for better gasoline mileage and, usually, lower interior noise.

POWER STEERING. It's standard equipment on large cars and most medium-sized models. Even many small cars offer it as an option. Power steering isn't necessary on most small cars, but it can provide a safety advantage on medium-sized cars.

SPARE TIRE. The temporary-use spare tire, common on many cars, is merely an emergency tire to get you to the nearest service station. We recommend a full-sized, conventional spare tire if it's available and will fit in the space provided for the spare.

AIR-CONDITIONING. Factory-installed air-conditioning is an expensive item on domestic cars, much more so on some imports. It will increase service costs and cut gasoline mileage. (Our readers have reported trouble with air-conditioning on a number of imported cars.) However, an integrated air-conditioner markedly improves window defogging and fresh-air ventilation. Beyond that, air-conditioning can delay the onset of driver fatigue by providing a comfortable, quiet environment.

TINTED GLASS helps reduce the heat load on the air-conditioner on a sunny day, but it also may reduce nighttime vision. Tall drivers may be bothered by the dark band at the top of the windshield of some domestic models. Domestic cars can usually be ordered with air-conditioning and clear glass.

SEATS. Front seats are usually available in a variety of special configurations and materials. A one-piece bench seat, standard in most large models, offers the best overall comfort when three people are sitting in front. A split bench seat offers improved side support and comfort for two, but less comfort for three; a split bench seat can also be adjusted to provide adequate leg room for a tall passenger who rides next to a short driver. Where possible, choose cloth upholstery rather than vinyl.

POWER WINDOWS. These extras offer real convenience. But they can be confusing to operate, and they might cause serious injury to children. They're also something else to break.

AUTOMATIC SPEED CONTROL. With this control, you can maintain a preset speed within a couple of miles per hour even over gently rolling terrain. (Car speed will usually tend to drop going up long expressway grades, however.) The control can help you stay within speed limits and may help improve gasoline mileage on trips.

CENTRAL LOCKING SYSTEM. Most medium-sized and large cars offer an option that enables you to lock all the doors at the touch of a button. Such systems provide increased occupant safety in high-crime areas: A lone driver can instantly lock out a would-be intruder.

"COURTESY" LIGHTS. Lights that go on when you open a door, the glove compartment, the trunk, or the hood are useful. But they may be sold as part of a package with options you don't want.

DEFOGGERS AND DEFROSTERS. Unless most of your driving is done in the arid regions of the Southwest, you will appreciate having a rear-window defogger or defroster. We recommend them.

OTHER REAR-VISION AIDS. A rear-window wiper/washer is desirable on most station wagons and hatchbacks. If one is not available, an air deflector can help keep the rear window clean. A deflector may decrease gasoline mileage slightly at expressway speeds.

INTERVAL WIPERS. Wipers that can be set to pause between strokes are useful in light rain or mist.

BODY TRIM. If protective vinyl strips, also called body side moldings, are not standard on the car you want, consider buying them. On the other hand, try to avoid expensive exterior trim packages with nonfunctional metal moldings and trim around doors and windows.

BUMPER PROTECTION. Full-width bumper facings and bumper guards can be useful if you drive or park in congested areas. Facings protect your bumpers, and guards help prevent the bumpers of other cars from riding over or under yours. Both are sometimes part of a deluxe bumper package.

VINYL ROOF. This frill is becoming deservedly less popular. It tends to age and deteriorate faster than a steel roof.

SUN ROOF. Despite its increasing popularity, this feature may reduce head room drastically.

ROOF RACK. This sometimes useful feature is available on many station wagons and small cars. But when you load up the rack, expect fuel economy and handling to suffer, especially at expressway speeds.

RADIO. You can buy an AM, AM/FM, AM/FM stereo, AM/FM stereo plus a tape player, or a CB transceiver. And you can buy it from the automaker, from the car dealer, or at a store that specializes in audio equipment for cars.

UNDERCOATING. Factory-applied undercoating is often included in a sound-deadening package, and indeed its chief value is insulating the car's interior from road noise. Heavy undercoating sprayed on by dealers may have some added sound-deadening effect, but its effectiveness as rust-proofing is questionable, and it adds undesirable weight. Sound-deadening packages are more effective; they contain acoustical insulation that is lighter and more effective than undercoating.

RUSTPROOFING. CU cannot support a general recommendation for extra rust-proofing. Indeed, all domestic cars and most imports now carry at least a three-year warranty on rust perforation.

After narrowing your choice to two or three models and choosing the options you feel are necessary, you're in a position to figure for yourself what price you'll have to pay. The "sticker" price on a new car normally represents a kind of upper limit of the car's price. You should have to pay the sticker price only for cars that have very high demand and short supply. A better benchmark to bargain from is the so-called "invoice" price—the price that the dealer had to pay for the car.

Although some dealers will reveal the invoice price for a car and make a deal for a stated mark-up over the inventory price, they are scarce. Even so, you can determine any dealer's cost quite precisely by using CU's Auto Price Service. For each of 647 cars and trucks on the market, CU makes available a computer printout listing the price shown on the sticker for the basic car and for every option available for it; next to that price, the printout shows the invoice price, which is the price the dealer paid the auto manufacturer. An order form for the service appears on page 400.

Add up the dealer's cost of the car and the options you want. To that base you could typically add about $200 to $400 for the dealer's expenses and profit. And you may find that your total, which represents a reasonable offering price, is hundreds of dollars below the sticker price. Of course, the most reasonable selling prices may be for cars that have been overstocked, especially if the factory adds a rebate to the deal. Cars in great demand may command pretty close to list prices, or well over list in some cases. Shop other dealers for comparison.

Beware of a sticker that some dealers paste on next to the official one. Such unofficial stickers may include dealer-added options (e.g., decorative wheel covers, undercoating, body protective coatings, and floor mats). But those items are not really necessary and should not have to be a part of your deal.

If you have a car to trade in or sell, try to get some real idea of what it's worth. One source of such information is a used-car price book; some newsstands carry them, or you could ask your bank's loan officer to look at his or her copy. Use the price-adjustment tables in the price book to adjust for low or high mileage and for special, extra-cost equipment.

Among the most numerous complaints that CU receives from readers are those concerning poor auto-warranty service. Since you must generally rely on the selling dealer to perform any necessary repairs on your new car—at least through the warranty period—you would be wise to check a dealer's reputation for service before concluding a deal. If you learn of a local dealer who gives unusually good service, you may be wise to buy your car there, even if you could get a slightly more advantageous deal elsewhere.

How to get a good used car

The average new car costs over $11,000 these days. The average used car costs closer to $5,000. That's why three out of four cars now sold are used cars.

Although you risk less money in buying a used car, the chances of getting stung are greater. If you buy from a private party, you get no warranty, unless there's leftover factory warranty. And most used-car dealers won't stand behind their wares for more than 30 days, if that. So you really have to watch out for yourself in the used-car market.

If you must stretch your used-car dollar the furthest, you can benefit some from quirks in the public's taste in used cars. Avoid the models that depreciate the most slowly. Flashy cars—sporty models, convertibles, luxury cars—cost more as used cars than family sedans that originally cost just as much. Flashy cars are also likely to have more elaborate options, like power seats and power windows, that are expensive to buy and expensive to keep up.

Another way to tip the scales in your direction is to take clues from the Frequency-of-Repair records that are published in this issue. The records are based on readers' recent repair experience with about 450,000 cars. Cars that are chronic trouble-makers show up clearly in the repair charts, as do the cars that purr along with little more attention than routine maintenance.

The charts identify individual trouble spots on the cars and give an overall trouble index of each model. In addition, we've worked out a cost index that compares a model's overall maintenance cost and repair with models of about the same mileage; it sheds a cautionary light on cars like the *BMW* and the *Mercedes-Benz* that run reliably but still cost more to own because their repairs are so expensive.

You can get some idea of which used cars are in your price range by scanning the classified advertisements in a large newspaper. A better source would be a used-car price guide such as the "N.A.D.A (National Automobile Dealers Association) Official Used Car Price Guide." That booklet is updated monthly and is available at some newsstands and public libraries.

Where you buy a used car also affects the price. New-car dealers who sell used cars often ask top dollar. On the other hand, those dealers generally keep the best cars they take in trade and wholesale the clunkers. They're usually equipped to service the used cars they sell, and they may offer a warranty.

Used-car dealers offer cars in a wider range of prices. (They wind up with the clunkers, among others.) Some dealers are equipped to service the cars that they sell; others aren't. Some dealers offer warranties; others don't.

Auto-rental agencies sell used cars that are fairly new and fairly well equipped. The cars may have a lot of miles on them, but they also have good maintenance records, which most agencies will let you see. Such cars usually come with a limited warranty.

Banks and other moneylenders sometimes sell fairly new, repossessed cars. Those cars are usually listed in a newspaper's classified section.

No matter where you buy a used car, make a careful inspection and take a test drive. Make your inspection on a clear day; rain or darkness, or even the glaring lights of a dealership lot, can hinder your ability to evaluate the car. You might need help in your inspection and test drive, so bring along a friend.

Here are the things to look for:

EXTERIOR. Check for rust, especially in the wheel wells and in the rocker panels below the doors. Check the paint. Uneven color, for example, suggests that the car was in an accident; ask the seller what happened.

TIRES. Look for excessive or uneven wear. Check the spare, too. (While you're looking in the trunk, make sure all the tire-changing gear is there, and look for stains that may indicate leaks.) Uneven tire wear suggests that the car has an alignment problem or that it was in an accident.

SUSPENSION. Push down hard on each corner of the car and release quickly. If it rebounds more than once, it may need new shock absorbers. Grab the top of each front tire and push and pull; if it moves or clunks, the bearings or joints may need replacement.

INTERIOR. Check the seats for comfort and broken springs. Compare general wear and tear inside against the number of miles on the odometer. Open and close the windows. Make sure that the seat belts work.

GAUGES, CONTROLS. Turn on the ignition and check the oil light, the wipers and washers, the radio, the heater, the air-conditioner. Have your friend outside check the lights and signals.

On the test drive, check the controls and gauges. And, as you travel a variety of roads, check the following:

ENGINE. It should start easily, and it should not make odd noises.

STEERING. Turn the wheel to either side to check for free play. When the car is in motion, check that the steering is smooth and precise, with no free play and no vibration.

BRAKES. With the engine running, step on the brake pedal and hold it for a minute. If it continues to sink, there may be a leak in the hydraulic system. Drive along a deserted road at 45 mph and brake fairly hard (but don't lock the wheels); the car shouldn't veer, and you shouldn't feel any vibration or grabbing in the brakes.

ALIGNMENT. On that deserted road, have your friend watch from behind as you drive straight ahead; he or she should make sure the car's front and rear wheels are properly lined up.

ACCELERATION. The car should accelerate smoothly. It should maintain power as it goes uphill. If you hear knocking or pinging, the car may simply need higher octane fuel; but it could also need a tune up—or more.

TRANSMISSION. This should work smoothly and quietly in reverse and all forward gears. If it's a manual, note how smoothly the clutch operates.

OIL CONSUMPTION. With the engine warm and while driving at highway speed, lift your foot off the accelerator for a few seconds, then press down hard. Have your friend watch for signs of exhaust smoke; blue smoke generally means the car is burning oil.

HANDLING, NOISE, COMFORT. Drive over a bumpy road at 30 to 40 mph. Note how well the car holds the road and how much it rattles. And, of course, note how the bumps affect comfort.

If the car has passed your road test, arrange with the seller to let you take it to a reliable, independent mechanic or a diagnostic center. Expect to pay $25 to $50 or more. Be sure that the mechanic checks the engine compression, brakes, wheel bearings, transmission, cooling system, exhaust system, and battery. Mention any oddity you noticed in your inspection and test drive. The mechanic should also look for any signs that the car had been hit (and check the repair job if it has been hit) and should note any oil leaks.

Get a written estimate for all needed repairs. It may be useful in bargaining with the seller.

1986 models as used cars

On the pages that follow, we tabulate the characteristics of the cars that CU has tested as new cars. If a model is not listed, it means that we have not tested it recently enough to report on it. Remember that these are comments about 1986 models as *used cars*, not previews of the new 1987 models.

We have listed the models in alphabetical order within general groups. We have indicated, with arrowheads, those models that we think will be the best to choose as used cars. These judgments are based on the performance of the car

Listed alphabetically
▶ designates models that deserve preference as used cars.

SMALL CARS

CHEVROLET CHEVETTE
2-door hatchback
4-door hatchback
PONTIAC 1000
2-door hatchback
4-door hatchback

Predicted reliability. For gasoline version, much worse than average.

Comfort and convenience. Uncomfortable front seats; cramped interior. Pedals too close to each other. Very uncomfortable rear seat. No detents to hold open rear doors. Fairly noisy. Unpleasant, choppy ride. Adequate heater, but mediocre fresh-air ventilation. Awkward and stiff climate controls. Gauges obscured by reflections in daytime.

▶CHEVROLET NOVA
4-door
4-door hatchback

Predicted reliability. No data; new model, but should be similar to that of the *Corolla*, which has been excellent.

Comfort and convenience. Excellent front seats and nearly ideal driving position. Uncomfortable, cramped rear seat, especially for three adults. Moderate noise level. Rode as comfortably as many larger models. Excellent climate-control system. Controls were generally easy to use, and displays were clear.

CHEVROLET SPECTRUM
2-door hatchback
4-door

Predicted reliability. No data; new model. This *Chevrolet* is built by Isuzu in Japan; their models have generally had good reliability.

Comfort and convenience. Fairly comfortable front seats, but cushions are narrow for wide people and short fore and aft for tall people. Some drivers wanted to sit higher. Tall drivers wanted more leg room. Uncomfortable rear seat; for two only. Fairly noisy, annoyingly so on coarse pavement. Basically well controlled-ride with light load, but harsh and jerky on rough roads. Strong ventilation, but anemic heating and windshield defrosting. Nicely designed controls except for horn buttons on the steering wheel spokes instead of hub. Clear displays. Annoyingly bright upshift light.

as we tested it when new, and on the Predicted Repair Incidence, which is very important, especially in a used car. Note that our information regarding engine and transmission availability and fuel mileage may not be applicable in California.

The fuel mileage given is for the car with the engine and transmission listed and was measured on the road. The cruising range given is computed by multiplying the mileage obtained on CU's 195-mile test trip by the fuel-tank refill capacity, less a 30-mile "cushion."

On the road. The 1.6-liter gasoline Four started easily and ran well, but acceleration was unresponsive. The automatic transmission shifted smoothly except when going into or out of lock-up. Competent handling, but the manual steering felt a bit heavy. Good brakes, but fairly long stopping distance and noticable fade from repeated stops.

Fuel economy. Mpg with gasoline Four and automatic transmission: city, 19; expressway, 37. Gallons used in 15,000 miles, 555. Cruising range, 370 miles.

Comments. Passenger space is tight, especially width; the 4-door has better seating than the 2-door. Reliability has been poor, though major components were not particularly troublesome. *Chevettes* may be a good used-car buy if their price is far enough below market competition. Service and parts should be readily available at low cost. *Chevettes* are widely used by fleets; those could be good buys as basic transportation.

On the road. The 1.6-liter Four started easily, but hesitated occasionally even after it warmed up. Smooth-shifting 5-speed manual transmission. Light clutch action. Handling of this front-wheel-drive model felt somewhat vague and sloppy, and the body leaned considerably during cornering. Excellent braking.

Fuel economy. Mpg with manual transmission: city, 24; highway, 46. Gallons used in 15,000 miles, 435. Cruising range, 530 miles.

Comments. The *Nova* tested out as a top-rated, high-quality car; it also has an identity crisis that could work to your advantage, since not everyone seems to know that it's essentially a *Toyota Corolla* in Chevrolet clothing. If you can find a used '86, its price may well be below the comparable *Corolla's;* that could be a good buy, and service would certainly be widely available. Bumper test damage: none.

On the road. The 1.5-liter Four bucked annoyingly under acceleration. When partly warm, it sometimes sagged severely and surged. Smooth-shifting 5-speed manual transmission. This front-wheel-drive car had very competent handling, excellent in emergency-type maneuvers. Touchy brakes; and the car swerved somewhat during very short stops.

Fuel economy. Mpg with manual transmission: city, 25; expressway, 48. Gallons used in 15,000 miles, 420. Cruising range, 445 miles.

Comments. The *Spectrum* didn't compete well with other small cars on the basis of CU's tests. Its mechanical reliability is yet unknown. Might be a serviceable used car at a favorable price. Bumper test damage: extensive.

Small cars (cont.)

►CHEVROLET SPRINT **2-door hatchback** **4-door hatchback**	**Predicted reliability.** Average for '85 models, the only year for which data is available; engine cooling was a particular problem.	**Comfort and convenience.** Very comfortable front seats, except for very large people. Nearly ideal driving position for most drivers. Very uncomfortable, skimpy rear seat. Fairly noisy. Ride is tiring on most roads, punishing on rough ones. Adequate air-conditioning, generous ventilation, and powerful heating and defrosting. Fussy controls and a poor radio. Clear displays.
►DODGE COLT **2-door hatchback** **4-door** **►PLYMOUTH COLT** **2-door hatchback** **4-door**	**Predicted reliability.** Much better than average, and repair costs are low.	**Comfort and convenience.** Exceptionally comfortable front seats, but too little leg room for tall drivers. Rear seat uncomfortable for two, very tight for three. Moderate noise level. Very good air-conditioning and ventilation; adequate windshield defrosting; weak heating. Very good controls, excellent displays.
DODGE OMNI/CHARGER **2-door hatchback, Charger** **4-door hatchback, Omni** **PLYMOUTH HORIZON/TURISMO** **2-door hatchback: Turismo** **4-door hatchback: Horizon**	**Predicted reliability.** Much worse than average.	**Comfort and convenience.** Fairly comfortable front seats. Awkward pedal placement gave tall drivers insufficient leg rooom in 4-door model. Very uncomfortable rear seat for two or for three. Moderate noise level. Ride was too busy although not uncomfortable; jerky on rough roads. Inconvenient climate controls. Poor placement of turn-signal lever. Weak ventilation in cars without air-conditioning.
FORD ESCORT **2-door hatchback** **4-door hatchback** **4-door wagon** **MERCURY LYNX** **2-door hatchback** **4-door hatchback** **4-door wagon**	**Predicted reliability.** Average for gasoline Four; insufficient data for diesel.	**Comfort and convenience.** Very good front seats. Awkward driving position, especially for tall people. Rear seat very uncomfortable for two. Moderate noise level, but espacially noisy on coarse pavement. Uncomfortable ride; frequent bobbing and tossing. Excellent climate-control system. Awkward controls. Displays could be a bit more legible.
►HONDA CIVIC **2-door hatchback** **4-door** **4-door wagon**	**Predicted reliability.** Much better than average.	**Comfort and convenience.** Fairly comfortable front seats. Uncomfortable rear seat for two, very uncomfortable for three. Moderate noise level. Fairly abrupt, stiff ride. Very good climate-control system. Excellent operating controls and displays.

On the road. The 1-liter Three started and ran flawlessly, and was as peppy as many 4-cylinder models. Silky-smooth 5-speed manual transmission; smooth, effortless clutch. This front-wheel-drive model gave agile, crisp, and safe handling. Excellent brakes.

Fuel economy. Mpg with manual transmission: city, 37; expressway, 59. Gallons used in 15,000 miles, 310. Cruising range, 445 miles.

Comments. The *Sprint* is a surprisingly competent minicar; it would make a good town car because it's small and gives superlative fuel economy, but its ride is punishing at times and its rear seat is only habitable, at best. A car this small and light is likely to come off second best in a crash with almost any other car. Bumper test damage: moderate.

On the road. The 1.5-liter Four ran well except for occasional stumbling during warm-up. Weak acceleration, especially in fourth and fifth gears. Crisp, easy-shifting manual 5-speed transmission. This front-wheel-drive model handled very precisely and responsively. Slight fade was the only problem with the brakes.

Fuel economy. MPG with manual transmission: city, 23; expressway, 45. Gallons used in 15,000 miles, 465. Cruising range, 410 miles.

Comments. The *Colt* is among the better small cars in overall quality, although its acceleration, ride, and heating system are a little below par. *Colts* are likely to be priced a bit below most top-selling small cars; if so, they would be good buys. Bumper test damage: none.

On the road. The 1.6-liter Four started and ran well, but the 4-speed manual transmission was balky and vague. The optional 2.2-liter Four ran well. The automatic transmission sometimes shifted abruptly. This front-wheel-drive model handled satisfactorily in normal driving, somewhat better than in previous years in emergency maneuvers. Very good power brakes.

Fuel economy. MPG with 1.6-liter Four and manual transmission: city, 22, expressway, 45. Gallons used in 15,000 miles, 475. Cruising range, 450 miles. Mpg with 2.2-liter 4 and automatic transmission: city, 19; expressway, 33. Gallons used in 15,000 miles, 595. Cruising range, 335 miles.

Comments. The repair record for these cars remains much worse than average up through CU's latest data; buy one only if the price and mileage are so low that coping with potential problems seems worth it.

On the road. The 1.9-liter Four started and ran well but buzzed and vibrated during acceleration. The 5-speed manual transmission wasn't crisp, and the clutch pedal required a long push. The automatic transmission shifted back and forth annoyingly often. Steering required frequent small corrections to maintain straight course. Sloppy but safe emergency handling. Brakes were somewhat hard to modulate, and the car nose-dived during hard stops.

Fuel economy. Mpg with gasoline engine and manual transmission: city, 21; expressway, 41. Gallons used in 15,000 miles, 505. Cruising range, 410 miles.

Comments. The *Escort/Lynx* is a better small-car choice than the traditional U.S. built small cars such as *Chevrolet Chevette* or the *Omni/Horizon* twins. Its repair history is better, and it performs somewhat better. But it doesn't have the passenger room and ride comfort of the high-rated small cars, and suffers from some poor design of its controls. These cars have been sold at the rate of a half-million per year; service and parts should be widely available and repair costs relatively low. Bumper test damage: none.

On the road. The 1.5-liter Four started easily and ran well. The automatic transmission did not shift very smoothly, but the lock-up mechanism worked well. This front-wheel-drive car handled nimbly and precisely; outstanding in our track tests. Excellent brakes.

Fuel economy. Mpg with automatic transmission: city, 22; expressway, 39. Gallons used in 15,000 miles, 505. Cruising range, 380 miles.

Comments. One of the better small cars; not quite up to the level of the *Toyota Corolla* in overall quality. Very reliable; at its best with a 5-speed manual transmission. Used models are likely to be scarce and expensive.

Small cars (cont.)

HYNDAI EXCEL **3-door hatchback** **4-door hatchback** **4-door sedan**	**Predicted reliability.** No data; new model.	**Comfort and convenience.** Firm and supportive front seats. Accelerator pedal too close to driver. Moderately noisy, annoyingly so on coarse surfaces. Adequate heater and fresh-air ventilation; detents for mode selection weak and vague. Gauges obscured by reflections in daytime.
►MAZDA 323 **2-door hatchback** **4-door**	**Predicted reliability.** No data; new model. The *323's* predessor, the *Mazda GLC,* has been much better than average.	**Comfort and convenience.** Very comfortable front seats; very good driving position. Uncomfortable rear seat. Moderate noise level. Typical small-car ride. Excellent climate-control system. Excellent controls and displays.
►MITSUBISHI TREDIA **4-door**	**Predicted reliability.** Better than average.	**Comfort and convenience.** Fairly comfortable front seats and driving position except for drivers over 5 feet 10 inches. Very uncomfortable rear seat for two or three. Moderate noise level. Reasonably comfortable ride. Excellent heating, very good ventilation, but rather weak air-conditioning. Excellent controls and displays.
►NISSAN SENTRA **2-door** **2-door hatchback** **4-door** **4-door wagon**	**Predicted reliability.** Better than average for gasoline version. Insufficient data for diesel.	**Comfort and convenience.** Very comfortable front seats and driving position. Uncomfortable rear seating for two, very uncomfortable for three. Moderate noise level. Stiff, jiggly ride. Excellent climate-control system. Excellent controls and displays.
RENAULT ALLIANCE **2-door** **2-door convertible** **4-door** **RENAULT ENCORE** **2-door hatchback** **4-door hatchback**	**Predicted reliability.** Much worse than average.	**Comfort and convenience.** The front seats were very comfortable except for tall people, who needed more leg room. Most drivers wanted to sit higher; the steering wheel was too high and horizontal. The *Alliance's* rear seat was uncomfortable for two or three; the *Encore's* rear seat was tighter and very uncomfortable for two or three. Fairly comfortable ride; among the best in small cars. Moderate noise level. Effective air-conditioning and ample ventilation, but slow, hard-to-modulate heating. Poorly designed horn control; not on steering wheel. Clear displays.

On the road. The 1.5-liter Four started quickly but sagged and hesitated during warm-up; surged during moderate acceleration. The 5-speed transmission generally shifted smoothly but often blocked engagement of reverse. Sluggish routine handling handling. sloppy but controllable emergency. Disappointing brakes with fairly long stopping distance and noticeable fade from repeated stops.

Fuel economy. Mpg with manual transmission; city, 23; expressway, 45. Gallons used in 15,000 miles, 465. Cruising range, 360.

Comments. New in the U.S., the '86 Hyundai's claim to fame was its unusually low price. Not up to the quality level of the better Japanese cars, its engine hesitated at times and acceleration, handling, braking and rear seat comfort were below par. Used specimens will be rare for a while; reliability is uncertain. If *Hyundai* becomes well established in the U.S., and its price stays below market, it could be a good used-car buy. Bumper test damage: none.

On the road. The 1.6-liter Four started and ran flawlessly; spirited acceleration. The 5-speed manual transmission shifted crisply and precisely. This front-wheel-drive model gave excellent routine handling. Sloppy but safe emergency handling. The brakes were a little difficult to modulate.

Fuel economy. Mpg with manual transmission: city, 22; expressway, 42. Gallons used in 15,000 miles, 480. Cruising range, 420 miles.

Comments. This front-wheel-drive model is an even better car than its predecessor. It gives both spirited acceleration and very good fuel economy. A good used-car buy when available at a competitive prices. Bumper test damage: none

---

On the road. The 2-liter Four started easily but sagged and hesitated. The 5-speed manual transmission shifted well except into fifth gear. This front-wheel-drive model handled very well in routine driving; somewhat sloppy but steady emergency handling. The brakes felt a bit touchy, and stops weren't always straight.

Fuel economy. Mpg with manual transmission: city, 21; expressway, 40. Gallons used in 15,000 miles, 510. Cruising range, 405 miles.

Comments. The *Tredia* is a satisfactory but not outstanding car: Its reliability should be good, but it's below par in accommodations and handling. Bumper test damage: none.

On the road. The 1.6-liter gasoline Four started easily and ran well except for occasional hesitation during acceleration. The engine buzzed and vibrated when revved. Smooth-shifting 5-speed manual transmission. Handling of this front-wheel-drive model was a bit vague but easily controllable. Brakes were somewhat difficult to modulate.

Fuel economy. Mpg with gasoline Four and manual transmission: city, 24; expressway, 45. Gallons used in 15,000 miles: 440. Cruising range, 510 miles. Mpg with gasoline Four and automatic transmission: city, 20; expressway, 36. Gallons used in 15,000 miles, 545. Cruising range, 390.

Comments. A competent car worth considering; it gives excellent fuel economy and rides more stiffly than most small cars. The redesigned 1986 version became available in midyear.

On the road. The 1.4-liter Four and the optional 1.7-liter Four started easily and ran well. The larger Four's extra power was welcome. The 5-speed manual transmission shifted smoothly into the first four gears, but was awkward going into fifth and sometimes balked going into reverse. The automatic transmission shifted smoothly. Acceleration with the automatic and 1.4-liter Four was weak. This front-wheel-drive car handled very well in normal driving but somewhat imprecisely in abrupt maneuvers. Excellent braking.

Fuel economy. Mpg with 1.4-liter Four and 5-speed manual transmission: city, 21; expressway, 45. Gallons used in 15,000 miles, 495. Cruising range, 395 miles. Mpg with 1.4-liter Four and automatic transmission: city, 22; expressway, 37. Gallons used in 15,000 miles, 520. Cruising range, 370 miles. Mpg with 1.7-liter Four and manual transmission: city, 25; expressway, 44. Gallons used in 15,000 miles, 445. Cruising range, 445 miles.

Comments. The *Alliance/Encore* tested out reasonably well, but the driving position, controls, and rear seating were not good. Because their repair records have worsened to much-worse-than-average, *Alliance/Encores* are not apt to be good buys. Bumper test damage: minor.

Small cars (cont.)

►**SUBARU** **2-door hatchback** **4-door** **4-door wagon**	**Predicted reliability.** Much better than average, but 1985 models have shown a significant decline.	**Comfort and convenience.** Very comfortable front seats and driving position. Rear seat comfortable for two, cramped for three. Moderate noise level. Fairly pleasant ride except with full load. Excellent heating, but rather weak air-conditioning. Poor ventilation with air-conditioning. Excellent controls and displays.
►**TOYOTA COROLLA** **4-door** **4-door hatchback**	**Predicted reliability.** Much better than average. Low maintenance and repair costs.	**Comfort and convenience.** Exceptionally comfortable front seats. Excellent driving position. Uncomfortable rear seat for two, very uncomfortable for three. Moderate noise level. Rode well for a small car except when carrying full load. Excellent climate-control system, operating controls, and displays.
►**TOYOTA TERCEL** **2-door hatchback** **4-door hatchback** **4-door wagon** **4-wheel-drive wagon**	**Predicted reliability.** Much better than average.	**Comfort and convenience.** Very comfortable front seats. Very good driving position. Uncomfortable rear seat for two, very uncomfortable for three. Fairly noisy. Good ride for a small car. Excellent climate-control system and operating controls.
►**VOLKSWAGEN GOLF** **2-door hatchback** **4-door hatchback**	**Predicted reliability.** Average.	**Comfort and convenience.** Exceptionally comfortable front seats and a nearly ideal driving position. Fairly comfortable rear seat, even for three adults. Moderate noise level. Firm ride, seldom harsh. Powerful air-conditioning and generous ventilation, but heating and front and rear defrosting were marginal. Generally clear gauges, but controls could be improved.
►**VOLKSWAGEN JETTA** **2-door** **4-door**	**Predicted reliability.** Much better than average.	**Comfort and convenience.** Very comfortable front seats. Fairly comfortable driving position. The rear seat was uncomfortable for two or three people. Stiff, busy, and fairly noisy ride. Excellent climate-control system. Excellent controls and displays. Unusually large trunk.

On the road. The 1.8-liter Four started easily but surged briefly during sharp acceleration and deceleration. The 5-speed manual transmission shifted smoothly, though not as precisely as some. A "hill-holder" feature keeps the car from rolling back when starting uphill. This front-wheel-drive model was easy to control, but steering was a bit sluggish. Excellent brakes.

Fuel economy. Mpg with manual transmission: city, 21; expressway, 45. Gallons used in 15,000 miles, 485. Cruising range, 555 miles.

Comments. The *Subaru* sedan and wagon are definitely worthy of consideration as used cars. They provide good seating, very good handling, and good gas mileage. On the bad side, fresh-air-ventilation with air-conditioning is poor, and the engine growls noticeably when acceleratng. Bumper test damage: extensive.

On the road. The 1.6-liter Four started easily and ran well except for occasional hesitation during acceleration from standstill. Crisp-shifting 5-speed manual transmission. Smooth automatic transmission. This front-wheel-drive model gave excellent routine handling, very good emergency handling. Excellent brakes.

Fuel economy. Mpg with manual transmission: city, 23; expressway, 48. Gallons used in 15,000 miles, 445. Cruising range, 500 miles. Mpg with 3-speed automatic transmission: city, 21; expressway, 43. Gallons used in 15,000 miles, 495. Cruising range, 445 miles.

Comments. Still one of the best all-around small cars tested, with few vices. Excellent reliability and low repair costs. Strong demand will create high prices for used *Corollas.* You could look for a *Chevrolet Nova* at the same time. The two cars are very similar. Bumper test damage: none.

On the road. The 1.5-liter Four usually stalled once when started from cold, then ran well. The 5-speed manual transmission shifted very easily. The automatic transmission shifted smoothly. Though not necessary, optional power steering didn't adversely affect handling of this front-wheel-drive car. Very good brakes.

Fuel economy. Mpg with 5-speed manual transmission: city, 23, expressway, 46. Gallons used in 15,00 miles, 460. Cruising range, 420 miles. Mpg with 6-speed, four-wheel-drive transmission: city, 22; expressway, 38. Gallons used in 15,00 miles, 520. Cruising range, 380 miles. Mpg with automatic transmission: city, 23; expressway, 42. Gallons used in 15,000 miles, 475. Cruising range, 445 miles.

Comments. The *Tercel,* along with the *Corolla,* is a top-choice in the small-car field. The *Tercel* is less expensive and more modestly trimmed than the *Corolla.* Both are reliable and have low operating costs. The *Tercel* station wagon model is quite roomy and, with four-wheel-drive, is an excellent performer.

On the road. The 1.8-liter gasoline Four started easily and ran flawlessly. Responsive acceleration. Crisp but unpleasantly stiff 5-speed manual transmission. This front-wheel-drive model handled very precisely, but some drivers may want the optional power steering for easier parking. Noticable brake fade after a series of fairly hard stops.

Fuel economy. Mpg with gasoline Four and manual transmission: city, 21; expressway, 40. Gallons used in 15,000 miles, 500. Cruising range, 490 miles.

Comments. The *Golf* did very well in CU's tests. Most recent data indicates that the *Golf's* repair record is average. Its running mate, the European-built *Jetta,* has improved its repair record to much better than average. Some used '86 *Golfs* may have some of their 2-year unlimited-mileage warranty left; that would be a plus. Bumper test damage: extensive.

On the road. The 1.8-liter Four started and ran flawlessly. The 5-speed manual transmission shifted stiffly and, occasionally, reluctantly. This front-wheel-drive model handled responsively and controllably. The brakes were somewhat difficult to modulate.

Fuel economy. Mpg with gasoline Four and manual transmission: city, 20; expressway, 40. Gallons used in 15,000 miles, 520. Cruising range, 480 miles.

Comments. The European-built *Jetta,* like its less-expensive brother, the U.S.-built *Golf,* earned high marks in CU's performance tests, and it has an improved repair record. New *Jettas* have a 2-year unlimited-mileage warranty. If you can find one with some coverage left, so much the better; but expect these models to be expensive. Bumper test damage: extensive.

Small cars (cont.)

Yugo GV **2-door hatchback**	**Predicted reliability.** No data; new model. The *Yugo* is basically an old Fiat design—and Fiats weren't noted for their reliability.	**Comfort and convenience.** Small, insufficiently contoured front seats. Extremely awkward driving position. Very uncomfortable rear seat, unsuitable for adults. Noisy, harsh ride. Marginal heater and defroster. Modest ventilation. Poorly-designed controls. Generally easy-to-read displays.

SPORTY CARS

CHRYSLER LASER **2-door hatchback** **DODGE DAYTONA** **2-door hatchback**	**Predicted reliability.** Much worse than average.	**Comfort and convenience.** Exceptionally comfortable front seats. Very good driving position. Awkward access. Very uncomfortable rear seat. Moderate noise level; noisy exhaust in *Turbo* model. Rode well on good roads, but suspension bottomed hard and often on poor roads. Very good climate-control system. Inconveniently located controls.
►HONDA CIVIC CRX **2-door hatchback**	**Predicted reliability.** Much better than average.	**Comfort and convenience.** The *CRX* is a low 2-seater and access is difficult. Fairly comfortable seats, but awkward pedal arrangement. Moderate noise level. Comfortable ride. Excellent climate-control system. Slightly awkward controls, but gauges and displays were easy to read.
►HONDA PRELUDE Si **2-door**	**Predicted reliability.** Much better than average.	**Comfort and convenience.** Very comfortable front seats. Driving position low and reclined. Drivers over six feet tall may have insufficient head room. Very cramped, uncomfortable rear seat. Moderate noise level. Ride was firm but not punishing. Fairly weak heating and defrosting; satisfactory air-conditioning. Excellent operating controls and displays.
ISUZU IMPULSE **2-door hatchback**	**Predicted reliability.** Average.	**Comfort and convenience.** Very comfortable front seats. Tight driving position for tall drivers. Very uncomfortable rear seat. Moderate noise level. Firm but reasonably steady ride; active on rough roads. Erratic automatic climate-control system; temperature control tended to overshoot. Unusual control layout.

On the road. The 1.1-liter Four started easily. Except for a slight hitch, it ran well, but the engine strained while climbing highway grades. The 4-speed manual transmission was very imprecise and often balky—the worst we've tested. In routine driving, the handling of this front-wheel-drive model wasn't as crisp as that of most small cars; the steering felt heavy during low-speed cornering. Excellent emergency handling. Excellent braking, despite spongy feel of the brake pedal.

Fuel economy. Mpg: city, 24; expressway, 42. Gallons used in 15,000 miles, 465. Cruising range, 255 miles.

Comments. The *Yugo's* remarkably low price as a new car can't make up for its serious shortcomings. Prices for used *Yugos* are likely to be extremely low, but in CU's opinion, one wouldn't be a good buy at any price. Bumper test damage: extensive.

On the road. The turbocharged 2.2-liter Four started and ran well. Strong acceleration. The 5-speed manual transmission shifted stiffly. The clutch was heavy and had a long travel. This front-wheel-drive car handled well during normal driving. At the track, it was less precise than the better sporty cars. Excellent brakes.

Fuel economy. Mpg with turbocharged Four and manual transmission: city, 16; expressway, 34. Gallons used in 15,000 miles, 640. Cruising range, 360 miles.

Comments. The *Laser* and *Daytona* performed fairly well in our tests, but were not up to the level of the better sporty models such as the *Honda Prelude* and *Toyota Celica*.

On the road. The 1.5-liter fuel-injected Four (standard in the *Si* model) started and ran flawlessly and accelerated briskly. The 5-speed manual transmission shifted quickly and smoothly. This front-wheel-drive model handled quickly and precisely. Excellent braking.

Fuel economy. Mpg with *Si* version: city, 27; expressway, 45. Gallons used in 15,000 miles, 415. Cruising range, 435 miles.

Comments. The *CRX* is a sporty, yet economical, two-seater package. Its nimble handling and snappy acceleration make it fun to drive. Used models will be hard to find and will demand a premium price.

On the road. The 2-liter Four started easily and was responsive once warm. The 5-speed manual transmission shifted very easily. This front-wheel-drive car handled pleasantly and responsively. Excellent brakes.

Fuel economy. Mpg with 2-liter Four and manual transmission: city, 21; expressway, 35. Gallons used in 15,000 miles, 535. Cruising range, 475 miles.

Comments. The *Prelude* is among our top choices in sporty cars. Responsive and peppy, it handles well also. The *Si* version provides more power, but the standard version has plenty of acceleration. Bumper test damage: none.

On the road. The 1.9-liter Four started and ran well. The 5-speed manual transmission shifted very smoothly through the forward gears, but reverse required a hard downward push. This model handled precisely, but rough pavement made it step to the side. Excellent brakes.

Fuel economy. Mpg with manual transmission: city, 17; expressway, 37. Gallons used in 15,000 miles, 590. Cruising range, 440 miles.

Comments. The *Impulse* does not perform up to level of the better cars in this group.

Sporty cars (cont.)

▶**MAZDA RX-7** **2-door hatchback**	**Predicted reliability.** No data; new model. Previous *RX-7's* had a much better than average record.	**Comfort and convenience.** This 2-seater has a very comfortable front seat. Driving position too low for optimal comfort. Moderately high road noise. Very active and hard ride on all but the smoothest roads. Excellent heating and fresh air ventilation. Satisfactory air-conditioning. Controls are a bit unusual but easy to use. Excellent displays.
▶**MERKUR XR4Ti** **2-door hatchback**	**Predicted reliability.** Insufficient data.	**Comfort and convenience.** Exceptionally comfortable front seats; driver's seat can be raised or lowered. Excellent driving position. Uncomfortable rear seat; not too bad for three average-sized adults, but inadequate head room for six-footers. Moderate noise level. Well-controlled ride, even with full load. Excellent air-conditioning and ventilation; the heater was a bit weak, but defrosting was satisfactory. Controls are odd and needlessly confusing. Clear displays.
▶**MITSUBISHI CORDIA** **2-door hatchback**	**Predicted reliability.** Better than average.	**Comfort and convenience.** Fairly comfortable front seats. Leg room cramped for tall drivers. Very uncomfortable rear seat for two or three. Moderate noise level. Stiff, jiggly ride. Excellent climate-control system.
▶**MITSUBISHI STARION** **2-door hatchback** ▶**DODGE CONQUEST** **2-door hatchback** ▶**PLYMOUTH CONQUEST** **2-door hatchback**	**Predicted reliability.** Insufficient data.	**Comfort and convenience.** Very comfortable front seats. Tight leg room for tall drivers. Very uncomfortable rear seat for two or three. Moderate noise level. Busy ride; much worse with more than two occupants. Excellent climate-control system. Inconvenient controls.
▶**NISSAN 200SX** **2-door** **2-door hatchback**	**Predicted reliability.** Better than average.	**Comfort and convenience.** Very comfortable front seats. Generous leg room. Very uncomfortable rear seat. Moderate noise level. Fairly good ride for a sporty car, especially on rough roads. Excellent climate-control system, operating controls, and displays.
▶**NISSAN PULSAR NX** **2-door coupe**	**Predicted reliability.** Better than average.	**Comfort and convenience.** Very comfortable front seats. Very good driving position. Very uncomfortable rear seat for two or three. Moderate noise level. Fairly comfortable ride. Fairly weak climate-control.

On the road. The 1.3-liter twin chamber rotary started quickly and ran flawlessly when warm. In cold weather, idle during warm-up was rough. Acceleration was strong and smooth. The transmission shifted smoothly. Routine handling was excellent. Emergency handling, extremely controllable in hard turns. Excellent brakes.	**Fuel economy.** Mpg with manual transmission: city, 15; expressway, 30. Gallons used in 15,000 miles, 700. Cruising range, 385.	**Comments.** The *RX-7* was redesigned for the 1986 model year but still retains its basic chassis layout. Handling was very agile and precise. A very desirable sports car, bound to be expensive as a used car. Bumper test damage: none.
On the road. The 2.3-liter turbocharged Four started easily and ran well. We noted some turbo lag—a pause before the engine responded to the accelerator—but acceleration was very strong. Rather stiff-shifting 5-speed manual transmission, with high gearing that wasn't ideal for driving around town. This rear-wheel-drive model gave smooth and precise handling in routine driving. In hard cornering it tended to swing out its tail—a bit disconcerting, but not hard to control. Exceptional brakes.	**Fuel economy.** Mpg with manual transmission: city, 16; expressway, 31. Gallons used in 15,000 miles, 660. Cruising range, 375 miles.	**Comments.** The *Merkur* is German-made and sold through Lincoln/Mercury dealers. It's not well-known or sold in large numbers. But it's a good all-around performer and will be especially slick with an automatic transmission. Bumper test damage: moderate.
On the road. The 2-liter four started easily but sagged and hesitated. The 5-speed manual transmission shifted well. This front-wheel-drive model handled crisply in normal driving, not as well in abrupt maneuvers. Very good brakes.	**Fuel economy.** Mpg with manual transmission: city, 21; expressway, 40. Gallons used in 15,000 miles, 510. Cruising range, 405 miles.	**Comments.** The *Cordia* is the sporty version of the *Mitsubishi Tredia* sedan.
On the road. The 2.6-liter turbocharged Four started easily but sagged during warm-up if accelerated hard. The 5-speed manual transmission shifted smoothly. Very good handling, but the power steering lacked feel. Excellent brakes.	**Fuel economy.** Mpg with manual transmission: city, 17; expressway, 33. Gallons used in 15,000 miles, 625. Cruising range, 525 miles.	**Comments.** Good all-around performers, these triplets have strong turbocharged acceleration.
On the road. The 1.8-liter turbocharged Four started and ran flawlessly. The 5-speed manual transmission was easy to shift. Responsive and sporty handling. Excellent brakes.	**Fuel economy.** Mpg with turbocharged Four and manual transmission: city, 20; expressway, 39. Gallons used in 15,000 miles, 545. Cruising range, 405 miles.	**Comments.** The *200SX* is another good all-around performer. The turbo version has especially strong acceleration
On the road. The 1.6-liter Four started quickly but sagged and hesitated during warm-up. The 5-speed manual transmission shifted smoothly except into reverse. This front wheel drive model handled well, but was somewhat tricky in abrupt maneuvers. Very good brakes.	**Fuel economy.** Mpg with manual transmission: city, 26; expressway, 50. Gallons used in 15,000 miles, 410. Cruising range, 525 miles.	**Comments.** A good entry-level sporty car. The *Pulsar* is based on the *Nissan Sentra*.

Sporty cars (cont.)

PONTIAC FIERO
2-door

Predicted reliability. Much worse than average.

Comfort and convenience. This very low two-seater provides difficult access. Fairly comfortable seats. Awkward driving position for short drivers. Moderate noise level. Busy and jiggly ride, punishing on rough roads. Excellent climate-control system. Some important controls are hard to see behind the steering wheel. Gauges were clear except for daytime reflections. Minimal trunk space.

▶PORSCHE 944
2-door hatchback

Predicted reliability. Data over the past three years shows few trouble spots. But costs of maintenance and repairs have been very high.

Comfort and convenience. Awkward access to the low front seat. Very comfortable front seats. Awkward driving position for short drivers. Very uncomfortable rear seat. Moderate noise level. Stiff, harsh ride, especially over patched or broken pavement. Adequate climate-control system. Controls logical and easy to use. Some displays hidden by driver's hands on the wheel.

▶TOYOTA CELICA
2-door
2-door hatchback

Predicted reliability. No data; new front-wheel-drive model.

Comfort and convenience. Excellent driving position due to wide adjustability of seat. Extremely comfortable front seats. Awkward access. Rear seat unsuitable even for children. Moderate noise level; worse on coarse pavement. Generally stiff and nervous ride, but good for a sporty car. Excellent climate-control system; powerful and unobtrusive. Controls were good and worked well. Displays were extremely clear.

▶TOYOTA MR2
2-door

Predicted reliability. Much better than average.

Comfort and convenience. The *MR2* is a 2-seater. Low but comfortable seats. Very good driving position. Awkward access. Fairly noisy but comfortable ride. Excellent climate-control system. Very good controls; excellent displays. Minimal trunk space.

On the road. The 2.5-liter Four started and ran well. The 2.8-liter V6, standard in the *GT*, started and ran faultlessly and gave powerful acceleration. Shifting the 4-speed manual transmission and depressing the clutch pedal required lots of effort. The 4-cylinder version of this mid-engine, rear-wheel-drive model has a 5-speed manual transmission, not tested. Handling in the standard version was tricky, especially on wet or snowy roads. The *GT's* performance suspension gave very good routine handling and excellent emergency handling. Excellent brakes.

Fuel economy. Mpg with 2.5-liter Four and 4-speed manual transmission: city, 20; expressway, 38. Gallons used in 15,000 miles, 535. Cruising range, 305 miles. Mpg with V6 and 4-speed manual transmission: city, 17; expressway, 31. Gallons used in 15,000 miles, 635. Cruising range, 255 miles.

Comments. The *Fiero* is much improved over the basic model we tested in 1984. Try to find one with the performance suspension, if possible. Bumper test damage: none.

On the road. The 2.5-liter Four started and ran flawlessly. Strong acceleration. The 5-speed manual transmission shifted competently. Routine handling was excellent; response was smooth and very predictable. Emergency handling was excellent. Extremely short, straight, and controllable brake stops.

Fuel economy. Mpg with manual transmission: city, 16; expressway, 35. Gallons used in 15,000 miles, 635. Cruising range, 560.

Comments. The *944* behaved as a true sports car should. It stopped, accelerated; and handled extremely well and without fuss. Price, even as a used car, will be high. Bumper test damage: none.

On the road. The 2-liter Four started and ran flawlessly. The 5-speed manual transmission shifted quickly and precisely. Excellent routine handling with quick and precise steering response. Excellent emergency handling; close to perfect around the test track. Extremely short, straight, and controllable brake stops.

Fuel economy. Mpg with manual transmission: city, 19; expressway, 35. Gallons used in 15,000 miles, 565. Cruising range, 465.

Comments. One of our top choices in the sporty car group. The *Celica* was redesigned for 1986 and is now front-wheel-drive. Our tested *GT-S* should be plenty responsive. Bumper test damage: none.

On the road. The 1.6-liter Four, a high-revving and responsive engine, started and ran faultlessly. The 5-speed manual transmission was the best we've ever used. This mid-engined, rear-wheel-drive model had excellent routine handling. Very good emergency handling—a bit tricky, but very responsive. Excellent braking, with very short, straight stops.

Fuel economy. Mpg with manual transmission: city, 25; expressway, 45. Gallons used in 15,000 miles, 435. Cruising range, 415 miles.

Comments. The *MR2* is a fine little sports car, as agile and responsive as one of the breed should be. Very little room inside. Bumper test damage: none.

COMPACT CARS

►ACURA LEGEND **4-door**	**Predicted reliability.** No data; new model. If the *Legend* is like other models made by Honda, reliability should be excellent.	**Comfort and convenience.** Exceptionally comfortable front seats; driver's seat has manual adjustments for lumbar and thigh support. Headroom tight for tall drivers. Rear seat fairly comfortable for two, tight for three. Moderate noise level. Ride was taut but comfortable; suspension absorbed jolts from tar strips and sharp bumps well. Ample heater; it responded quickly and accurately to changes in temperature settings. Ample ventilation, free of drafts. Excellent controls; easy to see and use both day and night. Excellent gauges; simple, easy-to-read.
►AUDI 4000S **2-door** **4-door** **4-door Quattro**	**Predicted reliability.** Better than average. Repair costs above average.	**Comfort and convenience.** Exceptionally comfortable front seats; driver's seat can be adjusted up and down at rear. Rear seat fairly comfortable for two, tight for three. Moderate noise level; road noise worse on coarse pavement. Steady, smoothly controlled ride; harsh with full load. Powerful and versatile air-conditioning. Powerful heater, but slow to respond to temperature settings. Strong but noisy ventilation. Good controls; clear displays.
CADILLAC CIMARRON **4-door**	**Predicted reliability.** Worse than average.	**Comfort and convenience.** Exceptionally comfortable front seats and excellent driving position. Uncomfortable rear seat; cramped for three adults. Moderate noise level. Noticeable vibration from engine and road surface. Stiff, jiggly ride. Excellent climate-control system. Generally familiar, easy-to-use controls. Excellent displays.
CHEVROLET CAVALIER **2-door** **2-door hatchback** **2-door convertible** **4-door** **4-door wagon** **BUICK SKYHAWK** **2-door** **4-door** **4-door wagon** **OLDSMOBILE FIRENZA** **2-door** **4-door** **4-door wagon** **PONTIAC SUNBIRD** **2-door** **2-door hatchback** **2-door convertible** **4-door** **4-door wagon**	**Predicted reliability.** For Buick and Oldsmobile Four, worse than average. For Chevrolet and Pontiac Four, much worse than average. Insufficient data for V6 models.	**Comfort and convenience.** Fairly comfortable front seats; very good driving position. Uncomfortable rear seat for two, very uncomfortable for three. Moderate noise level. Generally soft ride, but abrupt on pavement joints and rough roads. Excellent climate-control system. Gauges were hard to read in daytime because of reflections. Most controls were convenient.

On the road. The 2.5-liter V6 started and ran flawlessly. Acceleration was very strong. The overdrive automatic transmission shifted harshly at times. Excellent routine handling. Emergency handling was very precise and crisp. Excellent brakes.	**Fuel economy.** Mpg with automatic transmission: city, 15; expressway, 33. Gallons used in 15,000 miles, 695. Cruising range, 400 miles.	**Comments.** The *Legend* is the senior model in a new line of cars made by Honda and marketed by Acura dealers. It compares very favorably to the better European sports sedans in ride and handling, and is roomy inside and quite comfortable. Expect used *Legends* to be very rare and expensive. Bumper test damage: none.
On the road. The 2.2-liter Five in the *Quattro* sometimes required long cranking to start, but it ran well. Very responsive acceleration. Hydraulic valve lifters sometimes clacked temporarily after a cold start. Smooth-shifting 5-speed manual transmission. The *Quattro's* full-time four-wheel drive gave precise, responsive handling and excellent traction on dry and slippery roads. Stops were short and straight.	**Fuel economy.** Mpg with 2.2-liter 5 and manual transmission: city, 18; expressway, 31. Gallons used in 15,000 miles, 625. Cruising range, 470 miles.	**Comments.** The basic *Audi 4000* uses the *VW* 1.8-liter Four; the *Quattro* and *Coupe GT* use the 5-cylinder engine from the *Audi 5000S*. Our tested *Quattro* was an excellent performer; the full-time four-wheel drive gave an extraordinary sense of control and security. Bumper test damage: extensive.
On the road. The optional 2.8-liter V6 started and ran flawslessly. Very responsive acceleration. The 3-speed automatic transmission, with lock-up feature, occasionally shifted abruptly during acceleration. Responsive, precise, and controllable handling. Very good brakes.	**Fuel economy.** Mpg with V6 and automatic transmission: city, 15; expressway, 28. Gallons used in 15,000 miles, 720. Cruising range, 295 miles.	**Comments.** The *Cimarron* has considerably more up-market content than the other J-cars (see below) from GM. Handling and comfort are quite good; ride is very harsh. Bumper test damage: moderate.
On the road. The 2-liter Four (not available in the *Sunbird*, standard in the other J-cars) started and ran well. The 1.8-liter Four (standard in the *Sunbird*, optional in *Skyhawk* and *Firenza*) started easily, but hesitated and surged until fully warmed up. The automatic transmission shifted smoothly. The 5-speed manual transmission was sometimes awkward to shift into first or second gear. Abrupt clutch. This front wheel drive model handled well in normal driving and emergency maneuvers. Good, but touchy, brakes.	**Fuel economy.** Mpg with 2-liter Four and automatic transmission: city, 16; expressway, 35. Gallons used in 15,000 miles, 640. Cruising range, 335 miles. Mpg with 1.8-liter Four and 5-speed manual transmission: city, 20; expressway, 42. Gallons used in 15,000 miles, 515. Cruising range, 445.	**Comments.** GM's J-cars continue to improve but are still not up to the level of their Japanese competitors. The N-cars (*Buick Skylark/Somerset, Oldsmobile Calais*, and *Pontiac Grand Am*) are better performers and are more comfortable.

Compact cars (cont.)

FORD TEMPO **2-door** **4-door** **MERCURY TOPAZ** **2-door** **4-door**	**Predicted reliability.** Much worse than average.	**Comfort and convenience.** Fairly comfortable front seats, but they lacked lower-back support. Awkard driving position. Uncomfortable rear seat; tight for six-footers. Moderate noise level. Firm, busy ride. Excellent climate-control system, even in cars without air-conditioning. Annoying pushbutton release for ignition key.
►HONDA ACCORD **2-door hatchback** **4-door**	**Predicted reliability.** Much better than average.	**Comfort and convenience.** The *Accord*, redesigned for 1986, has very comfortable front seats; low, sporty-car driving position. Uncomfortable rear seat for two or three. Moderate noise level. Firm ride with good control. Excellent climate-control system. Excellent controls and displays.
►MAZDA 626 **2-door** **4-door** **4-door hatchback**	**Predicted reliability.** Much better than average.	**Comfort and convenience.** Very comfortable front seats. Driving position cramped for tall people. Uncomfortable rear seat for two or three. Moderate noise level. Firm ride with good control. Very good heating; excellent ventilation and air-conditioning. Very good controls. Excellent displays.
►MERCEDES-BENZ 190 **4-door**	**Predicted reliability.** For gasoline version, much better than average. For diesel, insufficient data.	**Comfort and convenience.** Exceptionally comfortable front seats. Very good driving position; plenty of leg room for tall drivers. Uncomfortable rear seat for two or three. Gasoline version fairly quiet. Taut, very well-controlled ride. Very good climate-control system with automatic temperature control.
►MITSUBISHI GALANT **4-door**	**Predicted reliability.** Average.	**Comfort and convenience.** Exceptionally comfortable front seats; driver's seat is adjustable for height and lower back support. Very comfortable rear seat; remarkably roomy for a compact model, even with three adults sitting abreast. Quiet inside. Unusually pleasant ride for a compact. Excellent climate-control system. Unusual but well-designed controls; radio was hard to reach. Easy-to-read gauges.
►NISSAN MAXIMA **4-door** **4-door wagon**	**Predicted reliability.** Much better than average.	**Comfort and convenience.** Very comfortable front seats. Fairly comfortable driving position; tight leg room for tall drivers. Uncomfortable rear seat; cramped for three adults. Fairly quiet, but sharply busy, ride. Powerful climate control, but noisy heater. Well-designed but complicated controls; excellent displays.

On the road. The 2.3-liter Four started easily. When warm, it often idled unsteadily and occasionally stalled. Adequate acceleration; slower than that of many compacts. The automatic transmission, with partial lock-up in second and third gears, was unpleasant; premature upshifts often made the engine lug and the car vibrate. Downshifts were delayed and abrupt. The 5-speed manual transmission shifted fairly well. Handling of this front-wheel-drive model was somewhat sluggish and vague. Stops were a bit long but straight; fade was minimal.	**Fuel economy.** Mpg with gasoline engine and 5-speed manual transmission: city, 19; expressway, 41. Gallons used in 15,000 miles, 530. Cruising range, 445 miles. Mpg with gasoline engine and automatic transmission: city, 18; expressway, 34. Gallons used in 15,000 miles, 590. Cruising range, 425 miles.	**Comments.** The *Tempo/Topaz* are equivalent in performance to GM's J-cars, but their reliability has been poor both in 1984 and 1985. Bumper test damage: none.
On the road. The 2-liter Four sometimes stalled once after a cold start and occasionally hesitated while warming up. The overdrive automatic transmission usually shifted smoothly. This front-wheel-drive car handled very well. Very good brakes.	**Fuel economy.** Mpg with automatic transmission: city, 19; expressway, 40. Gallons used in 15,000 miles, 550. Cruising range, 460 miles.	**Comments.** Extensively redesigned for 1986, the *Accord* remains one of the better compact cars and a good dollar value. Bumper test damage: none.
On the road. The 2-liter Four started and ran well except for an occasionally shaky idle. The 5-speed manual transmission shifted smoothly but balked going into reverse. The automatic transmission shifted smoothly but often downshifted unexpectedly. This front-wheel-drive model handled very well. Excellent brakes.	**Fuel economy.** Mpg with 5-speed manual transmission: city, 20; expressway, 38. Gallons used in 15,000 miles, 530. Cruising range, 505 miles. Mpg with automatic transmission: city, 18; expressway, 33. Gallons used in 15,000 miles, 595. Cruising range, 445 miles.	**Comments.** The *626* is one of CU's top compacts. We suggest that the manual transmission version will offer considerably better overall performance than the automatic version. Bumper test damage: none.
On the road. The 2.3-liter gasoline Four started and ran well at all times. Responsive acceleration. The 4-speed automatic transmission shifted abruptly at times. Handling was smooth, responsive, and controllable. Excellent brakes.	**Fuel economy.** Mpg with gasoline Four and automatic transmission: city, 23; expressway, 33. Gallons used in 15,000 miles, 530. Cruising range, 420 miles.	**Comments.** This smaller Mercedes is an excellent performer but commands a high price. Rear seating comfort is not what it should be. Diesel version, revised for 1986, has a more powerful engine.
On the road. The 2.4-liter Four started easily and ran well. The electronically-controlled overdrive automatic transmission with lock-up feature shifted smoothly and did a good job of selecting the proper gear. This front-wheel-drive model's handling was almost flawless. Very good braking.	**Fuel economy.** Mpg: city, 17; expressway, 38. Gallons used in 15,000 miles, 590. Cruising range, 445 miles.	**Comments.** An excellent "high-tech" compact with an exceptionally roomy and comfortable rear seat. A fairly rare model. Bumper test damage: none.
On the road. The 3-liter V6 started and ran flawlessly and gave strong acceleration. Smooth-shifting overdrive automatic transmission. Fairly responsive routine handling; steady in hard turns, but tendency to fishtail during abrupt maneuvers. Some weaving during shortest stops.	**Fuel economy.** Mpg: city,15; expressway, 32. Gallons used in 15,000 miles, 680. Cruising range, 385 miles.	**Comments.** Top of the line for Nissan, the *Maxima* is a powerful performer. Its seating package, however, not the best. Bumper test damage: none.

Compact cars (cont.)

▶NISSAN STANZA
4-door
4-door wagon

Predicted reliability. Much better than average.

Comfort and convenience. The front seats were exceptionally comfortable in the wagon. Very good driving position. Fairly comfortable rear seat. Moderate noise level. Fairly comfortable ride. Excellent climate-controlled system. Excellent controls and displays.

OLDSMOBILE CALAIS
2-door
4-door
BUICK SKYLARK/SOMERSET
2-door Somerset
4-door Skylark
PONTIAC GRAND AM
2-door
4-door

Predicted reliability. For Four, average; for V6, much worse than average.

Comfort and convenience. Fairly comfortable front seats. Very good driving position. Very uncomfortable on poor roads. Generally quiet. Excellent climate-control system. Very good controls. Excellent displays.

PEUGOT 505
4-door
4-door wagon

Predicted reliability. Average to worse-than-average. Costs of maintenance and repairs have been fairly high.

Comfort and convenience. Very comfortable front seating. Driving position very good, except the pedals were a bit too close for tall drivers. Very comfortable rear seating for two or three. Moderate noise, mostly wind and gear whine. Very competent ride; it smoothed out most bumps. Satisfactory heating. Marginal windshield defrosting; wipers iced up easily in the winter. Weak air-conditioning; couldn't cope with sunny days in upper 70's. Controls better than in previous Peugots, but still confusing and awkward to use. Very legible displays.

▶SAAB 900
2-door
2-door hatchback
2-door hatchback Turbo
2-door convertible Turbo
4-door

Predicted reliability. Average for turbocharged models, better than average for non-turbo models.

Comfort and convenience. Extremely comfortable front seats, with thermostatically controlled heating. Some drivers would have preferred a higher seat or a lower steering wheel. Fairly comfortable rear seat, even for three. Moderate noise level; road noise was prominent over coarse pavement. The firm suspension absorbed large bumps, but transmitted harshness from minor pavement imperfections. A full load didn't worsen the ride much. Powerful, versatile air-conditioning and effective ventilation. The heater warmed up slowly. Competent windshield defroster; marginal rear defroster. Some controls (such as the ignition switch on the floor) are inconvenient. Displays were clear and easy to read.

On the road. The 2-liter Four in our tested station wagon started quickly and ran well, giving brisk accleration. The overdrive automatic transmission sometimes downshifted abruptly and unnecessarily during acceleration. The 5-speed manual transmission shifted easily. The front-wheel-drive wagon's handling was not crisp. Its brakes, however, were exceptional.	**Fuel economy.** Mpg, for wagon with automatic transmission: city, 15; expressway, 32. Gallons used in 15,000 miles, 675. Cruising range, 400 miles.	**Comments.** The sedan versions of the *Stanza* were extensively redesigned for mid-1986. Our tests were of the station wagon version. The *Stanza* wagon is very tall and of pillarless design, with sliding doors on each side and lots of head room and cargo volume. A four-wheel-drive version is also available. Bumper test damage: none:
On the road. The 2.5-liter Four started and ran well except for occasional hesitation during warm-up. The optional 3-liter V6 started easily but stumbled during warm-up. The automatic transmission with lock-up shifted smoothly; premature locking sometimes made the engine lug and vibrate. This front-wheel-drive model handled a bit sluggishly, but very safely. Very good brakes; short stopping distance, but some weaving during the hardest stops.	**Fuel economy.** Mpg with Four and automatic transmission; city, 18; expressway, 38. Gallons used in 15,000 miles, 565. Cruising range, 405 miles. Mpg with V6 and automatic transmission: city, 16; expressway, 32. Gallons used in 15,000 miles, 645. Cruising range, 350 miles.	**Comments.** These N-cars from GM test out quite well and, should their reliability improve, they will join our recommended list of compacts. Bumper test damage: moderate.
On the road. The 2-liter Four started easily and ran well. The overdrive automatic transmission shifted fairly smoothly, but occasionally delayed its upshifts too long. Handling was very precise and responsive. Excellent brakes.	**Fuel economy.** Mpg, for wagon with automatic transmission: city, 15; expressway, 28. Gallons used in 15,000 miles, 720. Cruising range, 400 miles.	**Comments.** The *505* wagon we tested was a real cargo hauler with a very large and useful volume. Fairly sluggish acceleration, but a turbocharged version is available for those who need to go faster. Bumper test damage: none.
On the road. The 2-liter, turbocharged, 16-valve Four started and ran without a hitch, and it gave more than ample acceleration. The 5-speed manual transmission occasionally balked when shifts were hurried. Steering response was a bit slow in this front-wheel-drive model, but emergency handling was very stable and precise. The brakes were somewhat difficult to modulate.	**Fuel economy.** Mpg with turbo engine and manual transmission: city, 18; expressway, 32. Gallons used in 15,000 miles, 620. Cruising range, 420 miles.	**Comments.** The *Saab Turbo* is a powerful performer, but the standard model is peppy as well. Both command high prices as used cars. Repair costs will be high also. Bumper test damage: none.

Compact cars (cont.)

►**TOYOTA CAMRY** **4-door** **4-door hatchback**	**Predicted reliability.** Much better than average.	**Comfort and convenience.** Exceptionally comfortable front seats. Excellent driving position. In sedan, very comfortable rear seat for two, comfortable for three. (The hatchback has less headroom and is less comfortable.) Fairly quiet in sedan; moderate noise level in hatchback. Comfortable ride on expressways; busy on secondary roads. Excellent climate-control system. Very good controls; excellent dislays.
►**TOYOTA CRESSIDA** **4-door** **4-door wagon**	**Predicted reliability.** Much better than average.	**Comfort and convenience.** Exceptionally comfortable front seats. Excellent driving position. Fairly comfortable rear seat for two, less so for three. Quiet inside. Smooth ride with light load; markedly worse with full load. Excellent automatic climate-control system. Well-designed but complicated controls. Very legible displays.
►**VOLKSWAGEN QUANTUM** **4-door** **4-door wagon**	**Predicted reliability.** Insufficient recent data. Older models have generally been average.	**Comfort and convenience.** Very comfortable front seats. Very good driving position. Uncomfortable rear seat for two or three. Moderate noise level. Engine and road noise were quite noticeable. Harsh ride, but well controlled on poor roads. Mediocre heater; ample but drafty ventilation; excellent air-conditioner. Disappointing controls. Excellent displays.
►**VOLVO 240** **4-door** **4-door wagon**	**Predicted reliability.** Average.	**Comfort and convenience.** Exceptionally comfortable front seats, with adjustment for lower-back support. Height and angle of driver's seat is adjustable. Uncomfortable driving position for tall people. Fairly comfortable rear seat; plenty of room for two six-footers; crowded for three adults. Firm, rather harsh ride. Moderate noise level; a loud exhaust boom and vibration in the driveline and steering wheel were problems. Very good climate-control system, but slow response to temperature setting. Well-designed controls.

MEDIUM CARS

►**AUDI 5000S** **4-door** **4-door wagon**	**Predicted reliability.** Has improved to average, though repair costs have been high.	**Comfort and convenience.** Exceptionally comfortable front seats. Generous leg room. Fairly comfortable rear seat for two or three. Fairly quiet. Very competent ride. Excellent automatic climate-control system. Mostly logical controls; clear displays.

On the road. The 2-liter gasoline Four started and ran flawlessly. The 5-speed manual transmission with lock-up shifted smoothly. This front-wheel-drive model handled safely, though somewhat sluggishly. Excellent brakes.	**Fuel economy.** Mpg with gasoline Four and 5-speed manual transmission: city, 23; expressway, 46. Gallons used in 15,000 miles, 455. Cruising range, 510 miles. Mpg with gasoline Four and automatic transmission: city, 19; expressway, 44. Gallons used in 15,000 miles, 515. Cruising range, 490 miles.	**Comments.** The *Camry* has been one of our top compacts for several years now, and the new models are no exception. A good all-around performer with excellent gasoline mileage and a comfortable rear seat. Owner satisfaction has been high, which means that used models will be hard to find. Bumper test damage: none.
On the road. The 2.8-liter Six started and ran perfectly and accelerated briskly. Smooth-shifting overdrive automatic transmission. Impressive handling in routine driving. Steady, though slightly vague-handling in emergency tests. Faultless braking.	**Fuel economy.** Mpg: city, 15; expressway, 29. Gallons used in 15,000 miles, 700. Cruising range, 450 miles.	**Comments.** The *Cressida* is a very powerful performer and feels superficially slick and luxurious, but it doesn't rate quite as high in our tests as the *Camry*. Bumper test damage: none.
On the road. The 2.2-liter Five started and ran solidly, but its valve lifters clattered briefly after a cold start. Smooth-shifting automatic transmission. Very good routine handling; excellent emergency handling. Excellent brakes; very short stops from 60 mph.	**Fuel economy.** Mpg with automatic transmission: city, 14; expressway, 26. Gallons used in 15,000 miles, 765. Cruising range, 335 miles.	**Comments.** The *Quantum* is typical of European sports sedans in its ride and handling qualities. It is basically an *Audi 4000* at a lower price. 1986 saw a mid-model-year redesign of the front end and the introduction of a station wagon and four-wheel-drive models called *Syncro*. Bumper test damage: moderate.
On the road. The 2.3-liter Four started easily and generally ran well. While warming up, it occasionally hesitated briefly on takeoff. The overdrive automatic transmission shifted smoothly. Stable handling; sloppy but safe in hard turns at the test track. The brakes felt oversensitive at the track, but the car stopped well.	**Fuel economy.** Mpg with automatic transmission: city, 18; expressway, 32. Gallons used in 15,000 miles, 620. Cruising range, 395 miles.	**Comments.** The compact *Volvo 240* series has continued to be a durable and competent, if somewhat stodgy, model. Its bumpers are claimed to have been strengthened for the 1986 model.
On the road. The 2.2-liter 5 started and ran well at all times, though vibration was noticeable at higher speeds and at idle. The automatic transmission shifted smoothly. This front-wheel-drive car handled with smooth precision. Excellent brakes even without optional antilock feature.	**Fuel economy.** Mpg with non-turbo engine and automatic transmission: city, 14; expressway, 28. Gallons used in 15,000 miles, 745. Cruising range, 475 miles.	**Comments.** The *Audi 5000S* performs as a European sports sedan should. Seating and ride comfort are good also. Be sure that all the factory recalls relating to the "sudden acceleration runaway" have been performed on any used model that you are considering. Bumper test damage: none.

Medium cars (cont.)

BUICK CENTURY **▶Four cylinder model** **2-door** **4-door** **4-door wagon** **CHEVROLET CELEBRITY** **2-door** **4-door** **4-door wagon** **OLDSMOBILE CUTLASS CIERA** **▶Four cylinder model** **2-door** **4-door** **4-door wagon** **PONTIAC 6000** **2-door** **4-door** **4-door wagon**	**Predicted reliability.** For Four, average. For V6, worse than average.	**Comfort and convenience.** Very comfortable front seats. Very good driving position. Fairly comfortable rear seat. Very quiet. Ride not well controlled. Excellent climate-control system. Generally good controls. Lots of glare from gauges.
BUICK REGAL **2-door** **OLDSMOBILE CUTLASS SUPREME** **2-door** **4-door** **PONTIAC BONNEVILLE** **4-door**	**Predicted reliability.** Much worse than average.	**Comfort and convenience.** Very comfortable front seat for two, uncomfortable for three. Rear seat fairly comfortable for two, uncomfortable for three. Fairly quiet. Fairly comfortable ride except over large bumps. Excellent climate-control system.
BUICK RIVIERA **2-door**	**Predicted reliability.** No data; new model. GM models have tended to be particularly unreliable in their first year.	**Comfort and convenience.** Excellent front seats with no fewer than 18 power adjustments. Driving position, excellent. Very uncomfortable rear seat. Access to rear seat especially awkward. Very stiff ride on back roads with *T-Type* suspension. Very quiet. Excellent heating, ventilation and air-conditioning. Controls are needlessly complex; the Graphic Control Center is a small video-display monitor in the center of the dash. Operation requires pushing various spots on the screen to call-up other screens and select desired activity. Digital displays are clear.
CHRYSLER FIFTH AVENUE **4-door** **DODGE DIPLOMAT** **4-door** **PLYMOUTH GRAN FURY** **4-door**	**Predicted reliability.** Much worse than average.	**Comfort and convenience.** Exceptionally comfortable split bench seat for two, but cramped for a third occupant in the center. Uncomfortable rear seat—just roomy enough for six-footers and just wide enough for three adults. Good ride on smooth roads, snappy on rough ones. Moderate noise level. Excellent climate-control system. Crowded controls, but within easy reach. Daytime reflections spoiled the clearly marked displays.

On the road. Both the 2.5-liter Four and the 2.8-liter V6 started and ran well. The automatic transmission with lock-up feature shifted smoothly, but it tended to lock up prematurely, making the engine lug. This front-wheel-drive car handled sluggishly, but safely. Disappointingly long stops from 60 mph.

Fuel economy. Mpg for sedan with Four and automatic transmission: city, 16; expressway, 37. Gallons used in 15,000 miles, 610. Cruising range, 455 miles. Mpg for wagon with V6 engine: city, 14; expressway, 33. Gallons used in 15,000 miles, 710. Cruising range, 365 miles.

Comments. These GM A-body models appear to be improving in quality and reliability; the *Buick* and *Oldsmobile* versions more so than the *Chevrolet* and *Pontiac* models. We recommend the 4-cylinder engine; it provides adequate acceleration and gives good mileage. The sedan versions will benefit from any of the heavy-duty or performance suspension options. Bumper test damage: moderate with sedans; none with wagons. (The *Pontiac 6000 STE* is a special version of the A-cars; see separate entry for this model.)

On the road. The 3.8-liter gasoline V6 started and ran well. The automatic transmission with lock-up feature shifted smoothly. Handling was sluggish and vague, with considerable step-off over small bumps. Good, but touchy, brakes.

Fuel economy. Mpg with 3.8-liter V6 and automatic transmission: city, 13; expressway, 28. Gallons used in 15,000 miles, 780. Cruising range, 385 miles.

Comments. These aging GM models have little going for them anymore, and their reliability has been poor.

On the road. The 3.8-liter V6 started and ran without a problem. The overdrive automatic transmission shifted smoothly. Very competent routine handling with T-Type suspension. Very controllable emergency handling. Excellent brakes.

Fuel economy. Mpg with V6 and automatic transmission: city, 13; expressway, 34. Gallons used in 15,000 miles, 750. Cruising range, 385 miles.

Comments. Newly downsized for 1986, the *Riviera* appears overpriced and overcomplicated. Getting repairs for a used *Riviera* could be worrisome. The *T-Type* version we tested is considerably more competent in ride and handling than the standard version. Bumper test damage: moderate.

On the road. The 5.2-liter V8 started and ran well. Very smooth-shifting automatic transmission. Constant steering corrections need to keep car from wandering on highways. In very short stops, a front or rear brake often locked, making the car weave.

Fuel economy. Mpg: city, 11; expressway, 26. Gallons used in 15,000 miles, 885. Cruising range, 350 miles.

Comments. These older-design Chrysler products are sold in the large-car market class but are really medium in size. The *Fifth Avenue* has been successful in sales; the *Dodge* and *Plymouth* versions are popular primarily as police and fleet cars.

Medium cars (cont.)

CHRYSLER LE BARON **2-door** **2-door convertible** **4-door** **4-door wagon** **DODGE 600** **2-door** **2-door convertible**	**Predicted reliability.** Worse than average.	**Comfort and convenience.** Front bench seat very comfortable for two, fairly comfortable for three. Rear seat uncomfortable for two or three. Moderate noise level. Ride was busy even on good roads. Excellent climate-control system.
CHRYSLER LE BARON GTS **4-door hatchback** **DODGE LANCER** **4-door hatchback**	**Predicted reliability.** Average for nonturbo models; better than average for turbo (data for 1985 models).	**Comfort and convenience.** Very comfortable front seats. Very good driving position except for very tall or very short people. Uncomfortable rear seat; cramped for three adults. Quiet but jittery ride. Excellent climate-control system. Generally logical controls. Clear and complete displays.
CHRYSLER NEW YORKER **4-door** **DODGE 600** **4-door** **PLYMOUTH CARAVELLE** **4-door**	**Predicted reliability.** Worse than average.	**Comfort and convenience.** Very comfortable front seat. Good driving position, but could use a tilt steering column. Uncomfortable rear seat. Moderate noise level. Heater is powerful and unobtrusive, but warm-air distribution was spotty. Fan-forced fresh-air ventilation flowed freely from the four dash outlets. Controls are adequate but not as convenient as most. Displays are very legible at night but obscured by reflections during the day.
DODGE ARIES **2-door** **4-door** **4-door wagon** **PLYMOUTH RELIANT** **2-door** **4-door** **4-door wagon**	**Predicted reliability.** Worse than average.	**Comfort and convenience.** Bench front seat fairly comfortable for two or three. Very comfortable individual front seats (an option); they were a bit narrow and firm. Some drivers wished they could sit higher. Rear seat uncomfortable for two or three. Moderate noise level. Ride was busy even on good roads. Sharp bumps caused pitching, tossing, and metal-to-metal crunches from the suspension. Excellent climate-control system in cars with air-conditioning.

On the road. The 2.2-liter Four started and ran well. The automatic transmission usually shifted smoothly. This front-wheel-drive model handled controllably but not crisply. Very good brakes.

Fuel economy. Mpg with 2.2-liter Four: city, 16, expressway, 34. Gallons used in 15,000 miles, 640. Cruising range, 360 miles.

Comments. It's very easy to confuse the many versions of Chrysler K-cars. The *Le Baron* and 2-door versions of the *Dodge 600* are essentially similar to the lower-priced *Dodge Aries* and *Plymouth Reliant*. All could benefit from a heavy-duty suspension to tame the tender ride. The standard 2.2-liter Four is adequate for these models; the optional 2.5-liter Four and Turbocharged Four provide extra punch.

On the road. When cold, the optional 2.5-liter Four required longer cranking than usual, but it ran well. The automatic transmission shifted smoothly during normal driving, but more abruptly during hard acceleration. Vague but controllable handling, much improved by optional performance suspension. Excellent braking.

Fuel economy. Mpg with 2.5-liter Four and automatic transmission: city, 16; expressway, 31. Gallons used in 15,000 miles, 665. Cruising range, 335 miles. Mpg with turbocharged Four and automatic transmission: city, 16; expressway, 29. Gallons used in 15,000 miles, 675. Cruising range, 335 miles.

Comments. These Chrysler products are the models of choice in their family-sized line. Their hatchback body gives added versatility and their suspension, even in the standard version, is more competent than the suspension in the K-cars. The turbo Four with the performance suspension is even more capable. Bumper test damage: minor.

On the road. The 2.2-liter Four started easily and ran well at all times. When the air-conditioner was in use, the idle speed dropped and caused annoying vibration. The automatic transmission generally shifted smoothly, with occasional abrupt down-shifts. Routine handling was slow and vague, and power steering numbed road feel. Emergency handling was vague and sluggish, with considerable body roll in hard turns. Short brake stops, but controlling stops was difficult.

Fuel economy. Mpg with 2.2-liter Four and automatic transmission: city, 16; expressway, 34. Gallons used in 15,000 miles, 640. Cruising range, 360 miles.

Comments. These models are stretched K-cars. They have a slightly longer wheelbase and more fore-and-aft room in the rear seat. As with the K-cars, the suspension is overly soft and can benefit from a heavy-duty option. We found our tested *Plymouth Caravelle* to be an unpleasant car, and much preferred the *Chrysler Le Baron GTS* or *Dodge Lancer*. Bumper test damage: moderate.

On the road. The 2.2-liter Four started and ran well. The automatic transmission usually shifted smoothly. This front-wheel-drive model handled adequately but tended to go off line on bumpy roads. Very good brakes.

Fuel economy. Mpg with 2.2-liter Four and automatic transmission: city, 16; expressway, 34. Gallons used in 15,000 miles, 640. Cruising range, 360 miles.

Comments. These are the basic K-cars. Low first cost is their primary advantage. The standard 2.2-liter Four is recommended for these models, as is the heavy-duty suspension. Bumper test damage: moderate.

Medium cars (cont.)

►**FORD TAURUS** **4-door** **4-door wagon** ►**MERCURY SABLE** **4-door** **4-door wagon**	**Predicted reliability.** No data; new model. In general, other Ford medium-sized models have been average.	**Comfort and convenience.** Exceptionally comfortable front seats. Excellent driving position with power seat, but without it, the seat was low and the steering wheel high. Fairly comfortable rear seat for two or three. Quiet inside. Stable, tightly controlled ride on all but the bumpiest roads. Excellent climate-control system. Excellent controls and displays.
►**LINCOLN MARK VII** **2-door**	**Predicted reliability.** Average, but 1985 model showed the suspension system as a serious trouble spot.	**Comfort and convenience.** Exceptionally comfortable front seats. Very good driving position. Uncomfortable rear seat for two or three. Very quiet. Unusually well-controlled, smooth ride with automatic-leveling air suspension. Excellent automatic climate-control system. Complicated controls; clear digital displays.
►**MERCURY COUGAR** **2-door** ►**FORD THUNDERBIRD** **2-door**	**Predicted reliability.** Average.	**Comfort and convenience.** Exceptionally comfortable front seats. Low driving position, helped by optional power driver's seat. Very uncomfortable rear seat for two or three. Quiet. Smooth and well-controlled ride, even when carrying a full load. Excellent climate-control system. Inconvenient windshield wiper/washer controls.
►**MERCEDES-BENZ 300** **4-door**	**Predicted reliability.** We expect the new 300E to be like other *Mercedes* models: much better than average.	**Comfort and convenience.** Exceptionally comfortable front seats with many power adjustments. Excellent driving position. Fairly comfortable rear seat, with ample room for three average adults. Quiet inside. Firm, well-controlled ride. Excellent automatic climate-control system. Excellent controls and displays.
OLDSMOBILE TORONADO **2-door**	**Predicted reliability.** No data; new model. GM models have tended to be particularly unreliable in their first year.	**Comfort and convenience.** Very comfortable front seats. Driving position nearly ideal for all but very short drivers. Uncomfortable rear seat; barely enough headroom for six-footers. The suspension gave a smooth ride on good roads, but topped and bottomed badly on back roads. Access to rear seat is awkward. Extremely quiet. Excellent heating, ventilation, and air-conditioning. Controls are of conventional type, but made up of too many tiny buttons. Digital displays are clear.

On the road. Both the 3-liter V6 and the 2.5-liter Four started and ran well. With the V6, the overdrive automatic transmission shifted very smoothly, most of the time. With the Four, the automatic transmission shifted smoothly but acceleration was no more than adequate. These front-wheel-drive models handled very well; the wagon version was especially competent. Fairly long stopping distances and considerable brake fade, but stops were straight.

Fuel economy. Sedan mpg with V6: city, 15; expressway, 35. Gallons used in 15,000 miles, 660. Cruising range, 400 miles. Wagon mpg: city, 13; expressway, 35. Gallons used in 15,000 miles, 730. Cruising range, 435 miles. Mpg with 2.5-liter 4 and automatic transmission: city, 14; expressway, 33. Gallons used in 15,000 miles, 700. Cruising range, 385 miles.

Comments. These new Ford models are the best-performing domestic products we've tested. They combine the comfort expected in a domestic car with the competent handling expected in European models. The V6 combined with the overdrive automatic transmission is preferred over the 4-cylinder version. Bumper test damage: none.

On the road. The 5-liter V8 started and ran well. The overdrive automatic transmission shifted very smoothly. Routine handling was clumsy. Emergency handling was sluggish and vague, but safe. Handling was much better in the LSC model. Very good antilock brakes, but stopping distances were somewhat long.

Fuel economy. Mpg: city, 12; expressway, 35. Gallons used in 15,000 miles, 770. Cruising range, 500 miles.

Comments. The *Mark VII* is of an older design, but the car delivers the luxury and smoothness that one expects of a car of this type. We much prefer the more-sporty *LSC* version because of its more-competent handling. Bumper test damage: moderate.

On the road. The 3.8-liter V6 started and ran well and delivered ample acceleration. The automatic transmission shifted fairly smoothly. Sluggish handling; rear end sometimes swung out during hard turns. Stops were straight and fairly short.

Fuel economy. Mpg with 3.8-liter V6 and automatic transmission: city, 16; expressway, 29. Gallons used in 15,000 miles, 675. Cruising range, 505 miles.

Comments. These rear-wheel-drive Ford products are our models of choice in the domestic specialty coupe field, primarily because of their relatively good overall repair records. Bumper test damage: none.

On the road. The 3-liter Six started and ran flawlessly and accelerated very quickly. The 4-speed automatic transmission usually shifted very smoothly. Impressively precise handling. The antilock braking system stopped the car short and straight even on slippery roads.

Fuel economy. Mpg with automatic transmission: city, 16; expressway, 28. Gallons used in 15,000 miles, 700. Cruising range, 415 miles.

Comments. The best car, overall, that we have tested. Needless to say, this model will be a very expensive used car, but it's likely to give good service for those who can afford it. Bumper test damage: extensive.

On the road. The 3.8-liter V6 started and ran without a problem. The overdrive automatic transmission shifted smoothly. Sluggish routine handling; car tended to shift direction slightly in bumpy turns. Emergency handling was sloppy and vague; tail wagged and steering response lagged during abrupt maneuvers. Mediocre brakes; excessive nosedive contributed to long stopping distances.

Fuel economy. Mgp: city, 13; expressway, 35. Gallons used in 15,000 miles, 735. Cruising range, 400 miles.

Comments. The *Toronado* is all-new and downsized for 1986. We found the standard suspension to be too soft for best handling; the performance option would be a better compromise. Bumper test damage: moderate.

Medium cars (cont.)

PONTIAC 6000 STE **4-door**	**Predicted reliability.** Worse than average.	**Comfort and convenience.** Exceptionally comfortable front seats and driving position. Very good rear seating for two or three. Moderate noise level; the "sporty" exhaust noise was irritating. Steady ride on fairly good roads; pitching on bad roads. Heater was slow to warm and slow to respond to temperature adjustments: Otherwise, the climate-control system was excellent. Pretentious but functional displays.
►VOLVO 740/760 **4-door 740** **4-door wagon 740** **4-door 760** **4-door wagon 760**	**Predicted reliability.** Average.	**Comfort and convenience.** Exceptionally comfortable front seats. Very good driving position. Fairly comfortable rear seat for two or three. Moderate noise level. Generally steady ride, but became busy and jiggly on secondary roads. Excellent automatic climate-control system, operating controls, and displays.

LARGE CARS

BUICK ELECTRA **2-door** **4-door** **OLDSMOBILE 98 REGENCY** **2-door** **4-door**	**Predicted reliability.** Much worse than average	**Comfort and convenience.** Front seating exceptionally comfortable for two or three. Rear seating very comfortable for two, uncomfortable for three on long trips. Ride very good on smooth roads; much worse on bumpy roads. Quiet inside; coarse pavement increased interior noise. Excellent climate-control system. Most controls were convenient and displays were mostly clear.
BUICK LE SABRE **2-door** **4-door** **OLDSMOBILE DELTA 88 ROYALE** **2-door** **4-door**	**Predicted reliability.** No data; new model. The reliability of essentially similar *Buick Electra* and *Oldsmobile 98* has been much worse than average in the first year after redesign.	**Comfort and convenience.** Very comfortable split bench front seat, roomy enough for three adults. Very comfortable, though rather low, driving position. Rear seat fairly comfortable even for three. Exceptionally quiet inside. Smooth ride on expressways; rough on secondary roads. Excellent climate control. Old-fashioned, familiar controls. Minimal displays.
CHEVROLET CAPRICE **2-door** **4-door** **4-door wagon** **PONTIAC PARISIENNE** **4-door** **4-door wagon**	**Predicted reliability.** Worse than average.	**Comfort and convenience.** Optional 50-50 split bench front seat was low, but very comfortable for two and fairly comfortable for three. Power driver's seat gives better height. Rear seat fairly comfortable for two or three. Quiet. Very good ride, but busy on rough roads. Excellent climate-control system. Clear displays. Logical controls.

On the road. The 2.8-liter HO V6 started and ran flawlessly. The automatic transmission, with lock-up feature, shifted smoothly. This front-wheel-drive model (with standard performance suspension and tires) gave very good routine handling and excellent emergency handling. Excellent 4-wheel-disk brakes produced short, straight stops.

Fuel economy Mpg: city, 15; expressway, 29. Gallons used in 15,000 miles, 705. Cruising range, 365 miles.

Comments. The *STE* is a unique version of the *Pontiac 6000.* We found to to be a good performer and much more interesting to drive than the usual GM family sedan.

On the road. The 2.8-liter V6 (*760* model) started and ran well, but idle was often unsteady. The overdrive automatic transmission shifted smoothly. Handling was very good. Very good brakes.

Fuel economy. Mpg with 2.8-liter V6 and automatic transmission: city, 14; expressway, 25. Gallons used in 15,000 miles, 785. Cruising range. 320 miles.

Comments. An excellent all-around car, comfortable and responsive. The wagons are especially large and well-shaped. The 4-cylinder *740* should perform adequately; our tested version was a *760* V6.

On the road. The 3.8-liter V6 always started and ran well. The smooth-shifting overdrive automatic transmission shifted into and out of overdrive lock-up too often. In this front-wheel-drive car, directional stability felt uncertain at times, and the rear wheels tended to step out in bumpy turns, but steering response was good. Very good braking, though abrupt in short stops.

Fuel economy. Mpg with 3.8-liter V6: city, 14; expressway, 33. Gallons used in 15,000 miles, 700. Cruising range, 440 miles.

Comments. These recently downsized models are considerably lighter and shorter than the previous rear-wheel-drive models, but are roomy inside and have comfortable seating. Their ride and handling, however, are not as good as they should be, especially on more-challenging roads or road surfaces. Bumper test damage: moderate.

On the road. The 3-liter V6 started easily, but it occasionally stuttered briefly during acceleration after idling. The overdrive automatic transmission shifted smoothly most of the time. Handling was sluggish and vague, but safe. Excellent braking.

Fuel economy. Mpg with 3-liter V6: city, 14; expressway, 33. Gallons used in 15,000 miles, 700. Cruising range, 440 miles.

Comments. These new-for-86 models are essentially the same cars as the more-expensive *Buick Electra* and *Olds 98,* and thus are better values because of their lower first cost. Power driver's seat and tilt steering column are good options to look for. Bumper test damage: moderate.

On the road. The optional 5-liter V8 in our *Chevrolet* started and ran well and provided ample acceleration. The overdrive automatic transmission shifted smoothly. Smooth and controllable handling. Very good brakes.

Fuel economy. Mpg with V8: city, 14; expressway, 31. Gallons used in 15,000 miles, 735. Cruising range, 545 miles.

Comments. These models are the last of the traditional large GM rear-wheel-drive cars. They are not as comfortable, especially in the rear seat, as the new front-wheel-drive GM models, but offer the familiar feel and the heavier trailer-towing capability of older models. The station wagon versions of *Buick Le Sabre* and *Olds 88* share this chassis.

Large cars (cont.)

►**MERCURY GRAND MARQUIS** **2-door** **4-door** **4-door wagon** ►**FORD LTD CROWN VICTORIA** **2-door** **4-door** **4-door wagon**	**Predicted reliability.** Better than average.	**Comfort and convenience.** Split front bench seat exceptionally comfortable for two and very comfortable for three. Rear seat very comfortable for two or three. Very quiet. Excellent ride; rode well even with full load. Excellent climate-control system. The *Mercury's* glittery gauges were hard to read; the *Ford's* are better. Awkward windshield wiper/washer control.

SMALL VANS

CHEVROLET ASTRO **Passenger van** **GMC SAFARI** **Passenger van**	**Predicted reliability** Average.	**Comfort and convenience.** Exceptionally comfortable front seats. High driving position would have been excellent except for awkward pedal placement and lack of foot space. Fairly comfortable center and rear seats in 8-person seating package. Moderate noise level; uncomfortable ride. Adequate heating, modest ventilation, and weak air-conditioning. Awkward controls. Clear displays.
FORD AEROSTAR **Passenger van**	**Predicted reliability.** No data; new model. Other Ford products have generally been average.	**Comfort and convenience.** Fairly comfortable front captain's chairs (included in seven-seat *XL* package). Awkward and uncomfortable driving position. (Tilt steering wheel recommended.) Fairly comfortable center and rear seats. Moderate noise level. Fairly well-controlled ride on good roads; punishing on poor roads. Excellent climate-control system. Awkward, inconvenient controls. Easy-to-read displays.
►**PLYMOUTH VOYAGER** **Passenger van** ►**DODGE CARAVAN** **Passenger van**	**Predicted reliability.** Average.	**Comfort and convenience.** Exceptionally comfortable front seats and driving position; passenger's seat is not adjustable. Fairly comfortable second seat for two. Fairly comfortable third seat for two or three. Moderate noise level. The *Voyager* rode more like a car than a truck. The ride was pleasant on good roads, but rough on back roads. Excellent climate-control system. Very good controls and displays.

On the road. The 5-liter V8 started and ran well. The overdrive automatic transmission shifted smoothly, but shifted into and out of overdrive too frequently. Handling was somewhat sluggish and clumsy, but safe. Very good brakes.

Fuel economy. Mpg: city, 11; expressway, 27. Gallons used in 15,000 miles, 880. Cruising range, 350 miles.

Comments. These large Ford models have consistantly had good overall repair records, and for that reason are the models of choice in this group. They are comfortable and smooth-riding, but are not as fuel-efficient as their front-wheel-drive competitors. Heavy trailer-towing ability. Bumper test damage: moderate.

On the road. The 4.3-liter V6 ran flawlessly except for an occasional stall after a cold start. The overdrive automatic transmission usually shifted abruptly from first to second, and it hunted in and out of lock-up on mild upgrades. Handling was sluggish and vague, but safe. Traction was below par on slippery roads. Very good brakes, though a bit hard to modulate.

Fuel economy. Mpg with V6 and automatic transmission: city, 12; expressway, 29. Gallons used in 15,000 miles, 825. Cruising range with optional 27-gallon tank, 535 miles.

Comments. The *Astro* is much more truck-like than the small vans from Chrysler Corp. Its rear-wheel-drive chassis is capable of towing much greater trailer loads, however. Bumper test damage: extensive.

On the road. The 2.8-liter V6 started and ran flawlessly. The overdrive automatic transmission usually shifted very smoothly. Sluggish and sloppy but controllable handling. Poor traction on slippery roads. Braking was poor; stopping distances without wheel locking were very long; when a wheel locked, the van often swerved to the side, sometimes severely.

Fuel economy. Mpg with V6 and automatic transmission: city, 11; expressway, 25. Gallons used in 15,000 miles, 905. Cruising range, 310 miles.

Comments The *Aerostar* is also more truck-like than the Chrysler vans, with its tall body and rear-wheel-drive chassis. We found the braking problem to be a severe shortcoming. Bumper test damage: extensive.

On the road. The optional 2.6-liter Four started and ran well. (A 2.2-liter Four is standard.) The automatic transmission shifted smoothly except in cold weather, when it occasionally delayed shifts into high gear. This front-wheel-drive van handled much like a passenger car in normal driving, but was sluggish and vague in emergency maneuvers. The front brakes locked a bit too soon, extending stopping distances, but fade was slight.

Fuel economy. Mpg with 2.6-liter Four and automatic transmission: city, 14; expressway, 30. Gallons used in 15,000 miles, 725. Cruising range with optional 20-gallon tank, 470 miles.

Comments. Our choices among the small passenger vans. These Chrysler products do not have the capability to tow heavy trailers, but they perform much more like passenger cars, especially in ride and handling, than the other vans. Bumper test damage: extensive.

Frequency-of-Repair records, 1980-1985

The charts on the following pages give detailed repair and expense histories for 252 domestic and foreign cars. This unique collection of information was drawn from some 450,000 responses to CU's 1985 Annual Questionnaire, in which readers answered questions on the most recent year of operation for their car. We combine these responses with those from earlier years to provide the predicted reliability judgments included in our report on the 1986 cars. (See pages 58 to 89.) New-car buyers can also check the repair records of earlier models for signs of the kinds of problems likely to crop up in a current model.

These records are particularly valuable for used-car buyers, who can check a specific model to find the trouble spots that may have plagued current owners. If the model is recent and the problems are with a major component—the engine or automatic transmission, say—then the car is probably not a good buy. With an older car, ask about such problems before buying. The necessary repair may have already been made.

TROUBLE SPOTS. The charts show the frequency with which a given problem occurred in each model as compared with the occurrence of the same problem in all cars of that model year reported in the survey.

Cars develop repair problems not only as a result of age, but also as a consequence of the number of miles driven. In general, the more miles driven, the faster things wear out or fail. We ask respondents to state the number of miles on the car, and we adjust our tallies to eliminate differences among models due solely to their different mileages.

A blank column in a chart means the model did not exist in that year. A column labeled "insufficient data" means we didn't have enough responses to evaluate that year's car. A blank square means that the car didn't have that feature or that we had insufficient data. Unless otherwise indicated, all body types of a given model are represented in its chart.

The specific categories we asked readers to comment on in the Annual Questionnaire were:

Air conditioning: compressor, expansion valve, fans.

Body exterior (paint): fading, discoloring, chalking, peeling.

Body exterior (rust): pitting, corrosion, perforation.

Body hardware: window, door, and seat mechanisms; locks; seat belts; head restraints.

Body integrity: air or water leaks, wind noise, rattles, and squeaks.

Brakes: hydraulic or power-boost systems, linings, and disks or drums.

Clutch: lining, pressure plate, release bearing, and linkage.

Driveline (except transmission): universal joints, axle, differential, wheel bearings, and drive shaft.

Electrical system (chassis): starter, alternator, battery, horn, switches, instruments, wiring, lights, radio, and accessory motors.

Engine cooling: radiator, heater core, water pump, and overheating.

Engine mechanical: rings, cylinders, pistons, engine bearings, valves, camshaft, oil leaks, and engine overhaul.

Exhaust system: exhaust manifold, muffler, catalytic converter, pipes, and leaks.

Fuel system: stalling or hesitation, carburetion (can't be set properly), choke, fuel injection (if any), fuel pump, fuel leaks, and emissions-control devices.

Ignition system: spark or glow plugs, coil, distributor, points, electronic ignition, timing, and too-frequent tuneups.

Suspension: wheel alignment, springs or torsion bars, ball joints, bushings, and shock absorbers.

Transmission (manual): gear-shifting linkage and transaxle.

Transmission (automatic): gear-shifting linkage and torque converter.

TROUBLE INDEX, COST INDEX. The charts also give an overall Trouble Index for each model year that compares the trouble experience of a given model with the experience of all cars for the same year. The Trouble Index is also adjusted for mileage.

The charts also give some indication of the average maintenance and repair costs faced by the current owners of that model. Such costs are particularly sensitive to the mileage driven; high-mileage cars have costs up to double those of low mileage cars. We adjust the Cost Index for each model to eliminate the bias caused by different mileage distributions among models.

The symbols in the cost-index now indicate how far a model departs from the average maintenance and repair costs for other models of that year, which were:

AVERAGE REPAIR COST PER MODEL YEAR.

1980	1981	1982	1983	1984
$410	$380	$300	$220	$120

To be labeled much worse (or much better) than average, a model had to have costs that were at least 35 percent higher (or lower) than the adjusted average for all cars reported in that model year, and had to meet other stringent statistical tests.

There's no Cost Index or average cost given for the 1985 models; most of their repair costs should be covered under warranty. The cost of accident repair, tires, and batteries are omitted.

Frequency-of-repair records begin on next page

Much better than average · Better than average · Average · Worse than average · Much worse than average · * Insufficient cost data

AMC Concord 6

TROUBLE SPOTS	'80	'81	'82	'83	'84	'85
Air-conditioning	Average	Average	Average	Insufficient data	Insufficient data	Insufficient data
Body exterior (paint)	Average	Average	Average			
Body exterior (rust)	Average	Average	Average			
Body hardware	Worse	Worse	Average			
Body integrity	Much worse	Worse	Average			
Brakes	Much worse	Much worse	Worse			
Clutch	Worse	Much worse	Worse			
Driveline	Average	Average	Average			
Electrical system (chassis)	Average	Worse	Average			
Engine cooling	Average	Worse	Average			
Engine mechanical	Average	Much worse	Much worse			
Exhaust system	Much worse	Average	Average			
Fuel system	Average	Average	Average			
Ignition system	Average	Average	Average			
Suspension	Much worse	Average	Average			
Transmission (manual)	Average	Average	Average			
Transmission (automatic)	Average	Average	Average			
TROUBLE INDEX	Worse	Much worse	Average			
COST INDEX	Average	Average	*			

AMC Eagle 6

TROUBLE SPOTS	'80	'81	'82	'83	'84	'85
Air-conditioning	Better	Average	Average	Average	Average	Insufficient data
Body exterior (paint)	Average	Average	Average	Worse	Average	
Body exterior (rust)	Worse	Average	Average	Worse	Worse	
Body hardware	Much worse	Much worse	Average	Average	Worse	
Body integrity	Much worse	Worse	Average	Much worse	Much worse	
Brakes	Much worse	Much worse	Much worse	Much worse	Worse	
Clutch		Much worse	Much worse	Much worse	Average	
Driveline	Much worse	Much worse	Much worse	Much worse	Average	
Electrical system (chassis)	Average	Much worse	Average	Worse	Average	
Engine cooling	Average	Much worse	Average	Average	Average	
Engine mechanical	Much worse	Average	Average	Average	Average	
Exhaust system	Much worse	Better	Average	Average	Average	
Fuel system	Average	Average	Average	Worse	Much worse	
Ignition system	Average	Average	Average	Worse	Much worse	
Suspension	Much worse	Worse	Average	Average	Worse	
Transmission (manual)		Much worse	Average	Average	Average	
Transmission (automatic)	Average	Worse	Average	Worse	Average	
TROUBLE INDEX	Much worse	Much worse	Worse	Much worse	Much worse	
COST INDEX	Average	Worse	Worse	Worse	Average	

Audi 4000, 4000S 4

TROUBLE SPOTS	'80	'81	'82	'83	'84	'85
Air-conditioning	Worse	Average	Average	Average	Average	Average
Body exterior (paint)	Much better	Much better	Better	Average	Better	Average
Body exterior (rust)	Better	Better	Better	Average	Average	Average
Body hardware	Average	Better	Better	Average	Average	Average
Body integrity	Much better	Much better	Average	Better	Much better	Average
Brakes	Average	Better	Better	Average	Average	Average
Clutch	Average	Much better	Better	Average	Average	Average
Driveline	Average	Average	Better	Average	Average	Average
Electrical system (chassis)	Much worse	Much worse	Much worse	Average	Average	Average
Engine cooling	Average	Average	Average	Average	Average	Average
Engine mechanical	Average	Average	Average	Average	Average	Average
Exhaust system	Much worse	Better	Better	Average	Average	Average
Fuel system	Average	Much better	Much better	Average	Much better	Average
Ignition system	Average	Better	Better	Better	Better	Average
Suspension	Better	Better	Better	Better	Average	Average
Transmission (manual)	Worse	Average	Average	Average	Average	Average
Transmission (automatic)	Average	Average	Average	Average	Average	Average
TROUBLE INDEX	Average	Better	Better	Much better	Better	Better
COST INDEX	Worse	Average	Average	Worse	Average	

Audi 4000, Audi Coupe 5

TROUBLE SPOTS	'80	'81	'82	'83	'84	'85
Air-conditioning	Insufficient data	Average	Average	Insufficient data	Insufficient data	Insufficient data
Body exterior (paint)		Average	Better			
Body exterior (rust)		Average	Average			
Body hardware		Average	Average			
Body integrity		Average	Average			
Brakes		Average	Average			
Clutch		Average	Better			
Driveline		Average	Average			
Electrical system (chassis)		Much worse	Worse			
Engine cooling		Average	Average			
Engine mechanical		Average	Better			
Exhaust system		Better	Average			
Fuel system		Average	Average			
Ignition system		Average	Average			
Suspension		Average	Better			
Transmission (manual)		Average	Average			
Transmission (automatic)		Average	Average			
TROUBLE INDEX		Average	Better			
COST INDEX		*	Worse			

Audi 4000S, Quattro (4-WD)

TROUBLE SPOTS	'80	'81	'82	'83	'84	'85
Air-conditioning					Average	Insufficient data
Body exterior (paint)					Average	
Body exterior (rust)					Average	
Body hardware					Average	
Body integrity					Better	
Brakes					Average	
Clutch					Average	
Driveline					Average	
Electrical system (chassis)					Average	
Engine cooling					Average	
Engine mechanical					Average	
Exhaust system					Average	
Fuel system					Better	
Ignition system					Average	
Suspension					Average	
Transmission (manual)					Average	
Transmission (automatic)					Average	
TROUBLE INDEX					Better	
COST INDEX					Worse	

Audi 5000, 5000S (gas)

TROUBLE SPOTS	'80	'81	'82	'83	'84	'85
Air-conditioning	Worse	Worse	Average	Better	Much worse	Average
Body exterior (paint)	Better	Much better	Better	Better	Better	Average
Body exterior (rust)	Much better	Much better	Average	Better	Average	Average
Body hardware	Worse	Average	Average	Much worse	Worse	Average
Body integrity	Better	Much better	Better	Much better	Much better	Better
Brakes	Much worse	Average	Average	Average	Worse	Average
Clutch	Worse	Worse	Average	Average	Better	Average
Driveline	Much worse	Average	Average	Average	Average	Average
Electrical system (chassis)	Worse	Much worse	Much worse	Much worse	Much worse	Average
Engine cooling	Worse	Average	Average	Average	Much worse	Average
Engine mechanical	Average	Average	Average	Average	Average	Average
Exhaust system	Average	Much better	Average	Average	Average	Average
Fuel system	Average	Better	Average	Average	Average	Average
Ignition system	Average	Better	Better	Average	Average	Average
Suspension	Average	Average	Average	Better	Better	Average
Transmission (manual)	Average	Average	Average	Average	Average	Average
Transmission (automatic)	Average	Average	Average	Average	Average	Average
TROUBLE INDEX	Worse	Average	Better	Average	Average	Average
COST INDEX	Much worse	Much worse	Much worse	Much worse	Worse	

Audi 5000, 5000S (diesel)

TROUBLE SPOTS	'80	'81	'82	'83	'84	'85
Air-conditioning	Average	Much worse				
Body exterior (paint)	Much better	Better				
Body exterior (rust)	Much better	Better				
Body hardware	Average	Average				
Body integrity	Better	Better				
Brakes	Average	Average				
Clutch	Much worse	Worse				
Driveline	Average	Average				
Electrical system (chassis)	Average	Much worse				
Engine cooling	Worse	Average				
Engine mechanical	Average	Average				
Exhaust system	Better	Much better				
Fuel system	Better	Much better				
Ignition system	Average	Average				
Suspension	Average	Average				
Transmission (manual)	Average	Average				
Transmission (automatic)						
TROUBLE INDEX	Average	Average				
COST INDEX	Much worse	Much worse				

Audi 5000, 5000S (Turbodiesel)

TROUBLE SPOTS	'80	'81	'82	'83	'84	'85
Air-conditioning				Average		
Body exterior (paint)				Average		
Body exterior (rust)				Average		
Body hardware				Much worse		
Body integrity				Average		
Brakes				Worse		
Clutch						
Driveline				Average		
Electrical system (chassis)				Worse		
Engine cooling				Average		
Engine mechanical				Average		
Exhaust system				Average		
Fuel system				Average		
Ignition system				Worse		
Suspension				Better		
Transmission (manual)						
Transmission (automatic)				Average		
TROUBLE INDEX				Average		
COST INDEX				Much worse		

BMW 320i, 318i — TROUBLE SPOTS	'80	'81	'82	'83	'84	'85
Air-conditioning	○	○	○	○	●	○
Body exterior (paint)	⊜	⊜	⊖	⊖	○	○
Body exterior (rust)	⊜	⊖	⊖	○	○	○
Body hardware	⊜	⊜	⊜	⊜	○	○
Body integrity	⊖	⊜	⊖	⊖	⊜	○
Brakes	○	○	●	●	○	○
Clutch	○	○	⊖	○	○	○
Driveline	⊖	⊖	⊖	○	○	○
Electrical system (chassis)	○	○	○	○	○	○
Engine cooling	⊖	⊖	○	○	○	○
Engine mechanical	⊜	⊜	⊖	○	○	○
Exhaust system	○	⊖	○	○	○	○
Fuel system	⊖	⊖	⊖	○	●	○
Ignition system	○	⊖	○	○	○	○
Suspension	⊖	⊜	⊖	⊖	⊖	○
Transmission (manual)	○	○	○	○	○	○
Transmission (automatic)	○	○	○	○	○	○
TROUBLE INDEX	⊜	⊜	⊖	⊖	○	○
COST INDEX	◒	◒	◒	●	●	

BMW 325e — TROUBLE SPOTS	'80	'81	'82	'83	'84	'85
Air-conditioning					○	○
Body exterior (paint)					⊖	○
Body exterior (rust)					○	○
Body hardware					○	○
Body integrity					⊜	○
Brakes					○	○
Clutch					○	○
Driveline					○	○
Electrical system (chassis)					○	○
Engine cooling					○	○
Engine mechanical					○	○
Exhaust system					○	○
Fuel system					○	○
Ignition system					○	○
Suspension					⊖	○
Transmission (manual)					○	○
Transmission (automatic)					○	○
TROUBLE INDEX					⊜	⊖
COST INDEX					●	

BMW 528e, 533i — TROUBLE SPOTS	'80	'81	'82	'83	'84	'85
Air-conditioning	Insufficient data	Insufficient data	○	●	◒	Insufficient data
Body exterior (paint)			⊖	⊜	⊖	
Body exterior (rust)			⊖	⊖	○	
Body hardware			○	○	○	
Body integrity			⊜	⊖	⊜	
Brakes			○	○	○	
Clutch			○	◒	○	
Driveline			○	○	○	
Electrical system (chassis)			○	○	○	
Engine cooling			◒	○	○	
Engine mechanical			○	○	○	
Exhaust system			⊖	○	○	
Fuel system			○	◒	○	
Ignition system			○	○	○	
Suspension			○	◒	⊖	
Transmission (manual)			○	○	○	
Transmission (automatic)			○	○	○	
TROUBLE INDEX			⊖	○	⊖	
COST INDEX			●	●	●	

Buick Century 4 (FWD) — TROUBLE SPOTS	'80	'81	'82	'83	'84	'85
Air-conditioning			●	○	○	○
Body exterior (paint)			○	⊖	○	○
Body exterior (rust)			⊖	○	○	○
Body hardware			○	⊖	⊖	○
Body integrity			○	○	⊖	○
Brakes			●	●	○	○
Clutch						
Driveline			○	○	○	○
Electrical system (chassis)			○	◒	○	○
Engine cooling			○	◒	◒	○
Engine mechanical			○	◒	◒	○
Exhaust system			○	○	○	○
Fuel system			○	⊖	⊖	⊖
Ignition system			○	○	◒	○
Suspension			◒	○	○	○
Transmission (manual)						
Transmission (automatic)			○	○	○	○
TROUBLE INDEX			◒	◒	○	○
COST INDEX			○	○	⊖	

Buick Century V6 (FWD) — TROUBLE SPOTS	'80	'81	'82	'83	'84	'85
Air-conditioning			●	◒	●	◒
Body exterior (paint)			○	○	○	○
Body exterior (rust)			○	○	○	○
Body hardware			◒	○	○	○
Body integrity			○	○	○	○
Brakes			●	●	○	○
Clutch						
Driveline			○	○	○	○
Electrical system (chassis)			◒	●	●	◒
Engine cooling			●	●	◒	◒
Engine mechanical			●	○	○	○
Exhaust system			⊖	○	○	○
Fuel system			◒	◒	◒	○
Ignition system			●	◒	○	○
Suspension			●	◒	◒	○
Transmission (manual)						
Transmission (automatic)			◒	○	○	○
TROUBLE INDEX			●	●	●	◒
COST INDEX			○	○	○	

Buick Century V6 — TROUBLE SPOTS	'80	'81	'82	'83	'84	'85
Air-conditioning	○	○				
Body exterior (paint)	○	○				
Body exterior (rust)	⊖	○				
Body hardware	○	○				
Body integrity	○	○				
Brakes	○	○				
Clutch						
Driveline	⊖	○				
Electrical system (chassis)	⊖	○				
Engine cooling	○	●				
Engine mechanical	○	◒				
Exhaust system	⊖	●				
Fuel system	○	●				
Ignition system	○	●				
Suspension	○	●				
Transmission (manual)						
Transmission (automatic)	○	○				
TROUBLE INDEX	⊖	◒				
COST INDEX	⊖	○				

Buick Electra V8 — TROUBLE SPOTS	'80	'81	'82	'83	'84	'85
Air-conditioning	○	○	○	○	○	
Body exterior (paint)	○	○	○	○	○	
Body exterior (rust)	○	○	○	○	○	
Body hardware	○	○	◒	○	◒	
Body integrity	○	○	○	○	●	
Brakes	○	○	○	⊖	○	
Clutch						
Driveline	⊖	○	○	○	○	
Electrical system (chassis)	○	○	●	○	○	
Engine cooling	○	○	○	⊖	○	
Engine mechanical	○	○	⊖	⊖	⊖	
Exhaust system	○	●	●	●	○	
Fuel system	⊜	○	○	⊖	⊖	
Ignition system	○	○	○	○	○	
Suspension	○	○	○	◒	◒	
Transmission (manual)						
Transmission (automatic)	○	○	○	○	○	
TROUBLE INDEX	⊖	○	◒	○	○	
COST INDEX	○	○	○	○	○	

Buick Electra, Park Ave, T-Type — TROUBLE SPOTS	'80	'81	'82	'83	'84	'85
Air-conditioning						◒
Body exterior (paint)						○
Body exterior (rust)						○
Body hardware						◒
Body integrity						◒
Brakes						○
Clutch						
Driveline						○
Electrical system (chassis)						●
Engine cooling						◒
Engine mechanical						○
Exhaust system						○
Fuel system						◒
Ignition system						○
Suspension						○
Transmission (manual)						
Transmission (automatic)						◒
TROUBLE INDEX						●
COST INDEX						

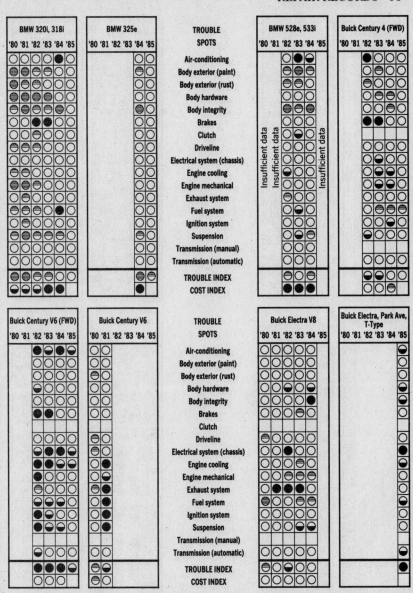

⊜ Much better than average · ◓ Better than average · ○ Average · ◒ Worse than average · ● Much worse than average · * Insufficient cost data

TROUBLE SPOTS	Buick LeSabre V6 '80	'81	'82	'83	'84	'85
Air-conditioning	○	○	●	○	○	Insufficient data
Body exterior (paint)	○	○	○	●	◒	
Body exterior (rust)	○	○	○	○	◒	
Body hardware	○	○	○	○	○	
Body integrity	○	○	○	○	○	
Brakes	○	○	○	◓	○	
Clutch						
Driveline	○	○	○	○	○	
Electrical system (chassis)	○	○	○	○	○	
Engine cooling	◒	●	●	●	○	
Engine mechanical	○	●	●	◒	○	
Exhaust system	◒	●	●	○	○	
Fuel system	○	◒	●	◒	○	
Ignition system	○	◒	○	◒	○	
Suspension	○	○	◒	●	●	
Transmission (manual)						
Transmission (automatic)	○	○	○	○	○	
TROUBLE INDEX	○	◒	●	◒	◒	
COST INDEX	○	○	○	◓	◓	

TROUBLE SPOTS	Buick LeSabre V8 '80	'81	'82	'83	'84	'85
Air-conditioning	○	○	◓	⊜	◓	○
Body exterior (paint)	○	○	○	◒	◒	◒
Body exterior (rust)	⊜	◓	○	○	◒	○
Body hardware	○	○	◒	○	○	○
Body integrity	⊜	○	○	○	◒	◒
Brakes	○	○	○	○	○	○
Clutch						
Driveline	○	○	○	○	○	○
Electrical system (chassis)	○	○	○	◓	○	○
Engine cooling	○	○	◓	○	○	○
Engine mechanical	◓	○	◓	◓	○	○
Exhaust system	○	●	●	●	○	○
Fuel system	◓	○	◓	○	◓	◓
Ignition system	○	◓	○	○	○	○
Suspension	○	○	●	●	●	◒
Transmission (manual)						
Transmission (automatic)	○	○	○	○	○	○
TROUBLE INDEX	◓	◓	○	○	○	◒
COST INDEX	○	○	○	○	○	

TROUBLE SPOTS	Buick Regal V6 '80	'81	'82	'83	'84	'85
Air-conditioning	○	◒	◒	○	○	○
Body exterior (paint)	◒	●	◒	◒	◒	◒
Body exterior (rust)	○	○	○	○	○	○
Body hardware	○	○	○	◒	○	●
Body integrity	◒	●	◒	●	●	●
Brakes	○	◒	○	◓	○	○
Clutch						
Driveline	○	○	○	○	○	○
Electrical system (chassis)	○	○	○	○	◒	○
Engine cooling	●	●	●	◒	○	◒
Engine mechanical	○	◒	◒	◒	○	○
Exhaust system	○	●	●	○	○	○
Fuel system	○	●	●	◒	◓	○
Ignition system	○	●	●	○	○	○
Suspension	◒	●	●	◒	◒	○
Transmission (manual)						
Transmission (automatic)	○	○	○	○	○	○
TROUBLE INDEX	○	●	●	◒	◒	●
COST INDEX	○	○	○	○	◓	

TROUBLE SPOTS	Buick Somerset Regal 4 '80	'81	'82	'83	'84	'85
Air-conditioning						○
Body exterior (paint)						○
Body exterior (rust)						○
Body hardware						○
Body integrity						○
Brakes						○
Clutch						○
Driveline						○
Electrical system (chassis)						●
Engine cooling						○
Engine mechanical						○
Exhaust system						○
Fuel system						○
Ignition system						○
Suspension						◒
Transmission (manual)						○
Transmission (automatic)						○
TROUBLE INDEX						○
COST INDEX						

TROUBLE SPOTS	Buick Somerset Regal V6 '80	'81	'82	'83	'84	'85
Air-conditioning						○
Body exterior (paint)						○
Body exterior (rust)						○
Body hardware						○
Body integrity						○
Brakes						○
Clutch						
Driveline						○
Electrical system (chassis)						◒
Engine cooling						○
Engine mechanical						○
Exhaust system						○
Fuel system						○
Ignition system						○
Suspension						◒
Transmission (manual)						
Transmission (automatic)						○
TROUBLE INDEX						○
COST INDEX						

TROUBLE SPOTS	Buick Riviera V8 '80	'81	'82	'83	'84	'85
Air-conditioning	○	○	○	○	○	○
Body exterior (paint)	●	○	○	○	○	○
Body exterior (rust)	◒	○	○	○	○	○
Body hardware	●	○	●	◒	○	○
Body integrity	○	○	○	○	○	○
Brakes	◒	○	◒	○	○	○
Clutch						
Driveline	●	○	◒	◒	○	○
Electrical system (chassis)	●	◒	●	●	●	○
Engine cooling	◒	○	○	○	○	○
Engine mechanical	○	○	○	◓	○	◒
Exhaust system	○	●	●	●	○	○
Fuel system	○	●	●	○	◓	○
Ignition system	○	○	○	○	○	○
Suspension	●	○	●	●	○	○
Transmission (manual)						
Transmission (automatic)	○	○	◒	○	○	●
TROUBLE INDEX	●	●	●	●	◒	◒
COST INDEX	◒	◒	◒	◒	○	

TROUBLE SPOTS	Buick Skyhawk 4 '80	'81	'82	'83	'84	'85
Air-conditioning			◒	◒	○	◒
Body exterior (paint)			○	○	○	○
Body exterior (rust)			○	○	○	○
Body hardware			○	○	○	○
Body integrity			○	○	○	○
Brakes			●	◒	◒	◒
Clutch			◒	○	◒	○
Driveline			○	○	○	○
Electrical system (chassis)			○	●	◒	○
Engine cooling			●	●	○	○
Engine mechanical			●	●	○	○
Exhaust system			●	●	○	○
Fuel system			◒	○	○	○
Ignition system			◒	●	○	○
Suspension			○	○	○	○
Transmission (manual)			◒	●	○	○
Transmission (automatic)			○	○	○	○
TROUBLE INDEX			●	●	◒	◒
COST INDEX			○	○	◓	

TROUBLE SPOTS	Buick Skylark 4 '80	'81	'82	'83	'84	'85
Air-conditioning	◒	○	●	●	○	○
Body exterior (paint)	●	●	●	◒	●	◒
Body exterior (rust)	◒	◒	◒	◒	○	○
Body hardware	○	○	○	○	○	○
Body integrity	○	○	○	○	○	○
Brakes	◒	◒	●	◒	○	○
Clutch	○	◒	○	○	○	
Driveline	○	◒	○	○	○	○
Electrical system (chassis)	○	○	○	○	○	◓
Engine cooling	○	◓	○	●	○	○
Engine mechanical	○	○	○	●	◒	○
Exhaust system	⊜	◒	○	○	○	○
Fuel system	○	○	○	○	○	○
Ignition system	○	○	●	◒	●	○
Suspension	○	○	◒	○	○	○
Transmission (manual)	◒	○	○	○	○	
Transmission (automatic)	○	○	○	○	○	○
TROUBLE INDEX	◒	◒	◒	●	◒	○
COST INDEX	○	○	○	○	○	

Buick Skylark V6

TROUBLE SPOTS	'80	'81	'82	'83	'84	'85
Air-conditioning	○	●	◒	◒	○	○
Body exterior (paint)	●	●	◒	●	◒	◒
Body exterior (rust)	○	◒	○	○	○	○
Body hardware	○	○	○	⊜	○	◒
Body integrity	○	○	○	○	○	○
Brakes	◒	◒	◒	◒	○	○
Clutch	○					
Driveline	◒	◒	○	○	○	○
Electrical system (chassis)	○	○	○	○	○	○
Engine cooling	◒	○	◒	○	○	○
Engine mechanical	○	○	○	○	○	○
Exhaust system	○	⊜	○	○	○	○
Fuel system	●	●	◒	○	○	○
Ignition system	○	○	○	○	○	○
Suspension	○	◒	◒	●	○	○
Transmission (manual)	○					
Transmission (automatic)	◒	○	◒	◒	○	○
TROUBLE INDEX	◒	◒	◒	◒	○	○
COST INDEX	○	○	○	○	○	

Cadillac Cimarron

TROUBLE SPOTS	'80	'81	'82	'83	'84	'85
Air-conditioning			○	○	○	Insufficient data
Body exterior (paint)			◒	◒	◒	
Body exterior (rust)			◒	○	○	
Body hardware			○	○	○	
Body integrity			○	○	○	
Brakes			◒	◒	◒	
Clutch			○	○	○	
Driveline			○	○	○	
Electrical system (chassis)			◒	●	◒	
Engine cooling			○	◒	○	
Engine mechanical			◒	○	○	
Exhaust system			○	◒	○	
Fuel system			○	○	○	
Ignition system			○	◒	○	
Suspension			○	○	◒	
Transmission (manual)			○	○	○	
Transmission (automatic)			○	○	○	
TROUBLE INDEX			◒	●	◒	
COST INDEX			○	◒	⊜	

Cadillac DeVille, Fleetwood V8 (gas)

TROUBLE SPOTS	'80	'81	'82	'83	'84	'85
Air-conditioning	◒	●	○	○	○	●
Body exterior (paint)	◒	○	○	○	○	○
Body exterior (rust)	○	○	○	○	○	○
Body hardware	●	◒	○	○	○	●
Body integrity	○	◒	○	○	◒	○
Brakes	○	◒	◒	○	○	◒
Clutch						
Driveline	○	○	○	○	○	○
Electrical system (chassis)	●	◒	●	●	◒	●
Engine cooling	⊜	○	●	○	○	●
Engine mechanical	○	◒	●	●	○	◒
Exhaust system	⊜	●	●	●	○	○
Fuel system	⊜	◒	○	○	⊜	○
Ignition system	○	○	●	○	○	○
Suspension	○	○	○	◒	○	○
Transmission (manual)						
Transmission (automatic)	○	○	○	○	○	○
TROUBLE INDEX	○	◒	●	●	○	●
COST INDEX	○	◒	●	◒	◒	

Cadillac Eldorado V8 (gas)

TROUBLE SPOTS	'80	'81	'82	'83	'84	'85
Air-conditioning	●	●	●	●	○	○
Body exterior (paint)	○	○	○	○	○	◒
Body exterior (rust)	○	○	○	○	○	○
Body hardware	○	○	◒	●	○	○
Body integrity	○	○	○	○	○	●
Brakes	●	●	◒	○	○	○
Clutch						
Driveline	○	○	●	○	○	○
Electrical system (chassis)	●	●	●	●	○	●
Engine cooling	○	○	◒	◒	○	○
Engine mechanical	○	◒	●	●	◒	○
Exhaust system	○	○	●	●	○	○
Fuel system	○	○	○	○	⊜	○
Ignition system	◒	○	◒	○	○	○
Suspension	○	○	◒	○	○	○
Transmission (manual)						
Transmission (automatic)	○	○	◒	○	○	○
TROUBLE INDEX	●	●	●	●	○	◒
COST INDEX	●	●	●	●	◒	

Cadillac Seville V8 (gas)

TROUBLE SPOTS	'80	'81	'82	'83	'84	'85
Air-conditioning	●	◒	●	●	○	○
Body exterior (paint)	○	◒	○	○	○	○
Body exterior (rust)	○	○	○	○	○	○
Body hardware	●	●	●	◒	○	○
Body integrity	○	◒	○	○	◒	○
Brakes	●	◒	◒	○	○	○
Clutch						
Driveline	○	○	◒	◒	○	○
Electrical system (chassis)	●	●	●	●	◒	◒
Engine cooling	○	○	○	○	◒	○
Engine mechanical	○	○	●	○	○	○
Exhaust system	○	○	●	●	○	○
Fuel system	◒	○	○	⊜	⊜	○
Ignition system	◒	○	○	○	○	○
Suspension	○	○	○	○	○	○
Transmission (manual)						
Transmission (automatic)	○	○	○	○	○	○
TROUBLE INDEX	●	●	●	●	◒	●
COST INDEX	●	●	●	●	◒	

Chevrolet Astro Van V6

TROUBLE SPOTS	'80	'81	'82	'83	'84	'85
Air-conditioning						○
Body exterior (paint)						○
Body exterior (rust)						○
Body hardware						○
Body integrity						○
Brakes						○
Clutch						
Driveline						○
Electrical system (chassis)						○
Engine cooling						○
Engine mechanical						○
Exhaust system						○
Fuel system						○
Ignition system						○
Suspension						○
Transmission (manual)						
Transmission (automatic)						○
TROUBLE INDEX						○
COST INDEX						

Chevrolet Blazer V8 (4-WD)

TROUBLE SPOTS	'80	'81	'82	'83	'84	'85
Air-conditioning	Insufficient data	Insufficient data	Insufficient data	○	○	○
Body exterior (paint)				●	●	●
Body exterior (rust)				○	◒	◒
Body hardware				●	●	○
Body integrity				○	●	◒
Brakes				○	●	◒
Clutch				○	○	○
Driveline				●	◒	●
Electrical system (chassis)				◒	○	○
Engine cooling				○	○	○
Engine mechanical				○	◒	●
Exhaust system				○	○	○
Fuel system				○	○	○
Ignition system				○	○	○
Suspension				○	◒	●
Transmission (manual)				○	○	○
Transmission (automatic)				●	●	◒
TROUBLE INDEX				●	●	●
COST INDEX				*	◒	

Chevrolet Camaro V6

TROUBLE SPOTS	'80	'81	'82	'83	'84	'85
Air-conditioning	○	○	●	○	○	○
Body exterior (paint)	◒	●	●	●	●	○
Body exterior (rust)	○	●	◒	○	◒	○
Body hardware	◒	◒	○	●	●	○
Body integrity	◒	●	●	●	●	○
Brakes	○	○	⊜	○	◒	○
Clutch		◒	●	●	●	○
Driveline	○	○	○	○	◒	○
Electrical system (chassis)	○	○	◒	◒	◒	●
Engine cooling	○	○	○	○	○	○
Engine mechanical	○	○	○	◒	●	○
Exhaust system	○	●	○	○	◒	◒
Fuel system	○	◒	○	○	●	○
Ignition system	○	◒	○	○	◒	○
Suspension	○	◒	○	◒	○	○
Transmission (manual)		◒	○	○	○	○
Transmission (automatic)	⊜	○	○	○	○	○
TROUBLE INDEX	◒	●	●	●	●	●
COST INDEX	○	○	○	○	○	

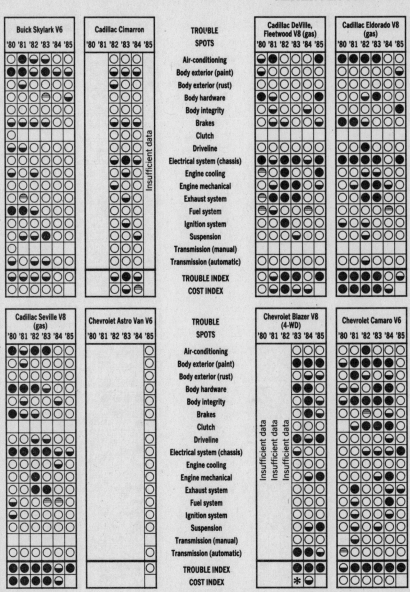

Key: ● Much better than average · ◓ Better than average · ○ Average · ◒ Worse than average · ● Much worse than average · * Insufficient cost data

Chevrolet Camaro V8

TROUBLE SPOTS	'80	'81	'82	'83	'84	'85
Air-conditioning	○	○	●	○	○	○
Body exterior (paint)	●	●	●	◒	●	●
Body exterior (rust)	○	○	◒	○	○	○
Body hardware	◒	◒	●	●	●	○
Body integrity	●	●	●	●	●	●
Brakes	○	○	⊜	○	◒	○
Clutch	◒	◒	●	◒	◒	○
Driveline	○	○	●	●	◒	○
Electrical system (chassis)	○	○	●	●	●	◒
Engine cooling	◒	◒	◒	○	○	○
Engine mechanical	○	○	○	◒	○	○
Exhaust system	○	●	◒	○	○	○
Fuel system	○	○	●	●	●	○
Ignition system	○	○	○	○	◒	○
Suspension	○	○	◒	●	◒	○
Transmission (manual)	○	○	○	○	○	○
Transmission (automatic)	○	○	○	○	○	○
TROUBLE INDEX	◒	●	●	●	●	●
COST INDEX	○	○	◒	◒	○	

Chevrolet Caprice, Impala V6

TROUBLE SPOTS	'80	'81	'82	'83	'84	'85
Air-conditioning	⊜	○	○	○	○	○
Body exterior (paint)	○	●	○	○	○	○
Body exterior (rust)	⊜	○	○	○	○	○
Body hardware	○	○	○	○	○	○
Body integrity	○	○	○	○	○	○
Brakes	⊜	⊜	○	○	○	○
Clutch						
Driveline	○	○	○	○	○	○
Electrical system (chassis)	○	○	◒	◒	○	○
Engine cooling	○	○	○	○	○	○
Engine mechanical	○	○	○	○	○	○
Exhaust system	○	●	●	○	○	○
Fuel system	○	●	●	◒	◒	◒
Ignition system	○	○	●	◒	○	○
Suspension	○	○	●	◒	○	○
Transmission (manual)						
Transmission (automatic)	○	○	○	○	○	○
TROUBLE INDEX	○	◒	◒	◒	◒	○
COST INDEX	⊜	○	○	○	○	

Chevrolet Caprice, Impala V8 (gas)

TROUBLE SPOTS	'80	'81	'82	'83	'84	'85
Air-conditioning	○	○	○	○	○	○
Body exterior (paint)	●	◒	○	◒	◒	○
Body exterior (rust)	●	○	○	○	○	○
Body hardware	○	○	◒	◒	◒	◒
Body integrity	○	⊜	○	○	○	○
Brakes	○	○	○	○	○	○
Clutch						
Driveline	○	○	○	○	○	○
Electrical system (chassis)	○	○	○	◒	○	○
Engine cooling	○	○	○	○	○	○
Engine mechanical	○	⊜	○	○	○	○
Exhaust system	○	●	◒	○	○	○
Fuel system	⊜	○	○	○	⊜	○
Ignition system	○	○	○	○	○	○
Suspension	◒	◒	◒	◒	○	○
Transmission (manual)						
Transmission (automatic)	◒	○	○	⊜	○	○
TROUBLE INDEX	○	○	○	○	○	◒
COST INDEX	○	⊜	○	○	⊜	

Chevrolet Cavalier 4

TROUBLE SPOTS	'80	'81	'82	'83	'84	'85
Air-conditioning			◒	○	○	○
Body exterior (paint)			●	○	○	○
Body exterior (rust)			◒	◒	○	○
Body hardware			◒	○	○	○
Body integrity			◒	○	○	○
Brakes			●	○	○	○
Clutch			◒	○	◒	○
Driveline			○	○	○	○
Electrical system (chassis)			●	○	○	○
Engine cooling			◒	◒	○	○
Engine mechanical			◒	◒	○	○
Exhaust system			●	◒	○	○
Fuel system			●	○	○	○
Ignition system			●	●	○	○
Suspension			○	⊜	●	●
Transmission (manual)			◒	◒	◒	○
Transmission (automatic)			○	○	○	○
TROUBLE INDEX			●	◒	◒	●
COST INDEX			○	⊜	⊜	

Chevrolet Celebrity 4

TROUBLE SPOTS	'80	'81	'82	'83	'84	'85
Air-conditioning			●	●	○	○
Body exterior (paint)			○	◒	○	○
Body exterior (rust)			○	○	○	○
Body hardware			○	●	○	○
Body integrity			○	○	○	○
Brakes			●	●	◒	○
Clutch					○	○
Driveline			○	○	○	○
Electrical system (chassis)			○	●	○	○
Engine cooling			○	●	◒	○
Engine mechanical			○	●	◒	○
Exhaust system			○	○	○	○
Fuel system			○	○	○	○
Ignition system			◒	○	●	○
Suspension			●	◒	○	○
Transmission (manual)					○	◒
Transmission (automatic)			●	○	○	○
TROUBLE INDEX			◒	●	◒	○
COST INDEX			○	○	⊜	

Chevrolet Celebrity V6

TROUBLE SPOTS	'80	'81	'82	'83	'84	'85
Air-conditioning			●	○	○	○
Body exterior (paint)			●	○	○	○
Body exterior (rust)			○	○	○	○
Body hardware			●	○	○	◒
Body integrity			○	○	○	○
Brakes			●	○	○	○
Clutch						
Driveline			○	○	○	○
Electrical system (chassis)			○	○	○	◒
Engine cooling			◒	○	○	○
Engine mechanical			○	○	○	○
Exhaust system			⊜	○	○	○
Fuel system			●	○	⊜	○
Ignition system			○	○	○	○
Suspension			●	◒	◒	○
Transmission (manual)						
Transmission (automatic)			◒	○	○	○
TROUBLE INDEX			◒	○	○	●
COST INDEX			○	⊜	⊜	

Chevrolet Chevette (gas)

TROUBLE SPOTS	'80	'81	'82	'83	'84	'85
Air-conditioning	⊜	○	⊜	○	○	Insufficient data
Body exterior (paint)	○	○	○	○	◒	
Body exterior (rust)	○	○	○	○	○	
Body hardware	○	◒	○	◒	●	
Body integrity	●	●	●	●	●	
Brakes	●	●	●	●	○	
Clutch	●	●	○	○	○	
Driveline	○	○	○	○	○	
Electrical system (chassis)	◒	●	◒	○	○	
Engine cooling	⊜	○	○	○	○	
Engine mechanical	○	○	⊜	○	○	
Exhaust system	○	●	●	◒	○	
Fuel system	○	◒	○	○	○	
Ignition system	○	◒	◒	○	◒	
Suspension	●	●	○	◒	○	
Transmission (manual)	○	○	○	○	○	
Transmission (automatic)	○	○	○	○	○	
TROUBLE INDEX	○	●	●	●	●	
COST INDEX	⊜	○	○	⊜	⊜	

Chevrolet Citation 4

TROUBLE SPOTS	'80	'81	'82	'83	'84	'85
Air-conditioning	●	◒	●	●	○	Insufficient data
Body exterior (paint)	●	◒	○	○	○	
Body exterior (rust)	●	●	○	○	○	
Body hardware	○	○	○	○	○	
Body integrity	◒	○	○	○	○	
Brakes	◒	◒	◒	◒	○	
Clutch	◒	●	○	○	○	
Driveline	○	○	○	○	○	
Electrical system (chassis)	⊜	○	○	○	○	
Engine cooling	○	○	◒	●	○	
Engine mechanical	⊜	○	○	○	○	
Exhaust system	○	●	○	○	○	
Fuel system	○	○	○	○	○	
Ignition system	○	○	◒	●	◒	
Suspension	○	◒	○	○	○	
Transmission (manual)	◒	●	◒	○	○	
Transmission (automatic)	◒	○	○	○	○	
TROUBLE INDEX	○	◒	◒	●	○	
COST INDEX	○	○	⊜	○	○	

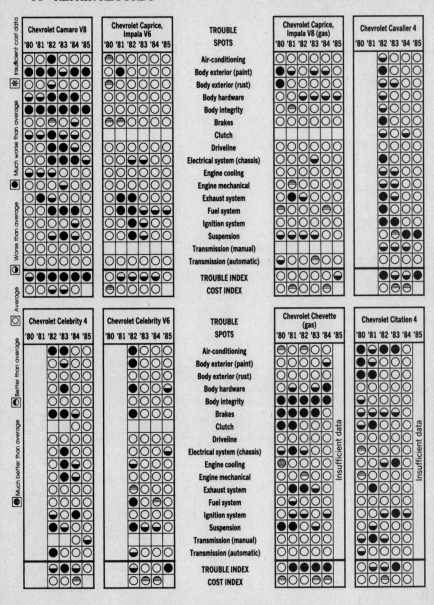

Chevrolet Citation V6 (Insufficient data)

TROUBLE SPOTS	'80	'81	'82	'83	'84	'85
Air-conditioning	○	●	●	●	○	
Body exterior (paint)	●	◒	○	○	◒	
Body exterior (rust)	●	●	○	◒	○	
Body hardware	○	○	○	○	○	
Body integrity	○	○	◒	○	⊜	
Brakes	◒	◒	◒	○	○	
Clutch	○	○	○	○	○	
Driveline	○	◒	○	○	○	
Electrical system (chassis)	○	○	○	○	○	
Engine cooling	◒	○	◒	◒	○	
Engine mechanical	○	○	○	○	○	
Exhaust system	○	⊜	○	○	○	
Fuel system	◒	◒	◒	○	○	
Ignition system	○	○	○	○	○	
Suspension	○	◒	◒	○	○	
Transmission (manual)	●	◒	○	○	◒	
Transmission (automatic)	○	○	○	◒	○	
TROUBLE INDEX	◒	◒	◒	◒	○	
COST INDEX	○	○	○	⊜	⊜	

Chevrolet Corvette (Insufficient data)

TROUBLE SPOTS	'80	'81	'82	'83	'84	'85
Air-conditioning	◒	○	◒		○	○
Body exterior (paint)	○	○	○		○	○
Body exterior (rust)	⊜	⊜	○		○	○
Body hardware	◒	○	○		●	○
Body integrity	◒	●	◒		●	○
Brakes	○	○	○		●	○
Clutch	◒	○			○	○
Driveline	○	●	○		●	○
Electrical system (chassis)	◒	○	○		●	○
Engine cooling	○	○	○		○	○
Engine mechanical	○	○	○		◒	◒
Exhaust system	○	○	○		○	○
Fuel system	○	⊜	○		⊜	◒
Ignition system	○	○	○		○	◒
Suspension	○	○	○		◒	○
Transmission (manual)	○	○			◒	○
Transmission (automatic)	○	○	○		○	○
TROUBLE INDEX	○	○	○		●	●
COST INDEX	*	*	*		◒	

Chevrolet Malibu V6

TROUBLE SPOTS	'80	'81	'82	'83	'84	'85
Air-conditioning	○	⊜	⊜	○		
Body exterior (paint)	○	◒	◒	◒		
Body exterior (rust)	○	○	◒	○		
Body hardware	○	○	○	○		
Body integrity	○	○	○	○		
Brakes	○	⊜	○	⊜		
Clutch	○					
Driveline	○	○	○	○		
Electrical system (chassis)	○	○	◒	◒		
Engine cooling	⊜	○	○	○		
Engine mechanical	○	○	○	○		
Exhaust system	○	●	●	○		
Fuel system	○	●	●	●		
Ignition system	○	◒	●	●		
Suspension	○	◒	●	●		
Transmission (manual)	○					
Transmission (automatic)	○	○	○	○		
TROUBLE INDEX	○	◒	●	◒		
COST INDEX	⊜	○	○	○		

Chevrolet Malibu V8

TROUBLE SPOTS	'80	'81	'82	'83	'84	'85
Air-conditioning	○	◒	○	⊜		
Body exterior (paint)	●	◒	○	●		
Body exterior (rust)	○	○	○	○		
Body hardware	○	○	○	○		
Body integrity	◒	◒	○	○		
Brakes	○	○	○	○		
Clutch						
Driveline	○	○	○	○		
Electrical system (chassis)	○	○	○	○		
Engine cooling	○	○	○	○		
Engine mechanical	○	○	○	○		
Exhaust system	○	●	●	○		
Fuel system	◒	●	○	○		
Ignition system	○	●	○	○		
Suspension	●	◒	◒	●		
Transmission (manual)						
Transmission (automatic)	○	○	○	○		
TROUBLE INDEX	◒	◒	○	○		
COST INDEX	○	○	*	⊜		

Chevrolet Monte Carlo V6 (Insufficient data)

TROUBLE SPOTS	'80	'81	'82	'83	'84	'85
Air-conditioning	○	○	○	○	◒	
Body exterior (paint)	●	●	●	◒	●	
Body exterior (rust)	○	○	○	○	○	
Body hardware	○	●	◒	○	●	
Body integrity	●	●	●	●	●	
Brakes	○	○	○	○	◒	
Clutch						
Driveline	○	○	○	○	◒	
Electrical system (chassis)	○	○	○	●	●	
Engine cooling	○	○	○	○	○	
Engine mechanical	○	○	○	○	●	
Exhaust system	○	●	●	○	○	
Fuel system	○	●	●	●	◒	
Ignition system	○	●	●	●	●	
Suspension	○	●	○	◒	●	
Transmission (manual)						
Transmission (automatic)	○	○	○	○	○	
TROUBLE INDEX	○	●	●	●	●	
COST INDEX	⊜	○	○	○	○	

Chevrolet Monte Carlo V8 (Insufficient data)

TROUBLE SPOTS	'80	'81	'82	'83	'84	'85
Air-conditioning	○	○		○	○	○
Body exterior (paint)	◒	●		●	●	●
Body exterior (rust)	○	○		○	○	○
Body hardware	●	◒		○	◒	○
Body integrity	●	●		◒	●	●
Brakes	○	○		○	○	◒
Clutch						
Driveline	○	○		○	○	◒
Electrical system (chassis)	◒	◒		●	●	●
Engine cooling	○	○		○	◒	◒
Engine mechanical	○	○		○	○	◒
Exhaust system	○	●		○	○	○
Fuel system	○	●		○	○	○
Ignition system	○	○		○	●	◒
Suspension	○	○		○	●	○
Transmission (manual)						
Transmission (automatic)	○	○		○	○	◒
TROUBLE INDEX	◒	●		◒	●	●
COST INDEX	○	○		⊜	○	

Chevrolet Pickup Truck 6, V6 (2-WD) (Insufficient data)

TROUBLE SPOTS	'80	'81	'82	'83	'84	'85
Air-conditioning	○	○	○	◒	○	
Body exterior (paint)	○	●	○	○	○	
Body exterior (rust)	○	●	◒	○	○	
Body hardware	○	○	○	○	○	
Body integrity	○	◒	○	○	○	
Brakes	⊜	⊜	⊜	○	○	
Clutch	○	○	○	○	◒	
Driveline	○	○	○	○	○	
Electrical system (chassis)	⊜	⊜	○	○	○	
Engine cooling	○	○	○	○	○	
Engine mechanical	○	⊜	○	○	●	
Exhaust system	○	○	○	○	○	
Fuel system	○	○	○	○	○	
Ignition system	○	○	○	○	○	
Suspension	○	○	○	○	○	
Transmission (manual)	○	○	○	○	○	
Transmission (automatic)	○	○	○	○	○	
TROUBLE INDEX	⊜	○	○	○	◒	
COST INDEX	⊜	⊜	○	*	*	

Chevrolet Pickup Truck V8 (gas, 2-WD)

TROUBLE SPOTS	'80	'81	'82	'83	'84	'85
Air-conditioning	○	◒	●	○	⊜	○
Body exterior (paint)	○	●	●	●	◒	◒
Body exterior (rust)	○	●	○	◒	○	○
Body hardware	⊜	○	○	○	○	◒
Body integrity	○	●	●	◒	◒	●
Brakes	⊜	○	○	○	◒	◒
Clutch	○	◒	○	◒	○	●
Driveline	◒	○	○	○	◒	○
Electrical system (chassis)	○	⊜	⊜	○	○	○
Engine cooling	○	○	○	○	○	○
Engine mechanical	○	○	◒	○	○	○
Exhaust system	○	○	○	○	○	○
Fuel system	◒	◒	●	●	○	○
Ignition system	○	○	◒	○	○	○
Suspension	⊜	○	○	○	◒	◒
Transmission (manual)	○	○	○	○	◒	○
Transmission (automatic)	○	○	◒	◒	○	○
TROUBLE INDEX	○	◒	◒	●	◒	●
COST INDEX	⊜	○	○	○	○	

⊖ Much better than average · ⊜ Better than average · ○ Average · ◒ Worse than average · ● Much worse than average · * Insufficient cost data

Chevrolet Pickup Truck V8 (gas, 4-WD)

TROUBLE SPOTS	'80	'81	'82	'83	'84	'85
Air-conditioning	○	●	○	○	○	○
Body exterior (paint)	○	●	●	●	●	●
Body exterior (rust)	◒	◒	○	○	○	○
Body hardware	○	○	○	○	○	○
Body integrity	○	○	○	○	●	○
Brakes	○	○	○	○	◒	◒
Clutch	○	◒	●	◒	●	○
Driveline	●	◒	●	●	◒	○
Electrical system (chassis)	○	○	○	○	○	●
Engine cooling	○	○	○	○	○	○
Engine mechanical	○	●	○	○	◒	◒
Exhaust system	○	○	⊜	○	○	○
Fuel system	○	○	○	○	○	○
Ignition system	○	○	○	○	○	○
Suspension	○	○	○	○	○	◒
Transmission (manual)	○	○	○	○	●	◒
Transmission (automatic)	◒	○	○	◒	○	◒
TROUBLE INDEX	◒	◒	◒	●	●	●
COST INDEX	*	*	*	*	○	

Chevrolet S10 Blazer V6 (4-WD)

TROUBLE SPOTS	'80	'81	'82	'83	'84	'85
Air-conditioning				●	○	○
Body exterior (paint)				◒	○	○
Body exterior (rust)				●	◒	○
Body hardware				●	◒	○
Body integrity				●	◒	○
Brakes				○	○	○
Clutch				●	◒	◒
Driveline				◒	◒	○
Electrical system (chassis)				◒	◒	○
Engine cooling				○	○	○
Engine mechanical				●	●	◒
Exhaust system				○	○	○
Fuel system				○	○	○
Ignition system				○	○	○
Suspension				○	○	○
Transmission (manual)				◒	○	◒
Transmission (automatic)				●	◒	◒
TROUBLE INDEX				●	●	◒
COST INDEX				○	○	

Chevrolet S10 Pickup Truck 4 (2-WD)

TROUBLE SPOTS	'80	'81	'82	'83	'84	'85
Air-conditioning			○	◒	○	○
Body exterior (paint)			○	○	○	○
Body exterior (rust)			○	○	○	○
Body hardware			○	○	⊜	○
Body integrity			○	○	○	○
Brakes			○	○	○	○
Clutch			◒	●	○	○
Driveline			○	○	○	○
Electrical system (chassis)			⊜	○	○	○
Engine cooling			○	○	○	○
Engine mechanical			○	◒	◒	○
Exhaust system			○	○	○	○
Fuel system			⊜	○	○	○
Ignition system			○	○	○	○
Suspension			⊜	○	○	○
Transmission (manual)			○	○	◒	○
Transmission (automatic)			○	●	○	○
TROUBLE INDEX			⊜	○	○	○
COST INDEX			⊜	*	*	

Chevrolet S10 Pickup Truck V6 (2-WD)

TROUBLE SPOTS	'80	'81	'82	'83	'84	'85
Air-conditioning			◒	●	○	○
Body exterior (paint)			○	○	○	○
Body exterior (rust)			○	○	○	○
Body hardware			⊜	○	○	⊜
Body integrity			⊜	⊜	○	○
Brakes			⊜	○	○	○
Clutch			●	●	●	○
Driveline			○	○	◒	○
Electrical system (chassis)			○	○	○	○
Engine cooling			○	○	○	○
Engine mechanical			○	●	●	◒
Exhaust system			⊜	○	○	○
Fuel system			○	○	⊜	○
Ignition system			○	○	○	○
Suspension			○	⊜	○	○
Transmission (manual)			●	○	○	○
Transmission (automatic)			●	◒	○	○
TROUBLE INDEX			○	○	○	○
COST INDEX			○	⊜	⊜	

Chevrolet S10 Pickup Truck V6 (4-WD)

TROUBLE SPOTS	'80	'81	'82	'83	'84	'85
Air-conditioning				●	○	○
Body exterior (paint)				○	○	○
Body exterior (rust)				○	○	○
Body hardware				○	○	○
Body integrity				○	⊜	○
Brakes				○	⊜	○
Clutch				●	○	○
Driveline				◒	◒	○
Electrical system (chassis)				○	○	○
Engine cooling				◒	○	○
Engine mechanical				●	●	○
Exhaust system				○	○	○
Fuel system				○	⊜	○
Ignition system				○	○	○
Suspension				○	○	○
Transmission (manual)				○	○	○
Transmission (automatic)				◒	○	○
TROUBLE INDEX				◒	○	○
COST INDEX				○	⊜	

Chevrolet Sportvan V8 (gas)

TROUBLE SPOTS	'80	'81	'82	'83	'84	'85
Air-conditioning	○	○	○	○	◒	○
Body exterior (paint)	○	○	○	○	●	◒
Body exterior (rust)	◒	○	○	○	○	◒
Body hardware	○	●	●	●	●	●
Body integrity	○	◒	●	●	●	◒
Brakes	⊜	○	○	○	○	○
Clutch	○					
Driveline	○	◒	○	◒	◒	○
Electrical system (chassis)	○	○	○	○	○	○
Engine cooling	○	○	○	○	○	◒
Engine mechanical	○	○	○	○	○	◒
Exhaust system	○	⊜	⊜	○	○	○
Fuel system	○	○	●	○	○	○
Ignition system	○	○	○	○	○	○
Suspension	○	●	◒	●	○	○
Transmission (manual)	○					
Transmission (automatic)	◒	○	◒	◒	○	○
TROUBLE INDEX	◒	◒	◒	●	●	●
COST INDEX	*	○	○	○	○	

Chevrolet Sprint

TROUBLE SPOTS	'80	'81	'82	'83	'84	'85
Air-conditioning						○
Body exterior (paint)						○
Body exterior (rust)						○
Body hardware						○
Body integrity						○
Brakes						○
Clutch						○
Driveline						○
Electrical system (chassis)						⊜
Engine cooling						●
Engine mechanical						○
Exhaust system						○
Fuel system						○
Ignition system						○
Suspension						○
Transmission (manual)						○
Transmission (automatic)						
TROUBLE INDEX						○
COST INDEX						

Chevrolet Suburban V8 (gas)

TROUBLE SPOTS	'80	'81	'82	'83	'84	'85
Air-conditioning	○	◒	○	○	○	●
Body exterior (paint)	○	◒	◒	○	●	●
Body exterior (rust)	●	◒	○	○	○	◒
Body hardware	◒	●	●	●	●	●
Body integrity	○	●	●	●	●	●
Brakes	⊜	○	○	○	●	◒
Clutch	○					
Driveline	○	●	○	○	●	○
Electrical system (chassis)	○	○	○	○	○	○
Engine cooling	○	○	○	○	◒	○
Engine mechanical	○	○	○	○	○	◒
Exhaust system	○	○	○	○	○	○
Fuel system	○	◒	○	○	○	○
Ignition system	○	○	○	○	○	○
Suspension	○	○	○	○	◒	◒
Transmission (manual)	○					
Transmission (automatic)	○	○	●	○	●	○
TROUBLE INDEX	○	●	◒	◒	●	●
COST INDEX	*	*	*	◒	◒	

TROUBLE SPOTS	Chrysler Laser (except Turbo) '80	'81	'82	'83	'84	'85
Air-conditioning					○	○
Body exterior (paint)					●	●
Body exterior (rust)					○	○
Body hardware					●	○
Body integrity					●	○
Brakes					○	○
Clutch					●	◒
Driveline					○	○
Electrical system (chassis)					●	◒
Engine cooling					○	○
Engine mechanical					○	○
Exhaust system					○	○
Fuel system					●	◒
Ignition system					○	○
Suspension					○	○
Transmission (manual)					○	○
Transmission (automatic)					○	○
TROUBLE INDEX					●	●
COST INDEX					○	

TROUBLE SPOTS	Chrysler Laser Turbo '80	'81	'82	'83	'84	'85
Air-conditioning					◒	○
Body exterior (paint)					◒	●
Body exterior (rust)					○	○
Body hardware					●	○
Body integrity					●	●
Brakes					○	○
Clutch					◒	●
Driveline					○	○
Electrical system (chassis)					●	●
Engine cooling					○	○
Engine mechanical					○	◒
Exhaust system					○	○
Fuel system					●	●
Ignition system					○	○
Suspension					○	○
Transmission (manual)					○	○
Transmission (automatic)					○	○
TROUBLE INDEX					●	●
COST INDEX					○	

TROUBLE SPOTS	Chrysler LeBaron 4 (except Turbo, FWD) '80	'81	'82	'83	'84	'85
Air-conditioning			⊜	○	○	○
Body exterior (paint)			○	◒	○	○
Body exterior (rust)			○	◒	○	○
Body hardware			◒	●	○	○
Body integrity			◒	◒	○	○
Brakes			◒	○	○	○
Clutch						
Driveline			○	○	○	○
Electrical system (chassis)			○	●	◒	◒
Engine cooling			⊜	○	○	○
Engine mechanical			○	○	○	○
Exhaust system			◒	○	○	○
Fuel system			○	●	●	○
Ignition system			○	○	○	○
Suspension			●	◒	○	○
Transmission (manual)						
Transmission (automatic)			○	○	○	○
TROUBLE INDEX			○	●	◒	○
COST INDEX			⊜	○	○	

TROUBLE SPOTS	Chrysler LeBaron 4 Turbo (FWD) '80	'81	'82	'83	'84	'85
Air-conditioning					○	○
Body exterior (paint)					○	○
Body exterior (rust)					○	○
Body hardware					○	○
Body integrity					○	○
Brakes					○	○
Clutch						
Driveline					○	○
Electrical system (chassis)					●	○
Engine cooling					○	○
Engine mechanical					○	○
Exhaust system					◒	○
Fuel system					○	○
Ignition system					○	○
Suspension					○	○
Transmission (manual)						
Transmission (automatic)					○	○
TROUBLE INDEX					●	○
COST INDEX					*	

TROUBLE SPOTS	Chrysler LeBaron GTS (except Turbo) '80	'81	'82	'83	'84	'85
Air-conditioning						○
Body exterior (paint)						○
Body exterior (rust)						○
Body hardware						◒
Body integrity						○
Brakes						○
Clutch						○
Driveline						○
Electrical system (chassis)						○
Engine cooling						○
Engine mechanical						○
Exhaust system						○
Fuel system						○
Ignition system						◒
Suspension						○
Transmission (manual)						○
Transmission (automatic)						○
TROUBLE INDEX						○
COST INDEX						

TROUBLE SPOTS	Chrysler LeBaron GTS Turbo '80	'81	'82	'83	'84	'85
Air-conditioning						○
Body exterior (paint)						○
Body exterior (rust)						○
Body hardware						○
Body integrity						○
Brakes						○
Clutch						○
Driveline						○
Electrical system (chassis)						○
Engine cooling						○
Engine mechanical						○
Exhaust system						○
Fuel system						○
Ignition system						○
Suspension						○
Transmission (manual)						○
Transmission (automatic)						○
TROUBLE INDEX						⊜
COST INDEX						

TROUBLE SPOTS	Chrysler New Yorker, New Yorker 5th Ave V8 '80	'81	'82	'83	'84	'85
Air-conditioning	Insufficient data	Insufficient data	○	⊜	○	○
Body exterior (paint)			○	○	○	○
Body exterior (rust)			○	○	○	○
Body hardware			○	⊜	◒	○
Body integrity			○	○	○	○
Brakes			○	○	○	○
Clutch						
Driveline			○	○	○	○
Electrical system (chassis)			●	◒	●	●
Engine cooling			○	○	○	○
Engine mechanical			○	○	○	○
Exhaust system			⊜	○	○	○
Fuel system			○	○	●	●
Ignition system			○	○	○	◒
Suspension			○	○	○	○
Transmission (manual)						
Transmission (automatic)			○	○	○	◒
TROUBLE INDEX			○	○	◒	●
COST INDEX			⊜	⊜	⊜	

TROUBLE SPOTS	Chrysler N. Y., E-Class 4 (except Turbo, FWD) '80	'81	'82	'83	'84	'85
Air-conditioning				○	○	○
Body exterior (paint)				○	○	○
Body exterior (rust)				○	○	○
Body hardware				◒	◒	○
Body integrity				●	●	○
Brakes				○	○	○
Clutch						
Driveline				○	○	○
Electrical system (chassis)				◒	●	◒
Engine cooling				○	○	○
Engine mechanical				○	○	○
Exhaust system				○	○	○
Fuel system				●	●	◒
Ignition system				○	○	○
Suspension				◒	◒	○
Transmission (manual)						
Transmission (automatic)				○	○	○
TROUBLE INDEX				◒	●	◒
COST INDEX				⊜	○	

⊜ Much better than average ⊖ Better than average ○ Average ◒ Worse than average ● Much worse than average * Insufficient cost data

Chrysler N.Y., E-Class 4 Turbo (FWD)

TROUBLE SPOTS	'80	'81	'82	'83	'84	'85
Air-conditioning					○	○
Body exterior (paint)					◒	○
Body exterior (rust)					○	○
Body hardware					◒	○
Body integrity					●	◒
Brakes					○	○
Clutch					○	
Driveline					○	○
Electrical system (chassis)					●	◒
Engine cooling					○	○
Engine mechanical					○	○
Exhaust system					○	○
Fuel system					○	◒
Ignition system					○	○
Suspension					◒	○
Transmission (manual)					○	
Transmission (automatic)					○	○
TROUBLE INDEX					●	◒
COST INDEX					○	

Datsun 200SX

TROUBLE SPOTS	'80	'81	'82	'83	'84	'85
Air-conditioning	○	⊜	⊜	⊖		
Body exterior (paint)	⊖	⊖	⊖	○		
Body exterior (rust)	⊖	⊖	⊖	○		
Body hardware	○	○	⊖	○		
Body integrity	○	○	○	○		
Brakes	●	●	●	◒		
Clutch	⊖	○	⊜	○		
Driveline	⊖	⊖	⊖	○		
Electrical system (chassis)	○	○	○	○		
Engine cooling	⊜	⊜	⊜	○		
Engine mechanical	⊜	⊜	⊜	⊖		
Exhaust system	○	⊖	⊖	○		
Fuel system	⊜	⊜	⊜	○		
Ignition system	⊜	⊜	⊜	⊖		
Suspension	⊖	⊖	⊖	○		
Transmission (manual)	○	○	○	○		
Transmission (automatic)	⊖	○	⊖	○		
TROUBLE INDEX	⊖	⊖	⊜	⊖		
COST INDEX	⊖	⊖	⊖	○		

Datsun 210

TROUBLE SPOTS	'80	'81	'82	'83	'84	'85
Air-conditioning	◒	●	●			
Body exterior (paint)	⊖	⊖	○			
Body exterior (rust)	○	●	●			
Body hardware	⊜	⊖	⊖			
Body integrity	⊖	⊖	○			
Brakes	○	○	●			
Clutch	○	○	○			
Driveline	⊖	○	○			
Electrical system (chassis)	⊜	⊜	⊖			
Engine cooling	⊜	○	○			
Engine mechanical	⊜	⊖	⊖			
Exhaust system	○	○	◒			
Fuel system	⊜	⊜	⊜			
Ignition system	⊜	⊜	⊜			
Suspension	⊖	⊖	○			
Transmission (manual)	○	○	○			
Transmission (automatic)	⊖	○	○			
TROUBLE INDEX	⊖	⊖	○			
COST INDEX	⊖	⊖	⊖			

Datsun 280ZX (except Turbo)

TROUBLE SPOTS	'80	'81	'82	'83	'84	'85
Air-conditioning	⊜	⊜	⊜	⊖		
Body exterior (paint)	○	○	○	○		
Body exterior (rust)	○	●	●	○		
Body hardware	⊖	⊜	⊜	⊜		
Body integrity	⊜	⊖	⊜	⊖		
Brakes	○	○	◒	⊖		
Clutch	⊖	⊜	⊖	⊖		
Driveline	⊖	○	⊖	○		
Electrical system (chassis)	⊖	⊖	⊖	⊖		
Engine cooling	○	⊖	⊜	⊖		
Engine mechanical	⊜	⊜	⊖	⊖		
Exhaust system	⊜	⊖	⊜	○		
Fuel system	⊜	⊜	⊜	⊖		
Ignition system	⊜	⊜	⊖	⊖		
Suspension	○	⊖	⊜	⊖		
Transmission (manual)	○	○	○	○		
Transmission (automatic)	○	○	○	○		
TROUBLE INDEX	⊖	⊖	⊜	⊜		
COST INDEX	○	○	○	○		

Datsun 280ZX Turbo

TROUBLE SPOTS	'80	'81	'82	'83	'84	'85
Air-conditioning	Insufficient data		⊖	○		
Body exterior (paint)			○	○		
Body exterior (rust)			○	○		
Body hardware			⊖	○		
Body integrity			○	○		
Brakes			○	○		
Clutch			○	○		
Driveline			○	○		
Electrical system (chassis)			○	○		
Engine cooling			○	○		
Engine mechanical			○	○		
Exhaust system			⊖	○		
Fuel system			○	○		
Ignition system			○	○		
Suspension			⊖	○		
Transmission (manual)			○	○		
Transmission (automatic)			○	○		
TROUBLE INDEX			⊜	⊖		
COST INDEX			*	*		

Datsun 310

TROUBLE SPOTS	'80	'81	'82	'83	'84	'85
Air-conditioning	●	○	○			
Body exterior (paint)	○	⊖	⊜			
Body exterior (rust)	●	●	○			
Body hardware	○	⊖	⊖			
Body integrity	○	○	⊖			
Brakes	●	●	●			
Clutch	◒	●	○			
Driveline	○	○	○			
Electrical system (chassis)	⊖	⊜	⊖			
Engine cooling	○	○	⊖			
Engine mechanical	⊜	○	⊖			
Exhaust system	◒	○	○			
Fuel system	⊜	⊜	⊜			
Ignition system	⊜	⊜	⊖			
Suspension	○	○	○			
Transmission (manual)	○	○	○			
Transmission (automatic)			○			
TROUBLE INDEX	○	○	⊖			
COST INDEX	○	○	⊖			

Datsun 510

TROUBLE SPOTS	'80	'81	'82	'83	'84	'85
Air-conditioning	⊖	○				
Body exterior (paint)	⊖	⊖				
Body exterior (rust)	●	●				
Body hardware	○	⊜				
Body integrity	⊖	⊜				
Brakes	⊖	○				
Clutch	⊖	⊜				
Driveline	⊖	⊖				
Electrical system (chassis)	⊜	⊜				
Engine cooling	⊜	⊜				
Engine mechanical	⊖	⊖				
Exhaust system	○	⊖				
Fuel system	⊜	⊜				
Ignition system	⊜	⊜				
Suspension	⊜	⊖				
Transmission (manual)	○	○				
Transmission (automatic)	⊖	○				
TROUBLE INDEX	⊖	⊜				
COST INDEX	⊜	⊜				

Datsun (Nissan) 810, Maxima (gas)

TROUBLE SPOTS	'80	'81	'82	'83	'84	'85
Air-conditioning	Insufficient data	⊜	⊜	⊜	⊖	
Body exterior (paint)		⊜	⊜	⊖	⊖	
Body exterior (rust)		○	○	○	○	
Body hardware		⊖	⊜	⊖	⊖	
Body integrity		○	⊜	⊜	⊖	
Brakes		○	⊖	○	○	
Clutch		○	○	○	⊖	
Driveline		○	○	○	○	
Electrical system (chassis)		○	⊖	⊖	⊜	
Engine cooling		○	⊖	⊖	○	
Engine mechanical		⊖	⊜	⊖	⊖	
Exhaust system		⊖	⊖	○	○	
Fuel system		○	⊜	○	○	
Ignition system		⊜	⊖	⊖	○	
Suspension		○	⊖	⊖	⊖	
Transmission (manual)		○	○	○	○	
Transmission (automatic)		⊖	⊖	○	○	
TROUBLE INDEX		⊖	⊜	⊜	⊜	
COST INDEX		○	⊖	○	○	

Datsun (Nissan) Pickup Truck (gas, 2-WD)

TROUBLE SPOTS	'80	'81	'82	'83	'84	'85
Air-conditioning	⊜	○	○	○	○	○
Body exterior (paint)	●	●	○	○	○	○
Body exterior (rust)	●	●	●	○	○	○
Body hardware	⊜	⊜	⊜	⊖	⊜	⊖
Body integrity	○	○	⊖	⊖	⊖	⊖
Brakes	⊖	○	◒	◒	◒	○
Clutch	⊜	⊜	⊜	⊜	○	○
Driveline	⊖	○	⊖	○	○	○
Electrical system (chassis)	⊖	⊜	⊜	⊜	⊜	⊖
Engine cooling	○	○	◒	○	○	○
Engine mechanical	○	○	●	⊖	○	○
Exhaust system	⊖	○	○	○	○	○
Fuel system	⊖	⊜	⊖	○	○	○
Ignition system	⊖	⊖	⊖	○	○	○
Suspension	◒	○	◒	○	○	○
Transmission (manual)	○	○	○	○	○	○
Transmission (automatic)	○	○	○	○	○	○
TROUBLE INDEX	○	○	○	⊜	⊜	⊜
COST INDEX	⊖	⊖	⊖	⊖	⊖	

Datsun (Nissan) Pickup Truck (4-WD)

TROUBLE SPOTS	'80	'81	'82	'83	'84	'85
Air-conditioning	Insufficient data	○	○	○	○	○
Body exterior (paint)		●	◒	○	○	○
Body exterior (rust)		●	●	○	○	○
Body hardware		⊖	○	⊖	○	○
Body integrity		○	○	⊖	○	○
Brakes		○	○	○	○	○
Clutch		⊖	○	○	○	○
Driveline		○	○	○	○	○
Electrical system (chassis)		○	⊜	⊖	⊜	○
Engine cooling		○	◒	○	○	○
Engine mechanical		○	●	⊖	○	○
Exhaust system		○	◒	○	○	○
Fuel system		⊜	○	○	○	○
Ignition system		○	○	○	○	○
Suspension		○	○	◒	●	○
Transmission (manual)		○	○	○	○	○
Transmission (automatic)						
TROUBLE INDEX		○	○	⊖	○	○
COST INDEX		○	○	⊖	○	

Dodge 400

TROUBLE SPOTS	'80	'81	'82	'83	'84	'85
Air-conditioning			⊖	○		
Body exterior (paint)			◒	○		
Body exterior (rust)			◒	○		
Body hardware			○	○		
Body integrity			○	○		
Brakes			○	○		
Clutch						
Driveline			○	○		
Electrical system (chassis)			○	◒		
Engine cooling			○	○		
Engine mechanical			◒	○		
Exhaust system			◒	○		
Fuel system			○	●		
Ignition system			○	◒		
Suspension			◒	◒		
Transmission (manual)						
Transmission (automatic)			○	○		
TROUBLE INDEX			◒	◒		
COST INDEX			○	○		

Dodge 600 (except Turbo)

TROUBLE SPOTS	'80	'81	'82	'83	'84	'85
Air-conditioning				○	○	○
Body exterior (paint)				○	○	○
Body exterior (rust)				○	○	○
Body hardware				◒	◒	○
Body integrity				●	●	○
Brakes				○	○	○
Clutch						
Driveline				○	○	○
Electrical system (chassis)				◒	●	◒
Engine cooling				○	○	○
Engine mechanical				○	○	○
Exhaust system				○	○	○
Fuel system				●	●	◒
Ignition system				○	○	○
Suspension				◒	◒	○
Transmission (manual)						
Transmission (automatic)				○	○	○
TROUBLE INDEX				◒	●	◒
COST INDEX				⊖	○	

Dodge 600 Turbo

TROUBLE SPOTS	'80	'81	'82	'83	'84	'85
Air-conditioning					○	○
Body exterior (paint)					◒	○
Body exterior (rust)					○	○
Body hardware					◒	○
Body integrity					●	◒
Brakes					○	○
Clutch					○	
Driveline					○	○
Electrical system (chassis)					●	◒
Engine cooling					○	○
Engine mechanical					○	○
Exhaust system					○	○
Fuel system					○	◒
Ignition system					○	○
Suspension					◒	○
Transmission (manual)					○	
Transmission (automatic)					○	○
TROUBLE INDEX					●	◒
COST INDEX					○	

Dodge Aries

TROUBLE SPOTS	'80	'81	'82	'83	'84	'85
Air-conditioning		○	⊖	○	○	○
Body exterior (paint)		○	◒	◒	○	○
Body exterior (rust)		◒	●	◒	○	○
Body hardware		●	●	○	○	◒
Body integrity		●	●	◒	●	◒
Brakes		○	○	○	○	○
Clutch		◒	●	●	○	
Driveline		○	○	○	○	○
Electrical system (chassis)		○	○	○	○	○
Engine cooling		○	⊖	○	○	○
Engine mechanical		●	◒	○	○	○
Exhaust system		●	●	○	○	○
Fuel system		○	◒	●	●	●
Ignition system		○	○	◒	◒	○
Suspension		●	●	○	○	○
Transmission (manual)		○	○	○	◒	
Transmission (automatic)		○	○	○	○	○
TROUBLE INDEX		◒	◒	◒	◒	●
COST INDEX		○	○	⊖	○	

Dodge Caravan

TROUBLE SPOTS	'80	'81	'82	'83	'84	'85
Air-conditioning					○	○
Body exterior (paint)					○	○
Body exterior (rust)					○	○
Body hardware					●	○
Body integrity					◒	○
Brakes					○	○
Clutch					○	○
Driveline					○	○
Electrical system (chassis)					○	○
Engine cooling					○	○
Engine mechanical					○	○
Exhaust system					○	○
Fuel system					◒	○
Ignition system					○	○
Suspension					○	○
Transmission (manual)					○	○
Transmission (automatic)					○	○
TROUBLE INDEX					◒	○
COST INDEX					⊖	

Dodge Challenger

TROUBLE SPOTS	'80	'81	'82	'83	'84	'85
Air-conditioning	○	○	○	○		
Body exterior (paint)	○	○	○	○		
Body exterior (rust)	⊖	○	○	○		
Body hardware	○	○	⊖	⊖		
Body integrity	○	○	⊖	○		
Brakes	○	○	○	○		
Clutch	○	●	●	○		
Driveline	○	○	○	○		
Electrical system (chassis)	⊖	○	○	⊖		
Engine cooling	⊖	⊖	○	○		
Engine mechanical	○	○	○	○		
Exhaust system	⊖	○	○	○		
Fuel system	◒	⊜	⊖	○		
Ignition system	○	○	⊖	⊖		
Suspension	○	⊖	⊖	⊖		
Transmission (manual)	○	○	○	○		
Transmission (automatic)	○	○	○	○		
TROUBLE INDEX	⊖	⊖	⊖	⊖		
COST INDEX	*	⊖	○	⊖		

⊜ Much better than average · ◓ Better than average · ○ Average · ◒ Worse than average · ● Much worse than average · * Insufficient cost data

Dodge Colt (except Turbo)	'80	'81	'82	'83	'84	'85
Air-conditioning	●	○	○	○	○	○
Body exterior (paint)	⊜	◓	○	◒	○	○
Body exterior (rust)	⊜	◓	○	●	○	○
Body hardware	◓	⊜	⊜	◓	◓	○
Body integrity	◓	◓	◓	○	○	○
Brakes	◓	◓	○	○	○	○
Clutch	○	◒	◒	○	○	○
Driveline	○	◓	○	○	○	○
Electrical system (chassis)	◓	◓	⊜	◓	⊜	○
Engine cooling	⊜	⊜	⊜	◓	○	○
Engine mechanical	◓	◓	⊜	◓	○	○
Exhaust system	○	○	○	○	○	○
Fuel system	●	⊜	⊜	⊜	◒	○
Ignition system	◒	◓	⊜	◓	○	○
Suspension	◓	◓	◓	○	○	○
Transmission (manual)	○	○	○	○	○	○
Transmission (automatic)	○	○	○	○	○	○
TROUBLE INDEX	◓	◓	◓	◓	◓	⊜
COST INDEX	◓	⊜	◓	⊜	◓	

Dodge Colt Vista Wagon	'80	'81	'82	'83	'84	'85
Air-conditioning					●	○
Body exterior (paint)					○	○
Body exterior (rust)					○	○
Body hardware					○	○
Body integrity					◓	○
Brakes					○	○
Clutch					○	○
Driveline					○	○
Electrical system (chassis)					◓	◓
Engine cooling					◓	○
Engine mechanical					○	○
Exhaust system					○	○
Fuel system					●	○
Ignition system					○	○
Suspension					○	○
Transmission (manual)					○	○
Transmission (automatic)					○	○
TROUBLE INDEX					○	○
COST INDEX					◓	

Dodge Daytona (except Turbo)	'80	'81	'82	'83	'84	'85
Air-conditioning					○	○
Body exterior (paint)					●	●
Body exterior (rust)					○	○
Body hardware					●	○
Body integrity					●	○
Brakes					○	○
Clutch					●	◒
Driveline					○	○
Electrical system (chassis)					●	◒
Engine cooling					○	○
Engine mechanical					○	○
Exhaust system					○	○
Fuel system					●	◒
Ignition system					○	○
Suspension					○	○
Transmission (manual)					○	○
Transmission (automatic)					○	○
TROUBLE INDEX					●	●
COST INDEX					○	

Dodge Daytona Turbo	'80	'81	'82	'83	'84	'85
Air-conditioning					◒	○
Body exterior (paint)					◒	●
Body exterior (rust)					○	○
Body hardware					●	○
Body integrity					●	●
Brakes					○	○
Clutch					◒	●
Driveline					○	○
Electrical system (chassis)					●	●
Engine cooling					○	○
Engine mechanical					○	◒
Exhaust system					○	○
Fuel system					●	●
Ignition system					○	○
Suspension					○	○
Transmission (manual)					○	○
Transmission (automatic)					○	○
TROUBLE INDEX					●	●
COST INDEX					○	

Dodge Lancer (except Turbo)	'80	'81	'82	'83	'84	'85
Air-conditioning						○
Body exterior (paint)						○
Body exterior (rust)						○
Body hardware						◒
Body integrity						○
Brakes						○
Clutch						○
Driveline						○
Electrical system (chassis)						○
Engine cooling						○
Engine mechanical						○
Exhaust system						○
Fuel system						○
Ignition system						◒
Suspension						○
Transmission (manual)						○
Transmission (automatic)						○
TROUBLE INDEX						○
COST INDEX						

Dodge Lancer Turbo	'80	'81	'82	'83	'84	'85
Air-conditioning						○
Body exterior (paint)						○
Body exterior (rust)						○
Body hardware						○
Body integrity						○
Brakes						○
Clutch						○
Driveline						○
Electrical system (chassis)						○
Engine cooling						○
Engine mechanical						○
Exhaust system						○
Fuel system						○
Ignition system						○
Suspension						○
Transmission (manual)						○
Transmission (automatic)						○
TROUBLE INDEX						◓
COST INDEX						

Dodge Omni, 024, Charger (except Turbo)	'80	'81	'82	'83	'84	'85
Air-conditioning	●	◒	○	○	○	○
Body exterior (paint)	○	●	●	●	◒	○
Body exterior (rust)	●	●	●	●	◒	○
Body hardware	●	●	●	○	◒	○
Body integrity	●	●	●	●	●	●
Brakes	○	○	○	○	○	○
Clutch	○	●	◒	◒	◒	◒
Driveline	●	○	○	○	○	○
Electrical system (chassis)	○	◒	●	◒	◒	○
Engine cooling	◒	○	○	○	○	○
Engine mechanical	○	◒	○	○	○	○
Exhaust system	●	●	●	◒	○	○
Fuel system	◒	●	●	●	●	●
Ignition system	●	●	○	◒	○	○
Suspension	●	○	○	○	○	○
Transmission (manual)	○	○	○	○	○	○
Transmission (automatic)	○	○	○	○	○	○
TROUBLE INDEX	●	●	●	●	●	●
COST INDEX	○	○	◓	◓	◓	

Dodge D100-D250 Pickup Truck 6	'80	'81	'82	'83	'84	'85
Air-conditioning	Insufficient data	Insufficient data	○	○	○	○
Body exterior (paint)			○	○	○	○
Body exterior (rust)			○	◒	○	○
Body hardware			○	○	○	○
Body integrity			○	○	●	○
Brakes			○	○	●	◒
Clutch			◒	○	○	◒
Driveline			○	○	○	◒
Electrical system (chassis)			○	○	○	○
Engine cooling			○	○	○	○
Engine mechanical			○	○	◒	○
Exhaust system			○	○	◒	○
Fuel system			○	●	◒	○
Ignition system			◒	◒	●	○
Suspension			○	◒	○	○
Transmission (manual)			○	○	○	○
Transmission (automatic)			○	○	○	○
TROUBLE INDEX			◒	●	●	●
COST INDEX			*	*	*	

Dodge D100-D250 Pickup Truck V8

'80, '81: Insufficient data

Trouble spots	'82	'83	'84	'85
Air-conditioning	○	○	○	○
Body exterior (paint)	○	○	○	○
Body exterior (rust)	○	○	○	○
Body hardware	○	○	○	○
Body integrity	◒	●	●	◒
Brakes	○	○	●	○
Clutch	○	○	●	◒
Driveline	◒	●	◒	○
Electrical system (chassis)	○	○	○	○
Engine cooling	○	○	○	○
Engine mechanical	○	○	○	○
Exhaust system	○	○	○	○
Fuel system	○	○	◒	○
Ignition system	○	○	◒	○
Suspension	○	○	○	○
Transmission (manual)	○	○	●	○
Transmission (automatic)	○	○	◒	○
TROUBLE INDEX	○	◒	●	◒
COST INDEX	*	*	○	

Dodge D50, Ram 50 Pickup Truck

Trouble spots	'80	'81	'82	'83	'84	'85
Air-conditioning	○	○	○	○	○	○
Body exterior (paint)	⊜	○	○	○	⊜	○
Body exterior (rust)	○	○	●	○	○	○
Body hardware	⊜	⊜	○	⊜	⊜	○
Body integrity	○	⊜	○	○	⊜	○
Brakes	⊜	⊜	⊜	⊜	○	○
Clutch	○	○	○	○	○	○
Driveline	○	○	○	○	○	○
Electrical system (chassis)	⊜	⊜	⊜	○	⊜	○
Engine cooling	⊜	⊜	⊜	⊜	○	○
Engine mechanical	⊜	○	○	○	○	○
Exhaust system	⊜	⊜	⊜	○	○	○
Fuel system	○	⊜	○	⊜	○	○
Ignition system	○	○	○	○	○	◒
Suspension	⊜	○	○	○	○	○
Transmission (manual)	○	○	◒	○	○	○
Transmission (automatic)	○	○	○	○	○	○
TROUBLE INDEX	⊜	⊜	⊜	⊜	⊜	○
COST INDEX	⊜	*	○	*	⊜	

Dodge Rampage Pickup Truck

Trouble spots	'80	'81	'82	'83	'84	'85
Air-conditioning			○	○	○	
Body exterior (paint)			○	○	○	
Body exterior (rust)			○	◒	○	
Body hardware			◒	○	○	
Body integrity			○	○	◒	
Brakes			○	○	○	
Clutch			○	○	○	
Driveline			○	○	○	
Electrical system (chassis)			○	○	○	
Engine cooling			○	○	○	
Engine mechanical			○	○	○	
Exhaust system			○	○	○	
Fuel system			○	○	○	
Ignition system			○	◒	○	
Suspension			⊜	○	○	
Transmission (manual)			◒	○	○	
Transmission (automatic)			○	○	○	
TROUBLE INDEX			○	●	◒	
COST INDEX			*	*	*	

Dodge Sportsman Wagon 6 (van)

'80, '81, '85: Insufficient data

Trouble spots	'82	'83	'84
Air-conditioning	○	○	◒
Body exterior (paint)	◒	●	○
Body exterior (rust)	●	●	○
Body hardware	○	○	○
Body integrity	◒	●	●
Brakes	○	○	○
Clutch	○	○	○
Driveline	◒	○	○
Electrical system (chassis)	○	○	○
Engine cooling	○	○	○
Engine mechanical	○	○	◒
Exhaust system	●	○	○
Fuel system	○	○	○
Ignition system	○	◒	○
Suspension	○	○	○
Transmission (manual)	○	◒	○
Transmission (automatic)	○	○	○
TROUBLE INDEX	●	●	●
COST INDEX	○	*	*

Dodge Sportsman Wagon V8 (van)

'81: Insufficient data

Trouble spots	'80	'82	'83	'84	'85
Air-conditioning	◒	◒	○	○	○
Body exterior (paint)	○	○	○	○	○
Body exterior (rust)	○	○	○	○	○
Body hardware	○	○	○	●	●
Body integrity	◒	●	●	●	●
Brakes	○	○	○	◒	○
Clutch	○				
Driveline	◒	○	◒	○	○
Electrical system (chassis)	○	○	○	◒	○
Engine cooling	○	○	○	○	○
Engine mechanical	○	○	○	○	○
Exhaust system	○	○	⊜	○	○
Fuel system	○	○	○	○	○
Ignition system	◒	○	○	○	○
Suspension	○	○	◒	○	◒
Transmission (manual)	○				
Transmission (automatic)	○	○	○	○	○
TROUBLE INDEX	◒	○	◒	●	●
COST INDEX	*	○	○	○	

Ford Bronco 6 (4-WD)

'82, '83: Insufficient data

Trouble spots	'80	'81	'84	'85
Air-conditioning			○	○
Body exterior (paint)			○	○
Body exterior (rust)			○	○
Body hardware			○	○
Body integrity			○	○
Brakes			○	○
Clutch			○	○
Driveline			○	○
Electrical system (chassis)			○	○
Engine cooling			○	○
Engine mechanical			○	○
Exhaust system			○	○
Fuel system			○	○
Ignition system			◒	○
Suspension			○	○
Transmission (manual)			○	○
Transmission (automatic)			○	○
TROUBLE INDEX			○	◒
COST INDEX			○	

Ford Bronco V8 (4-WD)

'81: Insufficient data

Trouble spots	'80	'82	'83	'84	'85
Air-conditioning	⊜	⊜	○	⊜	○
Body exterior (paint)	○	○	○	○	○
Body exterior (rust)	◒	○	○	○	◒
Body hardware	○	○	○	○	○
Body integrity	○	○	○	○	○
Brakes	◒	○	○	●	○
Clutch	○	○	○	○	
Driveline	●	●	◒	○	◒
Electrical system (chassis)	○	○	○	○	○
Engine cooling	⊜	○	○	○	○
Engine mechanical	○	○	○	○	○
Exhaust system	○	○	○	○	○
Fuel system	○	○	●	●	◒
Ignition system	○	○	◒	◒	○
Suspension	○	○	○	○	○
Transmission (manual)	○	○	○	○	
Transmission (automatic)	○	○	○	◒	○
TROUBLE INDEX	○	○	◒	◒	◒
COST INDEX	*	*	○	○	

Ford Bronco II V6 (4-WD)

Trouble spots	'80	'81	'82	'83	'84	'85
Air-conditioning					○	○
Body exterior (paint)					○	○
Body exterior (rust)					○	○
Body hardware					○	●
Body integrity					○	○
Brakes					○	○
Clutch					○	◒
Driveline					◒	○
Electrical system (chassis)					⊜	○
Engine cooling					○	○
Engine mechanical					○	○
Exhaust system					○	○
Fuel system					●	○
Ignition system					○	○
Suspension					○	○
Transmission (manual)					○	○
Transmission (automatic)					○	◒
TROUBLE INDEX					○	●
COST INDEX					⊜	

Key: Much better than average · Better than average · Average · Worse than average · Much worse than average · * Insufficient cost data

Ford Club Wagon 6 (van)

TROUBLE SPOTS	'80	'81	'82	'83	'84	'85
Air-conditioning	Insufficient data	Average	Average	Average	Average	Average
Body exterior (paint)		Average	Average	Average	Average	Average
Body exterior (rust)		Much worse	Average	Worse	Average	Average
Body hardware		Average	Average	Average	Average	Average
Body integrity		Average	Worse	Worse	Much worse	Average
Brakes		Worse	Worse	Worse	Average	Average
Clutch		Much worse	Average	Average	Average	Average
Driveline		Worse	Average	Average	Average	Worse
Electrical system (chassis)		Average	Average	Better	Average	Average
Engine cooling		Average	Average	Average	Average	Average
Engine mechanical		Average	Better	Average	Average	Average
Exhaust system		Better	Average	Average	Average	Worse
Fuel system		Average	Better	Average	Worse	Average
Ignition system		Average	Average	Average	Average	Average
Suspension		Average	Average	Average	Much worse	Average
Transmission (manual)		Worse	Average	Average	Average	Average
Transmission (automatic)		Average	Average	Average	Average	Average
TROUBLE INDEX		Worse	Average	Average	Worse	Much worse
COST INDEX		*	Average	*	*	

Ford Club Wagon V8 (Van)

TROUBLE SPOTS	'80	'81	'82	'83	'84	'85
Air-conditioning	Average	Average	Worse	Worse	Much worse	Average
Body exterior (paint)	Average	Average	Average	Average	Average	Average
Body exterior (rust)	Average	Average	Average	Average	Average	Worse
Body hardware	Average	Average	Average	Average	Much worse	Average
Body integrity	Worse	Average	Much worse	Much worse	Much worse	Much worse
Brakes	Average	Average	Average	Average	Average	Average
Clutch	Average	Average				
Driveline	Average	Average	Average	Worse	Average	Average
Electrical system (chassis)	Average	Average	Average	Much better	Better	Average
Engine cooling	Average	Average	Average	Average	Average	Average
Engine mechanical	Average	Average	Average	Average	Average	Average
Exhaust system	Average	Average	Better	Average	Average	Average
Fuel system	Average	Average	Average	Average	Worse	Average
Ignition system	Average	Average	Average	Average	Average	Worse
Suspension	Average	Average	Average	Worse	Much worse	Average
Transmission (manual)	Average	Average				
Transmission (automatic)	Average	Average	Average	Average	Average	Average
TROUBLE INDEX	Average	Average	Average	Average	Much worse	Much worse
COST INDEX	*	*	Average	Average	Average	

Ford Escort (gas)

TROUBLE SPOTS	'80	'81	'82	'83	'84	'85
Air-conditioning		Average	Average	Much better	Average	Average
Body exterior (paint)		Average	Average	Average	Average	Average
Body exterior (rust)		Much worse	Much worse	Average	Average	Average
Body hardware		Worse	Worse	Average	Average	Average
Body integrity		Average	Average	Average	Average	Average
Brakes		Better	Better	Better	Average	Average
Clutch		Much better	Much better	Better	Average	Average
Driveline		Average	Average	Average	Average	Average
Electrical system (chassis)		Average	Average	Average	Average	Better
Engine cooling		Worse	Average	Average	Average	Average
Engine mechanical		Much worse	Worse	Worse	Average	Average
Exhaust system		Worse	Worse	Worse	Average	Average
Fuel system		Average	Average	Much worse	Average	Average
Ignition system		Average	Worse	Much worse	Average	Average
Suspension		Average	Average	Average	Average	Average
Transmission (manual)		Average	Average	Average	Average	Average
Transmission (automatic)		Average	Average	Average	Average	Average
TROUBLE INDEX		Average	Average	Worse	Average	Average
COST INDEX		Average	Better	Better	Better	

Ford Escort (diesel)

TROUBLE SPOTS	'80	'81	'82	'83	'84	'85
Air-conditioning					Average	Insufficient data
Body exterior (paint)					Average	
Body exterior (rust)					Average	
Body hardware					Average	
Body integrity					Average	
Brakes					Average	
Clutch					Average	
Driveline					Average	
Electrical system (chassis)					Average	
Engine cooling					Worse	
Engine mechanical					Average	
Exhaust system					Average	
Fuel system					Much better	
Ignition system					Average	
Suspension					Much worse	
Transmission (manual)					Average	
Transmission (automatic)						
TROUBLE INDEX					Average	
COST INDEX					Better	

Ford EXP

TROUBLE SPOTS	'80	'81	'82	'83	'84	'85
Air-conditioning			Much worse	Average	Average	Insufficient data
Body exterior (paint)			Much worse	Worse	Worse	
Body exterior (rust)			Much worse	Average	Average	
Body hardware			Average	Average	Average	
Body integrity			Worse	Average	Average	
Brakes			Better	Average	Average	
Clutch			Much better	Average	Average	
Driveline			Average	Average	Average	
Electrical system (chassis)			Average	Average	Average	
Engine cooling			Much worse	Much worse	Worse	
Engine mechanical			Worse	Average	Average	
Exhaust system			Much worse	Worse	Worse	
Fuel system			Worse	Worse	Worse	
Ignition system			Average	Much worse	Average	
Suspension			Worse	Average	Average	
Transmission (manual)			Average	Average	Average	
Transmission (automatic)			Average	Much worse	Average	
TROUBLE INDEX			Much worse	Worse	Worse	
COST INDEX			Average	Average	*	

Ford Fairmont, Futura 4

TROUBLE SPOTS	'80	'81	'82	'83	'84	'85
Air-conditioning	Better	Average	Average	Insufficient data		
Body exterior (paint)	Average	Average	Average			
Body exterior (rust)	Average	Average	Worse			
Body hardware	Average	Average	Better			
Body integrity	Worse	Worse	Average			
Brakes	Average	Average	Average			
Clutch	Much worse	Worse	Average			
Driveline	Average	Average	Average			
Electrical system (chassis)	Average	Better	Average			
Engine cooling	Much better	Average	Average			
Engine mechanical	Worse	Average	Average			
Exhaust system	Worse	Average	Average			
Fuel system	Average	Average	Average			
Ignition system	Average	Average	Average			
Suspension	Worse	Average	Average			
Transmission (manual)	Average	Average	Average			
Transmission (automatic)	Better	Average	Average			
TROUBLE INDEX	Average	Average	Average			
COST INDEX	Better	Better	*			

Ford Fairmont, Futura 6

TROUBLE SPOTS	'80	'81	'82	'83	'84	'85
Air-conditioning	Much better	Much better	Better	Much better		
Body exterior (paint)	Average	Average	Average	Average		
Body exterior (rust)	Average	Average	Average	Average		
Body hardware	Average	Average	Average	Average		
Body integrity	Much worse	Average	Average	Average		
Brakes	Worse	Worse	Average	Average		
Clutch	Much worse					
Driveline	Average	Average	Average	Average		
Electrical system (chassis)	Average	Average	Average	Better		
Engine cooling	Average	Average	Better	Average		
Engine mechanical	Average	Average	Average	Average		
Exhaust system	Worse	Average	Average	Worse		
Fuel system	Much worse	Much worse	Much worse	Much worse		
Ignition system	Average	Average	Worse	Worse		
Suspension	Worse	Worse	Much worse	Average		
Transmission (manual)	Average					
Transmission (automatic)	Better	Average	Better	Better		
TROUBLE INDEX	Worse	Average	Average	Average		
COST INDEX	Average	Better	Better	Better		

Ford Fiesta

TROUBLE SPOTS	'80	'81	'82	'83	'84	'85
Air-conditioning	Average					
Body exterior (paint)	Much better					
Body exterior (rust)	Better					
Body hardware	Better					
Body integrity	Better					
Brakes	Much worse					
Clutch	Much better					
Driveline	Average					
Electrical system (chassis)	Average					
Engine cooling	Much worse					
Engine mechanical	Better					
Exhaust system	Average					
Fuel system	Better					
Ignition system	Better					
Suspension	Average					
Transmission (manual)	Average					
Transmission (automatic)						
TROUBLE INDEX	Average					
COST INDEX	Better					

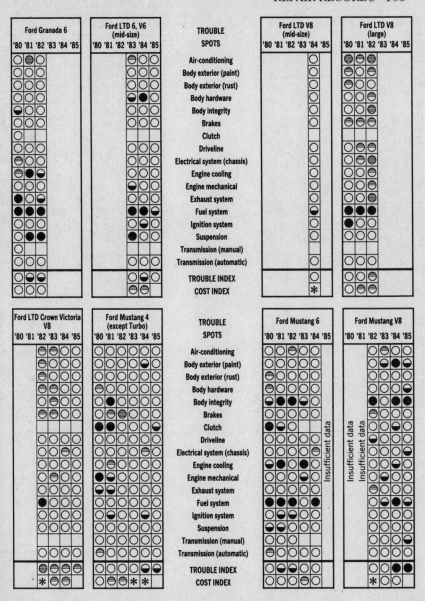

Ford Granada 6

TROUBLE SPOTS	'80	'81	'82	'83	'84	'85
Air-conditioning	○	⊜	○			
Body exterior (paint)	○	○	○			
Body exterior (rust)	○	○	○			
Body hardware	○	○	○			
Body integrity	◒	○	○			
Brakes	○	○	○			
Clutch	○					
Driveline	○	○	○			
Electrical system (chassis)	⊜	○	○			
Engine cooling	⊜	●	◒			
Engine mechanical	○	○	○			
Exhaust system	●	○	◒			
Fuel system	●	●	●			
Ignition system	○	○	○			
Suspension	○	●	●			
Transmission (manual)	○					
Transmission (automatic)	○	○	○			
TROUBLE INDEX	○	◒	◒			
COST INDEX	○	○	○			

Ford LTD 6, V6 (mid-size)

TROUBLE SPOTS	'80	'81	'82	'83	'84	'85
Air-conditioning				⊜	○	○
Body exterior (paint)				○	○	○
Body exterior (rust)				○	○	○
Body hardware				◒	●	○
Body integrity				○	○	○
Brakes				○	○	○
Clutch						
Driveline				○	○	○
Electrical system (chassis)				○	○	○
Engine cooling				○	○	○
Engine mechanical				◒	○	○
Exhaust system				○	○	○
Fuel system				●	●	◒
Ignition system				○	◒	○
Suspension				●	○	○
Transmission (manual)						
Transmission (automatic)				○	○	○
TROUBLE INDEX				○	◒	○
COST INDEX				⊜	⊜	

Ford LTD V8 (mid-size)

TROUBLE SPOTS	'80	'81	'82	'83	'84	'85
Air-conditioning					○	
Body exterior (paint)					○	
Body exterior (rust)					○	
Body hardware					○	
Body integrity					○	
Brakes					○	
Clutch						
Driveline					○	
Electrical system (chassis)					○	
Engine cooling					○	
Engine mechanical					○	
Exhaust system					○	
Fuel system					◒	
Ignition system					○	
Suspension					○	
Transmission (manual)						
Transmission (automatic)					○	
TROUBLE INDEX					○	
COST INDEX					*	

Ford LTD V8 (large)

TROUBLE SPOTS	'80	'81	'82	'83	'84	'85
Air-conditioning	⊜	⊜	⊜			
Body exterior (paint)	⊜	○	⊜			
Body exterior (rust)	⊜	○	○			
Body hardware	○	○	⊜			
Body integrity	○	○	⊜			
Brakes	⊜	⊜	⊜			
Clutch						
Driveline	○	⊜	⊜			
Electrical system (chassis)	○	⊜	⊜			
Engine cooling	○	○	⊜			
Engine mechanical	○	○	⊜			
Exhaust system	○	○	⊜			
Fuel system	●	●	●			
Ignition system	●	○	○			
Suspension	○	○	○			
Transmission (manual)						
Transmission (automatic)	○	○	○			
TROUBLE INDEX	○	○	⊜			
COST INDEX	○	⊜	⊜			

Ford LTD Crown Victoria V8

TROUBLE SPOTS	'80	'81	'82	'83	'84	'85
Air-conditioning			⊜	⊜	○	○
Body exterior (paint)			⊜	○	○	○
Body exterior (rust)			⊜	○	○	○
Body hardware			⊜	⊜	○	○
Body integrity			○	⊜	○	○
Brakes			⊜	⊜	○	○
Clutch						
Driveline			○	○	○	○
Electrical system (chassis)			○	○	⊜	○
Engine cooling			○	○	○	○
Engine mechanical			○	⊜	○	○
Exhaust system			○	○	○	○
Fuel system			●	○	○	○
Ignition system			○	○	○	○
Suspension			○	○	○	○
Transmission (manual)						
Transmission (automatic)			○	○	○	○
TROUBLE INDEX			⊜	⊜	⊜	⊜
COST INDEX			*	⊜	⊜	

Ford Mustang 4 (except Turbo)

TROUBLE SPOTS	'80	'81	'82	'83	'84	'85
Air-conditioning	○	○	○	○	○	○
Body exterior (paint)	○	○	○	○	◒	○
Body exterior (rust)	○	○	○	○	○	○
Body hardware	⊜	○	○	○	○	○
Body integrity	○	●	○	○	○	○
Brakes	○	⊜	⊜	○	○	○
Clutch	●	●	○	○	○	◒
Driveline	○	○	○	○	○	○
Electrical system (chassis)	○	○	○	○	⊜	○
Engine cooling	○	⊜	○	○	○	○
Engine mechanical	●	◒	○	○	○	○
Exhaust system	◒	◒	○	○	○	○
Fuel system	○	○	○	○	○	○
Ignition system	○	◒	○	○	◒	○
Suspension	○	○	○	○	○	○
Transmission (manual)	○	○	○	○	○	○
Transmission (automatic)	⊜	○	○	○	○	○
TROUBLE INDEX	○	○	○	○	◒	◒
COST INDEX	○	⊜	⊜	*	*	

Ford Mustang 6

TROUBLE SPOTS	'80	'81	'82	'83	'84	'85
Air-conditioning	○	○	⊜	○	○	Insufficient data
Body exterior (paint)	○	○	○	○	○	
Body exterior (rust)	⊜	○	○	○	○	
Body hardware	⊜	○	○	○	○	
Body integrity	◒	●	●	◒	○	
Brakes	○	○	○	○	○	
Clutch	●	◒	○			
Driveline	○	○	○	○	○	
Electrical system (chassis)	○	○	○	○	⊜	
Engine cooling	◒	●	○	●	○	
Engine mechanical	○	○	○	◒	○	
Exhaust system	○	○	○	○	○	
Fuel system	●	●	●	○	●	
Ignition system	○	◒	◒	○	○	
Suspension	◒	◒	○	○	○	
Transmission (manual)	○	○	○			
Transmission (automatic)	⊜	○	○	○	○	
TROUBLE INDEX	○	◒	◒	○	○	
COST INDEX	○	○	○	⊜	○	

Ford Mustang V8

TROUBLE SPOTS	'80	'81	'82	'83	'84	'85
Air-conditioning	Insufficient data	Insufficient data	○	⊜	○	○
Body exterior (paint)			○	◒	●	◒
Body exterior (rust)			○	○	○	○
Body hardware			○	○	○	◒
Body integrity			●	○	●	●
Brakes			⊜	○	○	○
Clutch			○	○	◒	○
Driveline			◒	○	○	○
Electrical system (chassis)			○	○	○	◒
Engine cooling			○	○	◒	○
Engine mechanical			○	◒	○	○
Exhaust system			⊜	○	○	○
Fuel system			○	◒	●	◒
Ignition system			○	○	○	○
Suspension			○	○	○	○
Transmission (manual)			○	○	○	◒
Transmission (automatic)			○	○	○	○
TROUBLE INDEX			○	○	●	●
COST INDEX			*	○	○	

- ⊜ Much better than average
- ⊖ Better than average
- ○ Average
- ◒ Worse than average
- ● Much worse than average
- * Insufficient cost data

Ford Pickup Truck 6, V6 (2-WD)

TROUBLE SPOTS	'80	'81	'82	'83	'84	'85
Air-conditioning	○	⊖	⊖	○	○	○
Body exterior (paint)	○	○	○	◒	○	○
Body exterior (rust)	○	○	○	○	○	○
Body hardware	⊖	⊜	⊜	⊖	⊖	○
Body integrity	○	⊖	○	○	○	○
Brakes	●	●	○	◒	◒	○
Clutch	○	○	○	○	○	○
Driveline	○	○	○	○	○	○
Electrical system (chassis)	⊖	⊜	⊜	⊜	⊜	○
Engine cooling	⊜	⊜	⊖	○	○	○
Engine mechanical	○	⊖	⊖	○	○	○
Exhaust system	○	⊖	⊜	○	○	○
Fuel system	⊖	⊜	⊜	○	○	◒
Ignition system	○	⊖	○	◒	◒	○
Suspension	○	○	◒	●	●	○
Transmission (manual)	●	○	○	○	○	○
Transmission (automatic)	○	○	○	◒	○	○
TROUBLE INDEX	○	⊖	⊖	◒	◒	○
COST INDEX	⊖	⊖	⊖	⊖	○	

Ford Pickup Truck V8 (gas, 2-WD)

TROUBLE SPOTS	'80	'81	'82	'83	'84	'85
Air-conditioning	○	⊖	○	○	○	○
Body exterior (paint)	○	○	○	○	○	○
Body exterior (rust)	○	⊖	○	○	○	○
Body hardware	○	⊖	⊜	⊖	⊖	○
Body integrity	○	○	○	○	○	○
Brakes	◒	●	◒	◒	○	○
Clutch	○	○	○	○	○	○
Driveline	○	◒	○	○	◒	○
Electrical system (chassis)	⊖	⊖	⊖	⊖	⊖	○
Engine cooling	⊖	○	○	○	○	○
Engine mechanical	○	○	○	○	○	○
Exhaust system	○	⊜	⊖	○	○	○
Fuel system	○	○	◒	●	●	◒
Ignition system	○	○	○	○	◒	○
Suspension	○	○	○	●	●	◒
Transmission (manual)	○	○	○	○	○	○
Transmission (automatic)	○	○	○	○	○	○
TROUBLE INDEX	○	○	○	○	◒	◒
COST INDEX	⊖	○	○	○	○	

Ford Pickup Truck V8 (gas, 4-WD)

TROUBLE SPOTS	'80	'81	'82	'83	'84	'85
Air-conditioning	○	○	○	○	○	○
Body exterior (paint)	○	○	○	○	○	○
Body exterior (rust)	○	○	○	◒	○	○
Body hardware	○	○	⊖	⊖	⊖	○
Body integrity	○	○	○	○	○	○
Brakes	○	○	○	●	◒	○
Clutch	○	○	◒	○	○	◒
Driveline	●	●	●	○	◒	○
Electrical system (chassis)	○	○	⊖	○	⊖	○
Engine cooling	○	○	⊖	○	○	○
Engine mechanical	◒	○	○	○	○	○
Exhaust system	○	⊖	○	○	○	○
Fuel system	○	○	○	◒	●	●
Ignition system	○	○	○	○	○	○
Suspension	○	○	○	○	◒	○
Transmission (manual)	○	◒	◒	○	○	○
Transmission (automatic)	○	○	○	○	○	○
TROUBLE INDEX	◒	○	○	◒	◒	●
COST INDEX	*	*	*	●	○	

Ford Ranger Pickup Truck 4 (2-WD)

TROUBLE SPOTS	'80	'81	'82	'83	'84	'85
Air-conditioning				⊖	○	○
Body exterior (paint)				○	⊖	○
Body exterior (rust)				○	○	○
Body hardware				⊜	⊖	⊖
Body integrity				○	○	○
Brakes				⊖	○	○
Clutch				○	○	○
Driveline				○	○	○
Electrical system (chassis)				⊜	⊜	⊖
Engine cooling				⊖	○	○
Engine mechanical				○	●	○
Exhaust system				◒	○	○
Fuel system				●	●	◒
Ignition system				●	●	○
Suspension				○	○	○
Transmission (manual)				○	○	○
Transmission (automatic)				○	○	○
TROUBLE INDEX				○	○	○
COST INDEX				⊖	⊖	

Ford Ranger Pickup Truck V6 (2-WD)

TROUBLE SPOTS	'80	'81	'82	'83	'84	'85
Air-conditioning					○	○
Body exterior (paint)					○	○
Body exterior (rust)					○	○
Body hardware					○	⊖
Body integrity					⊖	○
Brakes					○	○
Clutch					○	○
Driveline					○	○
Electrical system (chassis)					⊜	○
Engine cooling					○	○
Engine mechanical					○	○
Exhaust system					○	○
Fuel system					●	○
Ignition system					○	○
Suspension					○	○
Transmission (manual)					○	○
Transmission (automatic)					○	○
TROUBLE INDEX					○	○
COST INDEX					⊖	

Ford Pinto 4

TROUBLE SPOTS	'80	'81	'82	'83	'84	'85
Air-conditioning	●					
Body exterior (paint)	○					
Body exterior (rust)	○					
Body hardware	○					
Body integrity	●					
Brakes	○					
Clutch	○					
Driveline	○					
Electrical system (chassis)	⊖					
Engine cooling	⊖					
Engine mechanical	●					
Exhaust system	●					
Fuel system	○					
Ignition system	◒					
Suspension	○					
Transmission (manual)	○					
Transmission (automatic)	○					
TROUBLE INDEX	○					
COST INDEX	⊖					

Ford Tempo (gas)

TROUBLE SPOTS	'80	'81	'82	'83	'84	'85
Air-conditioning					○	○
Body exterior (paint)					○	○
Body exterior (rust)					○	○
Body hardware					○	○
Body integrity					○	○
Brakes					○	○
Clutch					⊖	○
Driveline					○	○
Electrical system (chassis)					○	○
Engine cooling					○	○
Engine mechanical					○	○
Exhaust system					○	○
Fuel system					●	●
Ignition system					◒	◒
Suspension					●	○
Transmission (manual)					○	○
Transmission (automatic)					○	○
TROUBLE INDEX					●	●
COST INDEX					⊖	

Ford Thunderbird 6, V6 (except Turbo)

TROUBLE SPOTS	'80	'81	'82	'83	'84	'85
Air-conditioning		○	⊖	⊖	○	○
Body exterior (paint)		○	○	○	○	○
Body exterior (rust)		○	○	○	○	○
Body hardware		○	○	○	○	○
Body integrity		◒	○	⊖	⊖	⊖
Brakes		○	○	○	○	○
Clutch						
Driveline		○	○	○	○	○
Electrical system (chassis)		○	○	○	○	○
Engine cooling		○	○	⊖	○	○
Engine mechanical		○	○	○	○	○
Exhaust system		○	○	○	○	○
Fuel system		●	●	○	●	◒
Ignition system		○	○	○	○	○
Suspension		●	◒	◒	○	○
Transmission (manual)						
Transmission (automatic)		○	○	○	○	○
TROUBLE INDEX		◒	○	⊖	○	○
COST INDEX		○	⊖	⊖	⊖	

Ford Thunderbird V8

TROUBLE SPOTS	'80	'81	'82	'83	'84	'85
Air-conditioning	⊜	◍	⊜	○	○	○
Body exterior (paint)	○	○	○	○	○	○
Body exterior (rust)	⊜	⊜	○	○	○	○
Body hardware	○	○	○	○	○	○
Body integrity	◒	○	○	○	⊜	○
Brakes	●	○	○	○	○	○
Clutch						
Driveline	○	○	○	○	○	○
Electrical system (chassis)	●	○	○	◒	○	○
Engine cooling	◒	○	○	○	○	○
Engine mechanical	●	○	○	⊜	⊜	○
Exhaust system	○	◍	○	○	○	○
Fuel system	◒	○	○	◒	○	○
Ignition system	●	○	○	○	○	○
Suspension	●	●	○	●	◒	○
Transmission (manual)						
Transmission (automatic)	⊜	○	○	○	○	○
TROUBLE INDEX	◒	○	○	○	○	○
COST INDEX	○	⊜	○	⊜	○	

GMC Pickup Truck V8 (gas, 2-WD)

TROUBLE SPOTS	'80	'81	'82	'83	'84	'85
Air-conditioning	Insufficient data	◒	○	○	○	◒
Body exterior (paint)		●	●	●	◒	●
Body exterior (rust)		○	○	○	○	○
Body hardware		○	○	○	○	○
Body integrity		○	◒	○	◒	●
Brakes		⊜	○	○	◒	○
Clutch		○	○	○	○	○
Driveline		○	●	○	○	○
Electrical system (chassis)		○	○	○	○	◒
Engine cooling		○	○	○	○	○
Engine mechanical		○	○	◒	○	○
Exhaust system		⊜	○	○	○	○
Fuel system		○	○	○	○	○
Ignition system		○	○	○	○	○
Suspension		○	○	○	◒	○
Transmission (manual)		○	○	○	○	○
Transmission (automatic)		○	○	◒	◒	○
TROUBLE INDEX		◒	◒	◒	◒	●
COST INDEX		*	*	*	*	

GMC S15 Jimmy V6 (4-WD)

TROUBLE SPOTS	'80	'81	'82	'83	'84	'85
Air-conditioning				○	○	○
Body exterior (paint)				○	○	○
Body exterior (rust)				◒	○	○
Body hardware				○	○	○
Body integrity				◒	○	○
Brakes				○	○	○
Clutch				●	○	○
Driveline				◒	◒	◒
Electrical system (chassis)				○	◒	○
Engine cooling				○	◒	○
Engine mechanical				◒	●	○
Exhaust system				○	○	○
Fuel system				○	○	○
Ignition system				○	○	○
Suspension				○	○	○
Transmission (manual)				○	○	○
Transmission (automatic)				◒	●	◒
TROUBLE INDEX				●	●	●
COST INDEX				*	○	

GMC S15 Pickup Truck V6 (2-WD)

TROUBLE SPOTS	'80	'81	'82	'83	'84	'85
Air-conditioning			○	○	○	
Body exterior (paint)			○	○	○	
Body exterior (rust)			○	○	○	
Body hardware			○	⊜	○	
Body integrity			○	○	○	
Brakes			○	○	○	
Clutch			●	●	○	
Driveline			○	○	◒	
Electrical system (chassis)			⊜	○	○	
Engine cooling			○	○	○	
Engine mechanical			○	○	●	
Exhaust system			○	○	○	
Fuel system			○	○	⊜	
Ignition system			○	○	○	
Suspension			⊜	○	○	
Transmission (manual)			◒	○	○	
Transmission (automatic)			◒	○	○	
TROUBLE INDEX			○	○	○	
COST INDEX			*	*	*	

Honda Accord

TROUBLE SPOTS	'80	'81	'82	'83	'84	'85
Air-conditioning	◍	◍	⊜	○	⊜	○
Body exterior (paint)	⊜	◍	◍	⊜	⊜	○
Body exterior (rust)	◒	○	⊜	○	○	○
Body hardware	◍	◍	◍	◍	⊜	⊜
Body integrity	◍	◍	◍	◍	◍	⊜
Brakes	●	●	○	◒	○	○
Clutch	⊜	○	⊜	⊜	●	○
Driveline	○	⊜	⊜	○	○	○
Electrical system (chassis)	◍	◍	○	◍	◍	◍
Engine cooling	⊜	⊜	⊜	⊜	○	○
Engine mechanical	◍	◍	◍	⊜	⊜	○
Exhaust system	◍	⊜	○	○	○	○
Fuel system	○	◍	⊜	◍	○	⊜
Ignition system	◍	◍	⊜	⊜	○	○
Suspension	◍	◍	◍	◍	⊜	○
Transmission (manual)	○	○	○	○	○	○
Transmission (automatic)	○	○	○	○	○	○
TROUBLE INDEX	⊜	◍	◍	◍	◍	◍
COST INDEX	⊜	⊜	⊜	⊜	○	

Honda Civic CRX

TROUBLE SPOTS	'80	'81	'82	'83	'84	'85
Air-conditioning					○	○
Body exterior (paint)					○	○
Body exterior (rust)					○	○
Body hardware					⊜	◍
Body integrity					◍	⊜
Brakes					⊜	○
Clutch					○	○
Driveline					○	○
Electrical system (chassis)					◍	⊜
Engine cooling					○	○
Engine mechanical					⊜	○
Exhaust system					○	○
Fuel system					⊜	○
Ignition system					○	○
Suspension					⊜	○
Transmission (manual)					○	○
Transmission (automatic)					○	○
TROUBLE INDEX					◍	◍
COST INDEX					⊜	

Honda Civic

TROUBLE SPOTS	'80	'81	'82	'83	'84	'85
Air-conditioning	⊜	◍	◍	○	○	○
Body exterior (paint)	○	○	⊜	⊜	○	○
Body exterior (rust)	●	●	◒	○	○	○
Body hardware	⊜	◍	◍	◍	⊜	⊜
Body integrity	◍	◍	◍	◍	⊜	⊜
Brakes	○	○	⊜	⊜	⊜	○
Clutch	⊜	◍	◍	⊜	◒	○
Driveline	⊜	○	⊜	○	○	○
Electrical system (chassis)	◍	◍	◍	◍	◍	◍
Engine cooling	○	◍	⊜	⊜	○	○
Engine mechanical	⊜	◍	◍	◍	⊜	○
Exhaust system	○	◍	◍	○	○	○
Fuel system	◍	◍	◍	◍	⊜	○
Ignition system	◍	◍	⊜	⊜	⊜	○
Suspension	⊜	⊜	◍	⊜	⊜	○
Transmission (manual)	○	○	○	○	○	○
Transmission (automatic)	○	○	⊜	○	○	○
TROUBLE INDEX	⊜	◍	◍	◍	◍	◍
COST INDEX	⊜	◍	◍	⊜	○	

Honda Prelude

TROUBLE SPOTS	'80	'81	'82	'83	'84	'85
Air-conditioning	⊜	◍	◍	◒	○	○
Body exterior (paint)	○	◍	◍	⊜	⊜	○
Body exterior (rust)	●	⊜	○	⊜	○	○
Body hardware	◍	◍	◍	○	◍	⊜
Body integrity	◍	◍	◍	⊜	◍	⊜
Brakes	●	●	◒	○	○	○
Clutch	○	○	●	○	●	○
Driveline	○	○	⊜	○	○	○
Electrical system (chassis)	◍	◍	◍	◍	◍	◍
Engine cooling	⊜	⊜	◍	○	○	○
Engine mechanical	◍	◍	◍	⊜	⊜	○
Exhaust system	◍	◍	◍	○	○	○
Fuel system	⊜	◍	◍	⊜	◍	⊜
Ignition system	◍	◍	⊜	⊜	⊜	○
Suspension	⊜	⊜	⊜	⊜	⊜	○
Transmission (manual)	○	○	○	○	○	○
Transmission (automatic)	○	○	○	○	○	○
TROUBLE INDEX	⊜	◍	◍	◍	◍	◍
COST INDEX	⊜	⊜	⊜	⊜	○	

⊜ Much better than average ◓ Better than average ○ Average ◒ Worse than average ● Much worse than average * Insufficient cost data

TROUBLE SPOTS	Isuzu Impulse '80	'81	'82	'83	'84	'85	Jeep (AMC) CJ Series 4 '80	'81	'82	'83	'84	'85
Air-conditioning				○	○	Insufficient data	○	○	○	○	○	Insufficient data
Body exterior (paint)				○	○		○	○	○	◒	◒	
Body exterior (rust)				○	○		●	●	●	●	◒	
Body hardware				○	○		◒	●	●	●	●	
Body integrity				○	○		●	●	◒	●	●	
Brakes				●	●		●	●	○	○	○	
Clutch				○	○		●	●	◒	○	○	
Driveline				○	○		○	●	○	●	◒	
Electrical system (chassis)				○	○		○	○	○	●	◒	
Engine cooling				○	○		○	○	○	◒	◒	
Engine mechanical				○	○		○	◒	○	◒	●	
Exhaust system				●	○		◒	●	○	○	○	
Fuel system				●	●		○	◒	○	◒	◒	
Ignition system				○	○		○	○	○	○	○	
Suspension				◓	○		○	○	○	○	○	
Transmission (manual)				○	○		◒	○	●	○	○	
Transmission (automatic)				○	○		○	○	○	○	○	
TROUBLE INDEX				○	○		◒	●	●	●	●	
COST INDEX				*	○		*	*	*	◒	*	

TROUBLE SPOTS	Jeep (AMC) Wagoneer, Cherokee '80	'81	'82	'83	'84	'85	Jeep (AMC) Wagoneer, Cherokee 4 '80	'81	'82	'83	'84	'85
Air-conditioning	○	Insufficient data	◓	◓							○	○
Body exterior (paint)	○		○	●							●	◒
Body exterior (rust)	●		○	●							○	○
Body hardware	●		●	●							●	◒
Body integrity	◒		●	●							◒	●
Brakes	○		○	○							○	○
Clutch	○		○	○							●	◒
Driveline	○		○	●							◒	◒
Electrical system (chassis)	○		◒	●							●	●
Engine cooling	◒		○	●							○	◒
Engine mechanical	○		◒	○							○	○
Exhaust system	○		○	○							○	○
Fuel system	○		○	◒							◒	◒
Ignition system	○		◒	●							○	○
Suspension	◓		○	○							○	○
Transmission (manual)	○		○	○							◒	○
Transmission (automatic)	○		○	◒							○	○
TROUBLE INDEX	◒		●	●							●	●
COST INDEX	*		*	●							○	

TROUBLE SPOTS	Jeep (AMC) Wagoneer, Cherokee V6 '80	'81	'82	'83	'84	'85	Lincoln Town Car (except Continental) '80	'81	'82	'83	'84	'85
Air-conditioning					○	○	○	◓	◓	○	○	○
Body exterior (paint)					●	○	○	◓	◓	◓	○	○
Body exterior (rust)					○	○	○	○	○	○	○	○
Body hardware					●	◒	◒	○	○	○	○	○
Body integrity					●	○	○	◓	○	○	◓	○
Brakes					○	○	○	○	◓	◓	◓	○
Clutch					●	○						
Driveline					●	○	○	○	○	○	○	○
Electrical system (chassis)					●	◒	○	○	○	○	○	○
Engine cooling					○	○	○	○	○	○	○	○
Engine mechanical					●	●	○	○	◓	◓	○	○
Exhaust system					○	○	◓	◓	◓	○	○	○
Fuel system					◒	◒	○	◓	◓	◓	◓	○
Ignition system					◒	○	○	○	○	○	○	○
Suspension					○	○	○	○	○	○	○	○
Transmission (manual)					◒	○						
Transmission (automatic)					●	◒	○	○	○	○	○	○
TROUBLE INDEX					●	●	◓	⊜	⊜	◓	◓	◓
COST INDEX					◒		◒	*	○	◓	◓	

TROUBLE SPOTS	Lincoln Continental '80	'81	'82	'83	'84	'85	Lincoln Continental Mark VI, Mark VII '80	'81	'82	'83	'84	'85
Air-conditioning			○	○	◓	○	◓	◓	◓	○	○	○
Body exterior (paint)			○	○	○	○	○	○	○	○	○	○
Body exterior (rust)			◓	○	○	○	○	○	○	○	○	○
Body hardware			○	○	○	○	●	○	○	○	○	◒
Body integrity			○	○	○	○	○	○	○	○	○	○
Brakes			○	○	○	○	○	○	○	○	○	○
Clutch												
Driveline			○	○	○	○	○	○	○	○	○	○
Electrical system (chassis)			●	○	●	○	◒	○	◒	○	◒	○
Engine cooling			◓	○	○	○	○	○	○	○	○	○
Engine mechanical			○	○	○	○	○	◓	◓	○	◓	○
Exhaust system			◓	○	○	○	○	◓	◓	○	○	○
Fuel system			●	○	○	○	○	○	○	○	◓	○
Ignition system			◒	○	○	○	○	◒	○	○	○	○
Suspension			○	○	◒	●	◓	○	◓	○	◒	●
Transmission (manual)												
Transmission (automatic)			○	○	○	○	○	○	○	○	○	○
TROUBLE INDEX			○	○	○	○	○	◓	◓	○	○	●
COST INDEX			○	*	◓		*	*	*	○	○	

Mazda 626

TROUBLE SPOTS	'80	'81	'82	'83	'84	'85
Air-conditioning	◒	○	⊖	●	○	○
Body exterior (paint)	⊜	⊜	⊖	⊖	⊖	○
Body exterior (rust)	⊖	⊜	⊖	⊖	○	○
Body hardware	⊖	⊖	⊖	○	⊖	⊖
Body integrity	⊜	⊖	⊖	⊖	⊜	⊖
Brakes	⊖	○	◒	⊖	⊖	○
Clutch	⊜	⊜	⊜	⊖	⊖	○
Driveline	○	○	○	○	○	○
Electrical system (chassis)	⊜	⊜	⊜	○	⊖	⊖
Engine cooling	⊖	⊖	○	○	○	○
Engine mechanical	○	○	○	⊖	⊖	○
Exhaust system	◒	●	●	○	○	○
Fuel system	⊜	⊜	⊜	⊜	⊜	○
Ignition system	⊜	⊜	⊖	⊖	⊖	○
Suspension	○	○	⊖	○	○	○
Transmission (manual)	○	○	○	○	○	○
Transmission (automatic)	○	○	○	○	○	○
TROUBLE INDEX	⊖	⊖	⊖	⊜	⊜	⊜
COST INDEX	⊖	⊖	○	⊖	⊖	

Mazda GLC (FWD)

TROUBLE SPOTS	'80	'81	'82	'83	'84	'85
Air-conditioning		●	●	●	◒	◒
Body exterior (paint)		⊜	⊖	⊖	⊖	⊖
Body exterior (rust)		⊖	○	○	○	○
Body hardware		⊖	⊖	⊖	⊖	○
Body integrity		○	○	⊖	⊖	○
Brakes		○	○	○	⊖	○
Clutch		⊜	⊜	⊖	⊖	○
Driveline		○	○	○	○	○
Electrical system (chassis)		⊜	⊜	⊜	⊜	⊖
Engine cooling		○	○	○	○	○
Engine mechanical		⊖	⊖	⊖	⊖	○
Exhaust system		●	●	○	○	○
Fuel system		○	○	●	○	○
Ignition system		⊖	⊖	⊖	○	○
Suspension		●	○	⊖	⊖	○
Transmission (manual)		○	○	○	○	○
Transmission (automatic)		○	○	○	○	○
TROUBLE INDEX		○	○	⊖	⊜	⊜
COST INDEX		⊖	○	⊖	⊖	

Mazda GLC (RWD)

TROUBLE SPOTS	'80	'81	'82	'83	'84	'85
Air-conditioning	◒	○	○			
Body exterior (paint)	⊜	⊖	○			
Body exterior (rust)	○	○	○			
Body hardware	⊜	⊖	○			
Body integrity	○	○	○			
Brakes	○	●	○			
Clutch	⊜	⊜	⊖			
Driveline	○	○	○			
Electrical system (chassis)	⊜	⊖	⊜			
Engine cooling	⊖	○	○			
Engine mechanical	⊜	○	⊖			
Exhaust system	○	●	●			
Fuel system	⊖	⊜	○			
Ignition system	⊖	○	○			
Suspension	⊜	⊖	○			
Transmission (manual)	○	○	○			
Transmission (automatic)	○	○	○			
TROUBLE INDEX	⊖	○	⊖			
COST INDEX	⊜	⊖	⊖			

Mazda RX-7

TROUBLE SPOTS	'80	'81	'82	'83	'84	'85
Air-conditioning	⊖	○	⊖	⊜	○	○
Body exterior (paint)	⊜	○	○	○	⊖	○
Body exterior (rust)	⊖	⊖	⊖	○	○	○
Body hardware	⊜	⊖	⊖	⊖	⊖	⊖
Body integrity	⊜	⊖	⊜	⊜	⊖	⊖
Brakes	⊖	⊖	⊖	⊖	○	○
Clutch	○	⊖	○	○	○	○
Driveline	⊖	○	○	○	○	○
Electrical system (chassis)	⊜	⊖	⊖	⊖	⊖	⊜
Engine cooling	○	○	○	○	○	○
Engine mechanical	⊜	⊜	⊜	⊖	⊖	○
Exhaust system	⊜	⊜	⊜	○	○	○
Fuel system	⊜	⊜	⊜	⊜	⊖	⊖
Ignition system	⊜	⊜	⊜	⊖	○	○
Suspension	⊖	⊖	⊖	⊖	○	○
Transmission (manual)	○	○	○	○	○	○
Transmission (automatic)	○	○	○	○	○	○
TROUBLE INDEX	⊜	⊜	⊜	⊜	⊜	⊜
COST INDEX	○	⊖	○	○	○	

Mercedes-Benz 190E

TROUBLE SPOTS	'80	'81	'82	'83	'84	'85
Air-conditioning					●	◒
Body exterior (paint)					⊖	○
Body exterior (rust)					○	○
Body hardware					○	⊖
Body integrity					⊜	⊖
Brakes					○	○
Clutch					○	○
Driveline					○	○
Electrical system (chassis)					○	○
Engine cooling					○	○
Engine mechanical					○	○
Exhaust system					○	○
Fuel system					⊖	○
Ignition system					⊖	○
Suspension					⊖	○
Transmission (manual)					○	○
Transmission (automatic)					○	○
TROUBLE INDEX					⊖	⊜
COST INDEX					◒	

Mercedes-Benz 240D

TROUBLE SPOTS	'80	'81	'82	'83	'84	'85
Air-conditioning	⊖	○	⊜	⊖		
Body exterior (paint)	⊜	⊜	⊜	⊖		
Body exterior (rust)	⊜	⊜	⊖	○		
Body hardware	⊜	⊜	⊖	○		
Body integrity	⊜	⊜	⊜	⊜		
Brakes	⊜	⊖	⊖	○		
Clutch	⊜	⊖	⊖	○		
Driveline	○	⊖	○	○		
Electrical system (chassis)	⊜	⊜	⊖	○		
Engine cooling	○	○	⊖	⊖		
Engine mechanical	⊜	⊜	⊖	⊖		
Exhaust system	⊜	⊜	⊜	○		
Fuel system	⊜	⊜	⊖	○		
Ignition system	⊖	⊖	⊖	○		
Suspension	⊖	⊜	⊜	○		
Transmission (manual)	○	○	○	○		
Transmission (automatic)	○	○	○	○		
TROUBLE INDEX	⊜	⊜	⊜	⊜		
COST INDEX	○	○	○	●		

Mercedes-Benz 300D 5 (except Turbodiesel)

TROUBLE SPOTS	'80	'81	'82	'83	'84	'85
Air-conditioning	◒	○				
Body exterior (paint)	⊜	⊜				
Body exterior (rust)	⊜	⊖				
Body hardware	⊜	⊖				
Body integrity	⊜	⊖				
Brakes	⊜	○				
Clutch						
Driveline	○	○				
Electrical system (chassis)	○	○				
Engine cooling	○	⊖				
Engine mechanical	⊖	⊖				
Exhaust system	⊜	⊜				
Fuel system	⊜	⊖				
Ignition system	⊖	⊖				
Suspension	⊖	⊖				
Transmission (manual)						
Transmission (automatic)	⊖	○				
TROUBLE INDEX	⊜	⊜				
COST INDEX	●	◒				

M-B Turbodiesel 5 (300D, CD, TD, SD)

TROUBLE SPOTS	'80	'81	'82	'83	'84	'85
Air-conditioning	●	○	○	⊖	○	○
Body exterior (paint)	⊜	⊖	⊜	⊜	⊖	⊖
Body exterior (rust)	⊜	⊖	⊜	⊖	○	○
Body hardware	⊖	○	⊖	⊖	⊖	○
Body integrity	⊜	⊜	⊜	⊜	⊜	⊖
Brakes	⊖	⊖	○	○	○	○
Clutch						
Driveline	⊖	○	⊖	○	○	○
Electrical system (chassis)	○	⊖	⊜	⊖	⊜	○
Engine cooling	⊖	⊖	⊜	⊖	○	○
Engine mechanical	○	○	⊖	⊖	⊖	○
Exhaust system	⊜	⊜	⊜	⊖	○	○
Fuel system	⊜	⊜	⊜	⊜	⊜	○
Ignition system	⊖	⊖	⊜	⊜	⊖	○
Suspension	○	⊖	⊜	⊖	⊖	○
Transmission (manual)						
Transmission (automatic)	⊖	○	○	○	○	○
TROUBLE INDEX	⊜	⊜	⊜	⊜	⊜	⊜
COST INDEX	◒	●	◒	●	●	

⊜ Much better than average | ⊖ Better than average | ○ Average | ◒ Worse than average | ● Much worse than average | * Insufficient cost data

Mercedes-Benz 380 Series V8

'80, '81: Insufficient data. '82: Insufficient data.

TROUBLE SPOTS	'80	'81	'82	'83	'84	'85
Air-conditioning				○	○	○
Body exterior (paint)				⊖	○	○
Body exterior (rust)				○	○	○
Body hardware				○	○	○
Body integrity				⊖	⊖	○
Brakes				○	○	○
Clutch						
Driveline				○	○	○
Electrical system (chassis)				○	○	○
Engine cooling				○	○	○
Engine mechanical				○	○	○
Exhaust system				○	○	○
Fuel system				○	○	○
Ignition system				○	○	○
Suspension				⊖	○	○
Transmission (manual)						
Transmission (automatic)				○	○	○
TROUBLE INDEX				⊜	⊜	○
COST INDEX				*	*	

Mercury Capri 4 (except Turbo)

TROUBLE SPOTS	'80	'81	'82	'83	'84	'85
Air-conditioning	○	○	○	○	○	○
Body exterior (paint)	○	○	○	○	◒	○
Body exterior (rust)	○	○	○	○	○	○
Body hardware	⊖	○	○	○	○	○
Body integrity	○	●	○	○	○	○
Brakes	○	⊖	⊜	○	○	○
Clutch	●	●	○	○	○	◒
Driveline	○	○	○	○	○	○
Electrical system (chassis)	○	○	○	○	⊖	○
Engine cooling	○	⊖	○	○	○	○
Engine mechanical	●	◒	○	○	○	○
Exhaust system	◒	◒	○	○	○	○
Fuel system	○	○	○	○	○	○
Ignition system	○	◒	○	○	◒	○
Suspension	○	○	○	○	○	○
Transmission (manual)	○	○	○	○	○	○
Transmission (automatic)	⊖	○	○	○	○	○
TROUBLE INDEX	○	○	○	○	◒	◒
COST INDEX	○	⊖	⊖	*	*	

Mercury Capri 6, V6

'85: Insufficient data.

TROUBLE SPOTS	'80	'81	'82	'83	'84	'85
Air-conditioning	○	○	⊖	○	○	
Body exterior (paint)	○	○	○	○	○	
Body exterior (rust)	⊖	○	○	○	○	
Body hardware	⊖	○	○	○	○	
Body integrity	◒	●	●	◒	○	
Brakes	○	○	○	○	○	
Clutch	●	◒	○			
Driveline	○	○	○	○	○	
Electrical system (chassis)	○	○	○	○	⊖	
Engine cooling	◒	●	○	●	○	
Engine mechanical	○	○	○	◒	○	
Exhaust system	○	○	○	○	○	
Fuel system	●	●	●	○	●	
Ignition system	○	◒	◒	○	○	
Suspension	◒	◒	○	○	○	
Transmission (manual)	○	○	○			
Transmission (automatic)	⊖	○	○	○	○	
TROUBLE INDEX	○	◒	◒	○	○	
COST INDEX	○	○	○	⊖	○	

Mercury Capri V8

TROUBLE SPOTS	'80	'81	'82	'83	'84	'85
Air-conditioning			○	⊖	○	○
Body exterior (paint)			○	◒	●	◒
Body exterior (rust)			○	○	○	○
Body hardware			○	○	○	◒
Body integrity			●	○	●	●
Brakes			⊖	○	○	○
Clutch			○	○	◒	○
Driveline			◒	○	○	○
Electrical system (chassis)			○	○	○	◒
Engine cooling			○	○	◒	○
Engine mechanical			○	◒	○	○
Exhaust system			⊖	○	○	○
Fuel system			○	◒	●	◒
Ignition system			○	○	○	○
Suspension			○	○	○	○
Transmission (manual)			○	○	○	◒
Transmission (automatic)			○	○	○	○
TROUBLE INDEX			○	○	●	●
COST INDEX			*	○	○	

Mercury Cougar 6, V6

TROUBLE SPOTS	'80	'81	'82	'83	'84	'85
Air-conditioning		○	⊖	⊖	○	○
Body exterior (paint)		○	○	○	○	○
Body exterior (rust)		○	○	○	○	○
Body hardware		○	○	○	○	○
Body integrity		◒	○	⊖	⊖	⊖
Brakes		○	○	○	○	○
Clutch						
Driveline		○	○	○	○	○
Electrical system (chassis)		○	○	○	○	○
Engine cooling		○	○	⊖	○	○
Engine mechanical		○	○	○	○	○
Exhaust system		○	○	○	○	○
Fuel system		●	●	○	●	◒
Ignition system		○	○	○	○	○
Suspension		●	◒	◒	○	○
Transmission (manual)						
Transmission (automatic)		○	○	○	○	○
TROUBLE INDEX		◒	○	⊖	○	○
COST INDEX		○	⊖	⊖	⊖	

Mercury Cougar XR-7 V8

TROUBLE SPOTS	'80	'81	'82	'83	'84	'85
Air-conditioning	⊖	⊜	⊖			
Body exterior (paint)	○	○	○			
Body exterior (rust)	⊖	⊖	○			
Body hardware	○	○	○			
Body integrity	◒	○	○			
Brakes	●	○	○			
Clutch						
Driveline	○	○	○			
Electrical system (chassis)	●	○	○			
Engine cooling	◒	○	○			
Engine mechanical	●	○	○			
Exhaust system	○	⊜	○			
Fuel system	◒	○	○			
Ignition system	●	○	○			
Suspension	●	●	○			
Transmission (manual)						
Transmission (automatic)	⊖	○	○			
TROUBLE INDEX	◒	○	○			
COST INDEX	○	⊖	○			

Mercury LN7

TROUBLE SPOTS	'80	'81	'82	'83	'84	'85
Air-conditioning			●	○		
Body exterior (paint)			●	◒		
Body exterior (rust)			●	○		
Body hardware			○	○		
Body integrity			◒	○		
Brakes			⊖	○		
Clutch			⊜	○		
Driveline			○	○		
Electrical system (chassis)			○	○		
Engine cooling			●	●		
Engine mechanical			◒	○		
Exhaust system			●	◒		
Fuel system			◒	◒		
Ignition system			○	●		
Suspension			◒	○		
Transmission (manual)			○	○		
Transmission (automatic)			○	●		
TROUBLE INDEX			●	◒		
COST INDEX			○	○		

Mercury Lynx (gas)

TROUBLE SPOTS	'80	'81	'82	'83	'84	'85
Air-conditioning		○	○	⊜	○	○
Body exterior (paint)		○	○	○	○	○
Body exterior (rust)		●	●	○	○	○
Body hardware		◒	◒	○	○	○
Body integrity		○	○	○	○	○
Brakes		⊖	⊖	⊖	○	○
Clutch		⊜	⊜	⊖	○	○
Driveline		○	○	○	○	○
Electrical system (chassis)		○	○	○	○	⊖
Engine cooling		◒	○	○	○	○
Engine mechanical		●	◒	◒	○	○
Exhaust system		◒	◒	◒	○	○
Fuel system		○	○	●	○	○
Ignition system		○	◒	●	○	○
Suspension		○	○	○	○	○
Transmission (manual)		○	○	○	○	○
Transmission (automatic)		○	○	○	○	○
TROUBLE INDEX		○	○	◒	○	○
COST INDEX		○	⊖	⊖	⊖	

Mercury Lynx (diesel) (Insufficient data for '85)

TROUBLE SPOTS	'80	'81	'82	'83	'84	'85
Air-conditioning					○	
Body exterior (paint)					○	
Body exterior (rust)					○	
Body hardware					○	
Body integrity					○	
Brakes					○	
Clutch					○	
Driveline					○	
Electrical system (chassis)					○	
Engine cooling					◒	
Engine mechanical					○	
Exhaust system					○	
Fuel system					⊜	
Ignition system					○	
Suspension					●	
Transmission (manual)					○	
Transmission (automatic)						
TROUBLE INDEX					○	
COST INDEX					⊖	

Mercury Marquis, Grand Marquis V8

TROUBLE SPOTS	'80	'81	'82	'83	'84	'85
Air-conditioning	○	⊜	⊜	⊖	○	○
Body exterior (paint)	○	⊖	⊖	○	○	○
Body exterior (rust)	○	○	○	○	○	○
Body hardware	○	○	⊜	⊖	○	○
Body integrity	○	○	⊖	⊖	⊖	○
Brakes	○	⊖	⊜	⊖	○	○
Clutch						
Driveline	○	○	○	○	○	○
Electrical system (chassis)	○	⊖	⊖	⊖	⊖	○
Engine cooling	○	⊖	⊖	○	○	○
Engine mechanical	○	⊖	⊖	⊖	⊖	○
Exhaust system	○	○	⊜	○	○	○
Fuel system	●	●	●	⊖	○	○
Ignition system	●	○	⊖	○	○	○
Suspension	○	○	⊖	○	○	○
Transmission (manual)						
Transmission (automatic)	○	○	○	○	○	○
TROUBLE INDEX	○	⊖	⊜	⊜	⊖	⊖
COST INDEX	○	⊖	⊖	⊖	⊖	

Mercury Marquis 6, V6

TROUBLE SPOTS	'80	'81	'82	'83	'84	'85
Air-conditioning				⊖	○	○
Body exterior (paint)				○	○	○
Body exterior (rust)				○	○	○
Body hardware				◒	●	○
Body integrity				○	○	○
Brakes				○	○	○
Clutch						
Driveline				○	○	○
Electrical system (chassis)				○	○	○
Engine cooling				○	○	○
Engine mechanical				◒	○	○
Exhaust system				○	○	○
Fuel system				●	●	◒
Ignition system				○	◒	○
Suspension				●	○	○
Transmission (manual)						
Transmission (automatic)				○	○	○
TROUBLE INDEX				○	◒	○
COST INDEX				⊖	⊖	

Mercury Topaz (gas)

TROUBLE SPOTS	'80	'81	'82	'83	'84	'85
Air-conditioning					○	○
Body exterior (paint)					○	○
Body exterior (rust)					○	○
Body hardware					○	○
Body integrity					○	○
Brakes					○	○
Clutch					⊖	○
Driveline					○	○
Electrical system (chassis)					○	○
Engine cooling					○	○
Engine mechanical					○	○
Exhaust system					○	○
Fuel system					●	●
Ignition system					◒	◒
Suspension					●	○
Transmission (manual)					○	○
Transmission (automatic)					○	○
TROUBLE INDEX					●	●
COST INDEX					⊖	

Mercury Zephyr, Z7 4 (Insufficient data for '83–'85)

TROUBLE SPOTS	'80	'81	'82	'83	'84	'85
Air-conditioning	⊖	○	○			
Body exterior (paint)	○	○	○			
Body exterior (rust)	○	○	◒			
Body hardware	○	○	⊖			
Body integrity	◒	◒	○			
Brakes	○	○	○			
Clutch	●	◒	○			
Driveline	○	○	○			
Electrical system (chassis)	○	⊖	○			
Engine cooling	⊜	○	○			
Engine mechanical	◒	○	○			
Exhaust system	◒	○	○			
Fuel system	○	○	○			
Ignition system	○	○	○			
Suspension	◒	○	○			
Transmission (manual)	○	○	○			
Transmission (automatic)	⊖	○	○			
TROUBLE INDEX	○	○	○			
COST INDEX	⊖	⊖	*			

Mercury Zephyr, Z7 6

TROUBLE SPOTS	'80	'81	'82	'83	'84	'85
Air-conditioning	⊜	⊜	⊖	⊜		
Body exterior (paint)	○	○	○	○		
Body exterior (rust)	○	○	○	○		
Body hardware	○	○	○	○		
Body integrity	●	○	○	○		
Brakes	◒	◒	○	○		
Clutch	●					
Driveline	○	○	○	○		
Electrical system (chassis)	○	○	○	⊖		
Engine cooling	○	○	⊖	○		
Engine mechanical	○	○	○	○		
Exhaust system	◒	○	○	◒		
Fuel system	●	●	●	●		
Ignition system	○	○	◒	◒		
Suspension	◒	◒	●	○		
Transmission (manual)	○					
Transmission (automatic)	⊖	○	⊖	⊖		
TROUBLE INDEX	◒	○	○	○		
COST INDEX	○	⊖	⊖	⊖		

Mitsubishi Cordia

TROUBLE SPOTS	'80	'81	'82	'83	'84	'85
Air-conditioning				○	○	
Body exterior (paint)				○	○	
Body exterior (rust)				○	○	
Body hardware				○	⊖	
Body integrity				○	⊜	
Brakes				○	○	
Clutch				○	○	
Driveline				○	○	
Electrical system (chassis)				○	⊜	
Engine cooling				○	○	
Engine mechanical				○	○	
Exhaust system				○	○	
Fuel system				○	◒	
Ignition system				○	○	
Suspension				○	○	
Transmission (manual)				○	○	
Transmission (automatic)				○	○	
TROUBLE INDEX				⊖	⊜	
COST INDEX				○	*	

Mitsubishi Galant

TROUBLE SPOTS	'80	'81	'82	'83	'84	'85
Air-conditioning						○
Body exterior (paint)						○
Body exterior (rust)						○
Body hardware						○
Body integrity						○
Brakes						○
Clutch						
Driveline						○
Electrical system (chassis)						○
Engine cooling						○
Engine mechanical						○
Exhaust system						○
Fuel system						○
Ignition system						○
Suspension						○
Transmission (manual)						
Transmission (automatic)						○
TROUBLE INDEX						○
COST INDEX						

⊜ Much better than average · ⊖ Better than average · ○ Average · ◒ Worse than average · ● Much worse than average · * Insufficient cost data

Mitsubishi Tredia (except Turbo)	'80	'81	'82	'83	'84	'85
Air-conditioning				⊖	○	Insufficient data
Body exterior (paint)				○	○	
Body exterior (rust)				○	○	
Body hardware				⊖	⊖	
Body integrity				○	○	
Brakes				○	○	
Clutch				⊖	○	
Driveline				○	○	
Electrical system (chassis)				⊜	⊖	
Engine cooling				○	○	
Engine mechanical				○	○	
Exhaust system				⊖	○	
Fuel system				⊖	○	
Ignition system				○	○	
Suspension				○	○	
Transmission (manual)				○	○	
Transmission (automatic)				○	○	
TROUBLE INDEX				⊜	⊜	
COST INDEX				○	*	

Nissan 200SX (except Turbo)	'80	'81	'82	'83	'84	'85
Air-conditioning					⊖	○
Body exterior (paint)					○	○
Body exterior (rust)					○	○
Body hardware					○	○
Body integrity					○	○
Brakes					⊖	○
Clutch					○	○
Driveline					○	○
Electrical system (chassis)					⊖	○
Engine cooling					○	○
Engine mechanical					○	○
Exhaust system					○	○
Fuel system					⊜	○
Ignition system					⊖	○
Suspension					○	○
Transmission (manual)					○	○
Transmission (automatic)					○	○
TROUBLE INDEX					⊖	⊖
COST INDEX					○	

Nissan 300ZX (except Turbo)	'80	'81	'82	'83	'84	'85
Air-conditioning					○	⊖
Body exterior (paint)					○	⊖
Body exterior (rust)					○	○
Body hardware					○	⊖
Body integrity					⊖	⊖
Brakes					⊖	○
Clutch					○	○
Driveline					○	○
Electrical system (chassis)					●	○
Engine cooling					○	○
Engine mechanical					⊖	○
Exhaust system					○	○
Fuel system					⊖	○
Ignition system					○	○
Suspension					○	○
Transmission (manual)					○	○
Transmission (automatic)					○	○
TROUBLE INDEX					⊖	⊜
COST INDEX					○	

Nissan 300ZX Turbo	'80	'81	'82	'83	'84	'85
Air-conditioning					○	Insufficient data
Body exterior (paint)					○	
Body exterior (rust)					○	
Body hardware					○	
Body integrity					○	
Brakes					⊖	
Clutch					○	
Driveline					○	
Electrical system (chassis)					●	
Engine cooling					○	
Engine mechanical					○	
Exhaust system					○	
Fuel system					○	
Ignition system					○	
Suspension					○	
Transmission (manual)					○	
Transmission (automatic)					○	
TROUBLE INDEX					○	
COST INDEX					◒	

Nissan Maxima	'80	'81	'82	'83	'84	'85
Air-conditioning						○
Body exterior (paint)						○
Body exterior (rust)						○
Body hardware						⊖
Body integrity						⊖
Brakes						○
Clutch						○
Driveline						○
Electrical system (chassis)						○
Engine cooling						○
Engine mechanical						○
Exhaust system						○
Fuel system						○
Ignition system						○
Suspension						○
Transmission (manual)						○
Transmission (automatic)						○
TROUBLE INDEX						⊜
COST INDEX						

Nissan Pulsar, NX (except Turbo)	'80	'81	'82	'83	'84	'85
Air-conditioning				⊜	○	○
Body exterior (paint)				⊖	○	○
Body exterior (rust)				○	○	○
Body hardware				○	○	○
Body integrity				⊖	○	⊖
Brakes				○	○	○
Clutch				⊖	⊖	○
Driveline				○	○	○
Electrical system (chassis)				⊜	⊜	○
Engine cooling				⊖	○	○
Engine mechanical				⊖	○	○
Exhaust system				○	○	○
Fuel system				○	●	○
Ignition system				⊖	○	○
Suspension				⊖	○	○
Transmission (manual)				○	○	○
Transmission (automatic)				○	○	○
TROUBLE INDEX				⊜	⊖	○
COST INDEX				⊖	○	

Nissan Sentra	'80	'81	'82	'83	'84	'85
Air-conditioning			⊖	⊖	○	○
Body exterior (paint)			⊖	○	⊖	○
Body exterior (rust)			○	○	○	○
Body hardware			○	○	⊖	○
Body integrity			○	○	○	○
Brakes			⊖	⊖	○	○
Clutch			⊖	○	○	○
Driveline			○	○	○	○
Electrical system (chassis)			⊖	⊜	⊜	○
Engine cooling			⊖	⊖	○	○
Engine mechanical			⊖	⊖	○	○
Exhaust system			⊖	○	○	○
Fuel system			○	○	●	○
Ignition system			○	⊖	○	○
Suspension			○	○	⊖	○
Transmission (manual)			○	○	○	○
Transmission (automatic)			○	○	○	○
TROUBLE INDEX			⊖	⊖	⊖	⊖
COST INDEX			⊖	⊖	○	

Nissan Stanza	'80	'81	'82	'83	'84	'85
Air-conditioning			⊖	⊖	○	○
Body exterior (paint)			⊖	⊖	⊖	○
Body exterior (rust)			○	○	○	○
Body hardware			⊜	⊜	⊖	○
Body integrity			⊜	⊖	⊜	○
Brakes			⊜	⊜	○	○
Clutch			⊖	○	⊖	○
Driveline			○	○	○	○
Electrical system (chassis)			○	○	⊜	⊖
Engine cooling			⊖	○	○	○
Engine mechanical			⊖	⊖	⊖	○
Exhaust system			⊜	⊖	○	○
Fuel system			⊖	○	⊖	⊖
Ignition system			●	○	○	○
Suspension			⊖	○	⊖	○
Transmission (manual)			○	○	○	○
Transmission (automatic)			○	○	○	○
TROUBLE INDEX			⊖	⊖	⊜	⊜
COST INDEX			○	⊖	⊖	

TROUBLE SPOTS	Oldsmobile 88 V6 '80	'81	'82	'83	'84	'85
Air-conditioning	Insufficient data	○	○	○	○	Insufficient data
Body exterior (paint)	Insufficient data	○	○	○	○	Insufficient data
Body exterior (rust)	Insufficient data	○	○	○	○	Insufficient data
Body hardware	Insufficient data	○	○	○	⊜	Insufficient data
Body integrity	Insufficient data	○	○	○	○	Insufficient data
Brakes	Insufficient data	○	⊜	○	○	Insufficient data
Clutch	Insufficient data					Insufficient data
Driveline	Insufficient data	○	○	○	○	Insufficient data
Electrical system (chassis)	Insufficient data	○	○	○	○	Insufficient data
Engine cooling	Insufficient data	○	○	○	○	Insufficient data
Engine mechanical	Insufficient data	○	○	○	○	Insufficient data
Exhaust system	Insufficient data	●	○	◒	○	Insufficient data
Fuel system	Insufficient data	○	◒	○	○	Insufficient data
Ignition system	Insufficient data	◒	○	◒	○	Insufficient data
Suspension	Insufficient data	○	○	○	◒	Insufficient data
Transmission (manual)	Insufficient data					Insufficient data
Transmission (automatic)	Insufficient data	○	○	○	◒	Insufficient data
TROUBLE INDEX		○	○	○	○	
COST INDEX		*	*	*	*	

TROUBLE SPOTS	Oldsmobile 88 V8 (gas) '80	'81	'82	'83	'84	'85
Air-conditioning	○	⊜	⊜	○	○	○
Body exterior (paint)	●	○	⊜	○	◒	◒
Body exterior (rust)	⊜	○	○	○	○	○
Body hardware	◒	○	○	○	○	◒
Body integrity	⊜	⊜	⊜	○	○	●
Brakes	○	⊜	⊜	○	○	○
Clutch						
Driveline	⊜	○	○	○	○	○
Electrical system (chassis)	○	○	○	○	○	○
Engine cooling	○	○	○	○	○	○
Engine mechanical	⊜	⊜	⊜	⊜	○	○
Exhaust system	⊜	●	●	●	○	○
Fuel system	⊜	○	○	○	⊜	○
Ignition system	○	⊜	○	○	○	○
Suspension	◒	○	●	◒	◒	○
Transmission (manual)						
Transmission (automatic)	◒	○	○	○	○	○
TROUBLE INDEX	○	○	○	○	○	◒
COST INDEX	○	⊜	⊜	⊜	⊜	

TROUBLE SPOTS	Oldsmobile 88 V8 (diesel) '80	'81	'82	'83	'84	'85
Air-conditioning	○	○	○	○	Insufficient data	Insufficient data
Body exterior (paint)	○	○	○	○	Insufficient data	Insufficient data
Body exterior (rust)	⊜	⊜	⊜	○	Insufficient data	Insufficient data
Body hardware	○	⊜	○	○	Insufficient data	Insufficient data
Body integrity	⊜	⊜	⊜	○	Insufficient data	Insufficient data
Brakes	⊜	⊜	⊜	○	Insufficient data	Insufficient data
Clutch					Insufficient data	Insufficient data
Driveline	○	○	○	○	Insufficient data	Insufficient data
Electrical system (chassis)	○	○	○	○	Insufficient data	Insufficient data
Engine cooling	⊜	⊜	○	○	Insufficient data	Insufficient data
Engine mechanical	●	●	●	◒	Insufficient data	Insufficient data
Exhaust system	⊜	⊜	⊜	○	Insufficient data	Insufficient data
Fuel system	●	●	●	◒	Insufficient data	Insufficient data
Ignition system	◒	○	○	○	Insufficient data	Insufficient data
Suspension	⊜	○	○	○	Insufficient data	Insufficient data
Transmission (manual)					Insufficient data	Insufficient data
Transmission (automatic)	◒	●	○	○	Insufficient data	Insufficient data
TROUBLE INDEX	○	○	○	○		
COST INDEX	●	◒	○	*		

TROUBLE SPOTS	Oldsmobile 98 V8 (gas) '80	'81	'82	'83	'84	'85
Air-conditioning	○	○	○	○	○	
Body exterior (paint)	◒	○	○	○	○	
Body exterior (rust)	○	⊜	○	○	○	
Body hardware	◒	○	◒	○	○	
Body integrity	○	○	○	⊜	○	
Brakes	○	○	○	○	○	
Clutch						
Driveline	⊜	○	○	○	○	
Electrical system (chassis)	○	○	◒	◒	◒	
Engine cooling	○	○	○	○	○	
Engine mechanical	○	○	○	⊜	○	
Exhaust system	○	●	●	●	○	
Fuel system	○	○	○	○	○	
Ignition system	○	○	○	○	○	
Suspension	○	◒	●	○	◒	
Transmission (manual)						
Transmission (automatic)	○	○	○	○	○	
TROUBLE INDEX	○	○	◒	○	○	
COST INDEX	○	○	○	○	○	

TROUBLE SPOTS	Oldsmobile 98 V6 '80	'81	'82	'83	'84	'85
Air-conditioning						◒
Body exterior (paint)						○
Body exterior (rust)						○
Body hardware						◒
Body integrity						●
Brakes						○
Clutch						
Driveline						○
Electrical system (chassis)						●
Engine cooling						◒
Engine mechanical						○
Exhaust system						○
Fuel system						◒
Ignition system						○
Suspension						○
Transmission (manual)						
Transmission (automatic)						○
TROUBLE INDEX						●
COST INDEX						

TROUBLE SPOTS	Oldsmobile Calais 4 '80	'81	'82	'83	'84	'85
Air-conditioning						○
Body exterior (paint)						○
Body exterior (rust)						○
Body hardware						○
Body integrity						○
Brakes						◒
Clutch						○
Driveline						○
Electrical system (chassis)						○
Engine cooling						○
Engine mechanical						○
Exhaust system						○
Fuel system						○
Ignition system						○
Suspension						○
Transmission (manual)						○
Transmission (automatic)						○
TROUBLE INDEX						○
COST INDEX						

TROUBLE SPOTS	Oldsmobile Calais V6 '80	'81	'82	'83	'84	'85
Air-conditioning						○
Body exterior (paint)						○
Body exterior (rust)						○
Body hardware						○
Body integrity						○
Brakes						◒
Clutch						
Driveline						○
Electrical system (chassis)						●
Engine cooling						◒
Engine mechanical						◒
Exhaust system						○
Fuel system						◒
Ignition system						◒
Suspension						◒
Transmission (manual)						
Transmission (automatic)						○
TROUBLE INDEX						●
COST INDEX						

TROUBLE SPOTS	Oldsmobile Cutlass, Cutlass Supreme V6 '80	'81	'82	'83	'84	'85
Air-conditioning	○	○	◒	○	○	○
Body exterior (paint)	○	◒	○	○	○	◒
Body exterior (rust)	⊜	○	○	○	○	○
Body hardware	⊜	○	○	○	○	○
Body integrity	○	●	◒	◒	●	●
Brakes	○	◒	○	○	○	○
Clutch						
Driveline	○	○	○	○	○	○
Electrical system (chassis)	⊜	○	○	○	○	○
Engine cooling	○	●	○	○	○	○
Engine mechanical	○	◒	○	◒	○	○
Exhaust system	⊜	●	●	○	○	○
Fuel system	○	●	●	○	○	○
Ignition system	○	●	●	◒	○	○
Suspension	◒	●	●	●	◒	○
Transmission (manual)						
Transmission (automatic)	○	○	○	○	○	○
TROUBLE INDEX	○	●	◒	○	◒	●
COST INDEX	⊜	○	○	○	○	

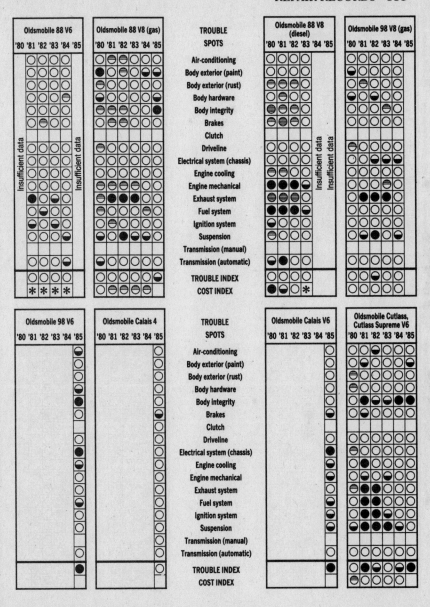

⊜ Much better than average ⊖ Better than average ○ Average ◒ Worse than average ● Much worse than average * Insufficient cost data

Olds Cutlass, Cutlass Supreme V8 (gas)

TROUBLE SPOTS	'80	'81	'82	'83	'84	'85
Air-conditioning	○	○	○	○	○	○
Body exterior (paint)	○	◒	○	○	◒	●
Body exterior (rust)	⊜	○	○	○	○	○
Body hardware	○	◒	○	◒	◒	○
Body integrity	○	◒	◒	◒	●	●
Brakes	○	○	○	○	○	○
Clutch						
Driveline	⊖	○	○	○	○	○
Electrical system (chassis)	○	○	○	◒	◒	○
Engine cooling	○	◒	○	○	○	○
Engine mechanical	○	○	○	○	○	○
Exhaust system	○	●	●	●	○	○
Fuel system	○	●	●	○	⊖	○
Ignition system	○	○	◒	○	○	○
Suspension	◒	◒	●	○	◒	○
Transmission (manual)						
Transmission (automatic)	○	○	○	○	○	○
TROUBLE INDEX	○	◒	●	◒	◒	●
COST INDEX	○	○	○	○	○	

Olds Cutlass, Cutlass Supreme V8 (diesel)

TROUBLE SPOTS	'80	'81	'82	'83	'84	'85
Air-conditioning	○	◒	○	Insufficient data	Insufficient data	Insufficient data
Body exterior (paint)	○	○	○			
Body exterior (rust)	⊜	⊜	○			
Body hardware	○	○	○			
Body integrity	○	○	○			
Brakes	⊖	⊜	○			
Clutch						
Driveline	○	○	○			
Electrical system (chassis)	◒	○	○			
Engine cooling	○	⊖	○			
Engine mechanical	●	●	●			
Exhaust system	⊜	⊜	⊖			
Fuel system	●	●	●			
Ignition system	●	○	○			
Suspension	○	◒	○			
Transmission (manual)						
Transmission (automatic)	●	●	○			
TROUBLE INDEX	◒	◒	○			
COST INDEX	◒	◒	○			

Oldsmobile Cutlass Ciera 4

TROUBLE SPOTS	'80	'81	'82	'83	'84	'85
Air-conditioning			●	○	○	○
Body exterior (paint)			○	○	○	○
Body exterior (rust)			○	○	○	○
Body hardware			○	○	⊖	○
Body integrity			○	○	○	⊖
Brakes			●	◒	◒	○
Clutch						
Driveline			○	○	○	○
Electrical system (chassis)			○	◒	○	○
Engine cooling			○	◒	○	○
Engine mechanical			○	◒	◒	○
Exhaust system			⊖	○	○	○
Fuel system			○	⊖	○	⊖
Ignition system			◒	◒	◒	○
Suspension			◒	○	○	○
Transmission (manual)						
Transmission (automatic)			○	○	○	○
TROUBLE INDEX			◒	◒	○	⊖
COST INDEX			○	⊖	⊖	

Oldsmobile Cutlass Ciera V6 (gas)

TROUBLE SPOTS	'80	'81	'82	'83	'84	'85
Air-conditioning			●	◒	●	○
Body exterior (paint)			○	○	○	○
Body exterior (rust)			○	○	○	○
Body hardware			◒	○	○	○
Body integrity			●	○	○	○
Brakes			●	●	◒	○
Clutch						
Driveline			○	○	○	○
Electrical system (chassis)			●	◒	●	○
Engine cooling			●	◒	◒	○
Engine mechanical			●	◒	○	○
Exhaust system			⊖	○	○	○
Fuel system			◒	◒	◒	○
Ignition system			●	○	○	○
Suspension			●	○	○	○
Transmission (manual)						
Transmission (automatic)			◒	○	○	○
TROUBLE INDEX			●	●	●	◒
COST INDEX			◒	○	○	

Oldsmobile Cutlass Ciera V6 (diesel)

TROUBLE SPOTS	'80	'81	'82	'83	'84	'85
Air-conditioning			○	○	○	Insufficient data
Body exterior (paint)			○	○	○	
Body exterior (rust)			○	⊖	○	
Body hardware			○	○	○	
Body integrity			○	○	○	
Brakes			●	●	◒	
Clutch						
Driveline			○	○	○	
Electrical system (chassis)			○	◒	○	
Engine cooling			◒	○	○	
Engine mechanical			●	◒	◒	
Exhaust system			⊖	○	○	
Fuel system			●	●	◒	
Ignition system			○	○	●	
Suspension			○	○	○	
Transmission (manual)						
Transmission (automatic)			●	◒	○	
TROUBLE INDEX			●	●	●	
COST INDEX			◒	○	*	

Oldsmobile Firenza 4

TROUBLE SPOTS	'80	'81	'82	'83	'84	'85
Air-conditioning			○	○	○	○
Body exterior (paint)			○	○	○	○
Body exterior (rust)			○	○	○	○
Body hardware			◒	○	○	○
Body integrity			◒	◒	○	○
Brakes			◒	○	○	○
Clutch			○	○	◒	○
Driveline			○	○	○	○
Electrical system (chassis)			◒	◒	●	○
Engine cooling			○	◒	○	○
Engine mechanical			●	◒	○	○
Exhaust system			●	●	○	○
Fuel system			●	○	○	○
Ignition system			◒	●	○	○
Suspension			○	○	○	○
Transmission (manual)			●	◒	○	◒
Transmission (automatic)			○	○	○	○
TROUBLE INDEX			●	●	◒	○
COST INDEX			○	○	⊖	

Oldsmobile Omega 4

TROUBLE SPOTS	'80	'81	'82	'83	'84	'85
Air-conditioning	◒	◒	●	●	○	
Body exterior (paint)	●	●	◒	●	●	
Body exterior (rust)	●	●	○	◒	◒	
Body hardware	○	○	○	○	○	
Body integrity	○	○	○	◒	○	
Brakes	●	◒	●	●	○	
Clutch	○	○	○	○		
Driveline	○	◒	○	◒	○	
Electrical system (chassis)	⊖	○	○	○	○	
Engine cooling	○	○	○	○	○	
Engine mechanical	○	○	○	◒	○	
Exhaust system	⊖	●	○	○	○	
Fuel system	○	◒	○	○	○	
Ignition system	○	○	○	○	●	
Suspension	○	○	◒	○	○	
Transmission (manual)	◒	●	◒	○		
Transmission (automatic)	●	○	○	○	○	
TROUBLE INDEX	◒	◒	◒	●	◒	
COST INDEX	○	○	○	○	⊖	

Oldsmobile Omega V6

TROUBLE SPOTS	'80	'81	'82	'83	'84	'85
Air-conditioning	○	●	●	◒	○	
Body exterior (paint)	●	●	◒	○	●	
Body exterior (rust)	●	●	○	○	●	
Body hardware	○	○	○	○	○	
Body integrity	○	○	○	○	○	
Brakes	○	○	◒	●	○	
Clutch	○		○	○	○	
Driveline	◒	○	○	○	○	
Electrical system (chassis)	○	○	○	⊖	○	
Engine cooling	○	○	○	◒	○	
Engine mechanical	○	○	○	○	○	
Exhaust system	○	⊜	○	○	○	
Fuel system	●	●	◒	○	○	
Ignition system	○	○	○	◒	○	
Suspension	○	○	○	○	○	
Transmission (manual)	●		○	○	○	
Transmission (automatic)	◒	◒	○	○	○	
TROUBLE INDEX	◒	◒	◒	○	●	
COST INDEX	○	○	○	*	*	

Oldsmobile Toronado V8 (gas)

TROUBLE SPOTS	'80	'81	'82	'83	'84	'85
Air-conditioning	○	○	○	○	○	○
Body exterior (paint)	◒	○	○	○	○	○
Body exterior (rust)	●	○	○	○	○	○
Body hardware	○	○	●	●	◒	○
Body integrity	○	○	○	○	○	○
Brakes	○	○	◒	○	○	○
Clutch	–	–	–	–	–	–
Driveline	○	○	●	○	○	○
Electrical system (chassis)	○	●	●	●	●	○
Engine cooling	◒	◒	◒	○	○	○
Engine mechanical	○	○	○	○	○	○
Exhaust system	○	●	●	●	○	○
Fuel system	⊜	◒	○	●	⊜	○
Ignition system	○	○	○	○	○	○
Suspension	○	◒	●	◒	⊜	○
Transmission (manual)	–	–	–	–	–	–
Transmission (automatic)	○	○	○	○	○	○
TROUBLE INDEX	◒	●	●	●	○	○
COST INDEX	●	*	●	◒	○	–

Peugeot 505

TROUBLE SPOTS	'80	'81	'82	'83	'84	'85
Air-conditioning	Insufficient data	Insufficient data	Insufficient data	○	○	○
Body exterior (paint)				○	○	○
Body exterior (rust)				○	○	○
Body hardware				○	○	○
Body integrity				○	○	○
Brakes				○	●	◒
Clutch				◒	○	○
Driveline				○	○	○
Electrical system (chassis)				○	●	○
Engine cooling				●	○	○
Engine mechanical				○	○	○
Exhaust system				○	○	○
Fuel system				○	●	●
Ignition system				○	○	○
Suspension				○	○	○
Transmission (manual)				○	○	○
Transmission (automatic)				○	○	○
TROUBLE INDEX				○	◒	○
COST INDEX				●	◒	–

Peugeot 505 (Turbodiesel)

TROUBLE SPOTS	'80	'81	'82	'83	'84	'85
Air-conditioning		◒	●	Insufficient data	Insufficient data	Insufficient data
Body exterior (paint)		○	○			
Body exterior (rust)		●	○			
Body hardware		◒	○			
Body integrity		○	○			
Brakes		◒	○			
Clutch		○	○			
Driveline		○	○			
Electrical system (chassis)		●	●			
Engine cooling		○	●			
Engine mechanical		○	○			
Exhaust system		⊜	⊜			
Fuel system		⊜	⊜			
Ignition system		○	◒			
Suspension		○	○			
Transmission (manual)		◒	○			
Transmission (automatic)		○	○			
TROUBLE INDEX		◒	○			
COST INDEX		●	●			

Plymouth Caravelle 4 (FWD)

TROUBLE SPOTS	'80	'81	'82	'83	'84	'85
Air-conditioning						○
Body exterior (paint)						○
Body exterior (rust)						○
Body hardware						○
Body integrity						○
Brakes						○
Clutch						–
Driveline						○
Electrical system (chassis)						◒
Engine cooling						○
Engine mechanical						○
Exhaust system						○
Fuel system						◒
Ignition system						○
Suspension						○
Transmission (manual)						–
Transmission (automatic)						○
TROUBLE INDEX						◒
COST INDEX						–

Plymouth Champ, Colt, Premier (except Turbo)

TROUBLE SPOTS	'80	'81	'82	'83	'84	'85
Air-conditioning	●	○	○	○	○	○
Body exterior (paint)	⊜	⊜	○	◒	○	○
Body exterior (rust)	⊜	⊜	○	●	○	○
Body hardware	⊜	⊜	⊜	⊜	⊜	○
Body integrity	⊜	⊜	⊜	○	○	○
Brakes	⊜	⊜	○	○	○	○
Clutch	○	◒	◒	○	○	○
Driveline	○	⊜	○	○	○	○
Electrical system (chassis)	⊜	⊜	⊜	⊜	⊜	○
Engine cooling	⊜	⊜	⊜	⊜	○	○
Engine mechanical	⊜	⊜	⊜	⊜	○	○
Exhaust system	○	○	○	○	○	○
Fuel system	●	⊜	⊜	⊜	◒	○
Ignition system	◒	⊜	⊜	⊜	○	○
Suspension	⊜	⊜	⊜	○	○	○
Transmission (manual)	○	○	○	○	○	○
Transmission (automatic)	○	○	○	○	○	○
TROUBLE INDEX	⊜	⊜	⊜	⊜	⊜	⊜
COST INDEX	⊜	⊜	⊜	⊜	⊜	–

Plymouth Colt Vista Wagon

TROUBLE SPOTS	'80	'81	'82	'83	'84	'85
Air-conditioning					○	Insufficient data
Body exterior (paint)					○	
Body exterior (rust)					○	
Body hardware					○	
Body integrity					○	
Brakes					○	
Clutch					○	
Driveline					○	
Electrical system (chassis)					○	
Engine cooling					○	
Engine mechanical					○	
Exhaust system					○	
Fuel system					●	
Ignition system					○	
Suspension					○	
Transmission (manual)					○	
Transmission (automatic)					○	
TROUBLE INDEX					○	
COST INDEX					*	

Plymouth Horizon, TC-3, Turismo (except Turbo)

TROUBLE SPOTS	'80	'81	'82	'83	'84	'85
Air-conditioning	●	◒	○	○	○	○
Body exterior (paint)	○	●	●	●	◒	○
Body exterior (rust)	●	●	●	●	◒	○
Body hardware	●	●	●	○	◒	○
Body integrity	●	●	●	●	●	●
Brakes	○	○	○	○	○	○
Clutch	○	●	◒	◒	◒	◒
Driveline	●	○	○	○	○	○
Electrical system (chassis)	○	◒	●	◒	◒	○
Engine cooling	◒	○	○	○	○	○
Engine mechanical	○	◒	○	○	○	○
Exhaust system	●	●	●	◒	○	○
Fuel system	◒	●	●	●	●	●
Ignition system	●	●	○	◒	○	○
Suspension	●	○	○	○	○	○
Transmission (manual)	○	○	○	○	○	○
Transmission (automatic)	○	○	○	○	○	○
TROUBLE INDEX	●	●	●	●	●	●
COST INDEX	○	○	⊜	⊜	⊜	–

Plymouth Reliant

TROUBLE SPOTS	'80	'81	'82	'83	'84	'85
Air-conditioning		○	⊜	○	○	○
Body exterior (paint)		○	◒	◒	○	○
Body exterior (rust)		◒	●	◒	○	○
Body hardware		●	●	○	○	◒
Body integrity		●	●	◒	●	◒
Brakes		○	○	○	○	○
Clutch		◒	●	●	○	–
Driveline		○	○	○	○	○
Electrical system (chassis)		○	○	○	○	○
Engine cooling		○	⊜	○	○	○
Engine mechanical		●	◒	○	○	○
Exhaust system		●	●	○	○	○
Fuel system		○	◒	●	●	●
Ignition system		○	○	◒	◒	○
Suspension		●	●	○	○	○
Transmission (manual)		○	○	○	◒	–
Transmission (automatic)		○	○	○	○	○
TROUBLE INDEX		◒	◒	◒	◒	●
COST INDEX		○	○	⊜	○	–

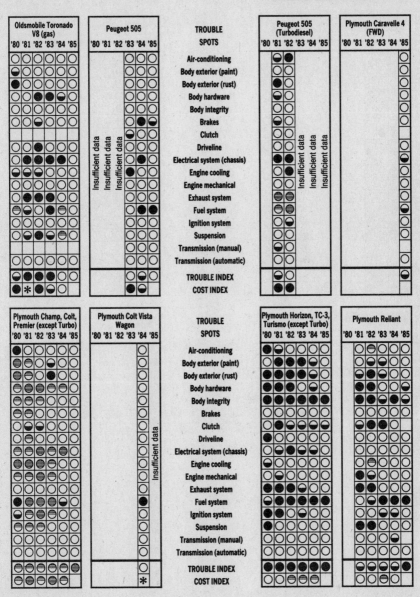

⊜ Much better than average ◓ Better than average ○ Average ◒ Worse than average ● Much worse than average * Insufficient cost data

Plymouth Sapporo

TROUBLE SPOTS	'80	'81	'82	'83	'84	'85
Air-conditioning	○	○	○	○		
Body exterior (paint)	○	○	○	○		
Body exterior (rust)	◓	○	○	○		
Body hardware	○	○	◓	◓		
Body integrity	○	○	◓	○		
Brakes	○	○	○	○		
Clutch	○	●	●	○		
Driveline	○	○	○	○		
Electrical system (chassis)	◓	○	○	◓		
Engine cooling	◓	◓	○	○		
Engine mechanical	○	○	○	○		
Exhaust system	◓	○	○	○		
Fuel system	◒	⊜	◓	○		
Ignition system	○	○	◓	◓		
Suspension	○	◓	◓	◓		
Transmission (manual)	○	○	○	○		
Transmission (automatic)	○	○	○	○		
TROUBLE INDEX	◓	◓	◓	◓		
COST INDEX	*	◓	○	◓		

Plymouth Voyager

TROUBLE SPOTS	'80	'81	'82	'83	'84	'85
Air-conditioning					○	○
Body exterior (paint)					○	○
Body exterior (rust)					○	○
Body hardware					●	○
Body integrity					◒	○
Brakes					○	○
Clutch					○	○
Driveline					○	○
Electrical system (chassis)					○	○
Engine cooling					○	○
Engine mechanical					○	○
Exhaust system					○	○
Fuel system					◒	○
Ignition system					○	○
Suspension					○	○
Transmission (manual)					○	○
Transmission (automatic)					○	○
TROUBLE INDEX					◒	○
COST INDEX					◓	

Pontiac 6000 4

TROUBLE SPOTS	'80	'81	'82	'83	'84	'85
Air-conditioning			●	○	○	○
Body exterior (paint)			○	◒	○	○
Body exterior (rust)			○	○	○	○
Body hardware			●	○	●	○
Body integrity			○	◒	○	○
Brakes			●	●	◒	○
Clutch						
Driveline			○	○	○	○
Electrical system (chassis)			○	◒	○	○
Engine cooling			○	●	●	◒
Engine mechanical			○	◒	◒	○
Exhaust system			◓	○	○	○
Fuel system			○	◓	○	◓
Ignition system			○	○	◒	○
Suspension			○	○	○	○
Transmission (manual)						
Transmission (automatic)			○	○	○	○
TROUBLE INDEX			◒	●	●	○
COST INDEX			○	◓	○	

Pontiac 6000, 6000STE V6

TROUBLE SPOTS	'80	'81	'82	'83	'84	'85
Air-conditioning			●	○	○	○
Body exterior (paint)			○	○	○	○
Body exterior (rust)			○	○	○	○
Body hardware			●	◒	◒	○
Body integrity			○	○	○	○
Brakes			●	◒	○	○
Clutch						
Driveline			○	○	○	○
Electrical system (chassis)			○	●	●	◒
Engine cooling			◒	●	○	○
Engine mechanical			○	○	○	○
Exhaust system			○	○	○	○
Fuel system			○	○	○	○
Ignition system			○	○	○	○
Suspension			◒	○	○	○
Transmission (manual)						
Transmission (automatic)			◒	◒	○	○
TROUBLE INDEX			●	◒	◒	○
COST INDEX			○	○	◓	

Pontiac Bonneville G V6

TROUBLE SPOTS	'80	'81	'82	'83	'84	'85
Air-conditioning			●	○	○	
Body exterior (paint)			○	○	◒	
Body exterior (rust)			◒	○	○	
Body hardware			○	○	○	
Body integrity			○	○	○	
Brakes			○	○	○	
Clutch						
Driveline			○	○	◒	
Electrical system (chassis)			○	○	●	
Engine cooling			●	●	○	
Engine mechanical			◒	◒	◒	
Exhaust system			●	○	○	
Fuel system			●	○	○	
Ignition system			●	◒	○	
Suspension			◒	●	●	
Transmission (manual)						
Transmission (automatic)			○	○	◒	
TROUBLE INDEX			●	○	◒	
COST INDEX			○	◓	◓	

Pontiac Bonneville G V8

TROUBLE SPOTS	'80	'81	'82	'83	'84	'85
Air-conditioning				●	○	
Body exterior (paint)				◒	○	
Body exterior (rust)				○	○	
Body hardware				○	○	
Body integrity				○	○	
Brakes				○	○	
Clutch						
Driveline				○	○	
Electrical system (chassis)				●	◒	
Engine cooling				○	○	
Engine mechanical				○	○	
Exhaust system				○	○	
Fuel system				○	○	
Ignition system				○	○	
Suspension				●	◒	
Transmission (manual)						
Transmission (automatic)				○	○	
TROUBLE INDEX				●	◒	
COST INDEX				○	*	

Pontiac Catalina, Bonneville V8 (gas)

TROUBLE SPOTS	'80	'81	'82	'83	'84	'85
Air-conditioning	○	◓				
Body exterior (paint)	●	○				
Body exterior (rust)	○	○				
Body hardware	○	○				
Body integrity	○	○				
Brakes	○	○				
Clutch						
Driveline	○	○				
Electrical system (chassis)	○	○				
Engine cooling	○	●				
Engine mechanical	◓	◓				
Exhaust system	○	●				
Fuel system	○	○				
Ignition system	○	○				
Suspension	○	○				
Transmission (manual)						
Transmission (automatic)	○	○				
TROUBLE INDEX	○	○				
COST INDEX	◓	◓				

Pontiac Fiero 4

TROUBLE SPOTS	'80	'81	'82	'83	'84	'85
Air-conditioning					●	Insufficient data
Body exterior (paint)					○	
Body exterior (rust)					○	
Body hardware					◒	
Body integrity					●	
Brakes					○	
Clutch					◒	
Driveline					○	
Electrical system (chassis)					●	
Engine cooling					●	
Engine mechanical					●	
Exhaust system					○	
Fuel system					●	
Ignition system					●	
Suspension					○	
Transmission (manual)					◒	
Transmission (automatic)					○	
TROUBLE INDEX					●	
COST INDEX					○	

Pontiac Firebird V6

TROUBLE SPOTS	'80	'81	'82	'83	'84	'85
Air-conditioning	○	○	●	○	○	○
Body exterior (paint)	◒	●	●	●	●	○
Body exterior (rust)	○	●	◒	○	◒	○
Body hardware	◒	◒	○	●	●	○
Body integrity	◒	●	●	●	●	○
Brakes	○	○	⊜	○	◒	○
Clutch		◒	●	●	●	○
Driveline	○	○	○	○	◒	○
Electrical system (chassis)	○	○	◒	◒	◒	●
Engine cooling	○	○	○	○	○	○
Engine mechanical	○	○	○	◒	●	○
Exhaust system	○	●	○	○	◒	◒
Fuel system	○	◒	○	○	●	○
Ignition system	○	◒	○	○	◒	○
Suspension	○	◒	○	◒	○	○
Transmission (manual)		◒	○	○	○	○
Transmission (automatic)	⊜	○	○	○	○	○
TROUBLE INDEX	◒	●	●	●	●	●
COST INDEX	○	○	○	○	○	

Pontiac Firebird V8

TROUBLE SPOTS	'80	'81	'82	'83	'84	'85
Air-conditioning	○	○	●	○	○	○
Body exterior (paint)	●	●	●	◒	●	●
Body exterior (rust)	○	○	◒	○	○	○
Body hardware	◒	◒	●	●	●	○
Body integrity	●	●	●	●	●	●
Brakes	○	○	⊜	○	◒	○
Clutch	◒	◒	●	◒	◒	○
Driveline	○	○	●	●	◒	○
Electrical system (chassis)	○	○	●	●	●	◒
Engine cooling	◒	◒	◒	○	○	○
Engine mechanical	○	○	○	◒	○	○
Exhaust system	○	●	◒	○	○	○
Fuel system	○	○	●	●	●	○
Ignition system	○	○	○	○	◒	○
Suspension	○	○	◒	●	◒	○
Transmission (manual)	○	○	○	○	○	○
Transmission (automatic)	○	○	○	○	○	○
TROUBLE INDEX	◒	●	●	●	●	●
COST INDEX	○	○	◒	◒	○	

Pontiac Grand Am 4

TROUBLE SPOTS	'80	'81	'82	'83	'84	'85
Air-conditioning						○
Body exterior (paint)						○
Body exterior (rust)						○
Body hardware						○
Body integrity						○
Brakes						◒
Clutch						○
Driveline						○
Electrical system (chassis)						◒
Engine cooling						○
Engine mechanical						○
Exhaust system						○
Fuel system						⊜
Ignition system						○
Suspension						○
Transmission (manual)						○
Transmission (automatic)						○
TROUBLE INDEX						◒
COST INDEX						

Pontiac Grand Am V6

TROUBLE SPOTS	'80	'81	'82	'83	'84	'85
Air-conditioning						○
Body exterior (paint)						○
Body exterior (rust)						○
Body hardware						●
Body integrity						○
Brakes						○
Clutch						
Driveline						○
Electrical system (chassis)						○
Engine cooling						◒
Engine mechanical						◒
Exhaust system						○
Fuel system						◒
Ignition system						○
Suspension						○
Transmission (manual)						
Transmission (automatic)						○
TROUBLE INDEX						●
COST INDEX						

Pontiac Grand Prix V6

TROUBLE SPOTS	'80	'81	'82	'83	'84	'85
Air-conditioning	○	◒	●	○	○	Insufficient data
Body exterior (paint)	●	●	●	●	◒	
Body exterior (rust)	⊜	◒	◒	◒	○	
Body hardware	○	◒	◒	◒	◒	
Body integrity	●	●	●	●	●	
Brakes	○	◒	○	○	○	
Clutch						
Driveline	○	○	○	○	○	
Electrical system (chassis)	○	○	●	◒	○	
Engine cooling	●	●	●	◒	○	
Engine mechanical	○	○	●	○	○	
Exhaust system	○	●	●	○	○	
Fuel system	○	●	●	○	○	
Ignition system	◒	●	●	○	○	
Suspension	◒	●	●	◒	○	
Transmission (manual)						
Transmission (automatic)	○	○	○	○	○	
TROUBLE INDEX	◒	●	●	●	●	
COST INDEX	○	○	○	○	*	

Pontiac Grand Prix V8 (gas)

TROUBLE SPOTS	'80	'81	'82	'83	'84	'85
Air-conditioning	○	○		●	○	Insufficient data
Body exterior (paint)	●	◒		◒	●	
Body exterior (rust)	○	○		○	○	
Body hardware	○	○		○	●	
Body integrity	●	○		●	●	
Brakes	○	○		○	◒	
Clutch			Insufficient data			
Driveline	○	○		○	○	
Electrical system (chassis)	○	○		◒	◒	
Engine cooling	◒	○		○	○	
Engine mechanical	○	○		○	○	
Exhaust system	○	●		○	○	
Fuel system	○	●		○	○	
Ignition system	○	○		○	○	
Suspension	◒	○		○	◒	
Transmission (manual)						
Transmission (automatic)	●	○		○	○	
TROUBLE INDEX	◒	●		●	●	
COST INDEX	○	*		○	○	

Pontiac J2000, Sunbird (except Turbo)

TROUBLE SPOTS	'80	'81	'82	'83	'84	'85
Air-conditioning			○	○	○	○
Body exterior (paint)			●	○	○	○
Body exterior (rust)			◒	○	○	○
Body hardware			○	○	○	○
Body integrity			○	○	○	○
Brakes			●	◒	○	◒
Clutch			○	○	○	○
Driveline			○	○	○	○
Electrical system (chassis)			●	○	○	○
Engine cooling			○	●	○	○
Engine mechanical			●	●	○	●
Exhaust system			●	●	◒	○
Fuel system			●	○	○	○
Ignition system			●	●	○	○
Suspension			○	○	◒	●
Transmission (manual)			○	◒	○	◒
Transmission (automatic)			○	○	○	○
TROUBLE INDEX			●	●	◒	●
COST INDEX			○	⊜	⊜	

Pontiac LeMans V6

TROUBLE SPOTS	'80	'81	'82	'83	'84	'85
Air-conditioning	○	○				
Body exterior (paint)	◒	◒				
Body exterior (rust)	⊜	○				
Body hardware	○	○				
Body integrity	○	○				
Brakes	○	○				
Clutch						
Driveline	○	○				
Electrical system (chassis)	◒	○				
Engine cooling	○	●				
Engine mechanical	◒	○				
Exhaust system	○	●				
Fuel system	○	●				
Ignition system	○	●				
Suspension	○	◒				
Transmission (manual)						
Transmission (automatic)	●	○				
TROUBLE INDEX	○	●				
COST INDEX	○	○				

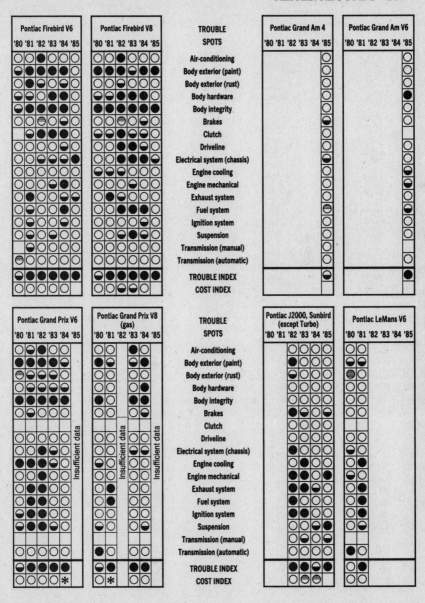

Key: ◍ Much better than average · ⊜ Better than average · ○ Average · ◒ Worse than average · ● Much worse than average · * Insufficient cost data

Pontiac Parisienne V6

TROUBLE SPOTS	'80	'81	'82	'83	'84	'85
Air-conditioning				○	○	○
Body exterior (paint)				○	○	○
Body exterior (rust)				○	○	○
Body hardware				○	○	○
Body integrity				○	○	○
Brakes				○	○	○
Clutch						
Driveline				○	○	○
Electrical system (chassis)				◒	○	○
Engine cooling				○	○	○
Engine mechanical				○	○	○
Exhaust system				○	○	○
Fuel system				◒	◒	◒
Ignition system				◒	○	○
Suspension				◒	○	○
Transmission (manual)						
Transmission (automatic)				○	○	○
TROUBLE INDEX				◒	◒	○
COST INDEX				○	○	

Pontiac Parisienne V8 (gas)

TROUBLE SPOTS	'80	'81	'82	'83	'84	'85
Air-conditioning				○	○	○
Body exterior (paint)				◒	◒	○
Body exterior (rust)				○	○	○
Body hardware				◒	◒	◒
Body integrity				○	○	○
Brakes				○	○	○
Clutch						
Driveline				○	○	○
Electrical system (chassis)				◒	○	○
Engine cooling				○	○	○
Engine mechanical				○	○	○
Exhaust system				○	○	○
Fuel system				○	⊜	○
Ignition system				○	○	○
Suspension				◒	○	○
Transmission (manual)						
Transmission (automatic)				⊜	○	○
TROUBLE INDEX				○	○	◒
COST INDEX				○	⊜	

Pontiac Phoenix 4

TROUBLE SPOTS	'80	'81	'82	'83	'84	'85
Air-conditioning	●	●	●	●	Insufficient data	
Body exterior (paint)	●	●	○	●		
Body exterior (rust)	●	●	○	○		
Body hardware	○	○	○	○		
Body integrity	◒	○	○	○		
Brakes	●	◒	●	○		
Clutch	◒	●	○	○		
Driveline	○	◒	○	○		
Electrical system (chassis)	○	○	◒	○		
Engine cooling	○	○	◒	●		
Engine mechanical	○	○	○	○		
Exhaust system	○	●	○	○		
Fuel system	●	◒	○	○		
Ignition system	○	○	○	○		
Suspension	○	○	○	○		
Transmission (manual)	●	○	◒	○		
Transmission (automatic)	◒	◒	○	○		
TROUBLE INDEX	◒	●	◒	●		
COST INDEX	○	○	○	*		

Pontiac Phoenix V6

TROUBLE SPOTS	'80	'81	'82	'83	'84	'85
Air-conditioning	◒	●	Insufficient data	Insufficient data	Insufficient data	
Body exterior (paint)	◒	●				
Body exterior (rust)	◒	●				
Body hardware	○	○				
Body integrity	◒	○				
Brakes	◒	●				
Clutch	○	○				
Driveline	●	●				
Electrical system (chassis)	◒	◒				
Engine cooling	●	◒				
Engine mechanical	○	○				
Exhaust system	○	○				
Fuel system	●	◒				
Ignition system	○	○				
Suspension	◒	○				
Transmission (manual)	●	○				
Transmission (automatic)	●	◒				
TROUBLE INDEX	●	●				
COST INDEX	○	○				

Pontiac Sunbird 4

TROUBLE SPOTS	'80	'81	'82	'83	'84	'85
Air-conditioning	●					
Body exterior (paint)	○					
Body exterior (rust)	○					
Body hardware	●					
Body integrity	●					
Brakes	○					
Clutch	●					
Driveline	⊜					
Electrical system (chassis)	○					
Engine cooling	◒					
Engine mechanical	○					
Exhaust system	○					
Fuel system	○					
Ignition system	○					
Suspension	●					
Transmission (manual)	○					
Transmission (automatic)	○					
TROUBLE INDEX	◒					
COST INDEX	○					

Pontiac T1000, 1000

TROUBLE SPOTS	'80	'81	'82	'83	'84	'85
Air-conditioning		○	⊜	○	○	Insufficient data
Body exterior (paint)		○	○	○	◒	
Body exterior (rust)		○	○	○	○	
Body hardware		◒	○	◒	●	
Body integrity		●	●	●	●	
Brakes		●	●	●	○	
Clutch		●	○	○	○	
Driveline		○	○	○	○	
Electrical system (chassis)		●	◒	○	○	
Engine cooling		○	○	○	○	
Engine mechanical		○	⊜	○	○	
Exhaust system		●	●	◒	○	
Fuel system		◒	○	○	○	
Ignition system		◒	◒	○	◒	
Suspension		●	○	◒	○	
Transmission (manual)		○	○	○	○	
Transmission (automatic)		○	○	○	○	
TROUBLE INDEX		●	●	●	●	
COST INDEX		○	○	⊜	⊜	

Porsche 944

TROUBLE SPOTS	'80	'81	'82	'83	'84	'85
Air-conditioning				⊜	○	○
Body exterior (paint)				○	○	○
Body exterior (rust)				○	○	○
Body hardware				○	○	○
Body integrity				⊜	○	○
Brakes				⊜	○	○
Clutch				○	⊜	○
Driveline				○	○	○
Electrical system (chassis)				○	○	○
Engine cooling				○	◒	○
Engine mechanical				◒	○	○
Exhaust system				○	○	○
Fuel system				⊜	○	○
Ignition system				⊜	○	○
Suspension				○	○	○
Transmission (manual)				○	○	○
Transmission (automatic)				○	○	○
TROUBLE INDEX				⊜	⊜	⊜
COST INDEX				●	●	

Renault Alliance, Encore

TROUBLE SPOTS	'80	'81	'82	'83	'84	'85
Air-conditioning				◒	◒	○
Body exterior (paint)				◒	◒	○
Body exterior (rust)				◒	○	○
Body hardware				●	●	●
Body integrity				●	●	◒
Brakes				●	●	○
Clutch				○	◒	○
Driveline				●	○	○
Electrical system (chassis)				◒	◒	○
Engine cooling				●	●	◒
Engine mechanical				●	○	○
Exhaust system				●	○	○
Fuel system				●	○	○
Ignition system				○	○	○
Suspension				◒	○	○
Transmission (manual)				●	◒	○
Transmission (automatic)				●	●	●
TROUBLE INDEX				●	●	●
COST INDEX				◒	○	

Renault LeCar	'80	'81	'82	'83	'84	'85
Air-conditioning	○	Insufficient data	○	Insufficient data		
Body exterior (paint)	●		○			
Body exterior (rust)	●		○			
Body hardware	●		○			
Body integrity	◒		○			
Brakes	●		●			
Clutch	○		○			
Driveline	○		○			
Electrical system (chassis)	●		○			
Engine cooling	●		●			
Engine mechanical	○		○			
Exhaust system	●		●			
Fuel system	◒		○			
Ignition system	○		○			
Suspension	○		○			
Transmission (manual)	○		○			
Transmission (automatic)						
TROUBLE INDEX	●		●			
COST INDEX	◒		●			

Saab 900	'80	'81	'82	'83	'84	'85
Air-conditioning	○	Insufficient data	○	○	◒	○
Body exterior (paint)	○		⊜	○	⊖	⊖
Body exterior (rust)	○		○	○	○	○
Body hardware	○		⊖	○	○	○
Body integrity	○		⊖	⊖	⊖	○
Brakes	○		○	○	○	○
Clutch	○		⊖	⊖	⊖	○
Driveline	○		○	○	○	○
Electrical system (chassis)	○		⊖	○	○	○
Engine cooling	○		●	◒	○	○
Engine mechanical	○		○	○	○	○
Exhaust system	●		●	●	○	○
Fuel system	○		○	○	○	○
Ignition system	○		○	○	○	○
Suspension	○		⊖	⊖	⊖	○
Transmission (manual)	○		○	○	○	○
Transmission (automatic)	○		○	○	○	○
TROUBLE INDEX	○		⊖	○	⊖	⊖
COST INDEX	●		●	●	●	

Saab 900 (Turbo)	'80	'81	'82	'83	'84	'85
Air-conditioning	Insufficient data	Insufficient data	○	○	○	○
Body exterior (paint)			⊜	⊖	⊖	○
Body exterior (rust)			⊖	○	○	○
Body hardware			○	○	○	○
Body integrity			⊖	⊖	○	○
Brakes			○	○	⊖	○
Clutch			○	○	○	○
Driveline			○	○	○	○
Electrical system (chassis)			○	◒	○	○
Engine cooling			●	●	○	○
Engine mechanical			○	○	○	○
Exhaust system			●	◒	○	○
Fuel system			○	⊜	⊖	○
Ignition system			○	⊖	○	○
Suspension			⊖	⊖	⊖	○
Transmission (manual)			○	◒	○	○
Transmission (automatic)			○	○	○	●
TROUBLE INDEX			○	○	⊖	○
COST INDEX			●	●	●	

Subaru (except 4-WD)	'80	'81	'82	'83	'84	'85
Air-conditioning	○	⊖	⊜	○	○	○
Body exterior (paint)	⊖	○	⊖	⊖	⊖	○
Body exterior (rust)	○	●	○	○	○	○
Body hardware	⊜	⊜	⊜	⊜	⊜	○
Body integrity	⊖	⊖	⊜	⊜	⊜	○
Brakes	●	●	●	◒	○	◒
Clutch	⊜	◒	◒	○	○	○
Driveline	◒	○	○	○	○	○
Electrical system (chassis)	⊜	⊜	⊜	⊜	⊜	○
Engine cooling	⊖	○	⊖	⊖	○	○
Engine mechanical	⊜	⊜	⊜	⊖	⊖	○
Exhaust system	○	⊖	⊖	○	○	○
Fuel system	⊜	⊜	⊖	⊖	⊖	○
Ignition system	⊜	⊜	⊖	⊖	○	○
Suspension	○	⊜	⊜	⊖	⊖	○
Transmission (manual)	○	○	○	○	○	○
Transmission (automatic)	○	○	●	◒	○	○
TROUBLE INDEX	⊖	⊖	⊜	⊜	⊜	○
COST INDEX	⊖	⊖	⊖	⊖	○	

Subaru (4-WD)	'80	'81	'82	'83	'84	'85
Air-conditioning	○	⊖	⊖	○	○	○
Body exterior (paint)	⊖	○	⊖	⊖	⊖	○
Body exterior (rust)	●	●	◒	○	○	○
Body hardware	⊜	⊜	⊜	⊜	⊜	○
Body integrity	⊖	⊖	⊜	⊜	⊜	○
Brakes	◒	○	○	○	○	○
Clutch	⊖	◒	●	⊖	○	○
Driveline	●	●	○	○	○	○
Electrical system (chassis)	⊜	⊜	⊜	⊜	⊜	○
Engine cooling	○	○	⊖	⊖	○	○
Engine mechanical	○	⊜	⊜	⊖	⊖	○
Exhaust system	○	○	⊖	○	○	○
Fuel system	⊜	⊖	⊖	⊜	⊜	○
Ignition system	⊖	⊜	⊖	⊖	⊖	○
Suspension	○	○	⊖	⊜	○	○
Transmission (manual)	○	○	○	○	○	○
Transmission (automatic)				○	◒	○
TROUBLE INDEX	○	○	⊖	⊜	⊜	○
COST INDEX	○	⊖	⊖	⊖	○	

Toyota Camry (gas)	'80	'81	'82	'83	'84	'85
Air-conditioning				⊖	⊖	○
Body exterior (paint)				⊖	⊖	⊖
Body exterior (rust)				○	○	○
Body hardware				⊜	⊜	⊖
Body integrity				⊜	⊜	⊖
Brakes				⊖	○	○
Clutch				⊖	○	○
Driveline				○	○	○
Electrical system (chassis)				⊜	⊜	⊜
Engine cooling				○	○	○
Engine mechanical				○	○	○
Exhaust system				◒	○	○
Fuel system				⊜	⊜	⊖
Ignition system				⊖	⊖	○
Suspension				⊖	⊖	○
Transmission (manual)				○	○	○
Transmission (automatic)				○	○	○
TROUBLE INDEX				⊜	⊜	⊜
COST INDEX				⊜	⊖	

Toyota Camry (diesel)	'80	'81	'82	'83	'84	'85
Air-conditioning					⊖	Insufficient data
Body exterior (paint)					⊖	
Body exterior (rust)					○	
Body hardware					⊜	
Body integrity					⊖	
Brakes					○	
Clutch					⊖	
Driveline					○	
Electrical system (chassis)					⊜	
Engine cooling					○	
Engine mechanical					⊖	
Exhaust system					○	
Fuel system					⊜	
Ignition system					○	
Suspension					⊖	
Transmission (manual)					○	
Transmission (automatic)						
TROUBLE INDEX					⊜	
COST INDEX					⊖	

Toyota Celica Supra, Supra 6	'80	'81	'82	'83	'84	'85
Air-conditioning	○	○	⊜	⊜	⊖	○
Body exterior (paint)	⊜	⊜	○	○	○	○
Body exterior (rust)	⊜	⊖	○	○	○	○
Body hardware	⊖	⊖	⊖	⊜	⊜	⊖
Body integrity	⊜	⊖	⊜	⊜	⊜	○
Brakes	○	⊖	⊜	⊜	⊖	○
Clutch	○	○	⊖	⊖	○	○
Driveline	○	○	○	○	○	○
Electrical system (chassis)	○	⊖	○	⊖	⊜	⊖
Engine cooling	○	◒	○	○	○	○
Engine mechanical	⊖	⊖	○	○	○	○
Exhaust system	⊖	○	⊜	○	○	○
Fuel system	⊜	⊜	⊜	⊜	⊜	⊖
Ignition system	⊜	⊖	⊜	⊖	⊖	○
Suspension	⊜	○	⊜	⊖	⊖	○
Transmission (manual)	○	○	○	○	○	○
Transmission (automatic)	○	○	○	○	○	○
TROUBLE INDEX	⊜	⊜	⊜	⊜	⊜	⊜
COST INDEX	○	○	⊖	⊖	⊖	

Legend: ◍ Much better than average · ◓ Better than average · ○ Average · ◒ Worse than average · ● Much worse than average · * Insufficient cost data

TROUBLE SPOTS	Toyota Celica 4 '80	'81	'82	'83	'84	'85
Air-conditioning	◍	◍	◍	◍	◓	○
Body exterior (paint)	◍	◍	○	◓	◓	○
Body exterior (rust)	◍	◍	◒	○	○	○
Body hardware	◍	◍	○	◓	◍	◓
Body integrity	◓	○	◓	◍	◍	◓
Brakes	○	◓	◍	◍	◓	○
Clutch	○	○	○	◓	◓	○
Driveline	◓	◓	○	○	○	○
Electrical system (chassis)	◍	◍	◍	○	◍	◍
Engine cooling	◍	◍	◓	○	○	○
Engine mechanical	◓	◍	◍	◓	◓	○
Exhaust system	◓	◓	◓	○	○	○
Fuel system	◍	◍	◍	◍	◍	◓
Ignition system	◍	◍	◍	○	◓	○
Suspension	◓	◓	◓	◓	◓	○
Transmission (manual)	○	○	○	○	○	○
Transmission (automatic)	◓	○	◓	○	○	○
TROUBLE INDEX	◍	◍	◍	◍	◍	◍
COST INDEX	◓	◍	◓	◓	◓	

TROUBLE SPOTS	Toyota Corolla (gas, FWD) '80	'81	'82	'83	'84	'85
Air-conditioning					◓	○
Body exterior (paint)					◓	◓
Body exterior (rust)					○	○
Body hardware					◍	◓
Body integrity					◍	◓
Brakes					◓	○
Clutch					◓	○
Driveline					○	○
Electrical system (chassis)					◍	◍
Engine cooling					○	○
Engine mechanical					◓	○
Exhaust system					○	○
Fuel system					◍	◓
Ignition system					◓	○
Suspension					○	○
Transmission (manual)					○	○
Transmission (automatic)					○	○
TROUBLE INDEX					◍	◍
COST INDEX					◓	

TROUBLE SPOTS	Toyota Corolla (RWD) '80	'81	'82	'83	'84	'85
Air-conditioning	◍	◍	◍	◍	○	◓
Body exterior (paint)	◍	◓	◓	◓	◓	○
Body exterior (rust)	◓	○	◒	○	○	○
Body hardware	◍	◍	◍	◍	◓	○
Body integrity	◍	◍	◍	◍	◍	◓
Brakes	◓	◓	◍	◍	◓	○
Clutch	◍	◍	◍	◓	◓	○
Driveline	◓	○	○	○	○	○
Electrical system (chassis)	◍	◍	◍	◍	◍	◓
Engine cooling	◓	○	◓	◓	○	○
Engine mechanical	◍	◓	◍	◓	◓	○
Exhaust system	◓	◓	○	○	○	○
Fuel system	◍	◍	◍	◍	◍	◓
Ignition system	◍	◍	◍	○	◓	○
Suspension	◍	◓	○	◓	◓	○
Transmission (manual)	○	○	○	○	○	○
Transmission (automatic)	◓	○	○	○	○	○
TROUBLE INDEX	◍	◍	◍	◍	◍	◍
COST INDEX	◍	◍	◍	◓	◓	

TROUBLE SPOTS	Toyota Corona '80	'81	'82	'83	'84	'85
Air-conditioning	◓	◍	◍			
Body exterior (paint)	◍	◍	◓			
Body exterior (rust)	◍	◍	○			
Body hardware	◍	◍	◍			
Body integrity	◍	◍	◓			
Brakes	○	○	○			
Clutch	○	○	○			
Driveline	◓	◓	○			
Electrical system (chassis)	◍	◍	○			
Engine cooling	◍	◍	○			
Engine mechanical	◍	◍	◓			
Exhaust system	○	○	○			
Fuel system	◍	◍	◍			
Ignition system	◍	◍	◓			
Suspension	◍	◍	○			
Transmission (manual)	○	○	○			
Transmission (automatic)	◓	◓	○			
TROUBLE INDEX	◍	◍	◍			
COST INDEX	◓	◍	◍			

TROUBLE SPOTS	Toyota Cressida '80	'81	'82	'83	'84	'85
Air-conditioning	◍	◓	◓	◓	◓	○
Body exterior (paint)	◍	◍	◍	◓	◓	○
Body exterior (rust)	◍	◍	◓	○	○	○
Body hardware	◍	◍	◍	◍	◍	◓
Body integrity	◍	◍	◍	◍	◍	◓
Brakes	○	◓	◍	◍	○	○
Clutch				○	○	○
Driveline	◓	○	○	○	○	○
Electrical system (chassis)	◍	○	○	◍	◍	◓
Engine cooling	◓	◍	◓	◓	○	○
Engine mechanical	◓	◍	◍	○	○	○
Exhaust system	○	○	○	○	○	○
Fuel system	◍	◍	◍	◍	◍	◓
Ignition system	◍	◍	◓	◓	◓	○
Suspension	◓	○	◓	◓	◍	○
Transmission (manual)				○	○	○
Transmission (automatic)	○	○	◓	○	○	○
TROUBLE INDEX	◍	◍	◍	◍	◍	◍
COST INDEX	◓	◓	◓	◓	◓	

TROUBLE SPOTS	Toyota MR2 '80	'81	'82	'83	'84	'85
Air-conditioning						○
Body exterior (paint)						○
Body exterior (rust)						○
Body hardware						○
Body integrity						○
Brakes						○
Clutch						○
Driveline						○
Electrical system (chassis)						◓
Engine cooling						○
Engine mechanical						○
Exhaust system						○
Fuel system						○
Ignition system						○
Suspension						○
Transmission (manual)						○
Transmission (automatic)						
TROUBLE INDEX						◍
COST INDEX						

TROUBLE SPOTS	Toyota Pickup Truck (gas, 2-WD) '80	'81	'82	'83	'84	'85
Air-conditioning	◓	◍	◍	◓	○	○
Body exterior (paint)	◓	◓	◓	○	○	○
Body exterior (rust)	●	○	○	○	○	○
Body hardware	◍	◍	◍	◍	◍	◓
Body integrity	◍	◍	◍	◓	◍	◓
Brakes	◍	◍	◍	◍	◓	○
Clutch	◍	◍	◍	◓	◓	○
Driveline	◓	◓	○	○	○	○
Electrical system (chassis)	◍	◍	◍	◍	◍	◍
Engine cooling	◍	◍	◓	○	○	○
Engine mechanical	◍	◍	◍	◓	◓	○
Exhaust system	◓	◍	◍	◓	○	○
Fuel system	◍	◍	◍	◍	◍	○
Ignition system	◍	◍	◍	◓	◓	○
Suspension	◍	◍	◍	◓	◓	○
Transmission (manual)	○	○	○	○	○	○
Transmission (automatic)		○	○	○	○	○
TROUBLE INDEX	◍	◍	◍	◍	◍	◍
COST INDEX	◍	◍	◍	◍	◓	

TROUBLE SPOTS	Toyota Pickup Truck (4-WD) '80	'81	'82	'83	'84	'85
Air-conditioning	◓	◓	◍	◓	◍	○
Body exterior (paint)	○	○	○	○	○	○
Body exterior (rust)	●	○	◒	●	◒	○
Body hardware	◍	◍	◍	◍	◍	◓
Body integrity	◍	◓	◍	◓	◓	◓
Brakes	◍	◍	◓	○	○	○
Clutch	○	○	◓	○	○	○
Driveline	○	◒	○	○	○	○
Electrical system (chassis)	◍	◍	◍	◍	◍	◍
Engine cooling	◍	◍	◍	○	○	○
Engine mechanical	◓	◍	◍	◓	◓	○
Exhaust system	●	◓	◍	○	○	○
Fuel system	◍	◍	◍	◍	◍	◓
Ignition system	◍	◓	◍	◓	◓	○
Suspension	◍	◓	◓	◓	◓	○
Transmission (manual)	○	●	◒	○	○	○
Transmission (automatic)						
TROUBLE INDEX	◍	◍	◍	◍	◍	◍
COST INDEX	◓	○	◓	◓	◓	

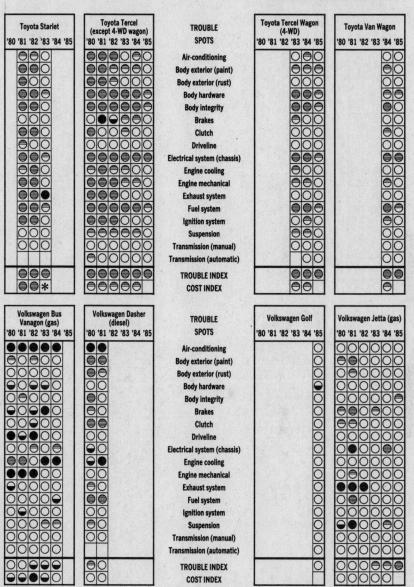

Toyota Starlet

Trouble spots	'80	'81	'82	'83	'84	'85
Air-conditioning		⊖	⊖	○		
Body exterior (paint)		◍	◍	○		
Body exterior (rust)		◍	○	○		
Body hardware		◍	◍	⊖		
Body integrity		◍	◍	○		
Brakes		○	○	○		
Clutch		◍	◍	○		
Driveline		⊖	○	○		
Electrical system (chassis)		◍	◍	⊖		
Engine cooling		⊖	◍	○		
Engine mechanical		◍	◍	○		
Exhaust system		◍	◍	●		
Fuel system		◍	◍	⊖		
Ignition system		◍	◍	○		
Suspension		○	○	○		
Transmission (manual)		○	○	○		
Transmission (automatic)						
TROUBLE INDEX		◍	◍	◍		
COST INDEX		◍	◍	*		

Toyota Tercel (except 4-WD wagon)

Trouble spots	'80	'81	'82	'83	'84	'85
Air-conditioning	◍	◍	◍	○	⊖	○
Body exterior (paint)	◍	◍	⊖	⊖	⊖	○
Body exterior (rust)	◍	◍	⊖	○	○	○
Body hardware	◍	◍	◍	◍	◍	⊖
Body integrity	◍	◍	◍	◍	◍	⊖
Brakes	○	●	◒	⊖	⊖	○
Clutch	◍	○	○	⊖	○	○
Driveline	○	○	○	○	○	○
Electrical system (chassis)	◍	◍	◍	◍	◍	◍
Engine cooling	⊖	◍	⊖	⊖	○	○
Engine mechanical	◍	◍	◍	⊖	⊖	○
Exhaust system	◍	◍	◍	○	○	○
Fuel system	◍	◍	◍	◍	◍	⊖
Ignition system	◍	◍	◍	○	○	○
Suspension	⊖	⊖	⊖	⊖	⊖	○
Transmission (manual)	○	○	○	○	○	○
Transmission (automatic)	⊖	○	○	○	○	○
TROUBLE INDEX	◍	◍	◍	◍	◍	◍
COST INDEX	⊖	⊖	⊖	⊖	⊖	

Toyota Tercel Wagon (4-WD)

Trouble spots	'80	'81	'82	'83	'84	'85
Air-conditioning				○	⊖	○
Body exterior (paint)				⊖	⊖	⊖
Body exterior (rust)				○	○	○
Body hardware				◍	◍	⊖
Body integrity				◍	◍	⊖
Brakes				⊖	○	○
Clutch				○	○	○
Driveline				○	○	○
Electrical system (chassis)				◍	◍	⊖
Engine cooling				⊖	○	○
Engine mechanical				⊖	⊖	○
Exhaust system				○	○	○
Fuel system				◍	◍	⊖
Ignition system				○	⊖	○
Suspension				⊖	⊖	○
Transmission (manual)				○	○	○
Transmission (automatic)					○	○
TROUBLE INDEX				◍	◍	◍
COST INDEX				⊖	⊖	

Toyota Van Wagon

Trouble spots	'80	'81	'82	'83	'84	'85
Air-conditioning					○	○
Body exterior (paint)					⊖	○
Body exterior (rust)					○	○
Body hardware					⊖	⊖
Body integrity					◍	○
Brakes					○	○
Clutch					⊖	○
Driveline					○	○
Electrical system (chassis)					◍	◍
Engine cooling					○	○
Engine mechanical					⊖	○
Exhaust system					○	○
Fuel system					◍	⊖
Ignition system					⊖	○
Suspension					○	○
Transmission (manual)					○	○
Transmission (automatic)					○	○
TROUBLE INDEX					◍	◍
COST INDEX					⊖	

Volkswagen Bus Vanagon (gas)

Trouble spots	'80	'81	'82	'83	'84	'85
Air-conditioning	●	●	●	●	●	
Body exterior (paint)	⊖	○	⊖	○	○	
Body exterior (rust)	○	○	○	○	○	
Body hardware	◒	○	◒	◒	○	
Body integrity	○	⊖	○	○	○	
Brakes	◒	○	◒	●	○	
Clutch	○	○	◒	○	○	
Driveline	●	◒	●	○	○	
Electrical system (chassis)	○	○	⊖	○	⊖	
Engine cooling	◍	◍	○	●	●	
Engine mechanical	●	●	●	○	○	
Exhaust system	◒	○	○	○	○	
Fuel system	○	○	○	○	◒	
Ignition system	○	◒	○	○	○	
Suspension	○	○	○	⊖	⊖	
Transmission (manual)	○	○	○	○	○	
Transmission (automatic)	○	○	○	○	○	
TROUBLE INDEX	○	○	◒	◒	◒	
COST INDEX	◒	◒	●	◒	○	

Volkswagen Dasher (diesel)

Trouble spots	'80	'81	'82	'83	'84	'85
Air-conditioning	●	●				
Body exterior (paint)	◍	◍				
Body exterior (rust)	◍	⊖				
Body hardware	○	○				
Body integrity	◍	○				
Brakes	⊖	○				
Clutch	◍	◍				
Driveline	○	○				
Electrical system (chassis)	◒	○				
Engine cooling	◒	●				
Engine mechanical	○	○				
Exhaust system	⊖	○				
Fuel system	◍	◍				
Ignition system	○	○				
Suspension	⊖	○				
Transmission (manual)	○	○				
Transmission (automatic)						
TROUBLE INDEX	⊖	○				
COST INDEX	○	○				

Volkswagen Golf

Trouble spots	'80	'81	'82	'83	'84	'85
Air-conditioning						○
Body exterior (paint)						○
Body exterior (rust)						○
Body hardware						◒
Body integrity						○
Brakes						○
Clutch						○
Driveline						○
Electrical system (chassis)						○
Engine cooling						○
Engine mechanical						○
Exhaust system						○
Fuel system						○
Ignition system						○
Suspension						○
Transmission (manual)						○
Transmission (automatic)						○
TROUBLE INDEX						○
COST INDEX						

Volkswagen Jetta (gas)

Trouble spots	'80	'81	'82	'83	'84	'85
Air-conditioning	○	○	○	○	○	○
Body exterior (paint)	⊖	◍	○	○	○	○
Body exterior (rust)	○	⊖	○	○	○	○
Body hardware	○	○	○	○	○	○
Body integrity	○	○	○	○	○	⊖
Brakes	⊖	◍	○	⊖	○	○
Clutch	⊖	⊖	○	○	○	○
Driveline	○	○	○	○	○	○
Electrical system (chassis)	○	●	○	○	◍	○
Engine cooling	○	○	○	○	○	○
Engine mechanical	○	⊖	○	○	○	○
Exhaust system	●	●	●	○	○	○
Fuel system	○	◍	○	○	○	○
Ignition system	○	○	○	○	○	○
Suspension	◒	●	○	○	⊖	○
Transmission (manual)	○	○	○	○	○	○
Transmission (automatic)	○	○	○	○	○	○
TROUBLE INDEX	○	○	○	⊖	⊖	◍
COST INDEX	○	○	○	○	○	

Key: MB = Much better than average; B = Better than average; A = Average; W = Worse than average; MW = Much worse than average; * = Insufficient cost data

Volkswagen Quantum (gas)

TROUBLE SPOTS	'80	'81	'82	'83	'84	'85
Air-conditioning			A	A	A	
Body exterior (paint)			B	A	A	
Body exterior (rust)			B	A	A	
Body hardware			A	A	A	
Body integrity			B	A	B	
Brakes			MB	A	A	
Clutch			B	A	A	
Driveline			A	A	A	
Electrical system (chassis)			A	W	A	
Engine cooling			MW	MW	MW	
Engine mechanical			MB	B	A	
Exhaust system			MB	A	A	
Fuel system			B	A	B	
Ignition system			B	A	B	
Suspension			A	A	A	
Transmission (manual)			A	A	A	
Transmission (automatic)			A	A	A	
TROUBLE INDEX			B	A	A	
COST INDEX			A	A	A	

'85: Insufficient data

Volkswagen Rabbit, GTI (gas)

TROUBLE SPOTS	'80	'81	'82	'83	'84	'85
Air-conditioning	MW	W	B	B	A	
Body exterior (paint)	B	B	B	A	A	
Body exterior (rust)	A	A	A	A	A	
Body hardware	MW	MW	W	A	A	
Body integrity	MW	MW	W	A	A	
Brakes	MB	B	MB	B	A	
Clutch	B	A	B	A	A	
Driveline	A	A	A	A	A	
Electrical system (chassis)	MW	W	MW	A	A	
Engine cooling	A	W	W	A	A	
Engine mechanical	A	A	B	B	A	
Exhaust system	MW	A	W	A	A	
Fuel system	MW	A	A	B	A	
Ignition system	W	A	A	B	A	
Suspension	W	W	A	A	A	
Transmission (manual)	A	A	A	A	A	
Transmission (automatic)	A	A	A	A	A	
TROUBLE INDEX	W	W	A	B	A	
COST INDEX	A	A	A	A	A	

Volkswagen Rabbit (diesel)

TROUBLE SPOTS	'80	'81	'82	'83	'84	'85
Air-conditioning	W	MW	MB	A	W	
Body exterior (paint)	B	MB	B	A	A	
Body exterior (rust)	A	B	B	A	A	
Body hardware	MW	MW	W	A	B	
Body integrity	W	W	A	A	A	
Brakes	MB	MB	MB	B	A	
Clutch	B	MB	MB	B	B	
Driveline	A	A	A	A	A	
Electrical system (chassis)	MW	A	A	B	B	
Engine cooling	A	A	MW	A	A	
Engine mechanical	W	A	A	A	A	
Exhaust system	MW	MB	MB	A	A	
Fuel system	MB	MB	MB	A	B	
Ignition system	MW	W	B	A	A	
Suspension	W	A	A	A	A	
Transmission (manual)	A	A	A	A	A	
Transmission (automatic)						
TROUBLE INDEX	A	A	B	B	MB	
COST INDEX	A	A	A	*	A	

Volkswagen Rabbit Pickup Truck (gas)

TROUBLE SPOTS	'80	'81	'82	'83	'84	'85
Air-conditioning		A				
Body exterior (paint)		A				
Body exterior (rust)		A				
Body hardware		W				
Body integrity		W				
Brakes		B				
Clutch		A				
Driveline		A				
Electrical system (chassis)		A				
Engine cooling		A				
Engine mechanical		A				
Exhaust system		A				
Fuel system		A				
Ignition system		A				
Suspension		A				
Transmission (manual)		A				
Transmission (automatic)						
TROUBLE INDEX		A				
COST INDEX		*				

'80: Insufficient data; '82: Insufficient data; '83: Insufficient data

Volkswagen Scirocco

TROUBLE SPOTS	'80	'81	'82	'83	'84	'85
Air-conditioning	A	A	A		A	
Body exterior (paint)	A	A	B		A	
Body exterior (rust)	A	MB	B		A	
Body hardware	A	A	A		A	
Body integrity	B	B	A		B	
Brakes	MB	B	MB		A	
Clutch	MB	A	B		A	
Driveline	A	A	A		A	
Electrical system (chassis)	MW	A	A		A	
Engine cooling	A	A	A		A	
Engine mechanical	A	B	B		B	
Exhaust system	MW	A	B		A	
Fuel system	A	A	B		B	
Ignition system	A	A	B		A	
Suspension	W	W	A		A	
Transmission (manual)	A	A	A		A	
Transmission (automatic)	A	A	A		A	
TROUBLE INDEX	A	B	B		MB	
COST INDEX	A	A	A		A	

Volvo 240 Series DL, GL 4 (gas, except Turbo)

TROUBLE SPOTS	'80	'81	'82	'83	'84	'85
Air-conditioning	W	A	A	B	A	W
Body exterior (paint)	MB	MB	MB	B	B	A
Body exterior (rust)	MB	MB	B	A	A	A
Body hardware	B	A	A	A	A	A
Body integrity	MB	MB	B	B	B	A
Brakes	A	W	A	MW	MW	A
Clutch	MB	A	B	A	A	A
Driveline	A	A	A	A	A	A
Electrical system (chassis)	B	B	W	A	B	A
Engine cooling	A	A	A	A	A	A
Engine mechanical	B	W	A	B	B	A
Exhaust system	MW	MW	MW	MW	MW	A
Fuel system	B	B	B	B	B	A
Ignition system	B	B	A	A	A	A
Suspension	B	MB	B	A	B	A
Transmission (manual)	A	A	A	A	A	A
Transmission (automatic)	A	A	A	A	A	A
TROUBLE INDEX	B	A	A	A	B	A
COST INDEX	W	W	W	W	MW	

Volvo 240 Series DL, GL 6 (Gas, Turbo)

TROUBLE SPOTS	'80	'81	'82	'83	'84	'85
Air-conditioning			A	B	A	
Body exterior (paint)			B	A	A	
Body exterior (rust)			B	A	A	
Body hardware			A	W	A	
Body integrity			B	A	A	
Brakes			A	MW	MW	
Clutch			B	A	A	
Driveline			A	A	A	
Electrical system (chassis)			A	A	A	
Engine cooling			A	MW	A	
Engine mechanical			MW	A	A	
Exhaust system			A	A	A	
Fuel system			B	A	A	
Ignition system			B	A	A	
Suspension			A	A	A	
Transmission (manual)			A	A	A	
Transmission (automatic)			A	A	A	
TROUBLE INDEX			B	A	A	
COST INDEX			MW	MW	MW	

'80–'81: Insufficient data; '85: Insufficient data

Volvo 240 Series DL, GL 6 (diesel)

TROUBLE SPOTS	'80	'81	'82	'83	'84	'85
Air-conditioning	A		A		A	
Body exterior (paint)	B		A		B	
Body exterior (rust)	B		A		A	
Body hardware	A		A		B	
Body integrity	A		A		B	
Brakes	A		A		A	
Clutch	A		A		A	
Driveline	A		A		A	
Electrical system (chassis)	A		A		A	
Engine cooling	A		B		A	
Engine mechanical	A		A		A	
Exhaust system	B		B		A	
Fuel system	MB		MB		B	
Ignition system	A		A		A	
Suspension	A		A		A	
Transmission (manual)	A		A		A	
Transmission (automatic)	A		A		A	
TROUBLE INDEX	MB		B		MB	
COST INDEX	*		W		W	

'83: Insufficient data

Much better than average — Better than average — Average — Worse than average — Much worse than average — * Insufficient cost data

Volvo 740 (except Turbo)

TROUBLE SPOTS	'80	'81	'82	'83	'84	'85
Air-conditioning						○
Body exterior (paint)						○
Body exterior (rust)						○
Body hardware						●
Body integrity						○
Brakes						◒
Clutch						○
Driveline						○
Electrical system (chassis)						○
Engine cooling						○
Engine mechanical						○
Exhaust system						○
Fuel system						○
Ignition system						○
Suspension						○
Transmission (manual)						○
Transmission (automatic)						○
TROUBLE INDEX						○
COST INDEX						

Volvo 760 (gas, except Turbo)

TROUBLE SPOTS	'80	'81	'82	'83	'84	'85
Air-conditioning				●	○	Insufficient data
Body exterior (paint)				○	○	
Body exterior (rust)				○	○	
Body hardware				●	○	
Body integrity				○	○	
Brakes				○	○	
Clutch					○	
Driveline				○	○	
Electrical system (chassis)				◒	○	
Engine cooling				●	○	
Engine mechanical				○	○	
Exhaust system				◒	○	
Fuel system				○	○	
Ignition system				○	○	
Suspension				○	⊜	
Transmission (manual)					○	
Transmission (automatic)				○	○	
TROUBLE INDEX				●	○	
COST INDEX				●	●	

Volvo 760 (gas, Turbo)

TROUBLE SPOTS	'80	'81	'82	'83	'84	'85
Air-conditioning					◒	Insufficient data
Body exterior (paint)					○	
Body exterior (rust)					○	
Body hardware					○	
Body integrity					○	
Brakes					○	
Clutch					○	
Driveline					○	
Electrical system (chassis)					○	
Engine cooling					◒	
Engine mechanical					○	
Exhaust system					○	
Fuel system					○	
Ignition system					○	
Suspension					○	
Transmission (manual)					○	
Transmission (automatic)					○	
TROUBLE INDEX					○	
COST INDEX					●	

Volvo 760 (Turbodiesel)

TROUBLE SPOTS	'80	'81	'82	'83	'84	'85
Air-conditioning					○	Insufficient data
Body exterior (paint)					⊜	
Body exterior (rust)					○	
Body hardware					○	
Body integrity					⊜	
Brakes					○	
Clutch					○	
Driveline					○	
Electrical system (chassis)					○	
Engine cooling					○	
Engine mechanical					○	
Exhaust system					○	
Fuel system					○	
Ignition system					○	
Suspension					○	
Transmission (manual)					○	
Transmission (automatic)					○	
TROUBLE INDEX					⊜	
COST INDEX					*	

Personal products

Men's and women's business suits

Condensed from CONSUMER REPORTS, August 1986

Although the price of a designer-labeled suit can be awe-inspiring, price and prestige are not faultless guides to quality. We learned that much and more while testing 29 men's suits and 10 women's suits, selected from all sorts of sources—discount outlets, suburban malls, and Fifth Avenue haberdashers.

For the men, we purchased traditional gray suits with a single-breasted jacket and, when possible, unpleated trousers. Our men's suits ranged in price from $70 to $715. They included familiar, moderately priced brands like *McGregor* and *Botany 500*, established store brands like the *Brooksgate* sold by Brooks Brothers, and high-fashion designer labels like *Giorgio Armani*.

We bought women's suits in a wider range of styles, but we tried to avoid extremes in favor of the traditional gray business suit. Our women's suits ranged in price from $58 (for a $140 suit bought at a discount store) to $320. The selection included a mail-order *Ashley Brooke* suit from Spiegel, department-store labels like *Saville*, separates by *Jones New York* and others, and designer labels like *Harvé Benard*.

Our project team, three members of which served as models, soon developed a practiced eye for differences in fabric quality, tailoring, and fit. They received coaching on the topic of modern suit manufacturing and in the fine points of fashion at a seminar given by the faculty of New York City's Fashion Institute of Technology. Tailoring consultants joined our project team and examined the suits to judge the quality of materials, tailoring, and detailing. But we left judgments about appearance to an inexpert panel of CU staffers, augmented by one fashion expert who joined the panelists at an informal fashion show.

FABRICS. The fabric, by industry estimates, accounts for one-third to one-half of the cost of manufacturing a suit. By far the most commonly used fabrics in our suits were wool and wool/polyester blends.

There are two basic types of wool fabrics: woolens and worsteds. Woolens are generally soft, with some bulkiness and often a noticeable nap. Tweeds and flannels are typical examples. Worsteds are very smooth fabrics. Because they're more tightly woven than woolens, they hold their shape (and a crease) better. And because they're generally lighter in weight than woolens, they're better able to span the seasons, especially into the warmer months.

Modern polyesters such as Dacron and Trevira can be woven to mimic wool and to avoid most of the snags and sags of earlier synthetics. But polyester lacks the soft drape of wool and can feel rather lifeless. Some polyester is so difficult to mold and shape that manufacturers sometimes cut armholes and other key areas larger than normal to provide comfort at the expense of fit.

When blended, wool and polyester can compensate for each other's shortcomings. Polyester adds strength, minimizes stretching and shrinkage, and helps a lightweight suit maintain a pressed look longer. Wool compensates for polyester's lack of absorption, allowing a garment to "breathe" so that it feels warmer in winter and cooler in summer.

Fabric, however, is not to be confused with weave. Many fabrics, be they wool, polyester, or a wool/polyester blend, are a simple "plain weave," with interlacing horizontal and vertical threads. Using threads of different colors produces patterns, such as a pinstripe or a glen plaid. "Hopsacking" is a plain weave that has a coarse look.

"Twill weaves," such as serge or gabardine, form diagonal ridges in the cloth. The twill weave is obvious in "herringbone" patterns, in which different-colored threads are often used. Another common twill weave is "sharkskin," which has a step-pattern.

Our experts and tailoring consultants found a wide variation in fabric quality among the men's suits. The better fabrics tended to have more body, and yet were soft without being spongy. The expensive *Oxxford* and *Giorgio Armani* suits used high-quality fabrics. But so did the moderately priced *Austin Reed*, at $325, and the *Yves Saint Laurent*, at $179.

The most expensive women's suit, the *Brooks Brothers*, at $320, was made of high-quality worsted. Several more moderately priced women's suits, including the *Harvé Benard*, at $195, were of fabric almost as good.

WRINKLES. Wool tends to wrinkle fairly easily. Polyester doesn't wrinkle easily but, once wrinkled, tends to stay that way till pressed. In tests for wrinkle resistance, we folded each suit into a small bundle, loaded it down with a five-pound weight, and exposed it for 24 hours to steamy weather (90°F heat with 85 percent relative humidity) in our environmental chamber. Then we put the rumpled suits on hangers.

A day later, most were still sorry-looking. The big change occurred when we hung the suits back in the environmental chamber at the same high heat and humidity for six more hours. The wools became wearable. The polyesters and some of the blends still needed pressing. In real life, though, suits aren't likely to be exposed to such severe crumpling. Hanging a rumpled suit in the bathroom while you shower may be all that's needed to make it presentable between dry-cleanings.

TAILORING AND FINISH. Our tailoring consultants inspected the sewing, construction, and details of all the tested suits with particular emphasis on jackets, which require the most adroit tailoring. They carefully opened seams to view the inner parts. And they evaluated 20 specific construction features and tailoring details in each of the men's jackets, and 10 features and details in the women's jackets, which are usually more simply tailored.

The best-made men's suits were expensive ones—the *Oxxford* and, a notch below, the *Giorgio Armani*. But not far behind those models in overall construction quality were several more reasonably priced suits, including the *Bur-*

Text continued on page 129

Ratings of business suits

Listed by types; within types, listed in order of estimated quality. Suits judged equal in quality are bracketed and listed alphabetically. Some suits were altered to fit CU models. Prices are those paid by CU in New York City area; + indicates shipping is extra.

◍ ⊖ ○ ◒ ●

Better ⟷ Worse

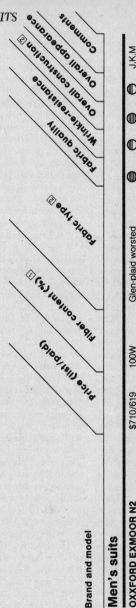

Brand and model	Price (list/paid)	Fiber content (%) [1]	Fabric type [2]	Fabric quality	Wrinkle-resistance	Overall construction [2]	Overall appearance	Comments
Men's suits								
OXXFORD EXMOOR N2	$710/619	100W	Glen-plaid worsted	◍	⊖	◍	⊖	J,K,M
GIORGIO ARMANI BOUTIQUE 45622	715	100W	Lightweight worsted	◍	⊖	⊖	⊖	B,Q
BURBERRYS STRATFORD	395	100W	Glen-plaid worsted	⊖	⊖	⊖	⊖	T,U
DAKS TYNE, A BEST BUY	300	100W	Slight-nap worsted	⊖	⊖	⊖	⊖	R,S,T,V
HART SCHAFFNER & MARX REGATTA I	395	45W, 55P	Medium-weight herringbone worsted	⊖	⊖	⊖	⊖	I
BILL BLASS ASCOT II	280	35W, 65P	Glen-plaid worsted	⊖	○	⊖	○	—
CLEEDS NOLAN 9619	375/235	100W	Flannel woolen	⊖	○	⊖	○	V
SAINT LAURIE CHAIRMAN	250/243	100W	Lightweight worsted	⊖	⊖	⊖	◒	J,R
AUSTIN REED MANCHESTER	325	100W	Medium-weight worsted	◍	⊖	○	⊖	I,V

BROOKS BROTHERS BROOKSGATE	280	100W	Flannel worsted	◍	◍	○	◍	A
PIERRE CARDIN VENDÔME 826	295	100W	Slight-nap worsted	◍	◍	○	◍	B
ADOLFO ALFRED 2000	350/199	100W	Flannel worsted	◍	◍	○	○	O
HARVÉ BENARD 732	300/219	100W	Flannel worsted	○	◍	○	◍	R
YVES SAINT LAURENT ST. HONORÉ 701	275/179	100W	Lightweight worsted	◍	○	○	○	B,P,Q
GIVENCHY	350/170	100W	Flannel worsted	○	◍	○	○	—
HALSTON KAVANAUGH	215/145	80W, 20S	Shadow-plaid worsted	◍	○	○	○	—
HARTMARX JOHNNY CARSON BRADLEY	229	45W, 55P	Medium-weight worsted	◍	○	○	○	I
CHRISTOPHER HAYES 663-CP	195/156	35W, 65P	Lightweight worsted	○	○	○	◒	J
CALVIN KLEIN 161	325/199	100W	Lightweight worsted	◍	◍	◒	○	L,P
EVAN-PICONE	245	100W	Herringbone worsted	◍	◍	◒	○	L
BOTANY 500 BENTLEY	275/169	35W, 65P	Flannel worsted	◍	○	◒	○	L
STAFFORD	180/135	45W, 55P	Lightweight worsted	◍	○	◒	○	L
JOHN ALEXANDER SUSSEX	210	45W, 55P	Lightweight worsted	○	○	◒	○	L
KUPPENHEIMER BRETT VI	140/100	35W, 65P	Lightweight worsted	○	○	◒	○	L
KUPPENHEIMER MARK VI	130/100	15W, 85P	Lightweight worsted	○	○	◒	○	L
KUPPENHEIMER BELMONT	160	100W	Lightweight worsted	○	○	◒	◒	L
HAGGAR MAGIC STRETCH	115	100P	Lightweight worsted	○	○	●	○	G,L,W
BLAIR PERSONAL CHOICE	70+	90P, 5N, 5R	Sharkskin-type	○	○	●	◒	L
MCGREGOR THE INTERNATIONAL COLLECTION	90	100P	Hopsacking	◒	◒	●	◒	H,L

[1] *Numbers indicate percentage of: W = wool; P = polyester; S = silk; N = nylon; R = rayon; O = other, as stated by manufacturer.*
[2] *As described by CU's consultants.*

Ratings continued on next page

Brand and model	Price (list/paid)	Fiber content (%) [1]	Fabric type [2]	Fabric quality	Wrinkle-resistance	Overall construction [2]	Overall appearance	Comments
Women's suits								
BROOKS BROTHERS 04-8507	320	100W	Plaid worsted	⬤	◓	⬤	◓	—
HARVÉ BENARD (JACKET: 54 402-3B; SKIRT: 54 114-3B), A BEST BUY	195	100W	Flannel woolen	◓	○	◓	○	—
ASHLEY BROOKE 1850 7160	99+	100W	Medium-weight tweed	○	⬤	○	○	F,I
JH COLLECTIBLES 04412 AND 04400	198	80W, 20P	Flannel woolen	◓	◓	○	○	E
JONES NEW YORK 60916	232	100W	Napped worsted	◓	◓	○	○	—
KIRKLAND HALL 2285	120	80W, 20P	Flannel woolen	○	◓	○	◓	E,F
LARRY LEVINE 75-331	195	100W	Plaid worsted	○	○	○	○	C
PEABODY HOUSE INTERNATIONAL 4479	140/58	100W	Flannel worsted	○	○	○	○	C,D,N
SASSON	130/100	40W, 55P, 5O	Napped woolen	○	○	○	○	F
SAVILLE 97027X	160	80W, 20P	Flannel woolen	○	○	○	○	—

[1] *Numbers indicate percentage of: W = wool; P = polyester; S = silk; N = nylon; R = rayon; O = other, as stated by manufacturer.*

[2] *As described by CU's consultants.*

FEATURES IN COMMON
All men's suits are single-breasted.
Except as noted, all men's suits: have 2-button front closure; have 1 center vent; have 2 rear pockets in trousers; are of year-round fabric weight.
Except as noted, all women's suits: are single-breasted; have jacket and skirt pockets; have slit or pleat in skirt; are year-round fabric weight.

KEY TO COMMENTS
A–3 jacket buttons.
B–No center vent in jacket; 1 rear pocket in trousers.
C–Double-breasted style.
D–No jacket pocket.
E–No skirt pocket.
F–No slit or pleat in skirt.
G–Washable.
H–Trousers are washable.
I–Fabric somewhat heavier than most.
J–More hand sewing than in most.
K–"Flower loop" behind and under lapel buttonhole.
L–Collar, lapel, and armhole construction judged of worse quality than that of most.
M–Pocket construction in jacket and trousers permits smoother fit than with most.
N–Open-pressed breast-pocket seam gives a clean, tailored appearance; has concealed skirt closure.
O–Extended facings inside jacket strengthen pocket and help jacket hold its shape.
P–Part of lining is fused, rather than sewn, at bottom of jacket.
Q–Lined trousers.
R–Trouser waistband permits expansion when wearer sits.
S–Waistband inserts keep trousers from slipping.
T–Adjustable waistband.
U–Waistband material and construction judged of better quality than most.
V–Trouser buttons for suspenders.
W–Edge on rear trouser pocket is fused, not sewn.

---

berrys, the *Daks*, and the *Hart Schaffner & Marx*.

We found less variation among the women's suits. Most of them were judged average in overall construction. The relatively expensive *Brooks Brothers* was the best made. The *Harvé Benard* was second best in that respect.

APPEARANCE. The three staff members to whom the suits had been fitted wore the suits day in and day out, forming their own opinions about what they liked. But they knew what they were wearing. To get an unbiased view, we arranged a fashion show—not when the suits were new, but after they had been worn, tested for wrinkle-resistance, and dry-cleaned three times.

The inexpert CU-staff panelists liked the looks of the *Daks* best among the men's suits. Other favorites: the *Hart Schaffner & Marx*, which drew praise for its excellent fit; the *Burberrys*, for its fabric, color, and fit; and the *Brooks Brothers Brooksgate*, for its color and fit.

Among the women's suits, the *Brooks Brothers* was favored by most panelists. One described it as "neat, clean, and polished." The *Kirkland Hall* was popular, too. It drew comment for its "clean lines" and "unfussy" collarless jacket.

By and large, the one fashion expert on the panel agreed with our lay panelists. But he liked the expensive men's *Oxxford* and *Armani* better than the others did. He remarked at the "very good drape" and "expensive look" of the *Oxxford*. He especially appreciated the fine fabric, lining, and detailing of the *Armani*. However, although we had removed the labels, he may have recognized the style of the *Armani*, a style that was too distinctively modern for some of the traditionalists on our judging panel.

RECOMMENDATIONS. The expensive men's *Oxxford* and *Giorgio Armani* suits measured up to our critical standards in nearly every way. But so did some suits that cost only half as much. The *Daks*, a Best Buy at $300, was above average in overall quality, and our fashion panelists applauded its appearance. Judged fully as good as the *Daks*, but more expensive, at $395, were the *Burberrys* and the *Hart Schaffner & Marx* suits.

The most expensive women's suit, at $320, the *Brooks Brothers*, scored higher than all the others. But also judged quite high in overall quality was the *Harvé Benard*, a Best Buy at $195.

We bought our suits in the fall of 1985, but, for all practical purposes, that shouldn't date them. Methods of manufacture don't change much from one year to the next. A good suit will last for years, and, if you choose a "classic" style, it should look good as long as it lasts.

Soft-sided luggage

Condensed from CONSUMER REPORTS, July 1985

Luggage manufacturers offer Pullman sizes that range from 24 to 32 inches long, as well as matching carry-on, overnight, and garment bags. Most of the soft-siders we tested for this project are 26 inches long. Shell fabrics include vinyl, regular nylon, tough Cordura nylon, cotton/linen, rayon, and canvas. Trim ranges from nylon to vinyl or leather. List prices run from $50 for a basic bag to more than $300 for a status model.

PROTECTION. The protectiveness of a piece of luggage depends largely on its framing. There are three categories: soft, partial-frame and full-frame. Soft cases are fine for stuffing in socks, shoes, and casual clothing. But they offer little protection for fragile items.

Only slightly more protective are partial-frame bags. Some of those have a stiff bottom panel and merely the ghost of a frame—springy wires encased in the bindings around their perimeter. Others have a narrow steel band around their middle that supports the handle. Like the soft bags, they leave it to the contents to expand them full width. But the contents are protected only at a few points.

As soft-siders go, bags with full-width framing give the best protection. They aren't necessarily stiff, however, nor is the full-frame effect necessarily caused by a full-frame. In some models, the frame is a band some six to eight inches wide protecting the full width of the bag. But in others, the frame is about two inches wide, with plastic inserts at the corners to hold the bag square (a design that can make the bag hard to close).

You can do a quick in-store check of a soft-sider's rigidity by pressing firmly, then releasing, the bag's top, sides, and corners. The less it yields and the faster it rebounds, the more protection it's likely to offer. You should be aware, though, that even the most rigid of the full-frame cases isn't firm enough to be stepped on or sat on.

CONVENIENCE. Most wheeled bags have two swiveling wheels at front and a fixed pair at the rear. They tend to trail you like a somewhat reluctant dog, pulling your arm straight behind you. Almost all wheeled bags are pulled by a leash 18 to 24 inches long.

For carrying purposes, bags have either one of two types of handle: top-mounted or side-attached. Top-mounted handles are single grips—sometimes a U-shaped piece of molded plastic, sometimes a single or doubled strap. Handles attached at the sides are twin looped straps, like those on a shopping bag, some with a small cover that snaps over the paired straps as cushioning. Try the handle to be sure it fits your hand and feels comfortable.

Text continued on page 133

Ratings of soft-sided luggage

Listed by types; within types, listed in order of estimated overall quality, based mainly on durability. Bracketed models were judged equal in quality and are listed in order of increasing price. Prices are list; + indicates plus shipping. Discounts are generally available. [D] indicates model was discontinued at original publication.

⊜ ⊖ ○ ◒ ●

Better ←——→ **Worse**

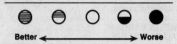

Brand and model	Price	Weight (lb.)	Volume (cu. ft.) [1]	Frame [2]	Shell material [3]	Impact resistance	Handle durability	Workmanship	Handle comfort	Packing	Pulling
Models with wheels											
SAMSONITE SERIES 2100	$ 80	$7\frac{3}{4}$	1.9	F	V	⊜	⊜	⊜	○	⊖	⊖
VENTURA SERIES 505026	125	$10\frac{1}{4}$	2.0	F	N	⊜	⊜	⊜	○	⊖	⊖
RICARDO OF BEVERLY HILLS BRENTWOOD COLL. 8326	130	$8\frac{1}{2}$	1.8	F	CL	⊜	⊜	⊖	○	⊖	○
SAMSONITE FREESTYLES 26 CARTWHEELS	130	$6\frac{1}{2}$	2.1	P	NC	⊜	⊜	⊜	○	○	○
HARTMANN 4200 SP26	215	$7\frac{1}{4}$	2.6	F	N	⊜	⊜	⊖	○	⊖	○
SEARS CAT. NO. 9006	60+	$7\frac{1}{2}$	1.8	F	V	⊖	⊜	⊖	○	⊖	○
AMERICAN TOURISTER 4826	85	$7\frac{3}{4}$	2.2	F	N	⊖	⊜	⊜	○	●	⊖
[D] SEWARD TRAVELWISE 308535	90	$7\frac{1}{4}$	1.8	F	A	⊖	⊜	⊖	○	◒	⊖
ATLANTIC GRASSHOPPER 2500-26	100	$7\frac{1}{2}$	2.3	F	N	⊖	⊜	⊖	◒	⊖	○
FRENCH 015	335	8	2.3	F	Ta	⊖	⊜	⊖	◒	⊖	○
PIERRE CARDIN TWEED 10026	115	6	1.8	F	Tw	○	⊜	○	○	●	◒
VENTURA PRESIDENTIAL W527A WHEEL-O-MATIC JUMBO PULLMAN	298	$11\frac{1}{4}$	2.2	F	Tw	○	⊖	⊖	⊖	⊖	⊖
CROWN OLYMPIAN 5626W	85	$6\frac{3}{4}$	1.8	F	N	◒	⊜	○	⊖	●	○
SASSON LE PRINT N775124	100	$7\frac{1}{2}$	2.0	F	N	◒	⊜	⊖	○	◒	◒
DIANE VON FURSTENBERG DUTY FREE 3926	95	$8\frac{1}{2}$	1.7	F	R	◒	⊜	●	○	◒	⊖

Ratings continued on next page

Ratings of soft-sided luggage continued

Brand and model	Price	Weight (lb.)	Volume (cu. ft.) [1]	Frame [2]	Shell material [3]	Impact resistance	Handle durability	Workmanship	Handle comfort	Packing	Pulling
AMELIA EARHART CIMARRON 1926	$ 90	$7\frac{3}{4}$	2.0	F	N	●	⊜	⊜	○	⊖	○
PEGASUS THE TAHOE COLLECTION 7728W	133	$7\frac{1}{4}$	2.4	F	NC	●	⊜	⊜	◒	⊖	⊖
VERDI SIMPATICO 626W26	100	$6\frac{1}{4}$	2.3	F	NC	○	◒	●	⊖	⊖	○
SKYWAY BALLISTIC 96426	133	$8\frac{1}{2}$	2.1	P	N	○	●	⊜	⊖	⊖	○
MONARCH HOLIDAY COLLECTION 13927	62	$6\frac{3}{4}$	1.9	F	N	○	●	●	⊖	⊖	○
Models without wheels											
[D] WINGS BUNK BAG COLLECTION 6526	140	5	1.7	P	NC	⊜	⊜	⊖	⊖	⊖	—
AMERICAN TOURISTER LEMANS 7426	105	$5\frac{1}{2}$	2.1	S	N	⊜	⊜	⊜	◒	○	—
JOHN WEITZ WAITLESS JW1680	90	$6\frac{1}{4}$	2.0	P	N	⊜	⊜	⊜	○	●	—
LONDON FOG 1103	110	$4\frac{1}{2}$	1.7	P	N	⊜	⊜	⊖	◒	○	—
OLEG CASSINI ELITE 040026	88	5	1.7	P	N	⊜	⊜	⊖	◒	◒	—
LARK PERMAMATIC SERIES 150 LPM	198	$7\frac{1}{4}$	2.0	P	N	⊖	⊜	⊖	⊖	⊖	—
AMELIA EARHART NONSTOP 926	80	$4\frac{1}{4}$	1.8	P	N	⊖	⊜	○	⊖	◒	—
YORK GATEWAY FORMULA ONE 4526	110	$4\frac{1}{2}$	2.1	P	N	○	⊜	⊖	○	◒	—
J.C. PENNEY NOMADS 26″	50	6	2.4	F	N	○	⊜	⊖	○	●	—
ANDIAMO LUGGAGE AP28	119	$3\frac{1}{4}$	2.2	S	NC	◒	○	⊜	●	○	—
VERDI CANNES 4827	65	$3\frac{1}{2}$	2.0	P	N	○	◒	⊖	◒	◒	—

[1] *Usable space, estimated with pockets empty.*

[2] *F = full; P = partial; S = soft.*

[3] *V = vinyl; N = nylon; CL = cotton/linen; NC = nylon Cordura; A = acrylic; Ta = tapestry pattern on canvas; R = rayon;*
Tw = tweed of olefin fiber **(Ventura Presidential)** or unspecified fiber **(Pierre Cardin 10026).**

Most models aren't overly helpful with organizing the major part of packing. They provide only one large compartment. But to satisfy special packing needs, many bags have outside and inside pockets. Outside pockets can be as wide and high as the entire suitcase or small enough to hold only a few airline tickets. A large inside pocket in the lid may help protect shirts and the like from wrinkles. Small inside pouches are handy for toiletries and such.

Locks serve mainly to keep a bag from opening accidentally as it's carried; they provide scarcely more than token security.

RECOMMENDATIONS. There's little price advantage in buying one of the wheelless models. Still, if you travel a lot by car, you may not want wheels on your luggage at all. Their somewhat hostile mountings may interfere with or damage other baggage in a tightly packed automobile trunk.

Hotel and motel chains

Condensed from CONSUMER REPORTS, July 1986

For this, our first report on hotel chains, we asked CONSUMER REPORTS subscribers to tell us in detail about the hotels and motels they had recently visited. (Any distinction there might once have been between hotels and motels has become blurred, so the word "hotel" in this report encompasses both meanings.) In our request, we focused on information about chain-affiliated hotels, since chains control more than three out of every five of the nation's guest rooms. In all, more than 150,000 readers obliged us by describing some 230,000 hotel stays.

As we pored over the data, we grew aware that expensive hotels generally were given better marks than cheaper hotels. That, we supposed, was as it should be, but it wasn't very fair or revealing for purposes of comparison. So we decided to group hotels by the rates our survey respondents had paid. We've sorted chains into three price tiers: under $40 a night; between $40 and $79; and $80 or more. Of the 24 chains we rated, 18 didn't fit neatly into a single price tier. We grouped visits to those chains by price and rated the chains twice, in each instance against competitors comparable in rates.

SATISFACTION. We asked our respondents to grade each hotel where they stayed according to nine factors: convenience of location, room comfort, climate control, staff helpfulness and efficiency, food quality and food value (if restaurant service was part of the hotel operation), swimming facilities (presence or absence and condition of), noise level, and overall value.

Also, we asked for an index of overall satisfaction on a 100-point scale. If everyone surveyed had been "completely satisfied" with the hotels of a given chain, that chain would have scored a perfect 100; had everyone been "very dissatisfied," the chain would have scored zero.

Holiday Corporation's *Embassy Suites* division, an upscale cousin to *Holiday Inn*, was the top-rated chain, leading among both mid-priced and higher-priced accommodations. It features

Text continued on page 137

Ratings of hotel and motel chains

Listed in groups by nightly room rates paid by survey respondents; within groups, listed in order of overall satisfaction expressed in responses to CU's 1985 Annual Questionnaire. Differences of fewer than 4 or 5 points on the satisfaction index were judged not very significant. A dash indicates insufficient data on which to base a judgment.

Hotel chain	Satisfaction index	Convenience of location	Room comfort [1]	Climate control [2]	Staff [3]	Food quality	Food value	Swimming facilities	Noise level	Value
Under $40										
LA QUINTA	77	⊖	○	⊖	⊖	○	⊖	○	○	⊜
RED ROOF INNS	75	⊖	⊖	⊖	⊖	–	–	●	⊖	⊜
SUPER 8	70	⊖	⊖	⊖	⊖	–	–	●	◒	⊖
COMFORT INNS	69	◒	○	○	○	–	–	–	○	⊖
HOWARD JOHNSON'S	69	○	○	◒	○	◒	○	○	○	⊖
BEST WESTERN	69	○	○	○	○	○	⊖	○	○	⊖
RODEWAY INNS	67	◒	◒	○	○	–	–	–	◒	⊖
FRIENDSHIP INNS	67	○	◒	○	○	–	–	–	◒	⊖
DAYS INNS	67	○	◒	◒	◒	●	○	○	◒	⊖
QUALITY INNS	65	◒	◒	◒	◒	○	○	○	◒	○
RAMADA INNS/HOTELS	64	◒	◒	◒	◒	◒	○	○	◒	○
ECONO LODGE	63	◒	◒	◒	◒	–	–	●	◒	○
TRAVELODGE	62	●	●	●	◒	–	–	●	◒	○
MOTEL 6	62	◒	●	●	●	–	–	◒	●	⊖
$40 to $79										
EMBASSY SUITES [4]	86	⊖	⊜	⊜	⊜	⊖	⊜	⊜	⊖	⊜
STOUFFER	80	⊖	⊜	⊜	⊜	⊜	○	–	⊜	⊖
RED LION INNS	80	⊖	⊖	⊖	⊖	⊜	⊖	○	⊖	○
MARRIOTT	79	⊜	⊖	⊜	⊜	⊜	○	⊜	⊖	⊖
WESTIN	79	⊜	⊖	⊖	⊖	⊜	○	⊖	⊜	⊖
HYATT	79	⊖	⊖	⊜	⊖	⊜	○	○	⊜	⊖

◍ ⊖ ○ ◒ ●

Better ←——→ **Worse**

Hotel chain	**Satisfaction index**	**Convenience of location**	**Room comfort** [1]	**Climate control** [2]	**Staff** [3]	**Food quality**	**Food value**	**Swimming facilities**	**Noise level**	**Value**
HOLIDAY INN CROWNE PLAZA	77	⊖	⊖	⊖	⊖	○	○	–	⊖	○
LA QUINTA	72	○	○	○	○	○	⊖	○	○	○
HILTON	70	○	○	○	○	○	◒	○	○	○
SHERATON	69	○	○	○	○	○	◒	○	○	○
BEST WESTERN	67	○	○	◒	○	○	○	○	◒	◒
COMFORT INNS	66	●	◒	○	●	–	–	–	◒	◒
HOWARD JOHNSON'S	65	○	○	◒	◒	◒	◒	○	○	◒
RODEWAY INNS	64	◒	◒	◒	◒	–	–	–	◒	◒
HOLIDAY INN	64	◒	◒	◒	◒	◒	◒	○	◒	●
QUALITY INNS	63	◒	◒	◒	◒	◒	○	◒	◒	◒
DAYS INNS	62	◒	◒	◒	●	●	◒	◒	◒	◒
RAMADA INNS/HOTELS	61	●	◒	◒	●	◒	◒	○	◒	●
ECONO LODGE	60	●	●	◒	●	–	–	–	◒	◒
TRAVELODGE	60	◒	◒	◒	◒	◒	◒	●	●	●
$80 and up										
EMBASSY SUITES [4]	85	⊖	◍	◍	◍	–	–	–	⊖	⊖
WESTIN	80	◍	◍	◍	◍	◍	○	⊖	◍	◒
HOLIDAY INN CROWNE PLAZA	79	⊖	◍	⊖	⊖	–	–	–	◍	◒
STOUFFER	79	⊖	⊖	⊖	◍	◍	○	–	◍	◒
HYATT	78	◍	⊖	◍	⊖	◍	○	⊖	⊖	◒
MARRIOTT	77	◍	⊖	⊖	⊖	⊖	○	◍	⊖	◒
SHERATON	70	○	○	○	○	○	◒	⊖	○	●
HILTON	68	⊖	○	○	○	○	●	⊖	○	●

[1] *In this judgment category, respondents were asked to consider the cleanliness, size, attractiveness, and general comfort of the room, as well as the comfort of the bed.*

[2] *Heating during cold weather and air-conditioning during warm weather.*

[3] *Respondents were asked to judge the staff in terms of helpfulness and efficiency.*

[4] *Chain was originally named* **Granada Royale.**

Table of Reservation Data

Hotel chain	Median room rate	Price tiers [1]	Geographical breakdown [2]	Siting [3]	Phone
BEST WESTERN	$40	Low/Mid	**NC**,SC,S,**W**	**U,S**,H,R	800-528-1234
COMFORT INNS	35	Low/Mid	SC,**S,W**	**U,S,H**,R	800-228-5150
DAYS INNS	35	Low/Mid	NC,SC,**S**	**U,S,H**,R	800-325-2525 [4]
ECONO LODGE	32	Low/Mid	NE,**S**	U,**S,H**,R	800-446-6900
EMBASSY SUITES	70	Mid/High	**NC,SC,W**	**U,S**	800-362-2779
FRIENDSHIP INNS	30	Low	**NC**,SC,**W**	**U,S**,H,R	800-453-4511
HILTON	75	Mid/High	NE,NC,SC,**S,W**	**U,S**,R	800-445-8667
HOLIDAY INN	50	Mid	NE,**NC**,SC,**S**,W	**U,S**,H,R	800-465-4329
HOLIDAY INN CROWNE PLAZA	75	Mid/High	**SC,S,W**	**U,S**	800-465-4329
HOWARD JOHNSON'S	46	Low/Mid	**NE**,NC,**S**	**U,S,H**,R	800-654-2000
HYATT	85	Mid/High	NE,**NC**,SC,**S,W**	**U**,S,R	800-228-9000 [5]
LA QUINTA	38	Low/Mid	NC,**SC**,S,W	**U,S**,H	800-531-5900
MARRIOTT	80	Mid/High	**NE**,NC,SC,**S,W**	**U**,S,R	800-228-9290
MOTEL 6	23	Low	NC,SC,**W**	**U,S,H**	[6]
QUALITY INNS	40	Low/Mid	NE,NC,SC,**S**,W	**U,S,H**,R	800-228-5151
RAMADA INNS/HOTELS	45	Low/Mid	NE,**NC**,SC,**S**,W	**U,S**,H	800-272-6232
RED LION INNS	55	Mid	**W**	**U,S**	800-547-8010
RED ROOF INNS	30	Low	**NE,NC,S**	**U,S,H**	800-848-7878
RODEWAY INNS	40	Low/Mid	NC,**SC**,S,**W**	**U,S**,H,R	800-228-2000 [7]
SHERATON	70	Mid/High	**NE**,NC,SC,**S,W**	**U,S**,R	800-325-3535
STOUFFER	80	Mid/High	**NE,NC,S**,W	U,S,R	800-468-3571
SUPER 8	28	Low	**NC,W**	U,**S,H**	800-843-1991
TRAVELODGE	40	Low/Mid	NE,NC,S,**W**	**U,S**,H,R	800-255-3050
WESTIN	90	Mid/High	NE,**NC**,SC,**W**	**U**	800-228-3000

[1] *Because room rates varied widely within many chains, the Ratings classify chains in three price tiers that are reflected here: Low (under $40 a night), Mid ($40 to $79), and High ($80 and up). Chains that bridged two price tiers were rated in both, against similarly priced competitors.*

[2] *NE = northeast; NC = north central; SC = south central; S = south; W = west. All regions thus abbreviated indicate that at least 10% of survey responses for a given chain came from that region; regions abbreviated in bold face type indicate that at least 20% of responses for the chain came from that region.*

[3] *U = site in major urban center; S = smaller-city or suburban site; H = highway site; R =*

two-room suites instead of individual rooms. (The *Embassy Suites* name is new. The chain was called *Granada Royale* during the time our respondents actually paid their overnight visits, and it was so listed on our survey. Holiday acquired Granada in 1984, changed the name, and has since added more hotels to the chain.)

Among the low-priced hotels (although here "motels" seems the *mot juste*), two chains—*La Quinta Motor Inns* and *Red Roof Inns*—achieved superior scores, both in the mid-70's. Both were judged significantly better than any others in the economy tier. Mid-priced hotels showed the widest range in satisfaction, a spread of more than 25 points between the top-rated *Embassy Suites* and the low-rated *Econo Lodge* and *TraveLodge*.

Comparing satisfaction indexes across price-tier lines, we noted a couple of surprises. The two leading low-priced chains surpassed *Hilton's* and *Sheraton's* scores, and a few other budget chains roughly equaled them. One mid-priced chain, *Red Lion Inns*, was judged as good as or better than every higher-priced hotel except *Embassy Suites*. We did consider the possibility that comparisons across price tiers might be less meaningful than comparisons within tiers, since people may expect less from less-expensive hotels and therefore be satisfied with less.

Nearly all the higher-priced chains quite evidently suffered somewhat in our respondents' value judgments. The real values emerged chiefly among the economy brand of lodgings. Ten of the low-priced chains received above-average grades for value. *La Quinta* and *Red Roof Inns* received the highest scores in that regard.

COMPLAINTS. On more than four out of five of their trips, respondents had made reservations. But about 6 percent reported suffering reservation foul-ups, such as overbooking. These problems tended to be concentrated in the higher-priced hotels. At *Hilton* and *Sheraton*, 8 percent of the travelers holding reservations reported that they had encountered difficulties.

Some travelers complained that long lines at the front desk delayed their checking out. That didn't happen often at budget chain hotels. But about 5 percent of respondents were irritated by delays at the checkout desks of higher-priced *Hiltons* and *Sheratons*.

More than 7 percent of the respondents encountered problems with their bills. The most commonly reported problem was an unfair or excessive charge for using the phone. Some hotels bill guests for calling toll-free numbers or for placing credit-card calls. Others charge for uncompleted calls. And most tack on sizable surcharges to normal phone rates.

We also learned of a problem involving credit cards. When you register, some hotels automatically freeze part of your card's credit line as a deposit against your bill. But when you leave, the desk clerk may neglect to notify the card company to free any unused credit

---

resort site. As above, abbreviations indicate at least a 10% response for a given chain; abbreviations in bold face type indicate at least a 20% response for the chain.

4 *In Georgia, call Days Inn at 800-320-2000.*

5 *In Nebraska, call Hyatt at 800-228-9001.*

6 *No toll-free line, but chain will send, on request, a free directory of their units. Write to Motel 6, 51 Hitchcock Way, Santa Barbara, Calif. 93105.*

7 *In Alaska and Nebraska, call Rodeway collect at 402-496-0101.*

(in the event, for instance, that you decide to pay in cash). If that happens often, you could find your credit line exhausted. So before you check out, make sure that the hotel clerk calls to release any unused holds on your card.

RECOMMENDATIONS. The first step in figuring out where to stay is to decide just what you want in hotel or motel accommodations. Are you looking for a full-service hotel with all the trimmings? Or will you be content with few amenities. And how much do you want to spend for a room?

After you've settled those questions, you might turn to the Ratings. Among the budget chains listed there, *La Quinta* and *Red Roof Inns* were the leaders. Both were judged excellent values. *Embassy Suites* led among the mid-priced and high-priced hotels—not only in satisfaction but, perhaps more impressively, in value as well.

Unfortunately, however, there's one more, far-from-foolproof step in this process of selection—to find out whether a unit of the hotel chain that you favor for overnight stays is on or close to your planned route. Many of the better-known chains in the Ratings are represented fairly widely on a national scale. But some tend to be regional, or at least tend to be distributed more densely in some areas than in others. Almost all are represented in urban areas, but some aren't often sited along major highways.

As an aid in preparing for trips, you may want to consult the table on page 136. It lists the median room rates paid by survey respondents for each rated chain; it gives an idea of each chain's geographical coverage and siting preferences; and, where possible, it gives the appropriate toll-free number to call for reservations.

Moving companies

Condensed from CONSUMER REPORTS, September 1986

According to the Interstate Commerce Commission, movers are on time for 98 percent of their pickups and 96 percent of their deliveries. Only 4 percent of all interstate moves provoke damage claims of more that $100, claimed the ICC in performance reports for the year 1985.

Ask 20,000 people who've recently moved, however, and a different picture emerges. Some 17 percent of the subscribers who responded to our 1985 Annual Questionnaire, describing the moves they had made in the previous three years, were dissatisfied with the way things had turned out. The van had arrived late for pickup on 8 percent of their moves and late for delivery on 15 percent of their moves. They had run about a fifty-fifty chance of seeing one or more of their possessions damaged during the move, with the median damage estimated at about $200.

ESTIMATES. It's possible to save money by getting multiple estimates before selecting a mover. But fewer than 40 percent of the people who move solicit even a single estimate, according to one national study. CU subscribers were more careful; two-thirds got at least one estimate, and almost a half said that they had collected two estimates or more.

There are three types of estimate—binding, nonbinding, and an interesting combination of the two. With a binding estimate, the estimated cost is final; the mover won't even weigh your things on

Text continued on page 140

Ratings of moving companies

Listed in order of overall satisfaction of surveyed respondents who had experienced moves during the period from 1982 to the beginning of 1985, based on responses to CU's 1985 Annual Questionnaire. Differences between closely ranked companies were judged not very significant. But differences of 6 points or more on the Satisfaction Index were judged meaningful.

⊜	⊖	○	◒	●
Better ←				→ **Worse**

Moving company	Satisfaction index	Number of moves	Accuracy of estimate [1]	On time pick-up/delivery	Frequency of damage claims [2]	Care in handling	Average number of days for claims settlement [3]	Comments
WHEATON	80	507	○	○	⊖	⊖	10.8	A,B,D
UNITED	79	3265	○	○	○	○	12	F
ALLIED	78	4105	⊖	○	○	○	17	—
NORTH AMERICAN	78	3540	○	○	○	○	12	—
ATLAS	77	1225	◒	○	○	○	14.6	G
AERO MAYFLOWER	77	3052	○	○	○	○	13.9	—
BEKINS [4]	77	2625	⊜	○	○	○	13	—
AMERICAN RED BALL	76	292	○	○	○	○	19	G
GLOBAL	74	663	○	○	○	◒	13.5	—
LYON	73	224	○	○	○	○	17	—
BURNHAM	71	211	[5]	○	●	●	9.1	C,E,G

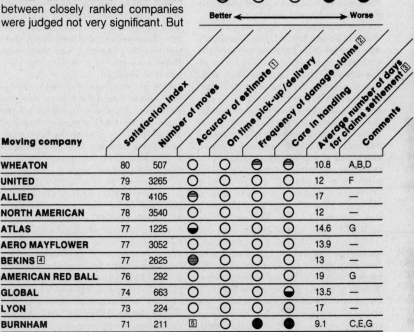

[1] *Based on the experience of respondents with prior written estimates.*

[2] *Based on number of claims, adjusted for distance and amount of furniture moved.*

[3] *Based on information from performance reports, dealing with claims of more than $100, prepared by the companies and submitted to the Interstate Commerce Commission.*

[4] ***Bekins** and **Neptune** merged in early 1985. Data is for **Bekins** only; data is insufficient to rate **Neptune.***

[5] Insufficient data.

KEY TO COMMENTS

A-Fewer unexpected or unreasonable charges than average.
B-Easier to contact than average.
C-Drivers, helpers, and sales representatives less courteous than average.
D-Drivers, helpers more helpful than average.
E-Drivers and helpers less helpful than average.
F-Sales representatives more informative than average.
G-Sales representatives less informative than average.

moving day. (ICC regulations allow movers to charge for binding estimates, but in practice most don't.) Nonbinding estimates tend to be lower, but they also have a way of erring on the low side. More than a fourth of our survey respondents who had gotten written, nonbinding estimates paid more than the estimate; a tenth of the respondents paid at least 10 percent extra.

Many movers also offer an estimate that binds them but not you: The mover issues a binding estimate but weighs your things on moving day anyway. If the actual weight is more than estimated, you pay only the estimated rate. If the weight is less than estimated, you pay only for the actual weight. Among the companies we rated, *Lyon* is the only one that doesn't offer that kind of estimate. But others may not tell you about that option unless you ask.

SEEDS OF DISSATISFACTION. We asked subscribers about 22 of the largest interstate van lines, which in total handle more than 90 percent of all interstate moves. In the Ratings, we've included only those companies for which we had at least 200 responses, narrowing the field to 11 companies. No company earned completely satisfactory marks. The top-rated mover, *Wheaton*, received a score of 80 on a 100-point "Satisfaction Index." (A score of 100 would mean that every respondent was "very satisfied," while a score of zero would mean that every respondent was "very dissatisfied.")

Although companies adjacent in the Ratings were quite close in overall satisfaction, the difference between the top and bottom of the list is meaningful, as is any difference of six points or more on the Satisfaction Index. Loss or damage contributed more to dissatisfaction than any other factor.

Respondents moved by *Wheaton* reported the least loss or damage, whereas *Burnham* clients told us that they suffered what amounted to much more loss or damage than average. Some 16 percent of our respondents complained of driver and helper carelessness. Drivers and helpers with *Wheaton* were the only ones rated more careful than average; those with *Global* were rated more careless than average; and those with *Burnham* were rated much more careless than average.

Our respondents also reported annoyance at final bills higher than the estimates. *Atlas* was found to be the worst at providing accurate estimates, and *Bekins* proved to be the best, much better than average. One reason *Bekins* scored so well in that respect could be that it issues more binding estimates—on almost 60 percent of its shipments, according to ICC figures—than other companies.

RECOMMENDATIONS. Although our survey may not provide hard-and-fast answers about which interstate movers are truly good, it does offer some reasonable basis for figuring which movers are more likely than others to cause you grief. Our respondents' comments were littered with negative notes. In that regard, incidentally, the ICC requires interstate movers to give clients the ICC pamphlet "Your Rights and Responsibilities When You Move" as well as a copy of the company's annual performance record. Despite the requirement, more than 25 percent of our respondents who moved across state lines said they never received any of that information.

Can't find it?

The index on page 388 lists all reports in this issue both alphabetically and by subject.

Innerspring mattress sets

Condensed from CONSUMER REPORTS, March 1986

An innerspring mattress consists of coiled metal springs sandwiched between layers of cushioning and sewn into a fabric cover known as ticking. The cushioning interposes a layer of yielding softness over the springs' sterner resiliency.

A foundation works in combination with its mated mattress. A box-spring foundation also has coil springs, or a version of them called torsion bars, on a wooden frame. Some other foundations are simply slabs of polyurethane foam secured to a wood frame. A few have steel components instead of wood slats.

We tested twin-sized mattresses and foundations for this report, but our durability judgments and our firmness and comfort descriptions should apply generally to their full-, queen-, and king-sized brandmates. Wider mattress sets, as a rule, are made with the same coil springs and other materials, though sometimes with additional strengthening features to counter the tendency of two sleepers to roll toward the middle.

DURABILITY. In matters of firmness and conformity to the body, the elements of personal comfort that count the most, mattress buyers must be the final arbiters. You want a mattress that feels comfortable, to be sure. But more than that, you want a mattress that retains its original good feel for a long time.

To explore that important matter of durability, we engaged the services of our mattress-tester, a machine that's equipped with a ram shaped like human buttocks. We set the machine to deliver 100,000 controlled strokes to the center of each mattress set, where a sleeper's weight is concentrated. Then we repositioned the set so that the machine could deliver 25,000 strokes to the edge, where a person might sit.

Only six of the 32 tested sets defiantly endured the abuse, suffering no structural damage and showing only minor changes in firmness. They make up our top Ratings group. The next 15 models suffered greater changes in their original firmness. And the 11 mattresses in the lowest Ratings group showed structural damage.

Many of the low-rated models were left with broken coils. Three suffered severe damage to their edges; the *Kingsdowns* helical wires (which keep the coil springs connected) broke at the edge; a torsion bar in the foundation of the *Penney 7141* failed; and the knotted end-coils of the *Sears-O-Pedic Luxury II* snapped.

COMFORT. At best, labeled descriptions of firmness—"extra," "super," "ultra," and so on—are helpful only in comparing models within a brand line, since different makers measure firmness in different ways. We tried to make some sense out of that confusion by running the mattress sets through an industry firmness test and then comparing the results with the subjective impressions of a panel of staffers. In the measured firmness test, we applied a load to the center of a mattress and measured the depression it made. The less the depression, the firmer it was judged.

Our panel of staffers had to judge firmness in much the same way consumers do while shopping. The panelists, however, were first given three benchmarks by which to judge firmness—the firmest mattress, the softest, and one of intermediate firmness, as judged in the other tests. In nearly every case, the

Text continued on page 145

Ratings of innerspring mattress sets

Listed by groups in order of estimated durability; within groups, listed in order of increasing price. Ratings apply to twin sets, but all the rated models are available in full, queen, and king sizes. Prices are list for twin sets; + indicates that shipping is extra. Substantial discounts are usually available in this product area. [D] indicates model was discontinued at original publication.

Brand and model	Price (set)	Mattress weight (lb.)	Foundation weight (lb.)	Mattress height at border (in.)	Center firmness [1]	Edge firmness [1]	Conformity [2]	Ticking [3]	Comments
■ *The following models sustained no structural damage in our tests and showed only minor changes in support firmness.*									
SIMMONS BEAUTYREST ROYALTY	$420	51	40	7	3	1	4	D	A,E,G,J,K
ETHAN ALLAN EXQUISITE	439	37	40	$5\frac{3}{4}$	2	1	3	D	B,D,G,K
BASSETT DREAMMAKER ULTIMA	440	56	40	7	2	2	2	D	B,J
RESTONIC VITALITY SUP-R-POSTURE	500	45	35	$6\frac{1}{2}$	5	5	3	D	A,F,G,J
SEARS-O-PEDIC IMPERIAL II CAT. NO. 73272	760+	46	44	$7\frac{1}{4}$	3	1	4	K	A,E,G,H,I,J,K
SEARS-O-PEDIC IMPERIAL ELITE CAT. NO. 73582	800+	45	43	7	1	1	3	D	A,E,G,H,J,K
■ *The following models sustained no structural damage in our tests but showed slightly greater changes in support firmness than those preceding.*									
SPRINGWALL CHIROPRACTIC	299	46	36	8	3	4	2	D	B,J,K
AIRELOOM GOODLIFE	380	59	51	$6\frac{1}{2}$	2	3	2	D	B,C,G,J,K
SERTA PERFECT SLEEPER AVANTI	400	38	39	$6\frac{3}{4}$	4	4	2	D	B,E,G,K
KING KOIL SPINAL GUARD	450	38	41	7	4	3	3	P	G,H,I,J
STEARNS & FOSTER REGENCY CLASSIC	460	47	39	$6\frac{1}{4}$	1	2	3	K	B,D,I,K

SIMMONS BEAUTYREST MONARCH	480	58	42	7¼	4	2	3	D	G,J,K
GOLD BOND SACRO-SUPPORT DELUXE	500	58	46	7	4	4	1	D	J
SERTA PERFECT SLEEPER MASTERPIECE	500	39	38	7¼	3	2	3	K	G,I,K
THER-A-PEDIC MEDI-COIL DELUXE	560	47	43	7¼	3	3	3	D	J,K
KING KOIL POSTUREBOND SPINE CARE	600	46	44	7½	4	3	4	D	G,J
[D] **J.C. PENNEY CAT. NO. 7224 (SEALY POSTUREPEDIC STERLING 300)**	640+	58	41	7½	3	4	2	D	J,K
SPRING AIR BACKSUPPORTER MAJESTIC	699	55	41	7¾	3	3	2	D	J,K
KING KOIL POSTUREBOND INTERNATIONAL	700	46	42	7¾	3	3	5	K	A,G,J
RESTONIC ORTHOTONIC KEEPSAKE	900	56	43	8	3	3	4	D	D,J,K
■ *The following model sustained no structural damage, but showed greater change in support firmness than those preceding*									
RESTONIC ORTHOTONIC STERLING	700	61	39	7¾	3	4	3	D	E,J,K
■ *The following sustained structural damage in our tests. They showed same range of changes in support firmness as second Ratings group.*									
SERTAPEDIC LUXURY	240	38	36	6¾	2	2	2	D	G
SIMMONS MAXIPEDIC DELUXE	260	50	41	7¼	3	3	2	D	G,J,K
J.C. PENNEY CAT. NO. 7141 (SEALY SLUMBER GUARD)	360+	49	31	6¾	2	3	2	D	D,J,L
SEARS-O-PEDIC LUXURY II CAT. NO. 73232	400+	41	36	6¾	2	1	2	D	B,G,H,J
SPRING AIR POSTURE COMFORT	459	38	36	7	4	4	3	D	A,J

[1] *Scale runs from 5 (most firm) to 1 (least firm).*

[2] *Scale runs from 5 (most conforming) to 1 (least conforming).*

[3] *D = damask; K = knit; P = plain weave.*

Ratings continued on next page

Ratings of innerspring mattress sets continued

Brand and model	Price (set)	Mattress weight (lb.)	Foundation weight (lb.)	Mattress height at border (in.)	Center firmness [1]	Edge firmness [1]	Conformity [2]	Ticking [3]	Comments
KINGSDOWN SLEEPING BEAUTY ORTHOPEDIC	$560	49	40	6½	3	2	2	P	G,H,I,J,K
SEARS-O-PEDIC DREAM VELVET II CAT. NO. 73242	560+	49	40	6½	2	3	3	D	B,G,H,J,K
SPRING AIR SPRING-O-PEDIC SUPREME	599	51	34	8	3	4	4	K	I,J
STEARNS & FOSTER CORRECT COMFORT DYNASTY PL. ULT. FIRM	680	51	41	6¼	4	4	2	D	E,K
SEALY POSTUREPEDIC STRATHMORE	720	61	41	7¼	3	4	3	D	J,K
MONTGOMERY WARD 470/1 (SEALY POSTUREPEDIC CLASSIC 300)	720	61	46	7¼	4	3	3	D	D,J,K

[1] *Scale runs from 5 (most firm) to 1 (least firm).*

[2] *Scale runs from 5 (most conforming) to 1 (least conforming).*

[3] *D = damask; K = knit; P = plain weave.*

FEATURES IN COMMON

Except as noted, all: had a firmness judged average to the touch; retained a constant level of firmness for light and heavy people alike; and lacked handles.

KEY TO COMMENTS

A–Somewhat firmer to the touch than most.
B–Somewhat softer to the touch than most.
C–Set became firmer with heavier weights.
D–Set became slightly firmer with heavier weights.
E–Set became slightly less firm with heavier weights.
F–Mattress made rustling noise when testers moved on it.
G–Foundation has nonslip material on top to prevent mattress from slipping.
H–Resisted spilled liquids better than others.
I–Ticking dye transferred slightly in rubbing.
J–Foundation has corner guards that help prevent wear.
K–Mattress has handles.
L–According to **J.C. Penney,** this model has been replaced by **Cat. No. 1110 (Sealy Posturepedic Slumber Guard Superba),** $380+, which has different ticking but is otherwise the same.

firmness they perceived paralleled our findings in the measured firmness test.

Note that, as some of the Ratings comments suggest, the firmness of a bed can vary with the weight of the sleeper. As heavier weights were applied during our firmness test, six mattress sets became progressively firmer; greater weights didn't produce correspondingly deeper depressions. On the other hand, six other sets "lost" firmness; greater weights made disproportionately deeper depressions. Those effects, which showed up in both firm and not-so-firm sets, will be of most relevance to heavyweight sleepers.

We also ran a firmness test along the edges of the mattress sets. About a third of the sets showed less firmness at the edges than at the center.

To judge conformity, we measured the independent action of different sections of the mattresses. We placed weighted boards about two feet apart on each set and observed the change in the area between them. If that area showed relatively little deflection, the mattress set in question was judged highly conforming.

RECOMMENDATIONS. The smartest way to start shopping for a mattress set is to try to make yourself as comfortable as possible in the store. You really do have to lie down on model after model to find out what level of firmness and conformity is right for you. If at all possible, lie down first on the six sets in the top Ratings group. Especially if they're to be used a lot, they should last the longest and retain the better part of their original firmness.

But the superior durability of the top-rated sets takes on less significance if they're for a relatively lightweight sleeper or for use in a guest room. Under those circumstances, mattress sets in the second group should also retain most of their original firmness for a long time.

Mattress sets seem to be always "on sale," so look for ads that show a substantial markdown. Try also to get a meaningful warranty from the store or the maker.

Child safety gates

Condensed from CONSUMER REPORTS, March 1986

The old accordion-style child safety gates, with large diamond- and V-shaped openings, were head-trappers and potentially lethal stranglers. They're no longer being made (although samples may still linger in stock in some stores). Most current gates have straight edges and either a flexible mesh screen, plastic grids, or vertical slats. And those accordion-style gates that are now being made have been redesigned in the interests of safety.

The 15 gate models that we tested are mainly of two kinds. Some are meant to be mounted permanently in a doorway, in a hall, or on a stair landing; they swing or slide open. Others are portable, made to be set up and removed quickly. All adjust for openings of varying widths.

SAFETY. A well-designed gate will block a child's movement out of a room or down the stairs. We tested each gate to find out how well it could resist various escape strategies.

The permanent gates, most of which are about two feet high, have a latch that's accessible to a child who stands

Text continued on page 147

Ratings of child safety gates

Listed by types; within types, except as noted, listed in order of estimated overall quality. Models judged equal are bracketed and listed alphabetically. Except where separated by heavy lines, closely ranked models differed little in quality. Prices are list.

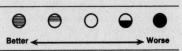

⊜ ⊖ ○ ◒ ●

Better ⟷ **Worse**

Brand and model	Price	Resistance to: Climbing	Steady push	Sudden impact	Quality of construction	Comments
Permanent models						
GERRY 505	$ 9	◒	⊜	⊜	⊖	*F,I,O,T*
NU-LINE 1048A	14	⊜	⊜	⊜	○	*D,U,Y,DD,EE*
PARIS 2448	20	⊜	⊖	⊖	⊖	*D,X,DD*
WORLDSBEST 46D	11	⊜	⊜	○	●	*D,O*
WORLDSBEST 36	14	◒	⊜	⊜	◒	*B,E,V,BB,EE*
MADISON MILL 23	13	◒	⊜	⊖	○	*A,E,Z,AA,BB*
Portable models						
NU-LINE 202	15	○	⊖	○	⊖	*J,K,R,W*
GERRY 525	18	◒	⊖	◒	⊖	*A,G,I,N,S,T*
NORTH STATES 3203	12	⊖	○	◒	○	*C,K,R,EE*
MAPES 13321	14	⊖	◒	◒	◒	*Q*
PARIS 300	15	⊖	◒	◒	○	*K*
GERRY 530	31	⊖	◒	●	⊖	*A,D,H,M,P,U*
WORLDSBEST 276	16	⊖	●	◒	●	—
NORTH STATES 8610 [1]	19	◒	●	◒	⊖	*A,F,I,L,T,CC*

Not Acceptable

■ *The following model was judged Not Acceptable because it repeatedly suffered permanent damage in attempts at mounting.*

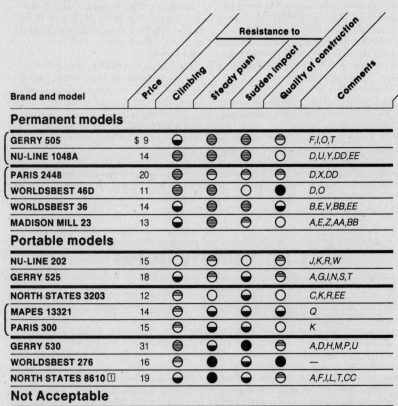

Brand and model	Price	Climbing	Steady push	Sudden impact	Quality of construction	Comments
MADISON MILL 3926	16	—	—	—	—	*C*

[1] *Although advertised as a "convertible," this model was judged by CU unsuitable for permanent installation.*

FEATURES IN COMMON

Except as noted, all: are intended for children no older than 2 yr., no taller than 34 in. and no heavier than 30 lb.; are about 24 in. high; fit opening width from about 27 to 42 in.; have wood frame.

Except as noted, all permanent gates: use mounting hardware consisting of eye bolts or brackets for installation (which was judged easy); use vertical wood slats as barrier material; cannot be removed without tools; have latch unlikely to be opened by a child; withstood 45-lb. horizontal push at all positions tested.

Except as noted, all portable gates: use flexible plastic mesh with relatively small openings as barrier material; weigh about 4 or 5 lb.; are installed by means of pressure bars (which was judged easy); showed significant inconsistency in gripping ability at varying door widths.

KEY TO COMMENTS

A-Height about 27 in.
B-Height about 30 in.
C-Fits openings about 25 to 39 in.
D-Fits openings about 27 to 47 in. (36 in. for Gerry 530).
E-Fits openings up to about 36 in.
F-All-plastic construction.
G-Plastic construction except for metal mounting bars; weighs about 6½ lb.
H-All-steel construction; weighs more than 16 lb.; has door that swings open.
I-Uses stiff plastic mesh as barrier material.
J-Uses coarse, flexible plastic mesh as barrier material.
K-Opening widths are clearly labeled on pressure bar, a convenience for installation.
L-Installation with locking lever and removal judged difficult.
M-Installation with adjustable cushions; readjusting width judged difficult.
N-Installation with spring-loaded bars judged difficult.
O-Removable without tools.
P-Door latch not stiff enough and handles not tight enough in some installations to be absolutely childproof.
Q-Reinstallation judged easier than with other portables, because setting holds when gate is removed.
R-**Nu-Line 202** gripped well in standard doorway openings (measured in even inches) but not openings a quarter-inch wider or narrower. **North States 3203** gripped much better in intermediate openings than in standard doorways.
S-Provided consistent grip at all opening widths within its range.
T-Finger-trapping judged possible at certain settings with children less than 12 mo. old.
U-Limb-trapping between slats judged possible.
V-Also available in 5-ft. width, model **60,** $21; 7 ft., **84**, $25; 9 ft., **108**, $35.
W-Also available in 26½-to-36-in. range.
X-Also available in 22-to-36-in. range.
Y-Also available in 23-to-36-in. range.
Z-Also available in 4-ft. width, model **24,** $14; 5 ft., **25,** $15; 6 ft., **26,** $16; 7 ft., **27,** $17.
AA-Latch judged very inconvenient to use.
BB-Accordion-style barrier with slanting wood slats.
CC-At original publication, this model was being changed. (See story for comments on replacement model.)
DD-Latch could pinch adult fingers.
EE-According to the company, this model is being changed.

---

taller than the gate itself. (The manufacturers say the gates aren't intended for children taller than 34 inches, heavier than 30 pounds, or more than two years old.) But the metal latch on most of the permanent gates is pretty stiff and shouldn't give way to prying fingers.

Most of the tested portables have no latch. Instead, they have rubber cushions. A child shouldn't be able to loosen them if the gate is properly installed. The *Gerry 530* is the only portable with a latch within reach of the child and openable by an average two-year-old.

It would be difficult for a child to climb most of the tested gates. Models with vertical slats provide no toeholds or handholds, so they offer the best protection against climbing. Mesh gates with small gaps are almost as good. A few models with wooden slats or stiff plastic mesh might trap arms, legs, or fingers.

We installed each model, extended to its fullest, in a doorway. We then exerted a horizontal push, steadily increasing the force to a maximum of 45 pounds—much more force than a two-year-old child is likely to muster, but a practical test to see how well the gate could stand up to abuse.

All but one of the permanent gates withstood the push. (The frame of the *Paris 2448* split at the latch.) The portables didn't have as much holding power. Typically, even under very low forces, the rubber cushions that hold a gate to the sides of a doorway often slid off and let the gate fall. When we narrowed the portable gates to span a three-foot door opening, the *Nu-Line 202* and the *Gerry 525* were able to resist a 45-pound push at top center and about 30 pounds near the other edges. Most other portables gave way under much less force.

We also tried all the portable gates in doorways whose width wasn't to the inch (as are most standard doorways) but to an odd quarter of an inch. The behavior of some models changed surprisingly. The *Nu-Line 202*, for example, which did well in standard-size doorways, gave way at its cushions under a mere 16-pound force. And the *North States 3203*, which didn't do well in standard doorways, became much more difficult to dislodge.

To see how the gates might stand up to sudden impact, we hung a 30-pound sandbag above the opening covered by the gate. Then we swung the bag into the gate from higher and higher starting points until the gate suffered damage or fell down.

The permanent gates generally stood up better than the portables. With any portable, it's necessary to follow the manufacturer's installation instructions to the letter to get reliable holding strength. But even then, there's no guarantee, because of sample-to-sample differences and different holding strengths at various door widths. We advise against depending on any portable model at the head of a staircase.

INSTALLATION. Setting up the permanent gates was fairly easy. Every model comes with the eye bolts or brackets needed for mounting in a doorway. All you need to finish the job are a few basic hand tools.

A portable model should be easy to set up quickly. Not all were. The cushioned steel tubes at the top and bottom of the *Gerry 525* give it superior holding power; but pulling on the tubes to install or remove the gate required undue effort. Installing the other *Gerry* portable was even more complicated.

The portable *Madison Mill 3926* was impossible to install in CU's 36-inch doorway; the pin that should link the pressure bars gouged out the wood adjacent to the hole, so the gate lost its grip. When we tried installing the gate at a 39-inch width, its advertised maximum, the same thing happened. In view of this model's tendency to self-destruct at standard door widths, we rated it Not Acceptable.

RECOMMENDATIONS. If you want the option of blocking the top of a stairway, the all-plastic *Gerry 505*, a permanent gate, should be a good bet. It's nicely constructed, removable without tools, impressively resistant to hard knocks and pushing, and, at $9, inexpensive. But if your child is a notorious climber, the *Nu-Line 1048A*, at $14, might be a better bet. Its wooden vertical slats would be much harder to climb than the stiff mesh of the *Gerry 505*.

Among the portable models, the *Nu-Line 202*, at $15, was our choice. It's well made; its opening-width numbers are clearly marked on its pressure bar as an aid to quick installation; and its grip in a standard doorway was better than that of most other portables.

(The *North States 8610*, advertised as a "convertible" gate, was rated only as a portable because it wasn't judged suitable for permanent installation. It has been replaced by model *8612*, which can also be installed as a permanent gate. As a portable model, it would rank almost on a par with the *Paris 300*. As a permanent gate, it would rank just below the *Madison Mill 23*.)

Hair conditioners

Condensed from CONSUMER REPORTS, January 1986

Americans spend more than half a billion dollars a year on various types of hair conditioners: conditioners for normal hair, oily hair, damaged hair, and hair that needs "extra body"; conditioners to be used with a companion shampoo; and conditioners sold merely as contributing elements of complete "hair-care systems."

Do those products really work, or is their appeal that same mixture of hope and dreams that sells so many cosmetics? To find out, we tested 47 instant conditioners, including expensive "prestige" brands as well as mass-marketed products.

WHAT SHOULD THEY DO? According to their advertising, conditioners make hair shine, give it body and bounce, make it soft, make it strong, make it more manageable, and make it tangle-free. To a greater or lesser extent, we found, most of them do.

Shampooing removes oil and dirt from hair. As a result, the scales that make up each hair's cuticle, as its outer layer is called, become ruffled. When the cuticles are ruffled, hair tangles easily and may look dull. Without its natural oily coating, hair can also become wild and frizzy.

The hair's natural protective coating—sebum, an oily substance released by the scalp's sebacious glands—eventually builds up to relieve the post-shampoo tangling and dryness. Usually, by the time it does, you're ready to wash your hair again. Conditioners have much the same effect as sebum—without the waiting.

Conditioners reduce the roughness of the cuticle, so hair combs easily, looks shinier, and feels softer. By coating each hair with a film that is electrically conductive, they counteract static electricity, so hair is more manageable. The coating also gives the effect of making hair strands slightly thicker; hence it can be described as giving extra body.

Conditioners that purport to remedy split ends, among other types of hair injury, aren't really anything special. The ingredients in many conditioners form a chemical bond to the hair, especially where the cuticle has been damaged. That may repair the damage temporarily, but the only way to eliminate split ends is to cut them off.

Products that purport to "nourish" hair may contain substances such as protein, wheat germ, milk, egg, or honey. But hair, once it's outside the scalp, isn't a living thing, and it can't be nourished (although it can be degraded by the poor diet of its wearer). Similarly, hair can't drink up the fatty substances in formulations labeled for dry hair; all it can do is wear the conditioner's coat for a while.

WHAT THEY DID DO. We had an expert consultant test the conditioners, working with 25 women over a period of 24 weeks. (Our survey of readers found that twice as many women use hair conditioners as men.) At each conditioning session, our consultant shampooed each woman's hair with *Johnsons Baby Shampoo*. Then, parting the hair down the middle, he applied about half an ounce of a different conditioner to each side of the woman's head, and left it on the hair for about a minute (the instruction given for most of the products) before rinsing the hair and toweling it dry.

Then our consultant judged each conditioner, using a checklist we had sup-

Text continued on page 151

Ratings of hair conditioners

Listed not in order of estimated overall quality but in decreasing order of conditioning effect; depending on hair characteristics, maximum conditioning effect may not be desirable (see story). All were judged effective in reducing tangling and improving softness and shine. Differences between closely ranked products were judged slight. Prices are the average paid by CU shoppers; cost per ounce is as calculated by CU.

◍	⊖	○	◒	●
More	←		→	**Less**

Product	Size, oz.	Price	Cost per oz.	Static reduction
WELLA BALSAM INSTANT REGULAR	8	$1.66	$.21	⊖
SUAVE BALSAM & PROTEIN EXTRA BODY	16	1.62	.10	⊖
SILKIENCE REGULAR	7	2.26	.32	⊖
L'ORÉAL REGULAR	15	2.61	.17	⊖
L'ORÉAL EXTRA BODY	15	2.48	.17	⊖
FINESSE REGULAR	7	2.44	.35	○
SUAVE BALSAM & PROTEIN REGULAR	16	1.57	.10	○
TAME EXTRA BODY	8	1.91	.24	○
SQUEEK NORMAL TO DRY	7	1.96	.28	○
FINESSE EXTRA BODY	7	2.47	.35	○
SILKIENCE EXTRA BODY	7	2.26	.32	○
CLAIROL CONDITION II EXTRA BODY	16	2.39	.15	○
WELLA BALSAM INSTANT EXTRA BODY	8	1.44	.18	○
VITAL CARE JOJOBA	16.9	1.59	.09	○
CLAIROL CONDITION II NORMAL	16	2.32	.15	○
AGREE EXTRA BODY	7	2.34	.33	⊖
TAME NORMAL/DRY	8	1.95	.25	⊖
ENHANCE NORMAL	8	2.19	.27	○
IVORY NORMAL	15	1.98	.13	○
CVS VARIABLE EXTRA BODY	18	1.99	.11	○
REVLON HDR EXTRA BODY	7	2.17	.31	○
AGREE REGULAR	7	2.24	.32	○
CVS MOISTURIZING NORMAL	16	1.67	.10	○

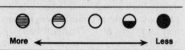

Product	Size, oz.	Price	Cost per oz.	Static reduction
REVLON HDR REGULAR	7	$2.29	$.33	○
VITAL CARE ALOE VERA	16.9	1.59	.09	○
VIDAL SASSOON EVERYDAY (TUBE)	2	2.41	1.21	○
ESTÉE LAUDER SWISS	6	6.50	1.08	○
ALBERTO VO5 EXTRA BODY	15	1.61	.11	○
ALBERTO VO5 NORMAL	15	1.54	.10	○
AVON NEW VITALITY EXTRA BODY NORMAL/DRY	8	2.49	.31	○
JHIRMACK GELÁVE NORMAL/OILY	8	2.88	.36	○
AVON ALOE VERA	8	2.49	.31	○
NATURE'S FAMILY ALOE VERA	18	1.99	.11	○
FREEMAN SEA KELP REGULAR	16	2.89	.18	○
VIDAL SASSOON EXTRA PROTECTION	12	3.99	.28	○
BRECK EXTRA BODY	16	2.73	.17	○
FABERGÉ ORGANICS WHEAT GERM & HONEY EXTRA BODY	15	2.11	.14	○
NUTRI-TONIC LIFE EXTRA BODY	12	2.87	.24	○
VIDAL SASSOON RE-MOISTURIZING	2	3.03	1.52	○
REVLON AQUAMARINE REGULAR	15	1.49	.10	○
REVLON AQUAMARINE EXTRA BODY	15	1.66	.11	○
FABERGÉ ORGANICS WHEAT GERM & HONEY	15	1.78	.12	○
BRECK NORMAL	16	2.73	.17	○
JHIRMACK GELÁVE EXTRA BODY	8	2.84	.36	○
FREEMAN SEA KELP EXTRA BODY	16	2.73	.17	○
NUTRI-TONIC LIFE REGULAR	12	3.37	.28	○
NATURE'S FAMILY JOJOBA	18	1.99	.11	○

plied. When the hair was wet, he evaluated how easy it was to comb and remove tangles. After drying the hair, he again noted how easy it was to comb. He also noted how much it showed the effects of static electricity, how soft it felt, and how shiny it was. And he evaluated three characteristics commonly referred to in the ads: body, fullness, and bounce. Over the weeks of the test, he used each of the 47 products at least 25 times.

His judgments indicated that hair conditioners indeed made hair softer and easier to comb. Some were a little better than others at controlling the static electricity that makes hair seem to stand on end. While all the tested products added body, fullness, and bounce to hair, some added more of the conditioning qualities than others. Those differences in the degree of conditioning form the basis of the Ratings order.

RECOMMENDATIONS. We don't necessarily recommend the hair conditioners listed at the top of the Ratings. We simply remark that they provide the greatest degree of conditioning, probably more conditioning than many types of hair need. Conditioners listed high in the Ratings should work best with hair that's dry or frizzy. Soft hair or oily hair, however, may look limp or greasy if overconditioned. And people with those types of hair might want to choose a conditioner from the bottom of the Ratings—if they care to choose a hair conditioner at all.

Toothpastes

Condensed from CONSUMER REPORTS, March 1986

To help remove plaque and stains, toothpastes all contain abrasives, such as hydrated silica or phosphate salts. Some, indeed, contain as much as 50 percent abrasives. But more isn't necessarily better.

Tooth enamel, the nonliving material that forms the visible crown of a tooth, is the hardest substance in the human body. It's virtually impervious to any wear imposed by brushing or dentifrices. But when gums recede with age or disease, softer dental tissues—dentin and cementum—become exposed. This soft tissue can be damaged by a toothpaste that's too abrasive.

PERFORMANCE. Accordingly, our main test of toothpastes was an abrasiveness test. For this report, we bought and tested 24 products, including some making enticing antiplaque and antitartar claims.

A consulting lab prepared extracted teeth so that the vulnerable dentin was exposed. The teeth were then bombarded with radiation and mounted in resin blocks. The blocks were placed in a brushing machine equipped with medium-hard toothbrushes. After the toothbrushes had been dosed with a watery mixture of each test toothpaste, the machine brushed 2000 strokes per tooth.

The lab gauged how much the teeth had worn away by measuring the radioactivity in the used dentifrice-water mixture; the more radioactivity, the harsher the toothpaste. The test results divided the products broadly into three groups. Least abrasive were several products from Colgate-Palmolive—*Peak*, *Colgate*, and *Dentagard*—and a desensitizing toothpaste called *Denquel*. Products scoring a notch lower in abrasiveness were about 40 percent harsher. The harshest products were almost twice as abrasive as the mildest products.

It's well known that the addition of fluoride to a toothpaste can reduce the incidence of cavities, but not necessarily any addition of fluoride. There may not be enough added, or some other ingredient in the toothpaste could render the fluoride useless. Because of those uncertainties, the American Dental Association has set up procedures whereby, to gain the ADA's antidecay "seal of acceptance," manufacturers have to present compelling evidence

Text continued on page 155

Ratings of toothpastes

Listed by types; within types, listed in order of increasing abrasiveness. Differences between closely ranked products are small. Prices are the average of those paid by CU shoppers in the New York City area.

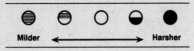

⊜	⊖	○	◒	●
Milder	←		→	Harsher

Product	Package type (tube or pump)	Price/size (oz.)	Cost per month [1]	Abrasiveness	Fluoride [2]
General-purpose products					
PEAK [3]	T	$2.19/6.3	$ .81	⊜	—
COLGATE REGULAR	T	1.87/7.0	.59	⊜	A
COLGATE REGULAR	P	1.49/4.5	.48	⊜	A
DENTAGARD	T	1.76/6.4	.48	⊜	A
DENTAGARD	P	1.86/4.5	.55	⊜	A
COLGATE WINTERFRESH GEL	T	1.87/6.4	.59	⊜	A
COLGATE WINTERFRESH GEL	P	1.49/4.5	.49	⊜	A
ULTRA BRITE [3]	T	1.99/6.0	.71	⊖	B
AQUA-FRESH FOR KIDS	P	1.67/4.6	.47	⊖	A
MACLEANS MILDMINT [3]	T	2.65/7.0	.81	⊖	A
CREST REGULAR	T	1.87/6.4	.50	⊖	A
CREST REGULAR	P	1.64/4.6	.59	⊖	A
AIM MINT	T	1.89/6.4	.41	⊖	A
AIM MINT	P	1.59/4.5	.37	⊖	A
CHECK-UP	T	2.66/6.4	.56	⊖	B

Ratings continued on next page

Ratings of toothpastes continued

Product	Package type (tube or pump)	Price/size (oz.)	Cost per month [1]	Abrasiveness	Fluoride [2]
CHECK-UP	P	$2.42/4.1	$ .62	◓	B
AIM REGULAR	T	1.71/6.4	.39	◓	A
AIM REGULAR	P	1.86/4.5	.52	◓	A
AQUA-FRESH	T	1.66/6.4	.54	◓	A
AQUA-FRESH	P	1.63/4.6	.53	◓	A
CHECK-UP GEL	T	2.43/6.4	.52	◓	B
CHECK-UP GEL	P	2.42/4.1	.56	◓	B
MACLEANS PEPPERMINT [3]	T	2.69/7.0	.86	○	A
CLOSE-UP FRESH MINT [3]	T	1.89/6.4	.65	○	B
Tartar-inhibiting products					
PREVENT ANTI-TARTAR [4]	T	2.22/2.7	1.27	◓	B
CREST TARTAR CONTROL FORMULA	T	1.79/6.4	.48	◓	A
CREST TARTAR CONTROL FORMULA	P	1.64/4.6	.54	○	A
Smokers' products					
PEARL DROPS SMOKER'S GEL	T	3.28/3.0	1.70	◓	B
TOPOL MINT [3]	T	5.99/7.0	1.89	○	—
TOPOL SMOKER'S GEL [5]	T	4.92/6.4	1.34	○	B
Desensitizing products [6]					
DENQUEL [3] [7]	T	2.55/3.0	1.63	●	—
THERMODENT [3]	T	3.25/4.0	1.21	○	—
SENSODYNE [3] [7]	T	2.99/4.0	1.21	○	—

1 *Based on roughly ½-in. of toothpaste used twice daily.*

2 *A: contains ADA-accepted fluoride formula. B: contains fluoride, but is not ADA-accepted for prevention of decay.*

3 *Test results are from Consumer Reports, March 1984; price is current.*

4 *Availability was limited in test market.*

5 *Contains FD&C Yellow No. 5, to which some aspirin-sensitive people may also be sensitive.*

6 *Should not be used for more than 2 weeks without consulting dentist.*

7 *ADA-accepted as effective in relieving sensitivity to hot and cold in otherwise normal teeth.*

---

that their products actually prevent decay. The Ratings indicate which fluoride-containing products have earned that seal and which have not.

A number of the tested products are self-styled plaque fighters, but none of those contain any special ingredients that would help them carry out their war on plaque. Three toothpastes, *Prevent* and two versions of *Crest*, make explicit antitartar claims, and they do indeed contain chemicals clinically proven to reduce tartar accumulation. Unfortunately, though, they can't dissolve tartar that's already on teeth; nor can they inhibit tartar buildup below the gum line, where it causes gum disease. Thus their benefits are strictly cosmetic and have no consequence for dental health.

Three products in the Ratings are formulated, or at least advertised, specifically for smokers. Abrasiveness is the chief weapon these toothpastes use to combat tobacco stains. But none of the smokers' toothpastes was particularly abrasive, although their relatively high prices may grate on sensitive shoppers' nerves.

Three products are billed as desensitizing toothpastes, and two of them, *Denquel* and *Sensodyne*, are accepted by the ADA as effective in relieving sensitivity to hot and cold in otherwise normal teeth. But before you try such a toothpaste, we suggest that you check with your dentist. Overly sensitive teeth could be a symptom of a serious dental problem that requires professional treatment.

One of the products we tested is *Aqua-Fresh for Kids*. We wondered whether kids would really like it, so we introduced it, along with ordinary *Aqua-Fresh*, to 69 grade-school children. Sure enough, they preferred the kids' version three to one. We suspect flavor made the difference. The kids' version has a flavor that's described by the manufacturer as tutti-frutti. The kids called the flavor bubble gum.

RECOMMENDATIONS. Our advice is to use the least abrasive toothpaste that gets your teeth clean. That strategy in favor of mildness is especially important if your gums have begun to recede. We'd also recommend using a toothpaste containing an ADA-accepted fluoride formulation. And of course, if only as encouragement to use it regularly, a toothpaste should taste good.

As the Ratings show, toothpaste manufacturers have introduced a new kind of dispenser, the pump, as an alternative to the tube. One might be half-prepared to disparage the pump, anticipating that it would prove to be merely an expensive packaging gimmick. But most price differences between tube and pump were trivial—and sometimes even to the advantage of the pump. And apart from the selling price, pumps may work out to be cheaper because they deliver a thinner ribbon of toothpaste and they're easier to empty completely. Tube and pump versions almost always performed alike in abrasiveness to dentin. The only exception was *Crest Tartar Control Formula*, whose pump version was harsher than its tube version.

Hand and bath soaps

Condensed from CONSUMER REPORTS, January 1985

One help out of the maze of soap prices, sizes, packages and shapes is unit pricing, which lets one compare price per ounce. Even at that, per-ounce prices may be misleading. A better measure is the number of hand-washings a soap delivers, or cost of use.

How many hand-washings you get from a soap depends on its dissolution rate—that is, how fast it disappears.

How fast liquid soap disappears depends largely on its container. Most have pump dispensers, which serve up varying amounts. A few liquid soaps come in a squeeze container, letting you squeeze out as much as you like.

Some soaps lather more profusely than others. But lathering has little to do with a soap's cleaning ability. Lathering is actually a result of the water interacting with the soap. Soft water, which contains few minerals, makes soap lather easily. Lathering also depends on the chemical makeup of the soap. Soaps containing detergent constituents lather more than plain soaps in hard water.

The fact is that soap is irritating to the skin, not soothing to it. Soap removes dirt and natural oil, which is very drying. In an attempt to make soap less drying and therefore less irritating, some makers add extra fats—such as lanolin, moisturizing cream, or cocoa butter.

But even a soap with extra fat is not a good moisturizer, since it has a drying effect. A moisturizing lotion applied right after bathing is better.

Ratings of hand and bath soaps

Listed by types. Within types, listed in order of increasing cost of use, based on test results and on average price paid for size given.

Bar soaps

P & Q Deodorant (A & P); Generic deodorant (Grand Union); Ivory Personal Size; Cashmere Bouquet Bath; Scotch Buy White Complexion (Safeway); Cost Cutter Deodorant W/Lanolin (Kroger); Generic deodorant (Lucky); LUX; Cashmere Bouquet Regular; Jergens Lotion Bath; No Frills Deodorant (Pathmark); Palmolive Gold Deodorant; Truly Fine Ocean Mist Deodorant (Safeway); Palmolive Mild Bath; Irish Spring Double Deodorant Bath; Dial Deodorant (Gold); Ivory Bath Size; Fiesta Deodorant; Gentle Touch Bath Bar With Baby Oil; Safeguard Deodorant; Lifebuoy Deodorant; Zest Deodorant; Coast Deodorant; Camay; Caress Body Bar With Bath Oil; Dove 1/4 Moisturizing Cream; Tone Glycerin and Cocoa Butter; No Frills Glycerin (Pathmark); Basis Superfatted; Yardley Cocoa Butter; Yardley English Lavender; Yardley Oatmeal; Shield Extra Strength Deodorant; Nivea Cream; Johnson's Baby Bar; Pears Transparent; Neutrogena Original Formula Unscented; Neutrogena Original Formula; CVS Glycerine; Roger & Gallet Savon Rose Thé; Myrurgia Jabon Maja; Jergens Medicated Clear Complexion Bar; Clinique Facial Mild; Estée Lauder Basic Cleansing Bar.

Liquid soaps

Ivory Liquid Soap Refill; Ivory Liquid Soap; Yardley English Lavender Liquid Soap; Showermate Liquid Shower Soap; Softsoap Original Formula Refill; Softsoap Liquid Soap; Liqua 4 Skin Cleansing System; Liquid Neutrogena.

Soap can irritate because it is alkaline. Most soaps are moderately alkaline, with a pH of about 10. But for most people pH doesn't matter. Normal skin returns to its natural acidic level quickly after encountering soap.

Granted, some people may be sensitive to an alkaline soap. Those individuals may want to consider an essentially neutral soap. A number of brands tested were either exactly neutral, with a pH of 7, or so close to neutral as to make no difference: *Caress Body Bar with Bath Oil*, *Dove* bar, *Estée Lauder* bar, *Johnson's Baby* bar, *Liqua 4* liquid, *Showermate* liquid, *Softsoap* liquid, and *Yardley* liquid.

Deodorant soaps contain antiseptics such as triclocarban or triclosan.

The antiseptics reduce skin bacteria and thereby slow the development of odor. Unfortunately, deodorant soaps may cause a rash or other allergic reaction in people with sensitive skin. Bathing with ordinary soap can usually be just as effective.

Perfume isn't new to soap. Since the beginning of soap-making, it has been used to mask the unpleasant odors of other ingredients. Of course, perfume is another way to get you to buy one brand over another. But even the strongest soap fragrance won't last long on your skin after bathing. The nature of soap is such that it removes most of its own traces from your skin when you rinse. If you want to smell nice, use a perfume or cologne.

RECOMMENDATIONS. Healthy skin can handle just about any soap. But sensitive or dry skin may fare better with soaps that do not have added perfume or antiseptics. (Many soaps have an ingredients list, so you may be able to avoid a brand that contains an ingredient to which you're allergic.) If you have oily skin, it's more important to keep your skin clean—no matter how often that means washing—than to use any particular brand of soap.

Whether you bargain-shop for soap or treat yourself to the most expensive, you can make a bar of soap last by minimizing the time it spends in water. Use a raised soap dish and remove a bar from the bath water promptly.

Shampoos

Condensed from CONSUMER REPORTS, September 1984

If the main function of a shampoo is to clean hair, just about every shampoo can do that well.

The men and women panelists enlisted by CU for this report often disagreed in their scores on the same product. Those sex-linked preferences may have been due to differences in men's and women's hair. Equally possible, we think, they may have been due to peripheral factors, such as preferences for different fragrances.

A panel test necessarily submerges individual preferences in favor of group preferences. But even on individual ballots, the panelists rarely said one product was *much* better than another.

PERSPECTIVE. Shampoo advertising seems to be highly charged with emotion and pseudoscience, obviously intended to establish a basis for preference. Yet we know from our tests that when the labels are removed from shampoo bottles, so are any strong preferences for one brand or another.

By the time hair emerges from the scalp, when shampoo can reach it, it's dead. It can't be "nourished" by sham-

Text continued on page 159

Ratings of shampoos

Listed alphabetically. All preferences were judged slight. Shampoo type is as claimed by the manufacturer.

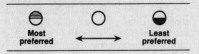

⊜ Most preferred ← ○ → ◒ Least preferred

Brand (and type) [1]	Panelists' preferences: Women	Panelists' preferences: Men
AGREE (XB)	○	○
AGREE (XC)	○	⊜
AGREE (R)	○	⊜
ALBERTO VO5 (XB)	○	○
ALBERTO VO5 (N)	○	○
AVON BODY BONUS (XB)	○	○
AVON NEW VITALITY (N/D)	◒	◒
BODY ON TAP (N)	○	○
BRECK (D)	⊜	○
BRECK (N)	○	○
BRECK (O)	○	○
CLAIROL CONDITION (D)	○	⊜
CLAIROL CONDITION (O)	○	○
CLAIROL CONDITION (N)	⊜	○
CLAIROL HERBAL ESSENCE (N)	○	⊜
CLAIROL HERBAL ESSENCE (O)	◒	○
COLGATE'S OCTAGON LIQUID DETERGENT	○	◒
CVS BALSAM & PROTEIN TREATMENT (N/D)	○	○
CVS CONCENTRATE	◒	○
DIMENSION	⊜	◒
ENHANCE (N)	○	○
FABERGE BRUT 33	◒	○
FABERGE ORGANICS (N)	○	○
FABERGE ORGANICS (XB)	○	◒
FINESSE (XB)	○	○
FINESSE (N)	○	○
FOR OILY HAIR ONLY (O)	⊜	⊜
GEE, YOUR HAIR SMELLS TERRIFIC (N/D)	○	○
HEAD & SHOULDERS (tube)	○	○
HEAD & SHOULDERS (C)	○	○
JHERI REDDING MILK'N HONEE (XB)	○	○
JHERI REDDING MILK'N HONEE (N)	◒	⊜
JHIRMACK E.F.A. (D)	⊜	○
JHIRMACK GELAVE (N)	◒	◒
JHIRMACK GELAVE (O)	○	○
JHIRMACK NUTRI-BODY (XB)	○	○
JOHNSON'S BABY SHAMPOO	◒	◒
KROGER FAMILY PRIDE EXTRA BALSAM & PROTEIN (N/D)	◒	○
L'OREAL ULTRA RICH (N)	○	◒
NATURAL'S (N)	◒	◒
PERT (D)	○	○
PERT (N)	○	○
PERT (O)	○	○
PRELL (N/D)	○	◒
PRELL (N/O)	○	⊜

Brand (and type) [1]	Panelists' preferences: Women	Panelists' preferences: Men
PRELL CONCENTRATE (N/D)	○	○
PRELL CONCENTRATE (N/O)	○	○
REVLON FLEX (XB)	⊜	○
REVLON FLEX (N/D)	○	○
REVLON FLEX (O)	⊜	⊜
REVLON MILK PLUS 6 (N)	○	○
SILKIENCE (R)	○	○
SUAVE BALSAM & PROTEIN (XB)	⊜	○
SUAVE BALSAM & PROTEIN (N/D)	⊜	○

Brand (and type) [1]	Panelists' preferences: Women	Panelists' preferences: Men
SUAVE BALSAM & PROTEIN (O)	◒	○
SUAVE FULL BODY (N/D)	○	○
TRULY FINE (Safeway) (N/D)	○	○
VIDAL SASSOON	○	○
WELLA BALSAM (N)	○	⊜
WELLA BALSAM (D)	○	○
WELLA BALSAM (XB)	⊜	⊜
WELLA BALSAM (O)	○	◒

[1] *XB = extra body; XC = extra cleansing; R = regular; N = normal; D = dry; O = oily; C = conditioning.*

poo (although its original growth may have been influenced by diet).

The outermost layer of a strand of hair is the cuticle, a series of minute, overlapping scales. The cuticle protects the cortex, a flexible inner structure that contains the pigment that gives hair color. A mild mix of chemicals, such as those in shampoos, can affect only the cuticle in normal hair.

Sebaceous glands in the scalp give hair a protective coat of oily sebum. Sebum gives hair shine and helps the scales of the cuticle lie flat. It also collects bacteria and dirt, which makes hair look dull. So a shampoo's primary function is to remove dirt and excess sebum from hair.

A manufacturer often alters ingredients to make its shampoos for dry, normal, and oily hair. At least, that's the theory. Whether you can truly perceive a difference in cleaning and conditioning ability between an "oily" formulation and a "dry" one is moot, judging by our penelists' responses.

If a shampoo stripped all the oil from hair—or failed to replace it with another oil—the scales of the cuticles would tend to flare out, like a feather ruffled backward.

Ruffled scales keep the hair from lying flat and reflect light unevenly so hair looks dull. Alkaline substances such as detergents tend to ruffle the scales. Acidic substances such as creme rinses or lemon juice tend to smooth the scales down.

RECOMMENDATIONS. If consumers thought of shampoo realistically—as nothing more than a hair detergent—they might not be so willing to pay 10 times more for it than they pay for liquid dishwashing detergents.

But consumers do think of shampoo as a personal product, yielding individual satisfaction. So if the brand you currently use makes you and your hair feel good, there's no reason to change. If you're looking for a new shampoo, you might try one that's cheaper and preferred by panelists of your sex.

Fade creams

Condensed from CONSUMER REPORTS, January 1985

A variety of natural shocks—chronic exposure to the sun, skin diseases, other diseases, pregnancy—can cause areas of hyperpigmentation, or excess darkening of the skin. Fade creams (more properly known as skin-bleaching creams) are intended to lighten the blemishes. At first blush, fade creams would seem to be cosmetics. But the U.S. Food and Drug Administration considers them drugs because they affect the body's structure (the skin) and function (pigment production).

Consumers Union's consultants also offer the following fade cream advice:

1. Fade creams, when they work at all, work only against flat brown blemishes such as freckles and age spots. They're useless on elevated lesions such as moles and red or blue pigmented areas such as scars or port-wine-stain birthmarks.

2. Fade creams are not "disappearing creams." It's highly unlikely that your blemishes will completely disappear.

3. Try to apply a fade cream only to the pigmented area, not to the surrounding normal skin. Depigmented skin can be just as unattractive as a brown spot.

4. If you've used a fade cream twice a day for three months and gotten no results, consider seeking professional treatment. Physicians can prescribe fade creams that are more potent than over-the-counter brands.

Dermatologists also can bleach dark areas permanently, using techniques such as cryosurgery (freezing the skin with liquid nitrogen) and laser surgery.

5. Most pigmented blemishes—freckles and flattened age spots or liver spots—result from exposure to the sun over many years. To help prevent excessive pigment production, try to protect your hands and face against excessive exposure to the sun. Cover the skin or use a sun-blocking lotion to prevent long exposures.

6. As an alternative to fade creams, foundation creams can cover up many skin biemishes.

Toilet paper

Condensed from CONSUMER REPORTS, August 1984

A lot of people resent spending any more than they have to for something that gets flushed down the toilet; they buy low-priced generic products. Other people put comfort and presumed quality above all else, including price; they buy premium brands. In a sense, both groups of people are right.

RECOMMENDATIONS. To a large degree, you do have to pay more to get higher-quality (soft yet sufficiently strong and absorbent) paper. But you don't have to buy the most expensive brands in order to get good quality. All the two-ply supermarket brands tested—*Truly Fine, Skaggs Alpha Beta, Pathmark,* and *Acme* were among the best-rated products. If you don't shop at those supermarkets, you might try your market's own two-ply brand.

Ratings of toilet paper

Listed in order of estimated overall quality. Differences between closely ranked products were slight.

Northern (Western version); Vanity Fair; Cottonelle; Truly Fine (Safeway); White Cloud; Pathmark (2-ply); Skaggs Alpha Beta (2-ply); Coronet; Delsey; Banner; Marina; Nice 'N Soft; Northern (Eastern version); Skaggs Alpha Beta (1-ply); Acme; Marcal Sofpac; Delta; Arrow; Basics (Grand Union); Lady Lee (Lucky); Scottissue; Charmin; No Frills (Pathmark); Econobuy (Acme); Lilac; Soft Weve; Waldorf; Econobuy (Skaggs Alpha Beta); Generic (First National); Hi-Dri; Hudson Mr. Big; Scotch Buy (Safeway); Pathmark (1-ply); Generic (Dublin); Marcal; P & Q (A & P); Cost Cutter (Kroger).

Electric shavers

Condensed from CONSUMER REPORTS, November 1984

Shavers are characterized by one of two designs. Foil heads, the most common design, have a thin, flexible screen over a cutter that shuttles underneath. Rotary heads have two or three spring-mounted guards that shield spinning cutters.

FEATURES. Most models have a trimmer, an auxiliary cutting edge at the side or top of the shaver. Some trimmers are fixed in position. Others conveniently retract and are moved up or flipped open for use. Out of respect to their separate function, most trimmers have their own on/off switch.

A number of models run or recharge only from regular 120-volt ac outlets. Most others can also be powered from the 240-volt circuits commonly found abroad. You can buy adapters at an electrical-supply shop.

Ratings on next page

What CU's Ratings mean

Products are rated, for the most part, in order of estimated overall quality, without regard to price.

Models are check-rated (✔) when the test samples prove to be of high overall quality and significantly superior to those of other models tested.

Best Buy Ratings are accorded to models which are not only rated high but also priced relatively low, and should give more quality per dollar than other Acceptable models.

A Rating of a given model should not be considered a Rating of other models sold under the same brand name unless so noted.

Ratings of electric shavers

Listed in order of overall preference of CU's test panelists. Except where separated by heavy lines, closely ranked models differed little in preference. Prices are suggested retail, rounded to nearest dollar; + indicates that shipping is extra; except for mail-order models, discounts are generally available. ◻D indicates that model was discontinued at original publication.

Brand and model	Price	Head type	Power	Advantages	Disadvantages	Comments
REMINGTON MICRO SCREEN XLR3000	$ 50	Foil	Recharge	E,F,I,O	b,o	*B,C,I,J*
HITACHI RM2530	50	Foil	Recharge	C,H,J,L	c	—
NORELCO ROTATRACT HP1606	80	Rotary	Plug-in	D,E,K,L,O	q	*B,E,G*
PANASONIC MR. WHISK ES827	43	Foil	Recharge	A,C,G,I,L	—	*B*
ELTRON 900	80	Foil	Plug-in	H,K,L,M	—	—
PANASONIC MR. WHISK WET/DRY ES869	60	Foil	Recharge	A,D,G,I,L	o	*B,C*
PANASONIC MR. WHISK ES889	24	Foil	Plug-in	A,L	p	*A*
SANYO SV3210	40	Foil	Plug-in	J	—	*I*
REMINGTON MICRO SCREEN XLR1000	40	Foil	Plug-in	F,I,O	b,d,f	*A,I,J*
NORELCO ROTATRACT HP1605	64	Rotary	Plug-in	D,K,L,O	q	*B,G*
ELTRON INTERNATIONAL	100	Foil	Recharge	B,C,H,K	—	*B,G,H,I*
◻D SCHICK FLEXAMATIC F45	75	Foil	Recharge	C,K	q	*J*
KRUPS FLEXONIC 488	60	Foil	Plug-in	I,J,L	d,f	*G*
◻D SCHICK FLEXAMATIC F20	35	Foil	Plug-in	--	p	*A,G*

D SCHICK FLEXAMATIC F33	50	Foil	Plug-in	—	p	*G*
HITACHI AV4500	35	Foil	Plug-in	J,L	—	*G,I*
NORELCO ROTATRACT HP 1328	100	Rotary	Recharge	B,C,D,K,L,O	q	*E,H*
ELTRON 660	65	Foil	Plug-in	H,K,M,N	—	*I*
REMINGTON MICRO SCREEN XLR800	32	Foil	Plug-in	I,O	b,e,f	*A,I,J*
SANYO SVM530	70	Foil	Recharge	H,K	o	*F*
NORELCO SPEEDRAZOR HP1620	26	Rotary	Plug-in	A,K,L,O	a,l,q	*A,G,J*
SEARS ROTOMATIC II Cat. No. 6835	50+	Rotary	Recharge	B,C,I,L	d,j,m,q	*A*
MITSUBISHI MICRO SHAVER SM600ST	90	Foil	Recharge	H,J,M,N	a,c,h,i,o	*A,D*
SEARS ROTOMATIC II Cat. No. 6834	40+	Rotary	Plug-in	I,L	d,f,g,h,i,k,n,q	*G*

FEATURES IN COMMON
Except as noted, all: have retractable trimmer; operate on either 120 or 240 volts ac; rechargeable models give about 1 week's worth of shaves; foil-head models have single head; rotary models have 3 heads; have 1-yr. parts-and-labor warranty that excludes cutter assembly.

KEY TO ADVANTAGES
A – Somewhat easier to manipulate than most.
B – More shaves per charge than most.
C – Can operate directly from power cord when battery is discharged.
D – Relatively free of noise and vibration.
E – Somewhat less likely than most to pull and nick skin.
F – Shaved somewhat closer than most.
G – Somewhat easier than most to use around mouth.
H – Mirror.
I – Soft case.
J – Semi-rigid case.
K – Hard case.
L – Warranty includes cutter assembly.
M – 3-yr. warranty on shaver.
N – 6-mo. warranty on cutter assembly.
O – 30-day money-back warranty.

KEY TO DISADVANTAGES
a – No trimmer.
b – Trimmer runs whenever shaver is on.
c – Fewer shaves per charge than most.
d – Judged somewhat unbalanced.
e – Judged unbalanced.
f – Somewhat harder to manipulate than most.
g – Somewhat more likely than most to pull and nick skin.
h – Somewhat slower than most.
i – Shaved somewhat less closely than most.
j – Somewhat harder than most to use around mouth.
k – Harder than most to use around mouth.
l – Somewhat less effective than most in trimming sideburns and mustaches.
m – Somewhat more irritating than most.
n – More irritating than most.
o – Will not operate directly from power cord.
p – No case.
q – Relatively hard to clean completely.

KEY TO COMMENTS
A – Runs only on 120 volts ac.
B – Automatic voltage converter.
C – Charger stand.
D – Charger built into case.
E – "Closeness/comfort" setting.
F – Cutter-speed control.
G – Coiled power cord.
H – Recharge indicator light.
I – Fixed trimmer.
J – 2 heads.

Telephones

Condensed from CONSUMER REPORTS, May 1986

Gone are the days when a telephone was merely a physical extension of the service provided by the phone company. Today, a phone is a basic home appliance, to be bought like any other appliance—with forethought and care.

Buying a phone presents some unaccustomed choices: Which of the scores of manufacturers and distributors makes the best, most reliable instrument? Should you buy the cheapest model around and throw it away when it stops working, or should you buy with durability in mind? And what about frills? What are they? Do you need them? Do you want them?

For this report, we tested telephones of the kind that the industry calls "enhanced basic." (That means, one may presume, that they're somewhat more elaborate than the simplest models and less elaborate than the fanciest models.) They came in three styles: console models, which have a roomy square base holding all controls and a separate handset; desk models, which are similar to consoles but have a smaller base; and compact models, styled like AT&T's popular *Trimline*, with controls incorporated into the handset. The tested models list for $30 to $120, but they're usually discounted. We paid $25 to $90 for our samples.

RECEPTION. The loudness of the signal heard at a telephone's receiver depends, in part, on the length of wire between the phone and the local phone company's switching station—the more wire, the softer the connection will sound. We measured our phones' reception by using lab equipment to mimic the effects of line distance. For short and moderate distances from a switching station, all the phones performed quite well. But sizable differences emerged in what amounted to our worst-case scenario, a setup equivalent to sending the signal over three miles of line (with two extensions to weaken the signal further). The Ratings judgments of listening and speaking loudness are based on that scenario.

A panel of listeners judged voice clarity, comparing each phone with a traditional AT&T desk phone. Most of the tested models outperformed the traditional one, no doubt due to newer and improved microphones.

The receivers of some telephones generate a magnetic field strong enough to "drive" many hearing aids magnetically. Models that produced the strongest magnetic field are noted in the Ratings as having superior hearing-aid compatibility. (But only actual try-outs with a phone can satisfy hearing-aid wearers entirely on that score.)

The Ringer Equivalence Number, or REN, given in the Ratings for each phone, is a measure of the current that the instrument's ringer draws. It's important if you have several extensions, because the REN's of all phones on a house line shouldn't total more than 5. If they do, the total current required will exceed the amount supplied on a standard line, and the phones might not ring at all.

DURABILITY. We abused the phones, electrically and physically, to see how well they would hold up. Typically, as a defense against electrical storms and the like, surge suppressors installed by the phone company protect the line where it enters a house. They work well with older phones, but the electronic circuitry in new phones is particularly vulnerable to transient voltage variations. Accordingly, we jolted each tested model with an 800-volt surge that might get by the suppressors. Five models, indicated in the Ratings, failed that test; their "brains" had been blown, so that they couldn't be dialed.

Since tiny sparks of static electricity are infamous for bringing microprocessors to ruin—and modern phones do have true microprocessors in them—we also shocked each tested model with an 8000-volt burst of static electricity. Three models couldn't be dialed after that. (But we didn't put a lot of weight on the results of that test, because the sparks, to do their damage, had to touch precisely the wrong spots.)

We repeatedly dropped each phone—handset and base separately—onto a concrete floor covered with asphalt tile. Half the phones showed no damage. Most others sustained only minor injury, such as split seams or a popped battery cover, and were easily put back together. But the *Telequest* was difficult to reassemble. And the *Sanyo* and the *Conair* were never again as loud and clear as before; they apparently had suffered microphone damage.

FEATURES. Most of our phones have push buttons. (The *AT&T Touch-a-Matic* has a flat "membrane" keypad for dialing, and the *Uniden* has a similar keypad for its memory buttons.) But even with buttons, a feature usually associated with Touch Tone dialing, a phone needn't be used as a tone dialer. All of ours switch easily between tone dialing and the older pulse-dialing system. That element of flexibility is very handy in areas as yet unconverted to the simplified long-distance dialing known as "Equal Access." It means that you can keep a low-cost pulse line for local calling and still switch to tone to complete non-AT&T long-distance calls.

However, in their tone setting, several phones emitted only a very brief tone, even when we held the key down. The short tones dialed calls well enough, but they may not last long enough to satisfy some answering devices or serve for some computerized phone applications, such as electronic banking.

All the tested phones, like many others on the market, excel at remembering frequently dialed numbers. Memory capacity ranged from just 9 phone numbers of 16 digits each to 33 numbers of 30 digits each. Most models have a pause button for inserting several necessary seconds of delay into a programmed dialing sequence, so a computer can answer. Some models can even remember whether a number was programmed to be dialed in pulse or tone, and they will dial it in the proper mode; they even allow the mode to be switched within a stored phone number, an ability pointed out in the Ratings Comments as "mixed-mode" dialing.

Three models boast one-touch dialing, meaning that there's a separate key for each phone number in memory. On phones without one-touch memory, numbers can be recalled from memory with the same keys used to dial; after a special memory button is pressed, a one- or two-digit code is used for the desired number. Nearly all the models are equipped with a small battery to retain their memories in case they're unplugged.

RECOMMENDATIONS. We were especially impressed with the *AT&T Touch-a-Matic 1600*, listing at $120, and the *ITT Medallion 2480*, at $70. Those and other high-rated models would make good replacements for a home's main telephone. But of course, when it comes to selecting features, only you can decide just how sophisticated and versatile a telephone you need.

Ratings on next page

Ratings of telephones

Listed in order of estimated overall quality; differences between closely ranked models were judged slight. Prices are list; + indicates shipping is extra. Discounts are usually available. D indicates model was discontinued at original publication.

⊜ ⊖ ○ ◒ ●

Better ⟷ Worse

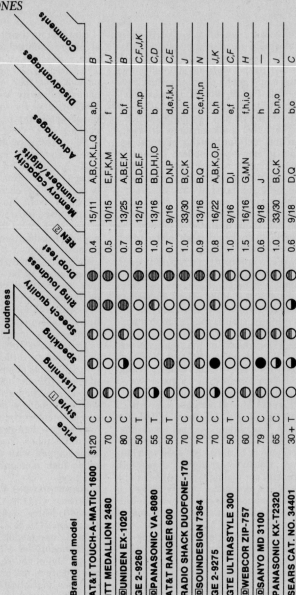

Brand and model	Price	Style [1]	Loudness: Listening	Loudness: Speaking	Speech quality	Ring loudness	Drop test	REN [2]	Memory capacity, numbers/digits	Advantages	Disadvantages	Comments
AT&T TOUCH-A-MATIC 1600	$120	C	⊖	⊖	⊖	⊜	⊜	0.4	15/11	A,B,C,K,L,Q	a,b	*B*
ITT MEDALLION 2480	70	C	⊜	○	○	⊜	⊜	0.5	10/15	E,F,K,M	f	*I,J*
D UNIDEN EX-1020	80	C	○	◒	⊖	⊜	○	0.7	13/25	A,B,E,K	b,f	*B*
GE 2-9260	50	T	⊜	○	○	○	⊜	0.9	12/15	B,D,E,F	e,m,p	*C,F,J,K*
D PANASONIC VA-8080	55	T	◒	○	○	⊖	⊜	1.0	13/16	B,D,H,I,O	b	*C,D*
AT&T RANGER 600	50	T	⊜	⊜	○	○	⊜	0.7	9/16	D,N,P	d,e,f,k,l	*C,E*
RADIO SHACK DUOFONE-170	70	C	○	○	○	○	⊜	1.0	33/30	B,C,K	b,n	*J*
D SOUNDESIGN 7364	70	C	⊜	⊖	⊜	○	⊜	0.9	13/16	B,Q	c,e,f,h,n	*N*
GE 2-9275	70	C	◒	●	○	⊖	⊖	0.8	16/22	A,B,K,O,P	b,h	*J,K*
GTE ULTRASTYLE 300	50	T	○	○	⊖	○	⊖	1.0	9/16	D,I	e,f	*C,F*
D WEBCOR ZIP-757	60	C	⊜	○	⊖	○	○	1.5	16/16	G,M,N	f,h,i,o	*H*
D SANYO MD 3100	79	C	⊜	●	⊖	○	○	0.6	9/18	J	h	—
PANASONIC KX-T2320	65	C	○	◒	⊖	○	⊖	1.0	33/30	B,C,K	b,n,o	*J*
SEARS CAT. NO. 34401	30+	T	○	◒	⊖	◒	⊖	0.6	9/18	D,Q	b,o	*C*

COBRA ST-410	55	T	○	◒	⊜	○	⊜	0.8	12/16	D,Q	a,e,k,p	*C,F,G*
CONAIR PRIMA PR1001	40	D	○	⊜	○	○	○	1.3	9/18	K	a,b,o,p	*L*
TELEQUEST GRAND PRIX PLUS 123	80	D	◒	●	⊜	○	◒	0.7	10/15	K	f,g,j,o	*A,J*

[1] *C = console model; T = Trimline-style model, with controls on handset; D = desk/table model, with controls on base.*

[2] *Ringer Equivalence Number; should total no more than 5 for all phones and extensions on standard line.*

FEATURES IN COMMON

All have: last number redial (for quick redialing after busy signals); switch for pulse or tone dialing; speed-dialing memory; chain-dialing capability (to recall 2 numbers from memory in sequence); volume and on/off switch for ringer. *Except as noted, all:* have pause feature (can be set to wait for computer tone or switchboard line when dialing automatically); have mute/hold button; can be used on desk or mounted on wall; carry 1-yr. warranty.

KEY TO ADVANTAGES

- A – 1-touch dialing for all numbers in memory.
- B – 3 keys for 1-touch dialing of 3 priority numbers.
- C – Low-battery indicator.
- D – Disconnect/flash button on handset.
- E – 2 speeds for pulse dialing: 10 and 20 pulses a second.
- F – Last number dialed can be stored in permanent memory.
- G – Can redial a number 15 times after busy signal.
- H – Volume control for earpiece.
- I – In-use light on back of handset.
- J – Very compact phone.
- K – Handset is of traditional, more-rounded design; may be more comfortable to cradle on shoulder than newer, flatter designs.
- L – Convenient digital display showing number dialed, low battery, ringer off, clock time, date, and call timer.
- M – Directory/index concealed for privacy.
- N – Pause feature more convenient than most.
- O – Somewhat louder reception than most, an advantage for those hard of hearing against noisy background.
- P – Better hearing-aid compatibility than most.
- Q – Better hearing-aid compatibility than many.

KEY TO DISADVANTAGES

- a – No pause control.
- b – No mute/hold button.
- c – Battery cannot be replaced by user.
- d – Phone must be turned on and off by hand.
- e – Last-number redial requires press of more than one button.
- f – Dialing tones are too short to work with some answering devices and other computerized equipment and phone services.
- g – Keyboard judged less convenient than others.
- h – Wire cannot be unplugged from phone base.
- i – Phone must be plugged into ac outlet.
- j – Inadequate battery cover; batteries fall out easily.
- k – Retains memory for shorter time than most when unplugged from phone line.
- l – Possible for phone to ring in ear; sound is jarring, but judged essentially harmless.
- m – User cannot hear tones when dialing.
- n – Sidetone (controlled feedback of speaker's voice through earpiece) judged deficient in conditions of weak reception.
- o – Damaged by voltage-surge test.
- p – Damaged by static-electricity test.

KEY TO COMMENTS

- *A* – Cannot be mounted on wall.
- *B* – Membrane keypad (only for memory keys on **Uniden**).
- *C* – Push buttons on front of handset.
- *D* – Push buttons on back of handset.
- *E* – Privacy feature; user can erase last number dialed.
- *F* – Lamp on keyboard side of handset.
- *G* – Ringer can be switched between bell and "chirp."
- *H* – Listen-only loudspeaker.
- *I* – Memo pad on phone.
- *J* – Memory recalls dialing mode (pulse or tone) for each number; allows "mixed-mode" dialing.
- *K* – 2-yr. warranty.
- *L* – 3-yr. warranty.

Phone-answering machines

Condensed from CONSUMER REPORTS, May 1986

Caller and users alike should find the new breed of answering machines friendlier and more sophisticated than their often surly and witless forebears. Most new machines, for instance, give callers ample time to leave a message. And their recording and playback circuitry is canny enough to pass over aborted calls and hang-ups, leaving only legitimate messages for users to review.

You can spend as little as $50 for a model that simply delivers a message to a caller. Or you can spend more than $300 for a unit with all the latest electronic wizardry. We split the difference, more or less, with the models tested for this report. Most are low- to moderate-priced units. All have voice activation (VOX) and remote control, two features that we consider highly desirable.

OPERATING CONVENIENCE. Many of the machines answer the phone with a greeting that's as short or as long (five minutes or more) as you like. The maximum length of greeting on other models ranges from 20 to 150 seconds.

After you have recorded your greeting, some units automatically replay your message for a final review. The others allow you to do that manually. A beep, to signal the caller to start speaking, is inserted automatically at greeting's end.

Nearly all answering machines let you select the number of rings before the call is answered. If you plan to be away from home, you might set the machine to pick up quickly. If you're home, you can leave it in the "answer" mode and set it to pick up after four rings or so. That gives you the luxury of screening calls. The models that made call-screening easiest automatically stop and reset to the answer mode when you pick up an extension.

Units with the feature known as VOX continue recording as long as they're activated by a voice. When the voice stops, they usually record for only a few seconds more before sensing silence or the disconnect signal. But some VOX circuits, we found, can be overly sensitive; the noise of an open phone line can keep them going long after a caller has hung up. Most machines give you the option of limiting time on incoming calls if you suspect that the voice-activation feature is being tricked.

All answering machines let you rewind the incoming-message tape to catch a garbled name or number. Most of them also allow you to run the tape fast-forward, so you can bypass a message. Some allow you to skip forward or back exactly one message. But many don't know when to stop playing back; they run past the last current message and treat you to ancient silence or the tail end of old, unerased messages.

SPEECH QUALITY. A listening panel had no difficulty understanding speech recorded on any model. They did find, however, that speech quality varied considerably from model to model. The most natural voices on both incoming and outgoing messages were those reproduced by the *Phone-Mate 8000*. Several other high-rated models were almost as good.

REMOTE CONTROL. In one way or another, all the tested models enable you to call home from a distant phone and listen to any messages that have come in. Generally, that remote control works like this: You call your answering machine, and, while your greeting plays, you signal the machine with a special sound code that identifies you as the owner.

To sound the code, about a third of our tested units require the use of a pocket-sized beeper. When it's held against a telephone mouthpiece, it plays a set of tones over the phone line. The other units employ tone-dialing. With that method, you punch a code number on the keypad of any tone-dialing phone. It's the more convenient method of establishing remote-control contact, in that you don't have to carry around and keep track of a beeper; but it's restrictive, in that you can't use just any old phone to get in touch with your machine.

Remote control entails the risk (if it is a risk) that others may also have access to your messages (if they have the signal or code). The least secure remote control is a single-tone beeper, such as the one for the *Cobra AN8400*. The other beeper remotes we tested emit a series of tones. Units with tone-dialing remote control provide security with a one- to three-digit number to be punched in. But some units, including the top-rated *Phone-Mate 8000*, use what we call "false" touch-tone signals; they allow keys in the same row as the code digit to work as well as the original code, and thus make the code easier to crack.

For all it may lack in security, though, the remote control of the *Phone-Mate 8000* more than makes up in clarity and convenience. It issues voice prompts to guide the user. If you call it to retrieve messages, for example, the voice might say, "Hello, you have two messages," and then gently prompt you through every step of getting your messages by remote operation.

As indicated by the table on page 172, many of the features with which answering machines are endowed are in some way associated with their remote-control systems. One such worthwhile feature is the "toll-saver." If there are no messages waiting on the tape, it delays picking up till the fourth ring. If you hear two or three rings while you're calling in, you can hang up before the call is completed, saving yourself a toll charge for the information that there are no calls. With other remote features, depending on the machine, you can phone in orders to change the outgoing greeting, and even to have the machine put itself in the answer mode (in case you had forgotten to turn it on at home). The features table also notes models whose remote control can be used, among other things, for monitoring sounds in a room at home (to keep tabs, say, on unsupervised children) or sending memos home.

RECOMMENDATIONS. Our first choice is the *Phone-Mate 8000*. It delivered natural-sounding speech, and its voice prompting made remote-control operations a snap. It does have its quirks—you must record your greeting very carefully to keep the machine from getting confused, and you can't reset the toll-saver remotely after taking your messages through another phone—but these are minor. The *8000* lists for $190, but it's often discounted by 30 percent. All the other models in the top two-thirds of the Ratings are also good machines, and any of them might be good buys if discounting makes the price right.

We also tested, but have not included in the Ratings, a number of answering machines that come with their own phones. Four of those combination units obviously grew from the addition of a phone to a rated answering machine. Hence, the *Phone-Mate 8000* grew into model *8050* ($230 list); the

Text continued on page 174

Ratings of phone-answering machines

Listed in order of estimated overall quality. Models judged equal in quality are bracketed and listed alphabetically. Ratings should be used in conjunction with the table on page 172. Except as noted, prices are list; * indicates price is that paid by CU. Discounts are usually available. [D] indicates model was discontinued at original publication.

⊜ ⊖ ○ ◒ ●

Better ⟵⟶ Worse

Brand and model	Price	Size [1]	Overall convenience	Speech quality: Owner's message	Speech quality: Caller's message	Control layout	Security of messages	Clarity of instructions	Advantages	Disadvantages	Comments
PHONE-MATE 8000	$190	S	⊜	⊜	⊜	⊜	●	⊖	A,B,E,G,H,J,K,L,M,P	—	B,C,D,L
PANASONIC KXT1421	120	M	○	○	⊜	○	⊜	⊜	F,P	b,i,k,l	A,C,F,G
PANASONIC KXT1625	170	S	○	⊖	⊖	⊖	⊜	⊜	F,P	i,k,l,u	C,F,G,H,O
UNIDEN EX9500	290	M	○	⊖	⊜	◒	⊜	⊜	A,E,L,N,O,P	e,f,g,i,k,l,r,u	B,G,H,K,L,O
CODE-A-PHONE 2530A	170	M	⊖	⊖	○	○	○	◒	A,F,L,O,P	—	A,F,M
AT&T 2500	230	L	○	○	⊖	●	○	⊖	F,G,L,M,O,P	c,e,f,i,l,q	A,C,L
AT&T 2300	160	L	◒	⊖	⊖	●	◒	⊜	C,D,O,Q	b,o,s	A
GE 29845	104	M	◒	⊖	⊖	⊖	○	○	F,L,P	b,i,k,l	A,G,I
GTE 7300	130	S	○	○	○	●	⊜	○	A,M,O	l	—
RECORD-A-CALL 675 [2]	110 [3]	L	○	○	◒	⊜	○	○	F,G,L,M,O,P	c,e,f,i,l,q	A,L,N
CODE-A-PHONE 2100	110	L	○	○	◒	⊜	◒	⊖	A,F,O	b,c	M
RECORD-A-CALL 655 [2]	90 [3]	M	◒	⊖	⊖	⊜	○	○	F,L,M,P	b,c,e,f,i,k,l,p	A,L,N
GTE 7200	120	S	◒	○	○	●	◒	○	A,M,O	h,l	—

(Rating symbols, from better to worse: ⊜ fully striped, ⊖ top half striped, ○ open, ◒ bottom half black, ● solid black.)

TOSHIBA TCD7020 [2]	150	M	○	●	◒	◒	○	⊜	D,G,I,O	e,f,l,u	*A,C,D*
COBRA AN8400	130	L	●	○	⊜	●	●	◒	—	b,c,d,l	*A*
MESSAGE-MINDER MM1850	157	L	●	○	⊜	⊜	◒	○	—	b,c,d,e,f,h,l,t	*A,L,N*
TOSHIBA TCD7010 [2]	127	M	◒	●	◒	◒	○	⊜	D,G,O	e,f,l,u	*A,C,D*
RADIO SHACK TAD212	120	M	●	⊜	⊜	⊜	◒	○	O,P	b,c,d,e,f,h,i,l,p,r,t	*A,E*
PHONE-MATE 5000	120	S	◒	○	●	◒	●	⊜	A,B,G,J,M,P	a,j,m,n,o,u	*J,L*
SANYO TAS3000 [2]	100	L	●	⊜	○	●	◒	●	M,O	b,d,e,f,l,s	*A,C,D,N*
RADIO SHACK TAD214	180	L	◒	◒	●	⊜	◒	○	D,O	b,c,d,e,f,h,i,p	*A*

[1] *S = small (approx. 6x8x2 in.); M = medium (approx. 8x9x2 in.); L = large (approx. 9x11x13 in.).*
[2] *Discontinued but may be available in some stores.*
[3] *Price CU paid.*

FEATURES IN COMMON
All have: voice-activated recording (VOX); phone-in remote playback of calls; telephone cord with modular plug and ac power cord; replaceable tapes; call-screening with adjustable volume.
Except as noted, all: use standard cassettes; have momentary rewind and fast-forward controls for caller's message; have built-in microphone for recording owner's message; have built-in jack for telephone connection; have variable-length owner's message; lose count of callers' messages when power is interrupted; require only 1 action to play owner's message and to reset for answering; allow erasing of callers' messages from tape; automatically stops or resets after last caller's message is played back; allow remote playback even if callers' message-tape becomes full; have ringer equivalence number (REN) of 1 or less (a REN total of more than 5 for all phones and machines on a standard home line may prevent instruments from ringing); have limited 1-yr. warranty on parts and labor.

KEY TO ADVANTAGES
A – Automatically enters answer mode when no other function is selected.
B – Automatically resets for new messages after playback.
C – Rewind backs up by 1 message when pressed during playback.
D – Fast-forward skips forward 1 message when pressed during playback.
E – Batteries preserve incoming-message count in case of momentary power loss.
F – Rewinds back over a portion of VOX delay; reduces time between callers' messages.
G – Answer mode cancels automatically if any phone is picked up.
H – Day and time is announced by voice after each message; voice judged to be clear.
I – Time is announced by voice before each message; voice judged to be not very clear.
J – Can be set to answer mode remotely by letting phone ring 10 or more times.
K – Prompts user with voice for most functions; judged a significant aid to use.
L – Hang-ups after the beep are not counted or recorded.
M – Automatically plays back owner's message for review after recordings.
N – Allows recording a second owner's message for optional use.
O – VOX can be overridden to limit length of callers' messages; can prevent tie-ups on noisy phone lines.
P – Hang-ups during greeting not counted.
Q – Answer cycle cancels automatically if connected phone is picked up.

KEY TO DISADVANTAGES
a – Uses single tape for both owner's and callers' messages; may create irksome delay for caller.
b – Requires endless-loop cassette for owner's message; replacements may be harder to find than standard cassettes.
c – Requires leaderless cassette for caller's message; replacements may be harder

Keys to Ratings continued on next page

Ratings Keys to phone-answering machines continued

to find than standard cassettes.

d – Recorder's heads do not retract between uses; may hasten tape wear.

e – Requires more than 1 action to play back callers' messages.

f – Callers' message tape must be rewound after playback before new messages can be recorded.

g – Requires more than 1 action (after coding) for remote playback of message.

h – Requires more than 1 action to reset machine after remote playback of callers' messages.

i – Rewind control locks when pressed; slightly less convenient than control activated only when held down.

j – No fast-forward.

k – Fast-forward control locks when pressed; slightly less convenient than control activated only when held down.

l – Does not automatically stop or reset after last message has played back.

m – Cannot erase previous messages; new messages are recorded over old ones.

n – Momentary power loss erases greeting.

o – Momentary power loss loses callers' messages up to point of outage.

p – No built-in jack for phone connection; 2-way adapter must be used if machine and phone share a jack.

q – Requires external microphone (supplied) for recording owner's message.

r – Phone line may be tied up for up to ½ hour if remote playback of callers' messages is interrupted.

s – Remote playback of callers' messages not possible after tape becomes full.

t – Length of owners' message is fixed by tape length: 20 sec. with tape supplied.

u – VOX circuit very sensitive; may continue to record on noisy phone lines after callers have hung up.

KEY TO COMMENTS

A – Controls arranged so that phone can rest on top of unit.

B – Batteries must be replaced yearly.

C – Can be used with multikey office phone system using A-A1 contacts.

D – Needs 2-line adapter for use with phone jacks supplying lighted-dial voltage or 2-line phones.

E – REN greater than 1.

F – Headphone jack.

G – Caller's message time can be fixed at 60 sec., except 30 sec. for **Uniden**.

H – Jack for remote-control microphone.

I – Line held briefly for call pick-up if machine is stopped manually during caller's message.

J – Caller's tape supplied holds only 15 min. of calls; longer tapes are readily available.

K – Includes coder, so remote control can work with non-touch-tone phones.

L – Remote control seems to need long tones; may not work on phones with short tones.

M – 2-yr. warranty on parts; 6 mo. on labor.

N – 1-yr warranty on parts; 3 mo. on labor.

O – Accepts external microphone with multiple functions for recording dictation.

Features of phone-answering machines

			Caller's message			Remote control								
Brand and model	**Tape size** [1]	**Maximum length of owner's message (sec.)** [2]	**Maximum time limit (min.)** [3]	**Call counter** [4]	**Playback stops at end of current messages**	**Activation** [5]	**Security-code**	**Message change**	**Toll-saver**	**Ring-number selection**	**Two-way record**	**Memo**	**Dictation**	**Comments**
PHONE-MATE 8000	M	Long	Long	D	✓	FT	—	✓	✓	1,4	✓	✓	—	*F,P,Q,S,U*
PANASONIC KXT1421	C	30	Long	B	—	T	✓	—	✓	2,4	—	✓	✓	*H,K,S,U*

PANASONIC KXT1625	M	Long	Long	B	—	T	✓	✓	✓	2,4	—	✓	✓	*C,D,F,H,K,O,S,T*
CODE-A-PHONE 2530A	M	150	Long	L	✓	T	—	✓	✓	1,4	✓	✓	—	*C,D,E,F,H,M,S,T,U*
UNIDEN EX9500	M	Long	Long	D	—	T	✓	—	—	1,4	✓	✓	✓	*C,D,E,F,H,K,M,N,T,U*
AT&T 2500	C	Long	Long	D	—	FT	—	✓	✓	1-6	✓	—	✓	*C,D,F,H,K,M,S,T,U*
AT&T 2300	C	20	Long	B	—	B	—	—	✓	2,4	✓	—	✓	*C,F,K,L,M,S,T,U*
GE 29845	C	30	Long	B	—	B	—	—	✓	2,4	—	—	—	*H,U*
GTE 7300	M	Long	Long	D	—	T	✓	✓	✓	2,4	✓	✓	—	*G,J,S*
RECORD-A-CALL 675	C	Long	Long	B	—	FT	—	✓	✓	4	✓	—	✓	*C,D,F,H,K,M,Q,S,U*
CODE-A-PHONE 2100	C	20	Long	L	✓	T	—	—	✓	2,4	—	✓	—	*H,M,S,U*
RECORD-A-CALL 655	C	20	3	L	—	FT	—	—	—	2,4	—	—	—	*C,M,S*
GTE 7200	M	Long	Long	B	—	B	—	—	✓	2,4	✓	✓	—	*G,J,S,U*
TOSHIBA TCD7020	C	90	Long	B	—	T	—	✓	✓	3-5	✓	—	✓	*K,M,P,Q,S,T,U*
COBRA AN8400	C	20	2	B	—	B	—	—	✓	2,4	—	✓	—	*B,U*
MESSAGE-MINDER MM1850	C	20	3.5	L	—	T	—	—	—	1-4	✓	—	—	*C,F,H,M,S,U*
TOSHIBA TCD7010	C	90	Long	B	—	T	—	—	✓	3-5	—	—	✓	*M,S,T,U*
RADIO SHACK TAD212	C	20	3	L	—	B	—	—	✓	1,4	—	—	—	*C,H,M*
PHONE-MATE 5000	M	60	3	B	✓	FT	—	—	✓	1,4	—	✓	—	*A,H,U*
SANYO TAS3000	C	30	Long	L	—	B	—	—	—	1-5	—	✓	✓	*C,K,L,M,S,U*
RADIO SHACK TAD214	C	30	3	L	✓	B	—	✓	✓	1,4	✓	—	—	*C,F,H,I,M,S,T,U*

[1] *M = microcassette; C = cassette.*
[2] *Long = 5 min. or more.*
[3] *Long = as long as rest of tape.*
[4] *L = light, no counter; B = blinking light indicates count; D = digital display of count.*
[5] *B = beeper; T = touch-tone; FT = "false" touch-tone, with less security than true touch-tone-activated models.*

Keys to Features Comments on next page

KEY TO FEATURES COMMENTS

A–Uses single cassette.
B–Phone available expressly for unit; hearing-aid compatible.
C–"Announce-only" mode; plays outgoing messages without recording incoming messages.
D–"Announce-only" message can be longer than 1 min.
E–"Announce-only" message can be interrupted to use remote features.
F–Records conversations without sounding warning beep.
G–Records conversations while sounding warning beep.
H–User can leave "marker" on tape as a reminder of messages already heard.
I–Tape counter.
J–Can fit on standard wall-telephone base.
K–Can be used for long dictation.
L–Will not answer if message tape is full.
M–Automatic "save" function.
N–Dual-greeting feature; plays one of two greetings.
O–Room-monitor feature (to check sounds from room in which machine is placed).
P–Time-stamping feature; includes time and (with **Phone-Mate 8000**) day-of-week with message playbacks.
Q–Tape-full message.
R–Answers 2 phone lines.
S–Remote erase of message tape.
T–Remote skip and/or fast-forward.
U–Remote backspace and/or repeat message.

Code-A-Phone 2530A became model *2555* ($180); the *Code-A-Phone 2100* became model *2150* ($150); and the *Phone-Mate 5000* became model *5050* ($160). The *Code-A-Phone 2555* was judged the best combination unit, overall (with its phone a bargain at only $10 extra, if you believe in list prices). The *Phone-Mate 8050* boasts the fine answering machine that we top-rated, but its phone wasn't up to the same high standard.

Telescopes

Condensed from CONSUMER REPORTS, November 1985

Distant and dim though it was on its last go-around through the inner solar system, Halley's Comet seemed to be a good omen for telescope makers. With comet hype soaring in late 1985, we figured it was high time to report on telescopes. We tested 16 models in a range of sizes, concentrating on inexpensive instruments (under $500) that might make good gifts for children, but touching on a few better-class models as well.

IMPORTANT OBJECTIVES. Our telescopes were of three types: refractors, long tubed instruments (descendents of the type that Galileo used) with an "objective" lens on one end to focus light into a small image, and an "eyepiece" lens at the other end to magnify that image; reflecting telescopes (descended from a design by Isaac Newton), which have a curved mirror for an objective to focus light into a small image for the eyepiece; and catadioptric telescopes, which combine the features of the other two types, having an objective that includes at least one lens and one or more mirrors (this permits even shorter barrels).

In any of those designs, the aperture, which is the diameter of the objective whether lens or mirror, is a vital measure. The aperture sets the limits of the instrument's light-gathering ability and its resolution, the primary optical properties of a telescope.

The bigger a telescope's objective, the more light it will collect and the brighter the image at a given magnification. A three-inch objective, for example, can gather about 100 times as much light as a human eye. Doubling that objective diameter would increase light-gathering ability fourfold.

Resolution refers to a telescope's ability to show as discrete images, separate objects that appear very close together. Note that both light-gathering and resolution are determined by the *effective* diameter of the objective, one of the important characteristics we've entered in the Ratings. The nominal, or physical, aperture of most of the lower-rated inexpensive models is higher than the figure that we give, but it's irrelevant. For instance, in the *Celestron Comet Watcher,* the telescope tube narrows a few inches behind the objective, cutting off about two-thirds of the light that the objective collects. The *Halleyscope,* our one zoom-lens model, didn't make the best use of its objective, either; at its lowest power, it uses only one-quarter of its objective's area.

USEFUL MAGNIFICATION. Deciding what magnification to use in a given situation depends, in very general terms, on the object you want to view. You usually begin with an eyepiece that has a fairly long focal length, then switch to shorter-length eyepieces if the object is bright enough to make the switch worthwhile. When viewing extended, dim objects such as galaxies, nebulae, and comets, image brightness often sets the limit on useful power.

The Ratings lists "power for bright image" for each telescope. That's the highest power that the telescope can use and still yield a maximum-brightness image of an extended object. Dividing that bright-image power into the telescope's focal length (the objective-to-eyepiece distance) in turn gives you the focal length the eyepiece must have to deliver an optimal image of extended *faint* objects.

The moon, the major planets, and other extended *bright* objects look best at higher magnifications (up to 1 times the objective diameter in millimeters). For resolving double stars, a magnification of 2 times the objective diameter is sometimes useful; that's listed as "maximum usable power" in the Ratings.

When viewing a pointlike object such as a star, you reach the upper limit of useful magnifying power when the image finally becomes large enough to see as a tiny disk rather than as an apparent point. There's no gain in using an even shorter eyepiece. In fact, greater magnification will make the image disk look worse—larger but dimmer.

A 60mm (2.4-in.) telescope can provide useful magnification no greater than about 120x. (That is, the object will appear to be 120 times larger than it would to the unaided eye.) As the Ratings indicate, a few models come with an eyepiece too powerful for the rest of the telescope.

Our tests evaluated the image each eyepiece provided of a pointlike "artificial star." The Ratings column headed "image quality" gives our judgments of the image each telescope's highest-power eyepiece provided in the center of the field of view. But image quality is limited by the light-gathering ability of the telescope. Our judgments, then, relate to the theoretical best to be expected from a telescope of a given objective size. An "excellent" image in a small-objective telescope will never be as good as an "excellent" image in a bigger model.

CONVENIENCE. Most of the inexpensive telescopes are cradled in simple "altazimuth" mounts that merely let the telescope swing up and down and from side to side. The "equatorial" mount found on the expensive models (and the inexpensive *Tasco 132T)* is greatly preferable. An equatorial mount has a polar axis and a declination axis (perpendicular to the polar axis). With the polar axis properly aligned (parallel to the earth's

Text continued on page 178

Ratings of telescopes

Listed in price groups; within groups, listed in order of estimated overall quality. Prices are list; + indicates shipping is extra. Substantial discounts may be available.

Excellent	Very good	Good	Fair	Poor
⊜ (fully hatched)	⊖ (partly hatched)	○	◒	●

Brand and model	List price	Type [1]	Weight (lb.) [2]	Effective objective diameter (mm)	Objective focal length (mm)	Power for bright image [3]	Max. usable power	Actual highest power	Image quality [4]	Tracking conven.	Focusing conven.	Advantages	Disadvantages	Comments
Inexpensive models (less than $500)														
EDMUND ASTROSCAN 2001	$ 299	NRF	13.8	105.1	445	15x	210x	16x	Good	Fair	Very good	—	—	G,I,M,Q
TASCO 132T	370	Cat 3	15.6	76	600	11x	150x	100x	Very good	Very good	Good	G,K,N	—	B,F,J,K
SELSI 241	289	Cat 3	7.1	76	600	11x	150x	100x	Very good	Fair	Good	G,K	—	B,D,J,K
JASON COMET CHASER 336	350	Cat 3	9.7	75.2	750	11x	150x	125x	Good	Good	Fair	G,K	—	B,D,J,H,K
BUSHNELL BANNER ASTRO 280	180	SRL	8.1	54	700	8x	110x	140x	Excellent	Fair	Poor	H,J	—	A,B,C,D
SELSI 274	184	SRL	9.0	51	800	7x	100x	160x	Very good	Good	Poor	C,H,I,J,L	—	A,B,C,D,K
MEADE COMETSCANNER 220	150	SRL	4.3	49.5	600	7x	100x	27x	Excellent	Fair	Good	—	—	C,G

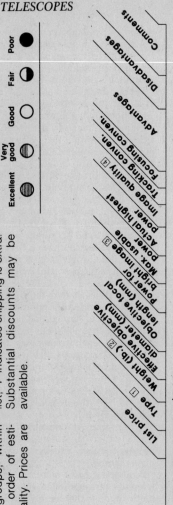

JASON 311	142	SRL	8.3	43	700	6x	90x	140x	⊜	◒	○	H,J	—	*A,B,C,D*
TASCO 49TR	300	SRL	12.5	40	800	6x	80x	160x	⊜	◒	◒	C,F,G,J	—	*B,C*
HALLEYSCOPE	240	SRZ	3.5	19.5-35	118-437	3x	40x	8-32x	⊖	◒	○	H,K	d	*C,J,N*
Not acceptable														
■ *The followingk model was rated Not Acceptable because of its inferior design and performance.*														
CELESTRON COMETRON COMET WATCHER	199	SRL	3.2	34.5	300	5x	70x	12x	○	●	◒	—	a	*C*
Expensive models (more than $500)														
CELESTRON SUPER C8 PLUS	2100	Cat 8	63.3	203	2000	29x	410x	286x	⊜	⊜	⊜	A,B,E,F,L,M,O	b,c	*E,M*
QUESTAR STANDARD 3.5	2483	Cat M	16.4	89.5	1300	13x	180x	81x	⊜	⊜	⊜	C,D,E,K,L,N,O	—	*B,C,D,J,N*
BAUSCH & LOMB CRITERION 4000	695	Cat M	15.8	101.6	1200	15x	200x	67x	⊖	⊜	⊜	A,C,E,L,N,P	—	*J,L,M*
CELESTRON C90 ASTRO	949	Cat M	17.3	91.6	1000	13x	180x	56x	⊖	⊜	○	E,L,P	a,b,e	*C,J,L,O*
MEADE 2045	995	Cat M	20.3	101.6	1000	15x	200x	111x	⊖	⊜	⊖	E,K,L,N	—	*J,L,M,P*

1 *NRF = 4⅛-in. Newtonian rich-field reflector. Cat 3 = 3-in. catadioptric, moderate resolution. Cat 8 = 8-in. catadioptric, high resolution. Cat M = 3½ to 4-in. catadioptric, moderate resolution.*

2 *Includes telescope, tripod, and storage box.*

3 *At 7mm exit pupil, the minimum-size output an eyepiece must have to magnify extended objects without loss of brightness.*

4 *Highest-power eyepiece. Judgments apply to center of image, and they are expressed in terms of the theoretical best that can be expected of a given size of objective lens. Thus, judgments of image quality for models with different objective diameters are not strictly comparable.*

Keys to Ratings on next page

Keys to Ratings for telescopes

FEATURES IN COMMON

All have star diagonal, or equivalent, and lens cap. *Except as noted, all have* altazimuth mount, table-top tripod, finderscope, and 0.96-in.-diameter eyepieces.

KEY TO ADVANTAGES

A – All appropriate optical surfaces have antireflection coatings.
B – Built-in spirit level.
C – Parfocal eyepieces; need not be refocussed when eyepieces are changed.
D – Carrying case judged very convenient.
E – Carrying case provided.
F – Comes with metal field tripod; judged more convenient than wooden tripod.
G – Moon filter provided.
H – Has erecting lens (to put image right side up) for viewing earth-surface objects.
I – Solar projection screen provided.
J – Tripod has tray for holding eyepieces.
K – Comes with adapter for camera.
L – Fine-motion controls.
M – Equatorial mount; alignment ease judged very good.
N – Equatorial mount; alignment ease judged good.
O – Clock drive; judged very good in smoothness.
P – Clock drive; judged good in smoothness.

KEY TO DISADVANTAGES

a – Tabletop tripod very unstable.
b – Does not fit easily into case.
c – Latitude scale inconveniently located.
d – No finderscope or sights.
e – Lens cap difficult to remove.

KEY TO COMMENTS

A – Has wooden field tripod.
B – Barlow lens provided (2x, except for **Questar,** which is 1.5x, and **Selsi 274,** which is 3x).
C – Dew cap.
D – Sun filter.
E – Comes with instruction tape.
F – Mount came incorrectly assembled.
G – Has sights in lieu of finderscope.
H – Although mount resembles equatorial type, it is actually altazimuth type.
I – Shoulder strap.
J – Can be used on camera tripod.
K – Lens cap has port for viewing sun.
L – Field tripod available.
M – Eyepieces are 1.25 in. in diameter.
N – Uses nonstandard, threaded eyepiece(s).
O – Equatorial mount; but its alignment ease was judged poor.
P – Clock drive was judged only fair.
Q – Available from Edmund Scientific, 101 East Gloucester Pike, Barrington, NJ 08007.

---

axis of rotation), you can follow a celestial object as it arcs across the heavens simply by turning the telescope about the polar axis. Celestial equivalents of latitude and longitude let you locate an object in the heavens by referring to a star chart and calculating the object's position at a particular time of night from a particular spot on earth.

All the equatorial-mount models except the *Tasco 132T* have a clock drive that turns the telescope about its polar axis at the same rate as the earth rotates. If the polar axis has been oriented properly, a smoothly running drive will automatically keep a celestial object in view.

A telescope's field of view at powers greater than about 60x is so small that it's difficult to locate a particular celestial object directly. Most models come with a finderscope, a small 5x or 6x wide-angle telescope attached to the main telescope's tube. It's used to locate and center the target object so that it appears within the narrower field of view of the main telescope.

A Barlow lens, provided with eight models, roughly doubles the magnification of a given eyepiece (although most models had eyepieces good enough to give adequate range and sharpness without the device). A Barlow lens can also help eyeglass wearers to see the entire field of view conveniently.

All the telescopes come with a "star diagonal" or its equivalent. A star diagonal contains a prism or mirror that permits viewing at right angles to the telescopes' line of sign (so you don't have to twist your neck when the scope is pointing high in the sky).

RECOMMENDATIONS. Our tests turned up one inexpensive model—the *Edmund Astroscan 2001*, listing at $299 plus shipping—that might make a natural gift for a youngster getting started in astronomy. The *Astroscan* is a 4 ½-inch Newtonian "rich-field" model that shows a relatively wide field (3 degrees) with an image brightness near the maximum possible. The spectacular star-packed view through a rich-field telescope can provide the beginner with an awesome introduction to the wonders of the sky. On the other hand, the *Astroscan's* low (16x) power suits it none too well for looking at small but larger-than-pointlike objects like planets. And its simple aiming system makes it difficult to track heavenly bodies conveniently.

Another interesting inexpensive model is the *Tasco 132T*. It lists at $370, but our sample cost $300. The *Tasco 132T* is optically respectable and has an equatorial mount.

If you're moved by a really serious interest in astronomy, the 8-inch catadioptric *Celestron Super C8 Plus* would make a fine choice. Its list price is high, $2100, but we were able to buy it for $1350 in a New York City camera store. If you find it at a similarly attractive discount, be sure that the price includes tripod and equatorial wedge (the latter needed for polar alignment.)

Running shoes

Condensed from CONSUMER REPORTS, October 1986

Modern running shoes are made of materials that are lighter yet sturdier and more durable than the sneakers that runners used to wear. And if they're well designed—according to the dictates of the relatively new science of biomechanics—modern running shoes cushion and cup the heel, support the arches, protect the ball of the foot, and flex easily in the forefoot to conserve momentum at the push-off of each new stride. As a result of such refinements in materials and design, people today can run farther, with less chance of injury, than they could have expected to a mere decade ago.

For this report, we tested 26 models of running shoes, 15 for men and 11 for women. Technically, the models are known as training shoes, which are supposed to have enough stability and cushioning to protect feet and legs over prolonged training periods, week in and week out. Having satisfied ourselves earlier that it's unwise to inflict cheap shoes on serious runners, we picked models priced for the most part from $45 to $80.

TEST RUNS. Our starting premise was simply to have a panel of serious runners do the testing, on grounds that no amount of lab analysis can tell how a shoe will actually feel on the road. To that end, we recruited 117 panelists, 77 men and 40 women, through a New York City area runner's club. The group represented a broad range in age, weight, running style, and miles usually logged per week. We assigned to each runner two models of shoes, and, to insure a good fit, we asked the runners to buy both pairs on their own, using CU funds.

The panelists alternated wearing test shoes daily for two to three months, accumulating about 200 miles on each

Text continued on page 182

Ratings of running shoes

Listed by types; within types, listed in order of preference of a panel of runners. Differences between closely ranked models were slight. Prices are list. Discounts are available.

◍	◓	○	◒	●
Better				Worse

Brand and model	Price	Weight per pair (oz.)	Materials: Midsole [1]	Materials: Outsole [2]	Type of last [3]	Panel preferences: Overall comfort	Shock absorption	Flexibility	Toe room	Overall stability [5]	Heel counter [5]	Sweat loss	Comments
Men's shoes													
NEW BALANCE 470	$53	24 oz.	SE,(M)	CR	C	◍	◓	◍	◍	○	○	◒	A,E
ASICS TIGER EPIRUS	80	20	ME,(M)	E	C	◍	◍	◍	◓	◓	◓	◍	B,D,E
TURNTEC QUANTUM PLUS	60	24	ME,(M)	E,(M)	S	◓	◓	◍	◍	◓	◓	◓	D
SAUCONY SHADOW	59	22	SE,(M)	CR	S	◍	◍	◍	◓	○	◓	◍	B,C
ASICS TIGER ULTRA 1000	57	19	ME,(M)	E	C	◍	◓	◍	◓	○	◓	◍	E
SAUCONY AMERICA	48	25	ME	CR	S	◓	◓	◓	◓	○	◓	◍	E
BROOKS TRILOGY	70	20	ME,(M)	E,CR,(M)	C	◍	◓	◓	◓	○	○	○	B,E,F
NEW BALANCE 1300	130	29	PE	CR	C	◓	◍	◓	◓	◓	◓	○	A,E
ADIDAS ZX500	75	26	SE,(M)	CR,(M)	S	◓	◓	○	○	◍	◓	◒	C,D
BROOKS CHARIOT	62	24	SE,(M)	E,CR,(M)	C	○	○	○	◓	◍	◍	○	B,D

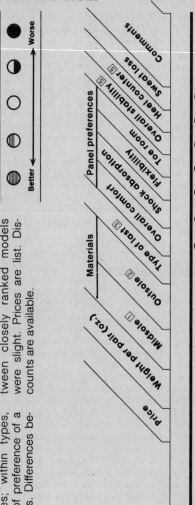

REEBOK DL5600	56	24	ME,(M)	E	C	◓	◓	●	◓	○	○	◓	B,E
NIKE VENUE	60	24	A,SE,(M)	CR	C	○	○	○	◓	◓	◓	◓	B,C,E
NIKE VORTEX	60	23	A,P	CR	S	○	○	◓	○	○	◓	○	B,E
NEW BALANCE 575	66	29	SE,PE, (M)	CR	C	○	◓	○	◓	◓	◓	◓	A
ETONIC MIRAGE	45	22	SE,(M)	CR	C	○	○	◓	◓	◒	◒	◓	E
Women's shoes													
ASICS TIGER LADY ALLIANCE	62	15	SE,(M)	E	C	●	◓	●	◓	◓	◓	●	B,E
ADIDAS HELSINKI	50	16	SE,(M)	(M)	B	●	◓	●	◓	○	◓	◓	B
NEW BALANCE 520	60	19	SE,(M), PE	CR	C	◓	◓	◓	◓	◓	◓	◓	A,B,E
SAUCONY LADY SHADOW	59	18	SE,(M)	CR	S	◓	●	◓	◓	○	◓	○	B,C
SAUCONY LADY AMERICA	48	19	ME	CR	S	◓	●	◓	●	○	◓	●	E
NIKE LADY VENUE	60	18	A,SE,(M)	CR	C	○	◓	◓	◓	◓	◓	○	B,C,E
BROOKS TRILOGY	70	16	ME,(M)	E,CR,(M)	C	◓	●	◓	◓	○	○	○	B,E,F
ETONIC MIRAGE	45	16	SE,(M)	CR	C	◓	◓	◓	●	◒	◒	◒	E
REEBOK DL5600	56	18	ME,(M)	E	C	◓	◓	◓	○	○	○	◓	B,E
NEW BALANCE 470	53	19	SE,(M)	CR	C	○	○	○	○	○	○	◒	A,E
TURNTEC LADY QUANTUM	50	18	ME,(M)	E,(M)	S	○	◓	◓	◓	◓	◓	○	E

[1] *SE = ethylene vinyl acetate (EVA) in sheet form; ME = molded EVA; P = polyurethane; PE = polyurethane encapsulating EVA; A = air-cushioned rubber; M in parentheses indicates multiple densities of materials.*

[2] *CR = carbon rubber (dense, hard, durable black rubber); E = EVA or expanded rubber (filled with tiny air bubbles for increased cushioning but less durable than carbon rubber); M in parentheses indicates multiple densities of materials.*

[3] *S = slip last; B = board=last; C = combination with board-lasted heel and slip-lasted forefoot.*

[4] *Composition unknown; appears to be hard and dense like carbon rubber but without the blackening of carbon.*

[5] *Consultants' judgments.*

Keys to Running-shoe Ratings continued on next page

Key to Ratings of running shoes

KEY TO COMMENTS

A - Available in several widths.
B - Safety reflective trim.
C - More aggressive outsole tread than most.
D - Plastic "speed lacing" eyelets.
E - Variable-width lacing (helpful for people with very wide or very narrow feet).

COMPANY NAMES AND ADDRESSES

Adidas, 1122 Rte. 22, Mountainside, N.J. 07092. **Asics Tiger Corp.,** 3030 S. Susan St., Santa Ana, Calif. 92704. **Brooks Shoes Inc.,** 9341 Courtland Dr., Rockford, Mich. 49351. **Etonic Inc.,** 147 Centre St., Brockton, Mass. 02134. **New Balance,** 38 Everett St., Boston, Mass. 02134. **Nike Inc.,** 9000 Southwest Nimbus Dr., Beaverton, Ore. 97005. **Reebok International,** 500 Bodwell St. Extension, Avon, Mass. 02322. **Saucony,** div. Hyde Athletic Industries, P.O. Box 6046, Peabody, Mass. 01961. **Lynx/Turntec,** American Sporting Goods, 1 World Trade Center, #8827, New York, N.Y. 10048.

---

pair. After every 40 miles or so, the panelists filled out questionnaires, indicating their degree of preference in several areas for one of the models they were testing over the other. The areas of preference included overall comfort, shock absorption (a combination of cushioning and firmness), flexibility, and toe room. We also asked each panelist which test shoe he or she preferred overall. The panelists' responses, reflecting the collective experience gained from more than 40,000 miles of running, formed the Ratings basis.

We also asked several marathoners—including a podiatrist and a physician who specializes in sports medicine—to act as consultants in assessing the overall stability of the shoes and the quality of the heel counter. Finally, our engineers devised a test to measure the speed with which each shoe model would allow moisture from within (such as sweat from feet) to evaporate.

MATCHING STRIDES. While we have confidence in the Ratings as a consensus determination of high-quality running shoes, we also recognize that there's an significant individual element to be considered, too. No single shoe model can be right for every runner, because runners display a variety of gaits. The most important variation concerns an element of stride called "pronation," the tendency of the foot to roll from the outside to the inside after it lands and as the runner's weight is transferred from heel to toe.

There are a couple of ways that you can analyze your own stride in that regard. The first has to do with the construction of your arches. Runners with high arches are considered likely to "underpronate"—that is, their feet roll only slightly on landing. Runners with low arches tend to have extremely flexible feet that roll from the outer heel on landing to the inner portion of the big toe on push-off; those runners are said to "overpronate."

To find out the condition of your arches, try standing barefoot in some water and then step out onto a flat surface where your footprints will be visible. If you have high arches, the heel and toe portions of the print will show separately or be joined by only a thin line. If you have normal arches, the middle of each foot will leave a wet mark that's about an inch to an inch and a half wide. If your arches are low, most or all of the middle of each foot will make a big wet blot.

The second way to check on your stride is to examine the wear pattern of your old running shoes. If you underpronate, heels and soles will be worn down along the outer edges; viewed from the back, the heel counters and the uppers will probably list to the outside. If you have normal feet and a normal stride, the heel counters will be worn on the outside and soles will show the wear near the inside ball of the foot. That's also basically the same wear pattern shown by overpronators, except that the degrees of wear on those portions of their shoes tend to be much more pronounced—the heel counters distorted and the midsoles compressed so that the shoes tilt inward. In extreme cases of overpronating, the entire area across the middle and the ball of each shoe may be heavily worn.

To accommodate individual differences in gait and stride, the makers of running shoes have adopted various methods of construction employing various materials. The Ratings, for example, give each model's type of "last"—the method of shaping a shoe and putting it together. There are two basic types. In a "board-lasted" shoe, the upper is fastened to a fiber board inside the shoe, thereby stiffening it. A "slip-lasted" shoe is made by fastening the upper around the shoemaking form in one piece; it's chief attribute is flexibility. Many of our models represented compromises between the two types, combining the stiffness of board-lasting in the heel with the flexibility of slip-lasting in the forefoot.

The materials used to form the midsole are the most critical in establishing the "feel" of the shoe. The principal cushioning material for midsoles is ethylene vinyl acetate (abbreviated EVA). Molded EVA is about the softest midsole material, but sheet EVA is more common and perhaps more suitable for the majority of runners.

Polyurethane is a heavier, firmer, and more durable material than EVA. When all or part of the EVA in a midsole is encapsulated in polyurethane, as it was in three of the tested shoes, the resulting midsole is claimed to possess the best properties of both materials. Three other shoes have midsoles made partly of rubber with chambers of air sealed inside. Such air cushioning is claimed to keep its shock-absorbing longer than other materials. In most of the running shoes, the materials of the midsole and the outsole are present in both lighter and heavier densities. Such multiple-density soles are designed to provide extra support or cushioning in different areas of the sole.

RECOMMENDATIONS. The shoes appearing in the top Ratings groups of the men's and women's models should satisfy most runners. They were, after all, the clear favorites of the fairly ample sampling of runners that comprised our panel. But runners who recognize in their own gaits certain divergences from the "normal" running stride may wish to consider some top-rated models ahead of others.

Runners who underpronate, for instance, need a cushioned shoe that doesn't restrict motion. They should look to the Ratings for slip-lasted (or combination-lasted) shoes with soft midsoles and high marks in shock absorption and flexibility. Runners who overpronate, however, need more motion control with good support. They should look to the Ratings for board-lasted (or combination-lasted) shoes with firm midsoles and high marks in stability and quality of heel counter. Note that not all of the desired qualities may be fully present in the top groups of both men's and women's shoes. (Thus combination-lasted shoes may have to serve as default choices.) Even so, in our judgment, there's enough variety of materials and construction among the top-rated shoes to please most runners.

Almost all the shoes we tested would be suitable for people who just want something comfortable to knock around in. But serious walkers should be as discriminating in their choice of shoes as serious runners.

Home exercise equipment

Condensed from CONSUMER REPORTS, August 1985

According to one study, nearly 10 million people work out with their home exercise equipment more than twice a week. One reason for all that activity may be the growing realization that an endurance exercise such as running isn't a "complete" workout. Running is an excellent aerobic exercise, conditioning the body to take in and use oxygen more efficiently, and it burns calories. But running doesn't do much to develop upper-body muscular endurance or all-round muscular strength. Those qualities come from working muscles against some form of resistance, as occurs in many exercises that can be performed with home gyms.

The most basic home gym might include a jump rope, a mat, and some dumbbells or ankle weights. Total cost: $50 to $70. A step up might include a stationary bike or rowing machine and a set of free weights or a "home gym" resistance machine. The cost of outfitting such a gym can range from $200 to $1000 or more.

ROWING MACHINES. All of these machines copy the sliding seat of the scull. Apart from that, their basic design diverges into three main branches: piston, oarlock, and flywheel machines.

What we call the piston rowing machine has two arms (the "oars") attached to the frame close to the seat track. The arms move only back and forth in a single plane, with a variable resistance provided by hydraulic pistons. These machines can provide a good workout, but they bear only a glancing resemblance to real rowing. Piston machines are usually compact and easy to store.

The arms of an oarlock rower are mounted about where the oarlocks of a real scull would be and are free to pivot as real oars would, with resistance supplied by some sort of friction or hydraulic device. Since the unrestricted arm movement better mimics actual rowing than the restricted motion of the piston machines, oarlock models can be not only more challenging to row but harder to master.

Some manufacturers configure and characterize their rowing machines as "multi-gyms." The typical multi-gym looks much like a regular piston-type rowing machine, except for the padded platform attached to the seat track. You set this platform on the floor and sit or lie on it to do "presses" and "lifts" with the rower arms. Or you can shift the position of the pistons to perform various other drills.

While the idea of a multi-gym is attractive, the reality was disappointing. The multi-gyms weren't very good resistance-training machines because pivoting arms (resistance that works well during rowing) create awkward an-

For the full story

The date of the original article in CONSUMER REPORTS appears directly below its title. For a more complete report, consult the original version. (For back issues, see page 5.)

gles of motion in other exercises. So paltry were the possible benefits of this gym work that we decided to rate the multi-gyms solely as rowing machines.

PERFORMANCE. In rating the rowing machines, we attached much importance to the quality of the stroke and the safeness of the position into which the machine puts your body, with some consideration given for the comfort of the seat. Those are the factors, we believe, that will contribute most to the success of a rowing exercise.

Quality of construction turned out to be a key in determining the quality of the stroke. The lightweight track on many models flexed enough under the weight of an average-sized rower to affect the seat's motion. (Two models were severely downrated because of the flimsy tubing of their seat tracks.) The quality and the number of seat rollers also affects the glide of the machine. Simple rollers tend to stick when there's weight on them. Better by far are seats that roll on ball bearings.

By and large, the more expensive models were the ones with the best strokes. Machines that are designed so that they produce a good stroke are also usually designed so they don't force the body to work in potentially harmful positions. The machine's arms have to be the right length and be positioned correctly in relation to the footrests; otherwise, they could cause back strain. The footrests should rotate a little, so that they don't force the ankle into a too-sharp angle; otherwise, they could cause shinsplints, foot strains, or overextension of the Achilles tendon.

HOME GYMS. The equipment sold as home gyms ranges from weight-stack machines to cable-strung racks. Despite the variation in design, however, these devices are all meant to substitute for, and presumably improve upon, free weights. One improvement—perhaps the only one—is that with a home gym, you can't drop a barbell on your chest or a dumbbell on your foot.

The weights in a weight-stack machine are safely contained on a column on which they slide up and down. You lift the weights by pulling on a bar, cuff, or handgrip. You can change the total weight being lifted by slipping out a pin and reinserting it elsewhere in the weight stack.

Weight-stack machines come with a bench; to set one up, you either attach it to a wall or use a special stand that costs extra.

PERFORMANCE. Since home gyms are meant to replace free weights, we compared what you could do on each home gym with a workout with dumbbells and barbells. Some machines worked certain parts of the body better than others, so separate judgments are given in the Ratings for the upper body, lower body, and torso.

Different parts of the body can do different amounts of work. During the course of a workout, therefore, you have to change the amount of weight you're lifting or the resistance you're pushing against. The relative convenience of that change was another important judgment, recorded in the Ratings as an advantage or disadvantage.

Home gyms that use springs were disappointing. The farther you stretch a spring, the higher its resistance. That made choosing the proper level of resistance throughout an exercise motion well-nigh impossible.

Although a home gym may make beginners feel safer and more comfortable, we feel that free weights are still the best equipment for building muscle strength and muscle endurance at home. Free weights take up much less space than any home gym, and you can get more and better equipment for the money.

Ratings begin on next page

Ratings of rowing machines

Listed in order of estimated overall quality. Except as noted, prices are list; * indicates approx. price; + indicates shipping is extra. Discounts are often available. [D] indicates model is discontinued.

◍ ◓ ○ ◒ ●
Better ⟷ Worse

Brand and model	Price	Type [1]	Dimensions (HxWxD, in.)	Stroke	Body position	Seat comfort	Advantages	Disadvantages	Comments
WALTON ROWBICISER 544	$349	Oarlock	21x73x56	◓	◓	◍	—	c,j	—
PRO FORM 520	349	Piston	9x31x50	◓	◍	◓	C,I	—	E
CONCEPT II ROWING ERGOMETER	595+	Flywheel	35x18x102	◍	◓	◓	G	a,j	G
PRECOR 612	285	Piston	9x28x50	◓	◓	◓	C,I	—	—
AVITA 950	350	Piston	10x29x52	◓	◍	◓	C,D,I	—	E,F
AMF BENCHMARK 920	595	Wheel	26x15x83	◓	○	◓	D,F	d,e,h	C
WALTON 577 DELUXE GYM SYSTEM	299	Piston/multi	35x30x50	◒	◓	◓	C,H,I	—	B
SEARS CAT. NO. 28772	280+	Piston/multi	35x32x52	◒	◓	◓	B,C,H	—	—
OMNIROW	299	Piston	9x30x50	◒	◓	○	C,I	—	B
HUFFY DELUXE 7010	200	Piston [2]	10x33x49	◒	◓	○	C,I	a,b	D
TUNTURI ATRM	199	Piston	11x29x54	◓	○	○	H,I	b,d,f	D
VITAMASTER RM11	270	Piston	9x33x49	○	◓	○	C,I	a,g	D,H
DP CARNIELLI SUPERSKIFF 160512	368	Oarlock	21x52x53	●	○	◒	A,E,J	d,f	E
AJAY OCTA-GYM 7180	149	Piston/multi	16x46x60	◒	○	◒	B	d,f,g,j	A

SEARS CAT. NO. 28751	170+	Oarlock	18x45x49	◒	○	●	A,I	b,c,f,j,k	*H*
[D]MCA SPORTS TR200	125	Piston	12x31x49	◒	●	◒	H,I	b,d,f	*H*
[D]SCANDIA 2226	100*	Piston	12x29x54	●	◒	◒	B,H,I	b,d	—
COLUMBIA 4872	135	Piston/multi	33x30x53	●	◒	●	H,I	c,t	—
[D]AJAY TRIMLINE 15248	60	Piston	16x30x57	●	◒	◒	B,H,I	b,d,f,g	—
COLUMBIA 4871	100	Piston	14x31x51	●	◒	●	H,I	c,f,g	—
[D]SCANDIA 2227	130*	Piston/multi	32x26x56	◒	●	●	B,H	a,b,d,f,i	—

[1] *Resistance provided in following ways: Oarlock, with friction or hydraulic device; piston, with modified shock absorbers; flywheel (and wheel) with weighted wheel (or wheel with electromagnetic brake); piston/multi, with modified shock absorbers for rowing and other exercises.*

[2] *Oars attached with universal joints, so they move more like real oars.*

FEATURES IN COMMON

Except as noted, all: have continuous resistance adjustment; have same height for storage as in use; require some simple assembly; come with 1-yr. warranty; are not adjustable for leg length.

KEY TO ADVANTAGES

A – Seat track adjusts for different leg lengths.
B – Uses pin fasteners rather than nuts and bolts to facilitate changing machine for different exercises.
C – Footrests rotate and have proper stop.
D – Has timer.
E – Has stroke counter.
F – Has calorie counter.
G – Has "speedometer."
H – Storage height between 10 and 15 in.
I – Stands on end for storage.
J – Can be quickly disassembled for storage.

KEY TO DISADVANTAGES

a – Number of resistance settings is limited.
b – Construction of seat track or seat insubstantial; under weight of average-sized user, track likely to bend and seat to stick.
c – Footrests rotate but have no stop; feet tend to be forced into too-sharp angle for safe use.
d – Only one strap for both feet.
e – Foot restraint is padded bar whose height cannot be adjusted.
f – Footrest angle forces feet into too-sharp angle for safe use.
g – Footrests are in awkward position; user is forced to lean too far forward at start of stroke.
h – Stroke starts with jerk that some users found objectionable.
i – Bench for auxiliary exercises is not removable.
j – Storage height is greater than 15 in.
k – Resistance, provided by friction device, was hard to set.

KEY TO COMMENTS

A – Instructional videotape available.
B – Comes assembled.
C – Resistance adjustments are not continuous, but number of settings was sufficient.
D – Comes with tools for assembly.
E – Comes partially assembled.
F – Limited 5-yr. warranty.
G – Limited lifetime warranty.
H – Limited 90-day warranty.

Ratings of home gyms

Listed in order of estimated quality, based mainly on ability to provide resistance training. Most require simple assembly. Except as noted, prices are list; * indicates approx. price; + indicates shipping is extra. Discounts are available. D indicates model is discontinued.

Better ◍ ◐ ○ ◑ ● Worse

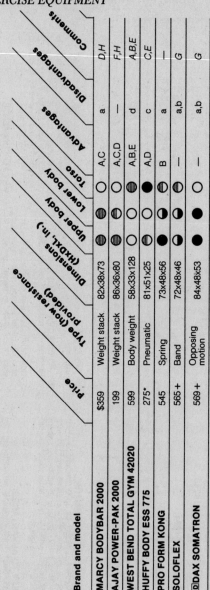

Brand and model	Price	Type (how resistance provided)	Dimensions (HxDxL, in.)	Upper body	Lower body	Torso	Advantages	Disadvantages	Comments
MARCY BODYBAR 2000	$359	Weight stack	82x38x73	◍	◍	○	A,C	a	*D,H*
AJAY POWER-PAK 2000	199	Weight stack	86x36x80	◍	◐	○	A,C,D	—	*F,H*
WEST BEND TOTAL GYM 42020	599	Body weight	58x33x128	○	○	◍	A,B,E	d	*A,B,E*
HUFFY BODY ESS 775	275*	Pneumatic	81x51x25	◐	○	●	A,D	c	*C,E*
PRO FORM KONG	545	Spring	73x48x56	●	◑	◐	B	a	—
SOLOFLEX	565+	Band	72x48x46	◑	◑	◐	—	a,b	*G*
D DAX SOMATRON	569+	Opposing motion	84x48x53	●	●	○	—	a,b	*G*

Keys to Ratings of home gyms

KEY TO ADVANTAGES

A-Relatively easy to change setup for various exercises.
B-Barbell weights can be used to increase weight resistance.
C-Extra weight kits available.
D-Bench and bars hang on frame for storage, reducing depth to less than 24 in..
E-Can be folded for storage (87x33x48 in.).

KEY TO DISADVANTAGES

a-Harder than most to store because of size and shape.
b-Bench judged less comfortable than most.
c-No pad or bench included.
d-Arm presses done lying head down on slant board can be unsafe for some users.

KEY TO COMMENTS

A-Instructional audio tape included.
B-Flip-card exercise guide available.
C-Comes with tools for assembly.
D-Limited 90-day warranty.
E-Limited 1-yr. warranty.
F-According to mfr., a later designation of this model is **Fitness Pak 200.**
G-Limited 10-yr. warranty.
H-Comes in many pieces; assembly is complex.

Exercise bikes

Condensed from CONSUMER REPORTS, August 1986

As a means of getting indoor exercise at home, an exercise bike is a good choice. Cycling strengthens the legs and makes certain leg and hip muscles more flexible. It burns lots of calories. It conditions the body aerobically, enabling it to use oxygen more efficiently and increasing overall endurance. Also, as exercises go, cycling is kind to those who are out of shape.

There are more than 100 brands and models of exercise bikes. They all work on the same principle. Pedaling moves the single wheel, which acts as a flywheel, against some form of resistance—rather like riding a regular bike with the brakes on. The resistance can be adjusted, making the bike harder or easier to pedal.

On relatively cheap exercise bikes, the wheel looks like the wheel on a regular bicycle. Such wheels develop little momentum and do little to make the exercise ride a smooth one. These bikes feel clumsy, and they're difficult to pedal. So, drawing from past experience with cheap bikes, we didn't bother to test any for this report. Instead, we looked for models with a heavy, solid flywheel, typically made of cast iron or steel. We selected 25 such models, ranging in price from $150 to $500.

PERFORMANCE. Since a good exercise device should interfere as little as possible with the hard work of conditioning, we considered smoothness of ride the most important attribute of an exercise bike. To that end, an exercise bike, like a regular bike, should have a rigid frame that doesn't wobble under the strain of pedaling. Many of the low-rated models flexed noticeably.

On the best bikes, the flywheel glides with a steady force as the pedals are pumped. The heavier the flywheel, the smoother the ride, as a rule. But the machining of the flywheel matters, too. Worst in that regard was the *Sears 28906*; its flywheel, made of welded plates, was enough out-of-round to produce a pulsing resistance.

We encountered three different

Text continued on page 192

Ratings of exercise bikes

Listed in order of estimated quality. Except where separated by heavy lines, closely ranked models differed little in quality. Unless otherwise indicated, prices are list; + indicates shipping is extra; * indicates approx. price. [D] indicates model is discontinued.

⊜	⊖	○	◒	●
Better				Worse

Brand and model	Price	Smoothness of operation	Noise	Seat comfort	Ease of adjusting resistance	Ease of reading instruments	Ease of adjusting seat height	Comments
TUNTURI EXECUTIVE ERGOMETER	$299	⊜	○	○	⊜	⊖	○	A,L,M,P,R,S,V
WALTON 490	399	⊜	⊜	⊖	○	○	○	A,I,J,M,P,R,S,V
[D] AJAY 520	210*	⊜	⊖	◒	⊜	○	○	A,J,M,P,R,S,V
OMNI 4000	450	⊖	⊖	◒	⊜	⊖	◒	A,M,P,R,S,V
AVITA 450	435	⊖	○	○	⊜	○	○	A,J,M,P,R,S,V
PRECOR 820e	500	⊖	⊜	◒	○	⊖	⊜	B,D,H,K,L,N,Q,T,U,V
MONARK 865 MK II	450	⊖	○	○	◒	○	⊜	B,G,N,P,S,V
AVITA 400	325	⊖	○	○	●	⊜	○	B,J,O,R,V
MONARK CRESCENT 888	199	○	◒	○	○	⊖	⊖	B,G,L,N,O,R,W
SCHWINN BD-3 BIO-DYNE	450	⊖	○	⊖	○	⊜	⊜	A,F,G,M,P,R,T,V
TUNTURI FAMILY CYCLE II	159	○	○	◒	⊜	○	○	B,L,O,S,V

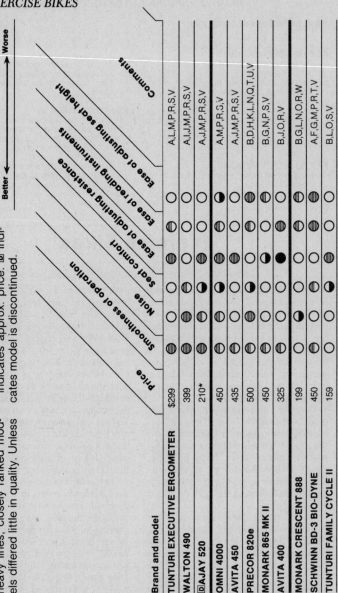

BODYGUARD 955	370*	○	⊜	○	◒	⊜	○	B,N,Q,S,V
[D]MONARK 875	299	○	○	○	○	◒	⊜	B,G,O
OMNI 2000	225	○	○	◒	⊜	◒	◒	B,O,R,S,V,W
SEARS CAT. NO. 29121	300+	○	⊜	○	◒	○	◒	A,I,M,P,Q,S,V,W
SCHWINN DX900	260	⊜	◒	○	○	⊜	⊜	A,F,G,M,R,T,U
WEST BEND 7200	500	○	●	◒	●	⊜	⊜	B,D,H,L,O,Q,T,V
KETTLER RECORD	150	◒	◒	◒	⊜	⊜	●	B,J,O,V
MCA FY 84	100	◒	◒	○	⊜	○	●	B,I,J,O,S,V
[D]WALTON 499B	399	◒	◒	⊜	○	○	◒	A,I,J,M,P,Q,S,V
SCHWINN XR100	190	◒	●	◒	◒	⊜	⊜	C,E,F,G,R,T,U
WALTON 474 TRAVELLER	189	◒	◒	●	⊜	○	●	B,J,O,R,S
[D]VITAMASTER FW-100	175	◒	○	●	⊜	○	◒	B,I,O,S,V
TUNTURI THC3 HOMECYCLE III	229	◒	◒	◒	⊜	●	⊜	B,V
SEARS CAT. NO. 28906	250+	●	◒	○	◒	○	◒	B,I,Q,S

FEATURES IN COMMON
All have an odometer, a speedometer or tachometer, and an adjustable seat.
Except as noted, all have a chain drive, adjustable handlebars, and a seat clamp that didn't slip.

KEY TO COMMENTS
A–Caliper resistance mechanism.
B–Strap resistance mechanism.
C–Single brake-shoe resistance mechanism.
D–Belt drive.
E–Gear drive.
F–Pedals do not stop as flywheel coasts, a disadvantage.
G–Seat held in place by screw pin, very secure.
H–Seat held in place by spring-loaded pin; can work loose (but did not in our tests).
I–Seat held in place by clamp, which may slip slowly.
J–Seat post not marked; difficult to reset height.
K–Handlebars cannot be adjusted.
L–Seat welded to post; cannot be replaced.
M–Tire on flywheel prevents bike from marking floor when being moved.
N–Wheels on frame help in moving bike.
O–Can be moved by rolling on flywheel.
P–Ergometer.
Q–Toe straps without weighted pedals.
R–Toe straps with weighted pedals.
S–Mechanical timer.
T–Electronic timer.
U–Electronic speedometer.
V–Calibrated resistance control, an aid in resetting resistance.
W–According to manufacturer, replaced by similar model: **Monark 888** by **Monark 805**, $199; **Omni 2000** by **Omni 1500EC**, $199; and **Sears 29121** by **Sears 29122**, $250+.

mechanisms used to drive the flywheel. Most models have a chain drive similar to that found on regular bikes. Two have a belt drive, and one uses gears. We also encountered three means of adjusting the resistance to pedaling. On some bikes, calipers with pads (like regular bicycle brakes) pinch the flywheel. On the *Schwinn XR100*, a single brake shoe pushes down on the wheel. And on the rest, a belt or strap cinched around the flywheel increases the pedaling resistance.

Most models allow the rider to coast—to stop pedaling while the flywheel keeps on turning. The *Schwinn* models won't coast, a failing of some consequence. It can add to the inconvenience of starting, since it's easier to begin pedaling if you can first backpedal to a comfortable position. And it could contribute some pain to your exercise; if your foot slipped off a pedal, you could get whomped on the leg.

FEATURES. Generally, wide seats were the most comfortable. The wide, firmly cushioned seat pads on the *Schwinn BD-3* felt as though they gave the best support. The seats were held in place in three ways: screw pins were judged the most secure, but spring-loaded pins and clamps were easier to adjust for seat height. Many models have a seat mounting like the one on regular bikes, so that the seat can be replaced if desired. The seats on some models, however, are welded on for good.

The resistance control, typically a knob or lever, is usually mounted on the handlebars, within easy reach. Most were easy to operate. But the control on the *Avita 400* and the *West Bend 7200* are mounted so low on the frame that a rider may have to stop pedaling to change the resistance, which would break the continuity of exercise.

Many exercise bikes have an ergometer, a device that measures how much energy you're spending in calories, watts, or newton-meters. It can help you to monitor your exercise levels (although some physical therapists contend that a more meaningful and precise monitor is your own pulse rate). Other gauges on the tested models include an odometer, to tell you how "far" you've traveled, and either a speedometer or tachometer, to tell you how fast you're pedaling. Timers are also common and useful, since many people plan to exercise for a certain amount of time rather than "travel" for a particular distance.

Most models have toe straps, which not only keep feet from slipping off the pedals but enable riders to maintain an evenness of exercise by working on both upstroke and downstoke. On some models, the pedals are weighted so that the toe straps always remain conveniently on top.

RECOMMENDATIONS. The three top-rated bikes were the smoothest to pedal, in addition to other virtues. We give a slight nod, overall, to the *Tunturi*, priced at $299.

How to use the Buying Guide

- Look in the index for specific reports.
- Look in the Contents for general subject areas.
- Look on pages 5 to 7 for explanations of check-ratings and Best Buys, and of why some products are included and others not.

Sailboards for beginners

Condensed from CONSUMER REPORTS, July 1985

One of the original practical problems in sailboarding remains a serious deterrent for beginners; they keep falling off, despite instruction to the contrary. Some experts contend that, given the proper lessons, beginners can learn the fundamentals of sailboarding in about six hours. That may be an overly optimistic view. Judging from the experience of two of our testers, who took sailboarding classes to prepare for this project, the typical beginner will need a day or two of instruction followed by 25 to 30 hours of sailing just to develop enough skill to perform the basic maneuvers with regularity, if not certainty. Only after a few months of sailing, can he or she expect to acquire a sense of proficiency.

The board itself may play the most important part in determining how quickly you can learn the sport. The boards that we favored are relatively stable, forgiving of mistakes, and easy to handle. Those are the qualities that we think will give beginners the most encouraging introduction to sailboarding, and, as their skills improve, sustain their pleasure over a wide range of recreational uses.

DESIGN. A board with a conventional sailing rig has difficulty collecting sufficient wind power to drive the hull fast enough to plane like a surfboard. That becomes possible with a novel type of sailing rig, the key elements of which are a pivoting mast and a "wishbone" boom. The mast is attached to the board with a universal joint so that it can pivot forward, back, or to the side. Underway, it's supported and hand-controlled directly by the sailor by means of a boom that wraps around the sail and can be grasped from either side. The pivoting mast and wishbone boom make possible techniques quite alien to those practiced in conventional sailboats.

Another unconventional function of the pivoting mast and wishbone boom is steering. Sailboards have no rudder, only a daggerboard and skeg to give them some lateral stability and reduce sideslippage. The sailor steers by tilting, or raking, the mast forward and back. Those actions change the position of the wind's "center of effort" on the sail—that is, a theoretical spot on the sail where all the wind forces can be said to be concentrated. When the mast is raked forward, the center of effort is moved toward the bow, so the board is forced to turn downwind. When the mast is raked back, the wind's thrust shoves the stern downwind, and the board must turn upwind.

Racing enthusiasts tend to choose long, thin boards with excellent planing characteristics. Trick artists perform most brilliantly on shorter, lighter boards. Unfortunately, there is as yet no firm convention about categorizing sailboards, so it's not always clear from the manufacturers' descriptions which boards are intended for beginners. Many models are described as "all-around" or "all-around fun" boards. The term "fun" seems to carry with it connotations of fancy or trick sailboard maneuvers.

PERFORMANCE. Early on, we established that most boards behaved reasonably well in light winds. And we found that with winds blowing upwards of 15 mph, a sailor's skills began to assume greater significance than the handling characteristics of the board. It was in moderate

Text continued on page 196

Ratings of sailboards for beginners

Listed in order of sailing performance judged most suitable for beginners. Prices are list; discounts may be available. D indicates model was discontinued at original publication.

Excellent	Very good	Good	Fair	Poor
⊜ (fully shaded)	⊖ (half shaded)	○	◒	●

Brand and model	Price	Length (ft./in.)	Hull weight (lb.)	Pointing	Tacking	Beam reaching	Bearing off	Running	Jibing	Static stability forward [2] (Midlewt. aboard [1])	Static stability aft [2] (Midlewt. aboard [1])	Static stability forward [2] (Hvywt. aboard [1])	Static stability aft [2] (Hvywt. aboard [1])	Daggerboard	Comments
				Sailing performance, lightweight/heavyweight sailor [1]											
WAYLER ONE DESIGN	$ 895	12/7	57	Excellent/Excellent	Excellent/Excellent	Very good/Very good	Excellent/Excellent	Very good/Very good	Very good/Very good	Excellent	Excellent	Very good	Excellent	Excellent	K
BIC DUFOUR 250 A Best Buy	599	12/6	46	Excellent/Excellent	Excellent/Excellent	Very good/Very good	Excellent/Excellent	Good/Good	Excellent/Excellent	Very good	Very good	Good	Very good	Good	A,G,K
SAILBOARD VARIO	1000	12/1	45	Fair/Fair	Good/Very good	Very good/Very good	Very good/Very good	Very good/Very good	Very good/Very good	Excellent	Excellent	Excellent	Excellent	Good	B,D,E,J,L
HIFLY 300CS	760	12/7	48	Good/Good	Good/Good	Very good/Very good	Very good/Very good	Excellent/Excellent	Very good/Very good	Excellent	Very good	Excellent	Very good	Excellent	C,E,G,J,L
AMF-TIGA ALL ROUND	749	12/9	52	Very good/Very good	Good/Good	Very good/Very good	Good/Good	Good/Good	Excellent/Good	Very good	Good	Very good	Good	Excellent	K,N
O'BRIEN FREESAIL ONE	599	12/4	51	Good/Good	Good/Good	Good/Fair	Good/Fair	Very good/Very good	Very good/Very good	Excellent	Excellent	Excellent	Excellent	Fair	D,K

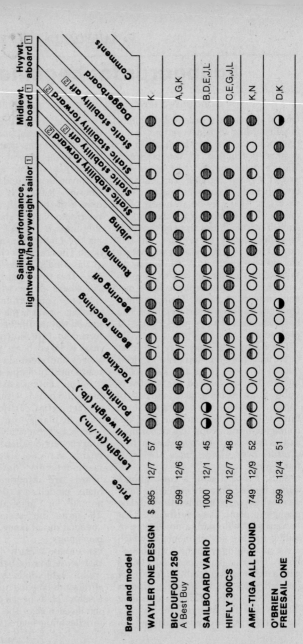

MISTRAL BERMUDA	1095	12/5	51	⊜/⊜	◒/◒	⊜/⊜	⊜/◒	⊜/⊜	○/●	⊜	⊜	⊜	⊜	⊜	D,E,K
MAGNUM 370	795	12/2	54	○/○	○/○	◒/◒	○/○	○/◒	○/◒	⊜	◒	⊜	● [3]	○	K
MISTRAL MAUI	1295	11/11	45	○/○	◒/◒	⊜/⊜	⊜/⊜	○/◒	◒/●	◒	●	● [3]	● [3]	○	D,E,I,L
WINDSURFER ONE DESIGN	899	12/0	49	○/●	⊜/●	⊜/●	⊜/●	⊜/◒	○/◒	◒	○	● [3]	○	●	H,I,K,M
[D] **WINDSURFER FREESTYLE**	899	12/0	48	○/●	⊜/●	⊜/●	⊜/●	⊜/◒	○/◒	◒	○	● [3]	○	—	F,H,I,K,M
BLUE MARLIN	650	12/7	47	○/○	◒/◒	◒/◒	⊜/○	●/●	●/●	◒	◒	◒	◒	○	B,E,J,L

[1] *Lightweight tester weighed 115 lb.; middleweight, 170 lb.; heavyweight, 215 lb.*

[2] *Static stability was judged with board at rest in calm water and with testers in forward (tacking) and aft (jibing) positions. With lightweight tester aboard, all models showed at least good static stability.*

[3] *No freeboard; deck awash.*

FEATURES IN COMMON

All have: beam (greatest hull width) of between 2 ft. 2 in. and 2 ft. 4 in.; "standard" sail of approx. 60 to 65 sq. ft.; adequately slip-resistant board surface.

Except as noted, all have: adjustable dagger-board that pivots back to lie parallel to or partly within hull at fullest retraction; bow eye for towing and mooring; safety leash to prevent hull and mast from separating.

KEY TO COMMENTS

A – Sailing rig relatively easy to raise.

B – Sailing rig harder to raise than most.

C – Sailing rig very hard to raise, even after it is out of water, because boom fills with water.

D – Surface of board judged more abrasive (and rougher on bare feet, legs, and knees) than most.

E – Daggerboard retracts fully inside hull.

F – Daggerboard is not adjustable, but drops in and lifts out of hull; when removed, it can be hung by strap from sailor's arm.

G – Skeg (stabilizing fin at stern of board) can be removed without tools, a convenience.

H – No bow eye for towing and mooring.

I – Footstraps (for sailing in high wind and rough water).

J – Provision to accept optional footstraps.

K – "Pinhead" sail with narrow top, which tends to be easier for novices to use.

L – "Fathead" sail with broad top, which tends to be harder for novices to use.

M – Not supplied with safety leash on sail rig; available as option.

N – According to the manufacturer, a later model is designated **AMF-Tiga One;** daggerboard, mast, wishbone boom, and sail are different from those on tested version.

air, 10 to 12 mph, that performance differences were most apparent in the various points of sail:.

Beam reaching, or sailing directly across the wind at a right angle to it, is generally the fastest and one of the more secure points of sail; the sail provides a good counterbalance to the sailor's weight and the daggerboard bites in hard against side forces to provide extra stability.

Pointing, or sailing close-hauled up into the wind is an important characteristic for any sailing craft. Those that did well held a high point with minimum effort.

Tacking on a sailboard is a "walk-around-the-mast" maneuver. Models that did well turned quickly and cleanly through the eye of the wind and maintained momentum for control throughout this upwind maneuver.

Bearing off to run, or turning downwind, is initiated by raking the mast forward, which puts demands on the board's stability as well as the sailor's balance.

In running, or sailing downwind, the stabilizing influence of the daggerboard is greatly reduced, and beginners find themselves uncomfortably dependent on the inherent stability of the board itself.

Jibing, another sail-shifting maneuver, is touchier than tacking because it's performed from a board at its most precarious point of sail, running downwind.

RECOMMENDATIONS. Our Ratings judgments were formed with the plight of newcomers to sailboarding foremost in mind. Expert sailors probably won't be bothered by the deficiences we observed and may even respect them as virtues.

Whatever board you choose—if you do choose to buy one—we suggest that sailboarding lessons should constitute a part of your initial investment in the sport. They may speed up the learning process for you. They should also acquaint you with vitally important safety practices and self-rescuing techniques. Although sailboarding is basically a safe sport, learning to avoid trouble is part of the game.

All-terrain bicycles

Condensed from CONSUMER REPORTS, February 1986

The all-terrain bike, or ATB, didn't spring fully grown from some marketing specialist's desk drawer. It was invented in the field by hobbyists, who borrowed parts and ideas from the whole world of cycling.

The handlebars and brake levers were inspired by motorcycles. The gearing came from lightweight racing and touring bikes, with extra gears added at the low end. The tires were patterned after versions of motocross "waffle-tread" tires. The frames were beefed-up likenesses of racer frames, almost invariably in the closed (or men's) frame design. Before long, home-built ATB's were boldly going where no bikes had gone before. And bike manufacturers, recognizing a solid trend in the making, began to build models of their own.

Although racing-style bikes still dominate the market, ATB's have become increasingly popular bikes for adults. They tend to be slightly more expensive than comparable touring bikes. The 15

ATB's we tested ranged in price from $120 to $399.

There's also a closely related product called the "city bike;" it shares so many features with the ATB that one can't always tell which is which. We tested four models described in their literature as city bikes, and we have entered them separately in the Ratings.

PERFORMANCE. We judged pedaling ease on a paved surface. For each bike, we used the gear that came closest to producing 10 mph at a cadence of 60 cranks per minute. The easiest bike to pedal, the top-rated *Bridgestone MB-2*, very nearly matched the ease of the top-rated touring bicycles that we last tested. (See the report beginning on page 202.) Eight other models, including three of the four city bikes, were almost as easy to pedal.

To assess road-handling ability, we ran each bike through slalom maneuvers at slow, medium, and high speeds. The better bikes felt nimble and tracked naturally. The worst felt numb and seemed to force our riders into making purely mechanical corrections.

We used two trails to evaluate off-road handling. The first was a path through the woods that was narrow, twisting, but reasonably firm. The best bikes on that trail felt surefooted; the worst felt vague and aimless.

We ran a sterner handling test on a motorcycle motocross course with all the usual motocross obstacles—ruts, rocks, steep inclines, and soft, sandy areas. (We excused most of our city bikes from that test because all but the *Motobecane City Becane* lack what we consider essential features for a true ATB.) The best bikes made the forbidding course seem easier than expected. The bikes with lower scores were either skittish and eager to oversteer or they seemed extremely numb, almost devoid of feel.

All ATB's and city bikes have derailleur gearing, the same type used on multispeed touring bikes. Bicycle gearing levels are expressed in numbers that are related to the number of inches the bike would travel with one full crank of the pedals. A 10-speed racing bike would typically have a gear range from around 33 at the low end to 100 or more at the high end. (Those numbers represent roughly a third of the actual number of inches travelled with each turn of the pedals.)

ATB's need more low-end power on the trail. They also can't make good use of very high gears. Our testers preferred gear ranges starting in the low-to-mid 20's and topping out in the 80's. Most ranges encompassed either 15 or 18 gears. The *Raleigh*, the *Columbia*, and the *Huffy*, all promoted as ATB's, had only 10 speeds, with gears tilted toward the higher numbers; those models were at a severe disadvantage on the trail. The city bikes had only 10 or 12 speeds, but those should be sufficient for around-town riding.

Most ATB's have the gearshift levers on the handlebars. That way, the shifting can all be done with only the thumbs. (The alternative is to have shift levers on the handlebar stem, which forces a rider to remove one hand from the handlebars at every shift.) The best bikes shifted easily and predictably; our riders didn't have to give gear shifts much thought. The shifts on other bikes felt vague or heavy, and they were slow and imprecise.

Bicycles for off-road use have usually been the first to carry new safety features, notably improved brakes. All but four of our ATB's came equipped with the new "cantilever" type of caliper brake, which is matched with heavy-duty motorcycle-type hand levers. The results of our braking tests on dry asphalt were generally excellent.

Text continued on page 201

Ratings of all-terrain and city bicycles

Listed by types; within types, listed in order of estimated overall quality. Ratings should be used in conjunction with the performance table on page 200. Except as noted, prices are list; * indicates price is approximate. Discounts may be available. D indicates model has been discontinued or replaced by a similar version.

Excellent	Very good	Good	Fair	Poor

Brand and model	Price	Weight (lb.)	Speeds	Gear range	Bearing quality: Head	Bearing quality: Crank	Bearing quality: Wheel	Frame rigidity	Pedal quality	Seat comfort	Features	Comments
All-terrain bicycles												
D BRIDGESTONE MB-2	$385	33	18	26-80	Very good	Fair	Fair	Excellent	Excellent	Excellent	A,B,C,D,E,F,H	—
PANASONIC ALL-TERRAIN	360	34	15	26-85	Very good	Very good	Good	Good	Very good	Excellent	A,B,C,D,E,F,H	—
D SCHWINN SIERRA	300	31	15	23-89	Very good	Very good	Good	Very good	Very good	Fair	A,B,C,D,E,F,H	—
UNIVEGA ALPINA UNO	330	33	15	23-89	Very good	Good	Good	Good	Excellent	Good	A,B,C,D,E,H	—
D NISHIKI CASCADE	349	33	15	23-89	Very good	Fair	Fair	Excellent	Excellent	Very good	B,C,D,E,G,H	—
D ROSS MT. HOOD	330	33	15	23-89	Very good	Very good	Very good	Excellent	Excellent	Good	B,C,D,E,G,H	—
PEUGEOT ORIENT EXPRESS	300	34	18	24-89	Good	Very good	Good	Good	Very good	Fair	B,C,D,E,F,G,H	—
D DIAMOND BACK TRAIL STREAK	285	33	15	23-82	Very good	Very good	Good	Good	Excellent	Fair	B,C,D,E,H	*E,G*

RALEIGH TETON	300	35	15	28-89	⊖	⊖	⊖	⊜	⊖	○	A,B,C,E,F,H	—
[D] TREK 830	389	31	15	23-85	⊖	⊖	○	○	⊖	○	A,B,C,D,E,F,H	—
RALEIGH GRAND MESA	220	36	10	39-100	⊖	⊖	⊖	◒	●	◒	A	*A,F*
MOTOBECANE MT. BECANE	399	34	18	21-92	⊖	⊖	◒	⊖	⊜	⊖	A,B,C,D,E,G,H	—
[D] VISTA MOUNTAINEER	390	33	18	21-92	⊖	⊖	◒	○	⊜	◒	B,C,D,E,G,H	*H*
[D] COLUMBIA TRAILRUNNER	199	40	10	38-96	●	●	◒	◒	●	●	D,E	*A,B,C,I*
HUFFY SCOUT	120	39	10	36-97	●	●	◒	○	●	●	G	*A,B,I*

City bicycles

PEUGEOT CITY EXPRESS	260	30	12	31-89	⊖	⊖	○	⊖	○	⊖	A,C,E,F,H	*A,F*
MOTOBECANE CITY BECANE	299	33	12	33-100	⊖	○	◒	⊖	⊖	⊖	C,D,E,F,G,H	—
PANASONIC VILLAGER DX	255	33	10	36-97	⊖	○	⊖	◒	○	⊜	E,F,H	*A,D,F*
[D] FUJI BOULEVARD	280	30	10	33-85	⊖	⊖	○	○	⊖	◒	A,E,H	*A,F*

FEATURES IN COMMON
All are closed-frame models and have wheels labeled as 26-in. in diameter.
Except as noted, all: come in 2 or more frame sizes in a range from at least 19 in. to 21 in.; have tires 2$^{1}/_{8}$-in. wide; and lack chain guard and fenders.

KEY TO FEATURES
A – Dual-pressure tires.
B – Extended gearing.
C – Cantilever brakes.
D – Seat quick-release.
E – Thumb shifters.
F – Non-serrated pedals.
G – Extra pedal clearance.
H – Aluminum rims.

KEY TO COMMENTS
A – Chain guard.
B – Kickstand.
C – Luggage carrier over rear wheel.
D – Fenders.
E – 1$^{3}/_{4}$-in.-wide tires.
F – 1$^{1}/_{2}$-in.-wide tires.
G – Only 1 frame size, 20$^{1}/_{2}$ in.
H – Only 1 frame size, 19$^{1}/_{2}$ in.
I – Only 1 frame size, 21 in.

Performance table: all-terrain and city bicycles

Excellent	Very good	Good	Fair	Poor
⊜ (fully striped)	⊖ (half striped)	○	◒	●

Brand and model	Pedalling ease	Handling			Shifting ease	Braking			
		Road	Mild trail	Rough trail		Dry	Wet	Trail	Control
All-terrain bicycles									
BRIDGESTONE MB-2	Excellent	Very good	Excellent	Excellent	Excellent	Excellent	Very good	Very good	Excellent
PANASONIC ALL-TERRAIN	Very good	Very good	Very good	Very good	Excellent	Excellent	Very good	Excellent	Very good
SCHWINN SIERRA	Good	Very good	Very good	Very good	Excellent	Excellent	Very good	Very good	Excellent
UNIVEGA ALPINA UNO	Very good	Very good	Very good	Very good	Very good	Excellent	Very good	Good	Excellent
NISHIKI CASCADE	Good	Very good	Very good	Very good	Excellent	Excellent	Good	Very good	Excellent
ROSS MT. HOOD	Good	Very good	Very good	Very good	Good	Excellent	Very good	Good	Excellent
PEUGEOT ORIENT EXPRESS	Good	Very good	Very good	Very good	Very good	Excellent	Very good	Excellent	Excellent
DIAMOND BACK TRAIL STREAK	Very good	Fair	Good	Good	Very good	Excellent	Very good	Good	Excellent
RALEIGH TETON	Good	Good	Good	Good	Fair	Excellent	Very good	Very good	Excellent
TREK 830	Very good	Good	Good	Good	Good	Excellent	Good	Fair	Fair
RALEIGH GRAND MESA	Very good	Very good	Good	Fair	Very good	Good	Poor	Fair	Excellent
MOTOBECANE MT. BECANE	Good	Very good	Good	Fair	Fair	Excellent	Very good	Fair	Good
VISTA MOUNTAINEER	Good	Good	Fair	Good	Good	Very good	Good	Good	Very good
COLUMBIA TRAILRUNNER	Fair	Fair	Fair	Fair	Poor	Excellent	Poor	Poor	Very good
HUFFY SCOUT	Fair	Fair	Fair	Fair	Poor	Very good	Poor	Poor	Very good
City bicycles									
PEUGEOT CITY EXPRESS	Very good	Excellent	Good	[1]	Very good	Excellent	Excellent	[1]	Excellent
MOTOBECANE CITY BECANE	Good	Good	Good	Very good	Fair	Excellent	Very good	Good	Good
PANASONIC VILLAGER DX	Very good	Very good	Good	[1]	Very good	Good	Fair	[1]	Very good
FUJI BOULEVARD	Very good	Good	Fair	[1]	Good	Good	Poor	[1]	Very good

[1] *Not subjected to rough-trail tests. Bicycle lacks features that would make it suitable for such use.*

Over the years, our tests have shown us that the metal used in the wheel rims largely determines how well the brakes will do when they're wet. Most of the ATB's were fitted with aluminum rims. When we rode them past 50 feet of perforated hose to wet the wheels, they required only a few feet farther to stop than they had needed on dry pavement. But the three models with steel rims—the *Raleigh*, the *Columbia*, and the *Huffy*—suffered a near-total loss of braking ability under wet conditions.

Our tests for trail braking were more subjective. A rider going downhill on a rough trail uses the rear brake almost exclusively, so our test was mainly a measure of the rear brake's grabbing power and of the hand pressure required to achieve the necessary braking response. (We excused most of our city bikes from this test.) On the best ATB's, the rear wheel could be controlled or even locked with a moderate squeeze on the brake lever. The bikes judged poor had feeble rear braking; with them, we judged, riders might have to use the front brake—with the attendant risk of skidding and taking a spill—just to keep the bike from picking up too much speed.

CONSTRUCTION. The quality of the bike bearings varied widely; some were crudely stamped pieces while others were lathe-turned or ground to a smooth finish. The head bearings, which support the connection between the front-wheel fork and the frame, can affect the steering when they become worn or deformed; those on the *Columbia* and the *Huffy* just weren't good enough for an ATB, in our opinion. The wheel and crank bearings aren't as directly related to safety, but they're important to the effort expended in pedaling.

Frame rigidity is another of the factors that determine how smoothly a bike will behave. As the Ratings show, some of the best and worst ATB's had pretty rigid frames, but the best combined rigidity with light weight.

Most of the tested bikes offer sturdy pedals with bearings that come apart for cleaning and repacking. Only a few have flimsy, easily damaged pedals that couldn't be dismantled for servicing. Several others have pedals of high enough quality, but with aggressive, sawtooth metal treads. Such pedals provide a fairly sure grip for shoes, but they also present a hazard, should a shoe be bounced off the pedal.

A bicycle seat isn't designed to be sat on in the usual sense. Rather it's a support that allows rider and machine to act in unison. The better seats on our bikes offer firm padding that conformed to the rider's anatomy at key places. The seats judged poor were quite hard and produced discomfort for the rider within minutes.

RECOMMENDATIONS. In our judgment, all-terrain bikes set a new high in ruggedness, controllability, pedaling ease, and safety both on and off the road. We might even venture to say that a good ATB is a better choice than a good lightweight racing-style bike for the recreational cyclist. The choice, however, is complicated by a young market, undecided and still in flux. Nearly half the all-terrain bikes that we tested have been discontinued.

Nevertheless, models at the top of the Ratings are fine examples of the breed. Any of them would be a good value at $300 or a little more, and would be equally adept in country or city riding. But we're not convinced that the three least-expensive models—the *Raleigh Grand Mesa*, the *Columbia Trailrunner*, and the *Huffy Scout*—belong in the same breed as most of the rugged, low-geared ATB's; they would really be more at home on city pavements.

Touring bicycles

Condensed from CONSUMER REPORTS, November 1985

In the early 1970's, when millions of adults took up cycling for fuel-saving transportation as well as for exercise, their clear favorite was the 10-speed touring bike with its distinctive handlebars, derailleur gear-changer, and skinny tires. That type of bike has remained the most popular one for adults.

We tested 28 touring models in what can be considered a low to moderate price range, from $100 to $319. All have a closed ("men's") frame, with racing-style handlebars and a slender seat. Most weigh between 25 and 30 pounds, although a few of the cheaper models weigh in at a truckish 35 pounds. Slightly more than half are 12-speed models; the rest are 10-speed models.

PERFORMANCE. Riding a well-made touring bike can be an exhilarating experience. In our two key performance tests, for pedaling ease and for handling, we attempted to quantify that feeling of exhilaration.

We tested the bikes for pedaling ease at a steady speed and in an acceleration run, using the gear that let us come closest to 10 mph at a pedaling cadence of 60 pedal revolutions per minute. Bikes that required no more than an extremely light push on the pedals to maintain a steady speed were judged excellent. In the acceleration test, bikes were judged excellent if they felt responsive, darting ahead cleanly with each pedal stroke.

To assess handling quality, we rode each bike, through slalom maneuvers at low, moderate, and high speeds. Models judged excellent were inherently stable and felt secure when we maneuvered them. A bike was downgraded if it tended to oversteer, or exaggerate turns, especially at low speed.

To test shifting ease, we ran each bike through its gears, both in the lab (on an off-the-floor stand) and on the road. We looked for derailleurs—mechanisms connected by cable to levers near the handlebars—that shifted the drive chain smoothly and predictably to the desired sprockets on the pedal axle and rear-wheel axle. The front derailleur on all the bikes moved the chains from one sprocket to the other quite well. But many of the rear derailleurs tended to overshoot an intermediate sprocket on the rear cluster of five or six sprockets.

Like nearly all touring bikes, the tested models have hand-operated caliper brakes. Our basic braking test involved stops from 15 mph on clean, level pavement. Our rider tried to stop the bike as quickly as possible, first using just the rear brake, then just the front brake, then both together.

Typically, the best stops were achieved with a hard squeeze on the front brake lever and a light squeeze on the rear brake lever. That helped prevent the rear tire from skidding and typically stopped the bike in about 15 feet. A few bikes, judged excellent, stopped in about 12 feet.

We then rode the bikes between 50-foot lengths of perforated hose that directed a fine spray at the wheels just prior to and during braking. Bikes with steel wheel rims usually showed an almost total loss of brake response. At 15 mph, it took more than 75 feet to stop most of them. The one exception was the *Peugeot P6;* its brake pads are impregnated with metal, a feature that greatly enhanced the bike's wet-braking ability. For much the same reason, bikes with aluminum rims did well in our wet-braking tests; fine aluminum particles rubbed off their rims and became embedded in the brake pads.

CONSTRUCTION. For smooth and easy riding, a bike should be lightweight and have high-quality bearings, a rigid frame, sturdy pedals, and a comfortable seat. Before we took the bikes on the road, we took each one apart and examined the quality of the bearings in the steering tube, pedal crank, and wheels. Steering bearings are particularly important because the slightest binding or looseness can cause unstable handling. Generally, but not unexceptionably, the more expensive the bike, the better the bearings.

When a cyclist exerts force on the pedals, the frame tends to flex under the stress. The flexing dissipates energy that could be spent on propelling the bike, and it detracts from handling precision and pedaling ease. That's why frame rigidity has traditionally been one hallmark of a good touring bike—but, as the Ratings indicate, not the only hallmark. The quality of the bearings and the weight of the bike may be more important factors.

(We tested only closed frames, which are the most rigid type. If you want a step-through "women's" frame, we recommend a "mixte" model, which has a pair of tubes slanting diagonally down from the steering tube, past the seat tube, and on to the rear axle. A well-made mixte frame is nearly as rigid as a closed frame.)

All the bikes have metal pedals with serrated metal edges that gripped rubber-soled shoes all right but gave little purchase for leather soles. Pedals judged excellent were sturdy, with high-quality bearings that come apart for cleaning and repacking. Pedals judged poor were flimsy and easily damaged; they'd readily bend if the bike fell over or banged against a curb.

The seat of a touring bike is designed more for leaning than for sitting, with the pedals and handlebars usually bearing most of the rider's weight. The only seat judged excellent, that of the *Wards*, has a flexible top under very good padding. Seats were downgraded for insufficient padding and resulting discomfort during riding.

RECOMMENDATIONS. The 10 bikes listed in the first Ratings group are all responsive, obedient cycles that earned high marks in our key tests for pedaling ease and handling. The *Lotus Challenger* ($215) was a match for the other top performers in most important respects, and it's $35 to $104 cheaper. We judged it a Best Buy.

Ratings on next page

What about prices?

The Buying Guide Issue usually notes prices as given in the full report cited at the beginning of each article. Unless otherwise stated, prices are list or suggested retail, current at the time of original publication. In many cases, inflation will have increased prices, but the price relationships among models is stable enough to be informative to consumers.

Ratings of touring bicycles

Listed in order of estimated overall quality. Except where separated by heavy lines, differences between closely ranked models were small. Except as noted, all were tested in 23-in. or 24-in. frame size (or metric equivalent thereof), with other available sizes ranging from at least 21 in. to 25 in. All have 27-in. wheels and closed frame; open ("mixte") frames may be available. Prices are list; + indicates shipping is extra. Discounts may be available.

◍ ⊖ ○ ◒ ●

Better ←→ Worse

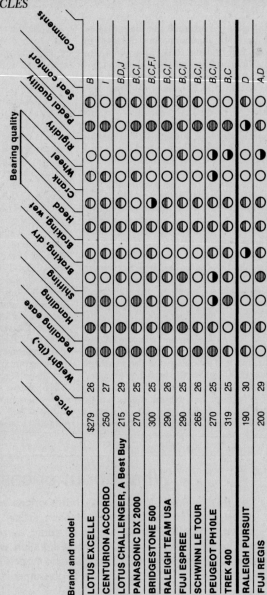

Brand and model	Price	Weight (lb.)	Pedaling ease	Handling	Shifting	Braking, dry	Braking, wet	Bearing quality: Head	Bearing quality: Crank	Bearing quality: Wheel	Rigidity	Pedal quality	Seat comfort	Comments
LOTUS EXCELLE	$279	26	◍	◍	◍	○	⊖	⊖	⊖	⊖	○	◍	⊖	B
CENTURION ACCORDO	250	27	◍	⊖	◍	○	⊖	⊖	⊖	⊖	○	◍	○	I
LOTUS CHALLENGER, A Best Buy	215	29	◍	◍	○	⊖	⊖	⊖	⊖	○	○	○	⊖	B,D,J
PANASONIC DX 2000	270	25	◍	⊖	◍	○	○	⊖	○	⊖	○	◍	⊖	B,C,I
BRIDGESTONE 500	300	25	◍	⊖	⊖	⊖	⊖	⊖	◒	○	○	◍	⊖	B,C,F,I
RALEIGH TEAM USA	290	26	⊖	◍	⊖	⊖	○	⊖	⊖	○	○	◍	⊖	B,C,I
FUJI ESPREE	290	25	⊖	◍	○	◍	○	⊖	⊖	○	⊖	⊖	⊖	B,C,I
SCHWINN LE TOUR	265	26	◍	⊖	○	○	○	⊖	⊖	○	○	◍	⊖	B,C,I
PEUGEOT PH10LE	270	25	◍	⊖	◒	◒	⊖	⊖	⊖	◒	◒	◍	○	B,C,I
TREK 400	319	25	⊖	○	◍	⊖	⊖	⊖	⊖	○	◒	◍	○	B,C
RALEIGH PURSUIT	190	30	⊖	⊖	○	○	◒	⊖	⊖	○	○	◒	⊖	D
FUJI REGIS	200	29	○	⊖	○	◍	⊖	⊖	⊖	○	◒	⊖	○	A,D

NISHIKI SPORT	210	29	⊜	⊜	○	○	◒	○	⊜	○	◒	◒	○	*A,I*
CENTURION CAVALETTO	179	32	○	⊜	○	⊜	●	⊜	⊜	⊜	⊜	○	○	*A,E,F,G*
MOTOBECANE MIRAGE	220	26	⊜	⊜	◒	◒	⊜	○	○	○	◒	○	⊜	*D,I*
NISHIKI RALLY	160	32	○	⊜	⊜	○	●	○	⊜	○	⊜	○	○	*A,E,G*
SCHWINN SPRINT	150	32	○	⊜	○	⊜	◒	○	⊜	○	○	○	●	*A,E,G*
PEUGEOT P6	180	29	○	⊜	○	○	⊜	⊜	⊜	◒	◒	⊜	⊜	*A,D,H*
SAINT TROPEZ CLASSIC	180	29	○	○	○	⊜	◒	○	⊜	○	○	⊜	⊜	*D*
MOTOBECANE LE VELO	165	29	○	⊜	◒	⊜	◒	○	◒	○	◒	◒	○	*A,E,G*
PANASONIC SPORT 500	160	32	○	○	⊜	⊜	●	⊜	○	◒	○	○	○	*A,E,F,G*
BRIDGESTONE 100	160	32	○	○	○	⊜	●	◒	○	◒	⊜	○	◒	*A,D,G*
ROSS ENHANCER	160	31	○	◒	⊜	⊜	●	⊜	⊜	◒	⊜	○	⊜	*A,E,G*
HUFFY 626	120	35	◒	◒	○	⊜	●	●	●	◒	⊜	●	⊜	*E,F,G,J*
MONTGOMERY WARD Cat. No. 80359	150+	35	◒	◒	⊜	⊜	●	●	●	◒	○	○	⊜	*A,E,F,G,J*
MURRAY CINTRO	170	32	◒	◒	◒	⊜	●	○	⊜	◒	○	●	○	*E,F,G,K*
SEARS FS-12 Cat. No. 47143	170+	32	◒	◒	◒	⊜	●	○	⊜	◒	⊜	●	●	*E,F,G,K*
COLUMBIA SHADOW	100	35	◒	◒	○	○	●	●	●	◒	○	●	◒	*A,E,F,G,I*

FEATURES IN COMMON
Except as noted all have: 12-speed derailleur; derailleur controls mounted on handlebar stem; auxiliary brake levers; quick-release cams on both wheels; brake release on both wheels; aluminum wheel rims; disk-type chain guard.

KEY TO COMMENTS
A–10-speed derailleur.
B–Derailleur controls on downtube.
C–No auxiliary brake levers.
D–Quick-release cam on front wheel only.
E–No quick-release cams.
F–No brake releases.
G–Steel wheel rims; judged undesirable for wet braking.
H–Has steel wheel rims, but brake pads are impregnated with metal, which enhanced wet braking in our tests.
I–No chain guard.
J–Tested in 22-in. frame size: 4 other sizes available for **Lotus Challenger**; only 1 other size (21 in.) available for Columbia Shadow; no other sizes available for **Huffy** and **Wards.**
K–Tested in 21-in. frame size: only 1 other size available for **Murray Cintro** (23 in.) and for **Sears** (19 in.).

Home care

Vacuum cleaners

Condensed from CONSUMER REPORTS, May 1986

Because household dust and dirt deposits itself in several ways about the house, no one type of vacuum cleaner excels at cleaning it all up. A brisk suction alone may remove the dirt that comes to rest on plain surfaces; a canister cleaner can provide such suction. Other dust particles burrow into the fibers of carpeting and can't be budged by suction unless they're first flushed into the open; the revolving beater brushes of an upright vacuum cleaner perform that service, busting the dust loose so that the free-floating particles can then be removed by merely a mild vacuum.

Thus, about the most effective way to clean house is to use two kinds of vacuum cleaner: an upright for rugs and carpeting, and a suction-only canister for other surfaces. There does exist a useful compromise alternative—the power-nozzle canister. It's essentially two vacuum cleaners in one; its power nozzle attachment has revolving brushes that mimic the action of an upright, while its other attachments work exactly like those of an ordinary canister.

Neither selection of house-cleaning gear—two vacuum cleaners or one—offers a great deal in the way of convenience. Most upright cleaners glide smoothly over expanses of carpeting, but they're out of their element anywhere else. Canister hoses and wands are usually easy to maneuver, as is the power nozzle on carpet, but there's always the canister itself trailing clumsily along. Neither type of full-size cleaner lends itself to graceful storage. And yet, anything less than a full-size cleaner won't do a satisfactory job, in our judgment. (Several compact uprights and compact canisters were among the models tested for this report.)

In all, we tested 51 vacuum-cleaner models. They ranged in price from $66 to $639.

CLEANING. We tested all the uprights and power-nozzle machines for removal of deeply embedded dirt in carpeting. Such deep cleaning is important because a carpet that looks well-groomed isn't necessarily clean; gritty soil that's allowed to accumulate in a carpet's nap will abrade and eventually cut carpet fibers. We excluded suction-only canisters from our deep-carpet-cleaning tests; they're not good at such tasks, we've learned from experience.

Most of the uprights did well in the test. So did many of the power-nozzle canisters. But, as the Ratings show, some expensive machines of both types failed to live up to their brand-name billing.

To check each machine's capability for surface cleaning, we strewed test carpeting with small items of debris: popcorn, peanut shells, pine needles, toothpicks, fabric threads, and polyester "angel hair." Given proper adjustment and sufficient patience, all models could consume the popcorn, peanut shells, and pine needles. A few canisters choked on toothpicks. Quite a number of uprights and power nozzles had trouble swallowing wisps of angel hair, which tended to stick in their brushes.

The strength of a vacuum cleaner's suction tells little about its carpet-cleaning abilities. But it's a good indicator of how well a cleaner and its attachments will do on bare floors and most other household surfaces. Starting with an empty bag, all the canisters had at least satisfactory suction. But some lost suction a lot faster than others as their bags filled. With uprights, suction usually isn't at issue, since they're generally awkward and unpleasant to use with attachments. Still, several uprights produced enough suction to make attachments useful. And on the most powerful of them, the *Kirby*, the beater brush can be conveniently turned off to make the machine suitable for bare-floor cleaning, a capability not shared by most uprights.

Most canisters have some sort of air-bleed control that opens a hole in the vacuum system and thereby reduces suction at the nozzle. The six models that lack such a control will be at a disadvantage in trying to clean drapes and scatter rugs.

CONVENIENCE. The handiest models to start and stop were those with a slide switch directly at hand when vacuuming. Judged almost as convenient were two uprights, the *Sears 34201* and the *Singer SST200*, which turn themselves on when their handle is lowered, and certain other models with a step-on switch or a well-placed toggle switch. The rest were awkward in one way or another.

Most uprights and a few power-nozzle canisters allow you to raise or lower the rug nozzle to suit carpets with high or low naps. Some models adjust "manually," with a foot lever or knob; others adjust automatically; a few permit manual adjustment or automatic settings.

Uprights generally hold more dirt than canisters—often twice as much. The *Electrolux* models, upright and canisters, came closest to our ideal for bag-changing; their self-sealing bags are easily popped in and out. Several other models have dust bags with plastic or cardboard collars to handle, instead of the bag itself. Less convenient were some uprights that oblige you to slip the bag's sleeve over the dirt tube and then stretch a garter spring around it.

A number of models were messy to empty. The *Hoover U4365*, for example, has a bag that fills from the bottom; the bag's open end is usually filled with dirt when its detached. Several models don't use disposable bags; the dirt receptacle has to be dumped out to empty them. The *Sears* and *Hoover* compact canisters have bags with wide-open mouths, which tended to spill dirt.

RECOMMENDATIONS. The range in prices among the tested vacuum cleaners was enormous. Even granting the prevalence of substantial discounts, it's difficult to escape the suspicion that some models simply aren't worth the prices being charged for them.

To be specific, it may not make economic sense to pay more than $400 for equipment that will do a good job with all house-vacuuming chores, whether you buy one machine or two. That limit

Text continued on page 213

Ratings of vacuum cleaners

Listed by types; within types, listed, except as noted, in order of estimated quality. Bracketed models were judged approximately equal in quality and are listed in order of increasing price. Weights are to nearest ½ lb.; those given for canisters include stored tools, hose, and nozzle. Unless otherwise indicated, prices are list; + indicates that shipping is extra; * indicates that price is approximate. Discounts are generally available. D indicates that model was discontinued at original publication.

◍ ⊖ ○ ◒ ●

Better ⟷ Worse

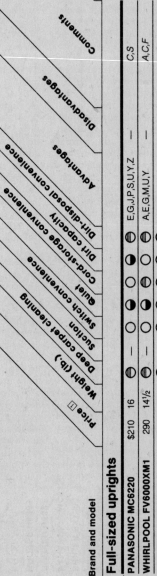

Brand and model	Price [1]	Weight (lb.)	Deep carpet cleaning	Suction	Switch convenience	Quiet	Cord-storage convenience	Dirt capacity	Dirt-disposal convenience	Advantages	Disadvantages	Comments
Full-sized uprights												
PANASONIC MC6220	$210	16	⊖	—	○	◒	○	◒	⊖	E,G,J,P,S,U,Y,Z	—	*C,S*
WHIRLPOOL FV6000XM1	290	14½	⊖	—	○	◒	⊖	○	⊖	A,E,G,M,U,Y	—	*A,C,F*
HOOVER U3305030	330	20½	⊖	—	○	◒	⊖	○	⊖	A,D,E	k	*A,C*
KIRBY HERITAGE II	499	20	⊖	—	⊖	◒	○	○	⊖	B,E,H,U,V,Y,Z	i	*C,D,P,R*
SEARS KENMORE Cat. No. 35401	148+	12½	⊖	—	◍	◒	○	⊖	○	E	—	*A,C*
WHIRLPOOL FV2000XM1	170	14½	⊖	—	○	◒	○	○	⊖	A,E,G,Y	—	*F*
HOOVER U4381930	200	16	⊖	—	◍	◒	○	○	⊖	C,U	—	*C,E,J,L*

EUREKA 5060F	310	17½	⊜	—	○	◒	◒	⊜	○	D,F,U	r	*C,E*
EUREKA 1425F	100	11½	⊜	—	○	◒	◒	⊜	○	V	q	*E,X*
HOOVER U4369	130	15½	⊜	—	○	◒	◒	○	⊜	C	—	*C,E*
EUREKA 1945A	150	13½	⊜	—	○	◒	◒	⊜	○	—	—	*C,E*
SINGER SST1000	170	14½	⊜	—	⊜	●	⊜	○	○	M	c	*A,C*
EUREKA 7575A	230	15	⊜	—	○	◒	◒	○	⊜	F	—	*C,E,S*
SEARS KENMORE Cat. No. 35951	270 + 15		⊜	—	⊜	◒	⊜	⊜	○	E	b	*A,C,S*
[D]ELECTROLUX 1451E	500	24	○	—	○	◒	○	○	⊜	G,M,S,T	v	*D,P*
SEARS KENMORE Cat. No. 34201	88 + 11		⊜	—	⊜	●	◒	⊜	○	—	q	*C*
SINGER SST200	100	11	⊜	—	⊜	●	◒	⊜	○	—	c,q	*C*
PANASONIC MC5130	150	12½	○	—	○	○	○	◒	⊜	G,P	—	*C,S*
HOOVER U4391	175	17½	⊜	—	○	◒	◒	◒	◒	C,P	—	*B,C,E*
HOOVER U4365	100	14	⊜	—	○	◒	◒	●	◒	C	q,x	*E*
ROYAL M880	486	14	◒	—	⊜	◒	◒	○	○	H,U,V	—	*C,D,P*
Compact uprights												
MIELE S125	215[2]	12	○	—	○	○	○	●	⊜	F,G,I,P,V	v	*P,S,V,W*
[D]ORECK XL100C	319	9½	◒	—	⊜	◒	◒	○	⊜	C,I,V	s,v	*C,D,K,P,S*
Power-nozzle canisters												
HOOVER S3281	460	30	⊜	⊜	⊜	◒	⊜	⊜	⊜	E,K,N,R,S,Y	—	*C,G,O*
PANASONIC MC9420	250	23½	⊜	⊜	⊜	⊜	⊜	⊜	⊜	E,H,P,S,X,Y	—	*A*
WHIRLPOOL FC7000	300	27½	⊜	⊜	⊜	◒	⊜	⊜	⊜	C,M,R,S,Y	—	*F,T*
SINGER CSS1000	270	25½	⊜	⊜	○	◒	⊜	○	⊜	C,R,S	u,z	—
MONTGOMERY WARD 5046	279	27½	⊜	⊜	◒	◒	⊜	⊜	⊜	H,O,P	u	*C*

Ratings continued on next page

Ratings of vacuum cleaners continued

Brand and model	Price [1]	Weight (lb.)	Deep carpet cleaning	Suction	Switch convenience	Quiet	Cord-storage convenience	Dirt capacity	Dirt-disposal convenience	Advantages	Disadvantages	Comments
HOOVER S3271	$280	22	◓	○	◓	◒	◍	○	◓	E,N,S,Y	—	*C*
SEARS KENMORE Cat. No. 24350	300+	24	◓	◓	◓	◒	◓	◓	◓	C,M,Y	y	*T*
EUREKA 1784B	370	28½	◓	◍	◒	◒	◓	◓	◓	H,O,P	k,u	*C*
EUREKA 1790A	430	29	◓	◓	◒	○	◓	◓	◓	O,S	—	*A,C*
MIELE S230i	435	23	◓	◓	◓	◒	◍	◍	◓	H,P	k,o,p,w	*H,I,P*
ELECTROLUX 1521 DIAMOND JUBILEE	639	26	○	◓	◓	◒	◓	●	◍	H,M,N,Q,T	j,m	*D,F,I,P*
[D] ELECTROLUX 1453 SPECIAL	349	23	○	◓	○	◒	◒	●	◍	H,M,N,T	j,m	*D,I,P*
ROYAL M401PN	456	21	○	○	◓	○	◒	○	◓	H,L	e,g,m,o,v	*D,P,R,T*
TOSHIBA VC222	120	14	◒	◓	◍	○	◓	◒	◒	P	a,e,g,n,p,v,z	*B,H,I,P,U*
SHARP EC7410	180	16	◒	◓	◍	○	◍	●	◒	J,S	a,e,h,n,p,v,w,z	*B,O,P,U*
Suction-only canisters												
PANASONIC MC7320	130	14	[3]	○	◓	○	◍	◒	◓	L,S,W	p,t	—
WHIRLPOOL FC5000XM	180	21½	[3]	◓	◓	◒	◍	◓	◓	—	h	*A,F*
[D] SEARS KENMORE 25022	130*	13	[3]	◓	◓	○	◍	◒	◓	P,S	a,p,t,w	—
HOOVER S3259	175	16	[3]	◒	◓	◒	◍	◒	◓	N,S,W	h	—
SANYO SCP2000	110	11½	[3]	○	◓	○	◍	○	◓	P,S	a,d,f,g,p,t	—

EUREKA 3336A	140	16	[3]	⊜	○	◒	◒	○	⊜	—	a,h,k,l,u	—
SINGER CSS500	150	18½	[3]	○	○	◒	⊜	○	⊜	H,J	f,h,j,k,u	—
Compact canisters												
TOSHIBA VC420	100	9½	◒	⊜	⊜	○	○	●	●	H,W	a,f,g,h,n,p,u,v,z	*B,H,N,P,U*
HOOVER S1077033	110	12	[3]	◒	⊜	○	◒	●	◒	H,W	d,f,h,p,u	*N,Q*
EUREKA 3120B	120	11	[3]	○	⊜	○	○	◒	⊜	H	a,d,h,k,u	*N*
SHARP EC6310	100	9½	[3]	⊜	⊜	○	⊜	●	●	—	a,f,g,p,w,z	*B*
SEARS KENMORE Cat. No. 60531	78+9		[3]	○	⊜	●	◒	●	◒	J	a,d,h,p,z	*B,M,O*
PANASONIC MC104H	66	6½	[3]	◒	⊜	○	◒	●	●	—	a,d,f,g,h,p	*B,M*

[1] *Prices for canister include attachments, except as noted.*

[2] *Includes cost of optional power nozzle, which was used in tests.*

[3] *Judged unsuitable for deep carpet cleaning.*

FEATURES IN COMMON

Except as noted, all models: have 1-speed motor; cannot be used as blower; use disposable dust bags; come with 1-yr. warranty covering parts and labor.

Except as noted, all uprights: were awkward to use on stairs; require adjustment for carpet-pile height; have more than 2 pile-height adjustments; clean an 11-to-13-in. swath; need 6- to 7½-in. clearance to reach 1 ft. under furniture; have 20- to 25-ft. cord.

All canisters have 16- to 23-ft. cord.

Except as noted, all canisters: have control for reducing suction; require 3½-in. clearance or less to reach 1 ft. under furniture; are fairly convenient to use on stairs; come with reinforced hose, metal wands with positive lock, floor/rug nozzle or power nozzle, wall/floor brush, upholstery nozzle, dusting brush, and crevice tool; can store at least some tools in or on canister.

All power-nozzle canisters can run power nozzle on floor without brush revolving.

Except as noted, all power-nozzle canisters: require no adjustment for carpet-pile height; clean an 11- to 13-in. swath of carpet.

KEY TO ADVANTAGES

A – Has both manual and automatic pile-height adjustment.

B – Has convenient mechanism for adjusting nozzle for different pile heights while cleaner is running. Highest suction of all uprights, and judged most suitable of those models for use with above-floor attachments. (But attachments may bring total purchase price of machine to $700 or more.)

C – Revolving brush less likely than most to collect polyester "angel hair" or other fluff.

D – Power-assisted wheels; easier to push than most uprights.

E – Revolving brush is very close to 1 edge of nozzle housing, making it easier to clean carpet close to wall.

F – Somewhat higher suction than most other uprights.

G – Convenient, for an upright, to convert to suction-only use with optional tools.

H – Can be used as blower.

I – Requires less clearance than full-size uprights to reach under furniture, and was easier to use on stairs.

J – Multiple speeds; lowest setting judged significantly quieter than highest.

K – Has main on/off switch and air-flow and motor-power indicator lights on canister, and has separate on/off switch with indicator light on power-nozzle handle. Has setting that changes motor automatically in response to air-flow requirement. Handle judged very comfortable.

L – Resisted clogging better than most.

Keys to Ratings continued on next page

Keys to vacuum cleaner Ratings continued

M–Overload protector guards against damage to cleaner if brush is jammed.
N–Overload protector guards against motor's overheating from clog or overfull bag.
O–Power nozzle has window for monitoring condition of drive belt.
P–Has dirt-level indicator gauge or (on **Hoover U4391)** transparent dirt container.
Q–Light goes on and unit shuts off when bag fills to preset level (but at highest setting bag is filled to only about 1/3 of typical canister bag's capacity.)
R–Separate indicator shows blockage of wand, tool, or hose.
S–Indicator signals when dust bag is full.
T–Interlock prevents machine from running without dust bag.
U–Long cord (30 ft. or more).
V–Brush is adjustable for wear.
W–Easier to push on high-pile carpet than most suction-only models.
X–Red flag next to on/off switch indicates whether unit is switched on or off.
Y–Cleans wide swath (13½ to 14½ in.).
Z–1 of 2 uprights with convenient way to stop brush for bare-floor cleaning.

KEY TO DISADVANTAGES

a–Friction-fit wands may be hard to part.
b–Hard to push on high-pile carpet.
c–Changing pile-height setting judged inconvenient; control-knob settings not marked for height or carpet type.
d–Did not readily pick up thread from carpet.
e–Had difficulty with toothpicks on carpet.
f–No means of reducing suction.
g–Tools cannot be stored in or on canister.
h–Tended to clog with many kinds of litter.
i–Requires more clearance than other uprights to reach 1 ft. under furniture.
j–Stiff hose makes machine awkward to use in tight quarters and to store.
k–Flimsy, unreinforced hose; tended to kink on **Miele S230I** and **Eureka 1784B, 3336A,** and **3120B.**
l–Canister does not stand on end; awkward to use on staircases and to store.
m–Power nozzle has no detent to hold handle upright; handle often fell over.
n–Power nozzle's handle has no upright position; may be difficult to store.
o–No positive lock between power-nozzle wand and hose; can come apart easily while vacuuming.
p–Lacks wide, bristled brush for walls and bare floors; available as option for **Hoover S1077033.**
q–Short cord for an upright (15 to 18 ft.).
r–Hard to wheel about, especially on high-pile carpet.
s–Revolving brush is farther from edge of housing than in other models; cannot clean carpet as close to walls.
t–Controls for turning unit on and off and for rewinding cord are poorly differentiated.
u–Exhaust poorly diffused and directed; likely to blow dirt about.
v–Cleans narrow swath (9½ to 10½ in.).
w–Dusting brush judged likely to clog.
x–Only 2 pile-height settings.
y–Hose may be hard to detach from canister.
z–Suction fell off relatively rapidly as bag or dirt compartment filled.

KEY TO COMMENTS

A–Multiple speeds, but lowest setting judged not much quieter than highest.
B–Uses dust bin instead of bags.
C–Head lamp.
D–2-yr. parts and labor warranty (5-yr. on **Royal M880**).
E–5-yr. warranty on upright base.
F–5-yr. warranty on fan and motor assembly.
G–5-yr. warranty on circuit board for solid-state control.
H–Comes with wall tool rack (**Toshiba VC222** and **VC420**) or special radiator brush (**Miele S230i**).
I–Comes with suction-only floor/rug nozzle in addition to power nozzle.
J–Comes with adapter, hose, and tools.
K–Assembly hampered by tight-fitting parts.
L–Momentary extra-power setting.
M–Machine does not wheel about; most conveniently used by holding motor unit in 1 hand and hose in other.
N–Machine tends to fall over if wheeled about; most conveniently used by holding motor unit in 1 hand and hose in other.
O–No bleed-type suction control; suction can be reduced by lowering motor speed.
P–Brush-strip not replaceable; roller assembly must be replaced when bristles wear out.
Q–Plastic wands with locking clamps.
R–**Royal M401PN** comes with cloth filter bag; cloth filter bag is optional with **Kirby**.
S–Automatic pile-height adjustment.
T–Requires adjustment for cleaning carpets of different pile heights.
U–Power nozzle powered by air flow.
V–Hybrid model; comes with bare-floor, upholstery, and crevice-tool attachments that fit on end of motor or wands.
W–Available without power nozzle for $135.
X–Now designated **1425G**.

might just barely justify the purchase of the top-rated power-nozzle canister, the *Hoover S3281*, which lists at $460 before any possible discount. It's a fine machine, but there may well be less expensive ways to achieve the same level of performance.

There is, for example, the *Panasonic MC9420*, another power-nozzle canister rated almost as high but listing at $250. And there are plenty of combinations of uprights and suction-only canisters that should perform well for a good deal less than $400 total. One attractively priced team might be formed, for another example, by pairing the the *Panasonic MC7320* ($130 list) with the *Eureka 1425F* ($100); the former is the top-rated suction-only canister, and the latter is a no-frills upright that cleaned carpeting about as thoroughly as any other model.

Hand-held cordless vacuum cleaners

Condensed from CONSUMER REPORTS, January 1986

After developing a series of cordless outdoor appliances—electric hedge trimmers, power drills, and the like—Black & Decker also led the power-tool industry in bringing the new technology indoors. Its 1979 *Dustbuster* was the first of a breed of cordless minivacuums, a breed now numbering at least the 10 models tested for this report.

Like many another cordless device, the minivacuum owes its existence to the rechargeable battery. Aside from its charging stand, a cordless vacuum typically consists of two elements: a motor/handle unit that holds the battery, and a nozzle/collector unit that sucks up and stores the dirt. To empty most models, one simply pushes a release button, separates the two units, and shakes out the collector.

When not in use, the minivac belongs on its combined battery charger/holder, which can be mounted on a wall. Plugged into a wall outlet, the chargers draw less than five watts. Before we tested, we gave each model a 16-hour charge, as the manufacturers recommend. Next, to condition the battery and break in the motor, we completely discharged and recharged every battery at least three times. (All the minivacs will perform better if their batteries are totally discharged and recharged now and again.) Then and only then did we begin testing to see how well each model could remove debris.

PICKING UP AT HOME. Good cleaning depends partly on the strength of a vac's suction. It also depends on how long a vacuum cleaner can maintain suction without significant drop-off. Judged by those two criteria, the *Black & Decker Dustbuster Plus* easily outclassed the field. But don't look to any of the cordless vacs for prolonged cleaning power. Even the *Dustbuster Plus* managed only a bit more than 15 minutes of sustained effort. Middling performers averaged 10 minutes or so.

To measure dirt capacity, we used each vac to pick up as much barley as its dust collector could hold. Then, in a much tougher test, we fed the vacuums their fill of very fine sawdust. Again, the *Dustbuster Plus* did best. But neither it nor any of the others did an adequate job of cleaning up an even finer dust, talcum powder. They picked up the

Text continued on page 215

Ratings of hand-held vacuum cleaners

Listed in order of estimated quality. Prices are list; + indicates shipping is extra. Discounts may be available.

⊜ ⊖ ○ ◒ ●

Better ⟵ ⟶ Worse

Brand and model	Price	Initial suction	Effective running time	Effective capacity	Car-interior cleaning	Advantages	Disadvantages
BLACK & DECKER DUSTBUSTER PLUS	$60	⊜	⊜	⊜	⊜ [1]	B,C,E,J	a,d
NORELCO CLEAN-UP MACHINE 2 HV1020	47	⊖	⊖	○	⊜	A,B,C,D,G,H,K	—
EUREKA MINI MITE	40	⊜	⊖	○	⊖	A,F,J,K	g
DOUGLAS READIVAC 6.0	40	◒	⊖	○	⊜	A,B,C,G,H,I,J,K	b
SANYO PORTA BUTLER PC3	35	⊜	⊖	○	⊖	A,C,K	b,d,i
SEARS Cat. No. 17832 CORDLESS VAC	25+	○	○	⊖	⊖ [1]	J	a,d
BLACK & DECKER DUSTBUSTER	46	○	○	⊖	⊖ [1]	J	a,d
DOUGLAS READIVAC 3.6	30	◒	◒	◒	⊖	H,I,J,K	b
NORELCO CLEAN-UP MACHINE	38	⊖	◒	●	○	G,H,K	—
CONAIR KWIK SWEEP [2]	25	●	●	●	●	A	b,c,d,e,f,g,h,i

[1] *But see Disadvantage a.* [2] *Now designated* **Conair Kleen Sweep.**

FEATURES IN COMMON

All: are battery-operated; measure about 15 in. long and weigh less than 2 lb.; have a plastic body; separate into 2 pieces, motor/handle unit and nozzle/collector unit; have a replaceable filter, a charger and holder for wall mounting, and a warranty of at least 1 year.

KEY TO ADVANTAGES

A – Charge-indicator light.
B – Brush attachment.
C – Crevice-tool attachment.
D – Rack for attachments.
E – Comes with spare filter.
F – Built-in nozzle extension.
G – Better than most at picking up cigarette butts.
H – Better than most at picking up hair.
I – Better than most at picking up sand.
J – Better than most at picking up potting soil.
K – Among the best at picking up cornflakes.

KEY TO DISADVANTAGES

a – May eject sand particles from exhaust with considerable force. We recommend wearing eye protection.
b – Parts and service may be inconvenient to obtain.
c – Instructions judged poor.
d – Hangs with nozzle down; can spill debris.
e – No provision for storing excess cord in back of holder.
f – Worse than most at picking up hair and cigarette butts.
g – Worse than most at picking up sand.
h – Worse than most at picking up cornflakes.
i – Worse than most at picking up potting soil.

powder readily enough, but they also ejected it readily through their exhaust ports.

Further cleaning tests showed important differences in performance, depending on the surfaces cleaned and on the material cleaned from them. We used various surfaces: tile, laminated plastic, upholstery, and a medium-pile rug. And from those surfaces, we tried to pick up assorted minor rubbish: potting soil, hair, cigarette butts, and cornflakes. The Ratings note better and worse performers. All the vacs, of course, did their jobs best when emptied of debris from earlier missions.

SPIFFING UP THE CAR. Cleaning car interiors was easiest with the *Dustbuster Plus*, the *Norelco 2*, and the *Douglas 6.0*, partly because of their superior staying power. More important still, each has a brush and a tapered nozzle extension, or crevice tool, which were very helpful when working inside a car.

Most of the other vacs cleaned well enough. But gravel, hair, and dried grass lodged in a car may be too much for some models, our tests indicate. And some models didn't have much appetite for sand. Both *Dustbuster* models and the *Sears* could gobble up sand easily, but occasionally they didn't care to swallow all of it. They tended instead to eject fine particles of sand through their air-exhaust ports with surprising force. We'd caution users of those three models, when working within the confines of a car's interior, to make some provision for protecting their eyes.

RECOMMENDATIONS. The *Black & Decker Dustbuster Plus* excelled at just about every test chore we could think up for minivacs, although its over-zealous disposal of sand seemed a little menacing at close quarters. The *Dustbuster Plus* lists for a relatively high price, $60, but it may be deeply discounted; CU's samples cost from $35 to $44.

Furniture polishes

Condensed from CONSUMER REPORTS, January 1986

According to one finishing school, the oil or lacquer treatment that's normally used on furniture protects the wood more or less permanently by sealing it; after that, the wood merely needs cleaning. Another school holds the opposite view: that the original finish itself needs a protective layer, usually wax, that should be renewed periodically.

Followers of contemporary advertising may recognize that difference of opinion in the to-wax-or-not-to-wax colloquy held occasionally by actors in TV commercials. The makers of furniture polish try not to take sides; they try to please everyone—no-wax, pro-wax, and undecided. So some furniture polishes contain no wax at all; others are part wax; and still others are nearly solid wax.

Which should you choose and use? As a rule, we don't think it matters much if your only aim is to keep ordinary furniture presentable. The rule obviously doesn't apply if you're dealing with worn wood that badly needs some sort of finish or with antique furniture that needs special treatment. You may also have reason to combat wax buildup on frequently polished pieces. Aside from those considerations, though, you should attempt to choose a polish that's easy to apply and that imparts only as much gloss as you want.

PERFORMANCE. We tested 34 popular furniture polishes on wood panels fin-

Text continued on page 218

Ratings of furniture polishes

Listed, overall, not in order of estimated quality, but rather in groups according to increase of gloss given to surface of unsealed, oil-finished wood; within groups, listed in order of estimated quality. Prices are the average paid by CU shoppers.

Key: Excellent, Very good, Good, Fair, Poor

Brand	Price	Size (oz. or fl. oz.)	Type [1]	Resistance to water: Oil finish	Resistance to water: High-gloss lacquer	Resistance to alcohol: Oil finish	Resistance to alcohol: High-gloss lacquer	Comments
■ *The following showed a moderate increase in gloss on oil-finished wood.*								
FAVOR LEMON	$1.49	7	A	Very good	Excellent	Good	Very good	C,D
BEHOLD LEMON	1.38	7	A	Good	Excellent	Good	Excellent	C,E
JOHNSON PASTE WAX	3.39	16	P	Good	Excellent	Poor	Excellent	C,L
BUTCHER'S BOWLING ALLEY	3.59	16	P	Good	Excellent	Poor	Excellent	C,M
OLD ENGLISH LEMON CREME	1.56	9	A	Very good	Excellent	Good	Very good	C,E
PLEDGE LEMON	1.63	7	A	Very good	Excellent	Good	Excellent	C,E,O
PLEDGE ORIGINAL	1.72	7	A	Good	Excellent	Good	Excellent	C,E,O
■ *The following showed a slight increase in gloss on oil-finished wood.*								
HAGERTY VERNAX	6.22	16	L	Very good	Excellent	Good	Excellent	C
PARKER'S LEMON OIL	4.25	16	L	Very good	Excellent	Good	Excellent	A,M
WOOLWORTH LEMON	1.46	14	A	Very good	Excellent	Good	Excellent	C,D
OLD ENGLISH LEMON	1.99	12	S	Very good	Excellent	Very good	Excellent	C,E
GODDARD'S WITH LEMON BEES WAX	4.49	10	A	Very good	Excellent	Very good	Excellent	C,D,O

PLEDGE LEMON	2.26	12	S	⊖	◍	⊖	◍	*B,D,O*
OLD ENGLISH SCRATCH COVER	2.86	8	L	⊖	◍	○	◍	*B,I,L,R*
KLEEN GUARD WITH LEMON	1.19	7	A	⊖	◍	⊖	◍	*C,E,H,O*
SCOTT'S LIQUID GOLD	3.51	14	A	⊖	◍	⊖	◍	*A,G,Q*
SCOTT'S LIQUID GOLD	4.16	16	L	⊖	◍	⊖	◍	*A,G,Q*
TREWAX TRES BIEN LEMON OIL	3.39	14	A	⊖	⊖	○	●	*B,F,L,N*
GUARDSMAN WOODSCENT	3.99	16	L	⊖	◍	⊖	○	*B,F,M,N,P*
GUARDSMAN LEMON	2.89	14	A	⊖	○	○	●	*B,F,N,P,R*
WEIMAN WITH LEMON	3.02	12	A	⊖	○	○	●	*C,F,M,N,P*
■ *The following showed no or almost no gloss increase on all-finished wood.*								
COMPLETE	2.36	16	S	⊖	◍	⊖	◍	*B,K*
A&P LEMON	1.38	14	A	⊖	◍	⊖	◍	*C,D*
TARGET WITH LEMON OIL	1.59	14	A	⊖	◍	⊖	◍	*B,D*
WOOD PLUS LEMON SCENT	1.89	16	S	⊖	◍	⊖	◍	*B,D,K*
ENDUST	1.87	6	A	⊖	◍	⊖	◍	*A,S*
AMWAY BUFF-UP	6.75	12	A	⊖	◍	◒	◍	*C*
WILBERT DRI-FINISH LEMON OIL	1.66	12	L	⊖	◍	⊖	◍	*A,M,S*
FURNITURE MAGIC WITH LEMON	2.79	13	A	⊖	◍	○	◍	*A,S*
SAFEWAY WHITE MAGIC LEMON	2.09	14	A	○	◍	◒	◍	*B*
OLD ENGLISH LEMON CREAM WAX	2.56	8	L	⊖	◍	⊖	◍	*C,D,O*
FORMBY'S LEMON OIL FURNITURE TREATMENT	2.86	8	L	⊖	◍	⊖	◍	*A,J,Q*
WEIMAN CREAM LEMON	2.96	8	L	⊖	◍	⊖	◍	*A,M,N,P*
GUARDSMAN LEMON	3.24	16	S	⊖	○	○	●	*B,F,N,P*

[1] *A = Aerosol spray. L = Liquid. S = Spray pump. P = Paste wax.*

Keys to Ratings on next page

Keys to furniture polishes Ratings

KEY TO COMMENTS

A–Caused no gloss increase on lacquered semigloss finish.
B–Caused slight gloss increase on lacquered semigloss finish.
C–Caused moderate gloss increase on lacquered semigloss finish.
D–Polish smudged on high-gloss finish.
E–Polish smudged on lacquered semigloss and high-gloss finishes.
F–Polished surface would be marred when rubbed.
G–According to label, product is for most natural-finished wood, which apparently precludes use on lacquered wood.
H–According to label, product is not to be applied to unsealed wood, which apparently precludes use on oiled wood.
I–Contains dark pigment for help in hiding scratches; not for light-colored woods.
J–According to instructions, buffing is not required, but we found buffing necessary.
K–Trigger-type pump; judged easier to use than most other pump sprays.
L–Instructions call for separate application cloth.
M–Instructions call for separate, predampened application cloth.
N–Not as easy to buff as most.
O–Multiple coats tended to look uneven when applied to lacquered semigloss finish.
P–Tended to look scratchy when several coats were applied to high-gloss finish.
Q–Gloss diminished after 1 day on both oil and lacquered-semigloss finishes.
R–Gloss diminished after 1 day on oil-finished wood.
S–Gloss diminished after 1 day on lacquered semigloss finish.

---

ished in three ways: oiled walnut, similar to the finish found on much Danish Modern furniture; walnut sealed with a semigloss lacquer, the type of finish used on much of the moderately priced furniture made in this country; and mahogany lacquered and hand-rubbed to a mirrorlike gloss, the kind of finish found on grand pianos. We applied one coat to see how that compared with the bare finish, and then applied six coats at intervals to see if any problems developed from wax buildup.

The word "polish" implies that the product will impart a shine, but the truth is that the shine you get will depend not only on the nature of the polish, but also on the nature of the finish. No polish could increase the shine of our high-gloss mahogany.

Our lacquered walnut panels had a low luster that looked nice to begin with and a few polishes—especially those that described themselves as cleaners or "no wax" preparations—left the panels that way. Many polishes, including some no-wax products, imparted a little more gloss to the semigloss finish.

Our oiled-walnut panels had no gloss to begin with, just the warm look of natural wood. Although a product that simply restored the natural look would satisfy many people, a number of polishes gave the walnut slight or moderate degrees of gloss. For test purposes, at least, that wide range in gloss was what we were after, because it makes sense for consumers to choose polishes that will give them the gloss levels they want. So, in the Ratings, the products are grouped according to their effect on the gloss of our oiled-walnut panels. Comments in the Ratings identify the products that also made lacquered walnut appear glossier.

To test for stain resistance, we laid pieces of blotting paper, soaked in water or alcohol, on wood panels that had received six applications of polish. The next morning, we removed the paper and wiped each spot dry. Judging from our tests, we'd be skeptical of claims that a polish actually protects wood. It was the finish and not the polish, we found, that provided the protection.

We rubbed a piece of cardboard

across the polished surfaces to simulate the damage that could occur, for example, when someone drags a coaster loaded with a cup of coffee across a table. Only five products marred surfaces, and then only high-gloss surfaces. But the damage occurred as scratches that couldn't be wiped off.

We smudged our test panels by rubbing them lightly with a finger swathed in soft paper towel. A smudge would often appear; then it would quickly heal itself and disappear. The polishes that retained smudges could be restored with a couple of swipes of a cloth.

The polishes in aerosol containers were by far the easiest to apply—too easy, it seemed sometimes, leaving too much polish on the wood. Pump sprays required a little more effort but provided better control. The pourable liquids and the paste waxes are meant to be applied with one cloth fairly soaked with the product, then wiped and buffed with a separate dry cloth—a fair amount of messy work.

RECOMMENDATIONS. If the oil or lacquer finish on a piece of furniture is worn and shabby, the remedy doesn't lie with any of the products we tested. What it needs is refinishing. But if the finish is in good shape, many of the polishes we tested can help keep furniture looking well cared for. Our Ratings can help you pick out one that will give you the level of gloss you want.

Glass cleaners

Condensed from CONSUMER REPORTS, October 1986

There are an awful lot of commercial products contending merely for your glass-cleaning dollars. Our shoppers returned from a supermarket sweep with 23 widely distributed glass cleaners costing from about 5 cents to 15 cents an ounce or fluid ounce. We checked their cleaning ability against that of a venerable home formula we concocted ourselves for less than a penny per fluid ounce; it consisted of half a cup of sudsy ammonia, a pint of rubbing alcohol, a teaspoonful of liquid dishwashing detergent, and enough water to make a gallon of the stuff. We also compared the performance of the commercial and homemade cleaners with that of plain tap water.

CLEANING. The last time we tested glass cleaners, we, at first, made things too easy for them by pitting them against ordinary suburban dirt on CU's ordinary office windows. Even tap water did well on those windows. So we then devised the tough lab test we now use. We "smoked" dozens of dark cigars in a hookah-like rig, trapped the smoke in alcohol, painted the resulting tarry goo on glass panels, and heated the panels in an oven until the coatings turned into a tough brown glaze.

We masked off half of each panel and applied a cleaner to the exposed half, allowing each measured dose to sit undisturbed for a minute to give the ingredients a chance to start working. Then each panel went into a machine that scrubbed a cheesecloth pad back and forth on it six times. A fresh pad mopped up the cleaned surface with four more strokes. After we switched the masking and repeated the routine with another cleaner on the formerly concealed section, a six-member jury judged which side of each panel was the cleaner, and by how much. Each prod-

Ratings of glass cleaners

Listed in order of estimated glass-cleaning ability. Performance differences between closely ranked products were slight. Prices are the average of those paid by CU shoppers for the sizes indicated.

Product	Type [1]	Price	Size (oz. or fl. oz.)	Cost per oz. or fl. oz. [2]	Comments
SAVOGRAN DIRTEX SPRAY CLEANER	A	$2.18	15	14.5¢	—
K MART WINDOW CLEANER	VP	.97	12	8.1	E
SPARKLE GLASS CLEANER	A	1.54	20	7.7	—
LADY LEE WINDOW GLASS CLEANER	TP	1.29	22	5.9	A,E
A&P WINDOW CLEANER	TP	1.19	22	5.4	D,E
WALGREENS WINDOW CLEANER	VP	1.36	16	8.5	C
WINDEX GLASS CLEANER (blue liquid)	TP	1.98	22	9.0	B,E
TREWAX INDUSTRIAL STRENGTH WINDOW CLEANER	TP	2.06	32	6.4	A
REVCO WINDOW CLEANER	TP	1.11	22	5.0	A
GLASS WAX GLASS AND METAL CLEANER	P	2.26	16	14.1	—
WHITE MAGIC GLASS CLEANER (Safeway)	TP	1.69	22	7.7	A,E
ARROW WINDOW CLEANER	TP	1.09	22	5.0	D,E
TEXIZE GLASS PLUS	TP	1.56	22	7.1	A,E
WINDEX GLASS CLEANER	A	2.01	20	10.1	—
COST CUTTER WINDOW CLEANER (Kroger)	P	.79	22	3.6	—
SPARKLE GLASS CLEANER	TP	1.58	25	6.3	E
ALPHA BETA GLASS CLEANER	TP	1.49	24	6.2	A,E
ECKERD GLASS ETC.	TP	1.44	22	6.5	A,E
EASY-OFF GLASS LEMONIZED	TP	1.89	22	8.6	E
BRIGHT WINDOW CLEANER (Kroger)	TP	1.29	22	5.9	A,E
EASY-OFF GLASS CLEANER LEMONIZED	A	1.69	18¾	9.0	—
BON AMI GLASS CLEANER	A	1.19	15	7.9	—
WINDEX GLASS CLEANER LEMON FRESH	TP	1.71	22	7.8	A,E

[1] *A = aerosol; P = pourable; TP = trigger pump; VP = vertical plunger.*

[2] *About enough for a lightly soiled, double-hung 32×48-in. window.*

KEY TO COMMENTS
A-Nozzle has handy Stream, Spray, and Off positions.
B-Nozzle has On (spray) and Off positions.
C-Pump must be screwed down into Off position; emits a wasteful squirt in the process.
D-Nozzle cover is a small, press-fit cap; could be easily lost.
E-Money-saving refills available.

uct, commercial and otherwise, was put through eight of those trials.

Savogran Dirtex was judged best, but not by much. More than half of the products in the Ratings made fairly easy work of the tarry test film. Our home formula was judged an average performer. Water did a poor job.

CONVENIENCE AND COSTS. Many glass cleaners are probably bought for their handy packaging. Most of ours came in aerosol cans or spray bottles. We judged the push-button aerosols, as usual, very convenient. They can spray a whole window with one push of the finger. But some pump-spray bottles are quite easy to use, too. The best have a nozzle with three positions: Stream, Spray, and Off. Stream has a longer, more accurate range than Spray.

Further, most of the products packaged with pumps and plungers offer a secondary saving. Bottled refills may be available for 20 to 50 percent off.

To get an idea of costs per use, we conducted practical trials on windows along a corridor at CU. We estimated that it would take about one ounce or fluid ounce of cleaner to get light dirt off a 32x48-inch window. The Ratings note those costs, as calculated from the prices we paid for each cleaner.

RECOMMENDATIONS. If you ever need to clean wretchedly foul windows—like those simulated in our tests—by all means invest in a can or two of the top-rated *Savogran Dirtex* aerosol cleaner, even if it does cost 14.5 cents an ounce. Otherwise, for ordinarily soiled windows, it makes better sense to strike some sort of balance between effectiveness, convenience, and cost.

Bathroom cleaners

Condensed from CONSUMER REPORTS, May 1986

In this age of specialization, it may be asking too much of a household cleaning product to expect it to clean every room in the house equally well. At least, that appears to be the rationale of the soap-makers who produced the 14 bathroom cleaning compounds tested for this report. But the rationale simply won't wash, because none of the specialized bathroom products cleaned bathroom dirt any better than several all-purpose cleaners. And none fought mold and mildew as successfully as ordinary household bleach.

PERFORMANCE. To see how the cleaners would do the really tough jobs, we first prepared our version of bathroom dirt mainly in imitation of that old bathroom standby, soap scum. We mixed "artificial sebum" (a laboratory replica of human skin oil) with soap and soot, seeded the mixture with mineral salts, let it spread from solution on glass plates where it formed a nasty gray film, and fed the glass plates to our scrub-testing machine.

Most of the specialized bathroom cleaners proved fairly potent. The best of them—*Tough Act*, *Boraxo*, and *Fantastik*—removed the tough scum in a

Text continued on page 223

Ratings of bathroom cleaners

Listed in order of estimated overall quality, based primarily on cleaning ability. Prices are the average of those paid by CU shoppers.

◍ ⊖ ○ ◒ ●

Better ← → **Worse**

Product	Price/size (oz.)	Cost per oz.	Cleaning ability	Mold-fighting ability	May mar these surfaces if left unwiped	Comments
TOP JOB ALL-PURPOSE	$2.07/28	7¢	◍	○	a,b,d	A
TOUGH ACT BATHROOM	2.09/17	12	⊖	⊖	a,b,d,e	A,E
AJAX ALL-PURPOSE	1.59/28	6	⊖	⊖	a,b	A
MR. CLEAN ALL-PURPOSE	2.07/28	7	⊖	⊖	b	A
BORAXO BATHROOM	1.99/17	12	⊖	◒	b,e	A,E
FANTASTIK BATHROOM	1.84/16	12	⊖	◒	a,b	A,E
TILEX MILDEW STAIN REMOVER	2.54/16	16	○	◍	a,b,c,d,e	A,C,E
LYSOL BATHROOM	1.79/17	11	○	○	b,g	A,E
DOW BATHROOM	1.69/17	10	○	◒	a,b,e	A,B
K MART BATHROOM	1.38/17	8	○	◒	a,b,e	A,B
WOOLWORTH BATHROOM	1.20/17	7	○	◒	a,b	A,B
KROGER BRIGHT BASIN, TUB & TILE	1.09/16	7	○	●	a,b,d	A,E
CARBONA TILE & BATH	2.69/16	17	○	●	a,b	A,H
CHLORINE BLEACH	[1]/128	[1]	◒	◍	a,b,c,d,f	A,C
EASY-OFF MILDEW STAIN REMOVER	1.99/16	12	◒	⊖	a,b,d	A,C,E,F
X-14 MILDEW STAIN REMOVER	2.32/16	15	◒	⊖	a,b,c,d,f	A,C,E
LIME-A-WAY BATHROOM/KITCHEN	1.74/16	11	◒	◒	b,f,g	D,G
SCRUB FREE BATHROOM	2.39/16	15	●	◒	b,e	D,E

[1] *Price range: $.59 to $1.09; cost-per-oz. range: ½ to 1¢.*

KEY TO SURFACES

a – Aluminum.
b – Brass.
c – Chrome.
d – Semigloss enamel.
e – Fiberglass-reinforced plastic.
f – Phenolic laminate (such as Formica).
g – Stainless steel.

KEY TO COMMENTS

A – Strongly alkaline.
B – Aerosol.
C – Contains bleach.
D – Strongly acidic. (Should be somewhat better than most at removing hard-water stains.)
E – Pump-spray bottle.
F – Dual safety closures, on nozzle and on neck or bottle.
G – Flip-top squirt bottle.
H – Squeeze bottle with brush applicator.

few strokes. Indeed, *Tough Act* could remove much of the soil just by dribbling down the glass plates held at a slant. But two all-purpose cleaners we included in our tests—*Ajax*, and *Mr. Clean*—cleaned just as well, and another, *Top Job*, did the best job of all.

To see how effectively these products fight mold and mildew, we pitted them in a couple of ways against laboratory cultures of the common black mold frequently found inhabiting tile grout and the bottom edges of shower curtains. The cleaners that best inhibited mold growth kept it from filling a pattern coated with cleaner on a culture plate. And those cleaners that excelled at destroying mold turned furry fields of it white and broke it up quickly after they were applied. But none of the cleaners wiped out mold as effectively as undiluted household chlorine bleach, the liquid used with laundry.

While most of the tested cleaners may be classified as strongly alkaline or acidic, they're not really strong enough to corrode common bathroom surfaces on mere passing contact. But they may mar certain materials if they're allowed to rest on them for some length of time, as might happen with spatters that escape notice. None of the cleaners, we found, could do significant harm to ceramic tile and acrylic plastic. But many could leave spots and stains on other surfaces, especially the aluminum and brass of bathroom fixtures.

RECOMMENDATIONS. The three top-rated bathroom cleaners offer very respectable cleaning performance. And one of them, *Tough Act*, offers impressive mold-fighting ability, even though it contains no bleach. But *Tough Act*, like most of the specialty products, costs more per ounce than all-purpose cleaners such as *Top Job*. Besides, *Top Job* cleaned better.

We therefore recommend *Top Job* for bathrooms, just as we recommended it four years ago as one of the best cleaners for all around the house. (If you want a fancier applicator than a sponge from a pan, you might try putting *Top Job* in a used but well-rinsed spray bottle, appropriately labeled, and using it full strength.) But none of the high-rated products offered truly satisfactory relief from chronic case of hard-core mold and mildew. For that, you may want to seek recourse in the best and cheapest mold-fighter that we know of—ordinary household bleach.

A word of caution here, though. Since bleach by itself isn't a good cleaner, there's a temptation to mix it with other products. Resist the temptation; it could prove hazardous. Bleach reacts almost instantly with acid to produce chlorine gas; and it reacts with ammonia and related alkaline substances to produce a combination of chlorine and other noxious gases. That's not to say that you shouldn't also use bleach in a room regularly scrubbed down with a cleaner. Just use the two separately, and make sure that you thoroughly rinse surfaces washed with bleach—something you'll want to do anyway because unwiped bleach can mar almost any smooth surface.

For the full story

The date of the original article in CONSUMER REPORTS appears directly below its title. For a more complete report, consult the original version.

(For back issues, see page 5.)

Scouring cleansers

Condensed from CONSUMER REPORTS, September 1985

Most scouring powders contain silica, a quartz dust so hard it can scratch glass, plastic, and enamel surfaces. Many of the new "soft" liquid and powder cleansers contain milder abrasives, such as feldspar or calcium carbonate. But even the softest will do some damage.

Scouring cleansers also contain a combination of soaps, detergents, bleaches, and alkaline or acidic chemicals to help remove certain stains. Cleaning power, apart from abrasive effects, comes from the combined effects of all those ingredients.

PERFORMANCE. We first put the cleansers to the test on white vinyl floor tiles smeared with a mixture of margarine, petroleum jelly, lanolin, and carbon-black.

Overall, powders are more abrasive than liquids. All cleansing products tended to scratch acrylic, plastic, and aluminum; none can be safely used on mirror-finish metal.

A powerful, abrasive cleanser that's good for general cleaning may not have the chemical action necessary for getting at stubborn stains. Manufacturers add bleach to help.

RECOMMENDATIONS. One of the most effective, and yet one of the gentlest, products is *Bon Ami Polishing Cleanser* (not to be confused with regular *Bon Ami*, which contains no bleach).

Ratings of scouring cleansers

Listed in groups in order of cleaning ability; within groups, listed primarily in order of increasing abrasiveness. Liquid cleansers are indicated.

BON AMI POLISHING CLEANSER, A & P, AJAX (with phosphates), WHITE MAGIC (Safeway), BAB-O

COMET (new formula), SOFT SCRUB liquid, BRIGHT (Kroger), AJAX (without phosphates), WOOLWORTH, ACME

SIERRA liquid, COMET (with phosphates), OLD DUTCH, LADY LEE (Lucky)

COMET liquid, BON AMI, WOOLWORTH liquid, LADY LEE liquid (Lucky), SHINY SINKS liquid, COMET (without phosphates)

How to use the Buying Guide

- Look in the index for specific reports.
- Look in the Contents for general subject areas.
- Look on pages 5 to 7 for explanations of check-ratings and Best Buys, and of why some products are included and others not.

Smoke detectors

Condensed from CONSUMER REPORTS, October 1984

Ionization models are the first to detect smoke from the fast fires—but only by a few seconds in our tests.

In the tests involving slow fires, the photoelectric models and combination ionization/photoelectric models sounded off first. Since that proved to be the big difference between the two types, we have ranked the detectors in the Ratings on the basis of their response to slow fires.

CONSIDERATIONS. The power source for the detectors we tested is a single nine-volt battery. To keep a detector at the ready, you must know when the battery is failing. Each tested model signals impending battery failure with a gentle, periodic beep. How long it continues to beep a warning depends on the model.

All the detectors have a test button to let you check if the unit is functioning; the alarm sounds when the button is pressed.

Some detectors sound frequent false alarms because they're put in the wrong place. Avoid placing a detector near a kitchen or close to a fireplace or woodstove. Garages and furnace rooms are also poor locations. Even a bathroom shower can set off an alarm. To keep a detector operating properly, we recommend a yearly cleaning with a vacuum wand.

RECOMMENDATIONS. In our tests, the photoelectric and combination units re-

Text continued on page 227

Ratings of smoke detectors

Listed by groups in order of response to slow fires. All responded reasonably well to fast fires. Within groups, listed in order of increasing price. Prices are suggested retail, rounded to nearest dollar; + indicates shipping is extra. Discounts are generally available. [D] indicates product has been discontinued.

◉ ⊖ ○ ◒ ●

Better ⟵⟶ **Worse**

Brand and model	Price	Type [1]	Response to slow fires	Alarm loudness [2]	Low-battery signal duration (days)	Warranty (months)	Comments
[D]✔ **SEARS EARLY ONE Cat. No. 57307**	$20+	P	◉	◒	7	12	—
PITTWAY FIRST ALERT SA202	30	P	⊖	○	30	12	—
SEARS EARLY ONE Cat. No. 57363	30+	I/P	⊖	○	30	12	A
PITTWAY FIRST ALERT SA301	40	I/P	⊖	○	30	60	A

Ratings continued on next page

Ratings of smoke detectors continued

Brand and model	Price	Type [1]	Response to slow fires	Alarm loudness [2]	Low-battery signal duration (days)	Warranty (months)	Comments
[D] J.C. PENNEY Cat. No. 3421	$11+	I	○	⊜	30	12	F
SEARS EARLY ONE 57358	11+	I	○	○	7	12	—
EMHART 03591530	13	I	○	○	7	12	A
FAMILY GARD FG777C	13	I	○	⊜	30	36	A
JAMESON REACT RS1	13	I	○	○	7	12	—
[D] WARDS Cat. No. 61666	13+	I	○	⊜	30	12	A
JAMESON CODE ONE CD1	15	I	○	○	7	36	A,E
PITTWAY FIRST ALERT SA67	15	I	○	⊜	30	60	—
SUNBEAM CENTURION III 45061	15	I	○	○	7	12	A,E
RADIO SHACK SAFE HOUSE 49455	17	I	○	◒	7	3	—
[D] J.C. PENNEY Cat. No. 3223	17+	I	○	○	7	12	B
[D] WARDS Cat. No. 61659	18+	I	○	⊜	30	60	A,G
FYRNETICS LIFESAVER 0905	20	I	○	○	7	12	—
GENERAL ELECTRIC HOME SENTRY SMK6	20	I	○	○	30	12	C
PITTWAY FIRST ALERT SA76RC	20	I	○	⊜	30	60	A
RADIO SHACK SAFE HOUSE 49456	20	I	○	◒	7	3	E
SEARS EARLY ONE Cat. No. 57313	25+	I	○	○	30	12	A,D
[D] J.C. PENNEY Cat. No. 3102	30+	I	○	○	30	12	A,D
[D] WARDS Cat. No. 61626	30+	I	○	○	30	60	A,D,H
PITTWAY FIRST ALERT SA120	40	I	○	○	30	12	A,D

[1] *P = photoelectric; I = ionization; I/P = ionization/photoelectric.*

[2] *Measured after low-battery signal had finished.*

FEATURES IN COMMON

All have: test button; low-battery beep signal; instruction book judged good.

Except as noted, all: require one 9V battery; have a pulsing, high-pitched alarm.

KEY TO COMMENTS

A–Flashing red light indicates working battery.

B–Has "hush" feature to quiet nuisance alarms.

C–Alarm is a warbling sound.

D–Requires 2 9V batteries; second is for emergency light.

E–Portable. Can be mounted on door.

F–Sample we purchased was identified as **BRK 79P**.

G–Sample we purchased was identified as **Pittway First Alert SA80FC**.

H–Sample we purchased was identified as **Pittway First Alert SA130**.

sponded most quickly to all kinds of fires. But photoelectric smoke detectors aren't as readily available or as cheap as most ionization units.

If you can, it's best to buy more than one detector. For a multiple-detector system, we recommend that one detector be an ionization unit or a combination unit; the others should be photoelectric detectors.

Ultrasonic humidifiers

Condensed from CONSUMER REPORTS, November 1985

Among the latest entries in the "home health-care market," ultrasonic humidifiers offer a new way to raise the humidity of dry indoor air. To see how well they work, we tested 18 of the most popular and readily available models, priced from $70 to $140. All of those, we judged, can effectively humidify one or two large rooms, though not an entire house, as a few manufacturers claim.

Ultrasonic humidifiers are compact (about the size of a bread box), relatively lightweight (about 20 pounds, filled with water), and, compared with conventional humidifiers and vaporizers, decidedly high-tech. Instead of employing an impeller or rotating drum to turn water into mist, they use a small electronic component, called a transducer, which transforms electrical energy into mechanical (specifically vibrational) energy. The part that actually vibrates is the "nebulizer"—a disk about the size of a dime that oscillates some 1.7 million times a second, churning water into a very fine, cool mist. The oscillation is so rapid that it's ultrasonic—above the range of human hearing and therefore, for practical purposes, silent.

In addition, we confirmed, ultrasonic humidifiers enjoy another advantage over console humidifiers and cool-mist vaporizers: They apparently kill molds and bacteria that might grow in the water. We theorize that the ultrasonic vibrations destroy microbes by breaking them apart. Even so, bits and pieces of mold and bacteria may be spewed about, and while they may not cause infections, they could still trigger allergic reactions in sensitive individuals.

PERFORMANCE. The models with the highest output rate were the top-rated *Toshiba* and the *Quiet Mist*. They vaporized more than two cups of water per hour. The *Holmes* and the *Robeson 3004* had the lowest output, vaporizing less than a cup and a half per hour. The output of all models, with volume control set at minimum position, could be lowered to five ounces per hour or less.

(In this and other tests, we discovered a greater sample-to-sample variation than we usually find in performance tests of appliances. The listed results for all brands, therefore, are the averages of more than one sample, as we note in the Ratings.)

To figure the coverage of the ultrasonic humidifiers, we first calculated the humidification requirements for a typically weatherized house, one with a ventilation rate of one air change per hour. On that basis, the models we tested could effectively humidify anywhere from 3200 to 5200 cubic feet—as long as their tanks had water in them. Most models with a fairly high output would run for about 10 hours on a tankful at their highest setting. So, for maximum coverage in continuous use, most would need to be filled more than twice a day.

Text continued on page 230

Ratings of ultrasonic humidifiers

Listed, except as noted, in order of estimated overall quality; bracketed models are similar in most important respects and are listed alphabetically. Prices are list; discounts are generally available. D indicates model was discontinued at original publication.

◍ ⊖ ○ ◒ ●

Better ← → Worse

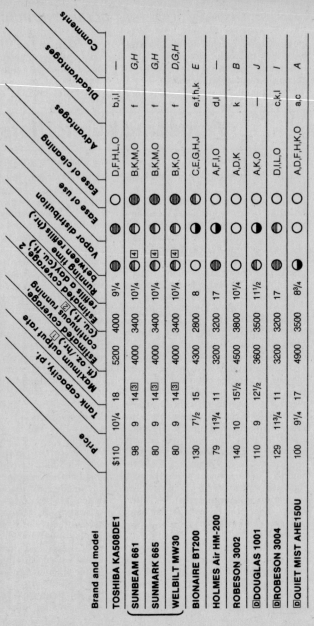

Brand and model	Price	Tank capacity, pt.	Maximum output rate (fl. oz./hr.) 1	Estimated coverage, continuous running (cu. ft.) 2	Estimated coverage, 2 refills a day (cu. ft.)	Running time between refills (hr.)	Vapor distribution	Ease of use	Ease of cleaning	Advantages	Disadvantages	Comments
TOSHIBA KA508DE1	$110	$10^1/_4$	18	5200	4000	$9^1/_4$	◍	◍	○	D,F,H,L,O	b,i,l	—
SUNBEAM 661	98	9	14 3	4000	3400	$10^1/_4$	⊖ 4	⊖	◍	B,K,M,O	f	*G,H*
SUNMARK 665	80	9	14 3	4000	3400	$10^1/_4$	⊖ 4	⊖	◍	B,K,M,O	f	*G,H*
WELBILT MW30	80	9	14 3	4000	3400	$10^1/_4$	⊖ 4	⊖	◍	B,K,O	f	*D,G,H*
BIONAIRE BT200	130	$7^1/_2$	15	4300	2800	8	○	◒	⊖	C,E,G,H,J	e,f,h,k	*E*
HOLMES Air HM-200	79	$11^3/_4$	11	3200	3200	17	◍	◒	○	A,F,I,O	d,l	—
ROBESON 3002	140	10	$15^1/_2$	4500	3800	$10^1/_4$	○	○	○	A,D,K	k	*B*
D DOUGLAS 1001	110	9	$12^1/_2$	3600	3500	$11^1/_2$	⊖	◒	○	A,K,O	—	*J*
D ROBESON 3004	129	$11^3/_4$	11	3200	3200	17	◍	⊖	○	D,I,L,O	c,k,l	*I*
D QUIET MIST AHE150U	100	$9^1/_4$	17	4900	3500	$8^3/_4$	◒	○	○	A,D,F,H,K,O	a,c	*A*

HANKSCRAFT 5930	99	$10^3/_4$	$15^1/_2$ [3]	4500	4100	11	○ [4]	○	○	O	k,l	*F*
SANYO CFK H501	140	$10^3/_4$	$15^1/_2$ [3]	4500	4100	11	○ [4]	○	○	O	k,l	—
CORONA UF40	135	$8^1/_2$	$14^1/_2$	4200	3200	$9^1/_4$	⊜ [4]	○	○	N,O	b,g	*K*
CORONA UF30	120	$8^1/_2$	$14^1/_2$	4200	3200	$9^1/_4$	⊜ [4]	○	○	N,O	a,b,g	*L*
SANYEI UH2	100	10	$14^1/_2$	4200	3900	11	◒	◒	○	—	k,l	—
WELBILT MW50H	90	$10^1/_2$	$12^1/_2$	3600	3600	$13^1/_2$	○ [4]	⊜	○	D,F,J	b,j,k	*C,D*
SEA MIST SM200H	70	8	$13^1/_2$ [3]	3900	3100	$9^1/_2$	⊜ [5]	◒	◒	—	b,i,k	*D*
TATUNG TUH400H	70	8	$13^1/_2$ [3]	3900	3100	$9^1/_2$	○ [5]	◒	◒	—	b,i,k	*D*

[1] *Average of 4 tests; 2 per sample, 2 samples per model.*
[2] *Assumes tank is never allowed to become empty.*
[3] *Results for bracketed models have been averaged together.*
[4] *Performance varied widely. Results are average of two samples and, where applicable, of similar models.*
[5] **Sea Mist** *and* **Tatung** *have different spray nozzles.*

FEATURES IN COMMON
All: measure about 10-12 in. high, 13-17 in. wide, and 6-8 in. deep; consumed 41-49 watts (about as much as a small light bulb); have volume control to regulate amount of mist; have automatic shut-off of transducer when water supply is depleted; have tank with top handle.
Except as noted, all have: humidistat to regulate room humidity automatically; a single nozzle that swivels 360 degrees; cleaning brush with storage provision; indicator light; 1-yr. warranty on parts and labor.

KEY TO ADVANTAGES
A – Has tip-over switch, which seemed to prevent damage to transducer in tip-over test.
B – Large filler allows easy filling and cleaning.
C – Built-in demineralization cartridge.
D – Additional handle on underside of tank.
E – Convenient carrying handle.
F – Convenient recess in base for carrying.
G – Fan shuts off when tank is empty.
H – Empty-tank indicator light.
I – Light indicates if air is too dry.
J – Separate power switch.
K – Safety interlock prevents access to mist chamber until tank is removed.
L – 2 nozzles.
M – Water level easier to see than in most.
N – External fuses, easy to replace.
O – Intake air filter.

KEY TO DISADVANTAGES
a – No humidistat.
b – No brush for cleaning.
c – No storage provision for brush.
d – Tank hard to remove and replace.
e – Tank harder to fill than most.
f – Tank hard to empty completely.
g – Nozzle hard to swivel.
h – Markings on controls hard to decipher.
i – Float more difficult to clean than most.
j – Slightly noisier than most.
k – Intake air vent located on bottom, where it may pick up dust or be obstructed by rug.
l – Volume and humidistat controls turn in opposite directions, a confusing arrangement.

KEY TO COMMENTS
A – No Warranty is specified. Manufacturer claims 90-day warranty on parts and labor.
B – Has humidity gauge, but it was inaccurate.
C – Has nozzle adapter; it evaporates room

Keys to Ratings continued on next page

Ratings keys for ultrasonic humidifiers continued

freshener or "medicated vapor" into mist.

D–Tank has water-level markings.

E–3-prong grounded plug.

F–No tip-over switch, but neither sample was damaged in tip-over test.

G–Can use **Sunbeam** demineralization filter.

H–Seems essentially similar to **Samsung HU701A,** which was received too late for testing.

I–Seems essentially similar to **Imarflex UH050,** which was received too late for testing.

J–Also available as **Sears Cat. No. 9361,** $85 plus shipping.

K–According to the manufacturer, this model has been replaced by essentially similar **Corona UF400,** $110.

L–According to the manufacturer, this model has been replaced by essentially similar **Corona UF300,** $100.

When run at their highest settings, some models sent all their mist upward into the air where it can evaporate before settling on anything, while some others let a lot of it drift downward where it can settle on and saturate surfaces nearby the vaporizer. If the vaporizer is placed on a wood floor or on a table top away from the edge, the settling mist could easily ruin the wood finish. Two of the best at vapor distribution, the *Toshiba* and the *Robeson 3004*, have two nozzles instead of one.

DUST DEVILS. All ultrasonic humidifiers are plagued by a common problem—at least it's a problem where the tap water is "hard," or has a high mineral content. They can deposit a coating of fine white dust onto furniture and other surfaces. The dust comes from minerals in the water, primarily calcium carbonate, which have little chance to come out of solution before they're ejected into the air as part of the mist. The dust is probably harmless to people, but it can harm sensitive electronic equipment. In any case, its a nuisance, and an expensive nuisance to reckon with.

One could, for example, skirt the problem by filling an ultrasonic humidifier only with distilled or demineralized water. That might cost more than a dollar a tankful, judging by distilled-water prices in our area.

The *Bionaire* incorporates in its tank a special demineralization cartridge that filters the water before it flows into the mist chamber. In our tests with hard water, the cartridge significantly reduced the amount of white dust that was deposited. A cartridge could treat about 30 gallons of relatively hard water; replacement cartridges cost $7.95.

The manufacturer of the *Sunbeam* sells a different style of filter, a resin-filled canister that fits over the filling hole of the tank. (It fits not only the *Sunbeam* but also two similar models, the *SunMark* and the *Welbilt MW30*; a funnel allows it to be used with other brands of ultrasonic humidifier as well.) In our tests, the filter eliminated virtually all white dust, but it made a chore of the filling operation. When last we checked, the price of the filter itself was $14.99. Replacement resin cost $9.99 for an amount that could purify about 35 gallons of hard water.

[Letters we have received since the original publication of this report indicate that the filters don't always eliminate or even reduce white dust. The types of minerals and other solid contaminants in the water supply vary widely throughout the country. Apparently the filters are effective in removing such common minerals as calcium carbonate but not so effective with others. Furthermore, even "soft" water can contain minerals that will be precipitated as white dust by the humidifiers. Although not regarded as harmful, the dust can have unexpected effects, such as changing the color of gas flames from blue to a yellow or orange.]

CONVENIENCE. Besides a volume control,

most models have a humidistat control that automatically turns them on and off when the room humidity reaches a preset level (a feature that's most useful in small rooms). All the models have an indicator that lights when the power goes on. The *Toshiba*, the *Bionaire*, and the *Quiet Mist* also have an indicator that signals for a tank refill.

The tanks with the largest filler hole—those on the *Sunbeam*, the *SunMark*, and the *Welbilt MW30*—were the quickest and easiest to refill, providing that they weren't equipped with the optional demineralization filter. But those tanks also seemed particularly susceptible to developing air locks that prevented water from flowing into the mist chamber. Resetting the tank on its base usually corrected that problem.

Ultrasonic humidifiers, like other types of humidifiers, require periodic cleaning. Soaking with various vinegar and bleach solutions, as recommended by the manufacturers, proved largely ineffective against mineral deposits. But we got excellent results from soaking with a half-strength solution of *Clean Away*, a product available by mail from Bionaire, P.O. Box 582, Franklin Lakes, N.J. 07417. A 16-ounce bottle of *Clean Away* costs $4.

Only four models—the *Holmes*, the *Robeson 3002*, the *Douglas*, and the *Quiet Mist*—have a tip-over switch that shuts off the power if the unit is picked up or knocked over. Such a switch isn't a critical safety feature, but it can save money. Most models without it needed transducer repairs after we had tipped them over while they were running.

RECOMMENDATIONS. All the models we tested performed satisfactorily. But the *Toshiba* ($110) clearly gave the best combination of performance and convenience. It had the highest output, so it could humidify the largest area—or humidify a single room the fastest. Its excellent vapor distribution means less chance of ruining surface finishes.

People who live where the tap water contains minerals, however, may be better off with a humidifier that offers a demineralization filter. The *Sunbeam*, *SunMark*, and *Welbilt MW30* models (which accept the *Sunbeam* filter) and the *Bionaire* (which comes with a built-in water filter) all scored respectably in our tests. However, as noted, you can't be sure what minerals your tap water may contain. We suggest that you shop in stores that allow a return. You will know within a couple of days of continuous running whether dust will be a problem. You may find that you would be best off using conventional humidifiers. Those appliances may have some internal difficulties with mineral deposits, but at least they won't mess up the house.

Console humidifiers

Condensed from CONSUMER REPORTS, September 1984

In houses with forced-air heating, the most convenient and often the most efficient kind of humidifier is one that's built right into the heating system and hooked up to the plumbing. But if you have hot-water, steam, or electric-resistance heating, you can't use a built-in humidifier. You can, however, use a plug-in, portable console model.

A portable humidifier may have to be refilled with water as often as three times a day. Usually, when a humidifier

Text continued on page 234

Ratings of console humidifiers

Listed, except as noted, in order of estimated overall quality. Closely ranked models differed little in quality. Prices are approximate retail; + indicates shipping is extra. Discounts may be available.

⊜ ⊖ ○ ◒ ●

Better ⟵⟶ Worse

Brand and model	Price	Weight, empty (lb.)	Weight, full (lb.) [1]	Evaporative capacity (gal. per 24 hr.) [2]	Fan speeds	Effective reservoir capacity (gal.) [3]	Convenience: Filling	Convenience: Mobility	Convenience: Emptying, cleaning	Convenience: Replacing belt or drum	Convenience: Humidistat marking	Advantages	Disadvantages	Comments
SEARS Cat. No. 7433	$130+	20	106	13	3	9	⊜	⊖	◒	◒	○	A,B,C,E,H, J,K,L,M,N	g,i	*A,B,D*
SEARS Cat. No. 7437	160+	22	110	15	[4]	9	⊜	⊖	◒	◒	○	A,B,C,E,F,H, J,K,L,M,N	g,i	*A,B,D*
■ *The following models had significantly lower effective reservoir capacity than those preceding and will require more frequent filling.*														
HERRMIDIFIER 130	175	23	98	12	3	6½	⊜	○	◒	◒	○	A,C,H,J,K, L,M,N	c,g,i	*A,B,D*
COMFORT-AIRE HCG15	155	34	83	15	[4]	4½	⊖	◒	⊜	⊜	◒	B,D,G,K	a,e,h	*D,E*
SEARS Cat. No. 7450	120+	16	61	10	2	5	⊜	◒	○	⊜	○	A,C,H,N	d,e,f,j,k	*C*
COMFORT-AIRE HCG12D	124	33	83	12	3	4½	⊖	◒	⊜	⊜	◒	B,D,G,K	a,e,h	*D,E*
EDISON 534121	155	21	73	12	3	5	◒	●	⊖	⊜	◒	B,H,N	d,l	*F*
WARDS Cat. No. 96082	80+	21	73	8	1	5½	●	◒	⊖	⊜	⊖	—	b,d	—
EDISON 534081	106	20	72	8	1	5½	●	[5]	⊖	⊜	◒	—	b	*F*

■ *The following models were judged very difficult to reassemble, which may be required frequently to maintain sanitation. Listed alphabetically.*

COMFORT-AIRE HCG7	81	15	82	7	1	6½	◐	◐	●	●	○	A,I,K,L	g,i,m	*B,E*
EMERSON HD071	106	15	81	7	1	6½	◐	◐	●	●	○	A,I,K,L	g,i,m	*B*
SEARS Cat. No. 7409	80 +	15	82	7	1	6½	◐	◐	●	●	○	A,I,K,L	g,i,m	*B*
SKUTTLE 411	158	15	82	7	1	6½	◐	◐	●	●	○	A,I,K,L	g,i,m	*B*

[1] *When filled to internal "full" mark, if clearly visible; otherwise, when filled to about 1 in. from top of reservoir.*

[2] *Capacity as certified by Assn. of Home Appliance Mfrs. and confirmed by CU tests. Capacity measured when unit is set to run continuously at maximum fan speed in chamber at 70°F and 30% relative humidity. Numbers are based on evaporation during 2-hr. period when unit is about half full.*

[3] *Excluding water left in reservoir when machine stops humidifying.*

[4] *Continuously variable fan speed.*

[5] *Lacks casters; mobility is worse than with any other model.*

FEATURES IN COMMON

All: are from about 23 to 28 in. high, 17 to 29 in. wide, and 12 to 17 in. deep; have adjustable humidistat; have 1-yr. parts warranty.

Except as noted, all: have casters; are "drum" models; have fixed louvers; have removable reservoir, judged reasonably easy to clean; tended to spill at least some water if moved when full; have 5- to 6-ft. power cord; have 1-yr. labor warranty.

KEY TO ADVANTAGES

A – Easy-to-see fixed "full" mark.
B – Gauge, regulated by float, indicates water level.
C – Large fill opening and interior baffling make unit relatively easy and tidy to fill.
D – Fill chute reduces chance of drips.
E – Comes with separate 7½-ft. fill hose, handy if unit is rolled to a faucet.
F – "On" light always indicates when unit is plugged in and turned on, even if humidistat cycles unit off.
G – Low-water shutoff and refill light that stays on even if humidistat cycles off.
H – Low-water shutoff and refill light that is on only while humidistat has cycled on.
I – Low-water shutoff but no refill light.
J – Judged less likely to spill when moved than most.
K – Evaporative pad or belt less apt to slip while in motion than others.
L – 8-ft. power cord.
M – Tilt-up lid, a convenience when filling.
N – Separate on/off control.

KEY TO DISADVANTAGES

a – Water level in reservoir difficult to see, and lack of fixed "full" mark makes float gauge's accuracy hard to check.
b – No low-water shutoff, refill light, water-level gauge, or visible "full" mark.
c – When full, unit may bind if moved over doorsills and deep-pile rugs.
d – When full, unit judged inconvenient to move over rug edges and doorsills.
e – Judged somewhat less stable than others when moved on rugs or over obstructions.
f – Pump judged likely to require periodic cleaning.
g – Fixed reservoir; relatively hard to clean.
h – Cool draft may be felt some 4 to 5 ft. from cabinet (but louver sections can be repositioned to redirect airflow).
i – Fan blades accessible to small fingers; model judged not suitable for use where small children have access to it.
j – Evaporative pad's mounting clips rusted heavily after relatively few uses.
k – After cleaning or replacement of pad, unit requires care in reassembly to avoid damage to float and pump.
l – Casters swiveled sluggishly.
m – Judged noisier than most.

KEY TO COMMENTS

A – Has very inconvenient drain.
B – Belt model.
C – Pump model.
D – Optional kit (not tested) allows permanent connection to house plumbing.
E – Warranty excludes labor.
F – Disposable plastic liners, **999040,** approx. $6 per doz., make reservoir easier to clean.

needs more water, its fan shuts off automatically and a signal light shines. Annoyingly, the automatic shutoffs tended to work prematurely, turning the unit off when there was still about 1 to 2½ gallons of water in the tank. For that reason, the Ratings list each model's *effective* capacity, the water actually available for putting moisture in the air.

Rolling an empty humidifier to the sink is easy, if it has casters. But a humidifier is much harder to push when filled, especially if you have to pilot it over doorsills or carpets.

CU's medical consultants recommend weekly cleaning to minimize the spread of molds and bacteria. In addition to the reservoir, the evaporation pad also needs regular cleaning, and it may need to be replaced annually.

RECOMMENDATIONS. Before you settle on a specific brand and model of humidifier, figure the maximum moisture output you're apt to need for your house. Here's an easy way to do it: Multiply the total floor area of the house (in square feet) by the ceiling height (in feet). Include closet space in your calculations. Also include the basement and attic unless vapor barriers separate them from the rest of the house. The result will be in cubic feet. For every 10,000 cubic feet, allow 6½ gallons per day of humidifying capacity.

Our way of estimating a humidifier's capacity assumes a house of typical "tightness." If you have a really tight house, with very snug storm windows and doors and dampered fireplaces, you'll need only about half the capacity our method indicates. In a loose house, with no storm windows, storm doors, weather stripping, or dampers, you may need half again the humidifying capacity arrived at through our method.

You should also correct your calculation for moisture given off inside the home by cooking, bathing, laundering, and the like. A typical family of four can deduct two gallons per day from their calculated capacity needs.

Dehumidifiers

Condensed from CONSUMER REPORTS, August 1984

Among dehumidifiers, the major variable is capacity: the amount of moisture a given model can take out of the air during a day. The Association of Home Appliance Manufacturers (AHAM) says that a model with a capacity of 25 pints a day should be able to handle most dampness problems. But we suggest that you favor a larger model. You can always turn a high-capacity model down if need be, but you can't turn an undersized unit up beyond its capacity.

PERFORMANCE. Most manufacturers base the capacity claims for their dehumidifiers on the results of a standardized test recommended by AHAM. The test checks performance when the temperature is 80°F and the relative humidity is 60 percent. When we duplicated those conditions in an environmental chamber, most models extracted at least as much moisture as claimed.

Under more typical conditions—70° and 70 percent relative humidity, a likely situation in a basement, performance dropped off a bit.

We then tested the dehumidifiers at 90° and 50 percent relative humidity, an extreme situation that you might find in say, the ground floor of a building without a basement. But all the dehumidifiers took those extreme conditions more or less in stride.

CONVENIENCE. On all the machines, a dial adjusts the humidistat, a device that senses humidity and cycles the dehumidifier's compressor and fan on and off accordingly. A switch on the *Comfort-Aire* and the *Dayton* lets the fan run even when the compressor is off; the air that continues to circulate through the machine lets the humidistat monitor the humidity level more closely.

As each dehumidifier works, moisture from the air condenses on the cooling coils and drips into a water container. When the container is full, the machine shuts off and a signal light prompts you to empty it. You'll usually have to do that once or twice a day.

Ratings of dehumidifiers

Listed in order of estimated overall quality. Models judged approximately equal in overall quality are bracketed and listed in alphabetical order. Prices are suggested retail, rounded to nearest dollar; + indicates shipping is extra. Except for mail-order brands, discounts are available.

Excellent	Very good	Good	Fair	Poor

				Moisture removal				
Brand and model	**Price**	**Mfr.'s stated capacity (pints per day)**	**Energy efficiency**	**At 80°F/60% humidity**	**At 70°F/70% humidity**	**At 90°F/50% humidity**	**At low temperature**	**At high temp., low volt.**
SEARS Cat. No. 5040	$275+	40	Very good	Excellent	Excellent	Very good	Very good	Very good
WHIRLPOOL AD0402XM0	289	40	Very good	Excellent	Excellent	Very good	Very good	Very good
OASIS OD3800L	386	38	Very good	Excellent	Very good	Excellent	Very good	Good
WARDS Cat. No. 93374	240+	37	Good	Very good	Good	Good	Excellent	Excellent
FRIGIDAIRE MR30A	239	30	Good	Good	Fair	Good	Good	Good
KELVINATOR DHC300A1	280	30	Good	Good	Fair	Good	Good	Good
J.C. PENNEY Cat. No. 1173	275+	35	Fair	Very good	Good	Very good	Fair	Good
WHITE WESTINGHOUSE ED358G	310	35	Fair	Very good	Good	Very good	Fair	Good
■ *The following models were downrated because of poor performance at high temperature/low voltage or at low temperature.*								
COMFORT-AIRE FDHD41	329	41	Good	Excellent	Very good	Very good	Very good	Poor
DAYTON 3H324	364	41	Good	Excellent	Very good	Very good	Very good	Poor
OASIS OD3800	359	38	Good	Very good	Very good	Very good	Poor	Good

Energy-saving thermostats

Condensed from CONSUMER REPORTS, October 1985

A "setback" thermostat lowers (sets back) the temperature setting at certain times of day. The tried-and-true setback thermostat is the electromechanical type, which uses a clock-timer to change the temperature settings at the times you designate. Newer, computerized thermostats may present problems of compatibility with particular heating systems. It may be better to focus on the less troublesome, though technologically inglorious, electromechanical models.

COMPUTERIZED MISFITS. Most of the computerized thermostats we looked at use low voltage not only to control the furnace but also to insure that their electronic clock maintains the correct time. Ironically, that special use of the control circuit often renders the thermostat's temperature-setback function useless.

In many heating systems, the voltage in the control circuit is interrupted during part of the furnace's cycle, cutting off power to the thermostat. When that happens to many computerized models, the clock fails to keep the correct time; it may lose or gain several minutes each time the furnace cycles on or off. Consequently, the setback cycles you've so carefully programmed will go awry.

With an electromechanical setback thermostat that draws its power from a battery, it doesn't matter if the low voltage is on or off for part of the cycle. But a computerized thermostat that uses the control circuit for timing must have that low voltage at all times. So you must buy the appropriate brand for your system, or hire a contractor to modify parts of the control circuit. We know of no simple way to tell if a given computerized thermostat will work with a given heating system.

For all their supposed versatility—the ability to handle several setback cycles each day, or a different set of cycles for each day of the week—the computerized thermostats lack flexibility in one key area. They may let the house warm up or cool down too much before turning the heat on or off.

In practice, a thermostat seldom shifts at precisely the temperature you've selected. But most conventional thermostats have what's known as an adjustable anticipator, a component that allows them to switch within, say, one-half degree above or below the temperature you want. The computerized thermostats we looked at have an electronic temperature sensor that's nonadjustable; it typically controls only to within two degrees above or below the chosen temperature. That four-degree "deadband" leads to unacceptably wide temperature swings.

CONVENTIONAL WISDOM. The conventional setback thermostats we tested have few of the shortcomings of their computerized cousins. They will work just fine with almost any oil-fired or gas-fired heating system.

All the thermostats work, and no one brand works better or worse than another. Ranking was thus largely a matter of assessing fine points of design and convenience.

All the conventional thermostats have a small clock wheel with slots around the rim for removable pins. By shifting the pins, you can set at least two setback cycles per day.

The *Emerson* and the *Honeywells* have a control that lets you override the thermostat and change to the alternate temperature setting in the middle of a cycle. All models but the *Robertshaws* have what's known as a half-cycle feature, a boon for people with erratic schedules. With a half-cycle, you switch to the setback temperature manually; the thermostat automatically switches back to the normal temperature at the set time.

Except for the *Honeywell* models, the tested thermostats may well pose installation problems. Their anticipators can handle only one ampere of current, which is less than some furnace controllers need. Check your existing thermostat or the furnace control box for a label that gives the anticipator setting in amps. If it's one amp or more, you'll have to use either a *Honeywell* or the *Autostat* described below.

(An interesting alternative that we found is a $50 add-on device called the *First Alert Autostat*, which can be mounted on the wall next to the existing thermostat. It's essentially a motor-driven hand, controlled by a computer chip, that reaches over to move the lever on the thermostat. The lever-moving mechanism was tricky to adjust at first, but, once that was done, the *Autostat* worked fine. It offers the intricate programming of a computerized model. Yet, because the *Autostat* uses alkaline

Ratings of energy-saving thermostats

Listed in order of estimated overall quality. Bracketed models were judged equal in overall quality. Prices are list; + indicates shipping is extra. Discounts are sometimes available.

Brand and model	Price	No. cycles per day	Minimum setting interval	Comments
EMERSON 1F76-353	$ 60	Up to 3	12 min.	C
SEARS Cat. No. 9101	50+	Up to 3	12	A,C,H
ROBERTSHAW T32-1042	60	1 or 2	12	A,B,C,E,G
ROBERTSHAW T33-1042	60	1 or 2	12	A,B,C,E
HONEYWELL T8085A	140	Up to 3	30	D
HONEYWELL T8082A	168	Up to 3	30	F

FEATURES IN COMMON

All: have adjustable anticipator; control same program each day; control 24-volt circuits.

Except as noted, all: have cycle-change switch, half-cycle capability, and independent high and low temperature settings; use replaceable alkaline battery; are for heating systems only (essentially similar versions are available for heating and cooling).

KEY TO COMMENTS

A–No cycle-change switch.
B–Only high-temperature setting is fully adjustable; setback temperature can be no more than 10 degrees below high setting.
C–Current capability limited to one amp; unit may be destroyed if control circuit shorts.
D–No battery. Requires third wire to furnace in order to power clock, which will lose time during power outages.
E–No half-cycle capability.
F–Uses built-in nickel-cadmium battery, which has unpredictable service life and cannot be easily replaced by owner.
G–Uses replaceable nickel-cadmium battery.
H–Heating/cooling version.

batteries, it's free of the electrical problems that are apt to plague computerized thermostats.)

All models but the *Honeywell* thermostats use a disposable, easily replaced battery. We downrated the *Honeywell T8082A* because it uses a built-in, rechargeable nickel-cadmium battery. That, our own tests and letters from many readers have convinced us, is of flawed design. Although Honeywell claims that the batteries will last for 10 to 12 years, our experience indicates that two to three years is closer to the mark—and then only if the furnace control circuit is left on during the summer. Finding a replacement and trying to change it yourself isn't easy.

The *Honeywell T8085A* doesn't use a battery; instead, it powers the clock with a third wire that bypasses the furnace control circuit. That design presents two problems: First, if the circuit doesn't already contain the third wire (and many don't), adding a wire can be difficult; second, a power failure would throw off the clock setting.

RECOMMENDATIONS. Among the electromechanical thermostats we tested, the *Emerson 1F76-353* ($60 list) and the *Sears 9101* ($50 plus shipping) get a slight nod. They have all the features that a setback thermostat should have, along with one problem: They can be used only in a heating or cooling system whose control circuit uses one amp or less. The *Robertshaw* models, which share that problem, are slightly less convenient.

The two *Honeywell* thermostats are fine in many ways. In fact, in previous reports, we have top-rated the *T8082A*. But the *Honeywells* are considerably more expensive than the others. And we have learned of so many problems concerned with supplying batteries for the *T8082A* that we can no longer encourage people to buy it.

Room air-conditioners

Condensed from CONSUMER REPORTS, July 1986

The air-conditioners tested for this report are well named. They have a cooling capacity of 5000 to 6000 Btu per hour, which is relatively low, but still enough to cool a small room in Florida or a large room in Maine.

Because the 10 models we selected for testing all have high energy-efficiency ratios (between 7.5 and 9), differences in operating costs are likely to be less significant than differences in purchase price. Running one of these units for a typical cooling season of 700 hours, at the national average electricity rate of 8.2 cents per kilowatt-hour, would cost about $35. The selling prices of the tested models averaged from $291 to $432.

PERFORMANCE. To test the air-conditioners, we used a heavily insulated chamber, partitioned and instrumented so that we could control the temperature in both the "room" on one side of the partition and the "outdoors" on the other side. The "room" was actually a box within a box so that we could set the temperature of the "house" around the room to represent the heat load from the rest of the living space. That house space was set at 90°F.

With a normal 120-volt power supply, all the units worked satisfactorily.

But the real test of an air-conditioner, we think, is under abnormal conditions, when so many air-conditioners are running that electric companies can't supply the normal voltage. For the sake of abnormality, we gave our units an outdoor temperature of 115° and reduced the voltage in 5-volt steps. All the units kept running, even down to 100 volts.

But when we turned them off and tried restarting them after a three-minute rest, a few machines labored so hard against compressor pressure that their circuit breakers shut them down again. The *Frigidaire* balked at 110 volts. Next to experience trouble was the *Airtemp*, at 105 volts. The *Friedrich* and the *Kelvinator* aborted at 100 volts when their fan was at its lowest setting; they started normally when the fan had been running at its highest setting. (Running any air-conditioner at its high setting helps relieve pressure on the compressor.)

Under less severe conditions (95° outdoor temperature), we checked to see how close to a set point each unit's thermostat would hold the indoor temperature. The *Carrier* had the most sensitive thermostat; it tried to hold the temperature to within a degree or so of a set point. (It may even prove too sensitive in small spaces exposed to severe heat loads.) The *Sanyo*, *Whirlpool*, *Kelvinator*, and the *Frigidaire* models fluctuated no more than 3°. The rest allowed wider temperature swings.

Typically, an air-conditioner's fan keeps running while its compressor cycles on and off under orders from the thermostat. But five models have an "automatic" or "energy-saver" setting in which the fan also cycles on and off along with the compressor. The feature isn't likely to save much electricity, though, because the compressor, not the fan, accounts for most of an air-conditioner's demand. And the feature usually exacts some penalty in discomfort in longer on-off cycles and hence bigger temperature swings.

All the machines except the *Kelvinator* have adjustable louvers to direct air flow. But none could be set to send the greatest cooling effect toward the right of the machine. Units with the lowest scores in temperature uniformity tended to throw lots of air toward their left, creating temperature differences of as much as 4° or 5° within the room.

Only four of the machines have adjustable horizontal louvers. The others have fixed louvers that pitch the air flow slightly upward. But as it turned out, a slight upward pitch gave the most even cooling distribution anyway.

As an air-conditioner cools, it also dehumidifies room air. Moisture from the air condenses on the cooling coils and dribbles down inside the machine to be disposed of, ideally, as a fine mist exhausted to the outdoors. When we cranked up the humidity, all but the *Emerson* and the *Whirlpool* dripped at least a little. The *GE* and the *Hotpoint* dripped a good bit, some of it inside the room.

INSTALLATION. The mounting panels and cabinets of air-conditioners offer small protection against cold weather. So people in cooler climes would be wise to remove their air-conditioners each winter and reinstall them each spring. That's not an easy task, even with small room models. Our units ranged in weight from 56 to 93 pounds.

The *Carrier*, the *Friedrich*, the *GE*, and the *Hotpoint*—the largest, heaviest units we tested—have a slide-out chassis, so that the empty cabinet can be mounted firmly before the hefty innards are slipped in. That eliminates a tricky balancing act on the windowsill.

Most units have a support bracket that helps to steady the machine until it's secured. The *Emerson* and the *Frigidaire* also have a helpful handle. The

Text continued on page 242

Ratings of room air-conditioners

Listed in order of estimated quality. Except where separated by heavy lines, closely ranked models differed little in quality. Prices are the average of those quoted to CU shoppers in a 10-city survey.

◍	⊖	○	◒	●
Better ←				→ Worse

Brand and model	Average price	Manufacturer's specifications: Btu/hr.	Manufacturer's specifications: Energy-efficiency ratio	Manufacturer's specifications: Dehumidification (pt./hr.)	Performance under adverse conditions [1]	Regular performance	'Energy-saver'	Temperature uniformity	Directional control	Moisture disposal	Cooling-speed settings	Weight (lb.)	Advantages	Disadvantages	Comments
CARRIER NTB7051	$310	5400	9.0	1.9	◍	◍	—	○	○	⊖	3	84	D,I,H	b,c	*C,D,H*
FRIEDRICH SP05G10	432	5250	8.7	1.2	⊖	○	◒	⊖	○	○	2	76	A,D,K,J	f	*A,B,E*
EMERSON QUIET KOOL 5LJ5E	303	5200	9.0	1.6	◍	○	○	⊖	●	◍	3	62	C,F	b,i,j	*B,I*
SANYO SA60U	333	5900	9.0	2.3	◍	⊖	—	●	●	◒	3	73	A,C,I,H	e,h	*A,C,G*
GENERAL ELECTRIC AJ906LV	389	5800	8.7	1.3	◍	◒	●	⊖	●	●	3	93	D,E	f	*A,B,F*
HOTPOINT KJ906LV	386	5800	8.7	1.3	◍	◒	●	⊖	●	●	3	92	D,E	f	*A,B,F*
WHIRLPOOL ACP552XR	291	5000	8.7	1.4	◍	⊖	—	●	○	◍	3	56	A	b,e,h	*B,E*

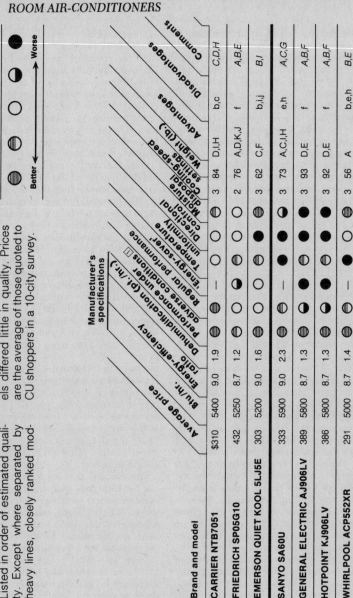

KELVINATOR SH206B1Q	298	5900	8.1	1.9	⊜	⊜	—	○	—	⊜	2	61	I,K		a,d,h,i	*E*
FRIGIDAIRE A6LECUD	373	5500	9.0	1.9	◒	⊜	●	○	◒	⊜	2	63	B,G,J		b,g,h	*B*
AIRTEMP LO61HKRNE	320	5900	7.5	—	○	○	—	◒	○	◒	3	63	—		b	*B,G*

[1] *115°F outdoor temperature and low voltage.*

FEATURES IN COMMON

All: are designed for installation in double-hung window; can be run, local codes permitting, on 15-amp branch circuit protected by circuit breaker or time-delay fuse; are rated at 5.2 to 7.5 amps but can draw more current under adverse conditions; should be used only with grounded outlet; have $5^1/_2$- to $6^1/_2$-ft. power cord; come with 1-yr. parts-and-labor warranty on entire unit, plus 4-yr. warranty coverage on part or all of sealed refrigeration system.

Except as noted, all have: adjustable vertical and horizontal louvers; barrier to prevent accidental contact with fan blade with servicing filter; sill bracket; leveling adjustment; expanding side panels with plastic framing; guard on outdoor end to protect cooling fins.

KEY TO ADVANTAGES

A – Expanding side panels have metal framing for added strength.
B – Signal lights for switch positions, providing useful reminder that unit is still on when dormant in Automatic cycle.
C – Framed pullout filter, access to which does not require removal of front panel; somewhat easier to clean than most.
D – Slide-out chassis makes installation relatively easy.
E – Installation allows for alternative mounting position to minimize either roomside or outdoor projection.
F – Security handle; helps steady unit during installation.
G – Carrying handle; also useful for steadying unit during installation.
H – Less noisy than most indoors on high setting.
I – Less noisy than most indoors on low setting.
J – Less noisy than most outdoors on high setting.
K – Less noisy than most outdoors on low setting.

KEY TO DISADVANTAGES

a – No louver adjustments.
b – Fixed horizontal louvers.
c – Thermostat control lacks reference numbers.
d – Screwdriver required to remove front panel when filter needs servicing.
e – No sill bracket or leveling provision; judged least secure of tested models during installation or removal.
f – No leveling provision.
g – No sill bracket.
h – No guard on outside coils.
i – No barrier to prevent contact with fan when filter is being serviced (although accidental contact judged unlikely).
j – Noisiest model indoors on low setting.

KEY TO COMMENTS

A – Horizontal louvers can be adjusted downward.
B – Has vent for exhaust air exchange; effect was minimal with **Airtemp, Emerson,** and **Whirlpool,** and somewhat greater with **Friedrich, General Electric, Hotpoint,** and **Frigidaire.**
C – Provision for drain-line connection to dispose of condensed moisture.
D – Sensitive thermostat (see story).
E – Manufacturer recommends oiling fan motor periodically.
F – Additional 1-yr. parts warranty on fan motor and 4-yr. warranty on sealed system.
G – Additional 4-yr. warranty on compressor.
H – Additional 4-yr. warranty, excluding labor, on compressor.
I – Additional 4-yr. warranty, excluding some labor, on entire unit.

Sanyo and the *Whirlpool* have neither, leaving one to balance the unit on the sill while trying to fasten the mounting hardware.

RECOMMENDATIONS. All the tested air-conditioners delivered cool air as they should. Most did fairly well under adverse conditions. The models at the top of the Ratings didn't get there by being perfect. Rather, they floated to the top because they weren't weighed down by nagging objections. But with most models so evenly matched in performance, an attractive sale price could well be enough to lift the burden from almost any objection.

Air cleaners

Condensed from CONSUMER REPORTS, January 1985

We found three types of air cleaners: simple filters, ion generators, and electrostatic precipitators.

FILTERS. Effectiveness depends on filter size and airflow. Pleated filters generally have the most area. Filters work best with dust and pollen; they work less well with smoke. Small desk models do little more than hum and dispense a little perfume.

ION GENERATORS. Electrically-charged pollutant particles adhere to room surfaces—walls, drapes, carpets, TV screens, etc. We downrated three small (desk-sized) fanless ion generators because they caused heavy soiling on nearby walls during our smoke-removal test. Some larger ion-generating models (about the size of a breadbox) have a fan and blow air through filter that can trap pollutants before they settle out on room surfaces.

ELECTROSTATIC PRECIPITATORS. Electrostatic precipitators work by drawing air past electrically charged wires and then through a collector that has the opposite charge. Usually, they are found built into the ductwork of central air-handling systems. There are also models (about the size of room air-conditioners) that are often sold on prescription for people with allergies; but these, too, are beyond the scope of our test project. We found one small electrostatic precipitator, the *Oster 402-06*, which was not quite as effective as some others we tested.

LIMITATIONS. Although airborne particles (smoke, dust, and pollen) can be swept from the air by the more effective of the models we tested, many other pollutants are unaffected. Gases such as combustion products from a gas range, formaldehyde from particle board and insulation, and radon from bedrock and stone foundations all pass through the sort of air cleaners we tested without significant reduction.

Newer homes that are made very tight to conserve heat may develop pollution problems. These homes should be ventilated sufficiently to keep the problems at bay.

RECOMMENDATIONS. If the object is to clear a space of frequent objectionable smells, consider improving the ventilation—open a window or install a small exhaust fan. If allergies are the problem, the air-cleaning requirements may well go beyond the capabilities of room air cleaners; really pollen-free air would probably call for an electrostatic precipitator in the air-supply ductwork (assuming forced-air heating) and an air-conditioner in the summer to keep the indoor air recirculating.

Ratings of air cleaners

Listed in order of estimated overall quality. Full test data are given only for the recommended models. Ratings order is based primarily on smoke-removal tests, which were performed at highest fan speed. Ion-generating models without fans were severely downrated because they badly soiled nearby walls. None were effective at removing gaseous pollutants. Prices are suggested retail, discounts are generally available.

⊜ ⊖ ○ ◒ ●

Better ⟷ Worse

Brand and model	Price (replacement filter)	Type [1]	Dimensions (HxWxD)	Weight	Smoke removal	Dust removal	Noise (high/low)
BIONAIRE 1000	$299(16)	ION/PF	9x14x8 in.	13 lb.	⊜	⊖	○/⊜
POLLENEX IONIZER 1801	100(15)	ION/FF	11x13x9	8	⊜	⊖	●/⊖
NORELCO HB9000	100(20)	PF	7x16x9	8	⊖	⊜	○/⊖
SPACE-GARD 2275	140(12)	PF	14x12x12	12	⊖	⊜	○/⊖
OSTER 402-06	158(7)	EP	6x14x11	8	⊖	○	◒/⊖
SEARS Cat. No. 7302	60+(10+)	PF	5x14x11	9	○	○	⊖/⊖
POLLENEX 1099	60(15)	FF	11x13x9	7	○	○	●/⊖
SEARS IONIZER Cat. No. 7305	100+(7+)	ION/FF	5x11x7	4	○	○	⊖/⊜

NORELCO HB1920; ECOLOGIZER 8005; NATURE FRESH AP30B1; CLEAN AIRE 3; ECOLOGIZER 97305; SUNBEAM 57-25; POLLENEX 699; SUNBEAM 57-16; NORELCO HB1900; ECOLOGIZER 3605; CONAIR E3A; CONAIR E1.

■ *The following models, all fanless ion generators, were severely downrated because they badly soiled nearby walls in CU's smoke-removal test.*
ENERGAIRE, ORBIT, AMCORE FRESHENAIRE.

[1] *ION = ion generator; PF = pleated filter; FF = flat filter; EP = electrostatic precipitator.*

Portable electric heaters

Condensed from CONSUMER REPORTS, October 1985

A great many electric heaters are the familiar boxy shape, but there are also baseboard units, radiator-style units, tall columns, and thin panels. Convection models slowly warm the air around them. Radiant models use a reflector to concentrate their heat on objects. Combination radiant/convection models use both methods. They warm a room faster than convection-only units.

Portable electric heaters may be called on for spot-heating—that is,

Ratings of portable electric heaters

Listed by types; within types, listed in order of estimated overall quality. Dimensions and weights are rounded. Prices are list; + indicates shipping is extra.

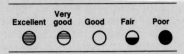

Excellent	Very good	Good	Fair	Poor
Excellent	Very good	Good	Fair	Poor

Brand and model	Price	Dimensions (HxWxD, in.)	Weight (lb.)	Temperature distrib. [1]	Temperature swing	Spot-heating	Safety	Control convenience	Portability
Convection models									
TPI 6LBB1	$185	11x72x5	23	Good	Excellent	Poor	Excellent	Very good	Poor
EDISON 324029G [2]	65	20x11x8	9	Good	Fair	Fair	Excellent	Very good	Good
PATTON FL15A	80	10x51x7	12	Fair	Excellent	Poor	Excellent	Excellent	Fair
INTERTHERM NP1500	139	10x74x6	24	Good	Excellent	Poor	Very good	Very good	Poor
PRESTO 07860	77	19x12x8	11	Good	Very good	Poor	Excellent	Very good	Good
TITAN T800	70	19x12x9	9	Good	Poor	Poor	Excellent	Excellent	Good
MARKEL 484T	79	8x49x6	11	Fair	Good	Poor	Very good	Excellent	Fair
SHETLAND OF8A	90	27x18x9	37	Fair	Excellent	Poor	Good	Very good	Poor
SLANT/FIN AQ1500	157	10x73x7	23	Good	Good	Poor	Excellent	Excellent	Poor
MARKEL 57TN	65	15x11x8	9	Very good	Good	Fair	Fair	Very good	Good
SEARS Cat. No. 7256 [3]	60+	17x13x9	10	Good	Poor	Fair	Excellent	Fair	Good
ARVIN 29H92	45	15x7x15	8	Fair	Good	Fair	Very good	Good	Very good
EMBASSY RAHX1500	99	10x49x7	14	Fair	Fair	Poor	Very good	Excellent	Poor
DELONGHI 5108	45	26x19x8	33	Good	Very good	Poor	Good	Very good	Poor
DIMPLEX 8115	168	27x20x9	38	Good	Excellent	Poor	Fair	Very good	Poor
THERMAL 695A	50	26x19x12	34	Fair	Very good	Poor	Fair	Very good	Poor
WELBILT 2001	50	19x23x10	12	Poor	Excellent	Poor	Fair	Very good	Fair
DELONGHI DF-15	69	17x23x7	11	Very good	Very good	Poor	Fair	Good	Fair
DIMPLEX 9215	241	24x58x9	48	Good	Good	Poor	Fair	Very good	Poor

[1] *At highest wattage setting.*
[2] *A later designation is* **Toastmaster 2529.**
[3] *A later designation is* **Cat. No. 36223.**
[4] *A later designation is* **36400.**
[5] *A later designation is* **Toastmaster 2453.**
[6] *A later designation is* **36003.**

Brand and model	Price	Dimensions (HxWxD, in.)	Weight (lb.)	Temperature distrib. [1]	Temperature swing	Spot-heating	Safety	Control convenience	Portability
Radiant and radiant/convection models									
TITAN BB42A	$70	9x39x6	10	○	⊖	◒	⊖	○	○
PRESTO 07875	98	31x15x16	9	○	◍	◍	◒	⊖	◒
ARVIN 49H2001	59	10x41x5	11	⊖	○	○	⊖	◒	○
SEARS Cat. No. 7206 [4]	50+	10x41x5	11	⊖	○	○	⊖	◒	○
PRESTO 07840	74	16x21x7	10	◒	⊖	◍	◒	○	◒
LAKEWOOD 415	35	13x19x10	8	○	○	⊖	◒	○	○
MARKEL 198TE	62	16x12x12	7	◒	⊖	○	◒	⊖	⊖
EDISON 324053C [5]	42	13x18x10	8	○	◒	○	◒	○	○
ARVIN 30H33	55	13x19x10	7	○	◒	⊖	◒	○	○
SEARS Cat. No. 7139 [6]	45+	13x19x6	7	○	◒	⊖	◒	○	○
TITAN RT26B1	47	13x17x12	8	○	●	⊖	◒	◒	○
TITAN RT40A1	70	14x21x12	9	◒	●	⊖	◒	○	○
LASKO 969	40	12x20x6	8	◒	◒	○	◒	◒	◒

Not acceptable—*The following models set ablaze fabric draped over the grille.*

ARVIN 30H1101; SEARS Cat. No. 7136; TOASTMASTER 2477

warming one area quickly. Radiant and radiant/convection units are better at spot-heating than convection heaters, because the reflectors in radiant models can beam the heat directly to objects in their path.

SAFETY. A fire hazard occurs when a portable heater, especially a radiant or radiant/convection heater, is placed near or actually touches curtains, bed linens, or flammables. Many heaters scorched fabric to varying degrees. But the *Arvin 30H1101*, the *Sears 7136*, and the *Toastmaster 2477* scorched a test fabric and then, within 15 minutes, set it ablaze. We rated them Not Acceptable.

On many heaters, a tipover switch automatically turns off the unit if it's pushed or it falls forward or backward. An even safer tipover switch turns off the heater no matter which way it happens to fall.

Burns are always a danger with heaters, especially with radiant models, whose surfaces can get quite hot. Most convection units pose less burn hazard because their surface temperatures are generally lower.

On some heaters, a potential for shock exists if a child pokes fingers or metallic objects through the grille to touch live electrical parts.

CONVENIENCE. The most convenient On/Off switch on a heater is one that's separate from the thermostat, so that you can turn the unit on and off without disturbing your thermostat setting. Most models, however, combine the two functions.

Thermostats lack actual temperature indications. Instead, most have numbers or simply marks for the purposes of setting.

The most unwieldy heaters are six-foot long baseboard heaters. The heaviest are radiator-style heaters, although they can be moved about fairly readily on their wheels.

RECOMMENDATIONS. The radiant and radiant/convection models have an edge in overall performance. But the convection-only models are safer to use, and the best of them can perform well at whole-room heating.

Tankless water heaters

Condensed from CONSUMER REPORTS, January 1986

Tankless water heaters have been in wide use for years in Europe and Japan, but the hot-water output of the foreign units is restricted, so they've never caught on in the U.S. where a hot deluge is regarded as practically a right of citizenship.

Now, distributors for at least four overseas manufacturers are trying to sell "American-style" water-heating systems that work on the same principle. The heart of such devices is a finned copper tube that passes over a gas burner. When a hot-water tap is turned up to anything above a moderate flow, the burner leaps to life, heating the water that passes through the tube. After a short delay, typically 10 to 15 seconds, the water leaving the heater becomes hot. When the tap is turned off, the unit shuts down.

Gas-fired tankless, or instantaneous, heaters come in two versions: those that run on natural gas, and those that run on propane (LP) gas. (There are electric models available, too, but none that we've seen can deliver water both hot enough and in sufficient volume to replace a conventional hot-water system.) Gas models also come in various sizes. We chose our samples from among the largest heaters currently available, the ones meant to replace conventional water heaters. Those models cost quite a lot—$400 to $680, compared with something on the order of $250 to $450 for a conventional hot-water heater.

LIMITED SAVINGS. Unlike a conventional water heater, an instantaneous heater doesn't keep a tank of hot water standing by all the time. Thus it suffers no energy "storage" loss. But the storage losses of a conventional heater aren't the dreadful waste they're sometimes made out to be; they generally account for only about 15 to 20 percent of the cost of running a water heater, which is typically a few hundred dollars per year. The potential saving from eliminating storage loss, then, is likely to be no more than about $50 a year, and it can be less.

Although tankless heaters eliminate storage losses, they don't eliminate all energy waste. There's a more or less continual loss from the burning pilot light, which, unlike the pilot on a conventional tank heater, provides no useful heating when the burner is off. In our tests, the pilot on one tankless heater, the *Paloma*, used twice as much gas as the others. That's the principal reason that the *Paloma* is rated lower than the other heaters.

UNLIMITED HOT WATER? In a sense, an instantaneous heater won't run out of hot water. A conventional heater can deliver 30 to 40 gallons of, say, 120°F water as fast as your house's plumbing will handle it. Some tankless heaters can deliver water at about the same maximum rate, but it won't be very hot. Others have internal restrictors that reduce the maximum flow to insure delivery of reasonably hot water when the tap is opened fully.

The Ratings indicate hot-water delivery (gallons per minute) for a 60° temperature rise. We use "temperature rise" rather than maximum temperature for a reason peculiar to tankless heaters: The temperature of the water they deliver depends on the temperature of the water that's supplied to them. While a storage-type heater set for 120° will deliver 120° water whether the inlet water is 45° or 70°, a tankless heater with a 60° temperature rise will deliver water at 105° or 130° under the same conditions.

With any of the models we tested, it's apt to take longer to run a hot bath or fill a clothes washer than you're used to.

Ratings of tankless water heaters

Listed in order of estimated overall quality. All are available in natural-gas and LP versions. Prices are list.

Brand and model	Price	Dimensions (H×W×D, in.)	Max. flow rate for 60-degree temp. rise	Min. flow, burner on	Max. water temp. at max. flow [1]	Comments
AQUASTAR 125VP	$599	26½×17×9½	3.1 gal./min.	0.6 gal./min.	124°F	A
BOSCH WR400	630	31½×17½×18¾	3.1	0.6	142	B
THERMAR TL200	399	34½×10½×16½	2.8	0.6	126	B
■ *The following model was downrated because its pilot light used more fuel than the others.*						
PALOMA PH16MD	680	39½×18½×10¾	[2]	[3]	144	C

[1] *With water entering at 60°*

[2] *Unit provides 60-degree temperature rise at 3 gal./min. by adding cold water to hot.*

[3] *Minimum flow depended on temperature setting. Warm: 1.1 gal./min.; Hot: .7 gal./min.*

KEY TO COMMENTS

A – LP version created with conversion kit supplied by the manufacturer.

B – Maximum flow rate can be changed by adjusting flow limiter valve, according to instructions.

C – Natural gas version requires special gas regulator valve, an extra-cost item.

A flow-reducing shower head is all but mandatory. Furthermore, you may not be able to use a dishwasher effectively. Many dishwashers require a 140° water supply. The *Aquastar* and the *Thermar* fell approximately 15 degrees short of that requirement. The Ratings note the maximum temperature to which each tested model could heat 60° incoming water when it was working at its maximum flow setting.

RECOMMENDATIONS. Ultimately, a tankless unit might justify its high price if it replaced a worn-out heater, but it's not an economically sensible replacement for a functioning gas heater. (Replacing an electric water heater with *any* gas model can usually produce meaningful savings.) Actually, a whole-house instantaneous unit is a good alternative to a conventional gas-fired unit only for those with special needs: for people who don't have room for a regular water heater, for instance, or for shower addicts who want an endless, if somewhat low-volume, flow of hot water. Another likely use would be in a lightly used vacation home, where easy start-up and shut-down of the water-heating system would be a big plus.

The *Aquastar* ($599 list) and the *Bosch* ($630) are the best choices, in our judgment. They produce the most hot water per minute, and their pilots are fairly frugal with gas. If you want to supply a dishwasher, however, the *Aquastar's* output might not be quite hot enough.

Burglar alarms

Condensed from CONSUMER REPORTS, October 1984

The typical burglar is an opportunist looking for easy pickings. If such a thief had to choose between a home with an alarm system and one without, he'd choose the one without.

The skill required to install a do-it-yourself system ranged from a little to a lot. The least expensive devices cost around $50; the more complex systems would cost upward of $300, depending on the layout of your home. That's still low compared with the cost of professionally installed systems, which typically start at around $1500.

SENSORS. There are two main types of sensor. Perimeter sensors guard the outside of your house—the windows and doors. Interior sensors detect movement or intrusion within specific areas inside of your house.

The main advantage of using a system based on perimeter sensors is that it sounds an alarm before an intruder has gotten very far inside. The main disadvantage is that such a system is hard to install.

Systems using interior sensors are easier to install. One interior sensor can often guard a lot more area than one perimeter sensor. But these systems have several disadvantages. They don't sound an alarm until an intruder is already inside. They restrict your own movements within the house when they're turned on. And many of them can be set off by innocent agents such as pets.

You can combine both types of sensor in the same system. In a two-story house with a basement and relatively inaccessible second-story windows, for example, you might use a perimeter system on the ground floor and interior sensors to guard the stairwells.

WIRING. Perimeter sensors have to be connected to a control unit, either with wires or with small radio transmitters. Most security experts consider a wired system the more reliable type and easier to service if something should go wrong. But in a large house, where wiring could be extensive, a "wireless" system using radio transmitters would be easier to install.

Wireless systems aren't entirely wireless; they merely do away with the long runs of wire from the sensors to the control unit. One or more sensors are attached to a battery-powered radio transmitter. When a sensor connected to the transmitter is disturbed, the transmitter sends a brief, coded signal to a receiver in the control unit. That triggers the alarm.

CONTROLS. A separate control unit is a necessary part of any perimeter system. Indeed, as the Ratings indicate, what you're buying with most of the "perimeter systems" we surveyed is just the control unit, with perhaps a token sensor and a siren thrown in. Additional sensors for these systems usually cost $4 to $5 each.

SWITCHES. Most systems allow you an enter and exit delay—some time (typically 10 to 30 seconds) to get in and out without setting off the alarm. Some of the delays can't be changed, while others are adjustable.

Obviously, a short delay means the access panel can't be very far from the door. If you want to hide the control unit, many systems allow separate "control stations" to be installed, either indoors or outdoors. With a control station outside the front door, you have no need for exit and enter delays; you turn the system on and off from outside. The controls of many systems come with or can be fitted with a "panic button." It's simply a direct-switch that sounds the alarm when you press it.

THE ALARM. One important feature of an audible alarm is the ability for it to silence itself. If it sounds for more than 15 minutes or so, you're likely to irritate both neighbors and the police. Most systems have an automatic silencing provision, shutting off the noise after 5 or 10 minutes.

Sophisticated systems can be hooked up directly to the police station (where allowed), to a monitoring service (commonly established by companies that install alarms), or to an automatic telephone dialer that will forward a recorded emergency message to a designated number. A truly comprehensive security system can protect against any number of things in addition to intruders. Smoke and heat detectors are commonly connected to a perimeter system. Other types of sensors are also available—temperature sensors to help protect against frozen pipes, for instance, or moisture detectors to warn of a burst water heater.

RECOMMENDATIONS. Before you spend the money for an expensive system, consider carefully whether you really need the added security it can provide.

No single alarm or system can possibly suit every requirement. A rambling colonial obviously needs a very different system from a studio apartment on the eighth floor. Pets can preclude using certain types of sensors. Most important, the type of equipment to choose also depends on whether your main intention is to protect yourself while you're at home or to protect your property while you're away. To protect yourself, you'd probably want some provision for summoning help. To safeguard your possessions, scare tactics may be sufficient.

In our opinion, the best and most reliable type of alarm system has as its heart a wired perimeter system. But because the installation of such a system can be difficult, especially on a large scale, it may be better left to a professional.

Text continued on page 252

Ratings of burglar alarms

Listed by types; within types, listed alphabetically. Prices are suggested retail; + indicates shipping is extra. Discounts may be available.

Brand and model	Price	Type [1]	No. sensors furnished	No. transmitters furnished	On/off capability [2]	Exit delay (sec.)	Entry delay (sec.)	Separate sensor zones	Auto-silencer	Advantages	Disadvantages	Comments
Perimeter systems												
AMWAY AMGARD E8496	$600	WL	2	3	S	45	12	1	✔	A,E,F,I,P,R	—	—
EICO FC-100 FAILSAFE	150	W	0	—	S or K	—	—	2	—	A,C	—	*C*
HEATHKIT GDA 2800-1	300+	WL	0	0	O	Adj.	Adj.	5	✔	A,F,H,I,P,R	—	*A,B,F*
LINEAR P-61	200	WL	0	0	S	50	12	1	✔	H,I	—	—
MASTER LOCK CRIME FIGHTER 2307	128	W	2	—	S or K	[3]	Adj.	1	✔	B,F,P	a,b	*C,D,F*
MOUNTAIN WEST MW-200	160	W	5	—	K	—	—	1	—	A,B,H	a,c	*E,F*
RADIO SHACK 49-401	160	WL	1	1	C	Adj.	Adj.	2	✔	A,D,F,G,I,P	—	—
RADIO SHACK 49-450	100	W	0	—	S or K	Adj.	Adj.	1	✔	A,B,F,H,P	—	*C*
UNIVERSAL PT-1000	200	WL	1	1	C	Adj.	Adj.	2	✔	A,D,F,G,I,P	—	—

SPECIFICATIONS FOR PERIMETER SYSTEMS

All: require purchase of additional sensors and/or transmitters; can use external horn. *Except as noted, all:* accept both normally closed and normally open sensors; normally operate on household current, with batteries for backup or transmitter power; require batteries to be purchased separately.

Brand and model	Price	Type [4]	Range (length x width, feet)	On/off switch [2]	Exit delay (sec.)	Entry delay (sec.)	Auto-silencer	Advantages	Disadvantages	Comments
Interior space-protector systems										
COLORADO 9435	$ 99	I	35x20	—	—	—	—	O	—	*G*
HEATHKIT GD-49	70+	U	25x25	S	10	20	✔	N	d,f,g	*A*
RADIO SHACK 49-303	60	U	30x20	S or K	20	15	✔	O,P	b,d	*C*
RADIO SHACK 49-304	100	U	30x20	S, K, or C	30	30	✔	J,K,M,O,P	d	*C*
RADIO SHACK 49-305	150	I	30x30	S, K, or C	30	30	✔	J,K,M,O,P,Q	d	*C*
SEARS Cat. No. 57159	50+	U	20x10	S	20	20	✔	J,L,P	d,e	—

[1] *W = wired; WL = wireless.*

[2] *S = simple on/off switch; K = key-operated; C = code punched in on keypad; O = other.*

[3] *No exit delay needed since system doesn't go on until door has been opened and closed.*

[4] *I = infrared; U = ultrasonic.*

SPECIFICATIONS FOR AREA SYSTEMS

Except as noted, all: can be attached to external horn; run on household current, with batteries for backup power; require batteries to be purchased separately.

KEY TO ADVANTAGES

A – Has lamp or light-emitting diode (LED) to indicate status of system.
B – Equipped with relay contacts for attaching auxiliary equipment such as automatic-dialer or lights.
C – Second zone has own alarm; intended for smoke detectors.
D – Transmitter has built-in magnetic switch; also accepts several additional sensors.
E – Transmitter has test LED.
F – Indicator shows whether alarm has gone off.
G – Transmitter includes panic button.
H – Can accept automatic dialer.
I – Signal receiver selective; should cut down on false alarms.
J – Can also perform as control unit for perimeter system.
K – Also accepts perimeter sensors of both normally open and normally closed types.
L – Also accepts perimeter sensors of normally closed type.
M – Area system can be switched off, leaving perimeter protection.
N – Unit disguised as book.
O – Has "walk test" indicator for adjusting sensitivity.
P – Alarm can be activated instantly or after delay period.
Q – Lower half of infrared beam can be switched off to accommodate pets.
R – Comes with built-in rechargeable battery.

Keys to Ratings continued on next page

Ratings keys for burglar alarms continued

KEY TO DISADVANTAGES

a – No provision for operating system on household current.
b – Battery cannot be housed in unit.
c – Installation instructions poor.
d – Controls on unit difficult to reach.
e – No "walk test" indicator, so sensitivity must be adjusted by trial and error.
f – System difficult to test.
g – No backup battery.

KEY TO COMMENTS

A – Comes as kit; requires assembly.
B – Uses special transmitter to turn system on and off (not included).
C – Switch must be bought separately.
D – Sensors and extension wires have plugs to facilitate making connections.
E – Includes window foil and foil-application tools; judged very difficult for amateur.
F – External horn included.
G – Device designed as component part of a wired perimeter system; it is hard-wired into that system, from which it gets power.

Of the various types of internal systems, we think the infrared type is the best. Infrared sensors are less prone to false alarms than ultrasonic or microwave sensors, as long as they don't point at objects that change temperature rapidly (such as radiators and air conditioners) and aren't in direct sunlight. You can aim sophisticated infrared sensors very precisely.

The Minolta Maxxum 7000

Condensed from CONSUMER REPORTS, March 1986

With the *Maxxum 7000*, Minolta has raised the level of 35mm camera design to unprecedented heights of automation. This new single-lens-reflex camera has automatic focus, automatic exposure setting, autoload, autowind, auto rewind, auto flash, and auto film-speed setting. It's not only fancy; it's among the best 35mm cameras we've tested in recent years. But it's expensive; it lists for more than $500, and its discounted price with a 50mm f/1.7 lens is approximately $330.

A computer within the *Maxxum* body masterminds its operation, and each of the dozen lenses available for it has a built-in semiconductor memory chip to feed the computer with information. There are 15 buttons and switches on the camera, but as long as it's in its programmed mode, most of those controls can be ignored. In hand, the *Maxxum* feels a bit heavy, but, at 29 ounces, it's no heavier than some manual-focus SLR's, and it's nicely balanced.

PERFORMANCE. Minolta calls the *Maxxum's* shutter release the "operating button," which is apt because it does a lot more than activate the shutter mechanism. The first touch activates the automated shutter-setting and its readouts; the camera chirps if it senses insufficient light to take a handheld picture. A bit of pressure on the button puts the autofocus to work, and gears buzz softly while a motor adjusts the lens. A successful focus evokes another chirp and the glow of a signal light in the viewfinder. At last, the button is depressed far enough to take the picture, which sets off another motor that advances the film.

Of course, all that happens pretty fast if you suddenly squeeze off a snapshot. For that fraction of a second, the camera seems like a live thing moving and buzzing in your hands.

We tested the autofocus system using the "normal" 50mm, f/1.7 lens and a 28mm-to-135mm, f/4 zoom lens. Except in the trickiest situations, the *Maxxum* produced a focus that we couldn't improve on by hand. We met with similar excellence when we tested the *Maxxum's* automatic exposure setting; its accuracy and consistency were among the best we've encountered.

The lenses we tested were typical of the general high quality of Minolta's lenses. Unfortunately, the *Maxxum* system employs a unique lens mount, so lenses from other *Minoltas* won't fit. *Maxxum* lenses cost more than comparable lenses that don't autofocus; the zoom lens that we tested sells for about $350.

RECOMMENDATIONS. With the *Maxxum*, Minolta has stolen a march on the rest of the photographic industry with a well-made, high-quality camera that approaches technical perfection in automation. But with "normal" lens and two zoom lenses (28-135mm and 70-210mm), the cost approaches $1000. Most people would consider that an awful lot of money for a camera outfit. So while the *Maxxum* may represent a uniquely ideal camera for point-and-shoot novice and enterprising amateur alike, it máy also illustrate the possibility that even a near-perfect product can cost too much.

Autofocus 35mm cameras

Condensed from CONSUMER REPORTS, September 1986

Today's typical compact, automated 35mm camera combines the simplicity of a point-and-shoot camera with the picture quality inherent in the relatively large 35mm film format. Automation takes care of all the basic functions: loading the film, advancing it between shots (and rewinding when the roll is used up), setting the lens opening and shutter speed, and firing the built-in flash, when necessary. The camera even focuses by itself to give clear, sharp snapshots under all but the trickiest conditions.

True, what you gain in ease with an autofocus 35, you give up in control. Those cameras will not so much as tell you what aperture or shutter-speed settings they've chosen, let alone allow you to disagree with their decisions. Yet they've become so popular that they've displaced single-lens reflex models as the most popular type of 35mm camera. And even Eastman Kodak, which abandoned its 35mm line in 1970, has introduced a batch of new autofocus 35's. We've included two of them among the 27 cameras tested for this report.

All the cameras come with flash. Most have motorized film-handling and automatic exposure metering. List prices ranged from about $100 to $300, but discounts of 40 percent or more are not uncommon.

PICTURE QUALITY. We rated each camera chiefly on how well it performed to give sharp, well-exposed pictures. The judgments of picture sharpness recorded in the Ratings are based on negatives taken of test patterns. The photos were taken with the camera's lens aperture wide open, where lenses are least sharp and least tolerant of misfocusing.

Autofocus 35's gauge the distance between camera and subject by bouncing a beam of infrared light off the subject. On the basis of that information, they decide which of their fixed "focus zones" will provide the best picture. All other things being equal, the more zones a camera has, the more precise its focusing can be.

On the whole, the autofocus performance of the cameras was remarkable. Rarely did they give us a poorly focused photo for any reasonable scene—even when we went out of our way to trick them. In one test, for example, we photographed a truck parked behind a chain-link fence to see if the camera would focus on the fence instead of the truck. Most often, the camera literally saw right through our ruse. In another test, we smeared fingerprints on the camera windows that emit and receive the autofocus beam. Even that didn't adversely affect pictures. The cameras can still be confounded by a few picture situations: glass or plastic windows that impose themselves in front of the subject, shiny subjects that deflect the infrared beam, or black subjects that absorb it. Usually, though, those peculiar picture-taking conditions are easily avoided or circumvented.

The exposure accuracy of the tested models—their ability to adjust aperture and shutter-speed to available light levels—was less impressive than their autofocusing. The majority overexposed pictures. The worst sometimes let in more than twice the light needed. Even such gross errors can produce acceptable pictures with print film. But if you regularly use slide film, which is much less tolerant of exposure errors, you should pay particular attention to models that excelled in exposure accuracy.

The Ratings column titled "Smallest field width" shows how wide a view each camera covers at its closest focusing distance (two to four feet away). The narrower the field width, the better-suited the camera is for taking close-ups. Models noted as having a built-in telephoto capability are also well-suited for taking portraits.

FEATURES. Most autofocus 35's are easy to load. They have a motor that automatically takes up the end of the film and pulls it through. Usually, you just open the camera, drop in the cassette, pull out enough film to reach the take-up spool, and close the camera. Some cameras finish loading automatically; others require you to click the shutter a few times. The motor also runs the "autowinder," which advances the film after each shot, and rewinds when the film is used up.

The top-rated *Fuji TW-300* reverses the usual film-advance process. It winds out the entire roll, and then rewinds as pictures are taken, shot by shot. That way, each picture is wound back into the film's light-tight cassette, where it can't be ruined if the camera is opened by mistake. Four models lack motorized film-handling. With those, the film is advanced with a lever or thumbwheel and rewound with a small crank.

A common mistake in loading 35mm cameras is to forget to set the camera's light meter to match the film's ISO sensitivity rating. That can make pictures from slide film turn out too light or too dark, and leave pictures from underexposed print film with too little contrast. Many autofocus 35's won't let you make that mistake. They set film speed automatically by "reading" it right off the cassette by means of what's called DX coding. Virtually all popular 35mm films are now DX-coded. But about a third of the tested cameras don't have DX sensing. They can take DX-coded film, but they can't read the code and must be set manually.

In the Ratings, we've shown the range of film speeds each camera can handle, automatically and manually. The DX ranges in most cases include only the widely used film speeds—ISO 25, 50 or 60, 100, 200, 400, 800 or 1000, 1600. Instead of relying on manufacturers' specifications for the film-speed data, we ran our own tests. The most striking discrepancy between their specs and our tests involves the *Olympus Trip*, which is claimed to handle print films with speeds from ISO 50 up to ISO 1600. Actually, we found, it has only two film-speed settings, ISO 100 for slower films and ISO 400 for faster films, regardless of the films' true speed.

The DX-equipped cameras can be set manually when using film that is not DX coded, but the range of settings may be limited, as indicated in the Ratings.

Text continued on page 260

Ratings of autofocus 35mm cameras

Listed in order of estimated quality. Except where separated by heavy lines, closely ranked models differed little in quality. Prices are list and also low quotes from advertisements placed by New

Brand and model	Price: List	Price: Low	ISO film speeds: DX system	ISO film speeds: Manual settings	Focus zones	Picture sharpness
FUJI TW-300	$290	$160	50 to 1600	100	11	◒
RICOH FF-90	265	140	25 to 1600 [1]	25 to 1600 [1]	10	◒
MINOLTA AF-TELE	291	170	25 to 1600 [1]	100	13	◒
CHINON AUTO 2001	250	150	50 to 1600	100 to 1000	8	◒
KODAK VR35 K12	207	127	100 to 1000	100	8	◒
NIKON ONE TOUCH	227	120	50 to 1600	100	9	◒
OLYMPUS QUICK SHOOTER	235	124	25 to 1600	100	8	◒
PENTAX SPORT 35 MOTOR	192	95	100 to 1000	100 to 1000	4	●
PENTAX SUPER SPORT 35	245	128	25 to 1600 [1]	100 to 1000	8	◒
RICOH AF-70	190	100	100 to 1000	100 to 1000	3	◒
KODAK VR35 K10	130	89	100 to 1000	100	3	◒
YASHICA T AF	290	99	—	50 to 1000	8	◒
MINOLTA TALKER	244	110	—	25 to 1000 [1]	7	◒
[D] CHINON 35 FS-A	160	—	100 to 1000	100 to 1000	3	◒
[D] NIKON L135AF	175	84	—	100,400,1000	3	●
VIVITAR PS:35	146	74	64 to 1600	100	2	●
YASHICA PARTNER AF	140	—	—	100 to 1000	4	●
VIVITAR TEC45	190	115	64 to 1600	100	6	◒
KONICA MG	181	79	—	50 to 1000	3	◒
MINOLTA FREEDOM II	193	99	100 to 1000	100 to 400	7	◒

York City camera stores, indicating that substantial discounts are often available. [D] indicates that model has been discontinued or was scheduled to be discontinued at original publication.

	Flash					Batteries				
Exposure accuracy	Smallest field width (in.)	Range (ft.) at ISO 400	Exposure uniformity	Film-loading ease	Type	Life, alkaline	Life, lithium	Advantages	Disadvantages	Comments
⊖	33	31	○	⊖	Built-in L	—	40	C,D,G,I,K,L	n	*E,I*
○	28	31	○	⊜	2 AA	16	—	A,C,D,F,G,I,J	—	*D*
⊖	25	33	○	⊜	2 AA [2] [3]	24	47	B,E,F,G	g,l,n	*D,I*
⊜	30	19	○	⊖	1 6V L	—	82	B,C,D,F,G,J	c,m	*D*
⊜	32	24	⊖	⊖	9V L [4]	36	250	B,C,D,F,G,H	c,n	*D*
○	24	32	○	⊖	2 AA	20	—	C,F,G	l,o	—
⊖	27	19	○	⊜	1 6V L	—	83	C,I	l,m	—
⊜	36	25	○	⊜	2 AA	23	—	K	c,o	*F*
⊖	24	31	○	⊜	2 AA	24	—	A,C	l,o	—
○	36	20	◒	⊜	2 AA	29	—	D,F,G,J	—	*D*
○	43	22	○	◒	9V L [4]	41	300	B,D,F,G,H,K	j	*A,C,F,H*
⊖	36	22	○	⊖	2 AA	26	—	C,D	—	—
⊖	29	37	○	⊜	2 AA [2]	24	—	E,G,K,M	h	*D,G*
⊜	43	27	◒	◒	2 AAA	11	—	D,J,K	j,l	*C*
○	43	25	○	○	2 AA	20	—	—	j	*A,F,H*
◒	44	20	○	○	2 AA	39	—	—	c,j	*F,H*
●	36	25	⊖	○	2 AA	23	—	K	e,j	*C,F*
○	32	22	○	⊖	2 AA [5]	22	—	F,G	c,l	—
○	39	24	○	⊖	2 AA	17	—	—	c	*G*
○	22	20	◒	⊖	2 AA [2]	28	—	F,J	g	*F,H*

Ratings continued on next page

Ratings of autofocus 35mm cameras continued

Brand and model	Price: List	Price: Low	ISO film speeds: DX system	ISO film speeds: Manual settings	Focus zones	Picture sharpness
CANON SURE SHOT	$240	$89	—	50 to 400 [1], 1000	7	⊖
CANON SPRINT	160	89	100,400	100	3	○
CANON MC	295	129	—	64 to 1000	7	○
[D] **KONICA AF-3**	175	70	—	25 to 400 [1]	7	⊖
OLYMPUS TRIP AF MOTOR	160	74	100,400	100	4	⊜
FUJI DL-50	160	75	—	100 to 400	2	◒
KEYSTONE EVERFLASH AF2	98	—	—	100,400	3	○

[1] *ISO film speeds are provided in 1/3-stop increments; e.g., 100, 125, 160, 200.*

[2] *Rechargeable nickel-cadmium batteries may be used instead.*

FEATURES IN COMMON
All have infrared autofocus, without aperture or shutter-speed indicators.
Except as noted, all have: antireflection coating on all lens surfaces; bright-frame viewfinder with parallax marks and autofocus frame; focus hold with indicator in viewfinder; low-light or slow-shutter-speed warning in viewfinder; electronic flash that user turns on; built-in lens cover; automatic film loading and film advance; film-advance indicator; motorized film rewind; self-timer that cancels after each use; shutter lock; tripod socket.
Except as noted, none have: backlight compensation control; warning that subject is too close for sharp focus; warning that subject is beyond flash range; warning of weak battery; focus-zone indicator.

KEY TO ADVANTAGES
A – Backlight compensation control.
B – Fill-flash switch.
C – Indicates focus zone before picture is taken.
D – Indicates when subject is too close.
E – Indicates when subject is too far for flash.
F – Flash turns on automatically when needed.
G – When flash is on, shutter locks until flash is ready.
H – Large lens/flash separation reduces chance of "red-eye" effect in eyes of pictured subjects.
I – Warns when batteries are weak.
J – Smaller and lighter unit than most.
K – Film advance slightly quieter than most.
L – Easier than most to use with eyeglasses.
M – Voice synthesizer provides 3 spoken messages; can be turned off.

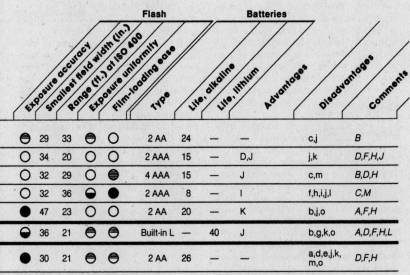

		Flash			Batteries					
Exposure accuracy	Smallest field width (in.)	Range (ft.) at ISO 400	Exposure uniformity	Film-loading ease	Type	Life, alkaline	Life, lithium	Advantages	Disadvantages	Comments
⊜	29	33	⊜	○	2 AA	24	—	—	c,j	*B*
○	34	20	○	○	2 AAA	15	—	D,J	j,k	*D,F,H,J*
○	32	29	○	⊜	4 AAA	15	—	J	c,m	*B,D,H*
○	32	36	◒	●	2 AAA	8	—	I	f,h,i,j,l	*C,M*
●	47	23	○	○	2 AA	20	—	K	b,j,o	*A,F,H*
◒	36	21	⊜	⊜	Built-in L	—	40	J	b,g,k,o	*A,D,F,H,L*
●	30	21	⊜	⊜	2 AA	26	—	—	a,d,e,j,k, m,o	*D,F,H*

[3] *Can use 6V lithium battery.*
[4] *Can use 9V alkaline battery.*
[5] *Also requires 2 LR44 "button" batteries.*

KEY TO DISADVANTAGES

a-No autoexposure control or low-light warning.
b-No focus hold; and viewfinder lacks bright picture and autofocus frames.
c-Part of lens not antireflection-coated.
d-Lens not antireflection coated.
e-May leak tight under severe conditions.
f-Film must be threaded manually.
g-Provision for checking flash-ready status works illogically (see text).
h-Detachable lens cover.
i-No shutter lock.
j-After loading, film must be advanced 3 times to reach first frame.
k-Film must be advanced to end of roll before it can be rewound.
l-Self-timer does not cancel automatically after use.
m-Battery-compartment cover can be mislaid.
n-Larger and heavier unit than most.
o-More difficult than most to use with eyeglasses.

KEY TO COMMENTS

A-No parallax marks for close-ups.
B-Indicates focus zone after picture has been taken.
C-No automatic film advance or rewind.
D-Rewind begins automatically at end of roll.
E-Winds film to end of roll before pictures are taken; then rewinds frame by frame.
F-No self-timer.
G-Once self-timer is set, it cannot be canceled without taking picture.
H-No tripod socket.
I-Built-in "telephoto" converter; useful for taking portraits and close-ups. With telephoto, smallest field is 18 in. (**Fuji**) and 15 in. (**Minolta**).
J-"Macro" setting for close-ups; with macro, smallest field width is 15 in.

After being aimed, most of the cameras confirm that they're focused, usually with a small light flashing or a tiny pictorial symbol in the viewfinder. Most models allow you to lock onto a focus setting by holding the shutter release part-way down. That permits you to place your subject off-center in the picture or get around some of the troublesome focusing situations described earlier. The *Olympus Trip* and the *Fuji DL-50* lack a focus hold.

All but one of the tested models have a built-in flash; the *Cannon MC's* flash is detachable. The exposure meter in some cameras automatically activates the flash in low light. Most other cameras light an indicator or beep to signal for the flash to be turned on. The flash unit on 10 cameras is interlocked with the shutter release. When a scene requires flash, the interlock prevents the picture from being snapped until the flash is charged and ready. Even when there's plenty of bright sunlight, it's sometimes advisable to use flash to fill in harsh shadows. Four models have a fill-flash switch.

On three cameras, noted in the Ratings, the flash system works illogically. Instead of the customary light indicating the flash is ready, these have a light indicating the flash *isn't* ready. The indicator light works when you press the shutter release part way. But when you do that, the flash *stops* charging until you let go.

Most models run on a pair of penlights (AA or AAA size). Other battery types include ultra-long-lasting lithium cells. The Ratings give the battery life, in numbers of 24-picture rolls, assuming the flash is used half the time.

RECOMMENDATIONS. We were especially pleased with the five highest-rated cameras. Their autofocus and light-metering systems delivered clear, sharp, and well-exposed photos. Beyond that, the *Fuji TW-3000* and the *Minolta AF-Tele* have a telephoto converter that's useful for taking portrait shots. The *Ricoh FF-90* is a fine, general-purpose camera with sensible features. The *Chinon Auto 2001* and the *Kodak VR35 K10* had the most accurate light metering among the five, an advantage with slide film.

But we wouldn't rule out any of the cameras in the top half of the Ratings. All of them performed well in most important respects. A particularly good price might provide incentive enough to choose any one of them, assuming that it has a mix of features you can use to advantage.

CU's objectivity

CU accepts no advertising; it accepts no samples of products; it does its utmost to stop use of its name or findings to promote any product or service. Ask anyone who claims that a CU Rating has been improperly influenced to write down the assertion and sign it. Then send the document to us. Consumers Union takes full responsibility for the integrity of its work.

Electronic flash units

Condensed from CONSUMER REPORTS, August 1984

All the flash units we tested are "dedicated"; that is, each unit is designed for one or several brands of 35mm single-lens reflex cameras, and it won't work entirely satisfactorily with cameras of other brands.

COMPATIBILITY. A flash unit, when mounted on a compatible camera, offers various conveniences. The flash unit may automatically set the camera's shutter speed, for example, so you don't inadvertently use a shutter speed that's too fast for flash. Or an indicator in the camera's viewfinder may show if the flash unit delivered enough light for proper exposure.

The models made by camera manufacturers (Canon, Minolta, Nikon, Olympus, Pentax) are dedicated only to the manufacturer's brand of camera. The remaining models are made by independent manufacturers. A few of them are immediately compatible with several camera brands; they adapt with the simple push of a switch to the proper position. But most of them achieve compatibility with a variety of adapter feet, each designed to work with a specific camera brand.

All the flash units we tested provide automatic exposure control. The units cut off the flash the instant that proper exposure has been achieved. Only the *Canon 011A* and the *Nikon SB-E* lack a manual exposure setting.

PERFORMANCE. Ideally, the flash should uniformly light all objects that are the same distance from the camera. In practice, however, objects at the edges of a photo receive somewhat less light than those at the center of the photo, so they look darker.

No matter how far away the subject is (within the flash unit's specified limits), it should receive the proper amount of light. The unit's automatic exposure control is supposed to provide such consistency, which is especially important with slide film.

A flash unit's guide number at a specified film speed is a convenient measure of its power. Our test numbers tended to be a bit lower than the manufacturers' numbers.

The manufacturers claim anywhere from 80 to 250 flashes on a set of alkaline batteries. In our tests, most models delivered at least the number of flashes claimed for them.

Most models allow you to tilt the flash head to bounce all or most of the light off the ceiling and onto the subject. A bounced flash tends to give softer, more diffused lighting. On about half the units, the flash head can turn sideways as well as tilt up, allowing you to bounce the flash off the ceiling while turning the camera for a vertical shot.

A number of units have a secondary (fill) flash or its equivalent (a small deflector of the primary flash) to provide some direct light on the subject while you bounce the main flash. Such a fill flash can increase the usable bounce range slightly, add desirable highlights, and soften shadows.

Partial-power flash setting gives faster recycling and is desirable for extreme close-ups.

RECOMMENDATIONS. The eleven highest-rated models are big, powerful, and expensive. They scored impressively in both uniformity and consistency of exposure. However, your choices may be limited by the brand of your camera.

Ratings on next page

Ratings of electronic flash units

Listed in order of estimated overall quality. Differences of less than 15 points in Overall Ratings Score were judged not very significant. Weights include adapter foot. Aperture settings in automatic mode and guide numbers are for ISO 100 film. Prices are suggested retail. Substantial discounts are generally available.

⊜ ⊖ ○ ◒ ●

Better ⟷ Worse

Brand and model	Overall Ratings Score	Price [1]	Weight (oz.)	Exposure uniformity	Exposure consistency	Control convenience	Measured guide no. (ft.)	Aperture settings, auto-mode (f-stop range)	Film speed range (ISO)	Shortest focal length covered (mm)	Battery life (no. of flashes) [2]	Advantages
MINOLTA 360PX	95	$176	17	⊜	⊜	⊜	93	2.8-11	25-400	28 [3]	100	A,B,C,F,G,H
OLYMPUS T32	85	175	14	⊖	⊜	⊜	88	4-8	25-1600	35 [3]	100	B,E,F,H
VIVITAR 5600 [4]	82	165	18	⊖	⊖	⊜	78	1.4-16	25-1000	28 [3]	(81)	B,C,D,E,F,G,H
METZ 32CT2	80	169	14	⊖	⊜	⊜	84	2-8	25-400	28	100	A,B,C,H
PENTAX AF280T	79	173	14	⊖	⊖	⊜	78	4-8	25-800	28 [3]	100	B,C,F,H
VIVITAR 5600 [5]	79	291	20	⊖	⊖	⊜	99	1.4-16	25-1000	28 [3]	(66)	B,C,E,F,G,H
VIVITAR 4600 [4]	79	158	17	⊖	⊜	⊜	76	2-8	25-800	28 [3]	90	B,C,D,E,G,H
SUNPAK 422D	77	166	15	⊖	⊜	⊜	81	2-8	25-800	35 [3]	110	A,B,C,F,H
NISSIN 360WXD	75	145	17	⊖	⊜	○	95	2.8-11	50-400	28	(118)	A,B,C,D,G
VIVITAR 4600 [5]	74	211	18	⊖	⊜	⊖	100	2-8	25-800	28 [3]	90	B,C,E,G,H
CANON 199A	73	167	16	⊖	⊖	○	88	2.8-11	25-800	24	100	B,G,H
NIKON SB-15	71	111	12	⊖	○	⊖	67	4-8	25-800	28	160	B,C,E,F,H
OLYMPUS T20	71	92	7	⊖	○	⊜	54	4-8	25-800	35	120	H

CANON 011A	70	30	6	◍	◍	◍	41	4	100-400	35	150	H
NIKON SB-E	69	56	6	◍	○	◍	50	5.6	25-400	35	80	—
BRAUN 340SCA	67	185	17	◍	◍	◍	85	4-8	25-800	28 [3]	120	B,C,D,G,H
POPULAR 30TBD	67	130	12	◍	◍	◍	80	2.8-11	25-400	35	120	B,H
SOLIGOR 30D	67	90	19	◍	◒	◍	81	2-8	25-800	28	130	A,B,C,E,F
STARBLITZ 3300DTS	67	110	15	◍	◍	●	80	2.8-5.6	25-800	28	120	A,B,C,D
AGFA 383CS	66	160	25	◍	◍	○	107	4-8	25-400	28	80	B,C,D,F,H
HANIMEX TZ236	63	83	13	○	○	◍	82	2.8-5.6	25-800	28	180	A,B,E,F
MINOLTA 118X	63	56	6	◍	○	◒	50	2-4	25-400	35	200	H
VIVITAR 3500	60	97	10	◍	●	◍	61	2-8	25-800	28	(137)	B,D,E,H
OSRAM VS250	60	100	12	○	◍	○	72	4-8	25-400	28	120	B,D,G,H
SIMON TSI 324	59	125	11	◍	○	○	90	2.8-5.6	25-1000	28	120	B,D
PENTAX AF160	59	50	5	◍	○	◒	45	2.8-4	25-400	28	200	—
ALFON 780MDZ	57	120	14	◍	○	●	74	2.8-5.6	25-400	30	150	B,D
HANIMEX TZ134	42	65	12	○	◒	◒	75	2.8-4	25-800	28	100	B,E
ACHIEVER 1850STW	38	120	17	●	◍	◍	109	2-8	25-800	25	100	A,B,C,D
SOLIGOR 24D	36	72	13	◒	●	◍	67	2-8	25-400	24	150	B

[1] *Includes, where applicable, price of most expensive adapter foot.*

[2] *As claimed by manufacturer, except where claim exceeded number of flashes recorded in CU's tests (which number is given in parentheses).*

[3] *Still shorter focal length is covered with optional adapter.*

[4] *With standard head.*

[5] *With "high power" zoom head.*

FEATURES IN COMMON

All have automatic exposure control and ready light.

KEY TO ADVANTAGES

A – Automatic battery-power shutoff.
B – Bounce-flash capability for horizontal pictures.
C – Bounce-flash capability for vertical pictures.
D – Fill flash.
E – Flash head can be tilted down for close-ups.
F – Partial power settings.
G – Illuminated scales.
H – Can use rechargeable batteries.

Home workshop

Snow throwers

Condensed from CONSUMER REPORTS, November 1985

In recent years, lightweight snow throwers, dubbed "compacts" by the manufacturers, have become more and more popular. Like larger "standard" models, compacts cut a 20-to-22-inch swath. But they usually have a less powerful engine (about 3 hp. versus about 5 hp.) and must be pushed by hand. Moreover, the front opening that bites into the snow isn't as high as that of standard models (about 10 inches versus 17 inches or so), so compacts are at a disadvantage in large accumulations or deep drifts.

Prices for compacts run from about $300 to $490. We bought 15 of those for testing. We also bought eight standard models. They're self-propelled and relatively heavy (well over 100 pounds), and most of them are priced from $500 to a little over $800. An exception is the *Honda*, which has rubber tank tracks instead of the wheels found on the other models; the *Honda* lists at a daunting $1100 (actually in the price range of still larger and heavier 7-hp. or 8-hp. machines).

Most standard models are of a "two-stage" design: A steel auger, like a corkscrew, turns slowly, gathering in snow and delivering it to a rapidly spinning impeller whose blades hurl the snow up and away through a chute. The standard *Atlas* and most of the compacts are "one-stage" machines. Because they have no impeller to throw the snow into the chute and away, their augers (made partly or entirely of rubber) must turn much faster than those in the two-stage design. The *Ariens ST2+2* is a two-stage thrower, but we list it with the compacts because it's a small, lightweight, hand-pushed machine.

Six compacts have neither auger nor impeller nor chute. Instead, a high-speed paddle wheel with rubber blades pulls snow into the machine, and then throws it upward and away through a series of plastic vanes.

The standard *Sears* comes with tire chains to improve traction. Since slipping tires can be a problem with larger machines, we decided to equip all the other self-propelled models with chains.

PERFORMANCE. Given their smaller front openings, even the best of the compacts couldn't match the performance of the standard machines. But in freshly fallen, powdery snow, four compacts were judged almost as good as the least capable standard models. Most models with a chute let you direct the snow to left, right, or front. The compacts with a paddle wheel give you much less control over where the snow goes, especially dry snow; most of the snow goes straight ahead, no matter how the vanes are positioned.

In heavy, wet snow, the standard *Toro* and *Sears* excelled; they went through about 15 inches of wet stuff without undue effort by the operator. The *Ariens* and *Atlas* standard models dealt creditably with a foot of snow. The other standard machines and the best of the compacts could handle perhaps six to eight inches of wet snow. The worst of the compacts lacked power to bite through and throw reasonably far away more than three inches of wet snow.

The *Toro 521* coped quite easily with 18-inch-deep packed snow. The *Ariens* and the *MTD Snowflite* could cut through about a foot of that hard stuff. The other standard machines and all the compacts tended to climb the packed snow rather than bite into it. When the compact *Penney* was pushed through packed snow, its handles broke. From then on, our testers were especially gentle with the *Atlas*, an essentially similar model.

Most standard models could hurl a six-to-eight-inch layer of snow more than 15 feet forward or to either side. The *Honda* exceeded 20 feet, and a couple of others almost matched it. The best compact machines could throw three-to-five-inch layers of snow 15 to 20 feet.

Some models did a more thorough job than others of leaving the surface clean and clear of loose snow. Best of all in that respect were the *Snapper 3201* and the compacts with paddles.

EASE OF USE. With their power on, the self-propelled models plowed ahead briskly, but they were cumbersome when pushed or turned with the motor off. Conversely, most of the compacts were very easy to maneuver with the motor off. But with the motor on, it took a fair amount of effort to push them straight ahead through snow.

Overall, the best controls were on three standard machines, the two *Toros* and the *MTD Snowflite*. Their gear selector was readily accessible and their "dead-man" controls were easy to hold in place. (Still, at least one gear speed on each of those models left something to be desired.) The controls on the compact models were simpler and, for the most part, convenient. However, the controls on three compact models were too simple for our liking. They lacked a dead-man control, thereby presenting a risk that's both serious and unnecessary. Therefore, we judged those three models, called out in the Ratings, Not Acceptable.

Our testers found big differences in the controls that operate the machines' chutes. All the standard machines and some of the compacts use a gearing system to move the chute around; the gears are worked by turning a crank handle. Instead of a gearing system, many of the compacts use some type of handle, lever, or rod to move the chute. Not all were convenient, as the Ratings indicate.

Snow throwers with a chute have an adjustable deflector at the chute's top to help angle the snow away from the machine. Those models can usually throw the snow far enough to the side so that it's possible to clear up and down the length of even a wide driveway in one series of passes. But the vanes of the paddle-wheel compacts can angle snow only slightly off to the side. To clear a wide driveway with one of them, the best tactic would be to aim the vanes straight ahead and run the machine from side to side—not very convenient, but better than building up higher and higher drifts to one side of each pass up and down the length of the driveway.

Text continued on page 268

Ratings of snow throwers

Listed by types; within types, listed except as noted in order of estimated quality. Except where models are separated by heavy lines, differences between closely ranked models were slight. Models judged equal are bracketed and listed alphabetically. Prices are list; + indicates shipping is extra. Unless otherwise indicated, standard models were tested with tire chains, which cost $30 to $40 extra. D indicates model has been discontinued and is not available under another model designation.

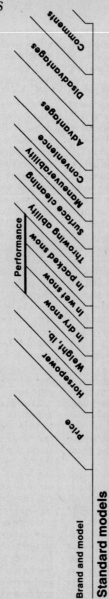

◍	⊖	○	◒	●
Better ←				→ Worse

Brand and model	Price	Horsepower	Weight, lb.	Performance: In dry snow	Performance: In wet snow	Performance: In packed snow	Throwing ability	Surface cleaning	Maneuverability	Convenience	Advantages	Disadvantages	Comments
Standard models													
TORO 521	$770	5	150	◍	◍	◍	◍	⊖	○	⊖	A,D,H	i,n,u	*P*
ARIENS ST350	649	3.5	127	◍	⊖	⊖	○	○	○	○	D,J	a	*Q*
MTD SNOWFLITE 315450	830	5	167	◍	○	⊖	◍	○	○	⊖	A,D,J	l	*Q*
SEARS Cat. No. 8825 [1]	700+	5	151	⊖	◍	○	⊖	○	◒	○	D,L	a,g,q,u	*M,Q*
TORO 3521	680	3.5	148	⊖	○	○	⊖	○	○	⊖	A,D,H	i,n,u	*P,Q*
HONDA HS55T	1100 [2]	5.5	171	◍	◒	◒	◍	⊖	●	○	A,C,D,E,F	b,t,x	*F*
ATLAS A5211B	500	5	120	⊖	⊖	◒	⊖	○	◒	●	B,G,J	c,h,k,s, v,y	*B,I,O,P,Q*
GILSON ST522	750	5	149	◍	[3]	◒	○	◒	◒	●	H,J	b,h,j,m,o,s	*P,Q*

Compact models

ARIENS ST2 + 2	489	2.7	94	○	○	○	○	⊖	○	◍	I,J,L	d	*C,D,G,Q*
SNAPPER 3201	380	3	47	◒	○	○	○	◍	◍	⊖	J,K,L	c,v	*Q*
HONDA HS35	469	3.5	97	○	◒	◒	○	⊖	○	◍	D,F,G,J	t,u,w,z	*D*
SUNBEAM AIRCAP 8430B	299	3	46	◒	◒	◒	◒	◍	◍	⊖	G,J,K,L	—	*E*
JOHN DEERE 322	380	3	45	◒	◒	◒	◒	◍	◍	⊖	J,K,L	e	*E,Q*
SIMPLICITY 0350E	430	3	47	◒	◒	◒	◒	◍	◍	⊖	J,K,L	e,w	*A,E,J*
ATLAS A3222	360	3	45	○	●	◒	●	⊖	◍	○	J,K,L	f,g,v	*Q*
J.C. PENNEY Cat. No. 8121030	280+	3	45	○	●	◒	●	⊖	◍	○	J,K,L	f,g,v	*Q*
GILSON ST320	390	3	41	◒	●	●	◒	⊖	◍	⊖	D,J,K	c,d,z	*F,Q*
SEARS Cat. No. 8823	330+	3	44	◒	◒	◒	◒	⊖	◍	◒	J,K,L	o,q,r,v	*H,K,R*
[D]**MTD 315160**	470	5	73	◒	◒	◒	◒	◒	●	⊖	I,J,K,L	g,n,p	*D,Q*
[D]**MTD 315151**	450+	3	66	●	●	●	◒	◒	●	○	J,K,L	c,g,n	*A,M,N*

Not Acceptable

■ *The following units were judged Not Acceptable because they lack a dead-man control, a serious safety deficiency.*

BOLENS 300E	470	3	53	◒	●	◒	●	◍	◍	⊖	J,K,L	—	*A,E,L*
TORO S620E	460	3	46	◒	●	◒	●	◍	◍	⊖	K	q,z	*A,E*
HOMELITE JACOBSEN 320E	410	3	53	◒	●	●	●	◒	◒	⊖	K	z	*A,E*

[1] *Comes with tire chains.* [2] *Rubber-tracked machine; does not need chains.* [3] *Machine was under repair at time of wet-snow tests.*

FEATURES IN COMMON
All standard models: are self-propelled; have 4-cycle engine and steel spiral auger; cut a swath 20 to 22 in. wide.
Except as noted, all standard models have: 2-stage snow-throwing mechanism; chute rotation of at least 180°; 2 dead-man controls (1 for the drive, 1 for auger rotation); 3 or more forward gears and 1 reverse gear; front opening about 16 to 18 in. high.
All compact models: must be pushed by hand; cut a swath 20 to 22 in. wide; have rubber auger or paddle wheel.
Except as noted, all compact models have: 1-stage snow-throwing mechanism; front opening about 9 to 11 in. high; 2-cycle engine; dead-man control for auger or paddle-wheel rotation.

Keys to Ratings on next page

Ratings keys for snow throwers

KEY TO ADVANTAGES
A-Gear-selector control very easy to use.
B-Throttle controls more convenient than most.
C-Both dead-man controls can be held in position by left hand.
D-Chute-rotation handle easy to use.
E-Reverse-gear speed judged suitably fast.
F-Starting easier than with most.
G-Relatively quiet.
H-Chute guarded by protective wire.
I-Has throttle control.
J-Can stand on end for storage.
K-Can hang on wall for storage.
L-Handle can fold for storage.

KEY TO DISADVANTAGES
a-Gear-selector control judged inconvenient.
b-Throttle and choke controls judged less convenient than most.
c-Choke judged less convenient than most.
d-Handle too high or narrow for some operators.
e-Handle too low for tall operators.
f-Flimsy handle. (It broke on the Penney.)
g-Deflector's angle hard to adjust.
h-Hand grips pulled off too easily, and handles were uncomfortably angled.
i-Reverse-gear speed judged too slow.
j-Spring-loaded reverse gear must be held by hand, reducing operator's control of machine.
k-Only 1 forward gear and no reverse, judged major deficiencies.
l-Lowest gear judged too fast for some conditions.
m-1 forward speed, judged much too fast.
n-Snow leaked at chute hinge.
o-Single dead-man control shuts off engine—for Gilson, complicating restart and operation in general.
p-Starting judged inconvenient.
q-Relatively noisy.
r-Chute and deflector failed to stay as set.
s-Fueling and adding oil judged inconvenient.
t-Adding oil judged inconvenient.
u-Chute rotates less than 180°.
v-Chute rotation judged inconvenient.
w-Dead-man control, held by left hand, judged uncomfortable.
x-Difficult to move with power off.
y-2 samples were defective, requiring major repair.
z-Lacks folding handles.

KEY TO COMMENTS
A-Electric start. (Essentially similar model without that provision available for $50 to $100 less.)
B-Only 1 stage.
C-2 stages.
D-4-cycle engine.
E-Paddle-wheel design.
F-Single, large 1-piece chute.
G-16-in. front opening.
H-7-in. front opening.
I-13-in. front opening.
J-Also available as **Deutz-Allis Snow-Wiz Electric Start**, $449.
K-Discontinued but still available as **Dynamark 535502** ($375) and as replacement models, **Sears Cat. No. 8833** ($340) and **Dynamark 535500** ($390), both identical except have electric start.
L-Discontinued but still available as **Bolens 300** ($380), essentially similar except has manual start.
M-Also available as **Dynamark 536076** ($810).
N-Also available as **White Sno Boss 350** ($380).
O-Also available as **J.C. Penney Cat. No. 8120735** ($400+).
P-Unlike most self-propelled models, has semi-pneumatic tires.
Q-Electric start available as option.
R-Also available as **Dynamark 535500** ($390).

RECOMMENDATIONS. People who rarely need to cope with a snowfall of more than 10 inches need not consider any snow thrower larger than a compact. The *Ariens ST2+2* ($489 list) and the *Snapper 3201* ($380) were by far the best of the small machines, with enough useful power to cope with almost any moderate snowfall.

For people who have more snow to deal with, the standard *Toro 521* ($770) is the clear first choice. The next five standard models in the Ratings are also worthy of consideration if you find one at a good price. But for most self-propelled snow throwers to perform at their best, we judged, they should be equipped with tire chains. As noted above, the *Sears* standard model came so equipped; the tank-tracked *Honda* didn't need any other help with its traction. Chains that are available for the rest of the self-propelled models cost $30 to $40 extra.

Low-priced lawn mowers

Condensed from CONSUMER REPORTS, June 1986

The lawn mowers tested for this report are the kind sold at the corner hardware store and the local discount house. They don't necessarily have a big brand name. They don't have an electric starter. They're not self-propelled. But they do cut grass. And they're priced at about $250 or less—in some cases, much less.

Like all new lawn mowers, these low-priced models have to comply with Federal safety standards requiring a "deadman" control on the handle. The idea is this: If a user lets go of the control, the lawn-mower blade must stop within three seconds.

All the tested mowers were reasonably easy to start with a yank or two on the starter cord. As a class, the Tecumseh engines on eight mowers started a bit more readily than did the Briggs & Stratton engines on the others. The Tecumsehs almost never needed more than one pull on the starter cord, while the Briggs engines often needed two.

We tested 31 side-discharge mowers and 11 rear-baggers. There's something to be said for each type. A side-discharge model offers the option of dispersing grass clippings over the lawn (which can partially feed the lawn if the clippings are cut fine and spread fairly evenly). But, with a bag in place at the side, the mower can be tough to maneuver in confined areas or around things. A rear-bagger never needs much more clearance than the width of its swath. But, unless it's a model that can accept a special deflector to aim its discharge away from the operator, it shouldn't be used without a bag.

MOWING. To determine the evenness of cut, we set the height of each mower at two inches, or as close as we could come to that height, and ran it through four-inch grass in two opposite directions. The *Homelite* gave an excellent cut—as smooth as a carpet, said our panel of judges. Seven other side-discharge models were judged very good, leaving only slight irregularities.

When a side-discharge mower is run without its bag, it should broadcast fine clippings evenly, so that they're biodegraded quickly and disappear into the lawn. The denser the rows of clippings a mower left behind, the lower we scored its dispersal of clippings.

A mower's spinning blade creates a vacuum effect that pulls up clippings, propelling them onto the lawn or into a bag. Machines whose swaths were virtually free of clippings were judged excellent in vacuuming. Those that left heavy accumulations were judged fair or poor.

Damp grass clippings tend to build up on the inside of the decks of some mowers. The models that best discouraged that buildup have a circular shroud open only for the discharge chute, with no places for the clippings to cling. But most models had only a partial shroud or none at all. They tended to let clippings collect in clumps, which dropped off in the mowers' wakes.

We found big differences in how competently the mowers filled their bags. (That's important because the bags are small—holding only about 1 ½ to 2 ½ cubic feet—and every time they have to be emptied, the mower has to be shut off and then restarted.) Models judged best in bagging hurled their clippings forcefully enough to fill the bag completely. Those judged poor in

Text continued on page 273

Ratings of low-priced lawn mowers

Listed by types; within types, listed in order of estimated quality. Models judged equal in quality are bracketed and listed alphabetically. Except where separated by heavy lines, differences between closely ranked models were judged slight. Prices are list. + indicates shipping is extra. Discounts may be available.

Excellent	Very good	Good	Fair	Poor
● (striped)	◒ (half striped)	○	◒ (half black)	●

Brand and model	Price [1]	Weight, lb. [2]	Blade size, in.	Evenness of cut	Dispersal of clippings	Vacuuming	Freedom from clumping	Bagging	Cutting tall grass	Overall handling	Stability across slopes	Ease of height adjustment	Comments
Side-discharge models													
HOMELITE/JACOBSEN SD20	$250	64	20	Excellent	Poor	Very good	Excellent	Excellent	Excellent	Good	Good	Excellent	F
MURRAY 20221, A Best Buy	120	56	20	Very good	Fair	Very good	Excellent	Excellent	Very good	Very good	Fair	Poor	D,H
LAWN CHIEF 51	170	59	20	Very good	Good	Very good	Fair	Excellent	Very good	Good	Good	Good	F
AIRCAP 4020, A Best Buy	120	49	20	Good	Fair	Very good	Fair	Excellent	Very good	Excellent	Poor	Poor	A,F,H,I,J
ATLAS 202021	190	60	20	Good	Very good	Very good	Excellent	Fair	Very good	Good	Good	Excellent	K
ATLAS 202221	180	65	22	Good	Fair	Good	Excellent	Very good	Very good	Good	Good	Excellent	K
ROPER RALLY A123	200	58	22	Very good	Very good	Very good	Poor	Fair	Very good	[3]	Poor	Excellent	C
ROPER RALLY A120	130	53	20	Very good	Excellent	Very good	Poor	Fair	Very good	[3]	Poor	Poor	C,D,H
MURRAY 22251	140	62	22	Good	Fair	Good	Excellent	Excellent	Fair	Good	Good	Poor	G
MTD LAWNFLITE 116062000	200	67	22	Good	Fair	Good	Excellent	Excellent	Fair	Fair	Good	Excellent	—

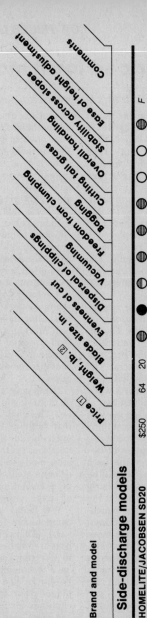

ATLAS 202001	130	55	20	○	⊜	⊜	◒	◒	◒	⊜	◒	●	D,H,K
CUB CADET 072	175	64	20	○	●	○	⊜	⊜	⊜	◒	○	⊜	—
MTD LAWNFLITE 116072000	200	64	20	○	●	○	⊜	⊜	⊜	◒	○	⊜	—
SEARS Cat. No. 3801	180+	55	20	○	●	○	◒	⊜	⊜	○	●	⊜	A,C,F
SERVISTAR 21657	146	57	20	○	●	○	◒	⊜	⊜	⊜	◒	●	D,H
SERVESS 50	145	55	20	⊜	●	○	◒	⊜	◒	○	○	●	D
DYNAMARK 223511	200	56	22	○	○	◒	●	●	◒	⊜	◒	⊜	—
VULCAN 92226	149	61	22	○	◒	◒	●	◒	⊜	○	○	○	—
MTD LAWNFLITE 116050000	170	57	20	○	●	○	◒	○	●	⊜	○	●	D,H
DYNAMARK 200306	165	52	20	○	○	●	●	◒	●	⊜	●	●	D,H
GARDEN PRIDE 30226	200	66	22	○	●	●	◒	⊜	◒	○	○	○	—
LAWN CHIEF 53	200	67	22	○	●	○	◒	⊜	◒	◒	○	○	—
WHEELER GRAN PRIX WB20	130	55	20	⊜	○	○	◒	●	●	○	◒	●	D,H
VULCAN 90206	130	54	20	○	◒	◒	●	●	◒	⊜	●	●	D,H
WHEELER GRAN PRIX WDE22	170	59	22	○	◒	○	◒	●	●	○	○	⊜	—
AIRCAP MASTERCUT 6020	150	56	20	○	●	○	◒	●	◒	○	○	⊜	—
YARD-MAN 11053	173	55	20	○	●	◒	●	◒	●	⊜	◒	●	A,E,H,J,L
ROPER RALLY A100	120	50	20	⊜	●	○	●	◒	●	○	●	●	C,D,H,I
AIRCAP MASTERCUT 6022	175	62	22	○	●	⊜	◒	○	◒	●	○	⊜	—
SEARS Cat. No. 3800	120+	48	20	○	●	○	●	●	○	○	●	●	A,C,E,H,I
SERVISTAR 21658	190	69	22	○	●	●	◒	●	●	●	○	⊜	—

Rear-bagging models

MURRAY 21851	190	73	21	⊜	—	⊜	◒	⊜	⊜	◒	⊜	⊜	—
SEARS Cat. No. 3831	240+	57	20	○	—	○	⊜	⊜	⊜	[4]	◒	⊜	B,C,F,J,M

Ratings continued on next page

Ratings of low-priced lawn mowers
continued

Brand and model	Price [1]	Weight, lb. [2]	Blade size, in.	Evenness of cut	Dispersal of clippings	Vacuuming	Freedom from clumping	Bagging	Cutting tall grass	Overall handling	Stability across slopes	Ease of height adjustment	Comments
SEARS Cat No. 3830	$190+	57	20	○	—	○	⊜	⊜	○	[4]	◒	⊜	*B,C,E,J,M*
ATLAS 202141	195	71	21	○	—	○	⊜	⊜	⊜	◒	⊜	○	—
LAWN CHIEF 81	220	71	21	○	—	○	⊜	⊜	⊜	◒	⊜	○	—
WHEELER GRAN PRIX WRB21	200	71	21	○	—	○	⊜	⊜	⊜	◒	⊜	○	—
YARDMASTER WRB21	200	71	21	○	—	○	⊜	⊜	⊜	◒	⊜	○	—
AIRCAP MASTERCUT 9321	199	73	21	○	—	○	◒	⊜	○	◒	⊜	⊜	*J,M*
ROPER RALLY B110	200	75	22	⊜	—	⊜	◒	◒	◒	○	⊜	⊜	*M*
DYNAMARK 213504	255	67	21	○	—	○	◒	◒	●	○	⊜	⊜	—
GARDEN PRIDE 42216	199	71	21	○	—	○	◒	●	●	●	⊜	○	—

[1] *Prices for side-discharge models do not include grass catcher bag (approx. $25 to $30). Prices for rear-bagging models include bag.*

[2] *Weight includes grass catcher bag.*

[3] *Judged excellent in maneuverability but poor in handling on straight runs; high handles caused arm fatigue.*

[4] *Judged excellent in maneuverability but fair in handling on straight runs; plastic wheels tracked vaguely. (Also see Comment B.)*

FEATURES IN COMMON

All: have engine kill/manual restart that stopped blade within 2 sec. after deadman control was released; cut to within 1 in. on left side.

All rear-bagger models can cut to within 1 in. on right side.

Except as noted, all: have 3½-hp **Briggs & Stratton** engine; have rubber wheels; have grass-catcher bag with capacity of at least 1½ cu. ft.; produce 86 to 90 decibels of sound.

Except as noted, all side-discharge models have hinged discharge chute that lifts to attach grass-catcher bag.

KEY TO COMMENTS

A–No throttle control, a minor inconvenience.
B–As grass catcher filled, front wheels tended to lift, causing bag problems.
C–Plastic wheels; tended to slip when mowing across a slope.
D–3-hp **Briggs & Stratton** engine.
E–3-hp **Tecumseh** engine.
F–3½-hp **Tecumseh** engine.
G–Adjusters for setting cutting height were very stiff.
H–Wheels must be unbolted to adjust cutting height.
I–Discharge chute must be unbolted before attaching bag.
J–Quite noisy; produced 91 to 93 decibels.
K–Grass bag smaller than most (1 cu. ft.).
L–Current designation of this model is **11051,** according to manufacturer.
M–Optional deflector available to allow use of mower without grass bag (not tested).

---

that regard filled only about a fourth of the bag before clogging. In cutting tall grass, six to seven inches high, the side-discharge mowers had a huge advantage; they didn't have to be weighted down with a grass bag.

HANDLING. Models judged excellent in overall handling felt relatively light and nimble, and their handle was at a comfortable height. Models judged poor had a very heavy, trucklike feel.

We couldn't assign a single handling score to the *Roper A123* and *A120.* Their long, high handles made them easy to maneuver, but they were tiring to push on straight runs. A similar problem bothered the two *Sears* rear-baggers; on straight runs, their plastic wheels tracked vaguely. Also, when the bags of those *Sears* models reached three-quarters full, their front wheels tended to lift, making them wander.

With their bags empty, none of the mowers was judged likely to tip sideways when run across the slope of inclines up to 15 degrees. (The safest way to mow a slope is from side to side; there's less chance of your feet slipping forward into the machine or the machine rolling back into your feet.) Models with plastic wheels tended to slide sideways. Most of the side-discharge models, with 15 pounds of grass in their bags, remained reasonably stable.

RECOMMENDATIONS. Some of the better low-priced mowers would be fine, we think, for taking care of small or medium-sized lawns. They're "manual" mowers, to a certain extent, but they're not really hard to start and push.

The top-rated side-discharge model, the *Homelite,* gave as smooth a cut as we've seen from any mower, no matter what the price. But it's more than twice the price of two other side-discharge models, the *Murray 20221* and the *Aircap 4020,* which we consider good enough to be named Best Buys.

Among the rear-baggers, the *Murray 21851,* which lists at $190, left the best-looking lawn, if you don't count assorted clumps here and there. But any of the top eight rear-bagging models can do about as good a job as any of the others. All are priced at close to $200, but bear in mind that those prices include bags. If you want a bag with any of the side-discharge models, you'll have to pay another $25 to $30 above the price for the machine alone.

Riding lawn mowers

Condensed from CONSUMER REPORTS, June 1985

According to Consumer Product Safety Commission estimates, riding mowers have been implicated in tens of thousands of injuries every year. The CPSC data indicate that the odds of being injured by a riding mower are significantly higher than those of being injured by a walk-behind mower.

Until the industry's voluntary safety standard's requirements are strengthened, we can only point out the safest mowers among the models we tested.

SAFETY. All the tested mowers have an interlock that keeps the engine from starting when the mower is in gear or when the blade is engaged. And the blade in all stops quickly when the driver disengages it; within three seconds with most models.

Six mowers have a "deadman switch" built into the seat. If you fall off or climb off the seat without disengaging the blade, the ignition shuts off and the engine and blade stop. The *Snapper* has, instead of a deadman seat switch, a pair of safety pedals; when they're released, the blade stops.

We think the deadman control for the blade is most important, and we downrated mowers that lack it. Those include three models that have, instead of a deadman control, a couple of other safety switches. One switch shuts off the engine when you shift into reverse with the blade engaged. The other shuts off the engine if you remove the discharge chute. Six models have neither a deadman control nor the safety switches.

In the course of our mowing tests, we discovered that one of the most important controls on a riding mower is its clutch. A clutch that engages smoothly provides the control needed to start off safely and to maneuver close to obstacles. But most of the mowers had a clutch that was abrupt and difficult to control.

CUTTING. For most of our cutting tests, we used a field of lush rye grass clipped to a four-inch height. We set each mower's cutting height at two inches and ran it at a moderate speed—2½ mph, or as close to it as the gears would allow.

We mowed side-by-side swaths with a bit of overlap. A smooth, carpet-like cut was judged excellent; a generally uniform cut with only occasional irregularities was judged very good; and a slightly mottled appearance was deemed good.

We drove each mower, with its grass catcher in place, into progressively heavier and taller grass until the engine lost power and the machine choked on the clippings.

CONTROL. Steering should be light and responsive, with a predictable and comfortable feel. Models that shifted best had a positive feel from one gear to the next, and their indicators showed at a glance what gear was in use. Those judged fair shifted vaguely—so much so that we had to count detents from the neutral setting to determine which gear we had engaged.

These mowers have a leisurely top speed of 3½ to 5½ mph, and they stop fairly quickly by themselves when the clutch is disengaged. So brakes aren't an important safety component. But all the brakes were able to hold on a 15-degree uphill slope. Most were reasonably easy to modulate.

To pass the industry's standards test for stability, a mower with rider must not tip sideways at a slant of 20 degrees

Text continued on page 278

Ratings of riding lawn mowers

Listed in groups in order of relative safety; within groups, listed in order of estimated overall quality. Bracketed models are essentially similar. Ratings should be used in conjunction with the performance table on page 276. Prices are list; + indicates shipping is extra. Discounts may be available. D indicates model has been discontinued.

Brand and model	Price: Mower	Price: Grass catcher	Overall width: Without catcher	Overall width: With catcher	Noise [1]	Comments
■ *The following models have a deadman control.*						
✓ **TORO 56145**	$1500	$200	38 in.	41 in.	91 dBA	E,J
JOHN DEERE R72	1339	215	41	40	90	—
TORO 56125	1220	200	34	32	91	A,D,O,Q
SNAPPER 28085S	1275	240	33	46	92	F,M,O
■ *The following models lack a deadman control, but have safety switches to shut off engine if operator tries to mow in reverse or if discharge chute is removed.*						
WARDS CAT. No. 34538	1150+	160+	38	39	93	L,N,Q
(**MTD LAWNFLITE 135-504**	1190	165	33	33	91	C,L,N,Q
(**YARD-MAN 13514**	1189	165	33	33	91	C,L,N,Q
■ *The following models lack a deadman control.*						
SIMPLICITY 3108E	1629	249	39	45	92	—
D **SEARS Cat. No. 25563**	1000+	230+	38	45	96	H,K,T
J.C. PENNEY Cat. No. 4175	1100+	150+	39	46	89	H,K,N
MURRAY 5-30705	944	120	32	32	90	C,H,K,N,Q,V
DYNAMARK 3280-00	1120	135	33	33	90	C,G,P
D **SEARS Cat. No. 25617**	1100+	230+	39	46	92	B,I,K,P,T

Conditionally Acceptable

Brand and model	Price: Mower	Price: Grass catcher	Overall width: Without catcher	Overall width: With catcher	Noise [1]	Comments
■ *The following models are judged Acceptable only if user equips them with a counterweight of approx. 40 lb. to control mower's tendency to rear up dangerously when catcher is full. Both have a deadman control.*						
ARIENS RM830E	1399	249	40	41	90	J,O,T
HOMELITE JACOBSEN RMX-8E	1469	130	34	34	92	O,S,T,U
■ *The following model is judged Acceptable only if equipped with a* **Bolens 6910** *counterweight basket holding 4 concrete patio blocks of approx. 20 lb. each to control mower's tendency to rear up dangerously when catcher is full. This model has a deadman control.*						
BOLENS 831	1525	197	42	45	92	R

[1] *Decibel level measured at operator's ear.*

Keys to Ratings on next page

Keys to riding lawn mowers Ratings

FEATURES IN COMMON

All have: interlock to keep engine from starting in gear or when blade is engaged; blade brake; deflector for grass chute.

Except as noted, all: are side-discharge models; weigh approx. 300 to 400 lb.; have electric-start 8-hp engine; cut a 30-in. swath with single rotary blade; have cutting heights of $1^1/_2$ or 2 in. up to $3^1/_2$ or $4^1/_2$ in.; have 5- or 6-speed transmission that provides speeds from 1 or $1^1/_2$ mph to 4 or 5 mph.

KEY TO COMMENTS

A – 7-hp engine with separate battery charger instead of an alternator; requires monthly charging.
B – 10-hp engine.
C – Rear-discharge model.
D – Cuts 25-in. swath.
E – Cuts 32-in. swath.
F – Cuts 28-in. swath.
G – Cuts 32-in. swath with twin blades.
H – 3-in. maximum cutting height.
I – 3-speed transmission.
J – Faster top speed than most, about $5^1/_2$ mph.
K – Slower top speed than most, about $3^1/_2$ mph.
L – Faster low speed than most, about 2 mph.
M – Handlebar-type steering.
N – Brakes were somewhat abrupt.
O – Has pull-cord starter as backup to electric start.
P – Semi-pneumatic tires in front.
Q – Dump-type grass catcher.
R – Combination dump-type and bag-type grass catcher.
S – Catcher unit uses garbage can (not included in catcher kit) as receptacle.
T – Rigid catcher receptacles, which can accept bags.
U – Safety switch for discharge chute.
V – Manual-start model.

Riding lawn mowers: performance table

Excellent · Very good · Good · Fair · Poor

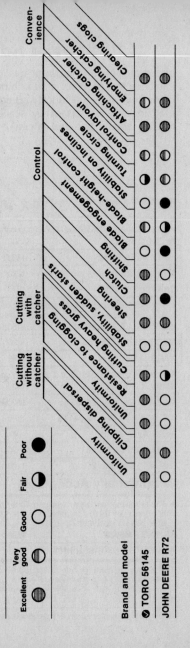

	Cutting without catcher		Cutting with catcher			Control									Convenience		
Brand and model	Uniformity	Clipping dispersal	Uniformity	Resistance to clogging	Cutting heavy grass	Stability, sudden starts	Steering	Clutch	Shifting	Blade engagement	Blade-height control	Stability on inclines	Turning circle	Control layout	Attaching catcher	Emptying catcher	Clearing clogs
✔ TORO 56145	Excellent	Excellent	Excellent	Excellent	Excellent	Good	Excellent	Excellent	Excellent	Good	Very good	Good	Fair	Very good	Excellent	Very good	Excellent
JOHN DEERE R72	Good	Excellent	Good	Good	Fair	Good	Excellent	Poor	Good	Poor	Fair	Poor	Very good	Very good	Excellent	Excellent	Excellent

TORO 56125	○	◒	○	◐	○	◒	○	◐	○	◐	◐	○	●	○	◒	◍	◍
SNAPPER 28085S	○	◐	○	◍	◐	◍	◒	◒	●	◐	◒	◒	◒	●	◐	◍	○
WARDS Cat. No. 34538	○	◒	○	◍	◐	◍	◒	○	◒	◐	◒	◐	◐	○	●	◐	○
MTD LAWNFLITE 135-504	◒	●	◐	◍	◐	◍	◒	○	◒	◐	◒	◐	◐	○	○	●	◍
YARD-MAN 13514	◒	●	◐	◍	◐	◍	◒	○	◒	◐	◒	◐	◐	○	○	●	◍
SIMPLICITY 3108E	◐	◍	◐	◍	◐	◒	◐	◒	◐	◐	●	○	◐	◐	◒	◍	◒
SEARS Cat. No. 25563	○	●	◐	◍	◐	◐	○	◐	◒	◍	○	◍	◍	◐	○	◐	◍
J.C. PENNEY Cat. No. 4175	◐	●	◐	●	●	◐	○	◒	◒	◍	○	◍	◍	○	◐	●	◒
MURRAY 5-30705	○	●	○	●	●	◐	○	◒	◒	◍	○	◍	◍	○	○	●	○
DYNAMARK 3280-00	●	●	◒	◒	◒	◍	◒	◐	◒	◍	●	○	◒	◒	[1]	◒	○
SEARS Cat. No. 25617	◐	●	○	●	●	○	◒	●	◒	◐	◒	◒	●	○	○	○	◍
Conditionally Acceptable (see Ratings and story)																	
ARIENS RM830E	◐	◍	◐	◍	◐	●	◍	○	◍	●	◒	○	○	◐	◐	◐	○
HOMELITE JACOBSEN RMX-8E	○	◐	◍	●	●	●	◐	○	◐	◍	◐	◒	○	○	◐	◐	◍
BOLENS 831	○	◐	○	○	◒	●	◒	◒	◐	◒	○	●	◒	◐	◒	◍	●

[1] *Has tow-behind sweeper, not grass catcher.*

or tip backward at a slant of 30 degrees. All the mowers passed that test.

In a final stability test, we drove machines straight up a 15-degree slope. (Straight up and down is the safest path to follow with a riding mower; traveling across a slope isn't recommended.) Even with a full grass catcher, some mowers felt stable and secure. But others lost almost all their steering, as their front wheels barely touched the ground, and felt as though they were about to tip over backwards at any moment.

Auto alarm systems

Condensed from CONSUMER REPORTS, October 1986

Thieves can attack a car on many fronts. They can steal engine components, tires, hi-fi equipment, and loose possessions inside the passenger compartment. They can pick, jimmy, or smash they way through door and ignition locks. They can try to start the engine and drive the car off. Not even the best auto alarm system can stop serious thieves, but it might slow them down enough to send them in search of more defenseless victims.

SYSTEM DEFENSES. The command post of an auto alarm system is an electronic control module, which typically uses the car's electrical system for both power and the first line of defense: the doors. By tapping into the electrical system, the control module senses when the dome light goes on and infers that a door has been opened. It delays several seconds, waiting to be disarmed; if it isn't, it assumes the door has not been opened legitimately, and then sounds its siren.

The second line of defense in a typical auto alarm system is composed of separate switches guarding the car's trunk and hood (unless, as on some cars, they too activate a light when they're opened). Such switches are designed to set off the siren instantly when they detect tampering with the truck or hood. Occasionally, they're installed on the passenger doors as well, to sound the alarm if any door but the driver's is opened first.

A third line of defense is something that senses an attack if a door is *not* opened. It might be a motion detector or a vibration sensor, for instance, which would be activated if the car was jacked up or moved or if a window was broken.

Yet another line of defense is a device that disables the car's engine. Most engine disablers interrupt current to the starter or the ignition, making it impossible to start the car. Another type of disabler, which we found in one system, shuts off the fuel line to stop the car after it's been driven a hundred yards or so.

Many auto alarm systems must be professionally installed. They're generally more comprehensive and often more convenient than user-installed systems—and they're always more expensive. The 18 professionally installed systems that we bought ranged in price from $260 to $550. The eight do-it-yourself kits that we bought ranged from about $80 to $220. Those price differences can be partly explained by the time and effort expended in doing it yourself. Considering the difficulties experienced by our technicians, figure on spending the better part of a day if you're installing a full system.

Because auto alarm systems are component systems, what you get as a "system" varies. Sometimes you get all four of the defense elements described above. Sometimes you have to buy some components separately. When we had to buy components separately, we stuck to a single brand. If a brand didn't include an engine disabler among its components, at least as an option, we didn't include it in the test program. While there are many such systems on the market, they don't provide what we consider adequate protection.

CONVENIENCE. Some features that add to car security may go unused because they're considered too much of a bother. That's why, in our judgment, convenience is a critical issue with these alarm systems. Some state insurance commissions apparently think so, too. Car owners in Illinois, Massachusetts, and New York are eligible for a 5 to 20 percent discount on their comprehensive insurance premium, depending on the system installed. (Michigan and Kentucky are soon to be included.)

Passive systems are obviously the most convenient because they arm and disarm themselves automatically. Active systems require some extra action on the part of the user. It might be the turn of an extra key, the entering of code into a key pad, the press of a remote-control device, or the flip of a toggle switch. As the Ratings show, some systems combine elements of passive and active controls.

Another convenience factor concerns the time allowed for normal entrance and exit. Actually, it's of no concern with the best passive systems, which don't start to arm themselves until the last door is shut. (Those are described in the Ratings as having "passive door" arming or disarming.) But most systems expect users to do something within a set period of time. Some systems don't leave enough time; the *Pioneer PAS 100*, for example, gives drivers only five seconds to get in and turn on the switch.

Engine disablers that are an integral part of the alarm system, as a majority of ours were, are easier to use than disablers that have to be activated separately. Often, the person who installs the disabler is given the choice between interrupting the starter motor or the ignition system. Attaching it to the starter is generally simpler. On the other hand, attaching the disabler to the ignition may void the warranty on cars with computerized ignition systems.

The Ratings note other features. Hood locks were part of three of our systems that came with separate engine disablers; they're deadbolt locks operated by a special key in the passenger compartment. Many systems have little light-emitting diodes that show whether the system is armed or not; such LED indicators are much more convenient than the warning chirps that sound when some systems are arming. All but two systems have a valet mode, which lets you turn over your car to garage or parking attendants without revealing security secrets. Ten systems have a panic switch, which allows someone in the car to sound the alarm without opening a door. One option that we favor is a backup battery, which can supply power to the alarm in the event that a thief disables the regular car battery. (That provision is standard with the *Multi Guard*.)

When sounding off, the alarm systems emitted warbling or staccato wails in varying degrees of stridency. We measured their output with a sound-level meter held five feet in front of the car. Most put out sound in the range of 92 to 96 decibels.

INSTALLATION PROBLEMS. At the outset, we asked the systems manufacturers for names of dealers in our area. We then sent out CU staff members, acting as

Ratings of auto alarm systems

Listed by types; within types, listed in order of estimated quality. Models judged equal in quality are bracketed and listed alphabetically. Except as noted, all have sirens that produced between 92 and 96 decibels at 5 ft. from front of car. Unless otherwise indicated, all do-it-yourself models lacked minor installation hardware. Prices of dealer-installed models are the total costs charged to CU shoppers. Prices of do-it-yourself models, including all parts bought separately, are list. D indicates model has been discontinued.

Excellent	Very good	Good	Fair	Poor
● (striped)	● (half-striped)	○	◒	●

Brand and model	Price	Convenience	Time limits (entry/exit, sec.)	Arming/disarming methods	Integral disabler [1]	Intrusion sensor	Features	Comments
Professionally installed								
CRIMESTOPPER HP2501	$399	Excellent	0-28/[3]	Passive door/passive	✓	Vibration	B,C,D,E	*C,D,E*
CLIFFORD SYSTEM III	550	Excellent	30/[2]	Passive door/ active remote	✓	Vibration	B,C,D,E	*A,B*
ALPINE 8101	400	Very good	0-45/5-45	Passive door/ active keypad	✓	Vibration, motion	B,C,D	*E*
MAXIGUARD P-1000; MAXI-LOK TUBAR 480	370	Very good	5-30/60	Passive/passive	—	Motion	A,C,D	*F*
TECHNE UNGO TL1600	485	Very good	[3]/32	Passive/active remote	✓	Vibration, motion	B,C,D,E	*B,I*
THUG BUG AVENGER 1001; 0825; 0826	450	Good	0-24/40	Passive/active keypad	✓	Motion	B,C	*A,F*
PARAGON KD6550; KPS9200	550	Good	13/65	Passive/passive	—	Optional	C,D	—
D VSE DIGIGUARD VS8200	450	Very good	5-30/60-180	Passive/active keypad	✓	Motion	B,C,E	—

CODE ALARM 1085	325	⊜	3-30/3-60	Passive/active keypad	✔	Optional	B,C,D,E	*A*
CHAPMAN-LOCK GENERATION III SYSTEM 400	375	⊜	11 or 18/60	Active key/active key	✔	Motion	A,B,C	*A,G*
Ⓓ MULTI GUARD MGB II	300	○	0-21/60	Active toggle/ active toggle	✔	Vibration	C,E	*A,G,H*
WATCHDOG TROOPER [4]; BM707R	260	○	12/55	Passive/passive	—	Vibration	C,D	*A,G*
ANES PRO 900; HL PRO 10	472	◒	15/110	Passive/passive	—	Sound	A	*A,K*
PIONEER PAS200; DISABLER	324	●	2-25/30	Active toggle/ active toggle	✔	Ultrasonic	C	*A,F,J*
HARRISON 7119; 7828	281	⊜	17/70	Passive/passive	—	Optional	C,D	*G,I*
AUTOMOTIVE SECURITY PRODUCTS K400-FS	455	○	16/45	Active keypad/ active keypad	✔	Optional	B,C,E	*G,L*
MCDERMOTT AK012; KP-1	467	●	13/30	Active toggle/passive	—	Motion	C,E	*G,J*
Do-it-yourself systems								
CRIMESTOPPER CS9502; CS8003	221	⊜	0-28/[2]	Passive/passive	—	Vibration	B,C	*M*
VSE THEFTRAP VS7810; SURESTOP VS3600	170	⊜	11/15	Passive/passive	—	Vibration	B,C	—
AUTO PAGE MA/07S	165	⊜	[3]/46	Passive/active remote	✔	Resonance	C	*B,N*
AUDIOVOX AA9135; AA7007	140	○	13/60	Passive/passive	—	Ultrasonic	A,C,D	*G,P*
Ⓓ SEARS Cat. No. 5980	100	◒	10 or 18/45	Passive/passive	—	Motion	—	*G,I*
ANES KD5000	99	●	14/55	Active toggle/ active toggle	✔	Motion	C	*A,G*
PIONEER PAS100	100	●	5/30	Active toggle/ active toggle	✔	Vibration	C	*G,J*
WOLO 612-XP	82	●	15/150	Active toggle/ active toggle	✔	Motion	C	*O*

[1] *If disabler is not integral with system, it will entail another step in arming/disarming procedure.*
[2] *No time limit; system arms when last door closes.*
[3] *No time limit; system disarms by remote control.*
[4] *Also sold as do-it-yourself model.*

Keys to Ratings on next page

Keys to auto alarms Ratings continued

KEY TO FEATURES
A-Hood lock.
B-LED indicator.
C-Valet mode.
D-Panic switch.
E-Backup battery.

KEY TO COMMENTS
A-Hood and trunk switches are extra-cost option.
B-Remote transmitter can arm and disarm system from outside car.
C-Needs battery to power memory; inconvenient to replace.
D-Parking lights flash when alarm sounds.
E-Override switch allows car to start if engine disabler malfunctions.
F-Headlights flash when alarm sounds.
G-Alarm stops too soon, after only 1 cycle, if entry point is left ajar.
H-Backup battery is standard.
I-Siren emits chirp at start of arming cycle.
J-Siren quieter than most.
K-Paging device beeps when alarm sounds.
L-Fuel-line cutoff switch acts as engine disabler as well as ignition cutoff.
M-All installation hardware was included.
N-Siren emits chirp at end of arming cycle.
O-Once triggered, alarm sounds until turned off or until battery is drained.
P-Hood lock installation judged relatively difficult.

ordinary consumers, to have the systems installed in their cars. But it seems that many of the dealers who were selected no longer handled the systems requested. Often, though, they tried to steer our staffers to "superior" and more expensive brands or models.

Our confidence in dealer installations was further diminished when we began receiving reports of wildly disparate installation fees. True, we had been alerted by manufacturers that fees might vary because installing a system might be trickier in some cars than in others. But our staffers got the different quotes for the same system in the same car. In one case, the installation charge doubled, from $125 at one shop to $250 at another. Clearly, in this product area, it pays to shop around.

Finding competent installers proved difficult, too. Two of the eighteen systems that we had installed in cars were plagued with false alarms and had to be completely dismantled and reinstalled. Other systems, we learned, had pieces missing, off-brand components used in defiance of our instructions, and unordered components added. Altogether, half our systems exhibited problems serious enough to require a second trip to the installer.

RECOMMENDATIONS. Of the dealer-installed systems we tested, we liked best the *Crimestopper HP-2501* (which cost us $399 installed) and the *Clifford System III* ($550 installed). Both arm themselves passively and have a lot of useful features. The top do-it-yourself systems were the *Crimestopper CS9502* ($221 list) and the *VSE Theftrap* ($170 list). But like most of the do-it-yourself kits, the *Theftrap* was missing some hardware needed for installation.

Auto-battery chargers

Condensed from CONSUMER REPORTS, February 1985

All of the tested chargers are for use on 12-volt batteries, which are the kind almost universally employed in modern cars. Most can also charge 6-volt batteries. The 10-amp models are claimed to be "automatic." The less powerful models are admittedly "manual," in that they should be monitored and

Text continued on page 284

Ratings of auto-battery chargers

Listed in groups by charging capacity; within groups, listed in order of overall quality based primarily on charging speed and performance. All tests were done at 12 volts. Prices are suggested retail; + indicates that shipping is extra. [D] indicates that model was discontinued at original publication. Discounts are generally available.

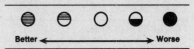

⊜ ⊖ ○ ◒ ●

Better ←→ Worse

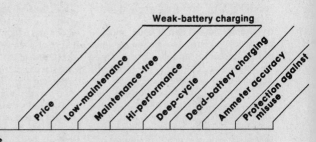

Brand and model	Price	Weak-battery charging: Low-maintenance	Weak-battery charging: Maintenance-free	Weak-battery charging: Hi-performance	Weak-battery charging: Deep-cycle	Dead-battery charging	Ammeter accuracy	Protection against misuse
10-ampere models								
▪ *Except as noted, the following 7 automatic models took 1½ to 3 hr. to charge a weak battery and 10 to 11 hr. to charge a dead battery: but most did not cut off completely when battery was fully charged.*								
✓ **SEARS Cat No. 71826**	$60+	⊜	⊜	⊜	⊜	⊜	◒	⊜
SCHUMACHER SE50M	70	⊖	⊜	⊖	⊜	⊜	⊜	○
ATEC BC91090	55	⊖	⊜	⊖	⊖	⊜	◒	⊜
CHRISTIE CA10	81	⊖	⊖	⊖	⊖	⊜	⊜	○
SCHAUER CRMF612	69	⊖	⊖	⊖	⊜	⊜	○	○
SOLAR 1014	50	⊖	⊖	⊖	⊖	⊜	○	○
[D]**RAY-O-VAC ROV10MA**	90	⊖	⊖	⊖	○	⊖	◒	○

6-ampere models

The following 7 manual models took 3 to 4 hr. to charge a weak battery and 15 to 17 hr. to charge a dead battery.

SEARS Cat. No. 71827, $35+; **CHRISTIE C6,** $52; **SCHUMACHER SE86,** $46; **SOLAR 1006,** $30; **ATEC BC91094,** $37; **SCHAUER B6612,** $44; [D]**RAY-O-VAC ROV6,** $52.

4-ampere models

The following 5 manual models took 4 to 5 hr. to charge a weak battery and 22 to 24 hr. to charge a dead battery.

SCHUMACHER SE84, $40; **ATEC BC91193,** $32; [D]**RAY-O-VAC ROV4,** $49; **SCHAUER A6612,** $39; **CHRISTIE C4,** $45.

Ratings continued on next page

Ratings of battery chargers continued

3-ampere model

The following manual model took 7 to 8 hr. to charge a weak battery and more than 24 hr. to charge a dead battery.

SOLAR 1003, $25.

FEATURES IN COMMON
All: weigh 12 lb. or less; measure at most 9 in. high, 11 in. wide, and 9 in. deep.

turned off by hand to prevent overcharging.

OVERCHARGING. When left on, most of the battery chargers—including most of the automatic models—overcharged the batteries. That can be especially damaging to a maintenance-free battery. Overcharging tends to boil off a battery's electrolyte, making it necessary to add distilled water. But many maintenance-free batteries have cells that are sealed and can't be topped off.

The manual units overcharged the quickest because their final charging current was higher than that of the automatic chargers. In most cases, the automatics tapered their current to zero or near zero as the batteries became charged.

SPEED. Most 10-amp models recharged weak batteries within 1½ to 3 hours; dead batteries within 10 to 11 hours. The 6-amp units needed 3 to 4 hours to recharge weak batteries and 15 to 17 hours to revitalize dead batteries. The weaker units took even longer.

Low line voltage took its toll on nearly all the chargers. It increased charging time for the 10-amp units by up to an hour and a half. The 6- and 4-amp units were also slowed.

RESISTING ABUSE. To round out our tests, we started doing everything wrong. We attached the clips to the wrong terminals, plugged the units into the electrical outlet before attaching their clips to the battery, and hooked the clips to each other. Most units produced sparks, but circuit breakers cycled off to protect user, charger, and battery.

When abused, two 10-amp chargers—the *Sears* and the *Atec*—did the best thing possible; they refused to turn on. In similar circumstances, two other units—the 6-amp *Ray-O-Vac* and the 4-amp *Christie*—failed permanently.

RECOMMENDATIONS. It's possible to live out all your driving days without really needing an auto-battery charger. But if your car gets only occasional exercise, if you live in an area where the winters are very cold, or if you have a lot of powered yard and recreational equipment, a charger may justify its cost.

Garage-door openers

Condensed from CONSUMER REPORTS, July 1985

Most garage-door openers use a bicycle-type chain and sprocket to hoist and lower the door; the chain is usually combined with a length of cable. Some models may use a narrow plastic strap instead of a chain. A third type uses a worm-screw drive. In our tests, we found no drive type to be inherently superior.

All 18 tested models are designed to

fit overhead doors with tracks—either solid, one-piece doors or hinged, segmented doors. Most models can also be installed on a trackless door; with a few brands, a special trackless-door version is available instead.

All the models passed our safety checks, which are in accord with Underwriters Laboratories standards. To qualify for the UL safety seal, a garage-door opener must automatically reverse if the door hits something while descending (except within an inch off the ground) or if for some other reason it can't manage to close the door within 30 seconds.

Indeed, all 18 of the garage-door openers we tested would work satisfactorily under normal circumstances. We found that the meaningful differences were chiefly features and conveniences.

Every model lets you operate the door by hand, as you'd have to do if the opener breaks or the power fails. To disconnect the door from the opener, you pull the disconnect cord, detaching some or all of the trolley from the motorized drive. A six-pound tug did the trick with most models.

CONVENIENCE. A wall switch, which you mount near the garage's entrance to the house, is standard equipment with a garage-door opener. So is one radio transmitter (a cigarette-pack-size unit that sends a coded signal to open or close the door). Additional transmitters may be bought for an extra $20 to $35.

The number of switches on the transmitter and the receiver determines the number of codes available. Eight two-position switches, for example, allow 256 (2^8) settings—which should be plenty to protect against someone breaking in by cracking the code. Nine three-position switches, found in a few models, allow 19,683 (3^9) settings. Most models have easy-to-set slide or rocker switches that can be changed over and over, if need be.

The transmitters run on a nine-volt battery. Most have a handy battery-strength indicator for trouble shooting.

Each opener automatically lights up the garage when you open or close the garage door. The light stays on for at least two minutes—ample time to park and get into the house. The Ratings note which lights can also be controlled independently at the wall switch and which wall switches are themselves lit for easy recognition in the dark.

Some models have a "vacation switch" on the receiver that makes it ignore signals from the transmitter. That's a convenience that may add to your sense of security when you're away. But by turning off the power to the opener, you can achieve the same effect. A key switch, which lets you work the garage-door opener from the outside, is available for most models as an option, at about $15. It can be handy, too, but it weakens security.

INSTALLATION. By one recent estimate, homeowners install four out of every five garage-door openers sold these days. (A professional may charge from $75 to $125.) The job should take four or five hours and calls for a screwdriver, a hammer, a few wrenches, a quarter-inch drill and assorted bits, a pair of pliers, a tape measure, and a step ladder. An assistant is also a big help.

Most models require some assembly. Typically you must bolt three or four rail sections together and attach the power head. A few models come fully assembled or with an assembled rail; they save an hour or two in installation time. All but a few models come with all the hardware needed to install them.

Before installing an opener, check the garage door itself. If you can't move it freely by hand, an opener won't perform well. To check the balance of a

Text continued on page 288

Ratings of garage-door openers

Listed in order of estimated overall quality; bracketed models were judged equal and are listed alphabetically. All models were judged satisfactory in opening and closing a properly balanced double-width garage door. Prices are list; + indicates that shipping is extra. D indicates that model has been discontinued.

◍	⊖	○	◒	●
Better ←				→ Worse

Brand and model	Price	Price of extra transmitter	Type of drive	Horsepower	Speed	Autoreverse sensitivity	Ease of assembly	Battery indicator	Independent light	Lighted wall-switch	Vacation switch	Door types	Comments
NORELCO GENIE GS940	$255	$30	Strap	1/2	◍	⊖	○	—	✓	✓	✓	A,B	*N*
MOORE-O-MATIC 838	199	35	Screw	1/3	◍	◒	⊖	✓	—	—	—	A,B	*B,C,E*
STANLEY 2200	185	35	Chain	1/3	◍	○	○	—	—	—	—	A,E	*D*
STANLEY 3200	195	35	Chain	1/2	◍	◒	○	✓	—	—	—	A,F	*D*
CHAMBEBRLAIN 350	150	30	Chain	1/3	⊖	○	○	✓	✓	✓	✓	A,B	*H*
CHAMBERLAIN 550	190	30	Chain	1/2	◒	○	○	✓	✓	✓	✓	A,B	*H*
D SEARS CAT. NO. 53400	225+	30+	Chain	1/3	⊖	○	○	✓	✓	✓	✓	A,B	*H*
SEARS CAT. NO. 53500	255+	30+	Chain	1/2	⊖	○	○	✓	✓	✓	✓	A,B	*H*
OVERHEAD TOUCH 'N GO 55A	169	25	Chain	1/3	⊖	◍	◍	✓	✓	—	—	A,B	*A,F,I,K,N*

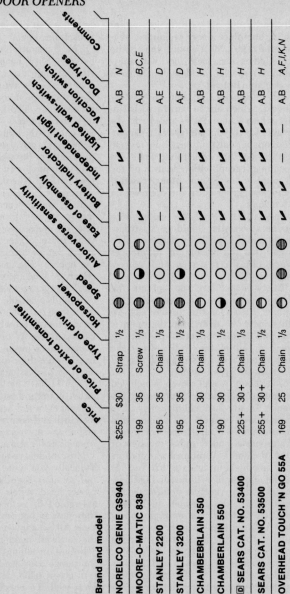

NORELCO GENIE GS850	220	30	Screw	1/3	○	⊜	◒	—	—	—	—	A,B	*M,N*
OVERHEAD TOUCH 'N GO 2000	240	25	Screw	1/3	○	⊜	⊜	✓	✓	—	—	A,B	*A,E,F,I,K,N*
MOORE-O-MATIC 727S	169	35	Chain	1/3	○	●	●	✓	—	—	—	A,C	*C*
CHAMBERLAIN 150	120	30	Chain	1/4	⊜	○	○	✓	—	✓	—	A,B	*G,H*
SEARS CAT. NO. 53100	135+	30+	Chain	1/4	⊜	○	○	✓	—	✓	—	A,B	*G,H*
CLOPAY 8100	185	20	Screw	1/3	○	○	⊜	✓	—	—	—	A,D	*B,F,J,K*
STANLEY 4100	185	35	Screw	1/3	◒	○	●	✓	—	—	—	A,B	*D*
NORELCO GENIE GS250	150	30	Strap	1/4	○	⊜	○	—	—	—	—	A,B	*G,L,N*
CLOPAY 2100	100	20	Chain	1/3	○	⊜	○	✓	—	—	—	A,D	*F,G,I,K*

FEATURES IN COMMON
All: come with 1 radio transmitter; automatically reverse when closing door is obstructed; can be controlled to stop or reverse a closing door; require 2 to 3 in. clearance above highest rise of door for installation; have a built-in light; have a time-delay switch that keeps light on for at least 2 min. after door starts to move.
Except as noted, all: require assembly, judged easy; provide key switch and key disconnect, features that allow operation without transmitter, as optional extras.

KEY TO DOOR TYPES
A – Fits sectional or 1-piece door with tracks.
B – Fits 1-piece trackless door.
C – Model **727J**, similar to model tested, fits 1-piece trackless door.
D – Requires extra-cost kit to fit 1-piece trackless door.
E – Model **2205**, similar to model tested, fits 1-piece trackless door.
F – Model **3205**, similar to model tested, fits 1-piece trackless door.

KEY TO COMMENTS
A – Comes completely assembled, which facilitates installation, but package is more than 10 ft. long and may be hard to transport.
B – Comes with assembled rail, which facilitates installation, but package is more than 9 ft. long and may be hard to transport.
C – Light flashes while door is closing.
D – Light flashes after door hits obstruction and automatically reverses.
E – Judged slightly quieter than most.
F – No brackets provided for hanging power head from garage ceiling.
G – No cover for light bulbs.
H – Manual disconnect takes greater force than most to operate and cannot be locked in disconnect position; contrary to company's claim, reconnection not always automatic.
I – If door is obstructed while opening, motor must overheat before it shuts off.
J – Code-changing procedure for radio transmitter judged awkward.
K – Power-head cover must be removed to change code, judged an inconvenience.
L – Fewer codes available than with others.
M – Can be wired so light stays on as long as door remains open.
N – No key switch or key disconnect available.

sectional door, raise it three or four feet and let go. If it doesn't stay still, it's out of balance, and the springs may need adjustment. That's a job for a professional, since the heavy springs are potentially hazardous.

RECOMMENDATIONS. All the tested openers worked well. The two models at the top of the Ratings got there not by being overwhelmingly superior, but by demonstrating small advantages and not possessing small inconveniences.

Concrete-floor paints

Condensed from CONSUMER REPORTS, March 1985

A coat or two of paint can help shield a concrete floor from oil, gasoline, and other stain-producing spills that a bare floor might absorb. And it can help hold down the dust that unpainted concrete floors seem to generate.

Applying paint to a smooth concrete surface is simple enough, though preparing the floor can entail some tedious, messy preliminaries (wire-brushing or sanding loose powder from the surface, scrubbing out oil stains with an appropriate solvent, vacuuming the surface meticulously clean). But getting the paint to stay down is another matter.

Concrete is inherently hard to paint because it changes in so many ways as it ages, or "cures." Even under ideal conditions, newly cast concrete needs a minimum of four weeks' curing time before it can take a coat of paint. Most paint manufacturers recommend treating bare concrete with muriatic acid to etch the surface so the paint will adhere well. As a nod to those recommendations, we bathed half of each test panel with muriatic acid and left the other half untreated. But since muriatic acid is one of the most hazardous products you can have around the house, we hesitate to recommend that etching procedure unless you've had some experience in handling strong acids or unless you have a qualified professional to do the work. (A safe alternative to acid-etching is time: If you're planning to paint an outdoor surface, you may want to let it go for a year or so, to let foot traffic and rain etch the surface.)

PERFORMANCE. After only two weeks, some paints on our outdoor walkway showed considerable degradation, usually in the form of blistering. The blisters were particularly noticeable on the concrete that hadn't been treated with muriatic acid. By contrast, the indoor walk looked almost as good as new after three months—even though it had seen heavier traffic. All the paints adhered better to acid-treated surfaces than to untreated ones.

The two epoxies were the best in adhesion, and the *Moore's* latex was nearly as tenacious. None of the oil-based paints adhered as well as the epoxies or the latexes.

When their surfaces were wetted, the epoxies and the oil-based paints were slippery to the point of being a hazard. The latex paints were a good deal less slippery.

When we spotted painted panels with motor oil, antifreeze, and gasoline, none of the tested paints suffered from short-term exposure to the liquids. Motor oil left the paints unscathed even when allowed to sit on the panels overnight. Overnight exposure to antifreeze also did no permanent damage; some paints softened to varying degrees, but recovered completely after a rinse with water and an overnight rest. The latex

Text continued on page 291

Ratings of concrete-floor paints

Listed by types; within types, listed in order of estimated quality. Models judged equal are bracketed and listed alphabetically. Prices are list; + indicates shipping is extra.

⊜ ⊖ ○ ◒ ●

Better ⟵⟶ **Worse**

Brand	Price per gal.	Adhesion: Treated concrete	Adhesion: Untreated concrete	Finish [1]	Stain resistance: Gasoline	Stain resistance: Antifreeze
Epoxy paints						
PITTSBURGH PAINTS AQUAPON POLYAMIDE Gray/Tile Red/Vista Green	$28	⊜	⊜	G	⊜	⊜
SEARS EPOXY (5550 SERIES) Natural Slate/Conch Red/Fern Green	33+	⊜	⊜	G	⊜	⊜
Latex paints						
MOORE'S FLOOR & PATIO Light Gray/Terra Red/Green	17	⊜	⊖	E	○	◒
BALTIMORE PAINT GOLDEN PREMIUM FLOOR & TRIM Brushed Pewter/Tile Red/Arbor	20	⊜	○	F	○	○
DEVOE PORCH & FLOOR ACRYLIC Airplane Gray/Seminole Red/Green Fairway	20	⊜	○	E	○	○
LUCITE FLOOR Gull Gray/Morocco Red/Pine Green	16	⊜	○	F	○	○
STANDARD BRANDS A-1 CONCRETE & PATIO Scotch Gray/Tile Red/Patio Green	12	⊜	○	E	○	○
COLONY SATINTONE FLOOR & PATIO French Gray/Tile Red/Terrace Green	24	⊜	○	E	◒	○
COOK LOCKSTEP FLOOR Blue Shale/Tile Red/Brier Green	21	⊜	○	E	◒	○
FULLER O'BRIEN FLOOR Light Gray/Tile Red/Patio Green	20	⊜	○	S	◒	○
TRU-TEST SUPREME FLOOR PORCH & PATIO Dark Gray/Tile Red/Spruce Green	18	⊜	○	S	○	◒
WARDS FLOOR & PATIO (1301 SERIES) Pewter Gray/Tile Red/Tile Green	14+	⊜	○	F	◒	◒

Ratings continued on next page

Ratings of concrete-floor paints continued

Brand	Price per gal.	Adhesion: Treated concrete	Adhesion: Untreated concrete	Finish [1]	Stain resistance: Gasoline	Stain resistance: Antifreeze
Oil-based paints						
STANDARD BRANDS A-1 FLOOR Medium Gray/Tile Red/Patio Green	$12	⊖	◒	G	⊖	⊜
WARDS FLOOR & PATIO (1400 SERIES) [2] [3] Pewter Gray/Tile Red/Tile	14+	⊖	◒	G	◒	⊜
PITTSBURGH PAINTS FLOOR & DECK [3] Dixie Gray/Tile Red/Meadow Green	19	⊖	◒	G	◒	⊖
TRU-TEST SUPREME POLYURETHANE FLOOR Dark Gray/Tile Red/Spruce Green	20	⊖	◒	G	◒	○
MOORE'S PORCH & FLOOR [3] Light Gray/Terra Red/Green	18	⊖	●	G	⊖	⊜
COLONY FLOOR & DECK French Gray/Tile Red/Terrace Green	24	◒	●	G	⊖	⊖
COOK SCUFFPROOF FLOOR Blue Shale/Tile Red/Brier Green	22	⊖	●	G	○	⊖
GLIDDEN SPRED URETHANE FLORENAMEL [3] Harbor Gray/Tile Red/Tile Green	25	⊖	●	G	◒	⊖
BALTIMORE PAINT GOLDEN PREMIUM FLOOR & TRIM Sky Gray/Spanish Tile/Tile Green	21	⊖	●	G	○	◒
FULLER O'BRIEN FLOOR & DECK [3] Light Gray/Tile Red/Patio Green	21	⊖	●	G	◒	○
DEVOE PORCH & FLOOR ALKYD-URETHANE [4] Airplane Gray/Seminole Red/Green Fairway	21	○	●	G	⊜	⊖
SEARS PORCH & FLOOR (5500R SERIES) [5] Natural Slate Gray/Conch Red/Emerald Green	16	○	●	G	◒	○

[1] *G = Gloss; E = Eggshell; F = Flat; S = Satin.*

[2] *Needed 5 hr. to dry tack-free.*

[3] *Permanently stained by gasoline.*

[4] *Price is for gray or red; green is $26/gal.*

[5] *Available only in Sears retail stores.*

OTHER TEST RESULTS

Slipperiness: All epoxy and oil-based paints were judged very slippery when wet. All latex paints were judged much less slippery when wet.

Drying time: All epoxy and most oil-based paints were dry to the touch (tack-free) in 4 hr. All latex paints were tack-free in 15 min.

Foot traffic: All paints were resistant to foot traffic when dry.

Stain-resistance: All were judged excellent in resisting motor-oil stains. Except as noted, all recovered overnight from gasoline and antifreeze spots.

paints tended to spread a little more easily than the oils and to penetrate somewhat better.

Though not nearly so hazardous as muriatic acid, the epoxies should still be treated very cautiously. If you fail to handle them precisely as their instructions recommend, the solvents and resins in the paints could irritate your skin, eyes, or respiratory tract. Until dry, epoxies emit fumes that are potentially toxic; they should be applied only where there's good cross ventilation and a breeze or some other plentiful source of fresh air.

When applied at the standard spreading rate, all the tested paints did an adequate job of hiding the bare concrete.

RECOMMENDATIONS. Your choice of a concrete-floor paint will be easiest if the floor is sound and will rarely be exposed to water. Virtually any of the paints we tested should work satisfactorily without resorting to muriatic-acid etching, and you can shop for the paint that has the best price. For outside use, choose among those with relatively good wet adhesion.

The toughest finish you can put on a concrete floor is a two-package epoxy. And, although we didn't test the epoxies for what happens when hot automobile tires are parked on them, we would judge that they're the paints of choice for garage floors. But the epoxy paints are rather slippery when their surfaces are wet, and their raw fumes can be hazardous.

If you don't require a glossy finish, a latex paint is doubtless the best choice. Latex paints go on easily and dry quickly. Their resistance to water is very good, and they're not very slippery when wet.

Interior latex paints

Condensed from CONSUMER REPORTS, May 1985

As a rule, glossier finishes cost a bit more than flat ones. Price, however, is a poor guide to determining if a paint will be easy to apply, spatter little, and cover and wear well.

In the Ratings, descriptions of gloss are based on our observations, rather than on label statements, which were frequently inaccurate.

HIDING POWER. The Ratings give our judgments of the hiding power of each paint in both one and two coats. With one coat, some of the paints covered only the first and lightest stripe on our hiding chart; those paints merited only a "1" in one-coat hiding power in the appropriate Ratings column. Several of the blue paints hid the chart's fourth stripe with one coat; those paints earned a "4" in one-coat hiding. All the paints hid more of the chart with two coats, although some hid only the second or third stripe, earning them only a "2" or "3" mark in two-coat hiding.

OTHER PROPERTIES. Some paints faded considerably when exposed to ultraviolet light. In general, the glossier paints were easier to clean. We also scrubbed the panels of paint to see which brands could stand up to harsh treatment with an abrasive cleaner.

RECOMMENDATIONS. Choose your color before you choose a brand. Look in the Ratings for the color you want and check the hiding ability of the various brands. (Note that the brands are listed alphabetically.) And, depending on the type of room you're painting, check for other properties that seem particularly appropriate.

Ratings on next page

Ratings of interior latex paints

Listed alphabetically. Branded-related properties apply to all colors tested. Colors cited by CU parade under a variety of brand-connected names (e.g., green as "Quintessence" and "Celery," among others); a few color names had been superseded at original publication, but whether that indicated a change in paint formulation was uncertain. Gloss judged by CU. Hiding scores ranged from 0 to 6 (worst to best, see story). Prices are list; custom colors may be higher. D indicates that the brand line was discontinued at original publication.

Excellent	Very good	Good	Fair	Poor
⊜ (Excellent)	⊖ (Very good)	○ (Good)	◒ (Fair)	● (Poor)

Brand line	Price per gallon	Gloss [1]	Ease of stain removal	Scrubbing resistance	Spatter resistance	White: Hiding—1 coat/2 coats	White: Fade resistance	Green: Hiding—1 coat/2 coats	Green: Fade resistance	Yellow: Hiding—1 coat/2 coats	Yellow: Fade resistance	Blue: Hiding—1 coat/2 coats	Blue: Fade resistance	Pink: Hiding—1 coat/2 coats	Pink: Fade resistance	Gold: Hiding—1 coat/2 coats	Gold: Fade resistance	Comments
BENJAMIN MOORE REGAL AQUAVELVET	$18	L	Excellent	Good	Good	1/4	Excellent	2/6	Good	1/2	Good	2/6	Excellent	1/3	Excellent	1/3	Poor	D,H,J
BENJAMIN MOORE REGAL WALL SATIN	14	F	Good	Fair	Good	2/6	Excellent	2/6	Excellent	1/5	Fair	3/6	Excellent	2/6	Excellent	2/6	Poor	F,I
DEVOE REGENCY HOUSE	21	L	Excellent	Good	Good	1/3	Excellent	2/6	Excellent	1/3	Fair	3/6	Good	2/6	Excellent	2/6	Poor	E,I
DEVOE WONDER-TONES	17	F	Good	Fair	Excellent	2/6	Excellent	2/6	Excellent	1/5	Fair	5/6	Excellent	2/6	Excellent	2/6	Good	J
DUTCH BOY DIRT FIGHTER LOW-LUSTRE	21	L	Excellent	Good	Good	1/4	Excellent	1/5	Very good	1/3	Fair	2/6	Excellent	1/4	Excellent	2/6	Good	B,H,J
DUTCH BOY DIRT FIGHTER FLAT	17	F	Good	Fair	Fair	1/2	Excellent	1/3	Fair	0/1	Fair	1/4	Very good	1/3	Excellent	2/6	Excellent	H
FULLER O'BRIEN FULLERGLO	16	S	Excellent	Excellent	Fair	1/2	Excellent	1/5	Excellent	0/1	Poor	2/6	Excellent	1/2	Excellent	1/3	Excellent	B,C

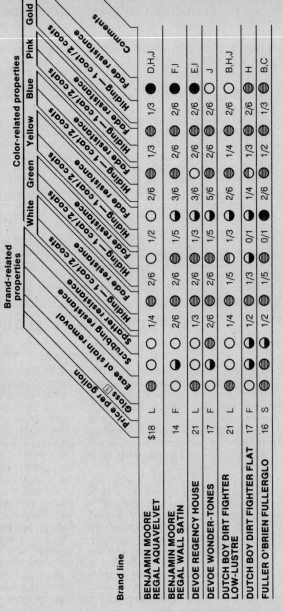

FULLER O'BRIEN LIQUID VELVET	16	F	○	◒	⊖	2/6	◍	2/6	◍	1/2	◒	2/6	◍	1/2	◍	1/5	◍	—
GLIDDEN COLOR NATURALS	20	L	⊖	○	⊖	1/3	◍	2/6	◍	1/3	◒	2/6	◍	1/4	⊖	2/6	○	F,I
GLIDDEN SPRED SATIN	16	F	○	◒	⊖	1/3	◍	1/4	○	1/3	●	2/6	◍	1/3	◍	2/6	⊖	F
KELLY-MOORE ACRY-PLEX	20	F	◍	○	⊖	1/2	◍	3/6	◍	1/2	◒	3/6	◍	1/4	◍	2/6	◒	J
KELLY-MOORE SAT-N-SHEEN	18	E	◍	⊖	⊖	1/2	◍	2/6	◍	1/2	●	3/6	◍	1/4	◍	2/6	●	B,I
K-MART THE FRESH LOOK FLAT	14	F	○	◒	◒	1/4	◍	1/3	◍	1/3	●	2/6	◍	1/4	⊖	1/4	◒	E
MAGICOLOR SATIN PLUS FLAT	15	F	◒	◒	○	1/4	◍	3/6	○	2/6	⊖	3/6	◍	—	—	3/6	◍	E
PITTSBURGH PAINTS MANOR HALL	16	L	◍	○	◒	2/6	◍	3/6	⊖	1/5	◒	4/6	◍	2/6	◍	3/6	⊖	—
PITTSBURGH PAINTS WALLHIDE	13	F	⊖	◒	○	1/3	◍	2/6	◒	1/3	●	2/6	◍	1/4	◍	2/6	⊖	F
PRATT & LAMBERT ACCOLADE	23	L	◍	○	◍	2/6	◍	2/6	◍	1/5	◒	2/6	◍	2/6	◍	1/2	○	A,G
PRATT & LAMBERT VAPEX	18	F	○	○	◍	2/6	◍	2/6	◍	2/6	◒	3/6	◍	2/6	⊖	1/2	○	—
SEARS EASY LIVING MATTE FLAT (9300 SERIES) [2]	16	F	⊖	◒	○	1/3	◍	1/4	◒	1/4	◒	1/2	◍	2/6	○	2/6	○	F
SEARS EASY LIVING SATIN FLAT (9100 SERIES) [3]	17	L	◍	○	○	2/6	◍	2/6	◒	1/5	◒	2/6	◍	2/6	○	3/6	○	B,I
SHERWIN-WILLIAMS CLASSIC 99	18	F	◍	◒	○	1/3	◍	1/5	◍	1/2	●	2/6	◍	2/6	◍	2/6	◍	—
SHERWIN-WILLIAMS SUPERPAINT	21	L	◍	◒	◒	2/6	◍	3/6	◍	1/5	●	4/6	◍	2/6	◍	2/6	◍	—
TRU-TEST SUPREME E-Z KARE	18	F	◍	◍	◍	1/5	◍	2/6	◍	2/6	●	4/6	◍	2/6	◍	3/6	◍	B
[D]TRU-TEST SUPREME SAT-N-HUE	15	F	○	◒	○	1/3	◍	1/3	◍	2/6	●	3/6	◍	2/6	◍	3/6	◍	—
VALSPAR OUR BEST QUALITY	16	F	◒	◒	◒	1/4	◍	2/6	◍	1/4	●	2/6	◍	1/5	◒	1/5	◒	F,I
VALSPAR PREMIUM	18	L	◍	○	●	1/3	◍	2/6	◍	1/3	●	2/6	◍	1/3	◒	1/3	○	F
MONTGOMERY WARD CUSTOM COLOR SERIES 4696	18	L	⊖	◍	○	1/2	◍	2/6	◍	1/4	◒	3/6	◍	1/4	◍	1/3	◒	B,K
MONTGOMERY WARD GREAT COAT SERIES 4200	15	F	◒	○	○	2/6	◍	2/6	◍	1/4	◒	2/6	◍	1/4	◍	2/6	◒	K

[1] *F = flat; L = low-luster; E = eggshell; S = satin.* [2] *Designation changed to* **9400 series.** [3] *Designation changed to* **9200 series.**

Keys to Ratings on next page

Keys to Ratings of interior latex paints

OTHER PERFORMANCE JUDGMENTS

Brand-related properties. All were judged excellent in ease of rolling. Except as noted, all were judged excellent in resistance to sticking after drying.

Color-related properties. All whites, blues, and pinks were judged excellent in color retention after scrubbing. Except as noted, all greens and golds were judged excellent in color retention after scrubbing, and all yellows were judged good in color retention after scrubbing.

KEY TO COMMENTS

Resistance to sticking:

A - Very good.
B - Poor.

Color retention after scrubbing:

C - Green, very good.
D - Green, fair.
E - Yellow, excellent.
F - Yellow, very good.
G - Yellow, good.
H - Yellow, fair.
I - Gold, very good.
J - Gold, good.
K - Gold, fair.

Extension ladders

Condensed from CONSUMER REPORTS, May 1985

An extension ladder is essentially two ladders combined. One, the base section, rests on the ground. The other, the fly section, slides up and down; typically, it's moved with a rope and pulley. Locks on one of the fly section's rungs keep the ladder extended.

To find the "standing height"—the maximum distance between the feet of the base section and the highest rung on which it's safe to stand—you have to allow for the overlap of the two ladder sections and the "unusable" top three rungs. Those allowances bring the standing height of a typical 24-foot ladder down to something less than 18 feet (down to about 9½ feet for a 16-foot ladder and about 25½ feet for a 32-footer). To figure out how far your feet will actually be above the ground, you'll also have to take into account the angle of the positioned ladder (ideally about 75° from horizontal). That accounting will locate your feet from 6 to 14 inches lower than the standing height, reducing the useful elevation of a nominal 24-footer to about 17 feet. To that height, add your own height and reach to find if a ladder meets your needs.

Most extension ladders are graded in three duty ratings: Type 1 (industrial), rated at a 250-pound load; Type II (commercial), 225 pounds; and Type III (household), 200 pounds. Keep in mind that the values are nominal, because the duty-rating standards call for a safety factor of four. Thus, ladders within the three types should be able to withstand maximum loads of 800 to 1000 pounds—well beyond the forces exerted by a normal climber, providing he or she doesn't generate extra forces by stomping on the rungs.

Ladders that conform to the requirements of Underwriters Laboratories (UL), the American National Standards Institute (ANSI), and the Occupational Safety & Health Administration (OSHA) are labeled to indicate that they meet the duty-rating standards.

RIGIDITY. For the 24-foot models at full extension, the best medium-duty, Type II ladders received average (and satisfactory) marks in resisting ladder motion. The best light-duty, Type III's gave a busier sensation, flexing and jiggling more. Most of the heavy-duty, Type I's were easily the steadiest.

Text continued on page 297

Ratings of extension ladders

Listed by duty-rating types; within types, listed in bracketed groups in order of estimated overall quality; within groups, listed in order of increasing price. Except for mail-order models, prices are mfr. suggested retail; + indicates shipping is extra.

⊜ ⊖ ○ ◒ ●

Better ←→ Worse

Brand and model	Price	Weight (lb.)	Standing height (ft./in.) [1]	Rigidity: Back-and-forth	Rigidity: Side-to-side	Ease of raising	Rung comfort	Rung traction	Comments
24-ft. Type II (medium-duty) ladders									
■ *The following 10 models are of the type CU recommends for 24-ft. ladders, as they represent a sensible compromise in rigidity, weight, and price.*									
WARDS CAT. NO. 6922	$120+	32	17/7	○	○	◒	⊖	⊖	I
WERNER D1224	126	33	17/7	○	○	◒	⊖	⊖	I
LOUISVILLE CLE24	130	36	17/9½	○	○	○	⊖	○	D,G
J.C. PENNEY Cat. No. 0242	130+	33	17/7	○	○	◒	⊖	⊖	E,I
FLINT VIKING	146	33	17/7¼	○	○	○	⊖	○	A,D,L
KELLER 3524	160	36	17/8½	○	○	⊜	⊖	○	F
WHITE METAL HEARTSAVER	140	30	17/9¾	◒	○	⊜	○	⊜	B,C,F,G,H,J
SCRANTON 1500-24	140	34	17/7	○	○	●	⊖	○	D,J
SEARS Cat. No. 42715	150+	32	17/9¾	◒	○	⊜	○	⊜	B,C,F,G,H,K
LINCOLN XMD24	175	33	17/10	○	◒	○	⊖	○	—

Ratings continued on next page

Ratings of extension ladders
continued

24-ft. Type I (heavy-duty) ladders

■ *The following 14 "contractors' " models are of a type that is generally heavier and more expensive than a 24-ft. ladder need be. However, the greater rigidity of models of this type may be a deciding factor in the selection of longer (say, 32-ft.) ladders.*

(**WARDS CAT. NO. 6903,** $150+; **WERNER D1524,** $160; **WHITE METAL ENDURALIGHT,** $175; **FLINTLITE,** $177; **J.C. PENNEY CAT. NO. 3931** [2], $180+; **SEARS CAT. NO. 42805,** $190+; **HOWARD 1153 ALUMAWOOD,** $200; **LINCOLN PR24,** $200; **KELLER 4024,** $230); (**GOLD MEDAL MDE24,** $155; **LOUISVILLE CDE24,** $170); (**FLINT YANKEE** (wood), $128; **GOLD MEDAL GEL24** (wood), $132; **SCRANTON 2000-24,** $140).

24-ft. Type III (light-duty) ladders

■ *The following 8 models are of a type that may not be rigid enough or feel secure enough for many users of 24-ft. ladders. However, the lighter weight and lower price of models of this type may be deciding factors in the selection of shorter (say, 16-ft.) ladders, which need less load-bearing strength to maintain rigidity and feel adequately secure.*

(**WERNER D1124,** $90; **WARDS CAT. NO. 6915,** $100+; **WHITE METAL EASYLIGHT,** $120; **KELLER 3224,** $140; **HOWARD 3050D,** $145); (**SCRANTON 1000-24,** $100; **FLINT SPARTAN 24,** $110); **LINCOLN WM24,** $145.

[1] *As measured by CU. Measurement is length from base of ladder to highest rung on which it is advisable to stand.*

[2] *Designation changed to* ***5886.***

KEY TO COMMENTS

A – No certification label, but CU's tests indicate that ladder would meet load-capacity requirements of standards.
B – Base and fly sections do not separate.
C – Box-shaped rungs.
D – Metal ladder lacks end caps at top of base section.
E – Designation changed to **Cat. No. 5951**.
F – Fly section slides in back of base section; judged slightly more convenient when ascending and descending or raising and lowering ladder.
G – Has limit lugs or stops to prevent fly section from being raised too far.
H – Has wall-wheels instead of end caps.
I – Rope forms closed loop; judged harder to grip for raising than with most others.
J – Sheet-metal rung-lock tongue bent out of shape or became loose enough to jam during use-tests.
K – Rung locks judged to have greater potential for malfunction than most.
L – Rung locks produced high friction as they moved past rungs, increasing effort required to raise ladder.

Our panelists judged the light-duty 16-footer that we sampled just about as rigid as the sturdiest 24-footers. On the other hand, the light-duty 32-footers shook so much when fully extended that some panelists were scared to climb them more than half-way.

CONVENIENCE. Most extension ladders are assembled so that the fly section rides in front of the base section with respect to the wall. Our testers preferred models with the fly in back because the transition while climbing or descending from one section to another was easier to make.

A ladder's size and weight assume critical importance when it comes to setting it up—wrestling it to the right spot on the ground, heaving it upright, and then raising the fly section to the proper height before easing it into position. With some of the taller and heavier ladders, our 110-pound tester simply couldn't manage the whole job alone. Our larger panelists could, although raising a long ladder can be such a strain of balance and control that anyone would be glad to have a helping hand.

The fly-in-back models were easiest to raise and lower because the rope hangs in front of the ladder. On a fly-in-front model, the rope hangs in back and can be harder to use.

RECOMMENDATIONS. Your first consideration in selecting an extension ladder will be its length. You don't want to pay for more ladder than you need. Most householders, we think, should do nicely with a 24-foot model. If you can get by comfortably with a 16-footer, all to the good. If you really need a 32-footer, so be it.

Personal computers

The IBM-PC computer & compatibles

Condensed from CONSUMER REPORTS, October 1985 and March 1986

For extensive business or professional work performed at home—work that requires a lot of typing, filing, or financial analysis—many people have good reason to choose the *IBM-PC* or a computer that's "compatible" with it, that is, one that will run the same programs that the *IBM-PC* will run. Not only do such people have general use for a computer with a large memory and at least two disk drives, they often have a specific need for a computer that can run the same IBM-compatible programs and read the same IBM-compatible data files that are used at the office.

The reason that many people don't buy the *IBM-PC* itself is that *IBM*-brand equipment tends to be more expensive than the equipment of IBM imitators—and not necessarily better. Indeed, some products of the imitators show improvements over the IBM originals in design particulars.

In all, we tested nine IBM-compatibles. Four of them —the *Compaq*, the *Kaypro 16*, the *Sanyo MBC-775*, and the *Panasonic Sr. Partner*—are "transportable" models; their components fold into a box about the size of a suitcase. The other five compatibles—the *Epson Equity I*, the *Kaypro PC*, the *Leading Edge Model D*, the *Tandy 1000*, and the *Zenith Z-148*—are desk-top models.

Equipped with 256K of memory, two disk drives, monitor, and a port for a printer, the compatibles ranged in discount price from $1350 for the *Leading Edge* to $2000 for the *Compaq*. A similarly configured *IBM-PC* would cost about $2100 at discount. (An *Apple Macintosh* prepared for the same level of work would cost $2400.)

MEMORY AND DRIVES. A memory of 256K (or some 256 *thousand* of the informational units known as bytes) has become standard memory for the *IBM-PC* and compatibles—since some popular word-processing and business programs require at least that much memory. And extra memory is always welcome, since it can simplify work with larger files, such as mailing lists and book-length manuscripts. The memories of all the tested units may be expanded to 640K for $200 or less.

As a minimum, two floppy-disk drives are all but essential for serious computer applications. Disks are used to store both programs and the data created with those programs. Unless a machine has at least two drives, you have to swap the program and data disks back and forth frequently in order to manipulate the large quantities of information used by big programs and data files. Each of the tested computers were equipped with two 360K-capacity floppy disk drives. That's adequate for most home offices.

But in more and more business offices, *IBM* users are moving to hard disk drives for convenience and greater operating speed. Those can hold so much information, 10 or 20 megabytes (that is, *millions* of bytes), that you can copy onto them all the programs that you regularly use and still have room for large data files, such as long mailing lists. Hard disk drives also let you manipulate large files much faster than is possible with floppy disks. A hard disk drive bought as an option adds about $500 to the price of a system.

IBM-COMPATIBILITY. There are hundreds of business programs available for the *IBM-PC*. No one uses hundreds of programs, of course; three good programs—for word processing, filing, and spread sheets—are enough to run a typical small business, and one or two selected programs might suffice for the concerns of a home office. But to take advantage of the choice offered by such a large software library, an IBM-compatible must be able to run all, or at least most, of the available programs without a lot of difficulty.

To check for IBM-compatibility, we tested each computer with 10 well-known programs designed to run on the *IBM-PC*. Our test library included two word-processing programs, *Microsoft Word* and *WordStar*; two highly regarded integrated spread-sheet programs, *SuperCalc 3* and *Lotus 1-2-3*; a real heavyweight database management program, *dBase III*; an outlining program called *ThinkTank*; a touch-typing drill called *Mastertype*; a home accounting program called *Managing Your Money*; and two versions of the aviation game *Flight Simulator*.

Most of the IBM-compatibles ran all those programs without difficulties. The *Leading Edge Model D* hit a snag while running an early version of *Flight Simulator*, but the error was harmless and easily correctable; Version 2 of *Microsoft Word* required a "patch" program from Leading Edge to get it running. The *Tandy 1000* ran all the programs, but it didn't seem perfectly suited for *ThinkTank* and *Flight Simulator*. Those programs utilize the plus and minus keys on the *IBM-PC* keypad, and the *Tandy* doesn't have those separate keys. We learned by experimenting, though, that we could substitute other keys. The *Sanyo* also failed to run *Mastertype* and stumbled on the early version of *Flight Simulator*.

A number of IBM-compatibles "bundle" programs into the selling price. If those programs are close to what you want—and they may include word-processing, spreadsheet, and filing programs that would otherwise sell for $100 to $400 apiece—the bundled package can be attractive. But if your goal is to acquire the latest and best from that big IBM library, then the value of bundled programs, which aren't always first rate, may diminish. Even the compatibles that aren't bundled with special programs come with the necessary "disk operating system" designed by Microsoft (MS-DOS) and patterned after the IBM disk operating system (PC-DOS). And all but the *Zenith* come with some form of the programming language known as BASIC.

DISPLAYS. The buyer of an *IBM-PC* usually chooses between two plug-in circuit boards. The *IBM Monochrome Display and Printer Adapter* board ($250) produces very sharp text, ideal for word processing. The *Color/Graphics Monitor Adapter* board ($244) produces color monochrome graphics, but only with medium resolution. Thus the text that it displays is comparatively coarse and hard on the eyes. Until fairly recently, IBM offered no way to get both graphics and high-resolution text within a single program. *IBM-PC* owners could, of course, buy both boards, but that would oblige them to buy two monitors as well, a monochrome monitor for sharp text and a color monitor for graphics and games.

The computer aftermarket—an aggressive sub-industry that attempts to capitalize upon every lapse by the computer manufacturers—was quick to contrive solutions to the dilemma of *IBM-PC* owners. The solutions appeared in the form of combination boards. But they can come at a shockingly steep price.

One board that we've looked at is the *Hercules* ($499), which combines high-resolution text with high-resolution monochrome graphics, close to the ideal solution. However, not all programs can be set up to recognize the *Hercules*. Another aftermarket board that we've looked at is the *STB Chauffeur* ($395), which produces sharp text but only medium-resolution graphics—more or less duplicating the performance of the two single *IBM* boards. Still another board represents IBM's belated effort to jump into its own aftermarket. Its *Enhanced Graphics Adapter* presumably provides high-resolution color graphics and text, but requires both a high-priced color monitor to derive maximum benefit.

Many IBM-compatibles offer even fewer display choices than the *IBM-PC*. Among those we tested, the *Kaypro 16*, the *Panasonic Sr. Partner*, the *Sanyo MBC-775*, the *Tandy 1000*, and the *Zenith Z-148* come with merely the equivalent of the medium-resolution graphics board. Unfortunately, various peculiarities in the hardware make it either impossible or fruitless to substitute or add a monochrome or aftermarket board. That means that, with those models, you can show monochrome graphics but must settle for a text display that's not very attractive or sharp. You can also show color on the *Sanyo*; it has a built-in RGB-color monitor. (All the other models come either with a monochrome monitor or—in the case of the *Epson Equity I*, the *Tandy*, and the *Zenith*—no monitor at all.)

The *Compaq* comes with both monochrome and graphics configurations installed. With some programs, it switches automatically between text and graphics. Otherwise, you can toggle back and forth between the two modes with a keyboard command. Like all transportable models, the *Compaq* has a small built-in monitor; it measures only nine inches diagonally. Some users may find that a bit too small.

The *Epson Equity I* is nominally sold with no display circuitry, as well as no monitor. Our sample came bundled with an optional *Epson Color Video* board ($149) that emulates IBM's medium-resolution graphics board. To see sharp text with the *Epson* you would need to substitute or add a monochrome board such as the *Epson Monochrome* ($129) or perhaps one of the aftermarket combination boards.

The *Kaypro PC* comes with a high-resolution monochrome monitor driven by a combination graphics and text board. The text display was excellent. However, the *Kaypro* isn't equipped to display graphics on the monitor included with the machine. For that you would need a second, color or monochrome monitor, and even then you would get only medium resolution.

With its *Hercules*-like capability, the *Leading Edge* offers the most versatile display possibilities. It incorporates circuitry for both high-resolution text and monochrome graphics. It also supports medium-resolution color, so you can display color on a separate color monitor, if you want to add one.

KEYBOARDS. Since its introduction, the *IBM-PC's* unconventional and often inconvenient keyboard has suffered criticism. Its shortcomings have, in fact, generated a thriving trade in aftermarket keyboards of improved design. Unfortunately, the designers of some compatible computers continue to copy IBM's flawed lead.

The *Leading Edge* keyboard lacks independent cursor-control keys but otherwise remedies most deficiencies of the IBM keyboard in one way or another. The *Epson*, *Tandy*, and *Zenith* keyboards were also improvements, in our judgment. The *Tandy* has separate cursor-control keys and 12 function keys, compared with the *IBM's* 10. The *Compaq* and *Kaypro* keyboards felt a little less crisp than the *IBM's*. The others were comparable.

PORTS AND SLOTS. Peripheral equipment such as printers must be connected to the computer through what are called ports. IBM followed the lead of *Apple II* computers by including spare expansion slots inside the central processing unit. Those slots are used to plug in a variety of accessory boards. Most IBM-compatibles have them as well. Commonly, the slots accommodate display circuit boards, printer-interface boards, or internal modems.

The IBM-compatibles that provide the most room for expansion are the *Leading Edge* (with four standard long slots free), the *Kaypro PC* (with three long and three short slots free), and the *Compaq* (with three long slots). The *IBM-PC* itself has three open board slots. The *Epson* has four slots in all, but one is needed for the monitor display and another is only for the manufacturer's memory upgrade. The *Sanyo* and the *Tandy* have two slots, but the *Tandy's* are only 10 inches long—not long enough to accept many boards made for the IBM-PC and compatibles. So, for some expansion needs, *Tandy* owners may be limited to using boards supplied by Radio Shack.

All the computers come equipped to accept a parallel printer, the type most likely to be used at home. The *Panasonic Sr. Partner* is unusual in that a small thermal printer is built in the housing. It's slow as printers go; it uses a roll of tear-off thermal paper; and its print quality is only fair. Despite its uses, it's not really an adequate substitute for the good-quality printer that most computer owners will probably want to add to their systems.

RECOMMENDATIONS. The Best Buy among IBM-compatibles, in our judgment, is the *Leading Edge Model D*. It comes with a high-resolution monitor and the circuitry necessary to display very sharp text as well as monochrome and color graphics. It's bundled with Leading Edge's own word-processing and spell-checking programs, which are good ones. And it has enough ports and expansion slots to build just about any computer system you might want in the future. We paid $1350 for our sample—some $250 to $700 less than for any of the other compatibles comparably equipped and about $750 less than for an *IBM-PC* configured for sharp text but without graphics.

Note that the distributor of the *Leading Edge* is one of the few sellers that has advertised our Ratings in deliberate defiance of CU's expressed request that no one use CONSUMER REPORTS for promotional purposes. Some buyers may wish to weigh the ethics of Leading Edge in making a buying decision.

If you want a computer that's fairly

easy to move from one place to another, consider the *Compaq Portable*. Like the *Leading Edge*, it delivers the excellent text display of the *IBM* monochrome board with the ability to switch to a graphics display as well. And it's well supplied with equipment ports and expansion slots. But make sure that you can work easily with the small screen that's typical of transportable models. We paid $2000 for the *Compaq*. That's about $100 under the discount price of similarly equipped *IBM-PC*, but still a hefty investment, considering the additional cost of software and a printer.

All the other IBM-compatibles performed all right. But only two of them—the *Epson Equity I* and the *Kaypro PC*—are capable of providing the sharp text display that's next to indispensable for serious business applications. Both models are relatively inexpensive. The *Epson* lists for $1424 with the monochrome board that's necessary for sharp text, but you have to make sure that you specify that configuration and, beyond that, you'll need a monitor that does justice to the display. That may cost $150 more, leaving you with a system that has no graphics capabilities. The *Kaypro PC*, which lists for $1595, comes complete with a monitor that shows off text to good advantage, but it can't display graphics either.

Commodore Amiga & Atari 520ST

Condensed from CONSUMER REPORTS, September 1986

The only major corporate survivors of the home-computer boom of the early 1980's—other than Apple—are Atari Inc. and Commodore Business Machines. In 1985, in a last-ditch effort to find something besides the purely professional or purely hobbyist niches for computers at home, the two companies introduced entirely new machines, the *Commodore Amiga* and the *Atari 520ST*.

(Actually, not long before that, Commodore had come out with its model *128*, an enhanced version of an old hobbyist's favorite. Our report on the *Commodore 128* begins on page 305.)

In price and in capabilities, the *Amiga* and the *520ST* attempt to straddle the two worlds of the cheap but fun and flashy "home" computer and the staid, sober, and suitably expensive "personal" or home/office computer. Both machines have obviously drawn for inspiration on the *Apple Macintosh* (reviewed in the report starting on page 312). Like the *Macintosh*, the *Amiga* and the *520ST* depend on the use of a mouse (a hand-held pointing device), menu windows (displaying choices available to the user), and iconography (symbols representing choices to be "clicked on" by the mouse). It's much easier to do than to describe—if the software is skillfully enough composed to take advantage of those "user friendly" devices. But to that largely graphic approach, Commodore and Atari have added lavish palettes of color. (The *Macintosh* cannot show color.)

Originally, it seemed, both companies tried to price their new models low enough to separate them from machines of the IBM stripe, most of which were then selling for close to $2000 with monochrome monitor. Commodore may have miscalculated at first. It set the *Amiga's* list price at $1295, but that was without an almost obligatory $500 color monitor. Later, the list price of the *Amiga* color system with one disk drive and 256K of random access memory (RAM) was reduced to $1095. (We've seen it discounted to $995.) The *Atari 520ST* with one disk drive, 512K RAM, and color monitor, lists for about $1000. (We've seen it discounted to about $750.) Meanwhile, though, competition has whittled away at whatever original price advantages those models may have enjoyed. Some IBM-compatibles began to appear with prices well under $1000, and versions of the *Macintosh* started going for close to $1600.

MEMORY AND DRIVES. We judged the *Amiga's* standard memory of 256K too limiting. Its operating system eats up 95K of RAM before any work program is loaded. The remaining 161K is plenty for most games, but when we loaded Commodore's *Textcraft* word-processing program, we found ourselves limited to producing documents of no more than four pages before running out of memory. Commodore offers a $200 upgrade card that boosts the machine's memory to 512K. We consider that upgrade all but essential for serious computer use.

The *Atari 520ST* comes with 512K of memory. In our first samples, however, the machine's operating system consumed a lot of it. A factory upgrade to later versions tucks the operating system out of the way in the machine's permanent read-only memory (ROM). That makes the *520ST* about equal in useful RAM with the upgraded *Amiga*. (Not long after the *520ST* came out, Atari introduced a "megabyte" offshoot, the *1040ST*, with more than 1000K of memory. It lists for about $1200 with a color monitor and for about $1000 with a monochrome monitor.)

The *Amiga's* one disk drive is double-sided and built into the main system unit. It can record up to 880K on a 3 ½-inch disk—the equivalent of about 300 typed pages. A second, external disk drive ($300 extra) can be connected through a port in the rear.

The *Atari's* single-sided disk drive, capable of writing 360K on a 3 ½-inch disk, is a separate, stand-alone unit. A double-sided disk drive, with a capacity of 720K, is available for an additional $300. (The *Atari 1040ST* comes with a built-in, double-sided drive.)

We ran a series of tests to gauge the useful calculating speed of each computer. The *Amiga* ran our BASIC programs very fast, considerably faster than an *IBM-PC* and about as fast as a good business-grade computer; writing to or reading from the disk drive was two to three times as fast as with an *IBM-PC*. The *Atari* processed information almost as quickly as the *Amiga*.

SOFTWARE PERFORMANCE. The graphics, color, and sound capabilities of the two new computers make them very fancy game machines indeed. In addition, the *Amiga* is capable of "multitasking," the ability to run more than one program at a time. As yet, not all programs for the *Amiga* take advantage of that ability.

Our *Amiga* came only with its operating system and a version of the Microsoft BASIC programming language, ABASIC. All the applications software we tested was bought separately. Commodore's *Textcraft* ($100) is a moderately full-featured word processor that makes good use of the mouse-and-icon pointing system. We tried two spreadsheets available for the *Amiga*. One, called *Unicalc* ($000), requires keyboarded commands. The other, *Analyze* ($000), works through the simpler icon-and-mouse arrangement. Both crunched numbers quite rapidly, if not as fast as a top spreadsheet program running on an *IBM-PC*.

Many video games have become

available for the *Amiga*. Those that we tried—*Hacker*, *Arctic Fox*, and *Skyfox*, among others—all displayed excellent color and sound. A drawing program that we looked at, *Deluxe Paint* ($100), taps the *Amiga's* highly sophisticated graphics abilities. Using the mouse, one can draw and fill in pictures in 32 colors, chosen from a palette of more than 4000 colors.

Included in the price of our newest sample of the *Atari 520ST* were two language programs (ST BASIC and LOGO), a word processor called *First Word*, and a "preview" version of a drawing program called *NEOchrome*. *First Word* makes good use of the drop-down menus, windows, and icons generated by the TOS operating system. On-screen functions go fairly fast. But certain "global" functions, such as reformatting a whole document, must be made paragraph by paragraph. The *Atari* spreadsheet we tried, *VIP Professional*, ran slowly and inefficiently, gobbling up big chunks of memory on its laggardly way.

The *Atari* games we played—including *King's Quest*, *Mudpies*, and *Time Bandits*—made excellent use of the graphics and sound potential of the *520ST*. In addition to the bundled *NEOchrome*, we tried another drawing program called *DEGAS* ($40). Neither proved as fancy or versatile as Commodore's *Deluxe Paint*, but both are impressive nonetheless. As many as 16 colors, from a palette of 512 colors, can be applied with the mouse in an impressive variety of brush sizes and fill patterns.

DISPLAY AND SOUND. The *Commodore* analog RGB monitor, model *1080*, that came with our *Amiga* can display 80 columns of text in its medium-resolution mode. The text, though readily legible, would be hard on the eyes over long periods, we feel. A high-resolution mode is available, but text displayed that way flickered disturbingly. The display was far better suited to games and paint programs.

The *Atari SC1224* analog RGB color monitor that came with our *520ST* was a cut above the *Amiga's*. It's text display, though also of only medium resolution, was more readable. We also looked at a monochrome *Atari* monitor, model *SM124*, which makes use of the *520ST's* high-resolution mode. That display was sharp enough for extended use, we judged, if not quite as sharp as an IBM monochrome display.

The *Amiga* has four electronic "voices" that it can reproduce over two channels. That gives it a potential stereo effect, which would require the addition of a stereo amplifier and loudspeaker to be realized. Another startling feature of the *Amiga* is a speech synthesizer that speaks typed words in either a male or female synthetic voice.

The *Atari* has three computer "voices" that it pipes over one channel. But it has no separate sound output. Instead, the sound comes out through the monitor speaker.

KEYBOARDS AND PORTS. The *Amiga* sports a full-size keyboard with standard typewriter layout, 10 function keys, separate numeric keypad, and a sensible diamond array of cursor keys on the right. The keyboard feel was very good.

The *Atari* keyboard is a part of the system unit, a low wedge-shaped affair. Above the typewriter layout is a slanted lineup of function keys. There's a separate numeric keypad, too, and cursor keys in a triangular pattern. But the keys felt soggier than the *Amiga's*.

Both computers come with one Centronics parallel and one RS232 serial port. Those ports, industry standards, let the machines run any standard brand of printer; the *Commodore* requires a special cable, though.

The *Atari* has a hard-disk interface, while the *Commodore* has a microprocessor bus output—a connector that allows installation of additioinal hardware such as a hard-disk drive or memory extensions

Both models have two joystick connections, and a TV output jack. The *Amiga* has two audio output jacks, for playing stereo. The *Atari* has a slot for plugging in program cartridges (if and when such cartridges become available) and MIDI (Musical Instrument Device Interface) ports for connecting a music synthesizer.

RECOMMENDATIONS. If the home-computer market can be reignited by entertainment values, the *Commodore Amiga* and the *Atari 520ST* (or *1040ST*) could be the machines to start the fire. They're easy to use and graphically dazzling. But whether the dazzle will actually make a difference to consumers remains to be seen. For the typical buyer, the decision may finally hinge on how well these computers perform the workaday tasks of dealing with words and numbers. And for those tasks, the color capability that makes these computers so attractive becomes a drawback. Their very dazzle obscures to some extent the words and numbers of practical programs.

From a technical standpoint, the *Amiga* outpoints the *Atari* simply because it has more of what makes both computers special—more colors in its color display, better animation potential, more voices, and more speed—and thus may appeal particularly to the "pro." Yet we lean slightly to the *Atari*. It's got plenty of color and sound and speed for ordinary home use. And its display is a lot better for prolonged text work. It enjoys a distinct price advantage, too. At latest check, not only does the color *520ST* system list for $300 less than a comparably equipped *Amiga* with the needed 512K of memory, but the *520ST's* price includes a fairly comprehensive starter set of applications software that the *Amiga* lacks.

The Commodore 128

Condensed from CONSUMER REPORTS, February 1986

A home computer, by our definition at least, is an inexpensive machine that's easy to use and runs a variety of educational and game programs as well as some slightly more businesslike programming having to do with word processing and money management. Few home computers survive—the *Apple II* family, the *Atari 800 XL*, and the *Commodore 64*—the majority having been shouldered aside by more powerful and more prestigious home/office machines (such as the IBM-compatibles discussed in the report beginning on page 298).

Apple cornered the best educational programs. Apple and Atari had the best games. But the *Commodore 64* has been the traditional favorite of hobbyists, who valued above all else its low price ($200 at any department store) for what seemed like a lot of power (64 kilobytes of memory at a time when most other computers could barely muster 16K). For those advantages, hobbyists were willing to overlook the *Commodore 64's* flaws: a limited screen display and, initially, a scarcity of programs.

Now Commodore has introduced a

new model, called the *Commodore 128*, which improves upon the old *64* in a number of ways. It has double the memory. It can run *Commodore 64* programs and CP/M programs, as well as programs written specifically for the *Commodore 128*. And it can produce 80 columns of text for word-processing and spread-sheet work.

PERFORMANCE. There are two central processing units inside the *Commodore 128*, which enable it to work like not two but three separate computers. When first powered up, the computer is in its "C128 mode," ready to run the small number of programs so far written for it. We tried using that mode with three word-processing programs—*Paperclip 128*, *WordPro 128*, and *Word Writer 128*. Only *Word Writer* produced text screens with varying margins (up to 80 characters) that approximated the appearance of the printed page. We also tried a spread-sheet program called *Swiftcalc 128*; it ran with acceptable speed.

As yet the software library available for the C128 mode is meager. But with simple keyboard commands, the computer converts to its C64 mode, in which it behaves exactly like a *Commodore 64*. So original owners of a *Commodore 64* can use their programs and files on the new machine, and newcomers will have access to the large library of "home-oriented" programs available for the *Commodore 64*.

Other keyboard commands put the *Commodore 128* under the control of a microprocessor that, in effect, turns it into a CP/M computer. In that mode, it gives access to the hundreds of business programs originally written for the CP/M operating system. We tried using it with two standard CP/M programs—*Wordstar* for word processing, and *Supercalc 2* as a spread sheet. Those programs ran, all right, but more slowly than on a standard CP/M machine such as a *Kaypro*.

The *Commodore 128* comes with an improved programming language called *Commodore BASIC Version 7*. Among other features, the new version generates "sprites" (movable objects on the screen), which make graphics easy to create and control. The machine also comes with a built-in sound synthesizer chip that can be activated with BASIC language commands or music-composition programs.

Connectors on the back of the *Commodore 128* allow hookups with a variety of display devices: a TV set, a composite color monitor, or a high-resolution RGB color monitor. But only the RGB port produces an 80-column signal, and most RGB monitors cost at least $500 to $700.

That leaves just a couple of practical choices for providing a satisfactory word-processing display. It's possible to connect a monochrome monitor to the RGB port using a $10 aftermarket cable, the *Cardco 128/80*. Perhaps a better choice for those who want both high-resolution color for games and educational programs and an 80-column display for businesslike programs is Commodore's own RGB monitor, the *1902* (at $300). We judged the 80-column display on both the monochrome and RGB monitors acceptably readable, though a trifle dotty in texture.

Commodore introduced a new disk drive, the *1571*, with the *128* computer. It can read and write disks in CP/M as well as in the two Commodore formats. Though faster than the old *1541* drive made for the *Commodore 64*, it's still a good bit slower than the standard drive for the *Apple IIc*, especially in writing data to disk.

The *Commodore 128* keyboard has all the keys of the *64's* keyboard in their familiar locations, plus a numeric keypad, eight function keys, and four cursor keys in a row at the top. The keys lack the crisp touch we've found on other keyboards, but the overall feel is still good.

Commodore provides only a proprietary serial port, for linking Commodore peripherals to the *128's* central processing unit in daisy-chain fashion. But a serial-to-parallel conversion interface, which turns the serial port into a parallel one, can be bought on the aftermarket for $50 or so. The advantage of a conversion interface is that it lets one reach outside the Commodore brand line for a better choice of printers and other peripheral equipment.

RECOMMENDATIONS. The *Commodore 128* would, in our judgment, make a nice step-up home computer for *Commodore 64* hobbyists. That is, they might well consider investing $300 in the *128* central processing unit and gradually replacing some software with versions that take advantage of the new model's expanded capabilities.

But scratch-built *Commodore 128*, system, including a *Commodore 1571* disk drive, a *Commodore 1902* RGB color monitor, and a decent printer, would cost in the neighborhood of $1100. For a low-priced home system, the *Atari 520ST* monochrome version would be a better choice. (See page 302.)

Apple IIe and Kaypro IIx computers

Condensed from CONSUMER REPORTS, August 1985

When the *IBM-PC* was introduced in 1981, it offered, in its expanded-memory versions, the opportunity to combine several programs into large, integrated, "office productivity" programs. The maneuver gave IBM a lead in the expanding office market and stranded a lot of decent little computers in the declining home market. In the ensuing shake out, many brand names became history, but a few popular little workhorses have kept chugging on.

One such computer, the *Apple IIe*, has an upgraded *Professional* model equipped with two disk drives and 128K of user memory (RAM). Another survivor is the portable *Kaypro IIx*, a leader in its day, like the *Apple II* series, and now the main inheritor of the huge body of mostly business and professional programs that were developed in the widely used CP/M operating system. Many time-tried CP/M programs require no more user memory than the *Kaypro's* 64K.

SOFTWARE. The *Apple* is sold with Apple's *BASIC* and operating system software only. You buy applications programs separately. One of *Apple's* appeals is that you can expand the range of the machine in many ways, including adding a Z-80 circuit card, which will give you access to *CP/M* programs.

There are many good word processors available for the *Apple*. Our readers have been especially well satisfied with *Word Juggler*, and the *Appleworks*, an integrated word processor, spreadsheet, and database. With the *CP/M* board added, you can also run *WordStar*.

The big name in database-management software is *dBase II*. But many find this a difficult program to learn and use. *Apple* users have expressed much higher levels of satisfaction with *Quickfile* and the combination of *PFS:File* and *PFS:Report*.

Bundled into the price of the *Kaypro* are programs for all likely small-business uses. In addition, there is a large number of similar (and sometimes better) programs available for the *CP/M* operating system.

WordStar, the program that often comes with the *Kaypro*, is not among the easiest word-processing programs to learn and use. It is, nevertheless, among the best.

The two spreadsheets that come with the *Kaypro* (*CalcStar* and *Profit Plan*) are second-rate examples of the type, judging by our readers' questionnaire responses and by our own struggles with these spreadsheets. If you expect to make heavy use of a spreadsheet, we recommend *SuperCalc* 2.

For filing, the combination of *Data Star* and *Report Star* comes in the package. The pair make a competent basic database-management system that works well with *WordStar*. And you can, of course, buy *dBase II* if you need heavyweight database management.

DISPLAYS. The 12-inch green-phosphor monitor that comes with the *Apple IIe Professional* is a separate unit that sits on top of the central processing unit. Although the *Apple* was able to deliver a legible display, the spacing of the scan lines on our *Apple* monitor lent the picture a certain "dottiness" that detracted from the overall effect.

The *Kaypro's* nine-inch green-on-black display was crisp and clear, although the far edges of the screen were a bit fuzzy. There's no external monitor jack to add an additional monitor with a larger screen, but the *Kaypro* display is about as good as any we've seen in a transportable computer.

DISK CAPACITY. The *Apple's* two drives are mounted in a low, separate horizontal enclosure that sits atop the system unit. The drives have a capacity of only 144K each—quite small by modern standards.

The *Kaypro's* two disk drives are mounted in the main system unit. These double-density, double-sided disk drives can handle 400K each, roughly equivalent to 200 typed pages. That's a lot, especially when one considers that the *IBM-PC's* drives have 360K.

KEYBOARDS. The *Apple's* 63-key keyboard is built onto the main system unit. That's a minor inconvenience for those who like to move the keyboard around. There's no integral numeric keypad, but you can buy a plug-in keypad separately for $100.

The *Kaypro's* keyboard is a detachable unit tethered to the machine with a coiled cord. During transport, the keyboard snaps onto the front of the machine to form a lid. The board has 76 keys, including a full numeric keypad. Cursor keys are located rather inconveniently at the top of the keyboard.

RECOMMENDATIONS. The *Apple IIe Professional* and the *Kaypro IIx* are dependable veterans with large libraries of available software and many user clubs whose members help each other along. The *Kaypro's* large disk capacity, built-in printer ports, and included software leads us to prefer it over the *Apple*, though not by much. At about the same price, however, you could bring home a *Leading Edge Model D* (see page 298), a very attractive *IBM-PC* clone at a very attractive price.

Can't find it?

The index on page 388 lists all reports in this issue both alphabetically and by subject.

Computer monitors

Condensed from CONSUMER REPORTS, July 1985

With a monitor, a computer isn't presented with the limitations of a TV tuner, so it can produce crisper signals. That allows the screen to display lines up to 80 characters (instead of 40) and thus mimic the final appearance of the printout on paper.

For a computer devoted to work, a monochrome monitor is all you are likely to need. Monochrome monitors are far less expensive than color monitors. And typically, though not invariably, monochrome monitors display 80-column text more clearly than color monitors do.

There are two common types of monochrome monitor. One type, introduced by IBM for its own personal computers, is called a Monochrome Display monitor—mainly to distinguish it from the other type, called "monochrome composite" monitors.

Games and educational programs don't absolutely require color graphics, but they are certainly enhanced by color. And there are certain specialized business and professional computer applications that absolutely do require color graphics.

Computer owners who need a color monitor have three basic choices:

First is a composite color monitor—similar to a color TV set in its limited resolution, but unable to receive a TV signal. Composite monitors are relatively inexpensive as color monitors go, and their display can offer some improvement over the display of the same signal routed through a TV tuner.

A second possibility is a monitor/receiver. As the name implies, it can both receive TV signals and produce computer-generated color graphics and—frequently—80 columns of text. A monitor/receiver could be the monitor of choice for computer owners who would rather watch TV where the computer is than use the computer where the TV is.

The third possibility is an RGB monitor. These are costly, high-resolution color monitors that can reproduce 80 characters of text clearly and provide the sharply defined color graphics necessary for a good display of tables and charts for business purposes or for using the computer as a design tool.

MONOCHROME MONITORS. The IBM Monochrome Display type achieves greater resolution than composite monitors, producing a text display that looks more like type than like an array of dots.

Not surprisingly, text looked better on most IBM Monochrome Display types than on composite monitors. Characters were more fully formed and the wide spacing between lines was more pleasing. But it's important to note here that you get that nice looking IBM text only when using an *IBM* or IBM-compatible computer with a *monochrome display* board. With a *color* board in the computer, you can reproduce monochrome graphics (Lotus 1-2-3 charts, for example), but you sacrifice the high-resolution text.

Ironically, the monochrome display sold under IBM's own brand name (the *IBM 5151*) appeared somewhat less crisp than the others of its type. It was about on a par with the best of the composite monochrome monitors. The *IBM 5151's* screen has long-persistence phosphors, which means that displayed text fades relatively slowly when the

Text continued on page 312

Ratings of computer monitors

Listed by types; within types, listed in order of estimated overall quality, based primarily on text and graphics appearance. Prices are list; deep discounts are generally available. D indicates that model was discontinued at original publication.

◍ ⊖ ○ ◒ ●
Better ⟷ Worse

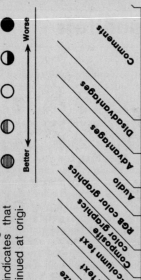

Brand and model	Price	Price paid	Weight	Measured screen size	80-column text	40-column text	Composite color graphics	RGB color graphics	Audio	Advantages	Disadvantages	Comments
IBM monochrome display-type monitors												
AMDEK VIDEO 310A	$230	$239	19 lb.	11¼ in.	◍	—	—	—	—	C,D	—	*C,H,I,R*
QUADRAM AMBERCHROME	250	189	19	11¼	◍	—	—	—	—	C,D	—	*C,H,I,R*
PGS MAX-12	249	189	25	11½	◍	—	—	—	—	—	—	*C,R*
IBM 5151	275	259	19	11¼	⊖	—	—	—	—	—	b	*C,S*
Monochrome composites												
AMDEK VIDEO 300	179	149	19	11¼	⊖	—	—	—	—	C,D	—	*H,S*
PANASONIC TR120M1PA	219	170	18	11½	⊖	—	—	—	✔	—	—	*B,H,S*
ZENITH ZVM123A	140	90	15	11½	○	—	—	—	—	C,E	—	*A,S*
ELECTROHOME EDM926	195	179	13	8½	○	—	—	—	—	—	—	*B,H,S*
NEC JB1201M(A)	179	149	16	11½	◒	—	—	—	✔	—	—	*B,H,S*

Color composites

AMDEK COLOR 300	349	269	24	13¼	—	⊜ [1]	⊜	—	✔	F,C	c	*J*
PANASONIC DTS101	339	269	16	10¼	—	⊜	⊜	—	✔	F,G	c	*B,H,K,L*
BMC BMAU9191U	370	289	26	13¼	—	○	⊜	—	✔	F	—	—
NEC JC1215MA	399	289	20	11¾	—	◒	⊜	—	✔	—	—	*B,H,K*
ZENITH ZVM131	379	310	35	13¼	●	◒	○	●	✔	—	—	*B,D,E,G,K*
[D] COMREX CR6500	399	279	26	13½	—	◒	◒	—	✔	—	—	*H*

Monitor/receivers

SEARS CAT. NO. 4084	340+	340+	27	13¼	○	⊜ [2]	⊜	◒	✔	E	—	*D,F,G,I,P*
PANASONIC CTF1465R	650	530	35	14	○	○	⊜	◒	✔	F	—	*B,F,G,H,K,N,O*
MITSUBISHI AM1301	520	449	31	13	○	○	⊜	○	✔	C	a	*G,J,K,M,N,P*
GE 13BC5509X	490	314	29	13	—	◒ [1]	⊜	—	✔	H	—	*B,K,Q*

RGB monitors

PANASONIC DTH103	749	599	21	10½	⊜ [3]	—	—	⊜	—	A,B,C, E,F,G	—	*E,F,G*
QUADRAM QUADCHROME II	599	519	30	12½	◒	—	—	⊜	—	C	—	*H*
IBM 5153	680	680	28	12¾	○	—	—	○	—	C,E	—	—
ZENITH ZVM136	799	629	32	13	○ [3]	—	—	◒	—	C	b	*D,G*
PGS HX12	695	489	28	11½	◒	—	—	○	—	—	—	*G,H*
AMDEK COLOR 700	649	519	28	13	◒ [3]	—	—	○	—	C	—	*D,E,H*

[1] *The* **GE** *and the* **Amdek Color 300** *yielded slightly improved graphics quality when their Luma/Chroma inputs were used.*

[2] *Judgment for the* **Sears** *is for its green-on-black mode.*

[3] *Differences in score between white-on-black and green-on-black modes were, in general, insignificant. Judgment for the* **Panasonic** *is for its reverse video mode (black-on-white), which was preferred.*

Keys to Ratings on next page

Ratings keys for computer monitors

KEY TO ADVANTAGES
A - Can be switched to reverse video.
B - Has swivel and tilt base for more-convenient viewing.
C - Has high-contrast screen.
D - Has matte-finish antiglare mesh over screen, which reduces glare significantly.
E - Has user control for adjusting height of display.
F - Has user control for centering display.
G - Has user adjustment for vertical centering.
H - Display width can be reduced by 10% to compensate for overscan.

KEY TO DISADVANTAGES
a - Cannot produce highlighted text, a significant disadvantage; can only reproduce 8 colors in IBM RGB signal; has annoying buzz in RGB mode even with volume at minimum.
b - Some users may find long-persistence screen annoying during scrolling.
c - Color and tint controls are inconveniently located.

KEY TO COMMENTS
A - Has 40/80 column switch.
B - Has a loop-through video input.
C - Designed to work only with **IBM PC** and **PC** compatibles.
D - Can be switched to green display.
E - Manufacturer says can directly reproduce color from RGB-equipped **Apple II** series computers with appropriate cable.
F - The "brown" in the 16 color IBM set displays as yellow.
G - RGB cable is optional accessory.
H - Display height adjustable with screwdriver (technician's adjustment).
I - Display centered with screwdriver (technician's adjustment).
J - Has headphone jack.
K - Has sharpness control.
L - Character mode judged of no advantage.
M - Has two sets of video/audio inputs.
N - Has a composite output derived from antenna (RF) signal.
O - Has a quartz tuner; full-function remote control; on-screen display of channel, time, and program source. Has a sleep timer, last-channel recall, and channel bypass; can receive 69 cable channels.
P - Has a varactor tuner.
Q - Has 2-knob mechanical tuner.
R - Amber display.
S - Green display.

---

screen changes. On that model, scrolling text left a "comet tail" that some of our testers found annoying. (The same effect occured on the *Zenith ZVM 136*.)

Among composite monochromes, the *Amdek Video 300* and the *Panasonic TR120M1PA* emerged as favorites. Even with fewer scanning lines than the IBM types (240 lines rather than 350 lines), their text looked quite sharp. Choose one of them for use with non-IBM computers.

COLOR MONITORS. In judging the various color monitors, we weighed their capacity to display both text and graphics. But note that the judgments for composite graphics are on a different scale from that for RGB graphics (RGB graphics are almost always sharper. Likewise, the judgments for 80-column text are not directly comparable to those for 40-column text.

Monitor/receivers are, in effect, composite monitors with a TV tuner. They differ from ordinary TV sets in that signals from a computer need not pass through the tuner.

RGB monitors take their name from the red, green, and blue color signals they use to display their wares. Their prices usually start around $500. The RGB video signal can have a broader bandwidth than a television video signal, since the color information doesn't have to be multiplexed. The practical result is a much sharper color display than is possible with a composite monitor receiving composite signals from the computer.

Apple Macintosh computer

Condensed from CONSUMER REPORTS, January 1985

Like driving a car or speaking French, operating a computer is a piece of cake, once you learn how. Once you learn how to navigate the keyboard. Once you learn how to negotiate the disk operating system. Once you learn what each applications program does—and how to generate the commands to get it to do those things.

The easiest programs to learn use a menu command system. The program presents you with a menu—a multiple-choice list of things you can do, written in plain English. By keying an item from the menu, you choose the function you want. In complex programs, you may be led step by step through a series of submenus, or prompted by yes/no choices.

Computer manufacturers help with expanded keyboards that may include keys programmed to generate a complex command or series of commands with a single stroke.

With all the help computer makers provide—all the "user friendliness," as the jargon has it—the newcomer to computing can look forward to a long period of study and of trial and error.

The *Macintosh* is Apple's idea of the ultimate user-friendly computer. To create this digital chum, the designers have in many places substituted symbols, called "icons," or menus for commands that must be explicitly typed in on other computers. They've boldly simplified the keyboard, replacing most function and special-purpose keys with a pointing device called a "mouse." And they have designed a unique operating system that invites all programmers for the *Macintosh* to integrate the mouse and the icons into the command structure of their programs.

The mouse is a hand-held unit about the size of a cigarette pack. Rolling it about on the tabletop next to the computer moves a cursor around on the screen. You move the mouse to position the cursor on an icon, and click a button on the mouse. That executes the chosen activity.

Bundled into the price of the *Macintosh* is a word-processing program called *Macwrite* and a drawing program called *Macpaint*. Those programs exemplify the ease of use designed into the *Macintosh*.

In the *Macintosh* system, a trash-can icon represents a delete-file command; a manila-folder icon represents data files; and a sheet-of-paper icon represents a text document. To delete a file, you "grab" its icon with the mouse, move it over to the trash can, and let it drop. Such tasks as taking letters you have written and grouping them into a single file folder is a simple matter of moving iconal symbols around on a screen that is itself an icon for a desk top. With other personal computers, moving or copying documents often requires you to wade through menus or enter special codes, while trying not to inadvertently delete the document you are moving.

Macintosh programs also use "windows." Windows show up as rectangular boxes that afford a glance at one or more projects at a time. For instance, you can display the contents of two files side by side, and cut and paste between them. Using the mouse, you can make the windows smaller or larger, or make them disappear. You can also use a window to display a working calculator or a clock somewhere on the screen while you work on another project.

Finally, *Macintosh* programs display a horizontal menu bar across the top of the screen. The bar contains headings naming the various menus. When you "click" one of these headings with the mouse, the menu "pulls down" like a window shade to reveal a series of choices. In word processing, there are menus for File, Edit, Fontsize, and Style, among others. Choose "Edit" with the mouse, and a menu pulls down with such choices as Cut, Copy, and Paste.

Instead of searching through an instruction manual, you can easily experiment with different commands to see their effects on the programs. If a command is not appropriate at a particular stage in the program, its menu listing is dimmed. This helps to remind novices what they might, and might not, do next. A handy "undo" feature allows you to rescind an order you made rashly. For instance, you can use it to restore the last thing you deleted. You can also retrieve things from the "trash can," provided that you haven't "emptied" it.

Accustomed as we are to operating computers by mastering an extensive keyboard, we were at first doubtful about a computer that made us leave the keyboard for the mouse. In word-processing, especially, we thought, one would want the fingers on the keys, in order to make corrections during the regular flow of typing.

We soon learned to abandon that way of working. When we typed first and made corrections later, we found it fast, natural, and pleasant to whip about the screen with the mouse.

There are drawbacks to the *Macintosh* system, however. All the little flourishes and frills that make the *Macintosh* such an inviting computer are extremely memory-intensive.

Although the *Macintosh* comes with 128K of temporary memory—a substantial amount—not much of that is left for actual data processing after the operating system and a program are loaded. For example, after you've loaded the *Macwrite* program and its operating system, there's only enough room left in the computer's memory for about 8½ single-spaced typewritten pages.

Once you have loaded up the memory with your 8½ pages, you have to end the document. To continue beyond that point, you must start a new document. Writing a lengthy term paper or article on a *Macintosh* is like writing it in bound nine-page notebooks.

Apple has apparently recognized that its *Macintosh* needs more than 128K for many serious business uses. It's offering the "Fat Mac," with a memory upgrade to 512K.

The "Fat Mac" can handle about 80 pages of text in a word-processig document. That's more than enough for most purposes.

The *Macintosh* has a standard 58 key typewriter-style keyboard with very few extra keys for computing. We judged the keyboard feel excellent. There are no cursor keys, since cursor functions are shouldered by the mouse. All the appropriate keys repeat when held down.

There is one function key that activates other keys to perform double duty. Most of these are short-cut keystrokes for common commands that can be a little wearisome to do, with the mouse.

There is no separate numeric keypad—something that will be missed by those who work a lot with numbers. You can buy one as an add-on for $99.

Most personal computers use 5¼-

inch floppy disks to store programs and data. The *Macintosh* uses a microfloppy disk sealed in a rigid, 3½-inch-wide plastic envelope. These disks have certain advantages over 5¼-inch disks. They are only about half the size; they fit into a shirt pocket; and they are somewhat easier to load and unload from the disk drive.

But most important, the hard-shell covering protects them from bending, fingerprints, and to some extent from dust and dirt—the bugbears of 5¼-inch disks.

The *Macintosh* comes with a single built-in disk drive—and therein lies another shortcoming. The diskettes can hold 400K (about 400,000 characters) of data. But, as with many other single-disk computer systems, you typically can't use all the disk to save your data.

When you load a program such as *Macwrite*, you must leave that program disk in the drive. You record data onto the part of the program disk that is not taken up by the program itself or by the operating system programs, called system files. The system files alone take up 212K of disk space. An applications program such as *Macwrite* takes up about 55K more. That leaves only about 146K of space on the disk for saving documents.

Once you've reached the limit of what you can save on the program disk (about 45 typewritten pages), the *Macwrite* and *Macprint* programs prompt you to change disks. Your document file or files will be copied onto the new disk. You can then erase them from the program disk and continue working. As an alternative, you can make several copies of the program disk, and simply use a new disk when the free space on the old one is filled up.

Although a single disk drive is adequate for home use, business users will no doubt want the added convenience of a two-drive system. A second disk drive is a $495 option.

The *Macintosh* comes equipped with a built-in high-resolution black-and-white monitor. It measures nine inches diagonally, compared with 11 inches for the typical computer monitor. The relatively small screen is no drawback, since both letters and pictures are unusually sharp—crisper even than the notably crisp monochrome display of the IBM-PC. Most computers address text to the screen using a mode known as block-mapping. But the *Macintosh* doesn't use a block-mapping text mode. Instead, all text as well as graphics are bit-mapped. In essence, each letter and line is drawn on the screen with lots of fine dots.

Block-mapped screens can display only those characters that are present in permanent memory, whereas bit-mapped screens can display a much wider variety of type styles. Thus, with the *Macintosh*, you can choose and see displayed something approaching the type selection available at a small print shop. If you want to italicize a word for emphasis, for example, the italics appear on the screen as italics. You can even create distinctive posters, if you wish.

An unusual feature of the *Macintosh* display is that it appears black-on-white rather than green (or amber) on black. Consequently, writing or drawing with the *Macintosh* is much more like working with a sheet of white paper, albeit a small one, than on the "blackboard" familiar to most computer-terminal users.

You can't use just any printer with the *Macintosh*. You need a graphics printer specially adapted to the computer. We used the *Apple Imagewriter*.

As we consider the printer to be an integral part of the system, you must take the cost of an *Imagewriter* (or similar printer) into account in any purchase decision. With *Macpaint* drawings, the printer made pictures that were near replicas of what was displayed on the screen.

Print generated by the *Macwrite* and *Macprint* programs does not try to imitate the standard "pica" typewriter print. The system's closet approximation of typewriter type is a bit larger. The print is proportional both on the screen and on paper, and we think it looks quite good.

Accessories are available that allow you to hook up the *Macintosh* to a formed-character "daisy wheel" printer, you won't be able to use the print enhancements that make *Macwrite so unusual.*

The Apple Macintosh comes with a tutorial audio tape cassette as well as three manuals. The tape and associated disks, called the "Guided Tour," demonstrate the machine step-by-step, much like a taped guided tour of a museum does.

The main manual, called "Macintosh," explains the system, how it works, and what to expect. It's a glossy, copiously illustrated spiral bound book that we found easy to follow and easy to understand.

Two companion booklets, which explain how to use *Macwrite* and *Macpaint*, are also clearly laid out and simple to follow. The manuals are structured in such a way that you are encouraged to use the machine and follow along with the manual, rather than reading the manuals through first.

RECOMMENDATIONS. The *Apple Macintosh* is far and away the easiest computer to learn and use that we have yet seen. The combination of mouse, pull-down menus, windows, and icons is more than a dazzling display of technical wizardry. It's a logically thought-out system that deserves the careful consideration of anyone about to buy a computer to work with at home or at a small business, away from formal training programs and office gurus.

But we say "work with," not "play with." Lacking color graphics, the *Macintosh* also lacks the many games and educational programs designed for use with a TV set or a color monitor. And the *Macintosh* is considerably more expensive than such all-purpose computers as the *Apple IIc*.

TV and audio

Large-screen TV sets

Condensed from CONSUMER REPORTS, January 1986

The large-screen TV sets of today aren't merely large; they're stylish, well-appointed, and designed to handle the rigorous demands of the modern video world—cable TV, video cassette recorders, laser disks, and stereo TV sound.

The 18 models tested for this report typify sets at or near the top of a brand line. All have the manufacturer's top-of-the-line chassis and a remote control, and all can reproduce stereo broadcasts. Most are also set up to serve as a color monitor for a computer or VCR. The majority have a 25-inch screen; the others are 26- and 27-inchers. List prices range from $750 to $1490, but they may be discounted by $200 to $400 or more.

PICTURE QUALITY. TV manufacturers offer a bewildering number of sets that differ in features, cabinet style, and price. However, our chief criterion for judging color TV's is picture quality, which is largely a function of picture clarity, color fidelity, and contrast.

Good picture clarity requires that images are rendered in fine detail, and edges appear crisp and natural. Good color fidelity demands that screen colors remain consistent and true to life. Picture contrast is governed primarily by the factors of black-level retention and screen reflectance.

We put our TV sets in a viewing room with what we consider typical household lighting conditions, and we had a panel of seasoned viewers judge the sets for clarity and color fidelity. Our statisticians then analyzed those assessments to produce the judgments shown in the Ratings. The sets judged to have the best picture quality were, by a small margin, the *Wards*, the *Philco*, the *Magnavox*, the *RCA*, and the *Sony*.

Nearly all the sets performed very well in our tests for secondary factors that influence picture quality: freedom from geometric distortion, interlace, overscan, automatic color control, adjacent-channel rejection, airplane-flutter rejection, VHF and UHF fringe reception, and spark rejection. Exceptions, for better or for worse, are called out in the Ratings.

SOUND QUALITY. In 1984, the FCC promulgated a broadcasting standard called MTS (for multi-channel television sound), which allows TV stations and cable companies to transmit stereo sound and other information along with the video signal. Although little pro-

Text continued on page 320

Ratings of large-screen TV sets

Listed in order of estimated overall quality. Differences of less than 7 points in Overall Ratings Score and 10 points in Tone Quality Accuracy Score were judged not very significant. Except as noted, prices are list; * indicates price CU paid, as no list price is available; + indicates shipping is extra. D indicates model is discontinued.

◉ ◐ ○ ◒ ●

Better ⟵⟶ Worse

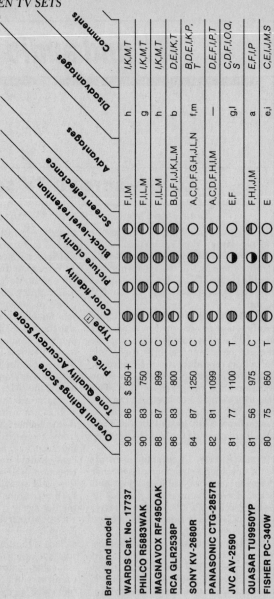

Brand and model	Overall Ratings Score	Tone Quality Accuracy Score	Price	Type [1]	Color fidelity	Picture clarity	Black-level retention	Screen reflectance	Advantages	Disadvantages	Comments
WARDS Cat. No. 17737	90	86	$ 850+	C	◉	◐	◉	◐	F,I,M	h	I,K,M,T
PHILCO R5883WAK	90	83	750	C	◐	◉	◉	◐	F,I,L,M	g	I,K,M,T
MAGNAVOX RF495OAK	88	87	899	C	◉	◐	◉	◐	F,I,L,M	h	I,K,M,T
RCA GLR2538P	86	83	800	C	◐	○	◉	◉	B,D,F,I,J,K,L,M	b	D,E,I,K,T
SONY KV-2680R	84	87	1250	C	◐	◐	◉	○	A,C,D,F,G,H,J,L,N	f,m	B,D,E,I,K,P,T
PANASONIC CTG-2857R	82	81	1099	C	◐	○	○	◐	A,C,D,F,H,I,M	—	D,E,F,I,P,T
JVC AV-2590	81	77	1100	T	◉	◉	◒	○	E,F	g,l	C,D,F,I,O,Q,S
QUASAR TU9950YP	81	56	975	C	◐	◐	◒	◐	F,H,I,J,M	a	E,F,I,P
FISHER PC-340W	80	75	850	T	◐	◐	◐	○	E	e,i	C,E,I,J,M,S

ⒹMITSUBISHI CK-2587R	80	81	1100	C	⊜	⊜	○	⊜	A,B,D,F,H,I	m	*D,F,I,M,P,Q,S*
TOSHIBA CZ2685	80	78	1490	T	◍	⊜	○	○	E,H,J	k,l	*A,C,D,E,I,J,O,R,S*
GE 26CP6869	79	78	899	T	⊜	⊜	⊜	◍	A,C,D,E,F,H,I	l,n	*A,C,D,G,I,M,P,S*
ZENITH SB2527P	77	88	960	C	○	⊜	◒	◍	B,C,D,F,I,M	d,g,n	*D,E,F,I,K,L,N,O,T*
ZENITH SB2729N	73	77	1080	C	○	⊜	◒	◍	B,C,D,F,I,M	d,k,n	*B,D,E,F,I,K,L,N,O,T*
SANYO AVM260	72	74	800	T	○	⊜	⊜	○	E,H	g,j	*C,E,I,J,M,S*
SEARS Cat. No. 4870	68	79	780+	C	⊜	○	●	⊜	B,D,H,I	f,i,m	*D,E,H,I,J,S*
CURTIS MATHES M2658RL	67	65	1250*	C	○	⊜	●	◍	A,B,D,F,G,H	c,f,g,l,n	*A,C,E,I,M,P,Q,S*
HITACHI CT-2559	65	72	1080	C	⊜	○	○	○	D,F,M	f,g,k,n	*D,I,S*

[1] *Type: C = console model; T = table model.*

FEATURES IN COMMON
All have: built-in stereo/SAP decoder and stereo speakers; quartz (frequency-synthesized) tuner; automatic fine tuning; sharpness control; VHF reception of channels 2 through 13, and UHF reception of channels 14 through 69, coaxial input connector for VHF and cable TV.
Except as noted, all were satisfactory in freedom from geometric distortion, interlace, and automatic color control; have cable-readiness for at least 42 channels; Have warranty of at least 12 mo. on parts, 3 mo. on labor, and 24 mo. on picture tube.
Unless otherwise indicated, all have: 25-in. screen; comb filter; tone and stereo-balance controls; vertical-hold control; illuminated channel numbers on control panel; room-light sensor.

KEY TO ADVANTAGES
A – 2 VHF inputs.
B – Built-in channel-selection keypad on receiver.
C – Channel censor; can be programmed to prevent viewing of selected channels.
D – Displays time of day on screen or on console.
E – Stereo headphone jack.
F – Scan feature with programmed channel bypass.
G – Capable of programming 1 on/off cycle.
H – Sleep timer.
I – Last-channel recall.
J – Better than most in airplane-flutter rejection.
K – Better than most in VHF fringe reception.
L – Better than most in UHF fringe reception.
M – Much better than most in spark rejection.
N – Most fully featured remote control of all tested models.

KEY TO DISADVANTAGES
a – No tone and stereo-balance controls.
b – No stereo-balance control.
c – Tone controls are on back of set.
d – Made crackling sound when set was turned on. According to Zenith, this problem affected early production runs, and models so afflicted will be repaired free.

Keys to Ratings continued on next page

Keys to Ratings of large-screen TV's continued

e-Worst interlace of models tested.
f-Somewhat worse than most in adjacent-channel rejection.
g-Worse than most in airplane-flutter rejection.
h-Much worse than most in airplane-flutter rejection.
i-Worse than most in VHF fringe reception.
j-Much worse than most in VHF fringe reception.
k-Worse than most in UHF fringe reception.
l-Worse than most in spark rejection.
m-Much worse than most in spark rejection.
n-Produced more than 12% overscan.

KEY TO COMMENTS

A-26-in. screen.
B-27-in. screen.
C-Removable pane of glass over screen.
D-Status of several controls can be displayed on screen.
E-1-button control.
F-AFT switch.
G-VIR system.
H-No comb filter.
I-No room-light sensor.
J-Scan stops automatically on next active channel.
K-No vertical-hold control (and none normally needed).
L-Switchable video filter.
M-Can also produce "pseudo stereo" sound from mono broadcasts; somewhat artificial effect, but can add sense of spaciousness to some programs.
N-Provision for 4-input remote RF switch.
O-Speaker jacks or terminals.
P-Retains channel and volume settings for at least 10 min. when unplugged.
Q-"Vacation" power switch turns off all power to set, but also causes set to lose time and other settings.
R-RGB input.
S-Can receive UHF channels 70 through 83.
T-Combination VHF/UHF coaxial input.

---

gramming now takes advantage of stereo (or a "second audio program," called SAP, used mainly for bilingual programming), the potential is surely there; some 200 TV stations plus the NBC and PBS networks have converted their equipment to allow broadcasting in stereo. But the full potential of TV stereo can't be realized, of course, until TV sets are converted to receive and play stereo (a conversion device has been marketed, but not tested by CU). Our expensive, large-screen sets, though, are thoroughly prepared for the flowering of network stereo. They're equipped with a built-in stereo/SAP decoder and stereo speakers. Their stereo effect is diminished, though, by the close spacing of the speakers.

We measured the frequency response of the sound delivered from each set's speakers in a typical listening environment, after adjusting the set's tone controls for the best test results. The Tone Quality Accuracy Scores in the Ratings are roughly analogous to the scores we use in our Ratings of audio loudspeakers. They show how close each television set came to producing a "flat" frequency response.

Sets with the best tone-quality scores were respectable performers—nearly what we would expect from a good set of low-priced audio components. The sets with the lowest scores could be improved by connecting them to a hi-fi system or a good set of speakers.

FEATURES. All the sets have a quartz frequency-synthesized tuner. That's the state-of-the-art in tuning technology, and it has the virtue of being easy to use. Channels are preprogrammed at the factory. You can change from one channel to any other channel simply at the touch of a button, while skipping any channels in between.

Until a few years ago, ordinary color TV sets couldn't rise to the standard of resolution maintained by the broadcast industry. But a device called a comb filter makes it possible for TV sets to increase resolution by about 20 percent to match the capability of broadcasters.

Of the tested sets, only the *Sears* lacks a comb filter.

All the sets come with an infrared wireless remote control, which, at the very least, lets you turn the set on and off, change the channel, and adjust the volume. Some remote controls let you do much more. The *Sony's* was the most versatile of those we tested.

Like most sets these days, the large-screen models are all cable-ready, set up to handle between 42 and 125 cable channels. But expanded cable-channel capability isn't the grand virtue it might appear, since most cable systems have a capacity of 53 channels or less. Also, the scrambling of signals that many cable companies employ to protect pay channels may thwart use of a set's cable-readiness on scrambled channels.

RECOMMENDATIONS. All the tested sets produced an acceptable picture. Accordingly, you might well extend the limits of your choice to models that occur anywhere in the Ratings if some feature or performance factor is important to you, or if you get an extremely advantageous price.

Readers' responses to our 1985 Annual Survey enabled us to compile reliability records for 11 brands of TV sets. Those records, reflecting TV purchases from 1980 on, show that sets from *Sony*, *Mitsubishi*, *Panasonic*, *Curtis Mathes*, and *Sears* have been more trouble-free than average. *Quasar*, *RCA*, and *GE* have been average. Sets from *Magnavox*, *Zenith*, and *Sylvania*, on the other hand, have been more trouble-prone than average.

Low-priced stereo receivers

Condensed from CONSUMER REPORTS, September 1985

The solid-state circuitry used in today's receivers virtually guarantees good performance from equipment at any price level. More money does buy more versatility in the form of higher power, more accomodations for other components, and more controls.

POWER. Low-priced receivers should deliver adequate amounts of power for relatively modest musical demands. On average, these receivers have about half the output power of mid-priced models, which we define as receivers priced in the neighborhood of $400.

If you try to push sound levels too high, you will overdrive the amplifier and produce a kind of distortion called clipping, which gives music a harsh, gritty sound and may damage the speakers. Any receiver rated to deliver about 35 watts or less may produce some degree of clipping, even well below the maximum volume setting. If you have reason to think your hi-fi system's power needs exceed a given receiver's output, you probably should play it safe by opting for extra power.

Some speakers rated at 8 ohms may actually present only 4 ohms for portions of the music spectrum, since impedance and frequency are interrelated. So it's desirable for an amplifier to have at least as much power available at 4 ohms as at 8 ohms. Some of the receivers we tested don't have the extra power, and the manufacturers of 13 tested models don't recommend using their receivers with speakers rated at 4 ohms.

If you want two pairs of speakers connected to your hi-fi system, the receiver's internal connection between the two speakers on each stereo channel is important. The connections are either

Text continued on page 326

Ratings of low-priced stereo receivers

Listed in order of estimated quality. Differences in score of 7 points or less are not very significant.

Prices are list; discounts are available.

◍ ⊖ ○ ◒ ●

Better ⟵⟶ Worse

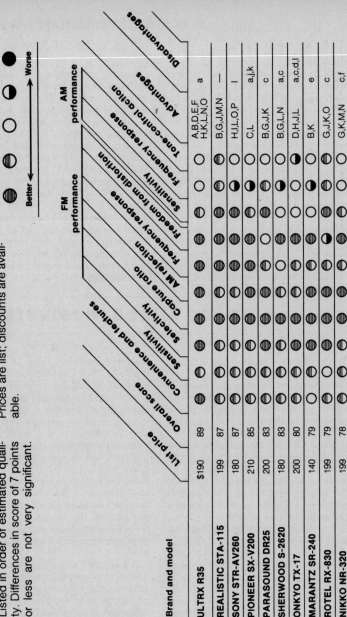

				FM performance						AM performance				
Brand and model	List price	Overall score	Convenience and features	Sensitivity	Selectivity	Capture ratio	AM rejection	Frequency response	Freedom from distortion	Sensitivity	Frequency response	Tone-control action	Advantages	Disadvantages
ULTRX R35	$190	89	◍	⊖	◍	◍	◍	◍	◍	⊖	○	○	A,B,D,E,F H,K,L,N,O	a
REALISTIC STA-115	199	87	⊖	⊖	⊖	◍	⊖	◍	◍	◍	⊖	⊖	B,G,J,M,N	—
SONY STR-AV260	180	87	⊖	⊖	⊖	◍	⊖	◍	◍	◍	◒	○	H,I,L,O,P	l
PIONEER SX-V200	210	85	⊖	⊖	⊖	◍	◍	◍	◍	⊖	◒	○	C,L	a,j,k
PARASOUND DR25	200	83	⊖	⊖	◍	◍	◍	⊖	○	◍	⊖	○	B,G,J,K	c
SHERWOOD S-2620	180	83	⊖	⊖	⊖	◍	⊖	○	◍	○	◒	○	B,G,L,N	a,c
ONKYO TX-17	200	80	⊖	⊖	◍	◍	⊖	⊖	◍	○	○	◒	D,H,J,L	a,c,d,l
MARANTZ SR-240	140	79	○	⊖	◍	◍	◍	⊖	◍	○	◒	○	B,K	e
ROTEL RX-830	199	79	⊖	○	◍	◍	◍	⊖	◒	◍	⊖	⊖	G,J,K,O	c
NIKKO NR-320	199	78	⊖	⊖	⊖	◍	◍	⊖	◍	⊖	○	○	G,K,M,N	c,f

ULTRX R25	140	78	○	○	●	●	◓	●	●	○	○	◓	B,J,K,M,O	a,i
JVC R-X110	175	77	◓	○	◓	●	◓	●	●	◓	○	○	J,L	b,l
SHERWOOD S-2610	150	77	◓	◓	◓	●	●	○	●	●	◒	○	B,G,J	c
TECHNICS SA-150	170	77	◓	○	◓	●	◓	◓	◓	◓	⬤	◓	J,L,P	b,c,g
AKAI AA-A1	170	76	○	○	◓	●	●	●	●	○	◒	◒	K,M,O	a,i,j
HITACHI HTA-25F	200	76	◓	◓	◓	●	◓	●	◓	○	◒	○	L,P	a,e,l
TECHNICS SA-120	150	76	○	○	◓	●	●	◓	○	●	◒	○	J,K	b
PIONEER SX-212	150	75	◒	○	◓	●	●	◓	●	●	○	◓	K	a,c,d,h,j
HITACHI HTA-2	150	74	○	○	◓	●	●	◓	◓	◓	◒	○	J,K,M	a,c
VECTOR RESEARCH VR-2200	150	74	◓	○	◓	◓	●	◓	◒	●	○	◓	G,J,K,O	c

KEY TO ADVANTAGES

A – Volume reduced on power-up if left too high.
B – Mono switch works for all sources.
C – Switching facility for 2 video sources.
D – Connection for second tape deck.
E – Can dub tape from either deck.
F – Can dub tape while listening to another source.
G – Speakers connected in parallel when 2 pairs used.
H – Shows which preset station is selected.
I – Provides front-panel labels for preset stations.
J – Allows listening in stereo to weak stations.
K – Tuning dial is readable from higher angle than most.
L – Has quartz tuning.
M – Slide-rule dial scale longer than most.
N – "Subsonic" filter reduces noise from record warp.
O – 2 auxiliary inputs.
P – Digital tuning "wraps" from top of band back to bottom.

KEY TO DISADVANTAGES

a – Accidental shorting of speaker output may require unit to be serviced.
b – Amplifier frequency response suffers because loudness compensation cannot be turned off.
c – Does not clearly show selected music source.
d – No auxiliary inputs—only tape input.
e – No connection for second pair of speakers.
f – Screw-type speaker connectors, judged somewhat inconvenient.
g – Preset station memory requires replaceable battery.
h – No interstation muting to reduce noise while tuning by knob.
i – Muting cannot be defeated for tuning weak station.
j – No FM mono switch to reduce noise on weak stations.
k – Tuning dial is visible only from lower angle than most.
l – Tuning auto-scan does not work on AM band.

Specifications and features on next page

Low-priced stereo receivers: specifications and features

Brand and model	Dimensions (HxWxD), in.	Amplifier power output (Watts) At 4 ohms	At 6 ohms	At 8 ohms	Tuning [1]	FM tuning step (kHz)	Warranty for labor (yr.)	Comments
ULTRX R35	5x16½x12½	49	46	41	DD;MS;AS;PS(7)	100	2	A,C,H,I,M,P
REALISTIC STA-115	4x16½x10¾	34	32	29	KO	—	2	B,L,M,P
SONY STR-AV260	4¼x17x12¼	36	36	35	DD;AS;DE;PS(10)	50	2	D,E,F,I,N,P
PIONEER SX-V200	3¾x16½x9¾	40	41	36	DD;MS;AS;PS(8)	100	2	H,I,O,P
PARASOUND DR25	3x17¼x14½	33	31	27	DD;KO	—	1	M,N,P
SHERWOOD S-2620	4½x17½x13½	31	29	24	MS;AS;PS(5)	200	3	M,N,P
ONKYO TX-17	4x17¼x13½	27	30	27	DD;MS;AS;PS(6)	100	2	I,P
MARANTZ SR-240	4¼x16½x13½	—	35	32	KO	—	3	I,L,M,N,P
ROTEL RX-830	3¾x17x11¾	30	27	24	KO	—	0	M,N
NIKKO NR-320	3¾x17¼x13	42	37	32	KO	—	2	L,M,N,P
ULTRX R25	4½x16½x11¼	25	28	27	KO	—	2	G,H,I,M,P
JVC R-X110	3¾x17¼x11½	26	28	29	DD;MS;PS(8)	100	2	I,M,Q
SHERWOOD S-2610	4¼x17½x12½	32	30	26	KO	—	3	M,N,P
TECHNICS SA-150	4x17x10¼	29	33	27	DD;MS;AS;PS(6)	100	2	I,P
AKAI AA-A1	3x17¼x12¼	33	40	37	KO	—	2	I,K,L,N,P

HITACHI HTA-25F	4¼x17¼x12¼	28	31	29	DD;MS;PS(7)	200	3	*I,M,P*
TECHNICS SA-120	3¾x17x11½	49	46	44	KO	—	2	*I,L,P*
PIONEER SX-212	3¾x16½x9¾	30	32	31	KO	—	2	*I,L,N,P*
HITACHI HTA-2	3¼x17¼x12	35	33	31	KO	—	3	*I,L,P*
VECTOR RESEARCH VR-2200	3¾x17x11¾	29	26	23	KO	—	2	*J,M,N,P*

[1] *DD: Digital display. KO: knob only. PS: preset (number). DE: direct entry. AS: auto scan. MS: manual stepped.*

PERFORMANCE NOTES

All were judged: excellent in FM stereo separation, amplifier signal-to-noise ratio, phono frequency response, phono freedom from distortion, and phono signal-to-noise ratio; excellent or very good in amplifier freedom from distortion.

Except as noted, all were judged: excellent in amplifier frequency response; good in strong-signal capability.

FEATURES IN COMMON

All have: FM and AM tuners; 1 phono input, volume and balance controls, and bass and treble tone controls; headphone jack; connection for 75-ohm FM antenna; AM loop antenna.

Except as noted, all have: switchable loudness compensation; 1 auxiliary input; connection for 1 tape deck; 1-way tape dubbing on models with 2 tape-deck connections; separately switched output for second pair of speakers; FM mono switch; interstation muting on knob-tuned models; speakers connected in series when 2 pairs are used; handy spring or twist-type speaker-wire connectors; clear indication of selected music source; connection for 300-ohm FM antenna.

KEY TO COMMENTS

A–Has push-button volume control.
B–Has switch to reduce high-frequency sounds and noise.
C–Has output-level display.
D–Scan tuning "samples" stations for a few seconds each.
E–Can sample-scan preset stations.
F–Preset button selects both band and station.
G–Has additional scale on slide-rule dial, numbered 0 to 10.
H–Has "matrix" switch to provide unusual acoustic effect.
I–Not recommended for 4-ohm speakers.
J–According to mfr., current designation is **VR-2200A**, identical to model tested except has 1 less a-c outlet.
K–No connection for 300-ohm FM antenna.
L–Knob-tuning aid; light shows when tuner is centered on desired frequency.
M–Signal-strength indicator.
N–1 switched a-c outlet.
O–2 switched a-c outlets.
P–1 unswitched a-c outlet.
Q–2 unswitched a-c outlets.

parallel or series. The parallel connection is preferable, because the signal reaching one speaker isn't degraded by the impedance of the other speaker on the same channel.

Some models will blow an internal fuse if you accidentally short circuit the speaker wires. Other models cope with a speaker-wire short in ways that don't require replacement parts.

FEATURES. Most low-priced receivers are tuned the old-fashioned way, using a knob to move a pointer across a dial. Precise tuning was easier with models that have a tuning light (which glows when the tuner is centered on the desired frequency) and a relatively long dial scale.

The ultimate in tuning ease is quartz tuning, which eliminates potential error by using a microprocessor. At the touch of a button, the microprocessor tunes unerringly to a station's center frequency, minimizing noise and distortion in the signal. Most quartz-tuned receivers show the frequency to which they're tuned on a digital display.

Thanks to the microprocessor, quartz-tuned models can be set to remember the frequency of from 10 to 16 stations, bringing in any one of them at the touch of a button. Even when you're searching for stations, there's no fiddling with a tuning knob. Instead, auto-scan tuning finds the next listenable station up or down the FM or AM band at the touch of another button. Because the auto-scan feature is unlikely to catch a weak station, quartz-tuned receivers let you tune manually by button; at each press, the receiver steps the tuning a discrete interval up or down the band. (It's best if the receiver steps exactly one FM "channel," a separation of 200 kilohertz, with each press of the button. Some models step only one-half or one-quarter channel to suit the FM channel-spacing that's conventional in other countries.)

Most models have a loudness switch to boost the bass and, usually, the treble. The boost varies with the volume setting and is meant to compensate for the ear's reduced sensitivity to bass sounds at low sound levels. It's an effect many listeners prefer.

Medium-priced loudspeakers

Condensed from CONSUMER REPORTS, October 1986

In recent years, we've tested a number of loudspeakers that delivered accurate sound for less than $300 a pair. (See the report beginning on page 330.) Some people, however, want more volume and more bass than such relatively inexpensive speakers can provide. The 21 medium-priced speakers tested for this report list from about $400 to $600 a pair. Scarcely anyone but a devout audio buff could ask for more fidelity, bass, or loudness than most of these speakers can provide.

PERFORMANCE TESTS. We put each speaker into CU's echo-free test chamber, fed it signals containing all the sounds of the musical spectrum, and collected computerized data on its output of acoustic power from about 30 Hz in the bass to about 14,000 Hz in the treble—the range over which most musical instruments put out their fundamental tones and combinations of overtones. Analysis of that data enabled us to score each speaker's accuracy as a percentage of "perfection."

The top-scoring models in accuracy—and thus, in our judgment, the top-rated models—were the *Advent Legacy*, the *Allison CD7*, and the *Infinity RS4000*, all with 92 out of a possible 100 points. But another 13 models came within eight points of the top three. And since past tests have shown that even experienced listeners can't consistently tell which of two speakers is the more accurate when their scores differ by eight points or less, we consider accuracy differences among the first 16 rated models not very significant. (But that doesn't mean that speakers with identical accuracy scores will sound alike; they may depart from accuracy at different points in the musical spectrum.)

To each speaker in our echo-free chamber, we then piped in increasingly loud low-frequency signals and measured any unwanted harmonics that the speaker put out. Nine models, including some fairly low-rated ones, were notably free of bass distortion. Those models would show to advantage in playing organ or synthesizer music very loud. Otherwise, they offer no special edge.

We calculated the power each model would need to produce fairly loud sound in a medium-sized (2500-cubic-foot) room with average acoustics. But if you have many compact discs or "audiophile" recordings and listen to them at loud levels, your amplifier will need to deliver twice or more the wattage we list in the Ratings, or more. Our measurements of impedance, another electrical factor determining whether an amplifier can adequately drive a pair of speakers, provide a margin of safety of about 25 percent. Thus, for example, speakers for which we measured 6 ohms of impedance would be compatible with an amplifier rated for 8 ohms or less.

LISTENING . To check the results of our performance tests, we listened to a variety of music played through each pair of speakers in a room furnished to match the acoustics of a typical listening room. Results tallied closely with our laboratory findings. At one point, for instance, our analysis of "directivity"—the way a speaker radiates sound at different frequencies—pointed to some acoustic anomalies with the *Pioneer CS605*. Those were confirmed when we auditioned each speaker for stereo imaging. The *Pioneer's* stereo image at different frequencies shifted noticeably and, some listeners judged, disconcertingly.

We listened with each pair of speakers about 10 feet apart, two feet from a wall, and five feet from the corner, with the tweeter (the treble element) at the ear level of a listener seated 10 feet away. Some manufacturers recommend positioning their speakers with the back close to a wall. But for some models, that position made the bass sound too loud and lowered the overall accuracy. We experimented to find a location that gave the best results, as you should when setting up your system.

With small speakers such as the *ADS L570*, ear-level installation is simple if you have adjustable shelving. Lacking shelves, you may want to get a stand to raise the speakers to ear level. The manufacturer of the *Mission 707* recommends an optional stand for use with that speaker, a recommendation that we followed. Some of the big speakers have a built-in base, but they sounded better on top of a stand that raised them still higher.

RECOMMENDATIONS. Theoretically, the closer a speaker is to the top of the Ratings, the smoother its overall frequency response should sound. In practice, however, any among the top 16 models in the Ratings may prove satisfactory. You might reasonably choose any one of them for considerations apart from sound quality.

Size is one such consideration. The *ADS L570* is the most compact model of the top 16, making it especially suitable for shelf installation. Or since a pair of larger speakers standing on the floor will constitute furniture of a sort, you might want to consider styling. The tall and narrow *Allison CD7* looks a little like a pedestal for a bust. (But anything placed on it will block one of the speaker elements, which plays through the cabinet top.) Some other models have a distinctly high-tech look that may or may not fit in with the decor of your listening room.

And then there's price. Theoretically, one of the top-scoring speakers, the *Advent Legacy*, was the cheapest. Its list price was $399. But in practice, the pricing of loudspeakers is exceedingly variable. Depending on the competitive situation in your area, you might find discounts as generous as 50 percent or as meager as 5 percent. We did, when we went shopping. In fact, one high-class store, a genteel component "salon," even charged us $50 *more* than list price for a pair of speakers.

Ratings of medium-priced loudspeakers

Listed, except as noted, in order of accuracy score; models with identical scores are listed alphabetically. Differences in score of 8 points or less were judged not very significant. Dimensions (HxWxD) are rounded to the higher 1/4 in. Impedance is rounded to the nearest ohm. Unless otherwise indicated, all have removable cloth grill, imitation or natural wood-grain finish, and spring-loaded push-on connectors for wiring to amplifier. Prices are list per pair; substantial discounts may be available.

ADVENT LEGACY. $399. 28¼×16¼×9¾ in. 41 lb. Accuracy: 92. Impedance: 6 ohms. Power required: 8 watts. Freedom from bass distortion: much better than average. Score was 88 when speaker was placed according to manufacturer's directions. Top and bottom are solid hardwood; rest of cabinet has wood-trim finish.

ALLISON CD7. $500. 27×9½×10¼ in. 24 lb. Accuracy 92. Impedance: 4 ohms. Power required: 13½ watts. Freedom from bass distortion: average. Score was 86 when speaker was placed according to manufactuer's directions. Has plastic-mesh grill.

INFINITY RS4000. $458. 22½×12½×9½ in. 25 lb. Accuracy: 92. Impedance: 4 ohms. Power required: 16 watts. Freedom from bass distortion: average. Has rotary level control.

AR AR38BXi. $470. 21¾×13×7½ in. 29 lb. Accuracy: 90. Impedance: 5 ohms. Power required: 13 watts. Freedom from bass distortion: much worse than average. Has "banana-plug" screw-type connectors. Score was 86 when speaker was placed close to wall according to manufacturer's directions.

CERWIN-VEGA D3. $530. 27¾×14×11½ in. 36 lb. Accuracy: 90. Impedance: 5 ohms. Power required 2½ watts. Freedom from bass distortion: much better than average. Has self-resetting tweeter protection.

EPI T/E 320. $500. 29×17×10½ in. 45 lb. Accuracy: 89. Impedance: 4 ohms. Power required: 11 watts. Freedom from bass distortion: better than average. Accuracy was 83 when speaker was placed close to wall according to manufacturer's directions. This model has been discontinued.

ADS L570. \$460. 18¾×11½×11 in. 21 lb. Accuracy: 88. Impedance: 4 ohms. Power required: 12½ watts. Freedom from bass distortion: better than average. Has metal-mesh grill and "banana-plug" screw-type connectors. Tweeter has protective fuse.

BOSTON ACOUSTICS A150 II. \$500. 32½×16×8¼ in. 42 lb. Accuracy: 88. Impedance: 4 ohms. Power required: 11 watts. Freedom from bass distortion: much better than average.

JBL L60T. \$590. 30½×12×11¾ in. 37 lb. Accuracy: 88. Impedance: 5 ohms. Power required: 11 watts. Freedom from bass distortion: better than average. Has "banana-plug" screw-type connectors. Cabinet has veneer finish.

SCOTT 311DC. \$500. 23×13×9¼ in. 22 lb. Accuracy: 88. Impedance: 6 ohms. Power required: 3½ watts. Freedom from bass distortion: much better than average. Has rotary level control. This model has been discontinued.

POLK AUDIO MONITOR 7C. \$500. 24×14×9½ in. 30 lb. Accuracy: 88. Impedance: 4 ohms. Power required: 9 watts. Freedom from bass distortion: much better than average. Has "banana-plug" screw-type connectors.

GENESIS 33. \$498. 31×16×8¾ in. 33 lb. Accuracy: 87. Impedance: 4 ohms. Power required: 16 watts. Freedom from bass distortion: better than average. Comes with stand assembly.

ELECTRO VOICE INTERFACE 2 Series II. \$546. 24¼×13¾×10¾ in. 30 lb. Accuracy: 86. Impedance: 5 ohms. Power required: 6 watts. Freedom from bass distortion: much better than average. Has rotary level control and screw-type connectors.

KEF C40. \$490. 25½×9¾×10¼ in. 20 lb. Accuracy: 86. Impedance: 6 ohms. Power required: 4¼ watts. Freedom from bass distortion: much worse than average. Has "banana-plug" connectors.

TECHNICS SBX700A. \$550. 27¼×15¼×13 in. 35 lb. Accuracy: 86. Impedance: 5 ohms. Power required: 11 watts. Freedom from bass distortion: much better than average. Has self-resetting speaker-overload protector, 2 rotary level controls, and screw-type connectors.

KLIPSCH KG4. \$600. 27½×15¾×11 in. 39 lb. Accuracy: 84. Impedance: 4 ohms. Power required: 5 watts. Freedom from bass distortion: average. Has "banana-plug" screw-type connectors. Accuracy was 76 when speaker was placed close to wall according to manufacturer's directions.

CELESTION DL8. \$550. 19¾×10¾×10¾ in. 22 lb. Accuracy: 80. Impedance: 7 ohms. Power required: 8 watts. Freedom from bass distortion: much worse than average. Has "banana-plug" screw-type connectors.

REALISTIC Mach Two. \$440. 28¼×17¼×12¼ in. 42 lb. Accuracy: 80. Impedance: 6 ohms. Power required: 5½ watts. Freedom from bass distortion: much better than average. Has 2 rotary level controls.

DALI VI. \$591 (including \$45 shipping). 30½×12×11¼ in. 37 lb. Accuracy: 79. Impedance: 4 ohms. Power required: 7 watts. Freedom from bass distortion: average. Accuracy was 77 when speaker was placed close to wall according to manufacturer's directions. Available from: Danish-American Ltd. Inc., P.O. Box 55386, Valencia, Calif. 91355.

Ratings continued on next page

Ratings of medium-priced loudspeakers continued

PIONEER CS605. $560. 25½×16×11 in. 35 lb. Accuracy: 82. Downrated because stereo-image shifting at different frequencies was quite noticeable and disconcerting to some listeners. Impedance: 4 ohms. Power required: 2 watts. Freedom from bass distortion: much better than average. Has level and overload power indicators and push-button level controls.

MISSION 707. $449. 18½×9¾×10¾ in. 16 lb. (21 lb. with optional stand, 7T, $59). Accuracy: 77. Impedance: 5 ohms. Power required: 5 watts. Freedom from bass distortion: worse than average. Has "banana-plug" screw-type connectors.

Low-priced loudspeakers

Condensed from CONSUMER REPORTS, August 1985 (and May 1984)

You may not be cutting corners when you buy inexpensive speakers—which we define, in a hi-fi context, as those priced at $200 or less per pair. You may quite sensibly be acknowledging that there's no requirement in your listening habits for the special virtues exhibited by more expensive speakers. Those special virtues confer two principal advantages: the ability to keep sound undistorted while filling a large room with sound; and the ability to reach deep into the bass to bring out the best in the low notes played by certain instruments (such as the organ) or rendered on certain demanding recordings (such as compact discs).

So-called budget speakers are satisfactory for a starter system in a small or medium-sized listening room, where volume demands are not great.

ACCURACY. The most meaningful standard for judging speaker performance is accuracy—the measure of a speaker's ability to produce sounds that are as close as possible to the message in the electrical signals delivered by the receiver or amplifier. A "perfectly" accurate speaker responds smoothly and uniformly to every sound in the music spectrum.

Our past tests have shown that even an experienced listener can't consistently tell which of two speakers is the more accurate when their scores differ by eight points or less. (That's not to say that they may not deviate from a uniform frequency response at different points in the music spectrum.)

Departures from accuracy were easy to hear in the treble and midrange of the less-accurate models. But the biggest differences were in bass response.

Bass response is also dependent on local effects: the room's size, shape, and acoustical properties, as well as the position of the speakers within the room. Most manufacturers recommend positioning the speakers away from corners and off the floor. Many recommend installing the speakers with the high-frequency tweeter element at the level of a seated listener's ear. Following those instructions usually gave us the best results.

Although most of the low-priced models are capable of filling a medium-sized listening room with sound as loud as any serious listener would want, none are suitable for playing music at anything like rock-concert levels. They lack built-in electrical protection from excessive power levels—a replaceable fuse, for example, that blows to cut off power from the amplifier. Be especially careful about volume levels if you use any of these speakers with a compact-disc player. Because compact discs have virtually no background noise, the tendency is to turn the volume up at the beginning of play.

Power requirements ranged from a low of 3 watts with the *JBL* to a high of 18½ watts with the *Infinity RS11*. If you have many "audiophile" recordings and compact discs, however, and if you listen to them at loud levels, you may need more than twice the wattage given for each speaker in the Ratings.

Impedance is important when connecting speakers to an amplifier or receiver. Some amplifiers may not be able to deliver adequate power if the speakers' impedance is much lower than the amp's minimum impedance rating. Our measurements, made across the entire audio spectrum, provide a safety margin of about 25 percent.

RECOMMENDATIONS. If your listening habits aren't demanding—that is, if you seldom turn the volume all the way up, or listen to recordings that are heavy on the bass—then you can safely shop for speakers according to price.

If your ear is a bit more critical, you should begin to wonder whether you would be satisfied with any low-priced speaker.

Ratings of low-priced loudspeakers

Listed, except as noted, in order of room-accuracy score; models with identical accuracy scores are listed alphabetically. Differences in score of 8 points or less were not judged very significant. Impedance is rounded to nearest ohm. Dimensions (HxWxD) are rounded to the higher ¼-in. Unless otherwise indicated, all are equipped with spring-loaded push-on connectors. Prices are list per pair; substantial discounts are generally available.

BOSTON ACOUSTICS A60. $200. 18x11½x7½ in. 15 lb. Accuracy: 85. Impedance: 6 ohms. Power required: 7½ watts. Freedom from bass distortion: much better than average.

BOSTON ACOUSTICS A40. $150. 13½x8¼x7¼ in. 8½ lb. Accuracy: 84. Impedance: 5 ohms. Power required: 13 watts. Freedom from bass distortion: average.

EPI T/E 70. $184. 16x10½x7¼ in. 14½ lb. Accuracy: 84. Impedance: 4 ohms. Power required: 11½ watts. Freedom from bass distortion: worse than average.

JBL J216A. $200. 14¾x10x9¼ in. 15½ lb. Accuracy: 84. Impedance: 7 ohms. Power required: 3 watts. Freedom from bass distortion: average.

PIONEER CSG201w. $200. 24x13¾x11¾ in. 20 lb. Accuracy: 84. Impedance: 7 ohms. Power required: 4½ watts. Freedom from bass distortion: much better than average. A later designation is **CSG201sw.**

AR 8BX. $200. 15½x9½x7½ in. 14 lb. Accuracy: 82. Impedance: 6 ohms. Power required: 15½ watts. Freedom from bass distortion: worse than average.

INFINITY RS10B. $170. 13½x8½x7¾ in. 11 lb. Accuracy: 81. Impedance: 4 ohms. Power required: 13 watts. Freedom from bass distortion: worse than average.

KLH 608. \$160. 21x12x9$^3/_4$ in. 18$^1/_2$ lb. Accuracy: 81. Impedance: 8 ohms. Power required: 6 watts. Freedom from bass distortion: worse than average.

MISSION 70. \$199. 13$^3/_4$x8$^1/_4$x8$^1/_4$ in. 10 lb. Accuracy: 80. Impedance: 4 ohms. Power required: 5$^1/_2$ watts. Freedom from bass distortion: worse than average. Grille not removable. Requires "banana-plug" speaker connections.

3D ACOUSTICS "THE CUBE." \$195. 10x9$^3/_4$x9$^3/_4$ in. 13 lb. Accuracy: 80. Impedance: 8 ohms. Power required: 7 watts. Freedom from bass distortion: much worse than average. Uses both "banana-plug" and screw-on connectors.

REALISTIC NOVA-15. \$160. 19x10$^3/_4$x7$^1/_2$ in. 12 lb. Accuracy: 80. Impedance: 7 ohms. Power required: 9$^1/_2$ watts. Freedom from bass distortion: better than average.

REALISTIC OPTIMUS 30. \$200. 22$^1/_2$x12$^1/_4$x9$^1/_2$ in. 16$^1/_2$ lb. Accuracy: 80. Impedance: 6 ohms. Power required: 7$^1/_2$ watts. Freedom from bass distortion: average.

INFINITY RS11. \$116. 12x7$^1/_2$x5$^3/_4$ in. 6 lb. Accuracy: 79. Impedance: 5 ohms. Power required: 18$^1/_2$ watts. Freedom from bass distortion: much worse than average.

PIONEER CSG101w. \$140. 22$^1/_2$x13x7$^3/_4$ in. 14$^1/_2$ lb. Accuracy: 78. Impedance: 6 ohms. Power required: 5 watts. Freedom from bass distortion: much better than average. A later designation is **CSG101wa.**

BABY ADVENT A1002. \$198. 16$^1/_4$x11x6$^1/_4$ in. 12 lb. Accuracy: 77. Impedance: 6 ohms. Power required: 18 watts. Freedom from bass distortion: worse than average.

YAMAHA NS10T. \$198. 16$^1/_4$x9$^3/_4$x8$^1/_4$ in. 14 lb. Accuracy: 77. Impedance: 6 ohms. Power required: 5$^1/_2$ watts. Freedom from bass distortion: worse than average.

MARANTZ HLM208. \$120. 18$^3/_4$x10$^3/_4$x8$^1/_2$ in. 11$^1/_2$ lb. Accuracy: 74. Impedance: 5 ohms. Power required: 5 watts. Freedom from bass distortion: worse than average. Grille not removable.

MARANTZ HE82. \$160. 18x11$^1/_4$x8$^1/_2$ in. 14 lb. Accuracy: 70. Impedance: 4 ohms. Power required: 6$^1/_2$ watts. Freedom from bass distortion: worse than average. Uses screw-on and phono-type speaker connectors.

MARANTZ HLM308. \$200. 28x13x9$^3/_4$ in. 19$^1/_2$ lb. Accuracy: 66. Impedance: 4 ohms. Power required: 10 watts. Freedom from bass distortion: worse than average. Grille not removable.

Auto receivers/cassette players

Condensed from CONSUMER REPORTS, March 1985

Some 50 companies sell aftermarket receivers/cassette players, and many sell dozens of different models. Two factors, price and fit, can eliminate a lot of those models from consideration right away.

Receivers/cassette players carry suggested retail prices from as little as \$70 or \$80 to well over \$1000. We wouldn't expect much in the way of sound or power from models at the low end of that range. And we wouldn't expect to get our money's worth for models at the high end of the range, for three reasons: First, road noise masks a lot of the low bass and high treble tones faithfully reproduced in expensive autosound equipment. Second, a sound system that wraps you solidly in sound could be dangerous. Third, an obviously expensive system makes a car a target for thieves, increasing the risk of loss, the price of insurance and the need for a good auto security system (another expense item).

The chassis of a receiver/cassette player must fit the cavity that's provided behind the dashboard of your car. Further, the knob shafts of the unit must correspond to the cutouts in the dashboard. Some models use an arrangement known as "DIN-mount," a standard agreed upon by the German car companies and increasingly found in other foreign cars as well. The entire DIN-mount component fits into a 2x7-inch squared cutout; depths vary but are usually around five inches.

RECEIVER PERFORMANCE. FM became music radio because it can produce better overall sound than AM. But FM can often sound a lot worse than AM in a car. The medium is not well suited for mobile reception.

Perhaps the most annoying problem, especially for urban and suburban drivers, is the interference called "multipath distortion." It's caused by the bounce of short-wavelength FM signals off objects as small as houses and cars and by their consequent arrival at the radio at different times. In a moving car, multipath can manifest itself as a rapid, rhythmic fading of the signal, at its weakest phase producing nothing but noise. The repeated fluctuation between noise-free and noisy reception, a pulsing pfft-pfft sound, is called "picket fencing."

Receivers now use three techniques to deal with the pulsing effects of multipath distortion. One automatically switches to mono from the inherently noisier stereo when the interference causes the signal to weaken. The second technique cuts down on the treble volume, and therefore hiss, when the signal weakens. (One way of doing that is called Dynamic Noise Reduction, or DNR, which also works when you play a tape.) Finally, some receivers reduce the entire audio level as the signal weakens, a technique known as "soft limiting." Although those three techniques have gone a long way toward improving the FM reception in cars, they don't conquer the garbling or the worst cases of picket-fencing.

After multipath distortion, perhaps the most annoying type of interference is front-end overload. When you're close to an FM transmitter, its signal can threaten to overwhelm other signals on the FM band. And the front-end electronics that normally screen out unwanted radio frequencies become overloaded (hence the name). The result is a buzzing and rasping noise, if not an actual breakthrough of the unwanted signal.

Radio signals can interfere in several other ways. A strong signal can intrude on a weak one adjacent to it on the FM band; a receiver's ability to keep the signals separate is measured as "FM selectivity." A receiver might pick up two FM signals being broadcast on the same frequency; its ability to ignore the weaker signal is measured as "FM capture ratio."

The key test for assessing a receiver's reception far from the radio station is "FM sensitivity"—a measure of the weakest radio signal that still gives noise-free sound.

Under most circumstances, the AM performance of most any model would be entirely satisfactory.

Text continued on page 336

Ratings of auto receivers/cassette players

Listed in order of estimated overall quality. Differences in overall score of 8 points or less were judged not significant. Prices are approximate retail; discounts are usually available. Ⓓ indicates model was discontinued at original publication.

⊜ ⊖ ○ ◒ ●

Better ⟵ ⟶ Worse

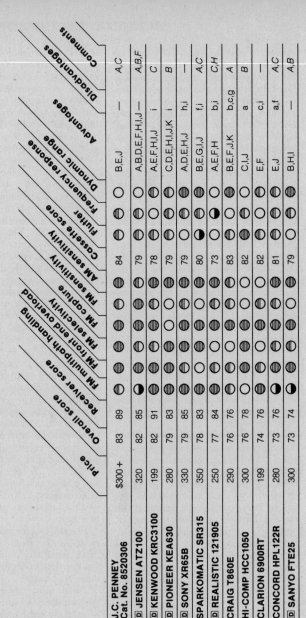

	Price	Overall score	Receiver score	FM multipath handling	FM front end overload	FM selectivity	FM capture	FM sensitivity	AM sensitivity	Cassette score	Flutter	Frequency response	Dynamic range	Advantages	Disadvantages	Comments
J.C. PENNEY Cat. No. 8520306	$300+	83	89	⊖	⊜	⊜	⊜	⊖	⊜	84	⊖	⊖	○	B,E,J	—	*A,C*
Ⓓ **JENSEN ATZ100**	320	82	85	◒	⊜	⊖	⊜	⊜	⊖	79	⊖	⊖	○	A,B,D,E,F,H,I,J	—	*A,B,F*
Ⓓ **KENWOOD KRC3100**	199	82	91	⊜	⊜	⊖	⊜	⊖	⊜	78	⊖	○	⊖	A,E,F,H,I,J	i	*C*
Ⓓ **PIONEER KEA630**	280	79	83	⊜	⊜	⊜	○	○	⊜	79	⊖	⊖	⊖	C,D,E,H,I,J,K	i	*B*
Ⓓ **SONY XR65B**	330	79	85	⊜	⊖	⊜	⊜	⊖	⊜	79	○	⊖	⊜	A,D,E,H,J	h,i	—
SPARKOMATIC SR315	350	78	83	⊜	○	⊜	⊜	○	⊜	80	◒	⊖	⊜	B,E,G,I,J	f,i	*A,C*
Ⓓ **REALISTIC 121905**	250	77	84	⊜	⊖	○	⊜	⊖	⊜	73	○	◒	○	A,E,F,H	b,i	*C,H*
CRAIG T860E	290	76	76	⊖	⊖	○	⊜	⊖	⊖	83	⊖	○	⊜	B,E,F,J,K	b,c,g	*A*
HI-COMP HCC1050	300	76	78	○	⊜	⊜	⊜	○	○	82	⊜	⊖	○	C,I,J	a	*B*
CLARION 6900RT	199	74	76	⊜	⊖	○	⊜	⊖	○	82	⊖	○	⊖	E,F	c,i	—
CONCORD HPL122R	280	73	76	◒	⊜	⊖	⊜	⊖	⊜	81	⊖	⊖	⊖	E,J	a,f	*A,C*
Ⓓ **SANYO FTE25**	300	73	74	◒	⊜	⊖	⊜	○	⊜	79	○	⊖	⊜	B,H,I	—	*A,B*

ALPINE 7154	330	71	74	◉	◓	○	○	○	◓	84	◉	◓	◓	F,I	a,d,e,g	*C*
SEARS Cat. No. 50029	240+	71	73	○	◓	◓	◓	○	◉	79	○	◓	◉	I,J	g	*B,D*
[D] BLAUPUNKT ASPEN SQR24	320	70	73	◓	○	◓	◓	○	◓	72	◒	○	◓	E,H,I	i	*C,G*
KRACO ETR1089	380	69	71	◒	◉	◉	◉	◒	◉	75	◒	◉	◓	E	a	*C,D*
[D] PANASONIC CQS804	250	69	73	◉	◓	○	◓	○	◓	73	◒	○	◓	E,H	b,c,i	*E*
AUDIOVOX AVX3500	280	60	58	◒	◓	◉	◓	◒	○	76	○	◓	◓	—	c,g	*D*

FEATURES IN COMMON

All have: FM stereo indicator light; locking fast-forward and rewind controls; automatic tape stop or play after fast-forward or rewind; "Motorola-type" antenna jacks; tone controls.

Except as noted, all: have a "local" switch to improve resistance to front-end overload.

KEY TO ADVANTAGES

A – Can play tape without radio on.
B – Cassette is easy to insert and eject.
C – Can skip weak stations in seek mode.
D – Seek mode works both up and down band.
E – Tone controls are easy to set.
F – Tone controls are hard to disturb.
G – Has bass-boost switches.
H – Good control layout.
I – Controls better lighted than on most.
J – Control settings are easy to check.
K – Panel brightness is adjustable with headlight switch.

KEY TO DISADVANTAGES

a – Cassette is difficult to insert or eject.
b – No "local" switch.
c – Tuner makes noise when changing stations.
d – Small slide controls are difficult to adjust.
e – Tone controls are difficult to set.
f – Tone controls are easy to disturb.
g – Controls poorly laid out.
h – Poor automatic volume control (a circuit intended to compensate for varying signal strength on AM).
i – Installation instructions judged sketchy.

KEY TO COMMENTS

A – "Slide-rule" dial display.
B – Liquid-crystal display with backlight.
C – Lighted-segment numeric display.
D – Includes device to check wiring-harness installation.
E – "Ambience" switch is claimed to expand the stereo effect.
F – Display lights go on when ignition is on.
G – "Automatic Radio Information" feature, to receive traffic and weather alerts broadcast by participating FM stations in some metropolitan areas, is available with $40 accessory box.

CASSETTE PERFORMANCE. The most important test of a cassette player is how much "flutter" it allows. Flutter, which makes music sound wavery, is caused primarily by mechanical imperfections in the tape-drive mechanism, but it can be exacerbated by the bumps and jolts of driving.

Next to flutter, "frequency response"—a measure of how accurately tones are reproduced—is the most important factor affecting sound quality. Another factor, "dynamic range," is a measure of how loudly and softly a tape player can reproduce a tone without the tone distorting or being submerged in tape hiss. Dynamic range is less important in an autosound system than in a home system because road and wind noise helps to mask tape hiss that would be objectionable elsewhere.

FEATURES. Some features affect both FM and cassette performance. With separate bass and treble controls, you can boost one range of frequencies without reducing the other. A loudness control boosts low bass and high treble—the frequencies most covered up by road noise. A "fader" adjusts the balance between front and rear speakers.

On receivers with a dial tuner, one way to change the station is to turn the knob. Another way is to use push buttons, or "presets," already tuned to preselected stations. Presets on a digital tuner are electronically "programmed." To roam around the dial on a digital tuner, you have to use "tuner seek." On some models, you have to keep pressing the seek button to move from one strong signal to the next up or down the band. On others, a variation called "tuner scan" samples successive stations for a few seconds apiece until you stop it.

Dial tuners show the frequency of the station being received with a "slide rule" type of display; it's easily visible in the dark, but hard to read accurately. Digital tuners present either a liquid-crystal display (LCD) or a lighted-segment display. LCD's don't wash out in bright light; lighted-segment displays show up better at night.

Important to cassette performance is some kind of noise reduction system to cut down on tape hiss. *Dolby B* is commonly offered; *Dolby C*, less so. To get the effect, the tapes you play have to have been recorded on a Dolby machine. An alternative system, DNR, works on all tapes, regardless of how they were taped, but at some sacrifice of treble at low volumes.

Some features add convenience to tape-playing. "Auto reverse" automatically plays the second side of a tape when the first side is finished. "Tape search" stops at each substantial blank portion on a tape during fast-forward or rewind, so you can quickly skip from selection to selection.

If a large part of your tape library is recorded on chrome or metal tape, look for a model with a "tape equalization" switch. Otherwise, metal tapes will sound extra bright.

A feature that can affect the way in which a cassette player will continue to perform is "pinch-roller release." With that, the pinch roller, which presses the tape against the capstan during play, automatically disengages when the cassette player is turned off. Otherwise, leaving the tape inside the unit could cause flat spots to develop on the roller and that could increase flutter. A variation on this feature is "automatic tape eject."

RECOMMENDATIONS. The first step in deciding which aftermarket receiver/cassette player is best for your car is to find out which ones will fit. Even then, be aware that installation isn't a trivial job, and most people should leave it to a professional.

Urban drivers need a model with a receiver that's good at handling multipath distortion and front-end overload. Rural drivers need a receiver with good FM sensitivity. Suburbanites need a model good at all three.

Bear in mind that a receiver/cassette player is only part of an autosound system. You need at least two other components—speakers and an antenna. Car speakers come in lots of shapes, from the common round to the severely flattened oval. So finding one to fit is usually not a problem.

A power antenna, which automatically retracts when the radio is turned off, should perform about the same as a regular whip antenna and be less vulnerable to vandals.

More elaborate components, such as graphic equalizers and power amplifiers, are also available. Attaching them to a receiver/cassette player is much easier if the unit has line-out jacks.

Mid-priced cassette decks

Condensed from CONSUMER REPORTS, June 1984

Modern mid-priced ($300 to $450) cassette decks are replete with sophisticated conveniences, partly because of increased use of microprocessors and partly from other technical refinements in their circuitry. These conveniences have not been incorporated at the expense of good audio performance.

PERFORMANCE. A noise-reduction system is used in one form or another in every deck tested. Although the Ratings give our evaluations for both Dolby B and C, we used only Dolby B in establishing the Ratings order. That's because Dolby B is the noise-reduction system that is most commonly found on prerecorded cassettes and is ordinarily used in making tapes to play on automobile tape decks.

FEATURES. All the decks let you go from one mode of action to another without first pressing the stop button. Special circuitry keeps track of the tape motion and acts to prevent the tape from snarling or breaking.

Some units have a "time-remaining" option that spares you from having to calculate remaining tape time. Other decks have a less desirable kind of time-remaining option that involves shuttling the tape forward to the end and then back to the record spot on the tape.

If you expect to do live recording, look for a deck with microphone jacks. Other features to look for: automatic reverse, which allows you to listen to both sides of a tape without interruption; automatic search and play, which senses gaps of silence in music and can be programmed to skip among recorded musical selections in various ways (although the feature may occasionally be fooled into interpreting a quiet passage as the end of a selection); and cue and review, which enables you to home in quickly on a desired section of tape by letting you hear recognizable "monkey chatter" as the machine speeds through the fast-forward or rewind mode.

RECOMMENDATIONS. Since good performance is a given with so many models, we suggest that you base your buying decision on the particular mix of features that best matches the way you're likely to use a tape-deck—and on price, of course.

Ratings on next page

Ratings of mid-priced cassette decks

Listed in order of estimated overall quality, based on performance with Dolby B noise reduction and on judgments of features and convenience. Differences in overall score of 8 points or less are judged not very significant. All will fit in a space 5 in. high, 18 in. wide, and 15 in. deep. Prices are approximate retail, rounded to nearest dollar; discounts are usually available.

⊜ ⊖ ○ ◒ ●

Better ⟷ Worse

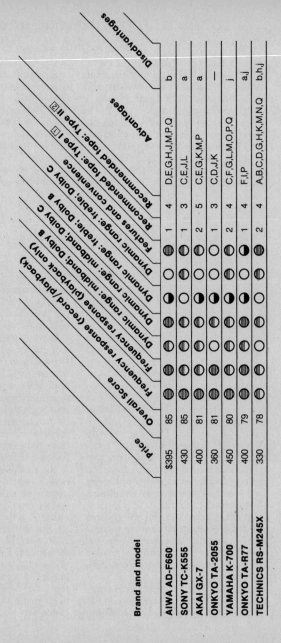

Brand and model	Price	Overall Score	Frequency response (record/playback)	Frequency response (playback only)	Dynamic range: midband; Dolby B	Dynamic range: midband; Dolby C	Dynamic range: treble; Dolby B	Dynamic range: treble; Dolby C	Features and convenience	Recommended tape: Type I [1]	Recommended tape: Type II [2]	Advantages	Disadvantages
AIWA AD-F660	$395	85	⊜	⊜	⊖	⊜	◒	○	⊜	1	4	D,E,G,H,J,M,P,Q	b
SONY TC-K555	430	85	⊜	⊖	⊖	⊖	○	⊖	⊖	1	3	C,E,J,L	a
AKAI GX-7	400	81	⊜	⊖	⊖	⊖	◒	○	⊖	2	5	C,E,G,K,M,P	a
ONKYO TA-2055	360	81	⊜	⊜	○	⊖	◒	○	○	1	3	C,D,J,K	—
YAMAHA K-700	450	80	⊜	⊖	⊖	⊖	◒	⊖	⊖	2	4	C,F,G,L,M,O,P,Q	j
ONKYO TA-R77	400	79	⊜	⊜	⊖	⊜	◒	○	◒	1	4	F,I,P	a,j
TECHNICS RS-M245X	330	78	⊖	⊖	○	⊖	○	⊖	⊜	2	4	A,B,C,D,G,H,K,M,N,Q	b,h,j

DENON DR-M2	400	77	⊖	⊖	⊖	⊖	○	⊖	○	2	3	D,E,G,K	j
TEAC V-500X	340	77	◍	⊖	○	⊖	○	⊖	◍	1	3	A,B,C,D,K,M,N,Q	i
HARMAN/KARDON OD291	435	76	◍	⊖	○	⊖	◒	⊖	○	2	3	J	c,g
SONY TC-V7	350	75	⊖	⊖	⊖	◍	◒	○	○	1	4	C,F,G,M,N	a,d,k
MARANTZ SD530	350	73	⊖	⊖	○	⊖	◒	⊖	◒	1	3	F,M,N,P	c,e
REALISTIC SCT-42	300	73	⊖	⊖	⊖	⊖	◒	○	○	1	3	F,G,M,O,P,Q	j
NIKKO ND-700II	300	72	⊖	⊖	○	—	◒	—	●	1	4	A,H,K	c,e,f,g
PIONEER CT-50R	310	70	⊖	○	○	⊖	◒	⊖	◒	1	3	F,G,M	c,i,j

[1] *1 = Maxell UDXL; 2 = TDK AD.*

[2] *3 = Maxell UDXL II; 4 = TDK SA; 5 = TDK SAX.*

FEATURES IN COMMON

All have: Dolby B noise reduction; provision for tapes of Types I, II, and IV; automatic stop; pause control; peak reading-bar graph-style recording indicators; ability to change tape motion without using stop button; tape-protection feature that will not record if cassette tabs have been punched out; button to mute recording momentarily.

Except as noted, all have: provision for timer control; Dolby C noise reduction; headphone jack; microphone jack; backlight for cassette compartment; electronic tape-counter display with tape-counter memory.

Keys for cassette deck Ratings

KEY TO ADVANTAGES

A – DBX noise reduction.
B – DBX noise reducer can be used to decode DBX records.
C – "Real time" tape counter indicates elapsed time in minutes and seconds.
D – Tape counter indicates time remaining on tape.
E – Three heads; (record, playback, erase) permit monitoring from tape while recording.
F – Automatic reverse.
G – Automatically adjusts for type of tape.
H – Cue/review.
I – Indicator shows status of record protection tabs on cassette.
J – Manually adjustable bias level control.
K – Output-level control, doubles as headphone-level control.
L – Separate headphone-level control.
M – Senses gaps in music to advance to next or replay current selection.
N – Senses gaps in music to skip multiple selections.
O – Senses gaps in music to play multiple randomly programmed selections.
P – Permits audible preview of selections.
Q – Can repeat a single selection.

KEY TO DISADVANTAGES

a – No built-in provision for recording from microphones.
b – Microphone jacks are located on rear of deck; judged inconvenient.
c – Mechanical tape counter; judged more difficult to read than electronic variety.
d – No headphone jack.
e – One-button record-control; judged more likely than most others to allow accidental erasures (if tape-protection feature is circumvented).
f – No Dolby C noise reduction.
g – No external-timer control.
h – Not recommended for use with external timer; timer may shut off power before tape is ended and damage machine.
i – Cassette compartment has no backlight.
j – No tape-counter memory.
k – Records only in forward direction.

Clock radios

Condensed from CONSUMER REPORTS, September 1986

Some manufacturers have tried to embellish the clock radio by combining it with other appliances, such as a tape deck, a television set, or a telephone. But most of the clock radios tested for this report are basic models, ranging in price from $20 to $60. For that kind of money, we found, you can expect to get a reliable clock, a good selection of features, and a radio that delivers fair-to-middling quality.

RADIO PERFORMANCE. Clock radios are usually more clock than radio. Because they're small, most sound tinny. However, two of our more expensive models, the *GE 74662* and the *Sony ICFC30W*, delivered better-than-average tone quality. And a few lower-price models were graced with tone quality judged least average.

Tone quality aside, it's reasonable to expect decent FM and AM performance: sensitivity, selectivity, ease of tuning, and image rejection. Those factors determine, for instance, how well the radio can pull in weak or distant stations, how easily it can tune in a weak station next to a strong one on the dial, if it will zoom in on a station's true signal (rather than spurious versions of that signal), and how well it can cope with interference generated by aircraft. The sums of those factors are collected in the Ratings in judgments of overall FM and AM performance.

FEATURES. All clock radios can give you drowse time, conferred by a button that, once pressed in the morning, gains a six- to eight-minute reprieve before the alarm sounds again. Another basic feature is sleep time; it lets you program the radio to play for a while at night. Still another near-standard feature is battery backup, which holds the time and alarm settings in the event of a power failure.

More than half the test models have reversible time-setting; if you overshoot the mark of your intended waking time, you can move the numbers backward instead of having to advance them through another forward cycle. Several offer two alarm settings so the radio can rouse two sleepers at separate times. The *General Electric 74662* has what amounts to a second alarm that grants up to an hour of extra nap time. The Ratings point out various options of settings and wake-up signals.

Electronic displays are easy to read at night, but they may wash out in bright daylight. Most models give a choice of two brightness levels; several offer more. The top-rated *General Electric* was the only model with a continuous brightness adjustment.

RECOMMENDATIONS. We check-rated the *General Electric 74662*, which lists at $55. It excelled in FM performance and is loaded with features.

Can't find it?

The index on page 388 lists all reports in this issue both alphabetically and by subject.

Ratings of clock radios

Listed in order of estimated quality. Except where separated by heavy lines, closely ranked models differed little in quality. Unless otherwise indicated, prices are list; * indicates that price is approximate; + indicates that shipping is extra. Ⓓ indicates that model was discontinued at original publication.

◍	⊜	○	◒	●
Better ←				→ Worse

Brand and model	Price	Dimensions, H×W×D (in.)	Overall FM performance	Overall AM performance	Tone quality	Features	Comments
✓ GENERAL ELECTRIC 74662	$55	3×11×8	◍	○	⊜	A,C,E,F,I,J,K M,N,O,Q,S,T,X	*D,H*
SOUNDESIGN 3789A	40	4×12×6	⊜	○	◒	A,B,E,M,S,T,V	*F,H*
PANASONIC RC6360	60	4×11×6	⊜	○	○	A,B,D,E,G,P,T,W	*D,E,G*
REALISTIC CHRONOMATIC-245	48	3×11×6	⊜	○	○	A,B,E,H,M, R,S,T,V	*G,I*
REALISTIC CHRONOMATIC-248	35	3×9×5	○	⊜	●	A,B,E,H, M,R,V	*D*
SONY ICFC30W	55	5×10×4	○	⊜	⊜	A,C,I,V	*H*
SANYO RM6600	30*	3×11×6	○	⊜	◒	A,B,S,T,V	*H*
ⒹSONY EZ3	60	4×10×3	○	⊜	◒	A,C,V	*D,F,H*
ⒹGE 74630	20*	3×11×7	○	◒	○	C,F,M,U	*B,C,F*

Ratings continued on next page

Ratings of clock radios continued

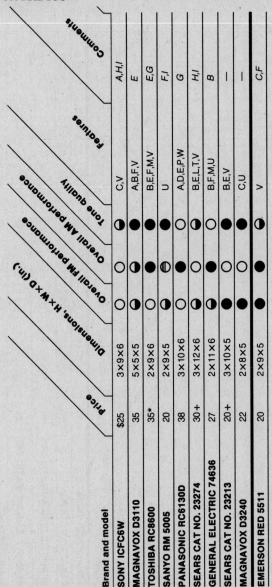

Brand and model	Price	Dimensions, H×W×D (in.)	Overall FM performance	Overall AM performance	Tone quality	Features	Comments
SONY ICFC6W	$25	3×9×6	○	○	◒	C,V	*A,H,I*
MAGNAVOX D3110	35	5×5×5	◒	◒	●	A,B,F,V	*E*
TOSHIBA RC8600	35*	2×9×6	○	●	●	B,E,F,M,V	*E,G*
SANYO RM 5005	20	2×9×5	◒	⊜	●	U	*F,I*
PANASONIC RC6130D	38	3×10×6	○	●	○	A,D,E,P,W	*G*
SEARS CAT NO. 23274	30+	3×12×6	◒	○	◒	B,E,L,T,V	*H,I*
GENERAL ELECTRIC 74636	27	2×11×6	◒	●	○	B,F,M,U	*B*
SEARS CAT NO. 23213	20+	3×10×5	●	○	●	B,E,V	—
MAGNAVOX D3240	22	2×8×5	●	○	●	C,U	—
EMERSON RED 5511	20	2×9×5	●	●	◒	V	*C,F*

FEATURES IN COMMON

All have: built-in wire antenna; drowse period of 6-10 min.; power-failure indicator.
Except as noted, all have: battery backup for alarm and clock memory; design to prevent user from resetting time accidentally; convenient push button or touch plate to reset alarm; red display digits $1/2$-in. high; sleep time feature, which provides radio-play period of up to 1 hr. before automatic shutoff.

KEY TO FEATURES

A – Reversible time-setting.
B – Double alarm setting.
C – Selectable alarm sound.
D – Pitch and tempo to tone alarm changes every min. for 5 min.

E - Alarm sounds during power failure.
F - Adjustable volume level to tone alarm.
G - Displays current time and 1 alarm setting simultaneously.
H - Earphone jack.
I - Treble-cut tone control; can improve tone quality of noisy transmission.
J - Drowse time can be set for 1 min. to 60 min.
K - Can use disposable or rechargeable battery.
L - Uses rechargeable battery. (Unit must be disassembled to replace battery.)
M - Automatic frequency control for FM.
N - Can be programmed for up to 60 min. of nap time.
O - Tone alarm can follow radio alarm with programmable delay of up to 60 min.
P - Tone alarm can follow radio alarm after 10 min.
Q - Radio can play on batteries for about 4 hr.
R - Battery-level indicator.
S - Larger-than-average digits on dial.
T - Illuminated radio dial.
U - 1 brightness level.
V - 2 brightness levels.
W - 5 brightness levels.
X - Continuous brightness adjustment.

KEY TO COMMENTS
A - No battery backup.
B - Time-setting control can be easily reset by accident.
C - Control to reset alarm is sliding switch.
D - Brightness control and/or time-setting controls located inconveniently on bottom or rear of unit.
E - Only pointer on radio dial is illuminated.
F - Radio can play for up to 2 hr. before automatic shutoff.
G - Green digits in display.
H - Blue digits in display.
I - Lowest brightness setting may be too bright at night.

Foods

Ice cream

Condensed from CONSUMER REPORTS, July 1986

Although some well-known brands of ice cream built their reputations by offering large varieties of fancy flavors, the nation's favorite ice-cream flavors remain vanilla and chocolate. So those, packaged under more than 20 brand names, are what we decided to test. We also tested a broad selection of strawberry ice cream, the first choice among fruit flavors. Our test roster of ice creams included supermarket house brands, national name brands, and rich, superpremium brands, as well as a few sold only by ice-cream chains. We bought our samples mainly in Texas and New York; a few of our samples were collected from California.

TASTE. Our trained panel of tasters evaluated unidentified samples of each ice cream in terms of flavor and texture. The flavor criteria varied, of course, with each ice-cream variety. But textural considerations were similar for all varieties. Overall, the panelists were looking for smooth (not counting strawberry lumps), creamy products with a rich mouthfeel. Specifically, the panelists assessed each product's fluffiness or density, the presence of ice crystals, the ease of melting, foaminess, graininess, viscosity, and residual mouthcoating. They even reported on "coldness"—not actual temperature but a sensory impression of it that can be conveyed more or less strongly by an ice cream's ingredients.

A fine vanilla ice cream should be pleasantly sweet, with a creamy, dairy flavor, a delicate vanilla bouquet, and an agreeable aftertaste. And, as a group, the vanillas were pretty fine. *Swensen's* was judged the finest, chiefly because its texture was given an edge over the rest. But the next eight brands of vanilla followed closely.

Ideally, a chocolate ice cream should have pronounced chocolate and cocoa flavors and be reasonably sweet, without harshness, bitterness, or any artificial flavor notes; some hint of milk, cream, or butter may come through. Nine ice creams and the *Light n' Lively* ice milk stood out from the rest in having a rich chocolate flavor; most of the nine scored high in cocoa flavor, too. But only *Breyers*, *Baskin-Robbins*, *Ben & Jerry's*, and *Friendly* combined superior flavor with very good texture.

Strawberry ice cream should be marked with the flavor of the fresh fruit. Dairy flavors should also be apparent, but all flavors must be balanced, without harshness or artificial notes suggesting something like strawberry

Text continued on page 349

Ratings of ice cream

Listed by flavors; within flavors, except as noted, listed in order of sensory quality. Closely ranked products differed little in quality; products grouped in brackets had identical sensory scores. Serving size is 4 fl. oz. (1/2 cup or approx. 2 scoops). Cost per serving are based on average prices paid by CU shoppers for, unless othewise indicated, 1/2 gal.

⊜ ⊖ ○ ◒ ●

Better ⟷ Worse

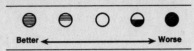

Product	Cost per serving	Weight of serving (oz.)	Flavor	Texture	Calories per serving	Butterfat (%)	Comments
Vanilla ice cream							
SWENSEN'S OLD FASHIONED	49¢ [1]	2.7	⊜	⊜	180	14	X,Z
DREYER'S FRENCH	26	2.3	⊜	⊖	160	15	R,T,Y
FRIENDLY	19	2.5	⊜	⊖	140	11	R,Y
LUCERNE NATURAL GOURMET	21	2.5	⊜	⊖	155	14	O,R,Y
BLUE BELL HOMEMADE	23	2.7	⊜	⊖	170	12	R,S,T
FRUSEN GLÄDJÉ	54 [1]	4.1	⊜	⊖	290	16	R,T,W
HÄAGEN-DAZS	56 [1]	3.8	⊜	⊖	265	17	R,T,W
HOWARD JOHNSON'S	43 [1]	3.0	⊜	⊖	200	16	R,T
SCHRAFFT'S	49 [1]	3.2	⊜	⊖	220	17	R
ABBOTT'S OLD PHILADELPHIA	20	2.4	⊜	○	160	12	R,T,U
BLUE BELL FRENCH	22	2.6	⊜	○	155	10	R,S,T
BREYERS	21	2.4	⊖	⊜	145	12	Q,R,W
DREYER'S	26	2.3	⊖	○	155	15	R,Y
SNOW STAR	12	2.3	⊖	⊜	130	11	J,R,V,Y
BEN & JERRY'S FRENCH	50 [1]	3.7	⊖	○	245	15	R,T
BORDEN OLD FASHIONED	15	2.4	⊖	○	140	10	R,S,V

Ratings continued on next page

Ratings of ice cream
continued

Product	Cost per serving	Weight of serving (oz.)	Flavor	Texture	Calories per serving	Butterfat (%)	Comments
COUNTRY CLUB	12¢	2.3	◓	○	125	10	*S,V,Y*
DOLLY MADISON ALL NATURAL	17	2.3	◓	○	130	10	*R*
SEALTEST ICE CREAM PARLOR TASTE	19	2.4	◓	○	140	11	*J,R,S, V,Y*
BASKIN-ROBBINS READY PACK	26	2.5	○	◓	150	12	*R,Y*
LUCERNE	15	2.4	○	◓	135	10	*R,S,V,Y*
SEALTEST FRENCH	17	2.3	◓	○	140	11	*N,R,S,T, V,Y*
KROGER DELUXE	15	2.5	○	○	140	11	*R,S,Y*
FOREMOST	17	2.3	○	◓	130	10	*O,R,S, V,Y*
LIGHT N' LIVELY [2]	15	2.3	○	○	110	5	*F,H,J,N, R,S,Y*
LOUIS SHERRY	16	2.4	○	○	135	10	*R*
ANN PAGE (A&P)	12	2.4	○	◒	135	10	*I,N,Q,R, S,V,Y*
Chocolate ice cream							
BREYERS	22	2.5	⊜	◓	170	12	*Q,R,W*
BASKIN-ROBBINS READY PACK	26	2.5	⊜	◓	165	11	*B,Q,V*
BEN & JERRY'S CHOCOLATE FUDGE	51 [1]	3.7	⊜	◓	250	13	*B,R,T*
SCHRAFFT'S	48 [1]	3.2	⊜	○	240	16	*B,Q,R*
LUCERNE NATURAL GOURMET (TEX.)	25 [1]	2.5	◓	⊜	155	14	—
ABBOTT'S DOUBLE	20	2.5	⊜	○	160	10	*B,Q,T,U*
FRIENDLY	19	2.5	⊜	◓	155	11	—
FRUSEN GLÄDJÉ	54 [1]	3.8	⊜	○	270	16	*N,P,T,W*
LUCERNE NATURAL GOURMET (CAL.)	25 [1]	2.5	◓	⊜	150	11	*X*
HÄAGEN-DAZS	56 [1]	3.8	⊜	○	275	17	*P,T,W*

Product	Cost per serving	Weight of serving (oz.)	Flavor	Texture	Calories per serving	Butterfat (%)	Comments
KROGER DUTCH	15¢	2.5	●	○	150	10	*V*
LIGHT N' LIVELY [2]	15	2.3	●	○	115	5	*Y*
HOWARD JOHNSON'S	43 [1]	2.9	◓	◓	205	16	*R,T*
BLUE BELL DUTCH	23	2.6	◓	●	165	11	*A,G,M,R*
DREYER'S	26	2.3	◓	●	155	15	—
FOREMOST	17	2.3	◓	●	135	9	*V*
ANN PAGE (A&P)	12	2.4	◓	○	135	10	*Q,R,V,Y*
COUNTRY CLUB	12	2.0	◓	◓	110	9	*V*
LADY BORDEN	21	2.6	◓	◓	165	13	—
DOLLY MADISON ALL NATURAL DUTCH	17	2.4	◓	◓	140	10	*Z*
LOUIS SHERRY	19	2.4	◓	◓	145	10	—
LUCERNE	17	2.4	◓	◓	120	9	*V*
SNOW STAR	12	2.2	◓	◓	115	9	*V*
SWENSEN'S	49 [1]	2.3	◓	○	155	13	*N,X,Z*
SEALTEST ICE CREAM PARLOR TASTE	17	2.3	◓	○	140	10	*Q,V,Y*
BORDEN DUTCH	16	2.4	○	◓	145	10	*A,C,G, S,V*
BLUE BELL MILK CHOCOLATE	23	3.1	○	○	185	9	*A,P,R,S*
Strawberry ice cream							
FRUSEN GLÄDJÉ	52 [1]	3.8	●	◓	270	16	*T,W*
HÄAGEN-DAZS	55 [1]	3.7	●	◓	255	16	*T,W*
BASKIN-ROBBINS READY PACK	57 [1]	3.1	◓	◓	175	9	*D,X*
FRIENDLY	19	2.5	◓	◓	135	9	*E,Y*
LOUIS SHERRY	16	2.4	◓	◓	140	10	—
BREYERS	22	2.4	◓	○	135	9	*W*
HOWARD JOHNSON'S	43 [1]	3.0	◓	○	180	12	*E,R,T*
SCHRAFFT'S	46 [1]	3.2	◓	◓	205	13	*R*

Ratings continued on next page

Ratings of ice cream continued

Product	Cost per serving	Weight of serving (oz.)	Flavor	Texture	Calories per serving	Butterfat (%)	Comments
KROGER CLASSIC	16¢	2.9	◒	⊜	150	8	*E,V,R*
SEALTEST ICE CREAM PARLOR TASTE	18	2.3	○	⊜	130	8	*E,I,V,Y*
BLUE BELL	26 [1]	2.7	⊜	◒	155	8	*E,L,N,R, S,T*
BORDEN	17	2.7	◒	○	170	10	*D,E,K,L, N,S,V*
DOLLY MADISON ALL NATURAL	18	2.3	◒	⊜	125	8	*D,E,R*
SWENSEN'S	49 [1]	1.9	◒	⊜	120	13	*E,X*
COUNTRY CLUB	12	2.4	◒	○	130	9	*E,S,V,Y*
FOREMOST	17	2.3	◒	○	115	8	*E,F,V,Y*
ANN PAGE (A&P)	12	2.4	◒	○	130	10	*E,I,N, V,Y*
SNOW STAR	12	2.2	◒	◒	120	10	*E,F,N, V,Y*

[1] *Bought in pints or quarts.* [2] *Ice milk.*

SENSORY CHARACTERISTICS

All left appropriate mouthcoating.

All vanillas: tasted slightly of cooked milk and egg; gave very "cold" sensory impression.

Except as noted, all vanillas: were very slightly grainy; were moderate in density, body, and dairy flavor; were slightly lacking in sweetness; had milky and very slightly sweet aftertaste.

All chocolates: tasted very slightly of cooked milk and malt; were slightly lacking in sweetness.

Except as noted, all chocolates: were slightly grainy; gave very "cold" sensory impression; were moderate in density and dairy flavor; were relatively thick in body; had slight chocolate aftertaste.

All strawberry flavors: tasted slightly of cooked milk and very slightly of vanilla, with very slightly sweet aftertaste; were slightly grainy and relatively thick in body.

Except as noted, all strawberry flavors: tasted very slightly of cooked strawberries; were moderate in dairy flavor; were appropriately sweet; gave very "cold" sensory impression.

KEY TO COMMENTS

A–Chocolate had some vanilla flavor notes (especially in **Borden Dutch**).
B–Among strongest in chocolate aftertaste.
C–Weakest in chocolate aftertaste.
D–Pronounced cooked-strawberry flavor (strongest in **Borden**).
E–Undesirable artificial-strawberry flavor (slight in **Dolly Madison, Friendly, Howard Johnson, Sealtest,** and **Borden,** and strong in **Country Club**).
F–Low dairy flavor.
G–More dairy flavor than in most other chocolate brands.
H–Low in milky aftertaste.
I–Too low in sweet taste.
J–Contains FD&C Yellow No. 5.
K–Slightly too sweet.
L–Gave less "cold" sensation than most.
M–Gave very "cold" sensation.
N–Less dense than other of its flavor.
O–Among thickest-bodied of vanilla brands.
P–Among thinnest-bodied of chocolate brands.

Q-Grainy and undesirably so except for Abbott's Double, which contains chocolate chips.
R-Natural flavor added.
S-Artificial flavor added (vanillin in **Lucerne, Borden,** and **Foremost**; unspecified in others noted).
T-Contains egg.
U-Contains honey.
V-Contains Polysorbate 80.
W-No added gums or other emulsifiers.
X-No ingredients list.
Y-Natural and artificial color added.
Z-Samples varied widely in calories and density.

---

candy or chewing gum. *Frusen Gladje* and *Haagen-Dazs* earned top honors by virtue of the intensity and freshness of their strawberry flavor. Six other brands were close runners-up.

Ice cream usually has air whipped into it. That practice, called "overrun" in the industry, has some value. Insufficient aeration makes ice cream heavy and soggy. Too much air, however, makes it fluffy or snowy—and short on real ingredients. As a minimum standard of density, the law requires that a gallon of ice cream weigh at least 4.5 pounds. That works out to 2.25 ounces per 4-fluid-ounce serving (the measure of ice cream used in the Ratings not because it's a constant quantity but because it represents the amount people are most likely to scoop or spoon out as a serving). As the Ratings show, several brands skirt close to the legal requirement for density. Our samples of *Country Club chocolate and Swensen's* strawberry were quite definitely under the minimum limit.

NUTRITION. Vanilla ice cream must contain at least 10 percent butterfat, according to Federal standards. Chocolate and strawberry ice cream need to have only 8 percent butterfat (and any flavor of ice milk only 2 percent). All the tested products met those standards, but the premium brands exceeded them generously. That, together with the fact that the premium brands tended to be the densest ice creams, gave them a relatively high caloric content per serving—something on the order of 200 to 250 calories compared with less than 160 for most other brands. But those servings, of course, not only contained more calories; they contained more ice cream, too.

After fat, carbohydrates—generally sugars—are the chief source of calories in ice cream. Milk and other dairy products contain sugar naturally, but much of ice cream's sugar has been added. Like other dairy products ice cream and ice milk contain a fair amount of protein. Salt also is a natural component of milk, although some producers may add a bit extra. Servings of our samples averaged 60 to 65 milligrams of salt.

Some other ingredients may find their way into commercial ice creams. Stabilizers, to improve smoothness and retard melting, are noted on labels as vegetable gums (guar, locust or carob bean, cellulose) or artificial substances (such as Polysorbate 80). Emulsifiers, also to improve smoothness and to enhance aeration, are noted as mono- and diglycerides, lecithin, and carrageenan. Colorings may be natural extracts or synthetic dyes (such as FD&C Yellow No. 5, an allergen to some people).

RECOMMENDATIONS. No brand did equally well in all the flavors we sampled. Nor did any brand distinguish itself as a bargain; the more expensive products on a volume basis usually compensated at least partly for that with their greater density. The Ratings nominate our choices for vanilla, chocolate, and strawberry. But if you fancy some other flavor, you might have the best luck trying *Abbott's, Breyers, Friendly, Frusen Gladje, Haagen-Dazs, Howard Johnson's, Lucerne Natural Gourmet,* or *Schrafft's.* The flavors that we tested from those brands all ranked fairly high, suggesting consistent quality.

Ready-to-eat cereals

Condensed from CONSUMER REPORTS, October 1986

Cereal grains are considered "nutrient dense," in the sense that they pack a good amount of food value for their calories. That food value includes complex carbohydrates (starches), fiber, B vitamins, and protein. In ready-to-eat cereals, however, processing removes some nutrients. Cereal makers can and do restore lost nutrients—sometimes to your benefit, sometimes not. And they can and do add fat, sodium, and sugar—never to your benefit.

For this report, we scored 59 cereals on their balance of five key components. In accordance with the 100-point Nutrition Index that we devised for Ratings purposes, we awarded points for dietary fiber and for protein, two desirable ingredients, and subtracted points for added sugars, sodium, and fat.

We found most of the data we needed for the Ratings right on the labels. Nutritional labeling has been standard on cereal boxes for years, and our spot checks indicated that the labeling is generally accurate.

Although fiber has become an important selling point for cereals, there's no requirement that manufacturers include fiber content in their labeling, and few do. So we analyzed all 59 products for fiber. We also performed a full analysis of the Swiss-made *Familia* cereals; those products do not carry nutritional labeling.

NUTRITION. In past times, bran, with its considerable "roughage," was promoted as a laxative. But dietary recommendations by the National Cancer Institute have urgently shifted consumers' concern from constipation to colon cancer. The NCI recommends the consumption of 20 to 35 grams of fiber daily from a variety of foods. Cereal grain is an excellent source of insoluble fiber, the type considered most helpful in preventing cancer of the colon.

The highest-fiber cereal in the Ratings is *Fiber One*, with 12 grams of fiber to the ounce or enough to supply about a third to a half of your fiber needs. (Kellogg has since topped *Fiber One* with its *All-Bran with Extra Fiber*, which contains 13 grams of fiber to the ounce. That brand appears and its Nutrition Index is given in the Listings of nonrated cereals beginning on page 356.) Kellogg's regular *All-Bran* contains nine grams of fiber to the ounce. The other bran cereals in the Ratings provide about five grams of fiber per one-ounce serving.

While you need not restrict to bran cereal, you should expect to get a fair part of your dietary fiber from the cereal you eat. Note that half the products in the Ratings don't even contain a gram of fiber per ounce.

The protein in grain is good but not what nutritionists term "complete." Unlike animal protein, cereal protein is deficient in certain essential amino acids. But thanks to the way most breakfast cereals are eaten, they can "borrow" nutrients from added milk to make their protein more complete.

Special K had more protein than any other cereal, six grams to the ounce. *Life* had five grams, and *All-Bran*, *Cheerios*, *Quaker 100% Natural Cereal*, and *Raisin Life* had four grams of protein per ounce. But more than half the brands offered only a gram or two of protein per serving.

Only 19 rated brands are very low in sugar, having three grams or less per ounce. (A teaspoon of table sugar weighs slightly more than four grams.) Four cereals, in fact, have no sugar at all; they're the three top-rated *Nabisco Shredded Wheat* and *Sun Flakes Crispy Wheat and Rice*. At the other extreme, nine cereals come loaded with 12 grams (three teaspoonfuls) or more of sugar per ounce.

Many Americans who try to limit their salt intake might not think to check their cereal bowl, since cereal grains themselves contain very little sodium. But many cereal makers routinely add some salt. General Mills adds so much salt to *Wheaties* (370 milligrams per serving) that, ounce for ounce, that cereal has about twice the sodium of potato chips. Four other rated cereals—*Cheerios*, *Corn Chex*, *Bran Chex*, and *Corn Bran*—contain 300 or more milligrams of sodium per ounce.

Some cereal makers add oils to soften the texture of their products—especially granola-type cereals, which are baked and can otherwise turn buckshot hard. *Quaker 100% Natural* in its two varieties, *Sun Country Granola*, and *Cracklin' Oat Bran* contain four or more grams of fat per ounce, the equivalent of more than a pat of butter.

Most cereal makers fortify their products with vitamins, but we didn't factor vitamins into our scores. Fortification is of dubious nutritional value. People who eat a reasonably varied diet will get sufficient vitamins whether or not they eat breakfast cereal. Our previous cereal tests—animal feeding studies—showed no consistent correlation between a cereal's fortification and the lab animals' health or growth.

TASTE. Though not a ranking factor, a brief sensory description accompanies the citation of each product in the Ratings. Our trained sensory panel evaluated the cereals with and without milk, first gauging their basic tastes: sweet, salty, sour, and bitter. Beyond that, the panelists sought to identify the specific grains, such as wheat, corn, or oats. And they noted other flavors: vanilla, brown sugar, caramelized sugar, brown spices (nutmeg, cinnamon, cloves, and allspice), cocoa, dried fruits, and nuts.

In a good cereal, one should be able to taste a rich, often nutlike grain flavor. Most of the "adult" cereals had a slight to moderate grain flavor; most were slightly sweet and just a bit sour. Many of the children's cereals at the bottom of the Ratings had hardly any grain flavor and had a candylike sweetness.

A good cereal should be moderately firm, crispy, and crunchy. Most were, our panelists said. They also scored each cereal for "toothpacking" and for residual particles. Toothpacking is the tendency of some cereals to stick between the teeth, residual particles are dry bits that stay in the mouth after swallowing. A good cereal may have both, in moderation. But some of the grittier cereals had our panelists wishing for toothbrush and floss.

RECOMMENDATIONS. Three varieties of *Nabisco Shredded Wheat* topped the Ratings; all three provided plenty of fiber and protein no sugar and very little sodium, or fat. Closely shadowing them were General Mills' *Fiber One* and Kellogg's *Frosted Mini-Wheats*. In the additional listing of other cereals for which we merely calculated Nutritional Indices, *Quaker Puffed Wheat* led all brands and varieties with a Nutrition Index of 78.

Our Nutrition Index scores weigh a cereal's virtues against its vices to find the best nutritional mix. But you may be concerned about one component in a cereal—sodium, say—and care little about others. The breakdown of key components in each Ratings entry will reveal, among other things, the number of grams of sodium in a one-ounce serving of that cereal.

Cereals are fairly low in calories—usually about 110 an ounce—but if you count calories, be sure to watch the amount of cereal you pour. Cereals have various densities. A bowl that holds exactly an ounce by weight of *Special K*, for example, will hold 3½ ounces of the denser *Quaker 100% Natural Raisin and Date Cereal*, with more than triple the calories—about 490.

The brands we rated ranged in cost from 10 to 20 cents per one-ounce serving. Add milk and a banana, and you can have a bowl of cereal for something like 35 to 45 cents. Pretty good, but it's still at least three times more than an egg would cost. To save a little, you might try sampling generic and supermarket brands. They're often 25 percent cheaper than major cereal brands.

We surveyed a variety of store brands and compared them nutritionally with similar brand-name products. We found that similar products scored virtually identically. Corn flakes, for instance, were equally nutritious whether the name on the box was Kellogg's or Safeway. The same held true for crisped-rice, puffed-oats, and shredded-wheat cereals.

Ratings of ready-to-eat cereals

Listed in order of CU's Nutrition Index; products with identical Index scores are listed alphabetically. Differences of 7 points or less are not nutritionally meaningful for most people. All values are for 1-oz. serving. Sensory comments are from panel tastings with milk. Costs are based on prices paid for 12-oz. package or closest available size.

NABISCO SHREDDED WHEAT 'N BRAN. Index: 73. Fiber: 4 gm. Protein: 3 gm. Sugar: none. Sodium: none. Fat: 1 gm. Calories: 110. Sensory comments: strong wheat flavor; less sweet than most. Cost: 14¢.

NABISCO SHREDDED WHEAT SPOON SIZE. Index: 73. Fiber: 3 gm. Protein: 3 gm. Sugar: none. Sodium: trace. Fat: 1 gm. Calories: 110. Sensory comments: strong wheat flavor; less sweet than most; no sourness. Cost: 12¢.

NABISCO SHREDDED WHEAT. Index: 71. Fiber: 3 gm. Protein: 2 gm. Sugar: none. Sodium: trace. Fat: 1 gm. Calories: 110. Sensory comments: slight to moderate wheat flavor; less sweet than most; no sourness. Cost: 12¢.

FIBER ONE (General Mills). Index: 67. Fiber: 12 gm. Protein: 3 gm. Sugar: 2 gm. Sodium: 220 mg. Fat: 1 gm. Calories: 60. Sensory comments: moderate bran and slight-to-moderate wheat flavors; left more residual particles than most. Cost: 12¢.

FROSTED MINI-WHEATS (Kellogg). Index: 62. Fiber: 3 gm. Protein: 3 gm. Sugar: 6 gm. Sodium: 5 mg. Fat: none. Calories: 110. Sensory comments: strong wheat flavor; caramelized-sugar flavor; sweeter than most. Cost: 13¢.

ALL-BRAND (Kellogg). Index: 60. Fiber: 9 gm. Protein: 4 gm. Sugar: 5 gm. Sodium: 270 mg. Fat: 1 gm. Calories: 70. Sensory comments: moderate bran and slight-to-moderate wheat flavors; less sweet than most; less crispy/crunchy than most; left more residual particles than most. Cost: 12¢.

NUTRI-GRAIN WHEAT (Kellogg). Index: 58. Fiber: 2 gm. Protein: 3 gm. Sugar: 2

gm. Sodium: 195 mg. Fat: none. Calories: 110. Sensory comments: slight-to moderate wheat flavor; less sweet than most. Cost 14¢.

FAMILIA GENUINE SWISS MUESLI (Biofamilia). Index: 56. Fiber: 3 gm. Protein: 3 gm. Sugar: 7 gm. Sodium: 2 mg. Fat: 2 gm. Calories: 105. Sensory comments: slight-to-moderate oat and wheat flavors; dried-fruit flavor; less crispy/crunchy than most. Cost: 15¢.

GRAPE-NUTS (Post). Index: 56. Fiber: 2 gm. Protein: 3 gm. Sugar: 3 gm. Sodium: 190 mg. Fat: none. Calories: 110. Sensory comments: Slight-to-moderate wheat flavor and very slight barley flavor; less sweet than most; firmer and more crispy/crunchy than most, even after chewing; more toothpacking and more residual particles than most. Cost: 10¢.

POST NATURAL BRAN FLAKES. Index: 56. Fiber: 5 gm. Protein: 3 gm. Sugar: 5 gm. Sodium: 230 mg. Fat: none. Calories: 90. Sensory comments: strong wheat flavor; less sweet than most. Cost: 10¢.

WHEAT CHEX (Ralston Purina). Index: 56. Fiber: 2 gm. Protein: 3 gm. Sugar: 2 gm. Sodium: 200 mg. Fat: none. Calories: 100. Sensory comments: Slight-to-moderate wheat flavor; less sweet than most. Cost: 11¢.

FAMILIA SWISS BIRCHERMUESLI (Biofamilia). Index: 53. Fiber: 4 gm. Protein: 3 gm. Sugar: 6 gm. Sodium: 60 mg. Fat: 2 gm. Calories: 100. Sensory comments: Slight-to-moderate wheat and oat flavors; dried-fruit and nut flavors; less crispy/crunchy than most; more residual particles than most. Cost: 20¢.

NUTRI-GRAIN CORN (Kellogg). Index: 53. Fiber: 2 gm. Protein: 2 gm. Sugar: 2 gm. Sodium: 185 mg. Fat: 1 gm. Calories: 110. Sensory comments: Slight-to-moderate wheat flavor; less sweet than most. Cost: 14¢.

SPECIAL K (Kellogg). Index: 53. Fiber: trace. Protein: 6 gm. Sugar: 3 gm. Sodium: 230 mg. Fat: none. Calories: 110. Sensory comments: mild corn and rice flavor; less sweet than most. Cost: 16¢.

BRAN CHEX (Ralston Purina). Index: 51. Fiber: 5 gm. Protein: 3 gm. Sugar: 5 gm. Sodium: 300 mg. Fat: none. Calories: 90. Sensory comments: slight-to-moderate wheat and slight bran flavors; less sweet than most. Cost: 12¢.

CHEERIOS (General Mills). Index: 51. Fiber: 2 gm. Protein: 4 gm. Sugar: 1 gm. Sodium: 330 mg. Fat: 2 gm. Calories: 110. Sensory comments: slight-to-moderate oat flavor; less sweet than most. Cost: 13¢.

NUTRI-GRAIN WHEAT & RAISINS (Kellogg). Index: 51. Fiber: 1 gm. Protein: 2 gm. Sugar: 6 gm. Sodium: 120 mg. Fat: none. Calories: 100. Sensory comments: slight-to-moderate wheat flavor; dried-fruit flavor. Cost: 15¢.

SUN COUNTRY GRANOLA WITH RAISINS (International MultiFoods). Index: 51. Fiber: 1 gm. Protein: 3 gm. Sugar: 6 gm. Sodium: 10 mg. Fat: 5 gm. Calories: 130. Sensory comments: slight-to-moderate oat and wheat flavors; caramelized-sugar, brown-sugar, honey, dried-fruit, and nut flavors; sweeter than most; firmer than most. Cost: 10¢.

GRAPE-NUTS FLAKES (Post). Index: 49. Fiber: 2 gm. Protein: 3 gm. Sugar: 5 gm. Sodium: 170 mg. Fat: 1 gm. Calories: 100. Sensory comments: slight-to-moderate wheat flavor. Cost: 12¢.

KELLOGG'S BRAN FLAKES. Index: 49. Fiber: 4 gm. Protein: 3 gm. Sugar: 5 gm. Sodium: 220 mg. Fat: none. Calories: 90. Sensory comments: slight-to-moderate wheat and slight bran flavors; less sweet than most. Cost: 11¢.

LIFE (Quaker Oats). Index: 49. Fiber: 1 gm. Protein: 5 gm. Sugar: 6 gm. Sodium:

Ratings continued on next page

Ratings of ready-to-eat cereals continued

180 mg. Fat: 2 gm. Calories: 120. Sensory comments: slight-to-moderate wheat flavor. Cost: 13¢.

SUN FLAKES CRISPY WHEAT & RICE FLAKES (Ralston Purina). Index: 49. Fiber: trace. Protein: 2 gm. Sugar: none. Sodium: 240 mg. Fat: 1 gm. Calories: 110. Sensory comments: slight-to-moderate wheat flavor; caramelized-sugar flavor; sweeter than most. Cost: 14¢.

TOTAL (General Mills). Index: 49: Fiber: 2 gm. Protein: 3 gm. Sugar: 3 gm. Sodium: 280 mg. Fat: 1 gm. Calories: 130. Sensory comments: slight-to-moderate wheat flavor; less sweet than most. Cost: 15¢.

100% NATURAL CEREAL RAISIN & DATE (Quaker Oats). Index: 47. Fiber: trace. Protein: 3 gm. Sugar: 5 gm. Sodium: 10 mg. Fat: 5 gm. Calories: 130. Sensory comments: slight-to-moderate oat and wheat flavors; brown-sugar, dried-fruit, coconut, and nut flavors: sweeter than most; firmer than most. Cost: 13¢.

WHEATIES (General Mills). Index: 47. Fiber: 2 gm. Protein: 3 gm. Sugar: 3 gm. Sodium: 370 mg. Fat: 1 gm. Calories: 110. Comments: slight-to-moderate wheat flavor; less sweet than most. Cost: 12¢.

CRISPIX (Kellogg). Index: 44. Fiber: trace. Protein: 2 gm. Sugar: 3 gm. Sodium: 220 mg. Fat: none. Calories: 110. Sensory comments: slight corn flavor; less sweet than most. Cost: 14¢.

FRUIT & FIBRE HARVEST MEDLEY (Post). Index: 44. Fiber: 4 gm. Protein: 3 gm. Sugar: 7 gm. Sodium: 190 mg. Fat: 1 gm. Calories: 90. Sensory comments: slight-to-moderate wheat flavor; dried-fruit flavor. Cost: 14¢.

FRUIT & FIBRE MOUNTAIN TRAIL (Post). Index: 44. Fiber: 4 gm. Protein: 3 gm. Sugar: 7 gm. Sodium: 180 mg. Fat: 1 gm. Calories: 90. Sensory comments: slight-to-moderate wheat and slight bran flavors; dried-fruit, coconut, and nut flavors. Cost: 13¢.

FRUIT & FIBRE TROPICAL FRUIT (Post). Index: 44. Fiber: 4 gm. Protein: 2 gm. Sugar: 6 gm. Sodium: 160 mg. Fat: 1 gm. Calories: 90. Sensory coments: slight-to-moderate wheat flavor; dried-fruit and coconut flavors. Cost: 13¢.

KELLOGG'S CORN FLAKES. Index: 44. Fiber: trace. Protein: 2 gm. Sugar: 2 gm. Sodium: 280 mg. Fat: none. Calories: 110. Sensory coments: moderate corn flavor; less sweet than most. Cost: 10¢.

100% NATURAL CEREAL (Quaker Oats). Index: 44. Fiber: trace. Protein: 4 gm. Sugar: 6 gm. Sodium: 15 mg. Fat: 6 gm. Calories: 140. Sensory comments: slight-to-moderate oat and wheat flavors; brown-sugar, honey, coconut, and nut flavors; sweeter than most; firmer than most; more toothpacking and more residual particles than most. Cost: 13¢.

QUAKER CORN BRAN. Index: 44. Fiber: 5 gm. Protein: 2 gm. Sugar: 6 gm. Sodium: 300 mg. Fat: 1 gm. Calories: 110. Sensory comments: slight-moderate wheat and slight corn flavors. Cost: 14¢.

FRUITFUL BRAN (Kellogg). Index: 42. Fiber: 4 gm. Protein: 2 gm. Sugar: 8 gm. Sodium: 170 mg. Fat: none. Calories: 90. Sensory comments: slight-to-moderate wheat and slight bran flavors; caramelized-sugar, dried-fruit flavors. Cost: 14¢.

PRODUCT 19 (Kellogg). Index. 42. Fiber: trace: Protein: 2 gm. Sugar; 3 gm. Sodium: 290 mg. Fat: none. Calories: 110. Sensory comments: slight-to-moderate corn flavor; less sweet than most. Cost 17¢.

RAISIN LIFE (Quaker Oats). Index: 42. Fiber: 1 gm. protein: 4 gm. Sugar: 10 gm. Sodium: 135 mg. Fat: 1 gm. Calories: 100. Sensory comments: slight-to-moderate wheat flavor; caramelized-sugar and dried-fruit flavors. Cost: 15¢.

RICE CHEX (Ralston Purina). Index: 42. Fiber: trace. Protein: 1 gm. Sugar: 2 gm. Sodium: 280 mg. Fat: none. Calories: 110.

Sensory comments: slight rice flavor; less sweet than most. Cost: 15¢.

RICE KRISPIES (Kellogg). Index: 42. Fiber: trace. Protein: 2 gm. Sugar: 3 gm. Sodium: 280 mg. Fat: none. Calories: 110. Sensory comments: slight rice flavor; less sweet than most; less toothpacking and fewer residual particles than most. Cost: 13¢.

SUPER GOLDEN CRISP (Post). Index: 42. Fiber: trace. Protein: 2 gm. Sugar: 14 gm. Sodium: 45 mg. Fat: none. Calories: 110. Sensory comments: slight-to-moderate wheat flavor; caramelized-sugar flavor; sweeter than most; no sourness. Cost: 14¢.

CORN CHEX (Ralston Purina). Index: 40. Fiber: trace. Protein: 2 gm. Sugar: 3 gm. Sodium: 310 mg. Fat: none. Calories: 110. Sensory comments: slight corn flavor; less sweet than most. Cost: 14¢.

HONEY SMACKS (Kellogg). Index: 40. Fiber: trace. Protein: 2 gm. Sugar: 16 gm. Sodium: 70 mg. Fat: none. Calories: 110. Sensory comments: slight-to-moderate wheat flavor; caramelized-sugar flavor; sweeter than most. Cost: 15¢.

POST NATURAL RAISIN BRAN. Index: 40. Fiber: 4 gm. Protein: 2 gm. Sugar: 9 gm. Sodium: 160 mg. Fat: none. Calories: 90. Sensory comments: slight-to-moderate wheat and slight bran flavors: dried-fruit flavors. Cost: 12¢.

KELLOGG'S RAISIN BRAN. Index: 38. Fiber: 4 gm. Protein: 2 gm. Sugar: 9 gm. Sodium: 150 mg. Fat: 1 gm. Calories: 80. Sensory comments: slight-to-moderate wheat and slight bran flavors; caramelized-sugar and dried-fruit flavors. Cost: 13¢.

ALMOND DELIGHT (Ralston Purina). Index: 36. Fiber: 1 gm. Protein: 2 gm. Sugar: 8 gm. Sodium: 200 mg. Fat: 2 gm. Calories: 110. Sensory comments: slight-to-moderate wheat flavor; caramelized-sugar, brown-sugar, and nut flavors; sweeter than most: more crispy/crunchy than most. Cost: 14¢.

CORN POPS (Kellogg). Index: 36. Fiber: trace. Protein: 1 gm. Sugar: 12 gm. Sodium: 90 mg. Fat: none. Calories: 110. Sensory comments: moderate corn flavor; caramelized-sugar flavor; sweeter than most. Cost: 15¢.

CRACKIN' OAT BRAN (Kellogg). Index: 36. Fiber: 4 gm. Protein: 3 gm. Sugar: 8 gm. Sodium: 190 mg. Fat: 4 gm. Calories: 120. Sensory comments: slight-to-moderate wheat and slight bran flavors; brown-sugar and coconut flavors; sweeter than most. Cost: 17¢.

APPLE JACKS (Kellogg). Index: 33. Fiber: trace. Protein: 2 gm. Sugar: 14 gm. Sodium: 125 mg. Fat: none. Calories: 110. Sensory comments: very low grain flavor; "fruity but artificial" and caramelized-sugar flavors: sweeter than most; less toothpacking and fewer residual particles than most. Cost: 16¢.

FROOT LOOPS (Kellogg). Index: 31. Fiber: trace. Protein: 2 gm. Sugar: 13 gm. Sodium: 125 mg. Fat: 1 gm. Calories: 110. Sensory comments: very low grain flavor; "fruity but artificial" and caramelized-sugar flavors; sweeter than most; less toothpacking and fewer residual particles than most. Cost. 15¢.

COCOA KRISPIES (Kellogg). Index: 29. Fiber: trace. Protien: 1 gm. Sugar: 10 gm. Sodium: 190 mg. Fat: none. Calories: 110. Sensory comments: very low grain flavor; cocoa and vanilla flavors; sweeter than most. Cost: 17¢.

CRISPY WHEATS 'N RAISINS (General Mills). Index: 29. Fiber: trace. Protein: 2 gm. Sugar: 10 gm. Sodium: 180 mg. Fat: 1 gm. Calories: 110. Sensory comments: slight-to-moderate wheat flavor; caramelized-sugar and dried-fruit flavors; sweeter than most. Cost: 14¢.

Ratings continued on next page

Ratings of ready-to-eat cereals continued

FROSTED FLAKES (Kellogg). Index: 29. Fiber: trace. Protein: 1 gm. Sugar: 11 gm. Sodium: 190 mg. Fat: none. Calories: 110. Sensory comments: moderate corn flavor; caramelized-sugar flavor; sweeter than most; more crispy/crunchy than most. Cost: 13¢.

HONEY-COMB (Post). Index: 29. Fiber: trace. Protein: 1 gm. Sugar: 11 gm. Sodium: 160 mg. Fat: none. Calories: 110. Sensory comments: slight-to-moderate oat flavor; sweeter than most. Cost: 17¢.

LUCKY CHARMS (General Mills). Index: 29. Fiber: trace. Protein: 2 gm. Sugar: 11 gm. Sodium: 180 mg. Fat: 1 gm. Calories: 110. Sensory comments: slight-to-moderate oat flavor; vanilla, "fruity but artificial" and caramelized-sugar flavors: sweeter than most. Cost: 17¢.

COCOA PEBBLES (Post). Index: 27. Fiber: trace. Protein: 1 gm. Sugar: 13 gm. Sodium: 160 mg. Fat: 1 gm. Calories: 110. Sensory comments: very low grain flavor; vanilla, cocoa, and caramelized-sugar flavors; sweeter than most. Cost: 17¢.

FRUITY PEBBLES (Post). Index: 27. Fiber: trace. Protein: 1 gm. Sugar: 12 gm. Sodium: 150 mg. Fat: 1 gm. Calories: 110. Sensory comments: very low grain flavor; "fruity but artificial" flavor; sweeter than most. Cost: 15¢.

GOLDEN GRAHAMS (General Mills). Index: 27. Fiber: trace. Protein: 2 gm. Sugar: 9 gm. Sodium: 280 mg. Fat: 1 gm. Calories: 110. Sensory comments: slight-to-moderate wheat flavor; brown-spice, caramelized-sugar, and brown-sugar flavors; sweeter than most. Cost: 15¢.

HONEY NUT CHEERIOS (General Mills). Index: 27. Fiber: trace. Protein: 3 gm. Sugar: 10 gm. Sodium: 255 mg. Fat: 1 gm. Calories: 110. Sensory comments: slight-to-moderate oat flavor; honey flavor; sweeter than most. Cost: 15¢.

TRIX (General Mills). Index: 27. Fiber: trace. Protein: 1 gm. Sugar: 12 gm. Sodium: 170 mg. Fat: 1 gm. Calories: 110. Comments: low grain flavor; "fruity" flavor; sweeter than most. Cost: 18¢.

COCOA PUFFS (General Mills). Index: 24. Fiber: trace. Protein: 1 gm. Sugar: 11 gm. Sodium: 200 mg. Fat: 1 gm. Calories: 110. Sensory comments: very low grain flavor; vanilla and cocoa flavors; sweeter than most. Cost: 18¢.

CAP'N CRUNCH (Quaker Oats). Index: 22. Fiber: trace. Protein: 1 gm. Sugar: 12 gm. Sodium: 220 mg. Fat: 2 gm. Calories: 120. Sensory comments: moderate corn flavor; caramelized-sugar flavor; sweeter than most; more crispy/crunchy than most. Cost: 16¢.

Listings of more ready-to-eat cereals

Listed, as with the regular story Ratings, in order of CU's Nutrition Index; products with identical scores are listed alphabetically. Differences of 7 points or less are not nutritionally meaningful for most people. Information about nutrient levels was taken from product labels and supplemented, in some cases, by information provided by manufacturers.

QUAKER PUFFED WHEAT. Index: 78

SUNSHINE SHREDDED WHEAT. Index: 69.

UNCLE SAM (U.S. Mills). Index: 69.

ALL-BRAN WITH EXTRA FIBER (Kellogg). Index: 67.

QUAKER PUFFED RICE. Index: 67

RAISIN SQUARES (Kellogg). Index: 62.

NABISCO TOASTED WHEAT & RAISINS. Index: 62.

NABISCO 100% BRAN. Index: 58.

TEAMFLAKE (Nabisco). Index: 53.

WHEAT GERM FLAKES WITH BRAN ADDED (International MultiFoods). Index: 53.

ALL-BRAN WITH FRUIT & ALMONDS (Kellogg). Index: 51.

BRAN BUDS (Kellogg). Index: 51.

CINNAMON LIFE (Quaker Oats). Index: 49.

JUST RIGHT (Kellogg). Index: 49.

NUTRI-GRAIN ALMOND RAISIN (Kellogg). Index: 49.

SUN FLAKES CRISPY CORN & RICE FLAKES (Ralston Purina). Index: 49.

SKINNER'S RAISIN BRAN (U.S. Mills). Index: 47.

FRUIT & FIBRE WITH DATES, RAISINS, & WALNUT (Post). Index: 42.

RAISIN NUT BRAN (General Mills). Index: 42.

RAISIN, RICE & RYE (Kellogg). Index: 42.

BRAN MUFFIN CRISP (General Mills). Index: 40.

HORIZON TRAIL MIX (Post). Index: 40.

KIX (General Mills). Index: 40.

APPLE RAISIN CRISP (Kellogg). Index: 36.

C.W. POST WITH RAISINS. Index: 36.

RAINBOW BRITE (Ralston Purina). Index: 36.

MARSHMALLOW KRISPIES (Kellogg). Index: 33.

GHOST BUSTERS (Ralston Purina). Index: 31.

KABOOM (General Mills). Index: 31.

KING VITAMIN (Quaker Oats). Index: 31.

ALPHA-BITS (Post). Index: 29.

HONEY & NUT CORN FLAKES (Kellogg). Index: 29.

OH'S CRUNCHY NUT (Quaker Oats). Index: 29.

OJ'S (Kellogg). Index: 29.

ROCKY ROAD (General Mills). Index: 29.

COOKIE-CRISP, CHOCOLATE CHIP (Ralston Purina). Index: 27.

COUNT CHOCULA (General Mills). Index: 27.

FROSTED KRISPIES (Kellogg). Index: 27.

PAC-MAN (General Mills). Index: 27.

COOKIE-CRISP, VANILLA WAFER (Ralston Purina). Index: 24.

FRANKENBERRY (General Mills). Index: 24.

CAP'N CRUNCH'S CRUNCH BERRIES (Quaker Oats). Index: 22.

CINNAMON TOAST CRUNCH (General Mills). Index: 22.

G.I. JOE (Ralston Purina). Index: 22.

S'MORES CRUNCH (General Mills). Index: 22.

CAP'N CRUNCH'S PEANUT BUTTER CRUNCH (Quaker Oats). Index: 20.

OH'S HONEY GRAHAM (Quaker Oats). Index: 18.

Hot dogs

Condensed from CONSUMER REPORTS, June 1986

Frankly, Americans eat too many hot dogs. An occasional frankfurter wouldn't upset an otherwise well-balanced diet, but Americans devour them in such numbers that hot dogs alone must unbalance a good many diets. Although they vary somewhat from brand to brand, hot dogs in general are low in protein and high in fat and sodium, exactly the opposite of a healthful diet. Further, our testing shows that the better-tasting brands are likely to be among the worst offenders.

Hot dogs are made of odds and ends of meat ground with water and spices, pumped into casings, cooked, and cured. The meat can be practically anything. Most hot dogs, or franks or wieners, are made with beef or a combination of beef and other meats. Some are made with chicken or turkey. We sampled all those kinds in our tests of 54 products.

Hot dog ingredients must be listed on the label in descending order by weight. If a hot dog is made from only one kind of meat or poultry, that must be entered as part of the product name, as in "beef franks" or "turkey wieners." "Meat" franks are predominantly beef and pork, although they may contain as much as 15 percent poultry meat.

NUTRITION. The typical cooked hot dog is a little more than half water. Most of that is water that's found naturally in meat, but the USDA allows manufacturers to add more, as much as 10 percent of the weight of the entire hot dog. The USDA also allows manufacturers to make hot dogs with up to 30 percent fat in them. And most of our samples did contain between 25 and 30 percent fat. The poultry products averaged about 20 percent fat.

With so much water and fat in hot dogs, there's not a lot of room for protein. Cooked steak and hamburger are almost 25 percent protein by weight, but today's hot dog averages only 13 percent. That, in a nutritional sense, makes hot dogs very expensive. In the samples we tested, protein cost an average of about $14.50 a pound, and it ran to a high of $30.65. By way of contrast, a pound of protein in ground sirloin costs about $12.50.

In general, because they contained more fat, the beef and meat hot dogs were highest in calories; most contained between 150 and 200 calories per frank. The poultry franks tended to be leaner; most of them contained between 100 and 150 calories, and a few contained less than 100. But we don't imagine that such caloric distinctions count for much, because we wouldn't expect to find many serious dieters or health-food enthusiasts among heavy hot-dog eaters. Nor should hot-dog eaters include people on low-sodium restrictions; most hot dogs contain 300 to 500 milligrams of sodium.

TASTE. Grilling can add a special flavor and crispness to hot dogs that many people like. But it would have been impossible for us to grill all our samples in precisely the same way. Besides, most people heat their franks in boiling water. So that's what we did to prepare for our taste tests, following label directions or, in their absence, a procedure recommended by the National Hot Dog and Sausage Council: putting the hot dogs in a pan of boiling water, covering them, removing the pan from the heat,

Text continued on page 362

Ratings of hot dogs

Listed by types; within types, listed in order of overall sensory quality. Differences between closely ranked products were judged slight. Costs are calculated from average prices paid.

Product	Overall sensory Rating	Price/weight (oz.) per package	Franks per package	Cost per ounce	Cost per pound of protein	Sensory comments
Beef hot dogs						
THORN APPLE VALLEY BRAND	◒	$1.77/16	8	11¢	$14.23	*A,B*
NATHAN'S FAMOUS SKINLESS BEEF	◒	2.79/16	8	17	21.70	*C,M*
SAFEWAY OUR PREMIUM BEEF	◒	1.74/16	8	11	14.49	—
ECKRICH BEEF	○	2.39/16	10	15	20.49	—
JOHN MORRELL JUMBO BEEF	○	1.62/16	8	10	14.47	*P*
KROGER JUMBO DINNER BEEF	○	1.69/16	8	11	15.45	*P*
SHOFAR KOSHER BEEF	○	2.54/12	7	21	25.25	*C,M*
MOGEN DAVID KOSHER SKINLESS BEEF	○	2.37/12	8	20	24.02	*M*
KAHN'S JUMBO BEEF	○	2.24/16	8	14	18.86	*C*
OSCAR MAYER BEEF	○	2.17/16	10	14	18.86	—
HEBREW NATIONAL KOSHER BEEF	○	2.74/12	7	23	30.65	*C,M*
BEST'S KOSHER BEEF LOWER FAT	○	2.94/12	8	25	25.62	*C,E*

[1] *Contains only one type of meat.*

[2] *Packages varied from 9.75 to 11.5 oz., and cost per pound from $2.75 to $2.99.*

[3] *Unlike other meat hot dogs, has more than 15% chicken.*

Ratings continued on next page

Ratings of hot dogs
continued

Product	Overall sensory Rating	Price/weight (oz.) per package	Franks per package	Cost per ounce	Cost per pound of protein	Sensory comments
SMOK-A-ROMA NATURAL SMOKE	○	$1.07/16	10	7	$8.12	—
WILSON BEEF	○	1.42/16	10	9	12.74	—
HYGRADE'S BEEF	○	1.57/16	8	10	14.21	*P*
A & P SKINLESS BEEF	○	1.52/16	10	10	13.39	*N*
BEST'S KOSHER BEEF	○	2.25/12	8	19	22.31	*G,J,M*
ARMOUR BEEF HOT DOGS	○	1.79/16	10	11	19.95	*D*
VIENNA BEEF	○	2.31/12	8	19	22.90	*G,J*
SINAI 48 KOSHER BEEF	◒	2.07/12	8	17	19.78	*C,G,M*
"Meat" hot dogs						
HORMEL 8 BIG	⊜	1.89/16	8	12	14.86	*O*
KAHN'S JUMBO	⊜	1.94/16	8	12	17.32	*B,P*
BALL PARK	⊜	1.86/16	8	12	15.20	*A,B*
KROGER JUMBO DINNER	⊜	1.59/16	8	10	14.01	—
SAFEWAY OUR PREMIUM	⊜	1.72/16	8	11	13.92	—
OSCAR MAYER WIENERS	⊜	2.04/16	10	13	18.24	*K*
ARMOUR HOT DOGS	○	1.57/16	10	10	14.12	—
FARMER JOHN WIENERS	○	1.46/16	10	9	11.83	*A*
BRYAN JUICY JUMBOS	○	1.79/16	8	11	15.41	—
ECKRICH LEAN SUPREME JUMBO	○	2.39/16	8	15	17.40	*A*

ECKRICH JUMBO	○	2.02/16	8	13	17.32	*A*
JOHN MORRELL	○	1.59/16	10	10	15.61	*O*
EAT SLIM VEAL [1]	○	1.80/10 [2]	7	18	20.40	*A,Q,R*
HYGRADE'S HOT DOGS [3]	○	1.44/16	8	9	12.65	*D,H,I,N*
SCOTCH BUY WITH CHICKEN & BEEF	◒	1.19/16	10	7	11.17	*D,H,I*
WILSON	◒	1.29/16	10	8	11.75	*D,H,I*
SMOK-A-ROMA NATURAL SMOKE	◒	.99/16	10	6	9.49	*D,G,O*
Poultry hot dogs						
WEAVER CHICKEN	⊜	1.29/16	10	8	10.21	*B,D*
SHORGOOD CHICKEN	○	.84/16	10	5	6.37	*A*
MR. TURKEY	○	1.14/16	10	7	8.42	*A*
LOUIS RICH TURKEY	○	1.22/16	10	8	9.37	*A*
LONGACRE FAMILY TURKEY	○	1.24/16	10	8	9.00	*A*
KROGER TURKEY	○	1.09/16	8	7	8.07	*A*
WEIGHT WATCHERS TURKEY	○	1.37/16	10	9	9.39	*A*
SHENANDOAH TURKEY LOWER FAT	○	.99/16	10	6	6.59	*A*
FOSTER FARMS JUMBO CHICKEN	○	1.14/16	8	7	8.43	*A*
MANOR HOUSE TURKEY (SAFEWAY)	○	1.24/16	8	8	8.63	*A*
LONGACRE FAMILY CHICKEN	○	1.19/16	8	7	7.39	*A*
HYGRADE'S GRILLMASTER CHICKEN	○	1.11/16	8	7	7.42	*A,F*
MANOR HOUSE CHICKEN (SAFEWAY)	○	.89/12	10	7	6.27	*A*
PERDUE CHICKEN	○	1.29/16	8	8	9.07	*A,F,K,L*
GWALTNEY'S GREAT DOGS CHICKEN	○	1.07/16	8	6	7.91	*A*
HOLLY FARMS 8 CHICKEN	○	1.14/16	8	7	8.79	*A*
TYSON BUTCHER'S BEST CHICKEN	◒	.99/16	8	6	7.18	*A,D,F,H,I,L*

Keys to Ratings on next page

Keys to Ratings of hot dogs

FOOTNOTES

1 *Contains only one type of meat.*

2 *Packages varied from 9.75 to 11.5 oz., and cost per pound from $2.75 to $2.99.*

3 *Unlike other meat hot dogs, has more than 15% chicken.*

SENSORY CHARACTERISTICS

Except as noted, all had: an average balance of meat and fat flavors, mild seasonings, a resilient "skin," and a juicy, firm interior.

KEY TO SENSORY COMMENTS

A–Not juicy when bitten into.
B–Better than average balance of meat and fat flavors.
C–More resilient than most at first bite.
D–Too soft.
E–Crumbled into pieces when chewed.
F–Not as dense as most.
G–Worse-than-average balance of meat and fat flavors.
H–Less resilient than most at first bite.
I–Softer "skin" than most.
J–Oily appearance.
K–Definite smoke flavor.
L–More peppery than most.
M–Spicier than most.
N–Sweeter than most.
O–Slightly sour.
P–Saltier than most.
Q–Least salty.
R–Slightly bitter.

and letting it stand for seven minutes.

An ideal hot dog, our trained sensory panelists agreed, should have a strong meaty flavor balanced by a slight but distinct fat flavor. The outside "skin" should resist just a bit when you bite into it. As your teeth break through that layer, your mouth should be rewarded with a spurt of meat-flavored juice. The meat at the center of a hot dog should be moist and firm.

Ten of the tested hot dogs came pretty close to the ideal. More combination meat franks earned our top score than did all-beef franks; only one poultry frank did. None of the kosher hot dogs, which sell at a premium price, tasted particularly good to our panelists.

Frozen pizza

Condensed from CONSUMER REPORTS, May 1986

We focused our testing on the three most popular types of frozen pizza—cheese, sausage, and pepperoni—and selected those types from brands found most frequently in a survey of frozen-food cases across the country. Our selection embraces 38 products, mostly round ones with thin crusts. We also included a square one with a thick, Sicilian-style crust and five pizzas with "French bread" crusts.

TASTE. Our Ratings are based on tasting by a panel of trained sensory testers. As they sampled each product, the tasters scored the dozens of properties that make up a pizza's flavor, aroma, and texture.

Freezing turns out to be a nasty way to treat mozzarella, the basic pizza cheese. (Maybe that's why most makers use a low-moisture, part-skim mozzarella cheese or cheese substitute in their frozen products.) Our sensory panelists didn't consistently detect more than a slight taste of mozzarella in any of the frozen pizzas. Nor did they unfailingly pick up the flavors of Romano, Parmesan, provolone, and even cheddar cheese in the products that list them as ingredients. If cheese flavor was largely absent, cheese texture was often found disagreeably chewy or crumbly; the preferred texture, in our tasters' judgment, is stringy and somewhat elastic.

Sauces, too, suffer from freezing; their subtle blend of distinct flavors drifts toward a musky garlic-tomato fog. No frozen pizza was judged more than moderately spicy. Sauces that scored highest in flavor combine fresh and cooked tomato flavors fairly successfully, in our judgment. Most of the sauces did have good body—not too thin or too pasty.

Both regular sausage and pepperoni sausage are spicy meat products; in the classic Italian versions, pork is the meat used. But a pizza fancier would be hard-pressed to identify the kind of meat used in the sausage of a pizzeria product, much less that used in a frozen pizza. Any differences in the meat flavor of our frozen pizzas were submerged under the spice flavors and sauces. The intensity of the meat-topping flavors was generally mild.

Although dough keeps well in freezing, no home ovens can match the 600°F-plus temperatures of a pizzeria oven. Hence, frozen-pizza makers have to compromise to come up with a decent approximation of freshly baked pizza crust. In general, the crusts of our samples were somewhat crackerlike or biscuitlike—crispy nearly all the way through when we finished cooking them and quite successful in imitating fresh pizza's moderate chewiness. The Ratings judgments for crusts indicate how well the flavor of the dough survived cooking; the poorest marks went to crusts with uncooked flavors.

NUTRITION. In evaluating the nutrition to be expected from a typical portion of frozen pizza, we ran into a snag: These products come in many sizes, and so yield different portions when sliced up. We decided that an appropriate snack or lunch portion would be six ounces or so, roughly the weight of a generous slice in a neighborhood pizzeria. So we took each brand's labeled weight and divided it into equal servings closest to six ounces. Portional data in the Ratings are based on those servings, which varied from about four to seven ounces.

As a snack or part of a quick meal, pizza fits nicely into a well-balanced diet. It's not a particularly thinning food, of course, but with an average of about 450 calories per portion, its not a great fattener, either. It supplies a fair amount of vitamins A and C, as well as iron. Pizzas with fairly thick crusts are decent sources of the B vitamins—niacin, thiamin, and riboflavin.

Pizza is also a good source of protein. On average, a slice of the meat-topped pizzas contained about 20 grams, more than a third of most people's Recommended Daily Allowance. The cheese pizzas shone in calcium; they averaged about 422 milligrams per slice, a half of most people's RDA. But people who need to be especially concerned about salt in their diet had better forget about commercial frozen pizza. Per slice, our samples averaged about 1000 milligrams of sodium, or the equivalent of about a half-teaspoonful of table salt.

RECOMMENDATIONS. As pizzas go, the products that top the various Ratings categories weren't really very good. Perhaps the best that can be said for any one of them is that their individual components—crust, cheese, sauce, and sometimes meat topping—each contributed a distinctive taste in good balance with the other components. On that basis, the *Celeste* and *Stouffer's French* products pretty consistently led the field.

Ratings begin on next page

Ratings of frozen pizza

Listed by types; within types, listed in order of sensory quality. Closely ranked products differed little in quality. Servings per package were determined by dividing labeled weight into equal slices closest to 6 oz. Calorie figures are per cooked serving. Prices are the averages of those paid by CU shoppers.

◍ ⊜ ○ ◒ ●
Better ⟷ Worse

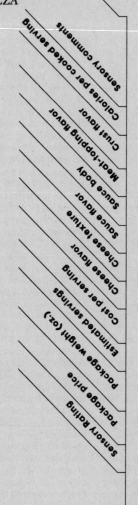

Product	Sensory Rating	Package price	Package weight (oz.)	Estimated servings	Cost per serving	Cheese flavor	Cheese texture	Sauce flavor	Sauce body	Meat-topping flavor	Crust flavor	Calories per cooked serving	Sensory comments
Cheese pizza													
CELESTE	⊜	$1.79	17.75	3	$0.60	⊜	⊜	○	◍	—	⊜	480	Q,W
STOUFFER'S FRENCH [1]	⊜	2.29	10.38	2	1.15	◒	⊜	⊜	◍	—	⊜	374	O,N
CHEF SALUTO	⊜	3.29	19.25	3	1.10	⊜	◒	○	◍	—	○	481	M,S
LA PIZZERIA	⊜	1.21	7.0	1	1.21	◒	◒	⊜	◍	–	⊜	459	L,M
TOTINO'S	⊜	1.57	10.5	2	1.57	◒	◒	○	◍	–	◍	401	E,P,Q
WEIGHT WATCHERS	⊜	1.96	6.0	1	1.96	◒	◒	⊜	◍	–	⊜	422	I,M,V
ELLIO'S	○	2.09	16.0	3	0.70	◒	●	⊜	◍	–	○	412	L,M
TREE TAVERN	○	2.19	16.0	3	0.73	◒	◒	◍	○	–	○	344	C,I,O,R
TOMBSTONE	○	2.87	20.0	3	0.96	◒	◒	⊜	○	–	⊜	526	A,C,H,L,M

PILLSBURY [2]	○	1.77	7.1	1	1.77	◒	◒	○	⊜	–	○	566	F,Q,U
CELENTANO [3]	○	1.81	13.0	2	0.91	◒	●	◓	◒	–	◓	449	C,O,R
JOHN'S	○	1.29	10.0	2	0.65	◒	◒	◒	○	–	○	418	T,X
JENO'S	○	1.41	10.1	2	0.71	◒	◒	◒	○	–	○	431	D,Q,T
Sausage pizza													
STOUFFER'S FRENCH [1]	◓	2.76	12.0	2	1.38	◒	◓	○	⊜	◓	◓	443	N,O
TONY'S	◓	2.23	16.0	3	0.74	◒	○	○	⊜	○	⊜	469	B,L,M
CELESTE	◓	3.61	20.0	3	1.20	◒	○	○	⊜	○	⊜	556	L,M
RED BARON	◓	3.18	22.0	4	0.80	◒	◓	○	⊜	○	○	478	B,L,M
RED BARON FRENCH [1]	◓	2.30	12.0	2	1.15	◒	◓	○	⊜	○	○	497	N,O
TOTINO'S	○	1.53	11.2	2	0.77	◒	◒	◒	⊜	○	⊜	492	B,Q,U
TOMBSTONE	○	2.40	13.0	2	1.20	◒	●	◓	⊜	○	◓	500	L,M
TOTINO'S [2]	○	0.96	4.8	1	0.96	◒	○	○	⊜	○	○	431	B,G,Q,U
PILLSBURY [2]	○	1.79	8.75	2	0.90	◒	○	○	⊜	○	○	357	G,Q,U
MR. P'S	○	0.79	9.0	2	0.40	◒	○	◒	◓	○	◓	371	Q,U
JENO'S	○	1.38	10.8	2	0.69	◒	○	◒	●	○	○	465	B,E,Q,T
Pepperoni pizza													
CELESTE	◓	3.48	19.0	3	1.16	◒	◓	◒	⊜	◓	⊜	557	B,D,J,L,M
STOUFFER'S FRENCH [1]	◓	2.77	11.25	2	1.39	◒	◓	◓	⊜	○	◓	440	J,N,O
TOMBSTONE [4]	◓	2.38	13.0	2	1.19	◒	○	○	⊜	◓	⊜	533	K,L,M
WEIGHT WATCHERS	◓	2.31	6.25	1	2.31	◒	○	○	⊜	○	⊜	411	J,L,M
TOTINO'S	◓	1.51	10.9	2	0.76	◒	○	◒	⊜	○	⊜	449	B,Q,U

[1] *2 pizzas per package; topping is on "French bread" crust.*
[2] *Microwave version; microwave-cooked for testing.*
[3] *Square with thick crust; similar to Sicilian-style pizza.*
[4] *Labeled Tombstone Smoked Sausage with Pepperoni Seasoning; sausage contains beef.*
[5] *4 "snack-sized" pizzas per package.*

Ratings continued on next page

Ratings of frozen pizza continued

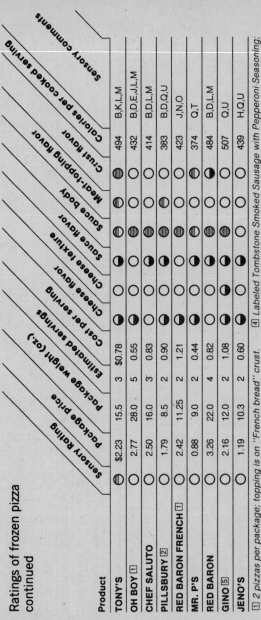

Product	Sensory Rating	Package price	Package weight (oz.)	Estimated servings	Cost per serving	Cheese flavor	Cheese texture	Sauce flavor	Sauce body	Meat-topping flavor	Crust flavor	Calories per cooked serving	Sensory comments
TONY'S	⊜	$2.23	15.5	3	$0.78	◒	○	◒	⊜	⊜	⊜	494	B,K,L,M
OH BOY [1]	○	2.77	28.0	5	0.55	◒	○	○	⊜	○	○	432	B,D,E,J,L,M
CHEF SALUTO	○	2.50	16.0	3	0.83	○	○	◒	⊜	○	○	414	B,D,L,M
PILLSBURY [2]	○	1.79	8.5	2	0.90	◒	○	◒	⊜	⊜	○	383	B,D,Q,U
RED BARON FRENCH [1]	○	2.42	11.25	2	1.21	◒	○	○	⊜	○	○	423	J,N,O
MR. P'S	○	0.88	9.0	2	0.44	◒	○	◒	⊜	○	⊜	374	Q,T
RED BARON	○	3.26	22.0	4	0.82	○	○	◒	⊜	○	◒	484	B,D,L,M
GINO [5]	○	2.16	12.0	2	1.08	◒	◒	◒	⊜	○	○	507	Q,U
JENO'S	○	1.19	10.3	2	0.60	◒	○	◒	○	○	○	439	H,Q,U

[1] *2 pizzas per package; topping is on "French bread" crust.*

[2] *Microwave version; microwave-cooked for testing.*

[3] *Square with thick crust; similar to Sicilian-style pizza.*

[4] *Labeled Tombstone Smoked Sausage with Pepperoni Seasoning; sausage contains beef.*

[5] *4 "snack-sized" pizzas per package.*

SENSORY CHARACTERISTICS
All: had a nicely chewey crust. *Except as noted, all:* tasted bland, with very slight spice/herb intensity, oily flavor, sweetness, saltiness, and sourness; had very slight-to-moderate meat/spice flavor; had slightly oily "mouthfeel".

KEY TO SENSORY COMMENTS
A – Cheddar-cheese flavor.
B – Slight-to-moderate oily flavor.
C – Very slight oily mouthfeel.
D – Moderate oily mouthfeel.
E – Slight-to-moderate spice/herb flavor.
F – Moderate spice/herb flavor.
G – Slight sweet flavor.
H – Slight-to-moderate salty flavor.
I – Very slight sour flavor.
J – Moderate meat/spice flavor.
K – Stronger meat/spice than most.
L – Biscuity crust flavor.
M – Biscuity crust texture.
N – Yeasty crust flavor.
O – Yeast-dough crust texture.
P – Cracker-crust flavor
Q – Cracker-crust texture.
R – Yeasty/biscuity crust flavor.
S – Biscuity/yeasty crust flavor.
T – Pastry/crackery crust flavor.
U – Crackery/pastry crust flavor.
V – Crackery/biscuity crust flavor.
W – Crackery/biscuity/pastry crust flavor.
X – Flaky pastry-crust texture.

Salad dressings

Condensed from CONSUMER REPORTS, February 1986

Some supermarket shelves groan not with food exactly but with bottles and packets of Russian, Thousand Island, Green Goddess, Roquefort, Blue Cheese, Taco, and many more mixtures formulated in the interest of making greens taste better. For this project, CU chose to test two of the most popular varieties, French and Italian dressings. From the more than 300 labels our shoppers found on supermarket shelves, we selected 64 widely advertised or widely available dressings in various formats.

Classically, both French and Italian dressings are vinaigrettes—sauces based on oil and vinegar, with herbs and spices added to give each dressing its special character. With a French dressing, those extras are typically salt, pepper, mustard, and garlic or onion. With an Italian dressing, the additions form a bolder array that includes basil, oregano, and garlic.

In America, however, the classic recipes have gone through some changes. "French" dressings usually contain tomato, which alters the flavor and color. And "Italian" dressings often come in "creamy" versions that may or may not contain dairy products. As a yardstick for testing, we concocted our own French and Italian dressings, incorporating in them appropriate aromas and flavors at the intensities that we consider ideal.

FRENCH. CU's French dressing has a moderate but not biting flavor and aroma of vinegar and onion, as well as a slight sourness and a hint of bitterness. The flavors are well blended, so that no one of them dominates. The dressing is devoid of gumminess.

Other qualities in a dressing are, within broad limits, a matter of personal preference, so we didn't score them. The Comments column in the Ratings notes products that differed somewhat from our dressing in oil and tomato aroma and flavor, as well as in sweetness, saltiness, oily texture, and the like. Our tolerance did have limits, though; *Richelieu Western*, for instance, was too sweet.

Two French dressings, *Kraft Catalina* and *Wish-Bone Sweet 'n Spicy*, were top-rated because they matched CU's recipe in all important respects, although they did differ in many minor ways. Both were slightly spicier, sweeter, and thicker than ours, as well as being a shade less oily.

ITALIAN. CU's recipe for Italian dressing is of the classic variety. It has a moderate level of the flavors and aromas of garlic and Italian herbs, a mild bite of vinegar, and a touch of sourness.

All the Italian products were rated on those factors. In addition, products that we categorize as "creamy" were expected to taste as if cream or mayonnaise has been added, with a creamy texture, moderate dairy flavors and aromas, and some mayonnaise taste. We didn't expect the Italian products to be "well blended," since it's appropriate for their hardier spicing to lend distinct flavor notes. Another variation of Italian dressing is a plainish vinaigrette compounded of red-wine vinegar and oil. We didn't expect those products to be quite as spicy as the rest.

Of the regular Italian dressings, seven commercial products held their own against our classic recipe. Two of them, *Good Seasons Mild* and *Lawry's*, are dry

Text continued on page 372

Ratings of salad dressings

Listed by types, within types, listed in order of overall sensory quality compared with CU's recipes for French and Italian dressings. Dressings judged equal in sensory quality are bracketed and listed alphabetically. Most are bottled; refrigerated products and dressings made from packets of mix are noted. Costs are calculated from the average prices paid by CU shoppers, and include any additional ingredients required, such as oil and vinegar.

Excellent | Very good | Good | Fair | Poor

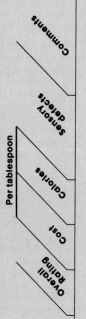

Product	Overall Rating	Cost (per tablespoon)	Calories (per tablespoon)	Sensory defects	Comments
French dressings					
KRAFT CATALINA	Excellent	6¢	70	—	C,D,E,F,H,I,J,K,M
WISH-BONE SWEET 'N SPICY	Excellent	6	70	—	C,D,E,H,I,J,K,M
HENRI'S ORIGINAL REDUCED CALORIE	Very good	7	35	h	B,C,D,E,H,I,J,K,M
LADY LEE	Very good	5	60	h	B,C,D,E,H,I,J,K,M
HAIN NATURALS CREAMY	Very good	10	60	c,h	B,C,D,E,G,H,I,J,K,M
NUMADE SAVORY (SAFEWAY)	Very good	6	55	c,h	B,C,D,E,H,I,J,K,M
PFEIFFER	Very good	6	80	a,h	B,C,D,E,H,I,J,M
WISH-BONE DELUXE	Very good	7	60	d,h	B,C,D,E,H,I,J,M
WISH-BONE LITE	Very good	7	30	a,h	B,C,D,E,G,H,I,J,K,M
FEATHERWEIGHT IMITATION	Very good	7	5	h,i	B,D,G,I,K
GIRARD'S ORIGINAL	Very good	7	65	a,i	F
GOOD SEASONS OLD FASHION (MIX)	Very good	7	85	a,d,h	A

KRAFT	◒	6	60	b,c,h	*B,C,D,E,H,I,J,K,M*
MILANI 1890	◒	8	60	c,f,h	*C,D,E,H,I,K,M*
A&P	◒	4	60	b,c,d,h	*B,D,E,H,I,J,K,M*
RICHELIEU WESTERN	◒	8	75	c,e,h,k	*B,C,D,G,H,I,J,K*
SEVEN SEAS CREAMY	◒	6	65	d,f,i	*B,C,D,F,H,I,J,M*
WALDEN FARMS REDUCED CALORIE	◒	7	30	b,h,i	*B,C,D,H,I,J,K,M*
KRAFT REDUCED CALORIE	◒	6	25	c,d,h,i	*B,C,D,E,G,H,I,J,K,M*
DIA-MEL LOW SODIUM/LOW CALORIE	○	8	1	d,f,g,h,i	*D,G,I,K*
PRITIKIN NO OIL	○	8	10	c,d,f,g,h,i	*B,C,D,G,H,I,K*
WEIGHT WATCHERS (MIX)	○	7	4	b,e,g,h,i,j	*B,D,E,G,I,J,K*

Italian dressings

GOOD SEASONS MILD (MIX)	●	7	80	—	*E*
KRAFT OIL-FREE	●	6	4	—	—
KRAFT PRESTO	●	6	70	—	*L*
LAWRY'S (MIX)	●	6	80	—	*L*
PFEIFFER	●	6	65	—	*D,L*
WISH-BONE	●	6	70	—	—
WISH-BONE HERBAL	●	6	70	—	*D,L*
BARÖNDORF NO OIL LITE	◒	5	4	f	—
CARDINI'S (NO SALT ADDED)	◒	8	65	h	*L*
DIA-MEL LOW SODIUM/LOW CALORIE	◒	7	1	h	—
GIRARD'S OLDE VENICE	◒	9	65	c	*D,L*
KROGER	◒	6	95	l	—
WALDEN FARMS REDUCED CALORIE CLASSICO	◒	6	10	c	*F*

Ratings continued on next page

Ratings of salad dressings continued

Product	Overall Rating	Cost (Per tablespoon)	Calories (Per tablespoon)	Sensory defects	Comments
BERNSTEIN'S RESTAURANT RECIPE	◓	6¢	65	f,m	*L*
EL MOLINO HERBAL SECRETS NO OIL	◓	9	2	c,h	—
FEATHERWEIGHT	◓	7	4	c,h	—
KRAFT ZESTY REDUCED CALORIE	◓	6	5	f,h	*F*
NUMADE TANGY (SAFEWAY)	◓	5	80	h,l	—
PRITIKIN NO OIL	◓	8	5	f,h	—
SEVEN SEAS VIVA	◓	6	75	d,f	*D,F*
WALDEN FARMS LOW SODIUM CLASSICO	◓	6	10	e,h	—
A&P	◓	4	75	c,d,l	*L*
CARDINI'S	◓	9	70	c,h,l	—
HENRI'S GOURMET	◓	8	95	c,l,m	—
KRAFT ZESTY	◓	6	80	c,l,m	—
TRADER VIC'S SAN FRANCISCO STYLE	◓	11	50	f,h,m	*L*
WISH-BONE LITE REDUCED CALORIE	◓	6	30	c,f,h	*D,I*
MILANI 1890	○	7	45	c,h,l,m	—
Creamy Italian dressings					
HIDDEN VALLEY RANCH SPICE (MIX)	◓	4	55	e,l,m,q	*D,I*
KRAFT CREAMY	◓	7	55	c,h,l,n,q	*D,E,I*
NATURALLY FRESH [2]	◓	6	80	c,e,h,l,n	*D,I,L*

PHILADELPHIA HERB	⊜	7	70	c,e,h,l,m	*D,I,L*
HOLLYWOOD CREAMY	⊜	7	75	c,h,n,o,p,q	*D,I*
MARIE'S CREAMY GARLIC [2]	⊜	8	95	c,e,h,l,m,n	*D,F,I,L*
WEIGHT WATCHERS CREAMY	⊜	4	50	c,h,l,m,n,o	*D,E,I,L*
HAIN NATURALS CREAMY (NO SALT ADDED)	○	9	80	f,h,n,o,p,q	*I*
SLIM-ETTE CREAMY LOW CALORIE NO SUGAR	○	6	4	h,n,o,p,q	*E,I*
HAIN NATURAL	○	9	75	c,h,l,n,o,p,q	—
Red-wine vinegar & oil					
SEVEN SEAS VIVA	⊜	6	85	—	—
PFEIFFER	⊜	6	65	c	*E*
KRAFT	⊜	7	75	c,h	*D,E,I*
NEWMAN'S OWN	⊜	8	85	c,f,h	*I*

[1] *Less than 1 gm.* [2] *Refrigerated.*

KEY TO DEFECTS
a – Too much vinegar aroma.
b – Not enough vinegar aroma.
c – Not enough onion or garlic aroma.
d – Too much vinegar flavor.
e – Not enough vinegar flavor.
f – Too sour.
g – Too bitter.
h – Not enough onion or garlic flavor.
i – Flavor not well blended.
j – Too gummy.
k – Too sweet.
l – Not enough Italian-seasoning aroma.
m – Not enough Italian-seasoning flavor.
n – Not enough dairy aroma.
o – Not enough dairy flavor.
p – Not enough mayonnaise flavor.
q – Not creamy enough in texture.

KEY TO COMMENTS
(All Comments are as compared with CU's recipes.)
A – More oil aroma.
B – Less oil aroma.
C – More tomato aroma.
D – Less oil flavor.
E – Sweeter.
F – Saltier.
G – Less salty.
H – More tomato flavor.
I – Less oily in texture.
J – Thicker.
K – Leaves less coating in mouth.
L – Leaves more coating in mouth.
M – Spicier.

mixes; we used vegetable oil and white distilled vinegar to make them up. Among the top-rated products, the only differences we noted from our recipe lay in such matters of preference as degrees of sweetness and oiliness.

No product stood out among the creamy Italian dressings. Many of them, indeed, seem to bear the "creamy" label simply because they're emulsified, to keep them from separating into oil and vinegar portions like a regular Italian dressing.

Of the four red-wine vinegar-and-oil products, one, *Seven Seas Viva*, was rated excellent. The rest were on the bland side.

CU's homemade dressings

FRENCH DRESSING

3/4 cup salad oil
2 tbsp. water
2 tbsp. white vinegar
1 tsp. dry mustard
1 tsp. sugar
1/2 tsp. salt
1/2 tsp. white pepper
1 tbsp. ketchup
2 tsp. finely chopped onion

After measuring out the oil and setting it aside, mix the water and vinegar in a cup and set that aside.Combine the mustard, sugar, salt, pepper, and ketchup in a small bowl. Into that bowl pour about a tbsp. of the oil and about 1/2 tbsp. of the water-vinegar mixture, beating with a wire whisk until the mixture is smooth and creamy. Continue beating while adding small amounts of the oil and the water-vinegar mixture alternately. Stir in the onion. Yield: one cup.

ITALIAN DRESSING

1/2 tsp. basil
1/2 tsp. oregano
3/4 tsp. salt
1/2 tsp. sugar
1/4 tsp. pepper
1/4 tsp. crushed garlic (1 medium clove)
3 tbsp. red-wine vinegar
1 tbsp. water
3/4 cup olive oil

Crumble the basil and oregano to release flavor, then drop the crushed herbs into a jar, along with the salt, sugar, pepper, garlic, vinegar, and water. Cap the jar tightly and shake well. Add the oil and shake again. Refrigerate between uses, but serve at room temperature. Yield: one cup.

Cottage cheeses

Condensed from CONSUMER REPORTS, March 1986

In the bucolic days when many families kept their own cow, cottage cheese was just that—a cheese made in the kitchen of a farm cottage. Whole milk or milk that had been skimmed for butter would be gently heated at the back of the stove. Left to itself, the milk would be curdled by bacteria from the air. Sometimes, a little acid (provided by lemon juice), buttermilk, or even a piece of a cow's stomach (rennet) would be added to speed the process.

When the milk curdled, the liquid whey would be poured off, leaving protein-rich curds, the basis of all cheeses. The curds would be strained off through cheesecloth the following morning and eaten for breakfast or lunch. The pigs would get the whey.

CURDS AND MILKFAT. Today's commer-

Text continued on page 375

Ratings of cottage cheeses

Listed by types; within types, listed in order of overall sensory quality; products with the same Overall Rating are listed alphabetically. Costs are based on average prices, except as noted, for 16-oz. size.

Excellent	Very good	Good	Fair	Poor
⊜ (Excellent)	⊖ (Very good)	○ (Good)	◒ (Fair)	● (Poor)

Product	Area	Cost [1]	Overall Rating	Calories [1]	Sensory defects	Comments
Low-fat (up to 2% milkfat)						
BORDEN LITE-LINE, 1½%	TX	20¢	Excellent	99	K	*A*
FOREMOST SO-LO, 2%	TX	45	Excellent	88	F,H,N	*A,C*
FRIENDSHIP 75% LACTOSE REDUCED, 1%	NY	32	Excellent	76	A,B,C,N	*C,D,G*
FRIENDSHIP, 1%	NY	34	Excellent	83	A,B,N	*C,G*
LUCERNE, 2%	CA	25	Excellent	92	M	*A,B*
LUCERNE, 2%	TX	36 [3]	Excellent	89	E,F,H,N	*C*
PATHMARK, 1%	NY	28	Excellent	81	N,R	*C*
SCHEPPS SLENDO, 2%	TX	36	Excellent	110	K	*C,E,G*
SUPERBRAND STA-FIT, 2%	TX	30	Excellent	89	K	*C*
WEIGHT WATCHERS, 1%	TX	25	Excellent	79	K	*E,G,I*
A&P LOOK-FIT, 1%	NY	26 [3]	Very good	75	F,K,M,O,R	*C*
ACME, 1%	NY	27 [3]	Very good	81	K,O,R	*C*
ALTA-DENA, 2%	CA	36	Very good	95	J	*A,B,J*
AXELROD'S EASY DIETER REDUCED SALT, 1%	NY	31	Very good	82	F,J,N,R	*C,G*
ALEXROD'S EASY DIETER, 1%	NY	34	Very good	79	F,K,M,O,R	*C*
BREAKSTONE'S SMOOTH AND CREAMY STYLE, 2%	NY	32	Very good	87	E,G,H,I,J,R	*C*
CROWLEY, 1%	NY	35 [3]	Very good	82	F,N,R	*C*
FRIENDSHIP NO SALT ADDED, 1%	NY	34	Very good	85	A,B,C,F I,J,N,S	*C,D,F*
GRAND UNION, 1%	NY	30	Very good	75	F,K,M,O,R	*C*

[1] Per 4-oz. serving. [2] Bought in 8-oz. container. [3] Bought in 12-oz. container.

Ratings continued on next page

Ratings of cottage cheeses continued

Product	Area	Cost [1]	Overall Rating	Calories [1]	Sensory defects	Comments
KNUDSEN 98% FAT FREE, 2%	CA	28¢	◓	93	H,J,R	—
KROGER, 1%	TX	32	◓	83	K	*C,E,G*
LADY LEE, 2%	CA	30[2]	◓	99	J,Q,R	—
SEALTEST LIGHT N' LIVELY, 1%	NY	33	◓	76	N,R	*C*
SHOPRITE, 1%	NY	27	◓	79	A,O,R	*C*
SKAGGS ALPHA BETA, 2%	CA	25	◓	90	J,R	—
WEIGHT WATCHERS, 1%	NY	32	◓	73	O,R	*C,I*
WEIGHT WATCHERS, 1%	CA	27	◓	84	K,M,O	*A,I*
ALTA-DENA LOW SODIUM DRY CURD, LESS THAN ½%	CA	53[3]	○	85	A,E,F,H,S	*C,D,G,J*
LUCERNE DRY CURD, LESS THAN ½%	CA	35	○	107	A,E,F,H, M,O,S	*C,D,G,J*
BREAKSTONE'S DRY CURD, NO SALT ADDED, LESS THAN ½%	NY	39[3]	◒	91	E,G,H,J, L,N,Q,S	*B,D,G*

Creamed (4% milkfat)

Product	Area	Cost [1]	Overall Rating	Calories [1]	Sensory defects	Comments
A&P	NY	27	⊜	113	N	*C,H*
ALBERTSONS	TX	27	⊜	98	F,H,N	*A*
ALTA-DENA FARMER STYLE	CA	36	⊜	123	R	*A,B,H,J*
AXELROD'S	NY	32	⊜	105	N,R	*C*
BORDEN	TX	48[2]	⊜	95	H,K,M,O	*C*
BREAKSTONE'S SMOOTH AND CREAMY	NY	32	⊜	107	N,R	*C*
CROWLEY	NY	30[3]	⊜	106	F,N,R	*C*
FOREMOST	TX	50[3]	⊜	100	F,N	*A,J*
KROGER	TX	26[3]	⊜	105	K	*A,C*
LUCERNE	CA	30[2]	⊜	108	K,M	*A,B,H*
LUCERNE	TX	32[3]	⊜	110	F,H,N	*C*
PATHMARK	NY	27	⊜	100	N,R	*C*
SCHEPPS	TX	36	⊜	109	K	*C*

Product	Area	Cost [1]	Overall Rating	Calories [1]	Sensory defects	Comments
SEALTEST	NY	31¢	●	107	N,R	*C*
SKAGGS ALPHA BETA	TX	42	●	97	F,H,N	*A,C*
SUPERBRAND SCHMIER-KÄSE COUNTRY STYLE	TX	30	●	106	K	*C*
ACME	NY	25	◓	103	K,M,O,R	*C*
AXELROD'S CREAMED, WHIPPED STYLE	NY	34	◓	118	D,I,J,N,P,R	*C*
FOREMOST	CA	30 [2]	◓	122	J,Q	—
KNUDSEN	CA	28	◓	116	J	*J*
LADY LEE	CA	30 [2]	◓	119	J	*J*
NANCY'S CULTURED RENNETLESS	CA	45 [2]	◓	113	A,H,J,L, N,P,Q	—
SKAGGS ALPHA BETA	CA	45	◓	107	H,J,R	—
BREAKSTONE'S NATURAL TANGY STYLE	NY	32	○	105	E,G,H,I J,N,Q,S	*B,D*

[1] *Per 4-oz. serving.* [2] *Bought in 8-oz. container.* [3] *Bought in 12-oz. container.*

SENSORY CHARACTERISTICS

Except as noted, all had: small curd; satisfactory dairy flavor; low dairy aroma; moderate cultured-milk flavors; the low sour aroma and flavor typical of cheeses; the very slight sweetness, saltiness, and chalkiness typical of milk; very slight aftertaste; curds slightly to moderately firm and slightly elastic; moderate-to-high moistness, slight graininess; and moderate body; slight-to-moderate mouthcoating.

KEY TO SENSORY DEFECTS

A – Slightly bitter.
B – Very slightly metallic.
C – Very slightly medicinal.
D – Curd too soft.
E – Curd too firm.
F – Somewhat too rubbery.
G – Very rubbery.
H – Curd too grainy.
I – Curd too dry.
J – Creaming mixture too grainy.
K – Creaming mixture too moist.
L – Creaming mixture too dry.
M – Body too thin.
N – Body too thick.
O – Somewhat watery.
P – Gummy.
Q – Slightly astringent.
R – Almost no milk aftertaste.
S – Dairy flavor to low.

KEY TO COMMENTS

A – Moderate dairy aroma.
B – Moderate dairy sourness.
C – Low in cultured-milk flavors.
D – Lacked sweetness.
E – Relatively sweet.
F – No salty taste.
G – Little salty taste.
H – Saltier than most.
I – Labeled serving size is 1 oz., whereas all others list 4 oz.
J – Contained less than 1 gm. of lactose per serving.

cial cottage cheese may still start out as the skim milk of yesteryear, but concentrated skim milk or nonfat dry milk can be used instead. The simplest version is "dry curd" cheese, essentially just the curds of Miss Muffet's nursery-rhyme snack. A dry-curd product contains less than ½-percent milkfat. We tested three dry-curd cheeses, which we've entered in the Ratings as extreme examples of "low-fat" cheeses.

Any cottage cheese but a dry-curd product has its milkfat content raised by a creaming mixture. Low-fat cottage cheese may contain anything up to 2 percent milkfat. We tested 27 low-fat products besides the dry-curd cheeses.

Conventional cottage cheeses (termed "creamed" in the Ratings) must contain at least 4 percent milkfat. The creaming mixture may be some sort of milk product—whole, skimmed, cream, or any combination thereof. The milk must be coagulated with rennet or another coagulating substance from a Federally approved list. The cheese's labeled ingredient list will note "enzymes" if a milk-clotting enzyme was used, or will say something like "cultured milk" if a bacterial culture was used. If acid was used to set the milk, the label should read "directly set" or "curd set by direct acidification." We tested 24 varieties of creamed cottage cheese.

Beyond the differences mentioned above, cottages cheeses differ in the size of their curds. We limited our testing mainly to the popular "small curd" variety, which contains lumps about the size of a corn kernel. There's also "large-curd" cottage cheese, with lumps about twice that size, and there's "chunky" cottage cheese, whose curds are larger yet. We did look at one "whipped" brand, with virtually no lumps.

Like most dairy products, cottage cheese is highly perishable and is generally made in local dairies. For that reason, we bought our samples in three far-flung venues—New York, Texas, and California—and had them tested on the spot. Our finding suggest that a brand name isn't always a sure guide to a dairy product's quality. Some *Foremost* cheeses bought in Texas, for example, tasted better than *Foremost* cheeses bought in California. TASTE. Like the milk from which it's extracted, cottage cheese is distinctly bland. Ideally, it should have a slightly acidic taste, as well as a hint of the fresh dairy flavors of butter, cream, and milk. The curds should be smooth, moist, and moderately chewy in texture, with enough integrity to hold their shape.

With an eye to those criteria, trained taste panels in New York, Texas, and California, sampled all the cottage cheeses bought in their area. The vast majority of products earned excellent or very good marks in taste. Only three cheeses were judged as low as good. The dry-curd *Breakstone's No Salt Added*, was judged fair—the lowest rating issued for any of the cottage cheeses.

All our samples were bought earlier than their expiration dates, but some products were moldy when we opened them nonetheless—possibly because they weren't stored properly in the supermarket. We rejected those samples, of course, and bought new containers of the brands in question. (If the cottage cheese you buy is moldy when you open it, don't hesitate to take it back for a refund.)

NUTRITION. Our tests confirmed a fact that dieters and the budget-conscious have long known: Cottage cheese is a reasonable protein substitute for meat. The cheese's protein quality is excellent, as good as that in fish and beef. And the protein in a four-ounce portion, generally about 14 grams, provides about one-quarter of an adult's recommended daily intake.

Furthermore, the cheese delivers its protein without meat's freight of calories. The creamed cottage cheeses averaged 108 calories per four-ounce serving—about half the calories in a cooked hamburger patty and about two-thirds the calories in a typical serving of tuna. The low-fat cottage cheeses were only slightly lower in calories than the creamed types.

You also get more calcium with cottage cheese than with most fish or meat; on average, the cheeses provided 74 milligrams of calcium in a four-ounce serving. (And you may get more salt than desired; most cheeses contained at least 300 milligrams of sodium per serving, and even most of the "no salt" products contained at least 80 mg.) In other respects, though, fish and meat provide more essential nutrients than cottage cheese.

Some 30 million Americans are unable to digest lactose, a sugar found naturally in milk. One New York brand, *Friendship 75% Reduced Lactose*, is being marketed for lactose-intolerant consumers. The reduced-lactose *Friendship* contained only three grams of carbohydrate per serving, of which about one gram was lactose. That's all very well, but there's better new yet for the lactose-intolerant: Seven other products, noted in the Ratings, contained less than one gram of lactose per serving.

Black teas

Condensed from CONSUMER REPORTS, January 1986

All teas sold in America are blends. *Lipton*, *Red Rose*, and other common domestic brands tend to be blends of black Indian or Ceylon teas. (The "orange pekoe" or "pekoe" on the label indicates the size of the leaf, not the type of the tea.) English brands, such as *Twinings* and *Jacksons*, offer a variety of black-tea blends with names like English Breakfast and Irish Breakfast (which indicate nothing about the tea aside from suggesting a good time to drink it) and Darjeeling (which refers to one variety of black Indian tea). We tested 25 imported and domestic blends.

Our taste-testers brewed the tea according to directions on the package, when there were any. When there weren't, the tasters poured six ounces of boiling water into a cup containing one tea bag. They let the bag steep (without covering) for four minutes, then removed it, and stirred the tea. They used a similar procedure in brewing the loose tea.

TASTE. An excellent black tea should be full-bodied, not thin. It should not be flat-tasting, but should have the character that tasters call "brisk" or "lively"; it should tingle on the tongue. It should have some pungency and bitterness. It might contain floral or malty notes, and sometimes both. (Maltiness in a tea refers to the actual aroma and flavor of malt, which can be described as cooked, sweetish, and reminiscent of caramel.) An excellent tea should have no off-flavors, such as notes of wood, hay, or fermented fruit. Unless it's smoky tea, it should have no smoke notes.

None of the tested teas measured up to the standard for a judgment of "excellent." All of them were somewhat bland. The best of the lot was the *Jacksons Darjeeling* loose tea, which we judged very good. It was livelier than most and relatively hearty, with slight but well-balanced malt flavors and aromas. Like all the tested teas, it was light-bodied and watery. But, to its credit, it had no off-flavors.

Continued on next page

Most of the other teas were judged good; they were less lively than the loose *Jacksons Darjeeling*. Many were low in malt or floral character. All were light-bodied.

Drinking tea almost certainly implies the intake of caffeine. Most brands contain from 40 to 80 milligrams of caffeine per cup. The *Lipton Decaffeinated* blend contains only 10 mg., but the *Salada Decaffeinated* has 41 mg. per cup.

Ratings of black teas

Listed in order of estimated overall sensory quality. Teas judged equal in sensory quality are bracketed and listed alphabetically. Except as noted, all teas come in bags. Costs per cup are based on prices CU paid.

Product	Cost per cup [1]	Sensory comments
■ *The following product was judged very good in sensory quality.*		
JACKSONS DARJEELING (loose)	5¢	A,C,E,H
■ *The following products were judged good in sensory quality.*		
COST CUTTER [2]	1	A,B,G,H
GRAND UNION	2	C,G,H
LIPTON	5	D,G,I,M
LIPTON DECAFF.	6	D,G,I,L
SALADA	2	C,E,I,O
A & P	3	C,F,H
CROWN COLONY [3]	5	B,G,H
EMBASSY [2]	2	C,F,H
LIPTON (loose)	2	A,C,F,I
RED ROSE	3	B,G,H
TWININGS DARJEELING	11	B,G,H
TWININGS ENGLISH BREAKFAST	10	B,G,H
JACKSONS DARJEELING	11¢	D,G,J,M
KROGER	5	B,F,H
LADY LEE [4]	2	C,F,I,L
P & Q [5]	1	C,E,J,P
SALADA DECAFF.	7	C,F,I,O
SCOTCH BUY [3]	2	D,E,K,J,P,S
SWEE-TOUCH-NEE	4	B,G,I,L
TETLEY	4	C,E,I,L
TWININGS IRISH BREAKFAST	10	B,G,I,L,Q
TWININGS	10	C,F,I,P
■ *The following products were judged fair in sensory quality.*		
JACKSONS ENGLISH BREAKFAST	12	C,F,J,M,Q,R
TWININGS ENGLISH BREAKFAST (loose)	5	B,F,J,N

[1] *Using one tea bag per cup, or, for loose tea, one level teaspoon per cup.*

[2] *Kroger.* [3] *Safeway.* [4] *Lucky.* [5] *A & P.*

SENSORY CHARACTERISTICS
All were judged light-bodied, relatively watery, and fairly smooth.
Except as noted, all had slight liveliness.

KEY TO COMMENTS
A - Livelier than most.
B - Very slight malt notes.
C - Slight malt notes.
D - No malt notes.
E - No floral notes.
F - Very slight floral notes.
G - Slight floral notes.
H - No defects.
I - Very slight defect level.
J - Low defect level.
K - Slight smoky traces, a defect.
L - Very slight hay traces, a defect.
M - Slight hay traces, a defect.
N - Some fermented flavor, a defect.
O - Very slight woody traces, a defect.
P - Slight woody traces, a defect.
Q - Grassy aftertaste.
R - Green aftertaste.
S - Smoky aftertaste.

Strawberry jams and preserves

Condensed from CONSUMER REPORTS, August 1985

Specialty labels such as *Trappist, Wilkin & Sons Ltd. Tiptree*, and *Crabtree & Evelyn* stand columns deep on shelves where jars of *Kraft, Smucker's*, and *Welch's* once ruled.

And what, one may ask, is the harm of gracing one's breakfast table with *Fortnum & Mason* preserves at 37 cents an ounce instead of *Smucker's* at 10 cents an ounce? No harm at all, but no good at all either unless the extra pennies lavished on the expensive preserves really buy something better.

To find out whether they do, we went shopping for jams and preserves in the most-popular flavor, strawberry. (The distinction between "jams" and "preserves" has been blurred. Historically, preserves usually contained larger pieces of fruit and were made with more sugar than jams. Now, the terms seem to be used interchangeably, so we'll call them all jams.)

TASTE. Some of the flavor of fresh strawberries is lost even if you "put up preserves" the old-fashioned way, by cooking with sugar and pouring it into jars. A lot more of the flavor is lost if the jam is made from frozen fruit, as it is by most commercial producers. A commercial strawberry jam, then, can't be expected to match a good homemade jam. Still, it should capture as much of the aroma and flavor of the berries as possible.

A good jam should also be sweet, but not *overwhelmingly* sweet. It may or may not contain large pieces of strawberry. The fruit pieces should be relatively firm, and the gel around the fruit should be soft yet cohesive. The jam should be easy to spread.

A jam lost points if our expert tasters detected the caramel flavor of overcooked strawberries; the flavor of any berry or fruit other than strawberry; or any bitter, or artificial, flavor.

The results of our taste tests may surprise devotees of "gourmet" brands. With two exceptions, the best jams were lower-priced ones.

The nine top-rated jams were judged very good—just a little short of the ideal. The *Knott's Berry Farm*, a high-priced domestic brand at 21¢ an ounce, was judged most successful at combining strong strawberry flavor, appropriate sweetness, and good texture. But two of the best-selling brands, *Kraft* and *Smucker's* preserves, were also judged very good. So were three preserves

Text continued on page 382

Ratings of strawberry jams

Listed, except as noted, in order of estimated overall quality. Products judged equal are bracketed and listed alphabetically. Prices are the average of those paid by CU shoppers for the size listed.

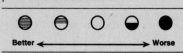

⊜ ⊖ ○ ◒ ●

Better ⟷ Worse

Brand	Type [1]	Price/size	Cost per ounce	Strawberry impact	Texture	Lack of defects	Comments
■ *The following jams were judged very good in overall quality.*							
KNOTT'S BERRY FARM	P	$2.09/10 oz.	21¢	⊖	⊜	⊜	C
POLANER	P	1.73/18	10	⊖	⊜	⊜	B
BONNE MAMAN	P	2.19/13	17	○	⊜	⊜	A
BAMA	P	2.79/32	9	⊖	⊜	⊖	A
KRAFT	P	1.56/18	9	○	⊖	⊜	B
EMBASSY (KROGER)	P	2.46/32	8	⊖	⊜	⊖	C
EMPRESS (SAFEWAY)	P	1.79/18	10	⊖	○	⊜	A
SCOTCH BUY (SAFEWAY)	P	2.14/32	7	○	⊜	⊖	C
SMUCKER'S	P	1.76/18	10	⊖	○	⊜	B
■ *The following jams were judged good in overall quality.*							
COUNTRY PURE BRAND	J	1.39/16	9	⊖	○	⊖	B
ALPHA BETA	P	1.55/18	9	○	○	⊖	B
CRABTREE & EVELYN	P	4.43/12	37	⊖	⊜	○	B
LADY LEE (LUCKY)	P	1.44/18	8	○	○	⊖	A
TRAPPIST	P	2.19/12	18	○	⊖	⊖	A
WELCH'S	P	1.86/18	10	○	○	⊖	B
A & P	P	2.02/32	6	○	⊖	⊖	A
BAMA	J	2.42/32	8	○	⊖	⊖	C
ECONO BUY (ALPHA BETA)	J	1.69/32	5	○	⊖	⊖	C
KROGER	P	1.59/18	9	○	⊜	⊖	A
POLANER LITE	D,P	.89/8.5	10	⊖	○	⊖	B

Brand	Type [1]	Price/size	Cost per ounce	Strawberry impact	Texture	Lack of defects	Comments
KRAFT	J	$2.29/32 oz.	7¢	○	◍	⊖	A
SMUCKER'S LOW-SUGAR	D,S	1.91/15.5	12	○	◍	⊖	B
WELCH'S	J	2.85/32	9	○	◍	⊖	C
FEATHERWEIGHT	D,P	1.11/8	14	○	○	◍	C
FRUITCREST	P	1.59/24	7	○	○	⊖	B
SMUCKER'S	J	2.56/32	8	⊖	◒	⊖	C
COST CUTTER (KROGER)	P	1.62/32	5	○	○	⊖	C
DICKINSON'S	P	1.95/12	16	○	○	⊖	A
HERO	P	2.46/12	21	○	○	⊖	A
SMUCKER'S SEEDLESS	J	1.94/18	11	○	◍	⊖	C
KERN'S	P	1.76/18	10	○	⊖	⊖	B
ACME	P	1.39/18	8	○	○	⊖	A
KNOTT'S BERRY FARM	J	1.69/16	11	○	○	⊖	C
P & Q (A & P)	P	1.29/32	4	○	○	⊖	A
WILKIN & SONS LTD TIPTREE	P	3.39/12	28	◒	⊖	⊖	A
RÉCOLTE	P	2.87/12	24	○	○	⊖	A
WELCH'S LITE	D,S	1.82/16	11	○	◒	⊖	C
DIA-MEL	D,P	1.22/8	15	○	◒	⊖	A
ROBERTSON'S	P	2.62/12	22	○	○	⊖	C
FORTNUM & MASON	P	4.44/12	37	○	○	○	A
■ *The following jams were judged fair in overall quality.*							
SMUCKER'S SLENDERELLA	D,J	1.08/8.5	13	○	●	⊖	A
NUTRADIET	D,J	1.02/8	13	◒	◒	⊖	C
LOUIS SHERRY	D,P	.85/8	11	◒	◒	○	A
SORRELL RIDGE	C	2.66/10	27	◒	◒	○	C

[1] *P = preserve; J = jam; D = diet; S = spread; C = conserve.*

KEY TO COMMENTS

A - Contains many large pieces.
B - Contains some large pieces.
C - Relatively smooth; contains no large pieces.

with supermarket labels—Kroger stores' *Embassy* and Safeway's *Empress* and *Scotch Buy*. The last is one of the cheapest jams tested, at 7¢ an ounce.

Jams are usually 60 to 65 percent sugar, a high level that retards spoilage but pours on the calories. Most of the regular jams have about 65 calories per one-tablespoon serving. Low-calorie jams contain less sugar, or sometimes substitute saccharin, and use common preservatives to retard spoilage. The best-tasting diet product was *Polaner Lite*, which contained 28 calories per tablespoon.

RECOMMENDATIONS. Forget the fancy labels and prices. Most of the expensive gourmet jams didn't distinguish themselves in our taste tests. But some humbler products of mass food preparation did.

Instant coffees

Condensed from CONSUMER REPORTS, May 1985

Coffee makers consistently claim that their instant brands are as good as high-quality ground coffee.

It seemed fair, then, to see how the instants stacked up against fresh-brewed coffee. Accordingly, we had expert tasters test them using *Brown Gold 100% Colombian* drip-grind coffee (high-rated in previous tests) as a standard for comparison. CU's taste consultants prepared all the coffees, instant and fresh-brewed, with bottled spring water.

None of the instant coffees equalled the fresh-brewed coffee they were measured against. But 13 instants did well enough to merit a Rating of very good. While the majority of our very good coffees were freeze-dried, the brand that topped the list, *Yuban*, was a regular (or spray-dried) instant. Decaffeinated products were also well represented; four made it into our top Ratings group.

Taste experts have finely honed palates. Could ordinary coffee drinkers detect the differences that caused some instants to rate high while other products trailed the pack? We invited 58 coffee-drinking CU staffers to help us answer that question.

In a comparison of a high-rated brand with a low-rated brand (top-rated *Yuban* vs. decaffeinated *Chock Full o'Nuts*), almost half the panelists were able to pick out the odd sample consistently. In a comparison of a high-brand with a middle-rated brand (*Yuban* vs. *Savarin*), only about one in five panelists identified the odd brand at both of two tastings. In a comparison of a middle-rated brand with a low-rated brand (*Savarin* vs. decaffeinated *Chock Full o' Nuts*), only a quarter of the panelists could tell the difference at both of two tastings.

RECOMMENDATIONS. A reasonably sensitive palate is a prerequisite to appreciating the advantages of the high-rated products.

Coffee drinkers with less-sensitive taste buds would do well to buy the cheapest instant coffee they can find; good and so-so are as one to them.

Ratings of instant coffees

Listed in order of estimated overall sensory quality. Coffees judged equal in sensory quality are bracketed and listed alphabetically. Prices are the average of those paid by CU for the size listed.

Product	Type [1]	Price/size, oz.	Cost per serving [2]	Caffeine, mg	Defects
■ *The following products were judged very good in sensory quality.*					
YUBAN	S	$4.63/8	4.9¢	62	e
BRIM	D,F	5.59/8	5.6	5	e
NESCAFÉ SILKA	S	3.79/8	3.9	57	a,d
SANKA	D,F	5.59/8	5.7	3	e
TASTER'S CHOICE	F	5.69/8	5.5	59	d
MAXIM	F	5.29/8	6.7	85	e
EDWARDS	D,F	2.49/4	5.4	5	a,f
KROGER	F	4.88/8	4.9	57	e
LADY LEE (LUCKY)	F	2.39/4	5.1	71	e
SANKA	D,S	4.79/8	4.9	5	a,d
BROWN GOLD	F	2.56/4	5.3	70	e
MAXWELL HOUSE	S	4.99/10	4.3	81	d
NESCAFÉ CLASSIC BLEND	S	4.85/10	4.1	78	a,e

The following products were judged good in sensory quality.

(HIGH POINT DECAFFEINATED, S&W), (EIGHT O'CLOCK, NESCAFÉ DECAF), (ANN PAGE DECAFFEINATED, LADY LEE DECAFFEINATED, SCOTCH BUY), (COST CUTTER, FOLGERS CRYSTALS DECAFFEINATED, KROGER CRYSTALS DECAFFEINATED, MJB DECAFFEINATED, SAVARIN), (EIGHT O'CLOCK, MJB), (ACME DECAF., LADY LEE).

The following products were judged fair in sensory quality.

(ECONO BUY, TASTER'S CHOICE DECAFFEINATED,) CHOCK FULL O'NUTS, P&Q, HILLS BROS., NESCAFÉ CLASSIC RICH & TRADITIONAL, ACME.

The following products were judged poor in sensory quality.

(HILLS BROS. DECAFFEINATED, SAFEWAY), KAVA, CHOCK FULL O'NUTS DECAFFEINATED, KROGER CRYSTALS.

[1] *D = decaffeinated; F = freeze-dried; S = Spray-dried.*

[2] *Based on 2 level tsp. per 6-oz. cup.*

KEY TO DEFECTS

a – Very slightly heavy/burnt flavor or aroma.
b – Slight heavy/burnt flavor or aroma.
c – Moderate heavy/burnt flavor or aroma.
d – Very slight aftertaste.
e – Slight aftertaste.
f – Moderate aftertaste.

Canned tuna

Condensed from CONSUMER REPORTS, March 1985

Only albacore can be labeled "white meat" tuna. White tuna has a light flesh and a characteristically mild flavor. Other tunas, such as yellowfish, bluefish, and skipjack, are darker, a bit more robust in flavor, and are labeled "light meat" tuna.

Generally, white tuna comes in solid style and, less often, in chunk style. Light tuna comes most often in chunk, occasionally in solid style or—less expensively—in grated or flaked styles. Many solid white tunas are labeled "fancy," "selected," or "first quality." But since there are no quality standards for canned tuna, those marketing commendations are meaningless.

In the past few years, water-packed tuna has come to dominate the market. (Water-packed tuna averages about 105 calories per half-can serving; oil-packed, tuna, 240 calories undrained, but that's reduced to 180 calories when the oil is drained off.)

TASTE AND TEXTURE. According to our taste experts, tuna should have a not-too-overpowering fishy flavor, moderate saltiness, and a firm but flaky texture. The meat should be moist, and it should remain moist in the mouth as it's being chewed.

Only one brand, American Stores' *Acme* solid white tuna in water, met that standard of excellence. Another 14 brands—most of them oil-packed—were judged very good.

While the top-rated *Acme* is a water-packed brand, most of the other water-packed brands were judged only good. Those brands suffered fairly serious defects, such as a pronounced dry or mealy texture, a tinny taste, excessive saltiness, and sourness.

Most of the low-salt brands were judged only good. None of them, by their very nature, had the moderately salty taste demanded by our standard of excellence.

RECOMMENDATIONS. What's the best tuna? Depending on what you're making, the best tuna may be the cheapest. If you plan to mix the tuna with mayonnaise and onion in a salad or with other ingredients in a casserole, any canned tuna should do.

If you like tuna straight, you'll probably be able to detect subtle differences between types and brands. You may prefer the moister-tasting oil-packed tunas, as our sensory experts did. You may prefer the milder taste of albacore to the stronger taste of light-meat tuna, although albacore averages about 30¢ extra per can.

How to use the Buying Guide

- Look in the index for specific reports.
- Look in the Contents for general subject areas.
- Look on pages 5 to 7 for explanations of check-ratings and Best Buys, and of why some products are included and others not.

Ratings of canned tuna

Listed by types; within types, listed in order of estimated overall sensory quality.

◍ ⊜ ○ ◒ ●

Better ←——→ **Worse**

Product	Type [1]	Overall rating
White tuna in oil		
3 DIAMONDS	S	⊜
GEISHA	S	⊜
GILL NETTERS BEST	S	⊜
BUMBLE BEE	S	⊜
CHICKEN OF THE SEA	C	⊜
BUMBLE BEE	C	⊜
STAR-KIST	S	⊜
SEASON	S	⊜
SEA TRADER [3]	S	⊜
GRAND UNION	C	○
CHICKEN OF THE SEA	S	○
GILL NETTERS BEST	C	○
GRAND UNION	S	○
A&P	S	○
Light tuna in oil		
CHICKEN OF THE SEA	C	⊜
3 DIAMONDS	C	⊜
BREAST O'CHICKEN	C	○
GEISHA	C	○
CARNATION	C	○
BUMBLE BEE	C	○
A&P	C	○
ACME [2]	C	○
COST CUTTER [5]	C	○
SEA TRADER [3]	C	○
ANN PAGE	F	○
GILL NETTERS BEST	C	○

Product	Type [1]	Overall rating
Light tuna in oil (cont.)		
KROGER	C	○
LADY LEE [4]	C	◒
SCOTCH BUY [3]	G	◒
Low-salt tuna		
STAR-KIST (LIGHT) [6]	C	○
STAR-KIST (WHITE) [7]	C	○
CHICKEN OF THE SEA (WHITE) [7]	C	○
FEATHERWEIGHT (LIGHT) [7]	C	○
CHICKEN OF THE SEA (LIGHT) [7]	C	○
STAR-KIST (LIGHT) [7]	C	◒
White tuna in water		
ACME [2]	S	◍
GILL NETTERS BEST	S	⊜
BUMBLE BEE	S	⊜
SEA TRADER [3]	S	⊜
A&P	S	○
GILL NETTERS BEST	C	○
GEISHA	S	○

[1] *S = solid tuna; C = chunk; F = flake; G = grated.*
[2] *American Stores.*
[3] *Safeway.*
[4] *Lucky.*
[5] *Kroger.*
[6] *Packed in oil*
[7] *Packed in water.*

Ratings continued on next page

Ratings of canned tuna continued

Product	Type [1]	Overall rating
CHICKEN OF THE SEA	S	○
3 DIAMONDS	S	○
KROGER	S	○
SEASON	S	○
STAR-KIST	S	○
LADY LEE [4]	S	○
GRAND UNION	S	○
BUMBLE BEE	C	○

Light tuna in water

Product	Type [1]	Overall rating
GEISHA	C	○
ACME [2]	C	○
LADY LEE [4]	C	○
EMPRESS	C	○
GILL NETTERS BEST	C	○
BUMBLE BEE	C	○
KROGER	C	○
A&P	C	○
3 DIAMONDS	C	○
CARNATION	C	○
CHICKEN OF THE SEA	C	○
STAR-KIST	S	○
DEEP BLUE	S	◒
ECONO BUY [2]	C	◒
BREAST O'CHICKEN	C	◒
SEA TRADER [3]	C	●

Spaghetti sauces

Condensed from CONSUMER REPORTS, October 1985

Most of the 50 commercial sauces we tested—meatless, marinara, meat-flavored, and meat sauces—list tomato paste as the main ingredient. To see what solids were in the products, we drained them through a sieve. Twenty ounces of heated sauce yielded, on average, only about two ounces of solids—tomato solids and skins, bits of onions, pieces of mushroom, and, in the meat and meat-flavored varieties, small remnants of meat. The chunkiest products were the two *Prego Plus* products; each had about five ounces of solids. The sauce with the least solids was *Acme* meatless, with only two-fifths of an ounce.

TASTE. An excellent spaghetti sauce should have a red to red-orange color and a moderately thick consistency. There should be a distinct fresh-tomato flavor. The sauce should be somewhat spicy, with a trace of herbs, typically oregano and basil. Meat sauces should have some fresh-meat flavor.

Only *Prego No Salt Added*, a meatless sauce, fully qualified under the standard of excellence for its type. We were surprised to find such zip in a no-salt product. Generous use of lemon juice plus herbs and spices apparently compensated for the lack of salt.

All the other sauces, including the best-selling *Ragu* products, lacked that fresh-tomato flavor and were rather bland. Most tasted overcooked. All the mushroom, meat, and meat-flavored sauces lacked the flavor associated with their types. The *Prego* products with salt had these defects to some extent, though less so than most of the other sauces. *Prego* sauces were the top-rated marinara, meat, and meat-flavored products.

NUTRITION. A meatless spaghetti sauce over pasta, sprinkled with Parmesan and served with a salad, is a relatively nutritious main dish that's not especially high in calories. A $3/4$-cup serving of an average meatless commercial sauce contained 145 calories, 3 grams of protein, 5 grams of fat, and 21 grams of carbohydrate. Except for the top-rated *Prego No Salt Added* (and the bottom-rated *Featherweight No Salt Added*), the commercial sauces were fairly high in sodium, providing an average of 800 milligrams per serving.

In the old days, simmering a sauce in an iron pot supposedly helped add iron to the daily diet. To test that, we checked the iron content of a meatless sauce before and after simmering it in a cast-iron pot for three minutes or so. Before simmering, the sauce contained about two milligrams of iron per $3/4$-cup serving. After cooking, the iron content had doubled.

RECOMMENDATIONS. If you value the convenience of a commercial sauce, try the *Prego No Salt Added*—or indeed any of the *Prego* sauces we tested. That brand was consistently among the higher-ranked products.

If you like meat or marinara sauce, you might want to buy a high-rated meatless sauce like the *Prego* and embellish it yourself. Using the sauce as a base, add fresh vegetables, mushrooms, meat, and spices as desired.

Ratings of spaghetti sauces

Listed by types; within types, listed in order of estimated overall quality based on sensory judgments by CU's consultants. Differences between closely ranked brands were judged slight.

Meatless sauces

Prego No Salt Added; Progresso; Golden Grain W/Mushrooms; Prego; A & P Premium; Prego W/Mushrooms; Prince; Ragu Old World Style; Kroger; Ragu W/Mushrooms; Acme; Francesco Rinaldi; Ragu Extra Thick; Town House; Town House W/Mushrooms; Alpha Beta; Buitoni; Lady Lee; Cost Cutter; Ronzoni; Aunt Millie's; Ronzoni W/Mushrooms; Featherweight No Salt Added.

Marinara sauces

Prego; Aunt Millie's; Newman's Own; Buitoni; Golden Grain; Ragu Old World Style; Ronzoni.

Meat and meat-flavored sauces

Prego Plus Veal And Mushrooms; Prego Plus Sausage And Peppers; Ragu Homestyle; Acme; Progresso; A & P Premium; Aunt Millie's; Aunt Millie's Sweet Peppers & Italian Sausage; Kroger; Town House; Buitoni; Prince; Alpha Beta; Francesco Rinaldi; Lady Lee; Ragu Extra Thick; Chef Boyardee; Cost Cutter; Ronzoni.

Buying Guide Index

and 5-year listing of Consumer Reports articles

This index lists articles that appeared in CONSUMER REPORTS from January 1982 to October 1986. Articles summarized for this edition of the Buying Guide appear in bold-face type. (•) indicates correction or follow-up.

Articles listed in bold type appear in this issue

Articles listed in bold type appear in this issue

Articles listed in bold type appear in this issue

Articles listed in bold type appear in this issue

Articles listed in bold type appear in this issue

STATEMENT OF OWNERSHIP MANAGEMENT AND CIRCULATION

(Required by 39 U.S.C. 3685)

1. Title of Publication: CONSUMER REPORTS. **1B.** Publication No: 00107174. **2.** Date of Filing: September 12, 1986. **3.** Frequency of Issue: Monthly. **3A.** No. of Issues Published Annually: 12. **3B.** Annual Subscription Price: $16.00. **4.** Complete Mailing Address of Known Office of Publication: 256 Washington St., Mt. Vernon, N.Y. 10553-1099. **6.** Full Names and Complete Mailing Address of Publisher, Editor, & Managing Editor. Publisher: Consumers Union of United States Inc., 256 Washington St., Mt. Vernon, N.Y. 10553-1099. Executive Director, Rhoda H. Karpatkin, 256 Washington St., Mt. Vernon, N.Y. 10553-1099. EDITOR: Irwin Landau, 256 Washington St., Mt. Vernon, N.Y. 10553-1099. Managing Editor: Eileen Denver, 256 Washington St., Mt. Vernon, N.Y. 10553-1099. **7.** OWNER (If owned by a corporation, its name and address must be stated and also immediately thereunder the names and addresses of stockholders owning or holding l percent or more of total amount of stock. If not owned by a corporation, the names and addresses of the individual owners must be given. If owned by a partnership or other unincorporated firm, its name and address, as well as that of each individual must be given. If the publication is published by a nonprofit organization, its name and address must be stated.) Name: Consumers Union of United States, Inc. A nonprofit organization. Address: 256 Washington Street, Mt. Vernon, N.Y. 10553-1099. **8.** Known Bondholders, Mortgagees, and Other Security Holders Owning or Holding 1 Percent or More of Total Amount of Bonds, Mortgages or Other Securities (If there are none, so state): None. **9.** For Completion by Nonprofit Organizations Authorized to Mail at Special Rates (Section 432.12 DMM only). The purpose, function, and nonprofit status of this organization and the exempt status for Federal income tax purposes has not changed during preceding 12 months.

10. Extent and Nature of Circulation:	Average No Copies Each Issue During Preceding 12 Months	Actual No. Copies of Single Issue Published Nearest to Filling Date
A. Total No. Copies (Net Press Run)	3,783,000	3,754,000
B. Paid and/or Requested Circulation		
1. Sales through dealers and carriers, street vendors and counter sales	166,000	157,000
2. Mail Subscription (Paid and/or requested)	3,412,000	3,424,000
C. Total Paid and/or Requested Circulation (Sum of 10B1 and 10B2)	3,578,000	3,581,000
D. Free Distribution by Mail, Carrier or Other Means Samples, Complimentary, and Other Free Copies	29,000	28,000
E. Total Distribution (Sum of C and D)	3,607,000	3,609,000
F. Copies Not Distributed		
1. Office use, left over, unaccounted, spoiled after printing	27,000	22,000
2. Return from News Agents	149,000	123,000
G. TOTAL *(Sum of E, F1 and 2—should equal net press run shown in A)*	3,783,000	3,754,000

11. I certify that the statements made by me above are correct and complete

Louis J. Milani, Business Manager